TAKING SIDES

Clashing Views on
Social Issues

SEVENTEENTH EDITION, EXPANDED

Selected, Edited, and with Introductions by

Kurt Finsterbusch
University of Maryland

Mc
Graw
Hill
Education

TAKING SIDES: CLASHING VIEWS ON SOCIAL ISSUES, SEVENTEENTH EDITION, EXPANDED

1 2 3 4 5 6 7 8 9 0 DOC/DOC 1 0 9 8 7 6 5 4 3

MHID: 0-07-813947-3
ISBN: 978-0-07-813947-5
ISSN: 95-83865

Acquisitions Editor: *Joan L. McNamara*
Marketing Director: *Adam Kloza*
Marketing Manager: *Nathan Edwards*
Developmental Editor: *Dave Welsh*
Project Manager: *Erin Melloy*
Buyer: *Jennifer Pickel*
Content Licensing Specialist: *Rita Hingtgen*
Cover Designer: *Studio Montage, St. Louis, MO.*
Media Project Manager: *Sridevi Palani*

Compositor: MPS Limited
Cover Image: © Design Pics RF

Editors/Academic Advisory Board

Members of the Academic Advisory Board are instrumental in the final selection of articles for each edition of TAKING SIDES. Their review of articles for content, level, and appropriateness provides critical direction to the editors and staff. We think that you will find their careful consideration well reflected in this volume.

TAKING SIDES: Clashing Views on SOCIAL ISSUES

Seventeenth Edition, Expanded

EDITOR

Kurt Finsterbusch
University of Maryland

ACADEMIC ADVISORY BOARD MEMBERS

Preface

The English word *fanatic* is derived from the Latin *fanum*, meaning temple. It refers to the kind of madmen often seen in the precincts of temples in ancient times, the kind presumed to be possessed by deities or demons. The term first came into English usage during the seventeenth century, when it was used to describe religious zealots. Soon after, its meaning was broadened to include a political and social context. We have come to associate the term *fanatic* with a person who acts as if his or her views were inspired, a person utterly incapable of appreciating opposing points of view. The nineteenth-century English novelist George Eliot put it precisely: "I call a man fanatical when . . . he . . . becomes unjust and unsympathetic to men who are out of his own track." A fanatic may hear but is unable to listen. Confronted with those who disagree, a fanatic immediately vilifies opponents.

Most of us would avoid the company of fanatics, but who among us is not tempted to caricature opponents instead of listening to them? Who does not put certain topics off limits for discussion? Who does not grasp at euphemisms to avoid facing inconvenient facts? Who has not, in George Eliot's language, sometimes been "unjust and unsympathetic" to those on a different track? Who is not, at least in certain very sensitive areas, a *little* fanatical? The counterweight to fanaticism is open discussion. The difficult issues that trouble us as a society have at least two sides, and we lose as a society if we hear only one side. At the individual level, the answer to fanaticism is listening. And that is the underlying purpose of this book: to encourage its readers to listen to opposing points of view.

This book contains 48 selections presented in a pro and con format. A total of 24 different controversial social issues are debated. The sociologists, political scientists, economists, and social critics whose views are debated here make their cases vigorously. In order to effectively read each selection, analyze the points raised, and debate the basic assumptions and values of each position, or, in other words, in order to think critically about what you are reading, you will first have to give each side a sympathetic hearing. John Stuart Mill, the nineteenth-century British philosopher, noted that the majority is not doing the minority a favor by listening to its views; it is doing *itself* a favor. By listening to contrasting points of view, we strengthen our own. In some cases, we change our viewpoints completely. But in most cases, we either incorporate some elements of the opposing view—thus making our own richer—or else learn how to answer the objections to our viewpoints. Either way, we gain from the experience.

Organization of the book Each issue has an issue *Introduction*, which sets the stage for the debate as it is argued in the YES and NO selections. *Learning Outcomes* further helps the reader to focus on just what he/she should "take away" from the issue debate. Each issue concludes with a section that explores the issue further and suggests questions which should help you to consider the issues from different angles. In reading the issue and forming your own opinions, you should not feel confined to adopt one or the other of the positions presented. There are positions in between the given views or totally outside them, and the suggestions for further reading that appear within the *Exploring the Issue* section at the end of each issue, that should help you find resources to continue your study of the subject. At the back of the book is a listing of all the *Contributors to This Volume,* which will give you information on the social scientists whose views are debated here. Also, on the *Internet References* page that accompanies each unit opener, you will find Internet site addresses (URLs) that are relevant to the issues in that unit.

A word to the instructor   An *Instructor's Resource Guide with Test Questions* (multiple-choice and essay) is available through the publisher for the instructor using *Taking Sides* in the classroom. A general guidebook, *Using Taking Sides in the Classroom,* which discusses methods and techniques for integrating the pro–con approach into any classroom setting, is also available. An online version of *Using Taking Sides in the Classroom* and a correspondence service for *Taking Sides* adopters can be found at www.mhhe.com/cls/UsingTS2.pdf.

Taking Sides: Clashing Views on Social Issues is only one title in the Taking Sides series. If you are interested in seeing the table of contents for any of the other titles, please visit the Contemporary Learning Series website at www.mhhe.com/cls/.

Kurt Finsterbusch
University of Maryland

Contents in Brief

Contents

Fred Barnes, journalist, executive editor of *The Weekly Standard* and TV commentator, argues that the mainstream media has a pronounced liberal bias. They do not hire conservatives, and an analysis of specific news stories shows their bias. Robert F. Kennedy Jr., environmentalist and political activist, agrees with Barnes that the media is biased but believes that it has a conservative bias. Surveys show that most Americans have many false beliefs that are fed to them by conservative talk radio shows and other conservative media outlets. Many media owners are very conservative and stifle investigative reporting.

Mark Krikorian, the executive director of the Center for Immigration Studies, presents the case against immigration. He emphasizes the changes in America that make immigration less beneficial for America. The current immigrants are not much different than immigrants in the past century, but they do not fit the new America as well as the past immigrants fit the old America. One part of the story is that the new America will not assimilate immigrants well. Jason L. Riley, an editor of the *Wall Street Journal*, applauds immigration because it will propel, not impede, economic growth. America has a flexible labor market, where both employers and employees can change the work situation as they need or desire. "In the end, employers, workers, and consumers are all better off." America has a labor shortage that immigrants help fill without taking jobs in the aggregate from Americans. Riley also argues that new immigrants assimilate much like the old immigrants did.

Elizabeth Marquardt, director of the Center for Marriage and Families, defends the common belief that divorce has devastating impacts on children and attacks Constance Ahrons's counter-thesis. Constance Ahrons, co-chair of the Council on Contemporary Families, found in her research on the children of divorced parents that they do quite well in later life, and most think that they were not harmed by the divorce.

Feminist scholar Linda Hirshman finds that successful and well-qualified women are "opting out" of work outside the home when their husbands' income is adequate for a rich lifestyle. Prioritizing parenthood over work is an affront to Hirshman's feminist values. Sociologist Pamela Stone reports on her survey research and finds a number of women who sacrificed careers for parenthood and thought it was their free choice. Her analysis, however, notes that they were tightly constrained by traditional gender roles and inflexible workplaces.

America's largest lesbian and gay organization, the Human Rights Campaign, presents many arguments for why same-sex couples should be able to marry. The main argument is fairness. Marriage confers many benefits that same-sex couples are deprived of. Researcher Peter Sprigg presents many arguments for why same-sex couples should not be able to marry. The main argument is that the state has the right and duty to specify who a person, whether straight or gay, can marry, so no rights are violated.

UNIT 3   STRATIFICATION AND INEQUALITY   103

James Kurth, Claude Smith Professor of Political Science at Swarthmore College, warns of very negative consequences for America of the growing income inequality from a conservative perspective. He also mentions the liberal criticisms of inequality but downplays their importance, because America has institutions that mitigate them. Gary S. Becker and Kevin M. Murphy, both economists teaching at the University of Chicago and senior fellows at the Hoover Institution, swim upstream on this issue by pointing out the positive consequences of the growing income inequality. The main reason for the increasing inequality is the increasing returns to education, which, in turn, inspire greater efforts by young people to increase their social capital.

Alvin Poussaint is a professor of psychiatry at the Harvard Medical School, with a focus on child psychiatry. He argues that the election of Barack Obama may indicate that America is approaching the mountaintop that King preached about. Lawrence D. Bobo, the W.E.B. Du Bois Professor of the Social Sciences at Harvard University, provides a scholarly analysis of racial inequalities. He explains how inequalities in America are constantly being recreated. Change occurs and is much celebrated, but change is successfully resisted in many subtle ways.

History Professor Barbara Epstein argues that the feminist movement has been highly successful in changing the consciousness of Americans to "an awareness of the inequality of women and a determination to resist it." She explains how feminists succeeded at the consciousness level but have declined as a movement for social change. Journalist Kate O'Beirne argues that feminism is unpopular with women and is pushing an agenda that most women do not support. She claims that most women have concluded "that the feminist movement is both socially destructive and personally disappointing."

UNIT 4 POLITICAL ECONOMY AND INSTITUTIONS 183

advance the general welfare. The political power of the corporations exceeds that of the people, so many nations with democratic elections do not function as democracies. Anthony B. Kim, a policy analyst at the Heritage Foundation's Center for International Trade and Economics, contends that economic progress through advancing economic freedom has allowed more people to discuss and adopt different views more candidly, ultimately leading societies to be more open, inclusive, and democratic.

Joseph E. Stiglitz, University Professor at Columbia University, argues that the government plays an essential role in enabling the market to work properly. Capitalism runs amok if it is not regulated to protect against abuse and ensure fairness. Walter Williams, professor of economics at George Mason University, argues that the founders defined a small role for government in the Constitution and protected the freedom of individuals. Now the role of government is increasing and individual freedoms are declining. The free market has achieved great prosperity for America and the intervention of government has had net negative impacts.

David Coates presents the argument for welfare reform, which is that most poverty is self-induced; the previous welfare program created poverty and many other problems; and the reform reduces poverty, improves the lives of the people who left welfare, and solves other problems. Stephanie Mencimer, staff reporter for *Mother Jones,* does not denigrate the current welfare law but documents the horrible way welfare is administered in many states. Many welfare workers deny many benefits to many people who qualify for welfare. Thus, many welfare benefits do not reach the poor.

Herbert Kleber, the executive vice president of the Center on Addiction and Substance Abuse (CASA), and Joseph Califano, founder of CASA, maintain that drug laws should remain restrictive because legalization would result in increased use, especially by children. Kleber and Califano contend that drug legalization would not eliminate drug-related violence and harm caused by drugs. Author Peter Gorman states that restrictive drug laws have been ineffective. He notes that drug use and drug addiction have increased since drug laws became more stringent. Despite the crackdown on drug use, the availability of drugs has increased while the cost of drugs has decreased. In addition, restrictive drug laws, says Gorman, are racist and endanger civil liberties.

Issue 18.   Are We Headed Toward a Nuclear 9/11?   354

Brian Michael Jenkins, senior advisor to the president of the Rand Corporation, in testimony before the U.S. Senate Committee on Homeland Security and Governmental Affairs, posited that a team of terrorists could be inserted into the United States and carry out a Mumbai-style attack, as terrorism has "increasingly become an effective strategic weapon." Graham Allison, Harvard professor and director of the Belfer Center for Science and International Affairs, affirms that we are not likely to experience a nuclear 9/11 because "nuclear terrorism is preventable by a feasible, affordable agenda of actions that . . . would shrink the risk of nuclear terrorism to nearly zero."

Issue 19.   Is Torture Ever Justified?   366

Bagaric and Clarke remind us, first of all, that torture, although prohibited by international law, is nevertheless widely practiced. A rational examination of torture and a consideration of hypothetical (but realistic) cases show that torture is justifiable in order to prevent great harm. Torture should be regulated and carefully practiced as an information-gathering technique in extreme cases. Philosopher Philip E. Devine argues for an absolute (or virtually absolute) position against torture. Devine suggests that the wrongness of torture and the repugnance that we feel toward it ultimately go beyond any moral theory. In addition, the examination of extreme cases should not inform our general thought about these and other matters.

Freelance writer Joshua Holland and Paul Krugman, Nobel laureate economist and professor of economics and international affairs at the Woodrow Wilson School of Public and International Affairs at Princeton University, argue that while unemployment is high, the government must stimulate the economy to produce many more jobs and thus more earnings, which will increase spending, which will stimulate more business and jobs and more spending, and so on. When the economy has recovered, the government should institute policies to reduce the debt. Dwight R. Lee, the O'Neil Professor of Global Markets and Freedom in the Cox School of Business at Southern Methodist University, argues that the Keynesian approach of Paul Krugman and others will have disastrous results for America. The Keynesian prescriptions are reasonable in the abstract, but when filtered through the political system controlled by special interests, the results are some short-run benefits but long-run costs including relative economic stagnation.

Aaron Smith, senior research specialist of the Pew Research Center, presents the findings of his research project based on interviews in 2011 of 1,015 networking site users who reported on how they used social media. Their major use was for keeping in touch with family and current friends, and 87 percent also used it to connect with out-of-touch old friends. Janna Quitney Anderson of Elon University and Lee Rainie, research specialist of the Pew Research Center's Internet and American Life Project, report the findings of an opt-in online survey in 2011 of a diverse but nonrandom sample of 2021 technology stakeholders and critics who report their expert opinion on the impacts of social media on the users. They report many positive and negative impacts.

Correlation Guide

The *Taking Sides* series presents current issues in a debate-style format designed to stimulate student interest and develop critical thinking skills. Each issue is thoughtfully framed with an issue summary, an issue introduction, and a postscript. The pro and con essays—selected for their liveliness and substance—represent the arguments of leading scholars and commentators in their fields.

Taking Sides: Clashing Views on Social Issues, 17/e, Expanded is an easy-to-use reader that presents issues on important topics such as *sex roles, stratification and inequality, political economy, crime,* and *social control.* For more information on *Taking Sides* and other *McGraw-Hill Contemporary Learning Series* titles, visit www.mhhe.com/cls.

This convenient guide matches the issues in **Taking Sides: Social Issues, 17/e, Expanded** with the corresponding chapters in three of our best-selling McGraw-Hill Sociology textbooks by Croteau/Hoynes, Witt, and Schaefer.

Taking Sides: Social Issues, 17/e, Expanded	Experience Sociology, by Croteau/Hoynes	SOC 2013, 3/e by Witt	Sociology Matters, 6/e by Schaefer
Issue 1: Does the Media Have a Liberal Bias?	**Chapter 14:** Media and Consumption	**Chapter 5:** Social Structure and Interaction	**Chapter 3:** Social Interaction, Groups, and Social Structure
Issue 2: Is Third World Immigration a Threat to America's Way of Life?	**Chapter 3:** Culture **Chapter 4:** Social Structure **Chapter 15:** Communities, the Environment, and Health **Chapter 17:** Social Change: Globalization, Population and Social Movements	**Chapter 3:** Culture **Chapter 9:** Government and Economy **Chapter 15:** Social Change	**Chapter 2:** Culture and Socialization **Chapter 9:** Social Institutions: Education, Government, and the Economy **Chapter 10:** Population, Community, Health, and the Environment **Chapter 11:** Social Movements, Social Change, and Technology
Issue 3: Does Divorce Have Long-Term Damaging Effects on Children?	**Chapter 12:** Family and Religion	**Chapter 7:** Families	**Chapter 8:** Social Institutions: Family and Religion
Issue 4: Are Professional Women "Opting Out" of Work by Choice?	**Chapter 1:** Sociology in Changing Times **Chapter 4:** Social Structure **Chapter 11:** Gender and Sexuality	**Chapter 10:** Social Class **Chapter 5:** Social Structure and Interaction **Chapter 12:** Gender and Sexuality	**Chapter 3:** Social Interaction, Groups, and Social Structure **Chapter 7:** Inequality by Gender

Taking Sides: Social Issues, 17/e, Expanded	Experience Sociology, by Croteau/Hoynes	SOC 2013, 3/e by Witt	Sociology Matters, 6/e by Schaefer
Issue 5: Should Same-Sex Marriages Be Legally Recognized?	**Chapter 1:** Sociology in Changing Times **Chapter 11:** Gender and Sexuality	**Chapter 12:** Gender and Sexuality **Chapter 15:** Social Change	**Chapter 7:** Inequality by Gender **Chapter 8:** Social Institutions: Family and Religion
Issue 6: Is Increasing Economic Inequality a Serious Problem?	**Chapter 9:** Class and Global Inequality **Chapter 16:** Politics and the Economy	**Chapter 9:** Government and Economy **Chapter 10:** Social Class **Chapter 11:** Global Inequality	**Chapter 5:** Stratification in the United States and Global Inequality **Chapter 9:** Social Institutions: Education, Government, and the Economy
Issue 7: Is America Close to Being a Post-Racial Society?	**Chapter 10:** Race and Ethnicity	**Chapter 13:** Race and Ethnicity	**Chapter 5:** Stratification in the United States and Global Inequality **Chapter 6:** Inequality by Race and Ethnicity
Issue 8: Has Feminism Benefited American Society?	**Chapter 11:** Gender and Sexuality	**Chapter 12:** Gender and Sexuality	**Chapter 3:** Social Interaction, Groups, and Social Structure **Chapter 5:** Stratification in the United States and Global Inequality **Chapter 7:** Inequality by Gender
Issue 9: Is the Gender Wage Gap Justified?	**Chapter 9:** Class and Global Inequality **Chapter 11:** Gender and Sexuality **Chapter 13:** Education and Work	**Chapter 10:** Social Class **Chapter 11:** Global Inequality **Chapter 12:** Gender and Sexuality	**Chapter 5:** Stratification in the United States and Global Inequality **Chapter 7:** Inequality by Gender **Chapter 9:** Social Institutions: Education, Government, and the Economy
Issue 10: Is Government Dominated by Big Business?	**Chapter 5:** Power **Chapter 16:** Politics and the Economy	**Chapter 9:** Government and Economy	**Chapter 9:** Social Institutions: Education, Government, and the Economy **Chapter 10:** Population, Community, Health, and the Environment
Issue 11: Does Capitalism Undermine Democracy?	**Chapter 16:** Politics and the Economy **Chapter 17:** Social Change: Globalization, Population and Social Movements	**Chapter 9:** Government and Economy	**Chapter 9:** Social Institutions: Education, Government, and the Economy **Chapter 10:** Population, Community, Health, and the Environment
Issue 12: Should Government Intervene in a Capitalist Economy?	**Chapter 16:** Politics and the Economy **Chapter 17:** Social Change: Globalization, Population and Social Movements	**Chapter 9:** Government and Economy	**Chapter 9:** Social Institutions: Education, Government, and the Economy **Chapter 10:** Population, Community, Health, and the Environment

(Continued)

Taking Sides: Social Issues, 17/e, Expanded	Experience Sociology, by Croteau/Hoynes	SOC 2013, 3/e by Witt	Sociology Matters, 6/e by Schaefer
Issue 13: Was the Welfare Reform the Right Approach to Poverty?	**Chapter 4:** Social Structure **Chapter 16:** Politics and the Economy **Chapter 17:** Social Change: Globalization, Population and Social Movements	**Chapter 5:** Social Structure and Interaction **Chapter 9:** Government and Economy	**Chapter 9:** Social Institutions: Education, Government, and the Economy **Chapter 11:** Social Movements, Social Change, and Technology
Issue 14: Is No Child Left Behind Irretrievably Flawed?	**Chapter 13:** Education and Work	**Chapter 8:** Education and Religion	**Chapter 9:** Social Institutions: Education, Government, and the Economy
Issue 15: Should Biotechnology Be Used to Alter and Enhance Humans?	**Chapter 2:** Understanding the Research Process	**Chapter 2:** Sociological Research **Chapter 14:** Health, Medicine and Environment	**Chapter 1:** The Sociological View **Chapter 11:** Social Movements, Social Change, and Technology
Issue 16: Is Street Crime More Harmful than White-collar Crime?	**Chapter 8:** Deviance and Social Control	**Chapter 6:** Deviance	**Chapter 4:** Deviance and Social Control
Issue 17: Should Laws Against Drug Use Remain Restrictive?	**Chapter 8:** Deviance and Social Control	**Chapter 6:** Deviance **Chapter 14:** Health, Medicine and Environment	**Chapter 4:** Deviance and Social Control
Issue 18: Are We Headed Toward a Nuclear 9/11?	**Chapter 16:** Politics and the Economy **Chapter 17:** Social Change: Globalization, Population and Social Movements	**Chapter 9:** Government and Economy **Chapter 15:** Social Change	**Chapter 9:** Social Institutions: Education, Government, and the Economy **Chapter 11:** Social Movements, Social Change, and Technology
Issue 19: Is Torture Ever Justified?	**Chapter 16:** Politics and the Economy **Chapter 17:** Social Change: Globalization, Population and Social Movements	**Chapter 9:** Government and Economy **Chapter 15:** Social Change	**Chapter 9:** Social Institutions: Education, Government, and the Economy **Chapter 11:** Social Movements, Social Change, and Technology
Issue 20: Does Immigration Benefit the Economy?	**Chapter 16:** Politics and the Economy **Chapter 17:** Social Change: Globalization, Population and Social Movements	**Chapter 9:** Government and Economy **Chapter 15:** Social Change	**Chapter 9:** Social Institutions: Education, Government, and the Economy **Chapter 10:** Population, Community, Health, and the Environment **Chapter 11:** Social Movements, Social Change, and Technology

Taking Sides: Social Issues, 17/e, Expanded	Experience Sociology, by Croteau/Hoynes	SOC 2013, 3/e by Witt	Sociology Matters, 6/e by Schaefer
Issue 21: Is Humankind Dangerously Harming the Environment?	**Chapter 15:** Communities, the Environment, and Health **Chapter 17:** Social Change: Globalization, Population and Social Movements	**Chapter 14:** Health, Medicine and Environment	**Chapter 10:** Population, Community, Health, and the Environment **Chapter 11:** Social Movements, Social Change, and Technology
Issue 22: Is Economic Globalization Good for Both Rich and Poor?	**Chapter 15:** Communities, the Environment, and Health **Chapter 16:** Politics and the Economy **Chapter 17:** Social Change: Globalization, Population and Social Movements	**Chapter 9:** Government and Economy **Chapter 10:** Social Class **Chapter 15:** Social Change	**Chapter 9:** Social Institutions: Education, Government, and the Economy **Chapter 9:** Social Institutions: Education, Government, and the Economy **Chapter 10:** Population, Community, Health, and the Environment **Chapter 11:** Social Movements, Social Change, and Technology
Issue 23: Is Stimulus the Best Way to Get the American Economy Back on Its Feet?	**Chapter 16:** Politics and the Economy	**Chapter 9:** Government and Economy	**Chapter 9:** Social Institutions: Education, Government, and the Economy
Issue 24: Does Social Media Have Largely Positive Impacts on Its Users?	**Chapter 14:** Media and Consumption **Chapter 17:** Social Change: Globalization, Population and Social Movements	**Chapter 3:** Culture **Chapter 15:** Social Change	**Chapter 11:** Social Movements, Social Change, and Technology

Topic Guide

This topic guide suggests how the selections in this book relate to the subjects covered in your course. You may want to use the topics listed on these pages to search the Web more easily. On the following pages a number of websites have been gathered specifically for this book. They are arranged to reflect the units of this *Taking Sides* reader. You can link to these sites by going to www.mhhe.com/cls/. All the articles that relate to each topic are listed below the bold-faced term.

Biology

15. Should Biotechnology Be Used to Alter and Enhance Humans?

Business

10. Is Government Dominated by Big Business?
16. Is Street Crime More Harmful Than White-Collar Crime?

Capitalism

10. Is Government Dominated by Big Business?
11. Does Capitalism Undermine Democracy?
12. Should Government Intervene in a Capitalist Economy?

Crime

16. Is Street Crime More Harmful Than White-Collar Crime?

Divorce

3. Does Divorce Have Long-Term Damaging Effects on Children?

Drugs

17. Should Laws Against Drug Use Remain Restrictive?

Economics

6. Is Increasing Economic Inequality a Serious Problem?
9. Is the Gender Wage Gap Justified?
20. Does Immigration Benefit the Economy?
22. Is Economic Globalization Good for Both Rich and Poor?

23. Is Stimulus the Best Way to Get the American Economy Back on Its Feet?

Education

14. Is No Child Left Behind Irretrievably Flawed?

Environment

21. Is Humankind Dangerously Harming the Environment?

Family

3. Does Divorce Have Long-Term Damaging Effects on Children?

Gender

4. Are Professional Women "Opting Out" of Work by Choice?
5. Should Same-Sex Marriages Be Legally Recognized?
8. Has Feminism Benefited American Society?
9. Is the Gender Wage Gap Justified?

Government/Politics

1. Does the Media Have a Liberal Bias?
2. Is Third World Immigration a Threat to America's Way of Life?
10. Is Government Dominated by Big Business?
11. Does Capitalism Undermine Democracy?
12. Should Government Intervene in a Capitalist Economy?
14. Is No Child Left Behind Irretrievably Flawed?
23. Is Stimulus the Best Way to Get the American Economy Back on Its Feet?

Immigration

Inequality

Legal Issues

Media

Nuclear War

Poverty

Racism

Science

Society

Technology

Welfare

Women's Issues

Torture

Introduction

Debating Social Issues

Kurt Finsterbusch

What Is Sociology?

"I have become a problem to myself," St. Augustine said. Put into a social and secular framework, St. Augustine's concern marks the starting point of sociology. We have become a problem to ourselves, and it is sociology that seeks to understand the problem and, perhaps, to find some solutions. The subject matter of sociology, then, is ourselves—people interacting with one another in groups and organizations.

Although the subject matter of sociology is very familiar, it is often useful to look at it in an unfamiliar light, one that involves a variety of theories and perceptual frameworks. In fact, to properly understand social phenomena, it *should* be looked at from several different points of view. In practice, however, this may lead to more friction than light, especially when each view proponent says, "I am right and you are wrong," rather than, "My view adds considerably to what your view has shown."

Sociology, as a science of society, was developed in the nineteenth century. Auguste Comte (1798–1857), the French mathematician and philosopher who is considered to be the father of sociology, had a vision of a well-run society based on social science knowledge. Sociologists (Comte coined the term) would discover the laws of social life and then determine how society should be structured and run. Society would not become perfect, because some problems are intractable, but he believed that a society guided by scientists and other experts was the best possible society.

Unfortunately, Comte's vision was extremely naive. For most matters of state there is no one best way of structuring or doing things that sociologists can discover and recommend. Instead, sociologists debate more social issues than they resolve.

The purpose of sociology is to throw light on social issues and their relationship to the complex, confusing, and dynamic social world around us. It seeks to describe how society is organized and how individuals fit into it. But neither the organization of society nor the fit of individuals is perfect. Social disorganization is a fact of life—at least in modern, complex societies such as the one we live in. Here, perfect harmony continues to elude us, and "social problems" are endemic. The very institutions, laws, and policies that produce benefits also produce what sociologists call "unintended effects"—unintended and undesirable. The changes that please one sector of the society may displease another, or the changes that seem so indisputably healthy at first turn out to have a dark underside to them. The examples are endless. Modern urban life gives people privacy and freedom from snooping neighbors that the small town never afforded; yet that very privacy seems to breed an uneasy sense of anonymity and loneliness. Take another example: Hierarchy is necessary for organizations to function efficiently, but hierarchy leads to the creation of a ruling elite. Flatten out the hierarchy and you may achieve social equality—but at the price of confusion, incompetence, and low productivity.

This is not to say that all efforts to effect social change are ultimately futile and that the only sound view is the tragic one that concludes "nothing works." We can be realistic without falling into despair. In many respects, the human condition has improved over the centuries and has improved as a result of conscious social policies. But improvements are purchased at a price—not only a monetary price but one involving human discomfort and discontent. The job of policymakers is to balance the anticipated benefits against the probable costs.

It can never hurt policymakers to know more about the society in which they work or the social issues they confront. That, broadly speaking, is the purpose of sociology. It is what this book is about. This volume examines issues that are central to the study of sociology.

Culture and Values

A common value system is the major mechanism for integrating a society, but modern societies contain so many different groups with differing ideas and values that integration must be built as much on tolerance of differences as on common values. Furthermore, technology and social conditions change, so values must adjust to new situations, often weakening old values. Some people (often called *conservatives*) will defend the old values. Others (often called *liberals*) will make concessions to allow for change. For example, the protection of human life is a sacred value to most people, but some would compromise that value when the life involved is a 90-year-old comatose man on life-support machines, who had signed a document indicating that he did not want to be kept alive under those conditions. The conservative would counter that once we make the value of human life relative, we become dangerously open to greater evils—that perhaps society will come to think it acceptable to terminate all sick, elderly people undergoing expensive treatments. This is only one example of how values are hotly debated today.

Two debates on values are presented in Unit 1. Issue 1 examines a major institution that can be seen as responsible for instilling values and culture in people—the media. This issue focuses in particular on whether the news reporters and anchorpersons report and comment on the news with professional objectivity and relatively bias free. Fred Barnes argues that the major news outlets are liberal and hire liberal journalists. The selection and reporting of news, therefore, has a liberal bias. In contrast, Robert F. Kennedy Jr. counters that most people get their news from conservative sources and believe many conservative myths as a result. Issue 2 concerns the cultural and economic impact of immigration. Mark Krikorian argues that America has changed in ways that make immigration less beneficial than in the past. The main problem is that America does not assimilate immigrants as well as in the past. Jason L. Riley, on the other hand, praises immigrants for the way they assimilate. They are like Americans in being hard working and strong on family values. Immigration also helps economic growth. America's flexible labor market enables newcomers to find jobs where they are needed. America also has had a labor shortage except in recessions like that happening currently, so immigrants generally take few jobs from American citizens.

Sex Roles, Gender, and the Family

An area that has experienced tremendous value change in the last several decades is sex roles and the family. Women in large numbers have rejected major aspects of their traditional gender roles and family roles while remaining strongly committed to much of the mother role and to many feminine characteristics. Men have changed much less, but their situation has changed considerably. Issue 3 examines the consequences of divorce on children, because it has become so common. Elizabeth Marquardt presents evidence that divorce damages children, but Constance Ahrons counters that her research with children of divorced parents shows otherwise. Issue 4 considers one of the current strains on mothers—the conflict between career and childrearing. Linda Hirshman argues that many professional women with husbands who are good providers "opt out" of work and focus on their family roles. This pattern suggests that many more women would do the same if their conditions allowed them this choice. If this is so, what is going on? Are women who can afford to leave work going home because the work situation is inadvertently pushing women home as Hirshman concludes or are women forced home because their husbands fail to pick up much of the parenting and home care work as Pamela Stone concludes? In either case women get the bad end of the deal. Issue 5 debates whether same-sex marriages should be legal. The Human Rights Campaign presents all the arguments in its favor and Peter Sprigg presents all the arguments against it.

Stratification and Inequality

Issue 6 centers around a sociological debate about whether or not increasing economic inequality is a serious problem. James Kurth asserts that it is, while Gary S. Becker and Kevin M. Murphy argue that the increasing inequality is largely the result of the education premium, which, in turn, encourages young people to get more education and better themselves. Today one of the most controversial issues regarding inequalities is the position of blacks in American society. Is the election of Barack Obama an indicator that America is now a post-racial society, meaning that blacks and whites are essentially on equal footing? In Issue 7, Alvin Poussaint interprets the election of Barack Obama as a sign that America has turned a significant corner in race relations and that now young blacks have a role model that allows them to dream the highest dreams. Lawrence D. Bobo looks under the surface reality and explains the many subtle ways that racism still operates in America. Issue 8 covers a major transformation in American stratification, which has been the dramatic change in women's position in society. The feminist movement was a major force in changing women's roles. Not all women, however, believe that the feminist movement has benefited society. In this vein, Kate O'Beirne blasts the feminist movement while Barbara Epstein praises feminists for the great things that they accomplished. Issue 9 deals with the gender wage gap. Why do full-time women workers make only 72 percent of men measured by median income? J. R. Shackleton argues that the wage gap is justified because it is the outcome of women's free choices. To have time and energy to be good mothers and housewives, many of them seek less demanding jobs. Hilary M. Lips rejects the supposition that women's choices cause the gap but blames it largely on discrimination, prejudice, and stereotypes.

Political Economy and Institutions

Sociologists study not only the poor, the workers, and the victims of discrimination but also those at the top of society—those who occupy what the late sociologist C. Wright Mills used to call "the command posts." The question is whether the "pluralist" model or the "power elite" model is the one that best fits the facts in America. Does a single power elite rule the United States, or do many groups contend for power and influence so that the political process is accessible to all? In Issue 10, G. William Domhoff argues that the "owners and top-level managers in large income-producing properties are far and away the dominant power figures in the United States" and have a dominating influence in government decisions. Sheldon Kamieniecki's research tells a different story. He finds that business interests do not participate at a high rate in policy issues that affect them, have mixed results when they do, and often lose out to opposing interest groups.

Another major political economy issue is whether capitalism supports or undermines democracy. In Issue 11, Robert B. Reich argues that capitalism undermines democracy by preventing the government from serving the public good and advancing the general welfare. The political power of the corporations is greater than the influence of the people, so nominal democracies do not function as democracies. Anthony B. Kim disagrees. Economic progress advances economic freedom, public discussion, multiplication of ideas, openness, and eventually democracy. He presents data to show this.

The United States is a capitalist welfare state, and the role of the state in capitalism (more precisely, the market) and in welfare is examined in the next two issues. Issue 12 considers whether or not the government should step in and attempt to correct for the failures of the market through regulations, policies, and programs. Joseph E. Stiglitz argues that government intervention is necessary to make markets work well and to prevent various harms to society. Walter Williams argues that the Constitution sought to protect the freedom of individuals, so it strictly limited the role of government. Regrettably the role of government has increased and individual freedoms have decreased. The free market has achieved great prosperity for America but the intervention of government has had net negative effects. One way in which the government intervenes in the economy is by providing welfare to people who cannot provide for their own needs in the labor market. Issue 13 debates the wisdom of the Work Opportunity Reconciliation Act of 1996, which ended Aid to Families of Dependent Children (which was what most people equated with welfare). David Coates presents the argument that the welfare reform was a great success because it greatly reduced welfare rolls and dramatically increased the employment of welfare mothers. Stephanie Mencimer tells a different story. She documents the horrible way welfare is administered in many states. Many welfare workers deny many benefits to many people who qualify for welfare. Thus, many welfare benefits do not reach the poor.

Education is one of the biggest jobs of the government as well as the key to individual prosperity and the success of the economy. For decades the American system of education has been severely criticized. Such an important institution is destined to be closely scrutinized, and many reforms have been attempted. The main policy that is trying to improve public schools today is No Child Left Behind (NCLB). Issue 14 debates whether this policy is improving or worsening America's schools. It was proposed by Bush in 2002 and passed with strong bipartisan support. It is based on high standards and measurable goals which are set and monitored by the states. The students' scores determine the performance scores of the schools, which are the basis for rewards and punishments for the schools including closing bad performing schools. Dianne Piché argues that NCLB is successful because test scores have noticeably improved. Sharon Nichols and David Berliner argue that teachers have to teach to the test and devote most of their attention to the slower students which debases the education of the better students.

The final issue in this section deals with a set of concerns about the use of present and soon-to-emerge biotechnologies. The value of biotechnologies for healing people is accepted by all. Issue 15, however, debates their use to alter and enhance humans. The President's Council on Bioethics describes how biotechnologies could improve the genes of babies and enhance everyone. The arguments against such practices are present by Michael Sandel.

Crime and Social Control

Crime is interesting to sociologists because crimes are those activities that society makes illegal and will use force to stop. Why are some acts made illegal and others (even those that may be more harmful) not made illegal? Surveys indicate that concern about crime is extremely high in America. Is the fear of crime, however, rightly placed? Americans fear mainly street crime, but Jeffrey Reiman argues in Issue 16 that corporate crime—also known as "white-collar crime"—causes far more death, harm, and financial loss to Americans than does street crime. In contrast, David A. Anderson calculates the full costs of crime, both direct and indirect, and concludes that the costs of murder and theft far exceed the cost of white-collar crime. These contradictory findings result from differing definitions of white-collar crime. A prominent aspect of the crime picture is the illegal drug trade. It has such bad consequences that some people are seriously talking about legalizing drugs in order to kill the illegal drug business. In Issue 17, Herbert Kleber and Joseph Califano disagree. They think that drug laws should remain restrictive because legalization would result in increased use, especially by children. They contend that drug legalization would not eliminate drug-related violence but would increase the harm caused by drugs. Peter Gorman thinks that the drug laws are harmful and should be repealed. Restrictive drug laws have been ineffective. He notes that drug use and drug addiction have increased since drug laws became more stringent. Despite the crackdown on drug use, the availability of drugs has increased while the cost of drugs has decreased. In addition, restrictive drug laws, says Gorman, are racist and endanger civil liberties.

Issue 18 deals with terrorism with weapons of mass destruction, perhaps the major problem in America today. According to Brian Michael Jenkins, a team of terrorists could easily be inserted into the United States and carry out a terrorist attack with a nuclear or radiological bomb. Graham Allison argues that we are not likely to experience a nuclear 9/11 because our counter-terrorist capacities have reduced the risk of nuclear terrorism to nearly zero.

Issue 19 takes up the current debate about torture. When national interest is threatened, is torture justified? The Bush administration thought so but argued that the torture that they used was not torture. According to Bagaric and Clarke, the Bush administration is not unique. Most nations use torture when needed. Their justification is that torture is needed to prevent great harm. Philip E. Devine argues that torture is wrong and the end does not justify evil means.

The Future: Population/Environment/Society

Issue 20 deals with population migration. Does the recent and current immigration into the United States benefit or harm our economy? The recent Bush administration needed to know the answer to this question and their research concluded that immigration had a positive impact on the American economy. Steven A. Camarota disagrees. He argues that immigration's benefit to the economy is too small to support a pro-immigration policy. Since immigration reduces the income of the poor with whom many immigrants compete for jobs, immigration should be minimized.

Many social commentators speculate on "the fate of the earth." Issue 21 on the state of the planet addresses this concern. Some environmentalists view the future in apocalyptic terms. They see the possibility that the human race could degrade the environment to the point that population growth and increasing economic production could overshoot the carrying capacity of the globe. The resulting collapse could lead to the extinction of much of the human race and the end of free societies. Other analysts believe that these fears are groundless. In Issue 21, Lester R. Brown shows how human actions are degrading the environment in ways that adversely affect humans. In contrast, Bjorn Lomborg argues that the environment is improving in many ways and that environmental problems are manageable or will have only mildly adverse effects.

Issue 22 assesses the benefits and costs of globalization. Staff members of the International Monetary Fund examine the effects of globalization and conclude that economic globalization contributes greatly to world prosperity. Ravinder Rena disagrees. Globalization does produce many benefits but also produces many negative impacts. The poor and poorer countries are the most harmed by globalization, so it should be restrained.

Bonus Issues—Special Topics for Today

Issue 23 addresses a major debate of the day: how to get the economy growing again. One side argues that more stimulus is needed, and the other side argues that cutting government expenditures will get the country back on its feet. The stimulus view is promoted by Paul Krugman, who advocates the Keynesian view that until unemployment drops and idled assets are put back into production, government expenditures and tax cuts are needed to stimulate the economy. When the economy is healthy again, then the government must work on reducing the debt. The anti-Keynesian view, presented by Dwight R. Lee, believes the Krugman proposal is fiscally irresponsible and leads to slower economic growth over the long run. The Republicans generally support Lee's view, and the Democrats generally support Krugman's view. It looks like neither side will get its way, and both will be dissatisfied with the policies that will be enacted.

Issue 24 deals with social media and discusses its positive and negative effects. The list of effects is quite long, and opinions differ on how beneficial it is overall. A major use of social media is to connect with friends and family. This positive benefit is tempered somewhat by the fact that heavy social media use is associated with fewer face-to-face interactions with these very people. Social media is also very useful for many instrumental purposes, including getting information and conducting one's affairs. The debate, however, arises over the many negative aspects of the social media and how much they subtract from the positive benefits. There is a debate over how much social media hurts social relations relative to how much it helps social relationships. We obtain much information from social media, but we also obtain much misinformation from it. It leads to social connections but also to social isolation and depression and even personality disorders in some people (though not often). Further the loss of privacy has badly hurt some people. It is very hard to pull all the effects of social media together and come up with a clear view of its overall impact on individuals and society.

The Social Construction of Reality

An important idea in sociology is that people construct social reality in the course of interaction by attaching social meanings to the reality they are experiencing and then responding to those meanings. Two people can walk down a city street and derive very different meanings from what they see around them. Both, for example, may see homeless people—but they may see them in different contexts. One fits them into a picture of once-vibrant cities dragged into decay and ruin because of permissive policies that have encouraged pathological types to harass citizens; the other observer fits them into a picture of an America that can no longer hide the wretchedness of its poor. Both feel that they are seeing something deplorable, but their views of what makes it deplorable are radically opposed. Their differing views of what they have seen will lead to very different prescriptions for what should be done about the problem.

The social construction of reality is an important idea for this book because each author is socially constructing reality and working hard to persuade you to see his or her point of view, that is, to see the definition of the situation and the set of meanings he or she has assigned to the situation. In doing this, each author presents a carefully selected set of facts, arguments, and values. The arguments contain assumptions or theories, some of which are spelled out and some of which are unspoken. The critical reader has to judge the evidence for the facts, the logic and soundness of the arguments, the importance of the values, and whether or not omitted facts, theories, and values invalidate the thesis. This book facilitates this critical thinking process by placing authors in opposition. This puts the reader in the position of critically evaluating two constructions of reality for each issue instead of one.

Conclusion

Writing in the 1950s, a period that was in some ways like our own, the sociologist C. Wright Mills said that Americans know a lot about their "troubles," but they cannot make the connections between seemingly personal concerns and the concerns of others in the world. If they could only learn to make those connections, they could turn their concerns into *issues*. An issue transcends the realm of the personal. According to Mills, "An issue is a public matter: some value cherished by publics is felt to be threatened. Often there is a debate about what the value really is and what it is that really threatens it." It is not primarily personal troubles but social issues that I have tried to present in this book. The variety of topics in it can be taken as an invitation to discover what Mills called "the sociological imagination." This imagination, said Mills, "is the capacity to shift from one perspective to another—from the political to the psychological; from examination of a single family to comparative assessment of the national budgets of the world. . . . It is the capacity to range from the most impersonal and remote transformations to the most intimate features of the human self—and to see the relations between the two." This book, with a range of issues well suited to the sociological imagination, is intended to enlarge that capacity.

Internet References . . .

Internet Philosophical Resources on Moral Relativism

This website for *Ethics Updates* offers discussion questions, a bibliographical guide, and a list of Internet resources concerning moral relativism.

http://ethics.sandiego.edu/

The National Institute on Media and the Family

The National Institute on Media and the Family website is a national resource for teachers, parents, community leaders, and others who are interested in the influence of electronic media on early childhood education, child development, academic performance, culture, and violence.

www.mediafamily.org

The International Center for Migration, Ethnicity, and Citizenship

The International Center for Migration, Ethnicity, and Citizenship is engaged in scholarly research and public policy analysis bearing on international migration, refugees, and the incorporation of newcomers in host countries.

www.newschool.edu/icmec/

National Immigrant Forum

The National Immigrant Forum is a pro-immigrant organization that examines the effects of immigration on U.S. society. Click on the links for discussion of underground economies, immigrant economies, race and ethnic relations, and other topics.

www.immigrationforum.org

The National Network for Immigrant and Refugee Rights (NNIRR)

The National Network for Immigrant and Refugee Rights (NNIRR) serves as a forum to share information and analysis, to educate communities and the general public, and to develop and coordinate plans of action on important immigrant and refugee issues.

www.nnirr.org

Culture and Values

*S*ociologists recognize that a fairly strong consensus on the basic values of a society contributes greatly to the smooth functioning of that society. The functioning of modern, complex urban societies, however, often depends on the tolerance of cultural differences and equal rights and protections for all cultural groups. In fact, such societies can be enriched by the contributions of different cultures. But at some point the cultural differences may result in a pulling apart that exceeds the pulling together. Another cultural problem in America is whether the media has a bias that is significantly removed from the epicenter of American culture. The final problem is whether current immigrants to the United States bring appropriate values and skills.

- Does the Media Have a Liberal Bias?
- Is Third World Immigration a Threat to America's Way of Life?

ISSUE 1

Does the Media Have a Liberal Bias?

YES: Fred Barnes, from "Is the Mainstream Media Fair and Balanced?" *Imprimis* (August 2006)

NO: Robert F. Kennedy Jr., from "The Disinformation Society," *Crimes Against Nature* (Harper Perennial, 2005)

Learning Outcomes
After reading this issue, you should be able to: <ul><li>Understand how the media can be biased even when the writers or newscasters are trying to be fair and unbiased.</li><li>Assess the thesis that money controls the message in the media.</li><li>Explain how the professional value system of journalists affects their reporting.</li><li>Assess the importance of a media company or individual journalist having a reputation for unbiased reporting. In other words, how much do they lose by losing their professional reputation.</li><li>Comment on why people listen to reporters or programs with known ideological biases that obviously provide biased opinions. Does their audience care about the truthfulness of their reporting? If not, why not?</li><li>Analyze what forces make reporters accountable. How well do they work? What are the consequences when they do not work well?</li><li>Evaluate the arguments for the media being liberal.</li><li>Evaluate the arguments for the media being conservative.</li></ul>

ISSUE SUMMARY

YES: Fred Barnes, journalist, executive editor of *The Weekly Standard* and TV commentator, argues that the mainstream media has a pronounced liberal bias. They do not hire conservatives, and an analysis of specific news stories shows their bias.

NO: Robert F. Kennedy Jr., environmentalist and political activist, agrees with Barnes that the media is biased but believes that it has a conservative bias. Surveys show that most Americans have many false beliefs that are fed to them by conservative talk radio shows and other conservative media outlets. Many media owners are very conservative and stifle investigative reporting.

"**A** small group of men, numbering perhaps no more than a dozen 'anchormen,' commentators and executive producers . . . decide what forty to fifty million Americans will learn of the day's events in the nation and the world." The speaker was Spiro Agnew, vice president of the United States during the Nixon administration. The thesis of Agnew's speech, delivered to an audience of midwestern Republicans in 1969, was that the television news media are controlled by a small group of liberals who foist their liberal opinions on viewers under the guise of "news." The upshot of this control, said Agnew, "is that a narrow and distorted picture of America often emerges from the televised news." Many Americans, even many of those who were later shocked by revelations that Agnew took bribes while serving in public office, agreed with Agnew's critique of the "liberal media."

Politicians' complaints about unfair news coverage go back much farther than Agnew and the Nixon administration. The third president of the United States, Thomas Jefferson, was an eloquent champion of the press, but after 6 years as president, he could hardly contain his bitterness. "The man who never looks into a newspaper," he wrote, "is better informed than he who reads them, inasmuch as he who knows nothing is nearer to truth than he whose mind is filled with falsehoods and errors."

The press today is much different than it was in Jefferson's day. Newspapers then were pressed in hand-operated frames in many little printing shops around the country; everything was local and decentralized, and each paper averaged a few hundred subscribers. Today, newspaper chains have taken over most of the once independent local newspapers. Other newspapers, like *The New York Times* and *The Washington Post*, enjoy nationwide prestige and help set the nation's news agenda. Geographical centralization is even more obvious in the case of television. About 70 percent of the national news on television comes from three networks whose programming originates in New York City.

A second important difference between the media of the eighteenth century and the media today has to do with the ideal of "objectivity." In past eras, newspapers were frankly partisan sheets, full of nasty barbs at the politicians and parties the editors did not like; they made no distinction between "news" and "editorials." The ideal of objective journalism is a relatively recent development, tracing back to the early years of the twentieth century. Disgusted with the sensationalist "yellow journalism" of the time, intellectual leaders urged newspapers to cultivate a core of professionals who would concentrate on accurate reporting and who would leave their opinions to the editorial page. Journalism schools cropped up around the country, helping to promote the ideal of objectivity. Although some journalists now openly scoff at it, the ideal still commands the respect—in theory, if not always in practice—of working reporters.

These two historical developments, news centralization and news professionalism, play off against one another in the current debate over news "bias." The question of bias was irrelevant when the press was a scatter of little independent newspapers. Bias started to become an important question when newspapers became dominated by chains, and airwaves by networks, and when a few national press leaders like *The New York Times* and *The Washington Post* began to emerge. Although these "mainstream" news outlets have been challenged in recent years by opinions expressed in a variety of alternative media—such as cable television, talk radio, newsletters, and computer mail—they still remain powerful conveyers of news.

Is media news reporting biased? The media constitutes a major socializing institution, so this is an important question. Defenders of the media usually hold that although journalists, like all human beings, have biases, their professionalism compels them to report news with considerable objectivity. Media critics insist that journalists constantly interject their biases into their news reports. The critics, however, often disagree about whether such bias is liberal or conservative, as is the case with this issue. In the following selections, Fred Barnes argues that the news media tilt to the left, whereas Robert F. Kennedy Jr. contends that the slant of the news media to which most people are exposed supports a conservative status quo.

Of course, a third possibility is that both views are right. Let's assume that there are biases on the left as Barnes argues and there are biases on the right as Kennedy argues. What is the net effect? One possibility is that biased people can find biased reporting to confirm their biases. That would make their biases stronger and people on opposite sides of issues would find it increasingly difficult to compromise with the other side. Ill will would also increase and possibly threaten the unifying forces that are essential to the survival of democracy. Many commentators today have expressed grave concerns about the level of hostility between Democrats and Republicans and between opponents on many issues. How much deeper can the chasms get? What can bring us back together and unite us?

YES

Fred Barnes

Is the Mainstream Media Fair and Balanced?

Let me begin by defining three terms that are thrown around in debates about the media today. The first is objectivity, which means reporting the news with none of your own political views or instincts slanting the story one way or another. Perfect objectivity is pretty hard for anyone to attain, but it can be approximated. Then there's fairness. Fairness concedes that there may be some slant in a news story, but requires that a reporter will be honest and not misleading with regard to those with whom he disagrees. And finally there's balance, which means that both sides on an issue or on politics in general—or more than two sides, when there are more than two—get a hearing.

My topic today is how the mainstream media—meaning nationally influential newspapers like the *Washington Post*, the *New York Times*, the *Wall Street Journal* and *USA Today*; influential regional papers like the *Miami Herald*, the *Chicago Tribune* and the *Los Angeles Times*; the broadcast networks and cable news stations like CNN; and the wire services, which now are pretty much reduced to the Associated Press—stacks up in terms of the latter two journalistic standards, fairness and balance. In my opinion, they don't stack up very well.

Twenty years ago I wrote a piece in *The New Republic* entitled "Media Realignment," and the thrust of it was that the mainstream media was shedding some of its liberal slant and moving more to the center. This was in the Reagan years, and I pointed to things like *USA Today*, which was then about five years old and was a champion of the Reagan economic recovery. CNN was younger then, too, and quite different from the way it is now; Ted Turner owned it, but he wasn't manipulating it the way he did later, which turned it into something quite different. Financial news was suddenly very big in the midst of the 401 (k) revolution, and the stock market boom was getting a lot of coverage. *The New Republic*, where I worked, had been pro-Stalin in the 1930s, but by the 1980s had become very pro-Reagan and anti-communist on foreign policy. I also cited a rise of new conservative columnists like George Will. But looking back on that piece now, I see that I couldn't have been more wrong. The idea that the mainstream media was moving to the center was a mirage. In fact, I would say that compared to what I was writing about back in the 1980s, the mainstream media today is more liberal, more elitist, more secular, more biased, more hostile to conservatives and Republicans, and more self-righteous.

Reprinted by permission from *Imprimis*, the national speech digest of Hillsdale College, www.hillsdale.edu. SUBSCRIPTION FREE UPON REQUEST. ISSN 0277-8432. Imprimis trademark registered in U.S. Patent and Trade Office #1563325.

Liberal and Impenetrable

Liberalism is endemic in the mainstream media today. Evan Thomas—the deputy editor of *Newsweek* and one of the honest liberals in the media—noted this very thing with regard to coverage of the 2004 presidential race, which I'll discuss later. It was obvious, he said, that the large majority in the media wanted John Kerry to win and that this bias slanted their coverage. And indeed, every poll of the media—and there have been a lot of them—shows that they're liberal, secular and so on. Polls of the Washington press corps, for instance, about who they voted for in 2004 always show that nine-to-one or ten-to-one of them voted Democratic. Peter Brown, a columnist who just recently left the *Orlando Sentinel*, conducted a poll a few years ago of newspaper staffs all around the country—not just at the big papers, but midsize papers and even some small papers—and found that this disparity existed everywhere.

Nor is this likely to change. Hugh Hewitt, the California lawyer and blogger and talk radio host, spent a few days recently at the Columbia Journalism School, supposedly the premiere journalism school in America. He spoke to a couple of classes there and polled them on who they had voted for. He found only one Bush voter in all the classes he spoke to. Steve Hayes, a fine young writer and reporter at *The Weekly Standard*, went to Columbia Journalism School and says that during his time there he was one of only two or three conservative students out of hundreds.

This is not to say that there aren't many fine young conservative journalists. But they aren't likely to be hired in the mainstream media. When I was at *The New Republic* for ten years—and *The New Republic* was quite liberal, despite its hawkish foreign policy—any young person who joined the staff and wrote stories that were interesting and demonstrated that he or she could write well was grabbed immediately by the *New York Times* or other big newspapers, *Newsweek*, *Time* or the networks. But that doesn't happen at *The Weekly Standard*, where I work now. Some of our young writers are the most talented I have ever met in my 30-plus years in journalism. But they don't get those phone calls. Why? Because they're with a conservative magazine. Of course there has been one famous exception—David Brooks, who is now the conservative columnist with the *New York Times*. But he was probably the least conservative person at *The Weekly Standard*. Conservatives are tokens on most editorial pages, just as they are on the broadcast networks and on cable news stations like CNN and MSNBC. Of course, I have a vested interest, since I work for FOX News; but if you compare the number of liberal commentators on FOX—and there are a lot of them—with the number of conservatives on those other stations, you'll see what I mean.

The fact is that the mainstream media doesn't want conservatives. It doesn't matter whether they're good reporters or writers. They go out of their way not to hire them. This was true 20 years ago, and it's true today. This impenetrability is why conservatives have had to erect the alternative media—talk radio, the blogs, conservative magazines and FOX News. Together, these form a real infrastructure that's an alternative to the mainstream media. But it's still a lot smaller, it's not as influential and it's largely reactive. It's not the equal of the mainstream media, that's for sure.

Powerful and Unfair

One way to see the unequaled power of the mainstream media is in how it is able to shape and create the stories that we're stuck talking about in America. A good example is Cindy Sheehan last summer. The Sheehan story was a total creation of the mainstream media. And in creating the story, the media shamelessly mischaracterized Sheehan. It portrayed her as simply a poor woman who wanted to see President Bush because her son had been killed in Iraq. Well, in the first place, she had already seen President Bush once. Also, though you would never know it from the dominant coverage, she was in favor of the Iraqi insurgency—the beheaders, the killers of innocent women and children. She was on their side, and she said so. She was also filled with a deep hatred of Israel. Yet the media treated her in a completely sympathetic manner, failing to report the beliefs that she made little attempt to hide. In any case, the Cindy Sheehan story came to dominate the news for the latter part of the summer; only the mainstream media still has the power to *make* stories big.

To see how distorted the mainstream media's view of the world can be, one need only compare its coverage of the Valerie Plame "leak" story with its coverage of the NSA surveillance leak story. Plame is the CIA agent whose name was written about by reporter Robert Novak in a column, following which the media portrayed her as having been outed as an undercover CIA agent. The simple facts from the beginning were that she was not an undercover agent any more; she was not even overseas. The story had no national security repercussions at all—none. But that didn't stop the media, which built the story up to great heights—apparently in the groundless hope that it would lead to an indictment of Karl Rove—and kept it front page news, at least intermittently, for what seemed like forever. The NSA surveillance story, on the other hand, also created by the media—this time pursuant to a real leak, and one that was clearly in violation of the law—had tremendous national security implications. After all, it revealed a secret and crucial program that was being used to uncover plots to bomb and massacre Americans and probably rendered that program no longer effective. Not only was this important story treated on an equal basis with the non-story of Valerie Plame, but the media was not interested, for the most part, in its national security repercussions. Instead the media mischaracterized the story as a "domestic spying scandal," suggesting constitutional overreach by the Bush administration. Well, a domestic spying story is exactly what the story was *not*. Those being spied on were Al-Qaeda members overseas who were using the telephone. If some of those calls were with people in the U.S., they were monitored for that reason only. But the media's stubborn mischaracterization of the story continued to frame the debate.

This brings me to the use of unfair and unbalanced labeling by the media. How often, if ever, have you heard or read the term "ultraliberal"? I don't think I've ever heard or read it. You'll hear and see the term "ultraconservative" a lot, but not "ultraliberal"—even though there are plenty of ultraliberals. Another widely used labeling term is "activist." If people are working to block a shopping center from being built or campaigning against Wal-Mart, they are called "activists." Of course, what the term "activist" means is *liberal*. But while conservatives are called conservatives by the media, liberals are "activists." For years we've seen something similar with regard to debates over judicial nominees. The Federalist Society, with which many conservative judicial nominees tend to be associated, is always referred to as the *conservative* Federalist Society, as if that's part of its name. But the groups opposing conservative nominees are rarely if ever labeled as liberal—giving the impression that they, unlike the Federalist Society, are somehow objective.

Related to this, I would mention that conservatives are often labeled in a way to suggest they are mean and hateful. Liberals criticize, but conservatives hate. Have you noticed that the media never characterizes individuals or groups as Bush haters? There are Bush critics, but there are no Bush haters—whereas in the Clinton years, critics of the president were often referred to as Clinton haters. I'm not saying that there weren't Clinton haters on the fringes in the 1990s. But far-left groups have been treated as acceptable . . . within the mainstream of American politics today by the media, while in truth they are as clearly animated by hatred as the most rabid anti-Clinton voices ever were.

Secular and Partisan Bias

With regard to religion, Christianity in particular—but also religious faith in general—is reflexively treated as something dangerous and pernicious by the mainstream media. Back in the early 1990s when I was still at *The New Republic*, I was invited to a dinner in Washington with Mario Cuomo. He was then governor of New York, and had invited several reporters to dinner because he was thinking about running for president. At one point that night he mentioned that he sent his children to Catholic schools in New York because he wanted them to be taught about a God-centered universe. This was in the context of expressing his whole-hearted support for public schools. But from the reaction, you would have thought he had said that one day a week he would bring out the snakes in his office and make policy decisions based on where they bit him. He was subsequently pummeled with stories about how improper it was for him, one, to send his kids to religious schools, and two, to talk about it. It was amazing. The most rigid form of secularism passes as the standard in mainstream journalism these days.

President Bush is similarly treated as someone who is obsessive about his religion. And what does he do? Well, he reads a devotional every day; he tries to get through the Bible, I think, once a year; and he prays. Now, I know many, many people who do this. Tens of millions of people do it. And yet the media treats Bush as some religious nut and pursues this story inaccurately. Again, it is clear that partisan bias is involved, too, because in fact, Bush talks publicly about his faith much less than other presidents have. There is a good book about Bush's religion by Paul Kengor, who went back to every word President Clinton spoke and found out that Clinton quoted scripture and mentioned God and Jesus Christ more than President Bush has. You would never get that from the mainstream media.

The partisan bias of the mainstream media has been at no time more evident than during the last presidential election. Presidential candidates used to be savaged equally by the media. No matter who—Republican or Democrat—they both used to take their hits. But that's not true any more. Robert Lichter, at the Center for Media and Public Affairs in Washington, measures the broadcast news for all sorts of things, including how they treat candidates. He's been doing it now for nearly 20 years. And would anyone care to guess what presidential candidate in all those years has gotten the most favorable treatment from the broadcast media? The answer is John Kerry, who got 77 percent favorable coverage in the stories regarding him on the three broadcast news shows. For Bush, it was 34 percent. This was true despite the fact that Kerry made his Vietnam service the motif of the Democratic National Convention, followed weeks later by 64 Swift Boat vets who served with Kerry in Vietnam claiming that he didn't do the things he said he did. It was a huge story, but the mainstream media didn't want to cover it and didn't cover it, for week after week after week.

There was an amazingly well documented book written by a man named John O'Neill—himself a Swift Boat vet—who went into great detail about why John Kerry didn't deserve his three Purple Hearts, etc. It might have been a right-wing screed, but if you actually read it, it wasn't a screed. It backed up its claims with evidence. Normally in journalism, when somebody makes some serious charges against a well-known person, reporters look into the charges to see if they're true or not. If they aren't, reporters look into the motives behind the false charges—for instance, to find out if someone paid the person making the false charges, and so on. But that's not what the media did in this case. The *New York Times* responded immediately by investigating the financing of the Swift Boat vets, rather than by trying to determine whether what they were saying was true. Ultimately, grudgingly—after bloggers and FOX News had covered the story sufficiently long that it couldn't be ignored—the mainstream media had to pick up on the story. But its whole effort was aimed at knocking down what the Swift Boat vets were saying.

Compare this with September 8, 2004, when Dan Rather reported on documents that he said showed not only that President Bush used preferential treatment to get into the Texas National Guard, but that he hadn't even done all his service. The very next morning, the whole story—because CBS put one of the documents on its Web site—was knocked down. It was knocked down because a blogger on a Web site called Little Green Footballs made a copy on his computer of the document that was supposedly made on a typewriter 30 years earlier and demonstrated that it was a fraud made on a modern computer. Then, only a few weeks after that embarrassment, CBS came up with a story, subsequently picked up by the *New York Times*, that an arms cache of 400 tons of ammunition in Iraq had been left unguarded by the American military and that the insurgents had gotten hold of it. Well, it turned out that they didn't know whether the insurgents had gotten that ammunition or not, or whether indeed the American military had possession of it. It was about a week before the election that these major news organizations broke this unsubstantiated story, something that would have been unimaginable in past campaigns. Why would they do that? Why would Dan Rather insist on releasing fraudulent documents when even his own experts recommended against it? Why would CBS and the *New York Times* come back with an explosive but unsubstantiated arms cache story only weeks later? They did it for one reason: They wanted to defeat President Bush for re-election. There is no other motive that would explain disregarding all the precautions you're taught you should have in journalism.

I'll wind up on a positive note, however. Forty years ago, John Kenneth Galbraith—the great liberal Harvard economist—said that he knew conservatism was dead because it was bookless. Conservatives didn't publish books. And to some extent, it was true at the time. But it's no longer true. Conservatives have become such prolific writers and consumers of books that Random House and other publishing companies have started separate conservative imprints. Nowadays it is common to see two or three or four conservative books—some of them kind of trashy, but some of them very good—on the bestseller list. Insofar as books are an indication of how well conservatives are doing—at least in the publishing part of the media world—I would say they're doing quite well. They're not winning, but they're much better off than they were before—something that can't be said about how they are faring in the unfair and unbalanced mainstream media.

Robert F. Kennedy Jr.  **NO**

The Disinformation Society

Many Democratic voters marveled at the election results. George W. Bush, they argued, has transformed a projected $5.6 trillion, 10-year Bill Clinton surplus into a projected $1.4 trillion deficit—a $7 trillion shift in wealth from our national treasury into the pockets of the wealthiest Americans, particularly the president's corporate paymasters. Any discerning observer, they argued, must acknowledge that the White House has repeatedly lied to the American people about critical policy issues—Medicare, education, the environment, the budget implications of its tax breaks, and the war in Iraq—with catastrophic results.

President Bush has opened our national lands and sacred places to the lowest bidder and launched a jihad against the American environment and public health to enrich his corporate sponsors. He has mired us in a costly, humiliating war that has killed more than 1,520 American soldiers and maimed 11,300. He has made America the target of Islamic hatred, caused thousands of new terrorists to be recruited to al-Qaeda, isolated us in the world, and drained our treasury of the funds necessary to rebuild Afghanistan and to finance our own vital homeland-security needs. He has shattered our traditional alliances and failed to protect vulnerable terrorist targets at home-chemical plants, nuclear facilities, air-cargo carriers, and ports. He has disgraced our nation and empowered tyrants with the unpunished excesses at Guantánamo and Abu Ghraib. These baffled Democrats were hard-pressed to believe that their fellow Americans would give a man like this a second term.

To explain the president's victory, political pundits posited a vast "values gap" between red states and blue states. They attributed the president's success in the polls, despite his tragic job failures, to the rise of religious fundamentalism. Heartland Americans, they suggested, are the soldiers in a new American Taliban, willing to vote against their own economic interests to promote "morality" issues that they see as the critical high ground in a life-or-death culture war.

I believe, however, that the Democrats lost the presidential contest not because of a philosophical chasm between red and blue states but due to an information deficit caused by a breakdown in our national media. Traditional broadcast networks have abandoned their former obligation to advance democracy and promote the public interest by informing the public about both sides of issues relevant to those goals. To attract viewers and advertising revenues, they entertain rather than inform. This threat to the flow of information, vital to democracy's survival, has been compounded in recent years by the growing power of right-wing media that twist the news and deliberately deceive the public to advance their radical agenda.

According to an October 2004 survey by the Program on International Policy Attitudes (PIPA), a joint program of the Center on Policy Attitudes, in Washington, D.C., and the Center for International and Security Studies at the University of Maryland:

- Seventy-two percent of Bush supporters believed Iraq had weapons of mass destruction (or a major program for developing them), versus 26 percent of Kerry voters. A seven-month search by 1,500 investigators led by David Kay, working for the C.I.A., found no such weapons.
- Seventy-five percent of Bush supporters believed that Iraq was providing substantial support to al-Qaeda, a view held by 30 percent of Kerry supporters. *The 9/11 Commission Report* concluded that there was no terrorist alliance between Iraq and al-Qaeda.
- Eighty-two percent of Bush supporters erroneously believed either that the rest of the world felt better about the U.S. thanks to its invasion of Iraq or that views were evenly divided. Eighty-six percent of Kerry supporters accurately understood that a majority of the world felt worse about our country.
- Most Bush supporters believed the Iraq war had strong support in the Islamic world. Kerry's supporters accurately estimated the low level of support in Islamic countries. Even Turkey, the most Westernized Islamic country, was 87 percent against the invasion.
- Most significant, the majority of Bush voters agreed with Kerry supporters that if Iraq did not have W.M.D. and was not providing assistance to al-Qaeda the U.S. should not have gone to war. Furthermore, most Bush supporters, according to PIPA, favored the Kyoto Protocol to fight global warming, the Mine Ban Treaty to ban land mines, and strong labor and environmental standards in trade agreements, and wrongly believed that their candidate favored these things. In other words, the values and principles were the same. Bush voters made their choice based on bad information.

It's no mystery where the false beliefs are coming from. Both Bush and Kerry supporters overwhelmingly believe that the Bush administration at the time of the 2004 U.S. election was telling the American people that Iraq had W.M.D. and that Saddam Hussein had strong links to al-Qaeda. The White House's false message was carried by right-wing media in bed with the administration. Prior to the election, Fox News reporters, for example, regularly made unsubstantiated claims about Iraq's W.M.D. Fox anchor Brit Hume, on his newscast in July 2004, announced that W.M.D. had actually been found. Sean Hannity repeatedly suggested without factual support that the phantom weapons had been moved to Syria and would soon be found. An October 2003 survey by PIPA showed that people who watch Fox News are disproportionately afflicted with the same misinformation evidenced by the 2004 PIPA report. The earlier study probed for the source of public misinformation about the Iraq war that might account for the common misperceptions that Saddam Hussein had been involved in the 9/11 attacks, that he supported al-Qaeda, that W.M.D. had been found, and that world opinion favored the U.S. invasion. The study discovered that "the extent of Americans' misperceptions vary significantly depending on their source of news. Those who receive most of their news from Fox News are more likely than average to have misperceptions."

Unfortunately for John Kerry, many Americans now do get their information from Fox—according to Nielsen Media Research, in February, Fox was the cable news leader, with an average of 1.57 million prime-time viewers, nearly 2.5 times CNN's average viewership in the same time slot— and from Fox's similarly biased cable colleagues, CNBC and MSNBC. Millions more tune to the Sinclair Broadcast Group—one of the nation's largest TV franchises. After 9/11, Sinclair forced its stations to broadcast spots pledging support for President Bush, and actively censored unfavorable coverage of the Iraq war—blacking out Ted Koppel's *Nightline* when it ran the names of the U.S. war dead. It retreated from its pre-election proposal to strong-arm its 62 TV stations into pre-empting their prime-time programming to air an erroneous and blatantly biased documentary about John Kerry's war record only when its stock dropped 17 percent due to Wall Street fears of sponsor boycotts and investor worries that Sinclair was putting its right-wing ideology ahead of shareholder profits.

Americans are also getting huge amounts of misinformation from talk radio, which is thoroughly dominated by the extreme right. A Gallup Poll conducted in December 2002 discovered that 22 percent of Americans receive their daily news from talk-radio programs. An estimated 15 million people listen to Rush Limbaugh alone, and on the top 45 AM radio stations in the country, listeners encounter 310 hours of conservative talk for every 5 hours of liberal talk. According to the nonprofit Democracy Radio, Inc., 90 percent of all political talk-radio programming is conservative, while only 10 percent is progressive. All the leading talk-show hosts are right-wing radicals—Rush Limbaugh, Sean Hannity, Michael Savage, Oliver North, G. Gordon Liddy, Bill O'Reilly, and Michael Reagan—and the same applies to local talk radio.

Alas, while the right-wing media are deliberately misleading the American people, the traditional corporately owned media—CBS, NBC, ABC, and CNN— are doing little to remedy those wrong impressions. They are, instead, focusing on expanding viewership by hawking irrelevant stories that appeal to our prurient interest in sex and celebrity gossip. None of the three major networks gave gavel-to-gavel coverage of the party conventions or more than an hour in prime time, opting instead to entertain the public with semi-pornographic reality shows. "We're about to elect a president of the United States at a time when we have young people dying in our name overseas, we just had a report from the 9/11 commission which says we are not safe as a nation, and one of these two groups of people is going to run our country," commented PBS newsman Jim Lehrer, in disgust at the lack of convention coverage. CBS anchor Dan Rather said that "I argued the conventions were part of the dance of democracy. I found myself increasingly like the Mohicans, forced farther and farther back into the wilderness and eventually eliminated."

The broadcast reporters participating in the presidential debates were apparently so uninterested in real issues that they neglected to ask the candidates a single question about the president's environmental record. CBS anchor Bob Schieffer, who M.C.'d the final debate, asked no questions about the environment, focusing instead on abortion, gay marriage, and the personal faith of the candidates, an agenda that could have been dictated by Karl Rove.

Where is that dreaded but impossible-to-find "liberal bias" that supposedly infects the American press? The erroneous impression that the American media have a liberal bias is itself a mark of the triumph of the right-wing propaganda machine.

•◆•

The Republican Noise Machine: Right-Wing Media and How It Corrupts Democracy, by David Brock—the president and C.E.O. of Media Matters for America, a watchdog group that documents misinformation in the right-wing media— traces the history of the "liberal bias" notion back to the Barry Goldwater presidential campaign, in 1964, in which aggrieved conservatives railed against Walter Cronkite and the "Eastern Liberal Press" at the Republican National Convention. In response to Spiro Agnew's 1969 attack on the networks as insufficiently supportive of Nixon's policies in Vietnam, conservatives formed an organization called Accuracy in Media, whose purpose was to discredit the media by tagging it as "liberal," and to market that idea with clever catchphrases. Polluter-funded foundations, including the Adolph Coors Foundation and the so-called four sisters—the Lynde and Harry Bradley Foundation, the John M. Olin Foundation, Richard Mellon Scaife's foundations, and the Smith Richardson Foundation—all of which funded the anti-environmental movement, spent hundreds of millions of dollars to perpetuate the big lie of liberal bias, to convince the conservative base that it should not believe the mainstream, to create a market for right-wing media, and to intimidate and discipline the mainstream press into being more accommodating to conservatism.

According to Brock, right-wing groups such as the Heritage Foundation and Scaife's Landmark Legal Foundation helped persuade Ronald Reagan and his Federal Communications Commission, in 1987, to eliminate the Fairness Doctrine—the F.C.C.'s 1949 rule which dictated that broadcasters provide equal time to both sides of controversial public questions. It was a "godsend for conservatives," according to religious-right pioneer and Moral Majority co-founder Richard Viguerie, opening up talk radio to one-sided, right-wing broadcasters. (Rush Limbaugh nationally launched his talk show the following year.) Radical ideologues, faced with Niagara-size flows of money from the Adolph Coors Foundation, the four sisters, and others, set up magazines and newspapers and cultivated a generation of young pundits, writers, and propagandists, giving them lucrative sinecures inside right-wing think tanks, now numbering more than 500, from which they bombard the media with carefully honed messages justifying corporate profit taking.

Brock himself was one of the young stars recruited to this movement, working in turn for the Heritage Foundation, the Reverend Sun Myung Moon's

Washington Times, and Scaife's *American Spectator.* "If you look at this history," Brock told me recently, "you will find that the conservative movement has in many ways purchased the debate. You have conservative media outlets day after day that are intentionally misinforming the public." Brock, who admits to participating in the deliberate deception while he was a so-called journalist on the right-wing payroll, worries that the right-wing media are systematically feeding the public "false and wrong information. It's a really significant problem for democracy.

"We're in a situation," continues Brock, "where you have 'red facts' and 'blue facts.' And I think the conservatives intentionally have done that to try to confuse and neutralize accurate information that may not serve the conservative agenda."

The consolidation of media ownership and its conservative drift are growing ever more severe. Following the election, Clear Channel, the biggest owner of radio stations in the country, announced that Fox News will now supply its news feed to many of the company's 1,240 stations, further amplifying the distorted drumbeat of right-wing propaganda that most Americans now take for news.

Sadly enough, right-wing radio and cable are increasingly driving the discussion in mainstream broadcasting as well. At a Harvard University symposium the day before the Democratic convention, three network anchors and a CNN anchor straightforwardly discussed the effects that right-wing broadcasters, conservative money, and organized pressure have on the networks. And in February 2005, Pat Mitchell announced her resignation as president of PBS, hounded from office by right-wing critics who felt her conciliatory efforts to conservatize the network—canceling a cartoon episode with a lesbian couple and adding talk shows by such right-wingers as Tucker Carlson and Paul Gigot—did not go far enough fast enough.

Furthermore, Fox's rating success has exerted irresistible gravities that have pulled its competitors' programming to starboard. In the days leading up to the Iraq war, MSNBC fired one of television's last liberal voices, Phil Donahue, who hosted its highest-rated show; an internal memo revealed that Donahue presented "a difficult public face for NBC in a time of war." CBS's post-election decision to retire Dan Rather, a lightning rod for right-wing wrath, coincided with Tom Brokaw's retirement from NBC. He was replaced by Brian Williams, who has said, "I think Rush [Limbaugh] has actually yet to get the credit he is due." According to NBC president Jeff Zucker, "No one understands this NASCAR nation more than Brian."

Conservative noise on cable and talk radio also has an echo effect on the rest of the media. One of the conservative talking points in the last election was that terrorists supported the candidacy of John Kerry. According to Media Matters, this pearl originated on Limbaugh's radio show in March 2004 and repeatedly surfaced in mainstream news. In May, CNN's Kelli Arena reported "speculation that al-Qaeda believes it has a better chance of winning in Iraq if John Kerry is in the White House"; in June it migrated to Dick Morris's *New York Post* column. Chris Matthews mentioned it in a July edition of *Hardball.* In September, Bill Schneider, CNN's senior political analyst, declared that al-Qaeda "would very much like to defeat President Bush," signaling that Limbaugh's contrivance was now embedded firmly in the national consciousness.

That "echo effect" is not random. Brock shows in his book how the cues by which mainstream news directors decide what is important to cover are no longer being suggested by *The New York Times* and other responsible media outlets, but rather by the "shadowy" participants of a Washington, D.C., meeting convened by Grover Norquist's Americans for Tax Reform, an anti-government organization that seeks to prevent federal regulation of business.

Every Wednesday morning the leaders of 80 conservative organizations meet in Washington in Norquist's boardroom. This radical cabal formulates policy with the Republican National Committee and the White House, developing talking points that go out to the conservative media via a sophisticated fax tree. Soon, millions of Americans are hearing the same message from cable news commentators and thousands of talk jocks across America. Their precisely crafted message and language then percolate through the mainstream media to form the underlying assumptions of our national debate.

This meeting has now grown to include more than 120 participants, including industry lobbyists and representatives of conservative media outlets such as *The Washington Times* and the *National Review.* According to Brock, columnist Bob Novak sends a researcher. *The Wall Street Journal*'s Peggy Noonan may attend in person. The lockstep coordination among right-wing political operatives and the press is new in American politics.

A typical meeting might focus on a new tax proposal released by President Bush. Following conference calls throughout the week, the decision will be made to call the plan "bold." Over the next 10 days, radio and cable will reiterate that it's "bold, bold, bold." The result, according to Brock, is that "people come to think that there must be something 'bold' about this plan."

This highly integrated network has given the right frightening power to disseminate its propaganda and has dramatically changed the way Americans get their information and formulate policy. In *The Republican Noise Machine,* Brock alleges routine fraud and systematically dishonest practices by his former employer the Reverend Sun Myung Moon's *Washington Times,* which is the primary propaganda organ for Moon's agenda to establish America as a Fascist theocracy. The paper doesn't reach more than a hundred thousand subscribers, but its articles are read on the air by Rush Limbaugh, reaching 15 million people, and are posted on Matt Drudge's Web site, to reach another 7 million people, and its writers regularly appear on *The O'Reilly Factor,* before another 2 million. Network TV talk-show producers and bookers use those appearances as a tip sheet for picking the subject matter and guests for their own shows. And so the capacity of the conservative movement to disseminate propaganda has increased exponentially.

This right-wing propaganda machine can quickly and indelibly brand Democratic candidates unfavorably—John Kerry as a flip-flopper, Al Gore as a liar. The machine is so powerful that it was able to orchestrate Clinton's impeachment despite the private and trivial nature of his "crime"—a lie about an extramarital tryst—when compared with President Bush's calamitous lies about Iraq, the budget, Medicare, education, and the environment. During the 2000 campaign, Al Gore was smeared as a liar—a charge that was completely false—by right-wing pundits such as gambling addict Bill Bennett and prescription-painkiller abuser Rush Limbaugh, both of whom the right wing has sold as moral paradigms. Meanwhile, George Bush's chronic problems with the truth during the three presidential debates that year were barely mentioned in the media, as Brock has noted. Americans accepted this negative characterization of Gore, and when they emerged from the voting booths in 2000, they told pollsters that Bush won their vote on "trust."

In the 2004 campaign, the so-called Swift Boat Veterans for Truth launched dishonest attacks which, amplified and repeated by the right-wing media, helped torpedo John Kerry's presidential ambitions. No matter who the Democratic nominee was, this machinery had the capacity to discredit and destroy him.

Meanwhile, there is a palpable absence of strong progressive voices on TV, unless one counts HBO's Bill Maher and Comedy Central's Jon Stewart—both comedians—or Fox's meek foil, Alan Colmes, who plays the ever losing Washington Generals to Scan Hannity's Harlem Globetrotters. There are no liberal equivalents to counterbalance Joe Scarborough, John Stossel, Bill O'Reilly, and Lawrence Kudlow. Brock points to the systematic structural imbalance in the panels that are featured across all of cable and on the networks' Sunday shows. Programs like *Meet the Press* and Chris Matthews's *Hardball* invariably pit conservative ideologues such as William Safire, Robert Novak, and Pat Buchanan against neutral, nonaligned reporters such as Andrea Mitchell, the diplomatic correspondent for NBC News, or *Los Angeles Times* reporter Ronald Brownstein in a rigged fight that leaves an empty chair for a strong progressive point of view.

There is still relevant information in the print media. But even that has been shamefully twisted by the pressures of the right. Both *The New York Times* and *The Washington Post,* which jumped on Scaife's bandwagon to lead the mainstream press in the Clinton-impeachment frenzy, have been forced to issue *mea culpas* for failing to ask the tough questions during the run-up to Bush's Iraq war.

Furthermore, America's newspapers, like most other media outlets, are owned predominantly by Republican conservatives. Newspapers endorsed Bush by two to one in the 2000 election. According to a recent survey, the op-ed columnists who appear in the most newspapers are conservatives Cal Thomas and George Will. Republican-owned newspapers often reprint misinformation from the right. And red-state journalists, whatever their personal political sympathies, are unlikely to offend their editors by spending inordinate energy exposing right-wing lies.

Print journalism is a victim of the same consolidation by a few large, profit-driven corporations that has affected the broadcasters. Today, a shrinking pool of owners—guided by big business rather than journalistic values—forces news executives to cut costs and seek the largest audience. The consolidation has led to demands on news organizations to return profits at rates never before expected of them. Last summer, just a few months after winning five Pulitzer

Prizes, the *Los Angeles Times* was asked by its parent company to drop 60 news-room positions.

The pressure for bottomline news leaves little incentive for investment in investigative reporting. Cost-cutting has liquidated news staffs, leaving reporters little time to research stories. According to an Ohio University study, the number of investigative reporters was cut almost in half between 1980 and 1995.

During the debate over the Radio Act of 1927, an early forerunner of the Fairness Doctrine, Texas congressman Luther Johnson warned Americans against the corporate and ideological consolidation of the national press that has now come to pass. "American thought and American politics will be largely at the mercy of those who operate these stations," he said. "For publicity is the most powerful weapon that can be wielded in a republic . . . and when a single selfish group is permitted to either tacitly or otherwise acquire ownership and dominate these broadcasting stations throughout the country, then woe be to those who dare to differ with them. It will be impossible to compete with them in reaching the ears of the American people."

The news isn't entirely bleak. Progressive voices are prevalent on the Internet, which is disproportionately utilized by the younger age groups that will exercise increasing influence in public affairs each year. The success of Air America Radio, the progressive network whose best-known host is Al Franken, offers great cause for optimism. Despite a shoestring budget and financial chaos at its inception, Air America has grown in one year to include 50 stations, from which it is accessible to half the American people. Most encouraging, a recent study shows that Air America personalities as a group rank second in popularity to Rush Limbaugh. Last fall in San Diego, a traditional Republican bastion, Air America was reported to be the No. 1 radio station among listeners 18 to 49 years old. But progressive activists need also to find a voice on television, and there the outlook is dark.

If there is a market for progressive voices, as the Air America experience suggests, why don't the big corporate owners leap in? A top industry executive recently told me that he was dead certain that there would be a large audience for a progressive TV news network to counterbalance the right-wing cable shows. "But," he said, "the corporate owners will never touch it. Multi-nationals, like Viacom, Disney, and General Electric, that rely on government business, contracts, and goodwill are not going to risk offending the Republicans who now control every branch of government."

This executive had recently spoken to Viacom chairman Sumner Redstone (a lifelong Democrat) about the corporation's open support of the Bush administration. "I said, 'Sumner, what about our children and what about our country?' He replied, 'Viacom is my life. I've got to do what's best for the company. I need to buy more stations, and the Republicans are going to let me do it. It's in the company's interest to support Republicans.'"

When veteran television journalist and former CBS news analyst Bill Moyers resigned as host of PBS's *Now* in December, he observed, "I think my peers in commercial television are talented and devoted journalists, but they've chosen to work in a corporate mainstream that trims their talent to fit the corporate nature of American life. And you do not get rewarded for telling the hard truths about America in a profit-seeking environment." Moyers called the decline in American journalism "the biggest story of our time." He added, "We have an ideological press that's interested in the election of Republicans, and a mainstream press that's interested in the bottom line. Therefore, we don't have a vigilant, independent press whose interest is the American people."

Moyers has elsewhere commented that "the quality of journalism and the quality of democracy are inextricably joined." By diminishing the capacity for voters to make rational choices, the breakdown of the American press is threatening not just our environment but our democracy.

EXPLORING THE ISSUE

Does the Media Have a Liberal Bias?

Critical Thinking and Reflection

1. Do you really want to hear both sides of hotly debated issues? What kind of media do you pay attention to and why? How unbiased are you in your selection of your news sources?
2. If you are biased in your selection of news sources, how do you justify your biased news gathering?
3. Evaluate the relative importance of information gathering versus entertainment in your choice of news sources.
4. How well does the current news system serve the public?
5. What changes in the current news system would serve the public better?
6. What is political correctness and are you for it or against it?
7. To what extent does money control the media and to what extent do professional norms have a strong influence on national media?

Is There Common Ground?

As the opposing arguments in this issue indicate, we can find critics on both the left and the right who agree that the media are biased. What divides such critics is the question of whether the bias is left-wing or right-wing. Defenders of the news media may seize upon this disagreement to bolster their own claim that "bias is in the eye of the beholder." But the case may be that the news media are unfair to both sides. If that were true, however, it would seem to take some of the force out of the argument that the news media have a distinct ideological tilt at all.

The problem of bias in news reporting has resulted in the emergence of fact checking groups that are used to determine what are the facts and the lies in the statements of politicians and sometimes commentators. Will they also become misused in biased ways?

Additional Resources

A number of works tend to support Barnes's contention that the media slant leftward, including Ann Coulter in *Slander: Liberal Lies about the American Right* (Crown Publishers, 2002); Bernard Goldberg in *Bias: A CBS Insider Exposes How the Media Distort the News* (Regency Publishing, 2002); and *Arrogance: Rescuing America from the Media Elite* (Warner Books, 2003). On the other hand, those who think the media are biased rightward include Ben Bagdikian, *The Media*

Monopoly, 6th ed. (Beacon Press, 2000); Eric Alterman, *What Liberal Media? The Truth about Bias and the News* (Basic Books, 2003); David Edwards and David Cromwell, *Guardians of Power: The Myth of the Liberal Media* (Pluto Press, 2006); Jeffery Klaehn, ed., *Bound by Power: Intended Consequences* (Black Rose Books, 2006); and Robert Waterman McChesney, *The Problem of the Media: U.S. Communication Politics in the Twenty-First Century* (Monthly Review Press, 2004). In *South Park Conservatives: The Revolt Against Liberal Media Bias* (Regnery, 2005), Brian C. Anderson observes that the media were very liberal but America revolted and now conservative voices are being heard. Lies in the media have along history as outlined by Eric Burns in *All the News Unfit to Print: A History of How Things Were—and How They Were Reported* (Wiley, 2009). Despite the prevalence of lies, Ronald N. Jacobs points out in *The Space of Opinion: Media Intellectuals and the Public Sphere* that objective journalism is also thriving (Oxford University Press, 2011).

There are many criticisms of the media besides its biases. Three interesting critiques are Chris Hedges, *Empire of Illusion: The End of Literacy and the Triumph of Spectacle* (Nation Books, 2009); Drew Curtis, *It's Not News, It's Fark: How Mass Media Tries to Pass Off Crap as News* (Gotham Books, 2007); and James Bowman, *Media Madness: The Corruption of Our Political Culture* (Encounter Books, 2008). Another connected issue is the concentration of the control of media outlets, which is addressed by C. Edwin Baker in *Media Concentration and Democracy: Why Ownership Matters* (Cambridge University Press, 2007). Several recent memoirs of journalists are very useful for the debate on media bias. See Tom Wicker's *On the Record* (Bedford/St. Martin's, 2002); Ted Koppel's *Off Camera* (Alfred A. Knopf, 2000); and Bill O'Reilly's *The No-Spin Zone* (Broadway Books, 2001). David Halberstam's *The Powers That Be* (Alfred A. Knopf, 1979), a historical study of CBS, *The Washington Post, Time* magazine, and the *Los Angeles Times,* describes some of the political and ideological struggles that have taken place within major media organizations.

ISSUE 2

Is Third World Immigration a Threat to America's Way of Life?

YES: **Mark Krikorian**, from *The New Case Against Immigration* (Sentinel, 2008)

NO: **Jason L. Riley**, from *Let Them In: The Case for Open Borders* (Gotham, 2008)

Learning Outcomes

After reading this issue, you should be able to:

- Articulate what American culture is and identify the aspects of American culture that are liable to be eroded by the current immigrant stream.
- Know how immigration in the past has impacted American culture.
- Identify different immigration streams by time periods, countries of origin, and types of people in the stream for their differential impacts.
- Evaluate how illegal immigration factors into this issue.
- Understand the relationship between secure borders and protection from terrorists.
- Understand the need for immigrants to increase the ratio of workers to retirees.
- Evaluate the role of fear in how people view immigration.

ISSUE SUMMARY

YES: Mark Krikorian, the executive director of the Center for Immigration Studies, presents the case against immigration. He emphasizes the changes in America that make immigration less beneficial for America. The current immigrants are not much different than immigrants in the past century but they do not fit the new America as well as the past immigrants fit the old America. One part of the story is that the new America will not assimilate immigrants well.

NO: Jason L. Riley, an editor of the *Wall Street Journal*, applauds immigration because it will propel, not impede, economic growth.

America has a flexible labor market, where both employers and employees can change the work situation as they need or desire. "In the end, employers, workers, and consumers are all better off." America has a labor shortage that immigrants help fill without taking jobs in the aggregate from Americans. Riley also argues that new immigrants assimilate much like the old immigrants did.

Before September 11, 2001, many Americans favored the reduction of immigration. After the terrorist attacks on the World Trade Center and the Pentagon by immigrants, some felt even stronger about limiting immigration. But is immigration bad for America, as this sentiment assumes, or does it strengthen America?

Today the number of legal immigrants to America is close to 1 million per year, and illegal ("undocumented") immigrants probably number well over that figure. In terms of numbers, immigration is now comparable to the level it reached during the early years of the twentieth century, when millions of immigrants arrived from southern and eastern Europe. A majority of the new immigrants, however, do not come from Europe but from what has been called the "Third World"—the underdeveloped nations. The largest percentages come from Mexico, the Philippines, Korea, and the islands of the Caribbean, while European immigration has shrunk to about 10 percent. Much of the reason for this shift has to do with changes made in U.S. immigration laws during the 1960s. Decades earlier, in the 1920s, America narrowed its gate to people from certain regions of the world by imposing quotas designed to preserve the balance of races in America. But in 1965, a series of amendments to the Immigration Act put all the world's people on an equal footing in terms of immigration. The result, wrote journalist Theodore H. White, was "a stampede, almost an invasion" of Third World immigrants. Indeed, the 1965 amendments made it even easier for Third World immigrants to enter the country because the new law gave preference to those with a family member already living in the United States. Because most of the European immigrants who settled in the early part of the century had died off, and few Europeans had immigrated in more recent years, a greater percentage of family-reuniting immigration came from the Third World. This shift in the backgrounds of immigrants to America raises a profound cultural question: Will these new immigrants add healthy new strains to America's cultural inheritance, broadening and revitalizing it? Or will they cause the country to break up into separate cultural units, destroying America's unity? Of all the questions relating to immigration, this one seems to be the most sensitive.

In 1992, conservative columnist Patrick Buchanan set off a firestorm of controversy when he raised this question: "If we had to take a million immigrants next year, say Zulus or Englishmen, and put them in Virginia, which group would be easier to assimilate and cause less problems for the people of Virginia?" Although Buchanan later explained that his intention was not to denigrate Zulus or any other racial group but simply to talk about assimilation into Anglo-American culture, his remarks were widely characterized as racist and xenophobic (related to a fear of foreigners). Whether or not that characterization is justified, Buchanan's question goes to the heart of the cultural debate over immigration—the tension between unity and diversity. In the selections that follow, Krikorian contends that immigrants are harming the United States both economically and culturally. He argues that America today does not assimilate immigrants very well, so more immigration will adversely affect American life. Riley counters that the accusations against immigrants are false and that immigrants contribute greatly to America.

An assumption common to both sides of the debate is that our culture is much better than other cultures. But is it? Many commentators complain that greed is elevated to the highest level in American culture. The superrich are supposedly willing to bankrupt America as long as they get their deals, big bonuses, and wealth. The unions are willing to screw the corporations and the public as long as they get what they want. Others are less guilty of screwing others but that is mainly because they lack the power to do so. I usually discount the critics because they tend to cherry-pick the evidence to make their case, but they have a valid point. Others complain that family values have declined to abysmal levels. The evidence is mixed on this issue, but most people accept the idea. We could go on to other values that Americans fall short on, but the point to bear in mind is that other cultures excel in many ways. It would seem that America would be benefited by the infusion of other cultures, especially if it is likely that the better aspects of other cultures would be acquired by America instead of the worse aspects.

YES

Mark Krikorian

The New Case Against Immigration

Introduction

It's not the immigrants—it's us.

What's different about immigration today as opposed to a century ago is not the characteristics of the newcomers but the characteristics of our society. Immigrants are what they've always been: not the poorest of the poor but one step up from the bottom, strivers looking for better lives for their children, coming from rural or small-town backgrounds in traditional—what we would call third-world—societies. But the changes that define modern America—in our society, economy, government, and technology, for example—are so fundamental that our past success in dealing with immigration is simply no longer relevant.

This is a new argument. It's not that previous critiques of immigration have been wrong—indeed, much of what follows in this book is based on the outstanding work of others over the years. Instead, the source of the problems created by immigration has usually been located in differences between *immigrants* past and present rather than in differences between *America* past and present. Immigrants in the past, it is said, were white, but now they're not; they used to want to assimilate, but now they don't; or they used to be self-sufficient, but now they seek out government assistance. We've all heard the laments: "My grandpa from Sicily learned English, and my grandma from Minsk got by without welfare—what's the problem with immigrants today?" The problem is that the America your grandparents immigrated to a century ago no longer exists. . . .

In short, mass immigration is incompatible with a modern society. As Hudson Institute scholar John Fonte has written, "It's not 1900 any more."

The subsequent chapters will spell out exactly how the changes that distinguish a modern, mature society are incompatible with continued immigration, but for now it will suffice to say that they paint a picture of a country fundamentally different from the past. Some examples:

ECONOMY. A century ago, what economists call the primary sector of the economy (farming, fishing, hunting, and herding) still employed more Americans than any other, as it had since the dawn of humankind. Today only 2 percent of our workforce occupies itself in this way. Meanwhile, the tertiary sector (service industries) now employs 80 percent of working Americans, and the percentage is climbing.

EDUCATION. Along with the change in the economy, education has become more widespread. Nearly a quarter of American adults had less than five years of schooling in 1910; as of 2000, that figure is less than 2 percent.

. . .

GOVERNMENT. In 1900, total government spending at all levels equaled about 5.5 percent of the economy; by 2003, it was more than 36 percent. Total government employment (federal, state, and local) went from a little more than 1 million in 1900 (about 4 percent of the workforce) to more than 22 million in 2000 (more than 16 percent of the workforce).

LIFESTYLE. America's population was still 60 percent rural in 1900; in 2000, only 21 percent of Americans lived in rural areas (and only a tiny fraction were involved in farming). The average household went from more than 4.5 people to a little more than 2.5, while the number of people per room in the average house fell from 1.1 in 1910 to 0.4 in 1997.

Other changes are harder to quantify but are just as real in marking modern society as a break with the past: a weakening sense of community and civic engagement, increased religious skepticism, a greater sense of responsibility for the less fortunate, rejection of racial and religious discrimination, and concern for our stewardship of the natural world.

. . .

These social changes marking national adulthood don't mean that mass immigration was out of place during our country's adolescence. America ended up a stronger nation because of the mass-immigration phase of our development, a phase that extended for seventy-odd years, from the late 1840s until the early 1920s. Had we not experienced that period of mass immigration, our population, derived mainly from descendants of a relatively small number of preindependence settlers, would still have grown rapidly, but it would have been smaller; in 1990, about half of America's population was attributable to post-1790 immigrants and their descendants. The first part of the immigration phase, dominated by northern Europeans, helped settle much of the land; this happened both because some immigrants went directly to the Midwest and West to establish farms and ranches and because others moved to eastern cities, filling in behind old-stock Americans who had moved west. The latter part of our nation's adolescent immigration phase was dominated by immigrants from eastern and southern Europe who settled mainly in the cities and contributed mightily to industrialization.

. . .

The closing of the frontier was irreversible—once it was gone, there was no way to get it back. But prospective immigrants continued to be available in abundance. And so, starting with the 1965 immigration law, America resumed its adolescent policy of immigration, leading to the largest wave of newcomers in its history. The total foreign-born population has ballooned, from fewer than

10 million in 1970 (less than 5 percent of the nation's population) to nearly 38 million in 2007 (12.6 percent of the population). Annual legal immigration—the number of people awarded permanent residency, potentially leading to citizenship—has gone from fewer than 400,000 in 1970 to nearly 1.3 million in 2006. And illegal immigration has become a major phenomenon, with today's illegal population totaling perhaps 12 million and growing by around half a million each year.

. . .

The objective of this book is to demonstrate how this new immigration wave clashes with modern America, how a policy that served us well in our adolescence is harmful in our maturity.

Assimilation: The Cracked Melting Pot

The most important long-term measure of success in immigration is assimilation. The American model of immigration has been based on turning immigrants and their descendants fully into Americans: Theodore Roosevelt summed up this Americanization tradition when he wrote that "if the immigrant who comes here does in good faith become an American and assimilates himself to us, he shall be treated on an exact equality with every one else, for it is an outrage to discriminate against any such man because of creed or birthplace or origin."

This is unlike the practice of other countries, such as Germany or the Persian Gulf sheikhdoms, and even our own historical lapses (African slavery, the Know-Nothing movement, and the Bracero program for Mexican guest workers), which all have one thing in common—the willingness to employ the labor of foreign workers without admitting them to membership in the society.

This process of Americanizing immigrants was tumultuous and wrenching for everyone involved but eventually very successful. The descendants of those who came in generations past—from Ireland or Poland, Mexico or Sweden, China or Germany, Britain or Armenia—have indeed become one people. This has been possible, of course, because American nationality is not based on blood relations, like a biological family, but is more like a family growing partly through adoption, where new immigrants attach themselves to their new country and embrace the cultural and civic values of their native-born brethren as their own.

. . .

But this offer of complete adoption into the American nation was always based on the requirement that the immigrant "assimilates himself to us." Such assimilation is more than the surface changes that are easily observed; future Supreme Court Justice Louis Brandeis put it well in a 1915 speech:

> But the adoption of our language, manners and customs is only a small part of the process. To become Americanized, the change wrought must be fundamental. However great his outward conformity, the immigrant is

not Americanized unless his interests and affections have become deeply rooted here. And we properly demand of the immigrant even more than this. He must be brought into complete harmony with our ideals and aspirations and cooperate with us for their attainment. Only when this has been done, will he possess the national consciousness of an American.

This adoption of "the national consciousness of an American" is what Hudson Institute scholar John Fonte calls patriotic assimilation—an identification with Americans as the immigrant's new countrymen, converting, in a secular sense, from membership in one national community to membership in another. . . .

Unfortunately, the conditions of modern society make such assimilation increasingly difficult. It is characteristic of modern societies that they have great difficulty in assimilating large numbers of newcomers into the model of a territorial nation-state, with a common language and civic culture helping to cultivate the patriotic solidarity necessary for both mutual sacrifice and respect for individual rights.

This is not because of any intrinsic differences between immigrants past and present; the simple fact that most immigrants now come from Latin America and Asia, rather than from Europe, is of less importance with regard to assimilation than some observers seem to think. Instead, it is *we* who have changed.

Our modern society is different in two major ways that relate to assimilation, one practical, the other political. The first, practical, difference is that modern technology now enables newcomers to retain ties to their homelands, even to the extent of living in both countries simultaneously; thus, becoming "deeply rooted here," in Brandeis's words, is simply less likely to happen. This leads to what scholars call transnationalism—living in such a way as not to be rooted in one nation, but rather living across two or more nations. As one student of the subject has put it, "Transnational communities are groups whose identity is not primarily based on attachment to a specific territory. They therefore present a powerful challenge to traditional ideas of nation-state belonging."

Second, and perhaps more important, is the political change. Elites in all modern societies, including ours, come to devalue their own nation and culture and thus recoil from the idea that newcomers should even be required to adopt "our language, manners and customs," let alone "be brought into complete harmony with our ideals and aspirations"—assuming we can even agree, in this contentious age, on what those ideals and aspirations are. This loss of confidence expresses itself in an ideology of multiculturalism, which rejects the idea of bonds tying together all members of a society.

The combination of these two modern traits—transnationalism and multiculturalism—means that mass immigration today is much less likely to result in the kind of deep assimilation of the vast majority of immigrants and their children that is necessary for immigration to be successful. This is true regardless of the characteristics of the immigrants—their legal status, country of origin, or even level of education—because the problem is inherent to modern society and the way that modernity limits our ability to replicate the successes of the past.

. . .

Either to maintain his own cognitive balance or preserve his professional viability in academia, [Robert Putnam, a political scientist and professor at Harvard University] tries to explain away the socially corrosive effects of mass immigration by arguing that in the long run "successful immigrant societies have overcome such fragmentation by creating new, cross-cutting forms of social solidarity and more encompassing identities." That is indeed what successful immigrant societies like ours have done—*in the past*. But these "cross-cutting forms of social solidarity and more encompassing identities"— in other words, an overarching American identity held by people of different ethnic groups and classes and regions and religions—are precisely what modern societies have greater trouble developing, for the reasons, both technological and ideological, that this chapter has explored.

In short, Americanization is much more difficult under modern conditions than in the past. Rather than turning out new Americans who are "blood of the blood, and flesh of the flesh of the men who wrote that Declaration," mass immigration today is helping transform the United States into what one anthropologist approvingly calls "one node in a post-national network of diasporas." Ending mass immigration does not guarantee the restoration of a common civic culture, but continuing it does guarantee that any attempt at such restoration will fail.

Economy: Cheap Labor versus Modern America

The key to the economic facet of the conflict between mass immigration and modern society is the fact that immigration floods the job market with low-skilled workers, creating what economists call a slack, or loose, labor market. This results in a buyer's market for labor, where employers can pick and choose among workers rather than having to compete with one another to attract and keep staff.

This has two major implications for the economy: First, a loose labor market reduces the bargaining power of workers compared to employers, resulting in lower earnings and less opportunity for advancement for the poorest and most marginal of Americans. And second, by artificially keeping wages lower than they would be otherwise, mass immigration reduces the incentives for more-efficient use of labor, slowing the natural progress of mechanization and other productivity increases in the low-wage industries where immigrants are concentrated.

In other words, while immigration certainly increases the overall size of our economy, it subverts the widely shared economic goals of a modern society: a large middle class open to all, working in high-wage, knowledge-intensive, and capital-intensive jobs exhibiting growing labor productivity and avoiding too skewed a distribution of income.

. . .

Economic Change

Immigration has always added workers to the economy, of course, but today is different because our economy has changed dramatically since the end of the first great immigration wave. When millions of Irish and Germans and Scandinavians and Italians and Jews and Slavs crossed the Atlantic, America was still settling vast swathes of empty land and undergoing the titanic process of industrialization. A century ago, what economists call the primary sector of the economy (farming, fishing, and so on) still employed more Americans than any other, as it had everywhere since the dawn of humankind. Today, only 2 percent of our workforce occupies itself in this way. Meanwhile, we've passed through the industrial phase of economic development and entered the postindustrial era, with the tertiary sector (the service industry overall) employing fully 80 percent of working Americans, and the percentage is climbing.

. . .

Into this twenty-first-century economy we have resumed the importation of what amounts to nineteenth-century foreign labor. Between 1980 and 2000, immigration increased the number of workers in the United States by nearly 10 percent and the number of high school dropouts by 20 percent, causing what economists call a supply shock—a sudden infusion of a particular resource (in this case, labor, especially low-skilled labor). And this shock to the labor market is likely to continue indefinitely, barring a change in federal policy; from 2000 to 2005, 8 million more immigrants arrived, the majority of them with no education beyond high school.

The contrast with American workers is stark: Only about 8 percent of native-born workers today have less than a high-school education, but almost 30 percent of immigrant workers do. What's more, while immigrants account for about 15 percent of all workers, they make up nearly 40 percent of workers lacking a high-school degree, resulting in an artificially bloated low-skilled labor force.

This gap between native and immigrant skills has been growing as the economy and society have modernized. In 1960, immigrant men were only about 25 percent more likely to be high-school dropouts than native-born men; by 1998, after the huge wave of low-skilled immigration, immigrants were nearly *four times* more likely to be dropouts. Of course, the process of modernization has been going on everywhere, so the proportion of immigrants who lack a high-school education has also been falling over the years, but much more slowly than among Americans, causing the gap to widen.

. . .

Reducing Wages

The effect of the ongoing surge of immigration on the income of low-skilled Americans is a textbook case of supply and demand. In fact, in his famous textbook, economist Paul Samuelson wrote specifically about the pre-1965 tight-border policies: "By keeping labor supply down, immigration policy tends to keep wages high." He stated the basic principle: "Limitation of the supply of any grade of labor relative to all other productive factors can be expected to raise its wage rate; an increase in supply will, other things being equal, tend to depress wage rates."

The National Research Council, in a wide-ranging study of immigration, concluded that in economic terms, immigration "harms workers who are substitutes for immigrants while benefiting workers who are complements to immigrants." In other words, since immigrants are disproportionately low skilled, it is low-skilled American workers who see their wages drop as immigrants expand the pool of people competing for jobs appropriate to their skill level. The NRC report estimated that immigration was responsible for nearly half the decline in wages of high-school dropouts between 1980 and 1994. At the same time, higher-skilled workers may gain, as the services that low-skilled workers provide (like lawn-mowing or valet parking) become cheaper and as the high skilled can specialize more.

In fact, immigration's overall economic benefit to Americans already here (as opposed to the simple increase in the total size of the economy) comes specifically from lowering the wages of American workers who compete with the immigrants. The National Research Council found that Americans as a whole received an economic benefit of between $1 billion and $10 billion per year from immigration, a tiny amount in what was, at the time of the report, an $8 trillion economy. But this small net economic benefit arises from the redistribution of wealth away from the poor and toward the rest of society; the report found that the poorest tenth of American workers (high-school dropouts who compete with immigrants) suffer a 5 percent cut in wages because of immigration, which is then redistributed to the rest of the American workforce, making the average person with at least a high-school education a minuscule two tenths of 1 percent richer.

In other words, immigration takes a figurative pound of flesh from one low-skilled American worker, who already has little to spare, and then slices it thinly among nine other better-educated Americans, who are more prosperous to begin with, giving each of them a barely noticeable benefit. And of course, even that small benefit is swamped by the extra cost in government services generated by low-skilled immigration, as discussed in the next chapter.

More recent research has found a quite pronounced loss to native-born American workers. Harvard economist George Borjas has found that the immigration wave of the 1980s and 1990s caused a drop in the annual earnings of all categories of American workers, including a 3.6 percent drop for male college graduates and a 7.4 percent drop for male high-school dropouts. Lest these numbers seem small, Borjas calculates that immigration reduced the average American high-school dropout's income in 2000 by about $1,800, while the American college graduate saw his salary reduced by $2,600.

Since education is not distributed evenly among Americans, some groups of American workers will experience a disproportionately large effect from immigration. Borjas found that the immigrant influx from 1980 to 2000 caused the annual wages of native-born white workers overall to fall 3.5 percent, but those of black workers fell 4.5 percent, and the wages of native-born Hispanic workers fell 5 percent. As he writes: "The adverse impact of immigration, therefore, is largest for the most disadvantaged native-born minorities."

Jason L. Riley  **NO**

Let Them In: The Case for Open Borders

. . . **T**his book expounds on two general themes. The first is that, contrary to received wisdom, today's Latino immigrants aren't "different," just newer. The second is that an open immigration policy is compatible with free-market conservatism and homeland security. I explain, from a conservative perspective, why the pessimists who say otherwise are mistaken. I argue that immigrants, including low-skill immigrants, are an asset to the United States, not a liability. Immigrants help keep our workforce younger and stronger than Asia's and Europe's. As entrepreneurs, they create jobs. As consumers, they generate economic activity that results in more overall economic growth. By taking jobs that over-qualified Americans spurn, they fill niches in the workforce that make our economy more efficient and allow for the upward mobility of the native population.

An immigration policy that acknowledges these economic realities would provide more, not fewer, legal ways for immigrants to enter the country. That, in turn, would go a long way toward reducing illegal entries. It would also alleviate pressure on the border and free up our overburdened patrols to track down terrorists, drug dealers, and other serious threats to our welfare. Unfortunately, as things stand, our border security officers spend most of their time chasing migrants who come north to mow our lawns and burp our babies. A guest-worker program for such individuals would help regulate the labor flow and isolate the criminals, thus making us much safer than any wall along the Rio Grande.

. . .

The reality is that America's foreign labor force helps to propel economic growth, not impede it, because the U.S. job market, properly understood, is not a zero-sum game. The number of jobs in the United States is not static. It's fluid, which is how we want it to be. In 2006, 55 million U.S. workers (or just less than 4.6 million per month) either quit their jobs or were fired. Yet 57 million people were hired over the same period. In a typical year, a third of our workforce is turning over. In about half of those cases the separation is voluntary; in the other half, the worker has been shown the door. But either way, this messy churn, which can disrupt lives and even make obsolete entire industries, has positive macroeconomic consequences in the long run.

From *Let Them In: The Case for Open Borders* (Gotham, 2008), pp. 12–13, 54–65, 145–147, 153–157. Copyright © 2008 by Jason L. Riley. Reprinted by permission of Penguin Group USA.

That's because flexible labor markets, the kind that minimize the costs to a business of hiring and firing employees, enable workers and employers alike to find the employment situation that suits them best. Flexible labor markets make it easier for an employee who doesn't like a job, is let go, or simply feels underappreciated by his boss to find another position somewhere else. And flexible labor markets make it more likely that an employer will expand his workforce, or take a chance on a job seeker who isn't very skilled or perhaps has a spotty record.

A better fit between employers and employees increases productivity and prosperity and makes markets more responsive to consumer demand. In the end, employers, workers, and consumers are all better off. Immigrants, be they Salvadoran dishwashers, Indian motel operators, or Russian microbiologists, increase the fluidity of U.S. labor markets. Access to fewer of them would reduce the flexibility that makes America so productive.

A nation's ability to produce goods and services determines its wealth. Productivity, defined as the quantity of goods and services produced from each hour of a worker's time, is why some nations are wealthier than others. It's a major reason why GDP per capita in the United States was $39,676 in 2007, but only $29,300 in France, $6,394 in Ukraine, and $1,237 in Mozambique. Productivity, writes Harvard economist N. Gregory Mankiw, "is the key determinant of living standards" and "the key determinant in growth of living standards." For our purposes, the question is whether immigrant labor ultimately contributes to America's productivity and economic growth, or detracts from it.

Fundamentally, immigration to the United States is a function of a labor shortage for certain kinds of jobs here. Of course, work is not the only reason foreigners migrate to America, but judging from their overrepresentation in the labor force, and the fact that immigrants (excluding refugees) resort to welfare less often than the native-born population, we know that work is the main reason they come.

Rather than appropriating jobs from natives, however, immigrants are more likely to be simply filling them—and often facilitating more employment opportunities in the process. The job-displacement myth, which fuels so much of the national immigration debate, can be rebutted empirically. In 2006, for example, there were around 146 million workers in the United States, and 15 percent, or 21 million, were foreign born. If immigrants are stealing jobs, 21 million U.S. natives, or something approximating that number, should have been out of work. But as economics reporter Roger Lowenstein noted in a July 2006 *New York Times Magazine* article, "the country has nothing close to that many unemployed. (The actual number is only seven million.) So the majority of immigrants can't literally have 'taken' jobs; they must be doing jobs that wouldn't have existed had the immigrants not been here."

The reason that immigrant workers tend not to elbow aside natives for jobs and depress wages has to do with the education and skills that foreigners typically bring to the U.S. labor market. Most immigrants fall into one of two categories: low-skilled laborers or high-skilled professionals. One-third of all immigrants have less than a high school education, and one-quarter hold a bachelor's or advanced degree. Most native workers, by contrast, are concentrated betwixt those two extremes. Hence, immigrant workers tend to act as complements to the native U.S. workforce rather than substitutes. There is some overlap, of course, but this skill distribution is the reason immigrants and natives for the most part aren't competing for the same positions.

. . .

A 2007 study published by economist Giovanni Peri analyzed the effects of immigrant labor on California, a state that wasn't chosen arbitrarily. The Golden State, the nation's most populous, is home to nearly a third of all foreign-born U.S. workers. Los Angeles, the nation's second-largest city after New York, is nearly half Hispanic. In the past decade, California's population growth has been almost entirely due to immigration, much of it illegal. The term "Mexifornia" has entered the lexicon. If, as conventional wisdom holds, immigration does in fact have a negative impact on the job security of Americans, California is one of the more likely places that the phenomenon would be manifest.

Yet Peri, a professor of economics at the University of California at Davis, found "no evidence that the inflow of immigrants over the period 1960–2004 worsened the employment opportunities of natives with similar education and experience." With respect to wages, he found that "during 1990–2004, immigration induced a 4 percent real wage increase for the average native worker. This effect ranged from near zero (+0.2 percent) for wages of native high school dropouts and between 3 and 7 percent for native workers with at least a high school diploma." In other words, immigrants tended to expand the economic pie, not displace native workers. These foreign workers lifted all socioeconomic boats; it was just a matter of how much.

At first blush, Peri's findings might seem counterintuitive. It's assumed that because immigrants increase the supply of labor, they necessarily decrease both the wages and the employment opportunities of the native workers. If most immigrant workers were interchangeable with U.S. natives, that might indeed be the case. But the assumption is problematic because immigrants on average aren't stand-ins for natives.

. . .

Peri found that since workers with different levels of education perform different tasks, the majority of native-born workers—high school graduates with some college—experience benefits, more than competition, from the foreign-born workers who are concentrated in high and low educational groups. The result is a more efficient domestic labor market, which leads to more capital investment, higher overall economic growth, and, ultimately, more choices for consumers.

But it also leads to better jobs and higher pay for American workers, explains Peri. "In nontechnical terms," he writes, "the wages of native workers could increase because the increased supply of migrants is likely to put native workers in jobs where they perform supervisory, managerial, training, and . . . coordinating tasks, which makes them more productive." More workers also means more consumers, "so that immigration might simply increase total production and demand without depressing wages."

. . .

In 1994 economist Richard Vedder of Ohio University, working with Lowell Gallaway and Stephen Moore, conducted a historical analysis of immigration's impact on the entire U.S. labor force. They found "no statistically reliable correlation between the percentage of the population that was foreign-born and the national unemployment rate over the period 1900–1989, or for just the postwar era (1947–1989)." Moreover, Vedder found that if there is any correlation between immigration and unemployment, it would appear to be negative. Which is to say that higher immigration is associated with lower unemployment.

. . .

Like Peri, Vedder concluded that the reason immigration doesn't cause unemployment is because immigrants help enlarge America's economic pie. "Immigrants expand total output and the demand for labor, offsetting the negative effects that a greater labor supply might have," he writes. "They fill vital niches at the ends of the skill spectrum, doing low-skilled jobs that native Americans rebuff (at prevailing wages) as well as sophisticated high-skill jobs."

Among high-skilled immigrant workers, these dots are perhaps easier to connect. Think of a silicon chip manufacturer in the United States that hires a bright immigrant engineer from China to redesign its products with the goal of making them more cost-efficient and marketable. If the hire is a success, the firm winds up making more chips, which requires more employees. These additional hires—from the managers to the secretaries—are all more likely to be U.S. natives. So are the additional advertisers and marketers who will be sought as the company expands. Why? In part because the skills necessary to do those jobs generally include a familiarity with the native language and culture that a recent immigrant is less likely to possess. As for the American consumer, he's now getting a better product, more choices, and lower prices. Thus has an immigrant hire resulted in more jobs for U.S. natives, not fewer, and increased overall productivity.

. . .

Of course, high-skill immigrants from Europe, Asia, and Southeast Asia do more than create extra jobs for U.S. employers. They also seem to have a knack for creating entirely new companies that employ thousands of people. Lucky for us. Technology firms, in particular, have made possible the U.S. productivity boom of the past decade. And immigrants have had a hand in starting a disproportionate number of the most successful ones—from Google and eBay to Yahoo! and Sun Microsystems.

A National Foundation for American Policy paper by Stuart Anderson and Michaela Platzer assessed the impact of immigrant entrepreneurs and professionals on U.S. competitiveness. Between 1991 and 2006, they discovered, immigrants started 25 percent of U.S. public companies that were venture-backed. These businesses employed some 220,000 people in the United States and boasted a market capitalization that "exceeds $500 billion, adding significant value to the American economy."

. . . Linguistic assimilation is key, not least because it amounts to a job skill that can increase earnings. And while restrictionists claim otherwise, there's simply no evidence that Latinos are rejecting English. "The model that we have from the European experience," sociologist Richard Alba told me in an interview, "is that the children of immigrants born in the U.S. grow up in homes where they learn, to some extent, the mother tongue. They understand it and may speak it, but they prefer English. And when they grow up, they establish homes where English is the dominant language."

According to 2005 census data, just one-third of immigrants who are in the country for less than a decade speak English well, but that fraction climbs to nearly three-quarters for those here thirty years or more. There may be more bilingualism today among the children of immigrants, but there's no indication that Spanish is dominant in the second generation. The 2000 census found that 91 percent of the children and 97 percent of the grandchildren of Mexican immigrants spoke English well. Nor are there signs, bilingual-education advocates notwithstanding, that immigrant parents *want* their children speaking Spanish. A 2002 Pew Hispanic Center/Kaiser Foundation survey found that 89 percent of Latinos "believe immigrants need to learn to speak English to succeed in the United States."

Longitudinal analyses also reveal that homeownership is up and poverty is down among the Latino immigrants. Using as his sample California, which has the country's largest concentration of Mexican foreign nationals, Myers notes that 16 percent of Latinos arriving in the Golden State in the 1970s owned homes by 1980. But more than 33 percent owned homes by 1990, and over half by 2000. The average rate of homeownership nationally was just over 66 percent in 2000.

The 2000 census found that the foreign-born poverty rate had fallen slightly, to 19.1 percent from 19.8 percent in. 1990. Myers reports that this small decrease was not due to an influx of more prosperous immigrant groups, such as Asians. The disaggregated data show that poverty fell among Latinos and Asians alike. Nor can it be attributed to a temporary upturn in the economy, since the economic conditions measured in the 1990 and 2000 censuses were similar. Again using as his sample California, Myers found that poverty reversal was directly attributable to the maturing of California's immigrant population. Longer-residing immigrants generally experience substantial improvements in poverty, but in the past those gains were overshadowed by the increasing numbers of newcomers. He explains: "Now that the longer-settled immigrants are beginning to outweigh the newcomers in number, the force of upward mobility is no longer being offset by the relatively high poverty of newcomers, and the total poverty rate of the foreign-born has turned around."

Myers is hardly the only social scientist to notice Latino upward mobility, and California isn't the only place it's happening. In a definitive longitudinal study in the 1990s, sociologists Alejandro Portes and Ruben Rumbaut found substantial second-generation progress among Latinos in Miami and Fort Lauderdale as well. Nationwide cross-generational studies show the same results. In 2006, economist James Smith of the RAND Corporation found that successive generations of Latinos have experienced significant improvements in wages relative both to their fathers and grandfathers and to the native whites with whom they compete for jobs. And Roger Waldinger and Renee Reichl, two UCLA social scientists, found that while first-generation Mexican men earned just half as much as white natives in 2000, the second generation had upped their earnings to three-quarters of their Anglo counterparts.

. . .

Assimilation is less about immigrants adopting our culture than about immigrants adopting our values. And America has been uniquely successful in this regard. Canada has utterly failed to bridge its linguistic divide. French Canadians in Quebec aren't just pro–French language but also anti-English. The United States has as many French Canadians as does Canada, and a large percentage of them live in New England, yet there has been no such tension on this side of the border.

. . .

The key to the success of the U.S. assimilation model, says Peter Salins, a senior fellow at the Manhattan Institute, is that "we put so much more stress on shared values rather than shared cultures." In an interview, Salins explained that immigrants find America's values and ideals as attractive as its economic opportunities. Yes, they come here to get rich, but it's more than that. It's also our value framework, with its emphasis on individual initiative and individual opportunity. Foreigners like the fact that you can make more money *because* you are hard-working or diligent or clever.

Salins says the other major value component is our civic institutions. We're the land of liberty and democracy. Here, people can say what they want, be what they want, do what they want. These are attractive values. And Americans are much more concerned about people sharing their values than sharing their cultural artifacts.

. . .

Key elements of America's Anglo-Protestant culture, [Salins] says, "include: the English language; Christianity; religious commitment; English concepts of the rule of law, the responsibility of rulers, and the rights of individuals; dissenting Protestant values of individualism, the work ethic, and the belief that humans have the ability and the duty to try to create a heaven on earth, a 'city on a hill.'"

Nothing indicates that today's immigrants, like those who came before them, don't share Huntington's commitment to those ideals.

. . .

For all the loud talk of late, the American public seems not to have lost confidence in the melting pot. If it had, you'd know it. There would be "English-only" signs and militarized border zones. There would be ubiquitous police checkpoints and far-right political parties like France's National Front. Michelle Malkin would be considered a serious pundit, not Ann Coulter without the nuance.

Of course, there is some bigotry and stupidity out there, which we'll always have. But when people really believe they can't live another day with other kinds of people, they don't send e-mails to *The O'Reilly Factor*. They engage in ethnic warfare. You get the Serbs and the Croats in the Balkans, the Hindus and the Muslims in India, the Hutus and the Tutsis in Rwanda. What we have in America is periodic grumpiness, short-lived sniffing about the most recent arrivals, a vague and ambivalent disdain that doesn't settle too deeply into the psyche. Americans still believe that our assimilationist model is working, even if the elites on the left and right who claim to speak on their behalf do not.

EXPLORING THE ISSUE

Is Third World Immigration a Threat to America's Way of Life?

Critical Thinking and Reflection

1. What are we afraid of when we oppose immigration? Is it that we assume that bad people will immigrate here?
2. Who are the people who want to leave their homeland and come to America?
3. To what extent are people pushed away from their countries by bad general conditions (dictatorship or economic depression) or by bad personal conditions (persecution or lack of opportunities)?
4. To what extent are people drawn to America by its values or its opportunities?
5. How does the process of assimilation work with various types of immigrants? Knowing English is very important to assimilation. What else is key?
6. Why do second-generation immigrants generally assimilate very successfully?
7. In what way does being embedded in an immigrant community facilitate assimilation and in what way does it hinder assimilation?

Is There Common Ground?

Former representative Silvio Conte (R-Massachusetts) said at a citizenship ceremony, "You can go to France, but you will never be a Frenchman. You can go to Germany, but you will never be a German. Today you are all Americans, and that is why this is the greatest country on the face of the earth." At one time, America's open door to immigrants was one of the prides of America. For some people, like Riley, it still is. He thinks that immigration is making America stronger. Many people disagree because they fear the consequences of today's immigration. Krikorian worries that the new immigrants will not assimilate very well in America as it is today. The results could be tragic. There are valid points on both sides. Does that mean that the truth lies in the middle—that immigration is both good and bad? This might very well be the case, but immigration policy is not likely to be very well balanced. The dominant mood today is anti-immigrant. Keep them out. Make illegal immigrants go home. But many immigrants have lived here a long time, so this is their home. Is America going to be compassionate? Is compassion a strong American value? But what about justice to those who are trying to get here legally? America will be having this debate for many decades.

Additional Resources

The following works describe or debate the immigration issue: Sarah Spencer, *The Migration Debate* (Policy Press, 2011); Mary C. Waters, Reed Ueda, and Helen B. Marrow, eds., *The New Americans: A Guide to Immigration Since 1965* (Harvard University Press, 2007); Jane Guskin and David L. Wilson, *The Politics of Immigration: Questions and Answers* (Monthly Review Press, 2007); Spencer Abraham and Lee H. Hamilton, *Immigration and America's Future: A New Chapter: Report of the Independent Task Force on Immigration and America's Future* (Migration Policy Institute, 2006); Nancy Foner, ed., *Not Just Black and White: Historical and Contemporary Perspectives on Immigration, Race, and Ethnicity in the United States* (Russell Sage Foundation, 2004); Carol M. Swain, ed., *Debating Immigration* (Cambridge University Press, 2007); and Lina Newton, *Illegal, Alien, or Immigrant: The Politics of Immigration Reform* (New York University Press, 2008).

Works that focus on assimilation and ethnic diversity include Ariane Chebel d'Appollonia and Simon Reich, eds., *Managing Ethnic Diversity after 9/11: Integration, Security, and Civil Liberties* (Rutgers University Press, 2010); David Trend, *A Culture Divided: America's Struggle for Unity* (Paradigm Publishers, 2009); Richard Alba and Mary C. Waters, eds., *The Next Generation: Immigrant Youth in a Comparative Perspective* (New York University, 2011); Kathleen R. Arnold, *American Immigration after 1996: The Shifting Ground of Political Inclusion* (Pennsylvania State University Press, 2011); Caroline L. Faulkner, *Economic Mobility and Cultural Assimilation among Children of Immigrants* (LFB Scholarly Publication, 2011); and Christina Slade and Martina Mollering, eds., *From Immigrant to Citizen: Texting Language, Testing Culture* (Palgrave Macmillan, 2010). Stanley Lieberson and Mary C. Waters, in *From Many Strands* (Russell Sage Foundation, 1988), argue that ethnic groups with European origins are assimilating, marrying outside their groups, and losing their ethnic identities. Richard D. Alba's study "Assimilation's Quiet Tide," *The Public Interest* (Spring 1995), confirms these findings. Latinos, however, are assimilating more slowly; see Jessica M. Vasquez, *Mexican Americans Across Generations: Immigrant Families, Racial Realities* (New York University Press, 2011); Paul R. Smokowski, *Becoming Bicultural: Risk, Resilience, and Latino Youth* (New York University Press, 2011); and Rosalyn Negron, *Ethnic Identification among Urban Latinos: Language and Flexibility* (LFB Scholarly Publishing, 2011). Susan F. Martin, *A Nation of Immigrants* (Oxford University Press, 2011), and Dowell Myers, in *Immigrants and Boomers: Forging a New Social Contract for the Future of America* (Russell Sage Foundation, 2007), emphasize the positive benefits of immigration for America. Several major works debate whether immigrants, on average, benefit America economically and whether they are assimilating. Sources that argue that immigrants largely benefit America include Julian L. Simon, *The Economic Consequences of Immigration*, 2nd ed. (University of Michigan Press, 1999), and *Immigration: The Demographic and Economic Facts* (Cato Institute, 1995), and Aviva Chomsky, *"They Take Our Jobs!": And 20 Other Myth about Immigration* (Beacon Press 2007). Sources that argue that immigrants have more negative than positive impacts include George Borjas, *Heaven's Door: Immigration Policy and the American Economy* (Princeton University Press, 1999); Roy Beck, *The Case Against Immigration* (W. W. Norton, 1996); Patrick Buchanan, *The Death of the West: How Dying Populations and Immigrant Invasions Imperil Our Country and Civilization* (Thomas Dunne Books, 2002); and Otis L. Graham, Jr., *Unguarded Gates: A History of American's Immigration Crisis* (Rowman & Littlefield, 2004). Thomas Sowell argues in *Dismantling America: And Other Controversial Essays* that immigration is one of several factors that are destroying American values (Basic Books, 2010).

Internet References . . .

American Men's Studies Association

The American Men's Studies Association is a not-for-profit professional organization of scholars, therapists, and others interested in the exploration of masculinity
in modern society.

http://mensstudies.org

Feminist Majority Foundation

The Feminist Majority Foundation website provides affirmative action links,
resources from women's professional organizations, information for empowering
women in business, sexual harassment information, and much more.

www.feminist.org

GLAAD: Gay and Lesbian Alliance Against Defamation

The Gay and Lesbian Alliance Against Defamation (GLAAD), formed in New York
in 1985, seeks to improve the public's attitudes toward homosexuality and to put
an end to discrimination against lesbians and gay men.

www.glaad.org

International Lesbian and Gay Association

The resources on the International Lesbian and Gay Association website are
provided by a worldwide network of lesbian, gay, bisexual, and transgendered
groups.

www.ilga.org

SocioSite: Feminism and Women's Issues

The Feminism and Women's Issues SocioSite provides insights into a number
of issues that affect family relationships. It covers wide-ranging issues regarding women and men, family and children, and much more.

www.sociosite.net/index.php

Sex Roles, Gender, and the Family

*T**he modern feminist movement has advanced the causes of women to the point where there are now more women in the workforce in the United States than ever before. Professions and trades that were traditionally regarded as the provinces of men have opened up to women, and women now have easier access to the education and training necessary to excel in these new areas. But what is happening to sex roles, and what are the effects of changing sex roles? How have men and women been affected by the stress caused by current sex roles, the demand for the right to same-sex marriages, and the deterioration of the traditional family structure? The issues in this part address these sorts of questions.*

- Does Divorce Have Long-Term Damaging Effects on Children?
- Are Professional Women "Opting Out" of Work by Choice?
- Should Same-Sex Marriages Be Legally Recognized?

ISSUE 3

Does Divorce Have Long-Term Damaging Effects on Children?

YES: Elizabeth Marquardt, from "The Bad Divorce," *First Things* (February 2005)

NO: Constance Ahrons, from "No Easy Answers: Why the Popular View of Divorce Is Wrong," *We're Still Family: What Grown Children Have to Say about Their Parents' Divorce* (HarperCollins, 2004)

Learning Outcomes

After reading this issue, you should be able to:

- Identify both the positive and negative impacts of the divorce on unhappily married couples and their children.
- Differentiate the short-term impacts from the long-term impacts of such divorces on children.
- Understand how children cope and adapt to traumatic family events generally and specifically to divorce.
- Understand how the economic situation generally changes for the children after the divorce.
- Separate out the economic consequences from other consequences in order to understand what the other consequences would be on children if their economic situation did not worsen.
- Understand how the postdivorce arrangements and ex-spouses' interpersonal behaviors affect the consequences of the divorce for the children.

ISSUE SUMMARY

YES: Elizabeth Marquardt, director of the Center for Marriage and Families, defends the common belief that divorce has devastating impacts on children and attacks Constance Ahrons's counter-thesis.

NO: Constance Ahrons, co-chair of the Council on Contemporary Families, found in her research on the children of divorced parents that they do quite well in later life and most think that they were not harmed by the divorce.

The state of the American family deeply concerns many Americans. About 40 percent of marriages end in divorce, and only 27 percent of children born in 1990 are expected to be living with both parents by the time they reach age 17. Most Americans, therefore, are affected personally or are close to people who are affected by structural changes in the family. Few people can avoid being exposed to the issue: violence in the family and celebrity divorces are standard fare for news programs, and magazine articles decrying the breakdown of the family appear frequently. Politicians today try to address the problems of the family. Academics have affirmed that the family crisis has numerous significant negative effects on children, spouses, and the rest of society.

But is the situation as bad as portrayed? Many of you reading this come from divorced homes and can evaluate how much you suffered and whether you have been scarred for life. All of you can look around you and judge for yourselves how your acquaintances have been affected by divorce. Obviously, divorce is much worse for children than a good marriage, but is it worse than a bad marriage? Because the answer is not obvious, the debate heats up.

One reason divorce is a very important issue is the important role that the family plays in the functioning of society. For a society to survive, its population must reproduce (or take in many immigrants), and its young must be trained to perform adult roles and to have the values and attitudes that will motivate them to contribute to society. Procreation and socialization are two vital roles that families traditionally have performed. In addition, the family provides economic and emotional support for its members, which is vital to their effective functioning in society. Stable, well-functioning families best perform these roles and divorce jeopardizes them.

Although most experts agree that the American family is in crisis, there is little agreement about what, if anything, should be done about it. After all, most of these problems result from the choices that people make to try to increase their happiness. People end unhappy marriages. When they do, most of them also carefully consider the best interests of the children. These considerations obviously prevent or delay many divorces and probably should prevent many more. Obviously, however, many situations are improved by divorce, especially if the divorce and aftermath arrangements are conducted in a compassionate manner. So which way is best is a judgment call, both by the potentially divorcing parents and by the academics who study the issue.

In the selections that follow, Constance Ahrons draws from her extensive work on the children of divorce to show that divorce has far fewer negative consequences on children than is commonly assumed. Elizabeth Marquardt's article is totally devoted to refuting Ahrons's thesis.

YES

Elizabeth Marquardt

The Bad Divorce

It is often said that those who are concerned about the social and personal effects of divorce are nostalgic for the 1950s, yearning for a mythical time when men worked, women happily stayed home baking cookies for the kids, and marriages never dissolved. Yet often the same people who make the charge of mythology are caught in a bit of nostalgia of their own, pining for the sexual liberationism of the 1970s, when many experts began to embrace unfettered divorce, confident that children, no less than adults, would thrive once "unhappy" marriages were brought to a speedy end.

Constance Ahrons, who coined the term "the good divorce" in the title of an influential 1992 book that examined ninety-eight divorcing couples, is very much a member of the latter camp. In her new book, *We're Still Family: What Grown Children Have to Say about Their Parents' Divorce,* Ahrons returns to those ninety-eight couples to survey their now-grown children. The result is a study based on telephone interviews with 173 young adults from eighty-nine families that tries to advance the idea it is not divorce itself that burdens children but rather the way in which parents divorce. As in her earlier book, Ahrons argues that the vocabulary we use to discuss divorce and remarriage is negative; she would prefer that we regard divorced families as "changed" or "rearranged" rather than broken, damaged, or destroyed. She claims that upbeat language will, above all, help children feel less stigmatized by divorce. Both of her books offer many new terms, such as "binuclear" and "tribe," to describe divorced families. The specific novelty of the new book is Ahrons' claim that her interviewees view their parents' divorces in a positive light.

It is with delight, then, that Ahrons shares surprising new findings from her on-going study. According to Ahrons, over three-quarters of the young people from divorced families who she interviewed do not wish their parents were still together. A similar proportion feel their parents' decision to divorce was a good one, that their parents are better off today, and that they themselves are either better off or not affected by the divorce. To general readers who have been following the debates about children of divorce in recent years, such findings might sound like big news. But there are problems.

According to Ahrons, over three-quarters of the young people whom she interviewed do not wish that their parents were still together. A similar proportion feel that their parents' decision to divorce was a good one, that their parents are better off today, and that they themselves are either better off because of the divorce or have not been affected by it. Statistically, that sounds overwhelmingly convincing. But an answer to a survey question tells us very little unless we have a context for interpreting it and some grasp of the actual experiences that gave rise to it.

Like those whom Ahrons interviewed, I grew up in a divorced family, my parents having split when I was two years old. Like Ahrons, I am a researcher in the field, having led, with Norval Glenn, a study of young adults from both divorced and intact families that included a nationally representative telephone survey of some 1,500 people. As someone who studies children of divorce and who is herself a grown child of divorce, I have noticed that the kinds of questions that get asked in such studies and the way the answers are interpreted often depend on whether the questioner views divorce from the standpoint of the child or the parent.

Take, for example, Ahrons' finding that the majority of people raised in divorced families do not wish that their parents were together. Ahrons did not ask whether as children these young people had hoped their parents would reunite. Instead, she asked if they wish today their parents were still together. She presents their negative answers as gratifying evidence that divorce is affirmed by children. But is that really the right conclusion to draw?

Imagine the following scenario. One day when you are a child your parents come to you and tell you they are splitting up. Your life suddenly changes in lots of ways. Dad leaves, or maybe Mom does. You may move or change schools or lose friendships, or all of the above. Money is suddenly very tight and stays that way for a long time. You may not see one set of grandparents, aunts, uncles, and cousins nearly as much as you used to. Then, Mom starts dating, or maybe Dad does. A boyfriend or girlfriend moves in, perhaps bringing along his or her own kids. You may see one or both of your parents marry again; you may see one or both of them get divorced a second time. You deal with the losses. You adjust as best you can. You grow up and try to figure out this "relationship" thing for yourself. Then, some interviewer on the telephone asks if you wish your parents were still together today. A lifetime of pain and anger and adjustment flashes before your eyes. Any memory of your parents together as a couple—if you can remember them together at all—is buried deep under all those feelings. Your divorced parents have always seemed like polar opposites to you. No one could be more different from your mother than your father, and vice versa. "No," you reply to the interviewer, "I don't wish my parents were still together." Of course, one cannot automatically attribute such a train of thought to all of Ahrons' interview subjects. Still, it is plausible, and it might explain at least some of the responses. But Ahrons does not even consider it.

Ahrons tells us that the vast majority of young people in her study feel that they are either better off or not affected by their parents' divorce. For a child of divorce there could hardly be a more loaded question than this one. The generation that Ahrons is interviewing grew up in a time of massive changes in family life, with experts assuring parents that if they became happier after divorce, their children would as well. There wasn't a lot of patience for people who felt otherwise—especially when those people were children, with their aggravating preference for conventional married life over the adventures of divorce, and their tendency to look askance at their parents' new love interests.

However, a child soon learns the natural lesson that complaining about a parent's choices is a surefire way to be ignored or worse, and that what parents want above all is praise for those choices. Few things inspire as much admiration among divorced parents and their friends as the words of a child reassuring them that the divorce was no big deal—or even better, that it gave the child something beneficial, like early independence, or a new brother or sister. Parents are proud of a resilient child. They are embarrassed and frustrated by a child who claims to be a victim. And who among us wants to be a victim? Who would not rather be a hero, or at least a well-adjusted and agreeable person? When the interviewer calls on the telephone, what will the young adult be more likely to say? Something like "I'm damaged goods"? Or "Yes, it was tough at times but I survived it, and I'm stronger for it today." It is the second reply that children of divorce have all their lives been encouraged to give; and the fact that they are willing to give it yet again is hardly, as Ahrons would have it, news.

Thus, Ahrons' statistics on their own hardly constitute three cheers for divorce. Far more meaningful and revealing are the extended quotations from interview subjects with which the book is liberally studded. She writes, for instance, that Andy, now thirty-two, sees "value" in his parents' divorce. Why? Because:

> "I learned a lot. I grew up a lot more quickly than a lot of my friends. Not that that's a good thing or a bad thing. People were always thinking I was older than I was because of the way I carried myself."

Treating a sad, unfortunate experience (like being forced to grow up more quickly than one's peers) as something neutral or even positive is merely one example of what can happen when a person attempts to conform to a culture that insists that divorce is no big deal. To take such an ambivalent response as clear evidence that divorce does no damage, as Ahrons does is inexcusable.

Ahrons cheerfully reports other "good" results of divorce. Here for example is Brian, whose parents split when he was five:

> "In general, I think [the divorce] has had very positive effects. I see what happens in divorces, and I have promised myself that I would do anything to not get a divorce. I don't want my kids to go through what I went through."

Tracy, whose parents divorced when she was twelve, sees a similar upside to divorce:

> "I saw some of the things my parents did and know not to do that in my marriage and see the way they treated each other and know not to do that to my spouse and my children. I know [the divorce] has made me more committed to my husband and my children."

These are ringing endorsements of divorce as a positive life event? Like the testimony of a child who's learned a painful but useful lesson about the dangers of playing with fire, such accounts indicate that the primary benefit of divorce is to encourage young people to avoid it in their own lives if at all possible.

Then there are the significant problems with the structure of Ahrons' study itself. While the original families were recruited using a randomized method, the study lacks any control group. In other words, Ahrons interviewed plenty of young people from divorced families but spoke to no one of similar ages from intact families. So she really can't tell us anything at all about how these young people might differ from their peers.

Rather than acknowledging that her lack of a control group is a serious limitation, Ahrons sidesteps the issue. In several places she compares her subjects to generalized "social trends" or "their contemporaries" and decides, not surprisingly, that they are not all that different. Thus, Ahrons notes that many of the young people from divorced families told her they frequently struggled with issues of "commitment, trust, and dealing with conflict," but on this finding she comments, "These issues are precisely the ones that most adults in this stage of their development grapple with, whether they grow up in a nuclear family or not." Never mind that she has not interviewed any of those other young people, or cited any studies to back up her contention, or acknowledged the possibility that, while all young people do have to deal with these kinds of interpersonal issues, some have a much harder time doing it than others. Ahrons instead wholly dismisses the pain expressed by the children of divorce and assures us that they are simply passing through a normal development phase.

When it comes to her conclusions, Ahrons claims that "if you had a devitalized or high-conflict marriage, you can take heart that the decision to divorce may have been the very best thing you could have done for your children." While research does show that children, on average, do better after a high-conflict marriage ends (the same research, by Paul Amato and Alan Booth, also shows that only one-third of divorces end high-conflict marriages), no one—Ahrons included—has shown that children do better when an adult ends a marriage he or she perceives as "devitalized." Children don't much care whether their parents have a "vital" marriage. They care whether their mother and father live with them, take care of them, and don't fight a lot. . . .

Ahrons also remains preoccupied with the concept of stigma. She writes, for instance, that we are seeing "progress" because a high divorce rate has the effect of reducing the stigma experienced by children of divorce. That's all well and good, but one wonders why Ahrons gives stigma so much attention while saying nothing about a far more damaging social problem for children of divorce—namely, silence. Consider my own experience. The type of family in which I grew up was radically different from the intact family model. Yet no one around me, not even therapists, ever once acknowledged that fact. Never mind that my beloved father lived hours away, or that the mother I adored was often stressed as she tried to earn a living while also acting as a single parent. I was left to assume, like many children of divorce, that whatever problems I struggled with were no one's fault but my own. The demand that children of divorce keep quiet and get with the program puts them in the position of protecting adults from guilt and further stress—effectively reversing the natural order of family life in which the adults are the protectors of children.

Ahrons is remarkably unsympathetic to the children on whom this burden is laid. What do children of divorce long for? According to Ahrons, they nurture unrealistic hopes for "tidy," "perfect" families. She uses these words so frequently—the first term appears at least six times in the book and the second at least four times—that she sometimes appears to be portraying children of divorce as weird obsessives. Speaking directly to children of divorce, Ahrons offers the following advice: "You may not have the idyllic family you dreamed of . . . [but] often the only thing within our control is how we perceive or interpret an event." "For example, you can choose to see your family as rearranged, or you can choose to see it as broken." Indeed, the curative powers of social constructivism are nothing short of miraculous. Encouraging readers to stop using the descriptive term "adult child of divorce," she asserts that "it's a stigmatizing label that presumes you are deficient or traumatized. . . . If you have fallen prey to using it to explain something about yourself, ask yourself if it is keeping you from making changes that might bring you more satisfaction in your life." Apparently, coming to grips with one's family history and the deepest sources of one's sadness and loneliness is the worst thing a child can do. . . .

Ahrons surely knows more about the tragedies of divorce than her thesis allows her to admit. She has studied divorced families for years. She has worked with them as a clinician. She has been through divorce herself. Yet she inevitably follows up heartbreaking observations of interviewees with the confident assertion that everyone involved would be so much happier if only they talked themselves out of—and even walked away from—their anguish. As she writes in one (unintentionally haunting) passage, "Over the years I have listened to many divorcing parents in my clinical practice talk about how much they look forward to the day when their children will be grown and they won't have to have anything more to do with their exes." Is it possible to image a sadder or more desperate desire than this one—the longing for one's children to grow up faster so that relations with one's ex-spouse can be more effectively severed? In such passages it becomes obvious that all of Ahrons' efforts to explain away the tragedy of divorce and its legacy are in vain. In the end, the theory collapses before reality.

Ahrons' poorly structured study and far too tendentious thesis are of no help to us in thinking through our approach to divorce and its consequences. Children of divorce are real, complex people who are deeply shaped by a new kind of fractured family life—one whose current prevalence is unprecedented in human history. These children are not nostalgic for "tidy," "perfect," "idyllic" families. They grieve the real losses that follow from their parents' divorce. They don't need new words to describe what they've been through. Ordinary words will serve quite well—provided that people are willing to listen to them.

No Easy Answers: Why the Popular View of Divorce Is Wrong

. . . **A**lthough it may appear strange, my exhusband's untimely death brought his second and first families closer together. I had mourned at his funeral and spent time with his family and friends for several days afterward. A different level of kinship formed, as we—his first and second families—shared our loss and sadness. Since then, we have chosen to join together at several family celebrations, which has added a deeper dimension to our feelings of family.

You may be thinking, "This is all so rational. There's no way my family could pull this off." Or perhaps, like the many people who have shared their stories with me over the years, you are nodding your head knowingly, remembering similar occasions in your own family. The truth is we are like many extended families rearranged by divorce. My ties to my exhusband's family are not close but we care about one another. We seldom have contact outside of family occasions, but we know we're family. We hear stories of each other's comings and goings, transmitted to us through our mutual ties to my daughters, and now, through grandchildren. But if many families, like my own, continue to have relationships years after divorce, why don't we hear more about them?

Quite simply, it's because this is not the way it's supposed to be. My family, and the many others like mine, don't fit the ideal images we have about families. They appear strange because they're not tidy. There are "extra" people and relationships that don't exist in nuclear families and are awkward to describe because we don't have familiar and socially defined kinship terms to do so. Although families rearranged and expanded by divorce are rapidly growing and increasingly common, our resistance to accepting them as normal makes them appear deviant.

Societal change is painfully slow, which results in the situation wherein the current realities of family life come into conflict with our valued images. Sociologists call this difference "cultural lag," the difference between what is real and what we hold as ideal. This lag occurs because of our powerful resistance to acknowledging changes that challenge our basic beliefs about what's good and what's bad in our society.

Why Good Divorces Are Invisible

Good divorces are those in which the divorce does not destroy meaningful family relationships. Parents maintain a sufficiently cooperative and supportive relationship that allows them to focus on the needs of their children. In good divorces children continue to have ties to both their mothers and their fathers, and each of their extended families, including those acquired when either parent remarries.

Good divorces have been well-kept secrets because to acknowledge them in mainstream life threatens our nostalgic images of family. If the secret got out that indeed many families that don't fit our "mom and pop" household ideal are healthy, we would have to question the basic societal premise that marriage and family are synonymous. And that reality upsets a lot of people, who then respond with familiar outcries that divorce is eroding our basic values and destroying society.

Although we view ourselves as a society in which nuclear families and life-long monogamous marriages predominate, the reality is that 43 percent of first marriages will end in divorce. Over half of new marriages are actually remarriages for at least one of the partners. Not only have either the bride or groom (or both) been divorced but increasingly one of them also has parents who are divorced.

Families are the way we organize to raise children. Although we hold the ideal image that marriage is a precursor to establishing a family, modern parents are increasingly challenging this traditional ideal. Families today arrange—and rearrange—themselves in many responsible ways that meet the needs of children for nurturance, guidance and economic support. Family historian Stephanie Coontz, in her book *The Way We Never Were*, shows how the "tremendous variety of workable childrearing patterns in history suggests that, with little effort, we should be able to forge new institutions and values."

One way we resist these needed societal changes is by denying that divorce is no longer deviant. We demean divorced families by clinging to the belief that families can't exist outside of marriage. It follows then that stories of healthy families that don't fit the tidy nuclear family package are rare and stories that show how divorce destroys families and harms children are common. In this way, bad divorces appear to represent the American way of divorce and good divorces become invisible.

Messages That Hinder Good Divorces

When the evils of divorce are all that families hear about, it makes coping with the normal transitions and changes that inevitably accompany divorce all the more difficult. Negative messages make children feel different and lesser, leading to feelings of shame and guilt. Parents who feel marginalized in this way are less likely to think about creative solutions to their problems. That all of this unnecessary anxiety is fueled by sensationalized reports of weak findings, half-truths and myths of devastation is deplorable. Only by sorting out the truths about divorce from the fiction can we be empowered to make better decisions, find healthy ways to maintain family relationships, and develop important family rituals after divorce. Let's take a close look at the most common misconceptions about divorce.

Misconception 1: Parents Should Stay Married for the Sake of the Kids

This is a message that pervades our culture, and it rests on a false duality: Marriage is good for kids, divorce is bad. Underlying this premise is the belief that parents who divorce are immature and selfish because they put their personal needs ahead of the needs of their children, that because divorce is too easy to get, spouses give up on their marriages too easily and that if you're thinking about divorcing your spouse, you should "stick it out till the kids are grown." A popular joke takes this message to its extreme. A couple in their nineties, married for seventy years, appears before a judge in their petition for a divorce. The judge looks at them quizzically and asks, "Why now, why after all these years?" The couple responds: "We waited until the children were dead."

The research findings are now very clear that reality is nowhere near as simple and tidy. Unresolved, open interparental conflict between married spouses that pervades day-to-day family life has been shown again and again to have negative effects on children. Most experts agree that when this is the case it is better for the children if parents divorce rather than stay married. Ironically, prior to the initiation of no-fault legislation over twenty years ago, in most states this kind of open conflict in the home was considered "cruel and inhumane" treatment and it was one of the few grounds on which a divorce would be granted—if it could be proved.

But the majority of unsatisfying marriages are not such clearcut cases. When most parents ask themselves if they should stay married for the sake of their children, they have clearly reached the point where they are miserable in their marriages but wouldn't necessarily categorize them as "high-conflict." And here is where, in spite of the societal message, there is no agreement in the research findings or among clinical experts. That's because it's extremely complex and each individual situation is too different to allow for a "one-size-fits-all" answer.

A huge list of factors comes into play when assessing whether staying married would be better for your kids. For example,

- Is the unhappiness in your marriage making you so depressed or angry that your children's needs go unmet because you can't parent effectively?
- Do you and your spouse have a cold and distant relationship that makes the atmosphere at home unhealthy for your children?
- Do you and your spouse lack mutual respect, caring or interests, setting a poor model for your children?
- Would the financial hardships be so dire that your children will experience a severely reduced standard of living?

Add to this your child's temperament, resources and degree of resilience, and then the personal and family changes that take place in the years after the divorce, and you can see how the complexities mount.

It is a rare parent who divorces *too easily*. Most parents are responsible adults who spend years struggling with the extremely difficult and complex decision of whether to divorce or stay married "for the sake of the children." The bottom line is that divorce is an adult decision, usually made by one spouse, entered into in the face of many unknowns. Without a crystal ball, no one knows whether their decision will be better for their children. As you read further in this book, however, you may gain some perspective on what will be most helpful in your situation, with your children, by listening carefully to the reactions and feelings of various children of divorce *as they have changed over twenty years*.

Misconception 2: "Adult Children of Divorce" Are Doomed to Have Lifelong Problems

. . . The truth is that, for the great majority of children who experience a parental divorce, the divorce becomes part of their history but it is not a defining factor. Like the rest of us, most of them reach adulthood to lead reasonably happy, successful lives. Although children who grew up with divorced parents certainly share an important common experience, their ability to form healthy relationships, be good parents, build careers, and so on, are far more determined by their individual temperaments, their sibling relationships, the dynamics within their parents' *marriages* and the climate of their *postdivorce* family lives.

Misconception 3: Divorce Means You Are No Longer a Family

There's this myth that as long as you stay married your family is good but as soon as you announce you're separating, your family is thrown into the bad zone. Your family goes from being "intact" to being "dissolved," from two-parent to single parent, from functional to dysfunctional. Even though we all know that people don't jump from happy marriages right into divorce, there is an assumption that the decision to separate is the critical marker. It doesn't seem to matter whether your marital relationship was terrible, whether you were miserable and your children troubled. Just as long as you are married and living together in one household, the sign over the front door clearly states to the world, "We're a normal family."

The inaccurate and misleading message that divorce destroys families is harmful to both parents and children because it hides and denies all the positive ways that families can be rearranged after divorce. It sends the destructive message to children that divorce means they only get to keep one parent and they will no longer be part of a family. Although two-parent first-married households now represent less than 25 percent of all households, and an increasing number of children each year are raised by unmarried adults, many people cling to the belief that healthy families can only be two-parent married families and social change is always bad and threatening to our very foundations. . . .

The truth is that although some divorces result in family breakdown, the vast majority do not. While divorce changes the form of the family from one household to two, from a nuclear family to a binuclear one, it does not need to change the way children think and feel about the significant relationships within their families. This does not mean that divorce is not painful or difficult, but over the years, as postdivorce families change and even expand, most remain capable of meeting children's needs for family.

Misconception 4: Divorce Leaves Children Without Fathers

This message is linked closely with the preceding one because when we say that divorce destroys families we really mean that fathers disappear from the family. The myths that accompany this message are that fathers are "deadbeat dads" who abandon their kids and leave their families impoverished. The message strongly implies that fathers don't care and are unwilling or unable to make continuing commitments to their children. While this reflects the reality for a minority of divorced fathers, the majority of fathers continue to have loving relationships with their children and contribute financially to their upbringing. . . .

Misconception 5: Exspouses Are Incapable of Getting Along

. . . Although we have come to realize that parents who divorce still need to have some relationship with one another, the belief that it's not really possible still lingers. In fact, when exspouses remain friends they are viewed as a little strange and their relationship is suspect. Yet, the truth is that many divorced parents *are* cooperative and effective coparents. Like good divorces and involved fathers, they are mostly invisible in the media. . . .

Misconception 6: Divorce Turns Everyone into Exfamily; In-Laws Become Outlaws

When it comes to the semantics of divorce-speak, all of the kinship ties that got established by marriage dissolve abruptly. On the day of the legal divorce, my husband and all of his relatives suddenly became exes. But even though the kinship is *legally* terminated, meaningful relationships often continue. My friend Jan, during her fifteen-year marriage, formed a very close relationship with her mother-in-law. Now, twenty years later, she still calls her eighty-two-year-old exmother-in-law "Mom," talks with her several times a week and has dinner with her weekly. Exmother-in-law is certainly not an adequate description of this ongoing relationship.

As a culture we continue to resist accepting divorce as a normal endpoint to marriage even though it is an option chosen by almost half of those who marry. It is this cultural lag, this denial of current realities that causes the inaccurate language, not only for the family ties that continue but also for the family we inherit when we, our former spouses, our parents or our children remarry. Kinship language is important because it provides a short-hand way for us to identify relationships without wading through tedious explanations. . . .

Misconception 7: Stepparents Aren't Real Parents

. . . Children and their new stepparents start off their relationships with two strikes against them. They have to fight an uphill battle to overcome negative expectations, and they have to do so without much help from society. Since almost 85 percent of the children with divorced parents will have a stepparent at some time in their lives, it is shocking that we know so little about how these relationships work. Clearly, societal resistance to recognizing the broad spectrum of postdivorce families has hindered the development of good role models for stepchildren and their stepparents.

Painting a False Picture

Taken together, these negative messages paint a false picture of divorce, one that assumes family ties are irretrievably broken so that postdivorce family relationships appear to be nonexistent. Despite these destructive messages, many divorced parents meet the needs of their children by creating strong families after divorce. Without a doubt, divorce is painful and creates stress for families, but it is important to remember that most recover, maintaining some of their kinship relationships and adding new ones over time.

By making good divorces invisible we have accepted bad divorces as the norm. In so doing, children and their divorced parents are being given inaccurate messages that conflict with the realities they live and make them feel deviant and stigmatized. It is time we challenge these outdated, ill-founded messages and replace them with new ones that acknowledge and accurately reflect current realities.

The Distortions of Oversimplifying

Just a little over a decade ago, in January 1989, the *New York Times Magazine* ran a cover story called "Children after Divorce," which created a wave of panic in divorced parents and their children. Judith Wallerstein and her coauthor, Sandra Blakeslee, a staff writer for the *New York Times*, noted their newest unexpected finding. Calling it the "sleeper effect," they concluded that only ten years after divorce did it become apparent that girls experience "serious effects of divorce at the time they are entering young adulthood."

When one of the most prestigious newspapers in the world highlights the findings of a study, most readers take it seriously. "That 66 percent of young women in our study between the ages of nineteen and twenty-three will suffer debilitating effects of their parents' divorce years later" immediately became generalized to the millions of female children with divorced parents. The message—just when you think everything may be okay, the doom of divorce will rear its ugly head—is based on a *mere eighteen out of the grand total of twenty-seven women* interviewed in this age group. This detail wasn't mentioned in the fine print of the article but is buried in the appendix of the book that was scheduled for publication a month after the *New York Times* story appeared. And it is on this slim data that the seeds of a myth are planted. We are still living with the fallout.

In sharp contrast to Wallerstein's view that parental divorce has a powerful devastating impact on children well into adulthood, another psychologist made headlines with a completely opposite thesis. In her book, *The Nurture Assumption: Why Children Turn Out the Way They Do*, Judith Rich Harris proposes that what parents do makes little difference in how their children's lives turn out. Half of the variation in children's behavior and personality is due to genes, claims Harris, and the other half to environmental factors, mainly their peer relationships. For this reason, Harris asserts parental divorce is not responsible for all the ills it is blamed for.

These extreme positions—of divorce as disaster and divorce as inconsequential—oversimplify the realities of our complex lives. Genes and contemporary relationships notwithstanding, we have strong evidence that parents still make a significant difference in their children's development. Genetic inheritance and peer relationships are part of the story but certainly not the whole story.

Sorting Out the Research Findings

Drawing conclusions across the large body of research on divorce is difficult. Studies with different paradigms ask different questions that lead to different answers. A classic wisdom story shows the problem. Three blind men bumped into an elephant as they walked through the woods. They didn't know what it was, but each prided himself on his skill at "seeing." So one blind man reached out and carefully explored the elephant's leg. He described in great detail the rough, scratchy surface that was huge and round. "Aha, this is an ancient mighty tree. We're in a new forest." "No, no," said the blind man who had taken hold of the elephant's trunk. "We're in great danger—this is a writhing snake, bigger than any in our hometown. Run!" The third man laughed at them both. He'd been touching the elephant's tusk, noticing the smooth hard surface, the gentle curve, the rounded end. "Nonsense! We have discovered an exquisitely carved horn for announcing the emperor's arrival."

The blind men described what they "saw" accurately. Their mistake was to claim that what they saw was the whole. Much like the three blind men, researchers see different parts of the divorce elephant, which then frames their investigations.

It should come, then, as no surprise that reports of the findings about divorce are often contradictory and confusing. It is impossible for any study to take account of all the complexities of real life, or of the individual differences that allow one family to thrive in a situation that would create enormous stress, and frayed relationships, in another. But it is in these variations that we can begin to make sense of how divorce impacts the lives of individuals and families.

Facing Reality

Hallmark Cards recently launched a line of greeting cards called "Ties That Bind" aimed at various nontraditional unions—from stepfamilies to adopted child households to unmarried partnerships. "Our cards reflect the times," says Marita Wesely-Clough, trend group manager at Hallmark. "Relationships today are so nebulous that they are hard to pin down, but in creating products, we have to be aware that they are there. Companies need to respect and be sensitive to how people are truly living their lives now, and not how they might wish or hope for them to live."

Advertising agencies and marketing services make it their business to assess social realities. To sell their products, they have to evaluate the needs and desires of their potential consumers. They do not share the popular cultural anxiety about the changes in families. Instead they study them and alter their products to suit. Policy makers would do well to take some lessons from them and alter their preconceived notions about families to reflect current realities.

While the political focus today is on saving marriages and preserving traditional family values, Americans in large numbers are dancing to their own drummers. They're cohabiting in increasingly large numbers, having more children "out of wedlock" and engaging in serial marriages. While the rates of divorce have come down from their 1981 highs, they have leveled off at a high rate that is predicted to remain stable. To meet the needs of children and parents, we need to burst the balloon about idealized families and support families as they really live their lives. And that means we have to face the true complexities of *our* families and not search for simple answers.

As you read this book, keep in mind that we can all look back on our childhoods and note something about our mothers or fathers or sisters or brothers that has had lasting effects on our personalities. If you are looking to answer the question of whether a parental divorce results in children having more or less problems than children who grew up in other living situations, you will be disappointed. Nor will you find answers to whether the stresses of divorce are worse for children than other stresses in life. However, you will find answers here to questions about how and why individual children respond in different ways to the variations in their divorced families.

Divorce is a stressful life event that requires increased focus on parenting. The effort and care that parents put into establishing their postdivorce families are crucial and will pay off over the years in their many benefits to the children. But remember, families are complex, and if you find easy answers, they are likely to be wrong.

EXPLORING THE ISSUE

Does Divorce Have Long-Term Damaging Effects on Children?

Critical Thinking and Reflection

1. Which is more hurtful for children, having their parents divorcing or having their parents frequently fighting and angry at each other? How does your judgment change if spouse abuse is part of the picture? How does your judgment change if child abuse is part of the picture?
2. To what extent do stepfathers fill the shoes of fathers when divorced mothers remarry? What about stepmother's integration with the children?
3. What are the psychological processes that can make it difficult for stepfathers or stepmothers to become well integrated into the step family? Are these difficulties lessening as stepfamilies are becoming more common?
4. Do you favor or oppose laws that make divorce easier and why?
5. What factors contribute to the current relatively high divorce rates? How can these factors be changed to reduce divorce rates?
6. What are the impacts of divorces on society?

Is There Common Ground?

Because about 45 percent of first marriages and about 60 percent of second marriages end in divorce, it is a major problem for the individuals involved and, potentially, for the society as a whole. Everyone agrees that happy marriages are far better than divorces. Everyone also agrees that the welfare of the children is critical to our judgments on the issue of divorce. The debate, therefore, is over which of two bad situations is the least bad. This is a difficult issue to clearly judge. Crucial to the answer is how bad is the marriage before the divorce and how bad are the arrangements after the divorce. Furthermore, many of the consequences of divorce are difficult to measure accurately.

Additional Resources

There was a deluge of books on families, divorce, and children in the 1990s and many fewer in the 2000s. Many of the earlier works are still very relevant. Most writings emphasize the negative effects of divorce, especially for the children. These include Maggie Gallagher, *The Abolition of Marriage: How We Destroy Lasting Love* (Regnery, 1996); Barbara Dafoe Whitehead, *The Divorce Culture: How Divorce Became an Entitlement and How It Is Blighting the Lives of Our Children* (Alfred A. Knopf, 1997); Richard T. Gill, *Posterity Lost: Progress,*

Ideology, and the Decline of the American Family (Rowman & Littlefield, 1997); James Q. Wilson, *The Marriage Problem: How Our Culture Has Weakened Families* (HarperCollins, 2002); Judith Wallerstein, *The Unexpected Legacy of Divorce* (Hyperion, 2000); Elizabeth Marquardt, *Between Two Worlds: The Inner Lives of Children of Divorce* (Crown, 2006); and Linda Waite and Maggie Gallagher, *The Case for Staying Married* (Oxford University Press, 2005).

The writings that minimize the harmful effects of divorce include John H. Harvey, *Children of Divorce: Stories of Loss and Growth* (Routledge, 2010); Constance Ahrons, *We're Still Family: What Grown Children Have to Say about Their Parents' Divorce* (HarperCollins, 2004); E. L. Kain, *The Myth of Family Decline* (D. C. Heath, 1990); and Mavis Hetherington and John Kelly, *For Better or for Worse: Divorce Reconsidered* (W. W. Norton, 2002). David Popenoe and Jean Bethke Elshtain's book *Promises to Keep: Decline and Renewal of Marriage in America* (Rowman & Littlefield, 1996) discusses the negative impacts of divorce but also discusses signs of the renewal of marriage. For a thorough treatment of divorce and its consequences, see Alison Clark-Stewart, *Divorce: Causes and Consequences* (Yale University Press, 2006). The legal aspects of divorce are covered by Joanna L. Grossman in *Inside the Castle: Law and the Family in 20th Century America* (Princeton University Press, 2011).

Works that analyze changes in marriage and the family along with divorce include Rebecca L. Davis, *More Perfect Unions: The American Search for Marital Bliss* (Harvard University Press, 2011); Tamara Metz, *Untying the Knot: Marriage, the State and the Case for Their Divorce* (Princeton University Press, 2010); Kristin Celello, *Making Marriage Work: A History of Marriage and Divorce in the Twentieth-Century United States* (University of North Carolina Press, 2009); Andrew J. Cherlin, *The Marriage-Go-Round: The State of Marriage and the Family in America Today* (Alfred A. Knopf, 2009); Betty Farrell's *Family: The Making of an Idea, an Institution, and a Controversy in American Culture* (Westview Press, 1999); Karla B. Hackstaff's *Marriage in a Culture of Divorce* (Temple University Press, 1999); Jessica Weiss's *To Have and to Hold: Marriage, the Baby Boom, and Social Change* (University of Chicago Press, 2000); Barbara J. Risman's *Gender Vertigo: American Families in Transition* (Yale University Press, 1998); Ronald D. Taylor and Margaret C. Wang, eds., *Resilience across Contexts: Family, Work, Culture, and Community* (Lawrence Erlbaum, 2000); Linda J. Waite and Maggie Gallagher, *The Case for Marriage: Why Married People Are Happier, Healthier, and Better Off Financially* (Doubleday, 2000); Daniel P. Moynihan et al., eds., *Future of the Family* (Russell Sage Foundation, 2004); and Lynne M. Casper and Suzanne M. Bianchi, *Continuity and Change in the American Family* (Sage, 2002). For counsel on how to strengthen marriages, see David P. Gushee, *Getting Marriage Right: Realistic Counsel for Saving and Strengthening Relationships* (Baker Books, 2004). For information on divorce among seniors, see Deirdre Bair, *Calling It Quits: Late-Life Divorce and Starting Over*, 1st ed. (Random House, 2007). For advice on handling divorce issues, see Mark A. Fine and John H. Harvey, eds., *Handbook of Divorce and Relationship Dissolution* (Lawrence Erlbaum, 2006). Finally, for information on the adjustment of children, see Robert E. Emery, *Marriage, Divorce, and Children's Adjustment*, 2nd ed. (Sage, 1999).

ISSUE 4

Are Professional Women "Opting Out" of Work by Choice?

YES: **Linda Hirshman,** from "Homeward Bound," *The American Prospect Online* (November 21, 2005)

NO: **Pamela Stone,** from "The Rhetoric and Reality of 'Opting Out,'" *Contexts* (Fall 2007)

Learning Outcomes

After reading this issue, you should be able to:

- Understand how people (in this case women) deal with the stress of situations involving the conflict between two very important values. Women have to make life-changing decisions regarding the balance of work and family responsibilities.
- Understand how the conditions affecting these choices have changed over time.
- Explore how the workplaces and family units are changing to accommodate women's needs in this conflict.
- Explain, if possible, why these institutions are not more accommodating.
- Form an opinion about whether this issue is largely an individual problem or largely an institutional problem or is both.
- Evaluate what the role of husbands is in this situation.

ISSUE SUMMARY

YES: Feminist scholar Linda Hirshman finds that successful and well-qualified women are "opting out" of work outside the home when their husbands' income is adequate for a rich lifestyle. Prioritizing parenthood over work is an affront to Hirshman's feminist values.

NO: Sociologist Pamela Stone reports on her survey research and finds a number of women who sacrificed careers for parenthood and thought it was their free choice. Her analysis, however, notes that they were tightly constrained by traditional gender roles and inflexible workplaces.

The fascinating aspect of social life is how many different trends and changes significantly affect how we live and the choices we make. For example, consider married women and their work–family choices. Ever since the 1950s, married women have increasingly participated in the labor force. Why? The reasons are numerous. Women want the money for themselves. Women need the money for the family. Women want the challenge of a career. Women want the social life that work provides. Women want independence. The list of reasons goes on and on. These reasons change, however, as the context changes. For example, since 1965 the median price of the one-family home compared to the average income of private nonagricultural workers had doubled before the housing market crashed. Thus, the single earner family is having much more difficulty buying a house. This trend helps explain why married women increasingly enter or stay in the labor force. Attitudes have also changed. In 1968, a large survey asked young people what they expected to be doing at age 35. About 30 percent of the 20- to 21-year-olds said that they would be working. Seven years later, 65 percent of 20- to 21-year-olds said they would be working. That is an astounding change. The statistical result is that in 1900, women 16 and over constituted 18 percent of the labor force; in 1950, women constituted 30 percent; and since 1995, women constituted 45–47 percent of the labor force.

Educational changes in the past half century have also been dramatic. Females have overtaken males in most aspects of education. Women are now outnumbering men in college and currently earn 57 percent of all bachelor degrees, 58 percent of all master degrees, and are rapidly closing the MD and PhD gaps. Women are also more focused on professional degrees while in college as demonstrated by their selection of majors. In 1966, 40 percent of college women graduates majored in education and 17 percent majored in English/literature, but only 2 percent majored in business. Women have stopped shying away from the business world. The percentage of female BA business degrees went from 9 percent in 1971 to 49 percent in 1997, while it went from 4 percent to 39 percent for MA business degrees and from 5 percent to 70 percent for law degrees. Another trend affecting choices and behaviors is the increasing scarcity of time. The percentage of males working more than 50 hours a week increased from 21.0 to 26.5 from 1970 to 2000 and for females from 5.2 to 11.3.

Two issues that have received major media attention explore the circumstances of the work–family choice. First, in the 1990s, employers talked about a mommy track for women employees who would be allowed an easier work load that would reduce the conflict between work and family but would slow down their advancement and hold down their income. Second, in the past decade investigators noticed that capable women with prosperous husbands "opted out" of the work world and stayed home with the kids. They had the circumstances that allowed them to make this choice. Could it be that if all women had such circumstances then the majority of them would make the same choice? This is the issue which is debated in the following selections. Linda Hirshman acknowledges in her title that women are tending homeward or "opting out," but largely blames this phenomenon on the near universal acceptance of men opting out of family responsibilities because they are the primary wage earner. On the other hand, Pamela Stone criticizes the structure of the work world that demands unreasonable commitment of workers, especially professional workers, to their careers and this negatively affects women more than men.

YES

Linda Hirshman

Homeward Bound

I. The Truth about Elite Women

Half the wealthiest, most-privileged, best-educated females in the country stay home with their babies rather than work in the market economy. When in September *The New York Times* featured an article exploring a piece of this story, **"Many Women at Elite Colleges Set Career Path to Motherhood,"** the blogosphere went ballistic, countering with anecdotes and sarcasm. *Slate's* Jack Shafer accused the *Times* of **"weasel-words"** and of **publishing the same story**—essentially, **"The Opt-Out Revolution"**—every few years, and, recently, every few weeks. . . . The colleges article provoked such fury that the *Times* had to post an *explanation* of the then–student journalist's methodology on its Web site.

There's only one problem: There is important truth in the dropout story. Even *though* it appeared in *The New York Times*.

I stumbled across the news three years ago when researching a book on marriage after feminism. I found that among the educated elite, who are the logical heirs of the agenda of empowering women, feminism has largely failed in its goals. There are few women in the corridors of power, and marriage is essentially unchanged. The number of women at universities exceeds the number of men. But, more than a generation after feminism, the number of women in elite jobs doesn't come close.

Why did this happen? The answer I discovered—an answer neither feminist leaders nor women themselves want to face—is that while the public world has changed, albeit imperfectly, to accommodate women among the elite, private lives have hardly budged. The real glass ceiling is at home.

Looking back, it seems obvious that the unreconstructed family was destined to re-emerge after the passage of feminism's storm of social change. Following the original impulse to address everything in the lives of women, feminism turned its focus to cracking open the doors of the public power structure. This was no small task. At the beginning, there were male juries and male Ivy League schools, sex-segregated want ads, discriminatory employers, harassing colleagues. As a result of feminist efforts—and larger economic trends—the percentage of women, even of mothers in full- or part-time employment, rose robustly through the 1980s and early '90s.

But then the pace slowed. The census numbers for all working mothers leveled off around 1990 and have fallen modestly since 1998. In interviews, women with enough money to quit work say they are "choosing" to opt out. Their words conceal a crucial reality: the belief that women are responsible for child-rearing and homemaking was largely untouched by decades of workplace feminism. Add to this the good evidence that the upper-class workplace has become more demanding and then mix in the successful conservative cultural campaign to reinforce traditional gender roles and you've got a perfect recipe for feminism's stall.

. . .

And there is more. In 2000, Harvard Business School professor Myra Hart surveyed the women of the classes of 1981, 1986, and 1991 and found that only 38 percent of female Harvard MBAs were working full time. A 2004 survey by the Center for Work-Life Policy of 2,443 women with a graduate degree or very prestigious bachelor's degree revealed that 43 percent of those women with children had taken a time out, primarily for family reasons. Richard Posner, federal appeals-court judge and occasional University of Chicago adjunct professor, reports that "the [*Times*] article confirms—what everyone associated with such institutions [elite law schools] has long known: that a vastly higher percentage of female than of male students will drop out of the workforce to take care of their children."

. . . The 2000 census showed a decline in the percentage of mothers of infants working full time, part time, or seeking employment. Starting at 31 percent in 1976, the percentage had gone up almost every year to 1992, hit a high of 58.7 percent in 1998, and then began to drop—to 55.2 percent in 2000, to 54.6 percent in 2002, to 53.7 percent in 2003. Statistics just released showed further decline to 52.9 percent in 2004. Even the percentage of working mothers with children who were not infants declined between 2000 and 2003, from 62.8 percent to 59.8 percent.

. . .

The arguments still do not explain the absence of women in elite workplaces. If these women were sticking it out in the business, law, and academic worlds, now, 30 years after feminism started filling the selective schools with women, the elite workplaces should be proportionately female. They are not. Law schools have been graduating classes around 40-percent female for decades—decades during which both schools and firms experienced enormous growth. And, although the legal population will not be 40-percent female until 2010, in 2003, the major law firms had only 16-percent female partners, according to the American Bar Association. It's important to note that elite workplaces like law firms grew in size during the very years that the percentage of female graduates was growing, leading you to expect a higher female employment than the pure graduation rate would indicate. The Harvard Business School has produced classes around 30-percent female. Yet only 10.6 percent of Wall Street's corporate officers are women, and a mere nine are Fortune 500 CEOs. Harvard Business School's dean, who extolled the virtues of interrupted careers on *60 Minutes*, has a 20-percent female academic faculty.

It is possible that the workplace is discriminatory and hostile to family life. If firms had hired every childless woman lawyer available, that alone would have been enough to raise the percentage of female law partners above 16 percent in 30 years. It is also possible that women are voluntarily taking themselves out of the elite job competition for lower status and lower-paying jobs. Women must take responsibility for the consequences of their decisions. It defies reason to claim that the falloff from 40 percent of the class at law school to 16 percent of the partners at all the big law firms is unrelated to half the mothers with graduate and professional degrees leaving full-time work at childbirth and staying away for several years after that, or possibly bidding down.

This isn't only about day care. Half my *Times* brides quit *before* the first baby came. In interviews, at least half of them expressed a hope never to work again. None had realistic plans to work. More importantly, when they quit, they were already alienated from their work or at least not committed to a life of work. One, a female MBA, said she could never figure out why the men at her workplace, which fired her, were so excited about making deals. "It's only money," she mused. Not surprisingly, even where employers offered them part-time work, they were not interested in taking it.

II. The Failure of Choice Feminism

What is going on? Most women hope to marry and have babies. If they resist the traditional female responsibilities of child-rearing and householding, what Arlie Hochschild called "The Second Shift," they are fixing for a fight. But elite women aren't resisting tradition. None of the stay-at-home brides I interviewed saw the second shift as unjust; they agree that the household is women's work. As one lawyer-bride put it in explaining her decision to quit practicing law after four years, "I had a wedding to plan." Another, an Ivy Leaguer with a master's degree, described it in management terms: "He's the CEO and I'm the CFO. He sees to it that the money rolls in and I decide how to spend it." It's their work, and they must do it perfectly. "We're all in here making fresh apple pie," said one, explaining her reluctance to leave her daughters in order to be interviewed. The family CFO described her activities at home: "I take my [3-year-old] daughter to all the major museums. We go to little movement classes."

Conservatives contend that the dropouts prove that feminism "failed" because it was too radical, because women didn't want what feminism had to offer. In fact, if half or more of feminism's heirs (85 percent of the women in my *Times* sample), are not working seriously, it's because feminism wasn't radical enough: It changed the workplace but it didn't change men, and, more importantly, it didn't fundamentally change how women related to men.

The movement did start out radical. Betty Friedan's original call to arms compared housework to animal life. In *The Feminine Mystique* she wrote, "[V]acuuming the living room floor—with or without makeup—is not work that takes enough thought or energy to challenge any woman's full capacity. . . . Down through the ages man has known that he was set apart from other animals by his mind's power to have an idea, a vision, and shape the future to it . . . when he discovers and creates and shapes a future different from his past, he is a man, a human being."

Thereafter, however, liberal feminists abandoned the judgmental starting point of the movement in favor of offering women "choices." The choice talk spilled over from people trying to avoid saying "abortion," and it provided an irresistible solution to feminists trying to duck the mommy wars. A woman could work, stay home, have 10 children or one, marry or stay single. It all counted as "feminist" as long as she *chose* it. (So dominant has the concept of choice become that when Charlotte, with a push from her insufferable first husband, quits her job, the writers at *Sex and the City* have her screaming, "I choose my choice! I choose my choice!")

Only the most radical fringes of feminism took on the issue of gender relations at home, and they put forth fruitless solutions like socialism and separatism. We know the story about socialism. Separatism ran right into heterosexuality and reproduction, to say nothing of the need to earn a living other than at a feminist bookstore. As feminist historian Alice Echols put it, "Rather than challenging their subordination in domestic life, the feminists of NOW committed themselves to fighting for women's integration into public life."

Great as liberal feminism was, once it retreated to choice the movement had no language to use on the gendered ideology of the family. Feminists could not say, "Housekeeping and child-rearing in the nuclear family is not interesting and not socially validated. Justice requires that it not be assigned to women on the basis of their gender and at the sacrifice of their access to money, power, and honor."

The 50 percent of census answerers and the 62 percent of Harvard MBAs and the 85 percent of my brides of the *Times* all think they are "choosing" their gendered lives. They don't know that feminism, in collusion with traditional society, just passed the gendered family on to them to choose. Even with all the day care in the world, the personal is still political. Much of the rest is the opt-out revolution.

III. What Is to Be Done?

Here's the feminist moral analysis that choice avoided: The family—with its repetitious, socially invisible, physical tasks—is a necessary part of life, but it allows fewer opportunities for full human flourishing than public spheres like the market or the government. This less-flourishing sphere is not the natural or moral responsibility only of women. Therefore, assigning it to women is unjust. Women assigning it to themselves is equally unjust. To paraphrase, as Mark Twain said, "A man who chooses not to read is just as ignorant as a man who cannot read."

. . . If women's flourishing does matter, feminists must acknowledge that the family is to 2005 what the workplace was to 1964 and the vote to 1920. Like the right to work and the right to vote, the right to have a flourishing life that includes but is not limited to family cannot be addressed with language of choice.

Women who want to have sex and children with men as well as good work in interesting jobs where they may occasionally wield real social power need guidance, and they need it early. Step one is simply to begin talking about flourishing. In so doing, feminism will be returning to its early, judgmental roots. This may anger some, but it should sound the alarm before the next generation winds up in the same situation. Next, feminists will have to start offering young women not choices and not utopian dreams but *solutions* they can enact on their own. Prying women out of their traditional roles is not going to be easy. It will require rules—rules like those in the widely derided book *The Rules*, which was never about dating but about behavior modification.

There are three rules: Prepare yourself to qualify for good work, treat work seriously, and don't put yourself in a position of unequal resources when you marry.

The preparation stage begins with college. It is shocking to think that girls cut off their options for a public life of work as early as college. But they do. The first pitfall is the liberal-arts curriculum, which women are good at, graduating in higher numbers than men. Although many really successful people start out studying liberal arts, the purpose of a liberal education is not, with the exception of a miniscule number of academic positions, job preparation.

So the first rule is to use your college education with an eye to career goals. Feminist organizations should produce each year a survey of the most common job opportunities for people with college degrees, along with the average lifetime earnings from each job category and the characteristics such jobs require. The point here is to help women see that yes, you can study art history, but only with the realistic understanding that one day soon you will need to use your arts education to support yourself and your family. . . .

After college comes on-the-job training or further education. Many of my *Times* brides—and grooms—did work when they finished their educations. Here's an anecdote about the difference: One couple, both lawyers, met at a firm. After a few years, the man moved from international business law into international business. The woman quit working altogether. "They told me law school could train you for anything," she told me. "But it doesn't prepare you to go into business. I should have gone to business school." Or rolled over and watched her husband the lawyer using his first few years of work to prepare to go into a related business. Every *Times* groom assumed he had to succeed in business, and was really trying. By contrast, a common thread among the women I interviewed was a self-important idealism about the kinds of intellectual, prestigious, socially meaningful, politics-free jobs worm their incalculably valuable presence. So the second rule is that women must treat the first few years after college as an opportunity to lose their capitalism virginity and prepare for good work, which they will then treat seriously.

The best way to treat work seriously is to find the money. Money is the marker of success in a market economy; it usually accompanies power, and it enables the bearer to wield power, including within the family. Almost without exception, the brides who opted out graduated with roughly the same degrees as their husbands. Yet somewhere along the way the women made decisions in the direction of less money. Part of the problem was idealism; idealism on the career trail usually leads to volunteer work, or indentured servitude in social-service jobs, which is nice but doesn't get you to money. Another big mistake involved changing jobs excessively. Without exception, the brides who eventually went home had much more job turnover than the grooms did. There's no such thing as a perfect job. Condoleezza Rice actually wanted to be a pianist, and Gary Graffman didn't want to give concerts.

If you are good at work you are in a position to address the third undertaking: the reproductive household. The rule here is to avoid taking on more than a fair share of the second shift. If this seems coldhearted, consider the survey by the Center for Work-Life Policy. Fully 40 percent of highly qualified women with spouses felt that their husbands create more work around the house than they perform. According to Phyllis Moen and Patricia Roehling's *Career Mystique,* "When couples marry, the amount of time that a woman spends doing housework increases by approximately 17 percent, while a man's decreases by 33 percent." Not a single *Times* groom was a stay-at-home dad. Several of them could hardly wait for Monday morning to come. None of my *Times* grooms took even brief paternity leave when his children were born.

How to avoid this kind of rut? You can either find a spouse with less social power than you or find one with an ideological commitment to gender equality. Taking the easier path first, marry down. Don't think of this as brutally strategic. If you are devoted to your career goals and would like a man who will support that, you're just doing what men throughout the ages have done: placing a safe bet.

In her 1995 book, *Kidding Ourselves: Babies, Breadwinning and Bargaining Power,* Rhona Mahoney recommended finding a sharing spouse by marrying younger or poorer, or someone in a dependent status, like a starving artist. Because money is such a marker of status and power, it's hard to persuade women to marry poorer. So here's an easier rule: Marry young or marry much older. Younger men are potential high-status companions. Much older men are sufficiently established so that they don't have to work so hard, and they often have enough money to provide unlimited household help. By contrast, slightly older men with bigger incomes are the most dangerous, but even a pure counterpart is risky. If you both are going through the elite-job hazing rituals simultaneously while having children, someone is going to have to give. Even the most devoted lawyers with the hardest-working nannies are going to have weeks when no one can get home other than to sleep. The odds are that when this happens, the woman is going to give up her ambitions and professional potential.

It is possible that marrying a liberal might be the better course. After all, conservatives justified the unequal family in two modes: "God ordained it" and "biology is destiny." Most men (and most women), including the liberals, think women are responsible for the home. But at least the liberal men should feel squeamish about it.

If you have carefully positioned yourself either by marrying down or finding someone untainted by gender ideology, you will be in a position to resist bearing an unfair share of the family. Even then you must be vigilant.

Bad deals come in two forms: economics and home economics. The economic temptation is to assign the cost of child care to the woman's income. If a woman making $50,000 per year whose husband makes $100,000 decides to have a baby, and the cost of a full-time nanny is $30,000, the couple reason that, after paying 40 percent in taxes, she makes $30,000, just enough to pay the nanny. So she might as well stay home. This totally ignores that both adults are in the enterprise together and the demonstrable future loss of income, power, and security for the woman who quits. Instead, calculate that all parents make a total of $150,000 and take home $90,000. After paying a full-time nanny, they have $60,000 left to live on.

The home-economics trap involves superior female knowledge and superior female sanitation. The solutions are ignorance and dust. Never figure out where the butter is. "Where's the butter?" Nora Ephron's legendary riff on marriage begins. In it, a man asks the question when looking directly at the butter container in the refrigerator. "Where's the butter?" actually means butter my toast, buy the butter, remember when we're out of butter. Next thing you know you're quitting your job at the law firm because you're so busy managing the butter. If women never start playing the household-manager role, the house will be dirty, but the realities of the physical world will trump the pull of gender ideology. Either the other adult in the family will take a hand or the children will grow up with robust immune systems.

If these prescriptions sound less than family-friendly, here's the last rule: Have a baby. Just don't have two. Mothers' Movement Online's Judith Stadtman Tucker reports that women who opt out for child-care reasons act only after the second child arrives. A second kid pressures the mother's organizational skills, doubles the demands for appointments, wildly raises the cost of education and housing, and drives the family to the suburbs. But cities, with their Chinese carryouts and all, are better for working mothers. . . .

IV. Why Do We Care?

The privileged brides of the *Times*—and their husbands—seem happy. Why do we care what they do? After all, most people aren't rich and white and heterosexual, and they couldn't quit working if they wanted to.

We care because what they do is bad for them, is certainly bad for society, and is widely imitated, even by people who never get their weddings in the *Times*. This last is called the "regime effect," and it means that even if women don't quit their jobs for their families, they think they should and feel guilty about not doing it. That regime effect created the mystique around *The Feminine Mystique,* too.

As for society, elites supply the labor for the decision-making classes—the senators, the newspaper editors, the research scientists, the entrepreneurs, the policy-makers, and the policy wonks. If the ruling class is overwhelmingly male, the rulers will make mistakes that benefit males, whether from ignorance or from indifference. Media surveys reveal that if only one member of a television show's creative staff is female, the percentage of women on-screen goes up from 36 percent to 42 percent. . . .

Worse, the behavior tarnishes every female with the knowledge that she is almost never going to be a ruler. Princeton President Shirley Tilghman described the elite colleges' self-image perfectly when she told her freshmen last year that they would be the nation's leaders, and she clearly did not have trophy wives in mind. Why should society spend resources educating women with only a 50-percent return rate on their stated goals? The American Conservative Union carried a column in 2004 recommending that employers stay away from such women or risk going out of business. Good psychological data show that the more women are treated with respect, the more ambition they have. And vice versa. The opt-out revolution is really a downward spiral.

Finally, these choices are bad for women individually. A good life for humans includes the classical standard of using one's capacities for speech and reason in a prudent way, the liberal requirement of having enough autonomy to direct one's own life, and the utilitarian test of doing more good than harm in the world. Measured against these time-tested standards, the expensively educated upper-class moms will be leading lesser lives. . . .

When she sounded the blast that revived the feminist movement 40 years after women received the vote, Betty Friedan spoke of lives of purpose and meaning, better lives and worse lives, and feminism went a long way toward shattering the glass ceilings that limited their prospects outside the home. Now the glass ceiling begins at home. Although it is harder to shatter a ceiling that is also the roof over your head, there is no other choice. . . .

Pamela Stone  **NO**

The Rhetoric and Reality of "Opting Out"

*P*rofessional women who leave the workforce may have fewer options than it seems. What does that tell us about work in America today?

As a senior publicist at a well-known media conglomerate, Regina Donofrio had one of the most coveted, glamorous jobs in New York. A typical workday might include "riding around Manhattan in limousines with movie stars." She loved her job, had worked "a long time," and felt "comfortable" in it. So when the time came to return to work after the birth of her first child, Regina did not hesitate. "I decided I would go back to work, because the job was great, basically," she told me.

Before long, Regina found herself "crying on the train," torn between wanting to be at home with her baby and wanting to keep up her successful, exciting career. She started feeling she was never in the right place at the right time. "When I was at work, I should have been at home. When I was at home, I felt guilty because I had left work a little early to see the baby, and I had maybe left some things undone." Ever resourceful, she devised a detailed job-share plan with a colleague who was also a first-time mother. But their proposal was denied. Instead, Regina's employer offered her more money to stay and work full time, and Regina left in a huff, incensed that her employer, with whom she had a great track record, would block her from doing what she wanted to do—continue with her career and combine it with family.

Despite mainstream media portrayals to the contrary, Regina's reasons for quitting are all too typical of what I found in my study of high-achieving, former professionals who are now at-home moms. While Regina did, in fact, feel a strong urge to care for her baby, she decided to quit because of an inflexible work-place, not because of her attraction to home and hearth. She gave up her high-powered career as a last resort, after agonized soul-searching and exhausting her options. Her story differs from the popular depiction of similar, high-achieving, professional women who have headed home. Media stories typically frame these women's decisions as choices about family and see them as symptomatic of a kind of sea-change among the daughters of the feminist revolution, a return to traditionalism and the resurgence of a new feminine mystique.

The quintessential article in this prevailing story line (and the one that gave the phenomenon its name) was published in 2003 by the *New York Times*'s work-life columnist, Lisa Belkin, titled "The Opt-Out Revolution."

From *Contexts,* vol. 6, no. 4, Fall 2007, pp. 14–19. Copyright © 2007 by University of California Press, Journals Division. Reprinted by permission via the Copyright Clearance Center.

"Opting out" is redolent with overtones of lifestyle preference and discretion, but Regina's experience counters this characterization; her decision to quit was not a lifestyle preference, nor a change in aspirations, nor a desire to return to the 1950s family. Regina did not "opt out" of the workplace because she chose to, but for precisely the opposite reason: because she had no real options and no choice.

High-achieving women's reasons for heading home are multilayered and complex, and generally counter the common view that they quit because of babies and family. This is what I found when I spoke to scores of women like Regina: highly educated, affluent, mostly white, married women with children who had previously worked as professionals or managers and whose husbands could support their being at home. Although many of these women speak the language of choice and privilege, their stories reveal a choice gap—the disjuncture between the rhetoric of choice and the reality of constraints like those Regina encountered. The choice gap reflects the extent to which high-achieving women like Regina are caught in a double bind: spiraling parenting (read "mothering") demands on the homefront collide with the increasing pace of work in the gilded cages of elite professions.

Some Skepticism

I approached these interviews with skepticism tempered by a recognition that there might be some truth to the popular image of the "new traditionalist." But to get beyond the predictable "family" explanation and the media drumbeat of choice, I thought it was important to interview women in some depth and to study women who, at least theoretically, could exercise choice. I also gave women full anonymity, creating fictitious names for them so they would speak to me as candidly as possible. The women I interviewed had outstanding educational credentials; more than half had graduate degrees in business, law, medicine, and other professions, and had once had thriving careers in which they had worked about a decade. By any measure, these were work-committed women, with strong reasons to continue with the careers in which they had invested so much. Moreover, they were in high-status fields where they had more control over their jobs and enjoyed (at least relative to workers in other fields) more family-friendly benefits.

While these women had compelling reasons to stay on the job, they also had the option not to, by virtue of their own past earnings and because their husbands were also high earners. To counter the potential criticism that they were quitting or being let go because they were not competent or up to the job, I expressly chose to study women with impeccable educational credentials, women who had navigated elite environments with competitive entry requirements. To ensure a diversity of perspectives, I conducted extensive, in-depth interviews with 54 women in a variety of professions—law, medicine, business, publishing, management consulting, nonprofit administration, and the like. . . .

To be sure, at-home moms are a distinct minority. Despite the many articles proclaiming a trend of women going home, among the demographic of media scrutiny—white, college-educated women, 30–54 years old—fully 84 percent are now in the workforce, up from 82 percent 20 years ago. And the much-discussed dip in the labor-force participation of mothers of young children, while real, appears to be largely a function of an economic downturn, which depresses employment for all workers.

Nevertheless, these women are important to study. Elite, educated, high-achieving women have historically been cultural arbiters, defining what is acceptable for all women in their work and family roles. This group's entrance into high-status, formerly male professions has been crucial to advancing gender parity and narrowing the wage gap, which stubbornly persists to this day. At home, moreover, they are rendered silent and invisible, so that it is easy to project and speculate about them. We can see in them whatever we want to, and perhaps that is why they have been the subject of endless speculation— about mommy wars, a return to traditionalism, and the like. While they do not represent all women, elite women's experiences provide a glimpse into the work-family negotiations that all women face. And their stories lead us to ask, "If the most privileged women of society cannot successfully combine work and family, who can?"

Motherhood Pulls

When Regina initially went back to work, she had "no clue" that she would feel so torn. She advises women not to set "too much in stone," because "you just don't know, when a human being comes out of your body, how you're going to feel." For some women, the pull of children was immediate and strong. Lauren Quattrone, a lawyer, found herself "absolutely besotted with this baby. . . . I realized that I just couldn't bear to leave him." Women such as Lauren tended to quit fairly soon after their first child was born. For others, like Diane Childs, formerly a nonprofit executive, the desire to be home with the kids came later. "I felt that it was easy to leave a baby for twelve hours a day. That I could do. But to leave a six-year-old, I just thought, was a whole different thing."

But none of these women made their decisions to quit in a vacuum. In fact, they did so during a cultural moment when norms and practices for parents—mothers—are very demanding. These women realized they would rear children very differently from the way their own mothers raised them, feeling an external, almost competitive pressure to do so. Middle- and upper-middle-class women tend to be particularly mindful of expert advice, and these women were acutely aware of a well-documented intensification in raising children, which sociologist Sharon Hays calls an "ideology of intensive mothering." This cultural imperative, felt by women of all kinds, "advises mothers to expend a tremendous amount of time, energy and money in raising their children."

A corollary is what Annette Lareau terms "concerted cultivation," a non-stop pace of organized activities scheduled by parents for school-age children. Among the women I spoke to, some, like Diane, felt the urgency of "concerted cultivation" and reevaluated their childcare as the more sophisticated needs of their older children superseded the simpler, more straightforward babysitting and physical care required for younger children. Marina Isherwood, a former executive in the health care industry, with children in the second and fourth grades, became convinced that caregivers could not replace her own parental influence:

> There isn't a substitute, no matter how good the child-care. When they're little, the fact that someone else is doing the stuff with them is fine. It wasn't the part that I loved anyway. But when they start asking you questions about values, you don't want your babysitter telling them. . . .

Because academic credentials were so important to these women's (and their husband's) career opportunities, formal schooling was a critical factor in their decisions to quit. For some, the premium they placed on education and values widened the gap between themselves and their less educated caregivers.

Depending on the woman, motherhood played a larger or smaller role in her decision whether and when to quit. Children were the main focus of women's caregiving, but other family members needed care as well, for which women felt responsible. About 10 percent of the women spoke of significant elder-care responsibilities, the need for which was especially unpredictable. This type of caregiving and mothering made up half of the family/career double bind. More important, though, motherhood influenced women's decision to quit as they came to see the rhythms and values of the workplace as antagonistic to family life.

Workplace Pushes

On top of their demanding mothering regime, these women received mixed messages from both their husbands and their employers. Husbands offered emotional support to wives who were juggling career and family. Emily Mitchell, an accountant, described her marriage to a CPA as "a pretty equal relationship," but when his career became more demanding, requiring long hours and Saturdays at work, he saw the downside of egalitarianism:

> I think he never minded taking my daughter to the sitter, that was never an issue, and when he would come home, we have a pretty equal relationship on that stuff. But getting her up, getting her ready, getting himself ready to go into work, me coming home, getting her, getting her to bed, getting unwound from work, and then he would come home, we'd try to do something for dinner, and then there was always something else to do—laundry, cleaning, whatever—I think he was feeling too much on a treadmill.

But husbands did little to share family responsibilities, instead maintaining their own demanding careers full-speed ahead.

Similarly, many workplaces claimed to be "family friendly" and offered a variety of supports. But for women who could take advantage of them, flexible work schedules (which usually meant working part-time) carried significant penalties. Women who shifted to part-time work typically saw their jobs gutted of significant responsibilities and their once-flourishing careers derailed. Worse, part-time hours often crept up to the equivalent of full time. When Diane Childs had children, she scaled back to part time and began to feel the pointlessness of continuing:

> And I'm never going to get anywhere—you have the feeling that you just plateaued professionally because you can't take on the extra projects; you can't travel at a moment's notice; you can't stay late; you're not flexible on the Friday thing because that could mean finding someone to take your kids. You really plateau for a much longer period of time than you ever realize when you first have a baby. It's like you're going to be plateaued for thirteen to fifteen years.

Lynn Hamilton, an M.D., met her husband at Princeton, where they were both undergraduates. Her story illustrates how family pulls and workplace pushes (from both her career and her husband's) interacted in a marriage that was founded on professional equality but then devolved to the detriment of her career:

> We met when we were 19 years old, and so, there I was, so naive, I thought, well, here we are, we have virtually identical credentials and comparable income earnings. That's an opportunity. And, in fact, I think our incomes were identical at the time I quit. To the extent to which we have articulated it, it was always understood, well, with both of us working, neither of us would have to be working these killer jobs. So, what was happening was, instead, we were both working these killer jobs. And I kept saying, "We need to reconfigure this." And what I realized was, he wasn't going to.

Meanwhile, her young daughter was having behavioral problems at school, and her job as a medical director for a biomedical start-up company had "the fax machine going, the three phone lines upstairs, they were going." Lynn slowly realized that the only reconfiguration possible, in the face of her husband's absence, was for her to quit.

Over half (60 percent) of the women I spoke to mentioned their husbands as one of the key reasons why they quit. That not all women talked about their husbands' involvement, or lack thereof, reveals the degree to which they perceived the work-family balancing act to be their responsibility alone. But women seldom mentioned their husbands for another reason: they were, quite literally, absent.

Helena Norton, an educational administrator who characterized her husband as a "workaholic," poignantly described a scenario that many others took for granted and which illustrates a pattern typical of many of these women's lives: "He was leaving early mornings; 6:00 or 6:30 before anyone was up, and then he was coming home late at night. So I felt this real emptiness, getting up in the morning to, not necessarily an empty house, because my children were there, but I did, I felt empty, and then going to bed, and he wasn't there."

In not being there to pick up the slack, many husbands had an important indirect impact on their wives' decisions to quit. Deferring to their husbands' careers and exempting them from household chores, these women tended to accept this situation. Indeed, privileging their husbands' careers was a pervasive, almost tacit undercurrent of their stories.

When talking about their husbands, women said the same things: variations on "he's supportive," and that he gave them a "choice." But this hands-off approach revealed husbands to be bystanders, not participants, in the work-family bind. "It's your choice" was code for "it's your problem." And husbands' absences, a direct result of their own high-powered careers, put a great deal of pressure on women to do it all, thus undermining the façade of egalitarianism.

Family pulls—from children and, as a result of their own long work hours, their husbands—exacerbated workplace pushes; and all but seven women cited features of their jobs—the long hours, the travel—as another major motivation in quitting. Marketing executive Nathalie Everett spoke for many women when she remarked that her full-time workweek was "really 60 hours, not 40. Nobody works nine-to-five anymore."

Surprisingly, the women I interviewed, like Nathalie, neither questioned nor showed much resentment toward the features of their jobs that kept them from fully integrating work and family. They routinely described their jobs as "all or nothing" and appeared to internalize what sociologists call the "ideal worker" model of a (typically male) worker unencumbered by family demands. This model was so influential that those working part time or in other flexible arrangements often felt stigmatized. Christine Thomas, a marketing executive and job-sharer, used imagery reminiscent of *The Scarlet Letter* to describe her experience: "When you job share, you have 'MOMMY' stamped in huge letters on your forehead."

While some women's decisions could be attributed to their unquestioning acceptance of the status quo or a lack of imagination, the unsuccessful attempts of others who tried to make it work by pursuing alternatives to full-time, like Diane, serve as cautionary tales. Women who made arrangements with bosses felt like they were being given special favors. Their part-time schedules were privately negotiated, hence fragile and unstable, and were especially vulnerable in the context of any kind of organizational restructuring such as mergers.

The Choice Gap

Given the incongruity of these women's experiences—they felt supported by "supportive" yet passive husbands and pushed out by workplaces that once prized their expertise—how did these women understand their situation? How did they make sense of professions that, on the one hand, gave them considerable status and rewards, and, on the other hand, seemed to marginalize them and force them to compromise their identity as mothers?

The overwhelming majority felt the same way as Melissa Wyatt, the 34-year-old who gave up a job as a fund-raiser: "I think today it's all about choices, and the choices we want to make. And I think that's great. I think it just depends where you want to spend your time." But a few shared the out-look of Olivia Pastore, a 42-year-old ex-lawyer:

> I've had a lot of women say to me, "Boy, if I had the choice of, if I could balance, if I could work part-time, if I could keep doing it." And there are some women who are going to stay home full-time no matter what and that's fine. But there are a number of women, I think, who are home because they're caught between a rock and a hard place. . . . There's a lot of talk about the individual decisions of individual women. "Is it good? Is it bad? She gave it up. She couldn't hack it," . . . And there's not enough blame, if you will, being laid at the feet of the culture, the jobs, society.

My findings show that Olivia's comments—about the disjuncture between the rhetoric of choice and the reality of constraint that shapes women's decisions to go home—are closer to the mark. Between trying to be the ideal mother (in an era of intensive mothering) and the ideal worker (a model based on a man with a stay-at-home wife), these high-flying women faced a double bind. Indeed, their options were much more limited than they seemed. Fundamentally, they faced a "choice gap": the difference between the decisions women could have made about their careers if they were not mothers or caregivers and the decisions they had to make in their circumstances as mothers married to high-octane husbands in ultimately unyielding professions. This choice gap obscures individual preferences, and thus reveals the things Olivia railed against—culture, jobs, society—the kinds of things sociologists call "structure."

Overall, women based their decisions on mutually reinforcing and interlocking factors. They confronted, for instance, two sets of trade-offs: kids versus careers, and their own careers versus those of their husbands. For many, circumstances beyond their control strongly influenced their decision to quit. On the family side of the equation, for example, women had to deal with caregiving for sick children and elderly parents, children's developmental problems, and special care needs. Such reasons figured in one-third of the sample. On the work side, women were denied part-time arrangements, a couple were laid off, and some had to relocate for their own careers or their husbands'. A total of 30 women, a little more than half the sample, mentioned at least one forced-choice consideration.

But even before women had children, the prospect of pregnancy loomed in the background, making women feel that they were perceived as flight risks. In her first day on the job as a marketing executive, for example, Patricia Lambert's boss asked her: "So, are you going to have kids?" And once women did get pregnant, they reported that they were often the first in their office, which made them feel more like outsiders. Some remarked that a dearth of role models created an atmosphere unsympathetic to work-family needs. And as these women navigated pregnancy and their lives beyond, their stories revealed a latent bias against mothers in their workplaces. What some women took from this was that pregnancy was a dirty little secret not to be openly discussed. The private nature of pregnancy thus complicated women's decisions regarding their careers once they became mothers, which is why they often waited until the last minute to figure out their next steps. Their experiences contrasted with the formal policies of their workplaces, which touted themselves as "family friendly."

The Rhetoric of Choice

Given the indisputable obstacles—hostile workplaces and absentee husbands—that stymied a full integration of work and family, it was ironic that most of the women invoked "choice" when relating the events surrounding their decision to exit their careers. Why were there not more women like Olivia, railing against the tyranny of an outmoded workplace that favored a 1950s-era employee or bemoaning their husbands' drive for achievement at the expense of their own?

I found that these women tended to use the rhetoric of choice in the service of their exceptionality. Women associated choice with privilege, feminism, and personal agency, and internalized it as a reflection of their own perfectionism. This was an attractive combination that played to their drive for achievement and also served to compensate for their loss of the careers they loved and the professional identities they valued. Some of these women bought into the media message that being an at-home mom was a status symbol, promoted by such cultural arbiters as *New York Magazine* and the *Wall Street Journal*. Their ability to go home reflected their husbands' career success, in which they and their children basked. Living out the traditional lifestyle, male breadwinner and stay-at-home-mom, which they were fortunate to be able to choose, they saw themselves as realizing the dreams of third-wave feminism. The goals of earlier, second-wave feminism, economic independence and gender equality, took a back seat, at least temporarily.

Challenging the Myth

These strategies and rhetoric, and the apparent invisibility of the choice gap, reveal how fully these high-achieving women internalized the double bind and the intensive-mothering and ideal-worker models on which it rests. The downside, of course, is that they blamed themselves for failing to "have it all" rather than any actual structural constraints. That work and family were incompatible was the overwhelming message they took from their experiences. And when they quit, not wanting to burn bridges, they cited family obligations as the reason, not their dissatisfaction with work, in accordance with social expectations. By adopting the socially desirable and gender-consistent explanation of "family," women often contributed to the larger misunderstanding surrounding their decision. Their own explanations endorsed the prevalent idea that quitting to go home is a choice. Employers rarely challenged women's explanations. Nor did they try to convince them to stay, thus reinforcing women's perception that their decision was the right thing to do as mothers, and perpetuating the reigning media image of these women as the new traditionalists.

Taken at face value, these women do seem to be traditional. But by rejecting an intransigent workplace, their quitting signifies a kind of silent strike.

They were not acquiescing to traditional gender roles by quitting, but voting with their feet against an outdated model of work. When women are not posing for the camera or worried about offending former employers (from whom they may need future references), they are able to share their stories candidly. From what I found, the truth is far different and certainly more nuanced than the media depiction.

The vast majority of the type of women I studied do not want to choose between career and family. The demanding nature of today's parenting puts added pressure on women. Women do indeed need to learn to be "good enough" mothers, and their husbands need to engage more equally in parenting. But on the basis of what they told me, women today "choose" to be home full-time not as much because of parenting overload as because of work overload, specifically long hours and the lack of flexible options in their high-status jobs. The popular media depiction of a return to traditionalism is wrong and misleading. Women are trying to achieve the feminist vision of a fully integrated life combining family and work. That so many attempt to remain in their careers when they do not "have to work" testifies strongly to their commitment to their careers, as does the difficulty they experience over their subsequent loss of identity. Their attempts at juggling and their plans to return to work in the future also indicate that their careers were not meant to be ephemeral and should not be treated as such. Rather, we should regard their exits as the miner's canary—a frontline indication that something is seriously amiss in many workplaces. Signs of toxic work environments and white-collar sweatshops are ubiquitous. We can glean from these women's experiences the true cost of these work conditions, which are personal and professional, and, ultimately, societal and economic.

Our current understanding of why high-achieving women quit—based as it is on choice and separate spheres—seriously undermines the will to change the contemporary workplace. The myth of opting out returns us to the days when educated women were barred from entering elite professions because "they'll only leave anyway." To the extent that elite women are arbiters of shifting gender norms, the opting out myth also has the potential to curtail women's aspirations and stigmatize those who challenge the separate-spheres ideology on which it is based. Current demographics make it clear that employers can hardly afford to lose the talents of high-achieving women. They can take a cue from at-home moms like the ones I studied: Forget opting out; the key to keeping professional women on the job is to create better, more flexible ways to work. . . .

EXPLORING THE ISSUE

Are Professional Women "Opting Out" of Work by Choice?

Critical Thinking and Reflection

1. The debate is limited to professional women because that is the group that can afford to choose to opt out. What hypotheses would you make about the desires of nonprofessional women based on the behavior of professional women?

2. Note two facts. First, the percentage of mothers with at-home children that were working in the labor force increased until the 1990s and then leveled off. Second, a noticeable number of professional women who could afford to were opting out. Linda Hirshman concludes from these facts that "the belief that women are responsible for child-rearing and homemaking was largely untouched by decades of workplace feminism." Critique this conclusion.

3. How does the fact that many mothers return to the labor force when their children are school age and more return when their children leave home impact your view of this debate?

4. What public policies would improve the lives of women with work–family tensions?

5. What is your judgment about the companies that have a "mommy tract" policy?

Is There Common Ground?

Both authors are feminists and upset about the situation that they analyze. Hirshman is angry that the culture has changed very little and still defines childrearing and home making as the mother's responsibility. The workplace has opened to women but the home has not changed. Stone is angry about how little the workplace has changed to accommodate mothers. Furthermore, both concur that work–family choices are often difficult, especially for working mothers who have to balance career and family. I know that I would feel very deprived if I had to quit my professor's job to raise children even though children are a great joy. But I do not have to make this choice. This is what is obviously unfair about this issue. It is mostly a female problem. Men are not expected to quit their jobs and stay home and raise their children. Some, in fact, are doing just this since their wives are making far more money than they are, but this is rare. Society and religious groups generally preach that the wife should put family before work, so the stress is generally on women.

Additional Resources

For analyses of the opt out phenomenon look at Pamela Stone, *Opting Out?: Why Women Really Quit Careers and Head Home* (University of California Press, 2007); Lisa A. Mainiero and Sherry E. Sullivan, *The Opt-Out Revolt* (Davies-Black, 2006); Phyllis Moen, *The Career Mystique* (Rowan & Littlefield, 2005); Ann Crittenden, *The Price of Motherhood* (Metropolitan Books, 2001); and Susan Chira, *A Mother's Place: Choosing Work and Family Without Guilt or Shame* (Perennial, 1999). Leslie Bennetts strongly advises women not to give up their careers in *The Feminine Mistake* (Voice/Hyperion, 2007), and Sylvia Ann Hewlett does the same in *Off-Ramps and On-Ramps: Keeping Talented Women on the Road to Success* (Harvard Business School Press, 2007).

For discussions of the demands of work and family on women, see Suzanne M. Bianchi, John P. Robinson, and Melissa Milkie, *Changing Rhythms of Family Life* (American Sociological Association, 2006); Susan Thistle, *From Marriage to the Market* (University of California Press, 2006); Arlie Russell Hochschild, *The Second Shift* (Penguin Books, 2003); and Anna Fels, *Necessary Dreams: Ambition in Women's Changing Lives* (Pantheon Book, 2004). Mary Eberstadt is the major critic of the working mothers who leave much of the childrearing to others. See her *Home-Alone America: The Hidden Toll of Daycare, Behavioral Drugs, and Other Parent Substitutes* (Penguin, 2004).

On the issue of time scarcity and time use, which factors into the debate on the tension between work and family, see *Fighting for Time: Shifting Boundaries of Work and Social Life,* edited by Cynthia Fuchs-Epstein and Arne L. Kalleberg (Russell Sage Foundation, 2004); Phyllis Moen, *It's About Time: Couples and Careers* (Cornell University Press, 2003); Harriet B. Presser, *Working in a 24/7 Economy: Challenges for American Families* (Russell Sage Foundation, 2003); John Robinson and Geoffrey Godbey, *Time for Life: The Surprising Ways Americans Use Their Time*, 2nd ed. (State University Press, 1999); Juliet Schor, *The Overworked American: The Unexpected Decline of Leisure* (Basic Books, 1991); and Jerry A. Jacobs and Kathleen Gerson, *The Time Divide: Work, Family, and Gender Inequality* (Harvard University Press, 2004).

ISSUE 5

Should Same-Sex Marriages Be Legally Recognized?

YES: Human Rights Campaign, from "Answers to Questions about Marriage Equality," *Human Rights Campaign Report* (Human Rights Campaign, 2009)

NO: Peter Sprigg, from "Questions and Answers: What's Wrong with Letting Same-Sex Couples 'Marry'?" *Family Research Council* (2004)

Learning Outcomes
After reading this issue, you should be able to: • Understand the potential force of traditions in delegitimizing proposed changes that counter them.   • Understand the importance of other traditions and strongly held values in supporting changes that seem to oppose accepted traditions.   • Observe how the way the issue is defined affects the success or failure of the change efforts.   • Analyze how the political system and its laws can be ahead of the public on changing institutions or can lag behind the public.   • Understand the arguments and the values that they are based upon for and against same-sex marriage.

YES: America's largest lesbian and gay organization, the Human Rights Campaign, presents many arguments for why same-sex couples should be able to marry. The main argument is fairness. Marriage confers many benefits that same-sex couples are deprived of.

NO: Researcher Peter Sprigg presents many arguments for why same-sex couples should not be able to marry. The main argument is that the state has the right and duty to specify who a person, whether straight or gay, can marry, so no rights are violated.

In 1979, in Sioux Falls, South Dakota, Randy Rohl and Grady Quinn became the first acknowledged homosexual couple in America to receive permission from their high school principal to attend the senior prom together. The National Gay Task Force hailed the event as a milestone in the progress of human rights. It is unclear what the voters of Sioux Falls thought about it, because it was not put up to a vote. However, if their views were similar to those of voters in Dade County, Florida; Houston, Texas; Wichita, Kansas; and various localities in the state of Oregon, they probably were not pleased. In referenda held in these and other areas, voters have reversed decisions by legislators and local boards that banned discrimination by sexual preference.

Yet the attitude of Americans toward the rights of homosexuals is not easy to pin down. Voters have also defeated resolutions such as the one in California in 1978 that would have banned the hiring of homosexual schoolteachers, or the one on the Oregon ballot in 1992 identifying homosexuality as "abnormal, wrong, unnatural and perverse." In some states, notably Colorado, voters have approved initiatives widely perceived as antihomosexual. But, almost invariably, these resolutions have been carefully worded so as to appear to oppose "special" rights for homosexuals. In general, polls show that a large majority of Americans believe that homosexuals should have equal rights with heterosexuals with regard to job opportunities. On the other hand, many view homosexuality as morally wrong. These developments have prompted President Bush to propose a constitutional amendment limiting marriage to the union of a man and a woman, but this law did not pass Congress.

Since 2001, ten countries have legalized same-sex marriages nationwide, but currently, same-sex marriages are not legally recognized by Congress. In the Defense of Marriage Act of 1996, Congress defined marriage as heterosexual. A state does not have to recognize another state's nonheterosexual marriage. The legal situation is constantly changing. The states that have legalized same-sex marriages are Connecticut, District of Columbia, Iowa, Massachusetts, New Hampshire, New York, Vermont, and most recently, Maryland. However, 31 states have constitutional restrictions limiting marriage to one man and one woman. By the time this book is published the situation will probably change. Activists on both sides are constantly introducing legislation on same-sex marriages and gay rights. This is not only a civil rights issue but also a moral, religious, social, and political issue that can be sliced and diced in many ways. President Obama prefers to keep the term marriage for heterosexual couples but to legalize same-sex civil unions with almost all the rights of married couples. There are many other positions as people try to balance their moral, religious, and political values. On the other hand, the issue is a legal matter and new legislation for or against same-sex marriages must conform to the constitution and various standing civil rights laws.

One argument in support of same-sex marriage is that marriage conveys many important benefits on the couple, and denying same-sex couples legal access to marriage represents discrimination based on sexual orientation, which should violate our civil rights laws. They would be denied many financial, psychological, and physical well-being benefits and their children would grow up in a less conducive atmosphere. A serious question is whether legalized civil unions would convey all these benefits or whether the word marriage is necessary. Of course, those who think that even civil unions for same-sex couples are morally and religiously wrong would oppose such civil unions.

The issue of same-sex marriage fascinates sociologists because it represents a basic change in a major social institution and is being played out on several fields: legal, cultural/moral, and behavioral. The legal debate will be decided by courts and legislatures; the cultural/moral debate is open to all of us; and the behavioral debate will be conducted by the activists on both sides. In the readings that follow, the Human Rights Campaign presents the major arguments for same-sex marriages, and Peter Sprigg argues that marriage must remain heterosexual.

YES  Human Rights Campaign

Answers to Questions about Marriage Equality

Why Same-Sex Couples Want to Marry

Many same-sex couples want the right to legally marry because they are in love—many, in fact, have spent the last 10, 20 or 50 years with that person—and they want to honor their relationship in the greatest way our society has to offer, by making a public commitment to stand together in good times and bad, through all the joys and challenges family life brings.

Many parents want the right to marry because they know it offers children a vital safety net and guarantees protections that unmarried parents cannot provide. And still other people—both gay and straight—are fighting for the right of same-sex couples to marry because they recognize that it is simply not fair to deny some families the protections all other families are eligible to enjoy. Currently in the United States, same-sex couples in long-term, committed relationships pay higher taxes and are denied basic protections and rights granted to married straight couples. Among them:

- **Hospital visitation.** Married couples have the automatic right to visit each other in the hospital and make medical decisions. Same-sex couples can be denied the right to visit a sick or injured loved one in the hospital.
- **Social Security benefits.** Married people receive Social Security payments upon the death of a spouse. Despite paying payroll taxes, gay and lesbian partners receive no Social Security survivor benefits—resulting in an average annual income loss of $5,528 upon the death of a partner.
- **Immigration.** Americans in bi-national relationships are not permitted to petition for their same-sex partners to immigrate. As a result, they are often forced to separate or move to another country.
- **Health insurance.** Many public and private employers provide medical coverage to the spouses of their employees, but most employers do not provide coverage to the life partners of gay and lesbian employees. Gay and lesbian employees who do receive health coverage for their partners must pay federal income taxes on the value of the insurance.
- **Estate taxes.** A married person automatically inherits all the property of his or her deceased spouse without paying estate taxes. A gay or

From *Human Rights Campaign Report,* 2009, pp. i, 1–17. Copyright © 2009 by Human Rights Campaign Foundation. Reprinted by permission.

lesbian taxpayer is forced to pay estate taxes on property inherited from a deceased partner.

- **Family leave.** Married workers are legally entitled to unpaid leave from their jobs to care for an ill spouse. Gay and lesbian workers are not entitled to family leave to care for their partners.
- **Nursing homes.** Married couples have a legal right to live together in nursing homes. The rights of elderly gay or lesbian couples are an uneven patchwork of state laws.
- **Home protection.** Laws protect married seniors from being forced to sell their homes to pay high nursing home bills; gay and lesbian seniors have no such protection.
- **Pensions.** After the death of a worker, most pension plans pay survivor benefits only to a legal spouse of the participant. Gay and lesbian partners are excluded from such pension benefits.

Why Civil Unions Aren't Enough

Comparing marriage to civil unions is a bit like comparing diamonds to rhinestones. One is, quite simply, the real deal; the other is not. Consider:

- Opposite-sex are couples who are eligible to marry may have their marriage performed in any state and have it recognized in every other state in the nation and every country in the world.
- Couples who are joined in a civil union, for example in Vermont, New Jersey or New Hampshire, have no guarantee that its protections will travel with them to other states. Moreover, even couples who have a civil union and remain in Vermont, New Jersey or New Hampshire receive only second-class protections in comparison to their married friends and neighbors. While they receive state-level protections, they do not receive any of the more than 1,100 federal benefits and protections of marriage.

In short, civil unions are not separate but equal—they are separate and unequal. And our society has tried separate before. It just doesn't work.

Marriage:

- State grants marriage licenses to couples.
- Religious institutions are not required to perform marriage ceremonies.

Civil unions:

- State would grant civil union licenses to couples.
- Couples receive legal protections and rights under state law only.
- Civil unions are not necessarily recognized by other states or the federal government.
- Religious institutions are not required to perform civil union ceremonies.

"I Believe God Meant Marriage for Men and Women. How Can I Support Marriage for Same-Sex Couples?"

Many people who believe in God—as well as fairness and justice for all—ask this question. They feel a tension between religious beliefs and democratic values that has been experienced in many different ways throughout our nation's history. That is why the framers of our Constitution established the principle of separation of church and state.

That principle applies no less to the marriage issue than it does to any other. Indeed, the answer to the apparent dilemma between religious beliefs and support for equal protections for all families lies in recognizing that marriage has a significant religious meaning for many people, but that it is also a legal contract. And it is strictly the legal—not the religious—dimension of marriage that is being debated now.

Granting marriage rights to same-sex couples would not require leaders of Christian, Jewish, Islamic or any other religious leaders to perform these marriages. It would not require religious institutions to permit these ceremonies to be held on their grounds. It would not even require that religious communities discuss the issue. People of faith would remain free to make their own judgments about what makes a marriage in the eyes of God—just as they are today.

Consider, for example, the difference in how the Roman Catholic Church and the U.S. government view couples who have divorced and remarried. Because church tenets do not sanction divorce, the second marriage is not valid in the church's view. The government, however, recognizes the marriage by extending to the remarried couple the same rights and protections as those granted to every other married couple in America. In this situation—as would be the case in marriage for same-sex couples—the church remains free to establish its own teachings on the religious dimension of marriage while the government upholds equality under law.

A growing number of religious communities bless same-sex unions, including Reform Judaism, the Unitarian Universalist Association and the Metropolitan Community Church. The Presbyterian Church (USA) allows ceremonies to be performed but they're not considered the same as marriage. The Episcopal Church, United Church of Christ and the United Synagogue of Conservative Judaism allow individual congregations to set their own policies on same-sex unions.

"This Is Different from Interracial Marriage. Sexual Orientation Is a Choice."

> "We cannot keep turning our backs on gay and lesbian Americans. I have fought too hard and too long against discrimination based on race and color not to stand up against discrimination based on sexual orientation. I've heard the reasons for opposing civil marriage for same-sex couples. Cut through the distractions, and they stink of the same fear, hatred, and intolerance I have known in racism and in bigotry."

> —*Rep. John Lewis, D-Ga., a leader of the black civil rights movement,*
> *writing in the Boston Globe, Nov. 25, 2003*

Decades of research all point to the fact that sexual orientation is not a choice, and that a person's sexual orientation cannot be changed. To whom one is drawn is a fundamental aspect of who we are. In this way, the struggle for marriage equality for same-sex couples is just as basic as the successful fight for interracial marriage. It recognizes that Americans should not be coerced into false and unhappy marriages but should be free to marry the person they love—thereby building marriage on a true and stable foundation.

"Won't This Create a Free-for-All and Make the Whole Idea of Marriage Meaningless?"

Many people share this concern because opponents of LGBT equality have used this argument as a scare tactic—but it is not true. Granting same-sex couples the right to marry would in no way change the number of people who could enter into a marriage (or eliminate restrictions on the age or familial relationships of those who may marry). Marriage would continue to recognize the highest possible commitment that can be made between two adults, plain and simple.

"I Strongly Believe Children Need a Mother and a Father."

Many of us grew up believing that everyone needs a mother and father, regardless of whether we ourselves happened to have two parents, or two good parents.

But as families have grown more diverse in recent decades, and researchers have studied how these different family relationships affect children, it has become clear that the quality of a family's relationship is more important than the particular structure of families that exist today. In other words, the qualities that help children grow into good and responsible adults—learning how to learn, to have compassion for others, to contribute to society and be respectful of others and their differences—do not depend on the sexual orientation of their parents but on their parents' ability to provide a loving, stable and happy home, something no class of Americans has an exclusive hold on. That is why research studies have consistently shown that children raised by gay and lesbian parents do just as well as children raised by straight parents in all conventional measures of child development, such as academic achievement, psychological well-being and social abilities.

That is also why the nation's leading child welfare organizations, including the American Academy of Pediatrics, the American Academy of Family Physicians and others, have issued statements that dismiss assertions that only straight couples can be good parents—and declare that the focus should now be on providing greater protections for the 1 million to 9 million children being raised by gay and lesbian parents in the United States today.

"How Could Marriage for Same-Sex Couples Possibly Be Good for the American Family—or Our Country?"

> "We shouldn't just allow gay marriage. We should insist on gay marriage. We should regard it as scandalous that two people could claim to love each other and not want to sanctify their love with marriage and fidelity."
>
> —*Conservative columnist David Brooks,*
> *writing in the New York Times, Nov. 22, 2003*

The prospect of a significant change in our laws and customs has often caused people to worry more about dire consequences that could result than about the potential positive outcomes. In fact, precisely the same anxiety arose when some people fought to overturn the laws prohibiting marriage between people of different races in the 1950s and 1960s. (One Virginia judge even declared, "God intended to separate the races.")

But in reality, opening marriage to couples who are so willing to fight for it could only strengthen the institution for all. It would open the doors to more supporters, not opponents. And it would help keep the age-old institution alive.

As history has repeatedly proven, institutions that fail to take account of the changing needs of the population are those that grow weak; those that recognize and accommodate changing needs grow strong. For example, the U.S. military, like American colleges and universities, grew stronger after permitting African Americans and women to join its ranks.

Similarly, granting same-sex couples the right to marry would strengthen the institution of marriage by allowing it to better meet the needs of the true diversity of family structures in America today.

"Can't Same-Sex Couples Go to a Lawyer to Secure All the Rights They Need?"

Not by a long shot. When a gay or lesbian person gets seriously ill, there is no legal document that can make their partner eligible to take leave from work under the federal Family and Medical Leave Act to provide care—because that law applies only to married couples.

When gay or lesbian people grow old and in need of nursing home care, there is no legal document that can give them the right to Medicaid coverage without potentially causing their partner to be forced from their home—because the federal Medicaid law only permits married spouses to keep their home without becoming ineligible for benefits.

And when a gay or lesbian person dies, there is no legal document that can extend Social Security survivor benefits or the right to inherit a retirement plan without severe tax burdens that stem from being "unmarried" in the eyes of the law.

These are only a few examples of the critical protections that are granted through more than 1,100 federal laws that protect only married couples.

In the absence of the right to marry, same-sex couples can only put in place a handful of the most basic arrangements, such as naming each other in a will or a power of attorney. And even these documents remain vulnerable to challenges in court by disgruntled family members.

"Won't This Cost Taxpayers Too Much Money?"

No, it wouldn't necessarily cost much at all. In fact, treating same-sex couples as families under law could even save taxpayers money because marriage would require them to assume legal responsibility for their joint living expenses and reduce their dependence on public assistance programs such as Medicaid, Temporary Assistance to Needy Families, Supplemental Security Income disability payments and food stamps.

Put another way, the money it would cost to extend benefits to same-sex couples could be outweighed by the money that would be saved as these families rely more fully on each other instead of state or federal government assistance.

For example, two studies conducted in 2003 by professors at the University of Massachusetts, Amherst, and the University of California, Los Angeles, found that extending domestic partner benefits to same-sex couples in California and New Jersey would save taxpayers millions of dollars a year.

Specifically, the studies projected that the California state budget would save an estimated $8.1 million to $10.6 million each year by enacting the most comprehensive domestic partner law in the nation. In New Jersey, which passed a new domestic partner law in 2004, the savings were projected to be even higher—more than $61 million each year.

(Sources: "Equal Rights, Fiscal Responsibility: The Impact of A.B. 205 on California's Budget," by M. V. Lee Badgett, Ph.D., IGLSS, Department of Economics, University of Massachusetts, Amherst, and R. Bradley Sears, J.D., Williams Project, UCLA School of Law, University of California, Los Angeles, May 2003, and "Supporting Families, Saving Funds: A Fiscal Analysis of New Jersey's Domestic Partnership Act," by Badgett and Sears with Suzanne Goldberg, J.D., Rutgers School of Law-Newark, December 2003.)

"Where Can Same-Sex Couples Marry Today?"

In 2001, the Netherlands became the first country to extend marriage rights to same-sex couples. Belgium passed a similar law two years later. Spain followed suit in July 2005, and in December 2005, the South African Supreme Court ruled that the country had to extend the rights of marriage to same-sex couples by the end of 2006. Some of these countries, however, have strict citizenship or residency requirements that do not permit American couples to take advantage of the protections provided. In 2003, Ontario became the first Canadian province to grant marriage to same-sex couples, and in July 2005, Canada's federal government passed a law extending marriage equality nationwide.

In November 2003, the Massachusetts Supreme Judicial Court recognized the right of same-sex couples to marry, giving the state six months to begin issuing marriage licenses to same-sex couples. It began issuing licenses May 17, 2004.

In October 2008, the Connecticut Supreme Court recognized the right of same-sex couples to marry. Connecticut began issuing licenses to same-sex couples Nov. 12, 2008.

On Nov. 4, 2008, California voters approved Proposition 8, which amends the state constitution to prohibit marriage by same-sex couples. The amendment overrules a May 2008 decision by the California Supreme Court recognizing marriage equality. California continues to provide rights and responsibilities to registered domestic partners.

Follow the latest developments in California, New Jersey, New Mexico, New York, Oregon, Washington and other communities across the country at the HRC Marriage Center. Other nations have also taken steps toward extending equal protections to all couples, though the protections they provide are more limited than marriage. Croatia, Denmark, Finland, France, Germany, Iceland, Israel, New Zealand, Norway, Portugal, Slovenia, Switzerland, Sweden and the United Kingdom all have nationwide laws that grant same-sex partners a range of important rights, protections and obligations.

Beginning in December 2005, same-sex couples in the United Kingdom have been able to apply for civil partnership licenses to certify their relationships before the government. These licenses provide same-sex couples hospital visitation rights, pension benefits, the ability to gain parental responsibility for a partner's children and other rights granted to opposite-sex couples.

"What Protections Other Than Marriage Are Available to Same-Sex Couples?"

At the federal level, there are no protections at all available to same-sex couples. In fact, a federal law called the "Defense of Marriage Act" says that the federal government will discriminate against same-sex couples who marry by refusing to recognize their marriages or providing them with the federal protections of marriage.

Some members of the U.S. Congress have tried to go even further by attempting to pass a federal marriage amendment that would write discrimination against same-sex couples into the U.S. Constitution. This was defeated twice, in 2004 and 2006.

At the state level, Vermont, New Jersey and New Hampshire offer civil unions (as of 2008), which provide important state benefits but no federal protections, such as Social Security survivor benefits. There is also no guarantee that civil unions will be recognized outside these states. Forty-four states also have laws or state constitutional amendments explicitly prohibiting the recognition of marriages between same-sex partners.

Domestic partner laws have been enacted in California, Maine, Hawaii, Oregon, Washington and the District of Columbia. The benefits conferred by these laws vary; some offer access to family health insurance, others confer co-parenting rights. Some offer a broad range of rights similar to civil unions.

10 FACTS

1. Same-sex couples live in 99.3 percent of all counties nationwide.
2. There are an estimated 3.1 million people living together in same-sex relationships in the United States.
3. Fifteen percent of these same-sex couples live in rural settings.
4. One out of three lesbian couples is raising children. One out of five gay male couples is raising children.
5. Between 1 million and 9 million children are being raised by lesbian, gay and bisexual parents in the United States today.
6. At least one same-sex couple is raising children in 96 percent of all counties nationwide.
7. The highest percentages of same-sex couples raising children live in the South.
8. Nearly one in four same-sex couples includes a partner 55 years old or older, and nearly one in five same-sex couples is composed of two people 55 or older.
9. More than one in 10 same-sex couples include a partner 65 years old or older, and nearly one in 10 same-sex couples is composed of two people 65 or older.
10. The states with the highest numbers of same-sex senior couples are also the most popular for straight senior couples: California, New York and Florida.

These facts are based on analyses of the 2000 Census conducted by the Urban Institute and the Human Rights Campaign. The estimated number of people in same-sex relationships has been adjusted by 62 percent to compensate for the widely reported undercount in the Census. (See "Gay and Lesbian Families in the United States: Same-Sex Unmarried Partner Households.")

Peter Sprigg  **NO**

Questions and Answers: What's Wrong with Letting Same-Sex Couples "Marry"?

What's Wrong with Letting Same-Sex Couples Legally "Marry"?
There are two key reasons why the legal rights, benefits, and responsibilities of civil marriage should not be extended to same-sex couples.

The first is that homosexual relationships are not marriage. That is, they simply do not fit the minimum necessary condition for a marriage to exist—namely, the union of a man and a woman.

The second is that homosexual relationships are harmful. Not only do they not provide the same benefits to society as heterosexual marriages, but their consequences are far more negative than positive.

Either argument, standing alone, is sufficient to reject the claim that same-sex unions should be granted the legal status of marriage.

Let's Look at the First Argument. Isn't Marriage Whatever the Law Says It Is?
No. Marriage is not a creation of the law. Marriage is a fundamental human institution that predates the law and the Constitution. At its heart, it is an anthropological and sociological reality, not a legal one. Laws relating to marriage merely recognize and regulate an institution that already exists.

But Isn't Marriage Just a Way of Recognizing People Who Love Each Other and Want to Spend Their Lives Together?
If love and companionship were sufficient to define marriage, then there would be no reason to deny "marriage" to unions of a child and an adult, or an adult child and his or her aging parent, or to roommates who have no sexual relationship, or to groups rather than couples. Love and companionship are usually considered integral to marriage in our culture, but they are not sufficient to define it as an institution. . . .

Why Should Homosexuals Be Denied the Right to Marry Like Anyone Else?
The fundamental "right to marry" is a right that rests with *individuals*, not with *couples*. Homosexual *individuals* already have exactly the same "right"

From *Family Research Council*, no. 256, 2004, pp. 173–179. Copyright © 2004 by Family Research Council. Reprinted by permission to marry as anyone else. Marriage license applications do not inquire as to a person's "sexual orientation.". . .

However, while every individual person is free to get married, *no* person, whether heterosexual or homosexual, has ever had a legal right to marry simply any willing partner. Every person, whether heterosexual or homosexual, is subject to legal restrictions as to whom they may marry. To be specific, every person, regardless of sexual preference, is legally barred from marrying a child, a close blood relative, a person who is already married, or a person of the same sex. There is no discrimination here, nor does such a policy deny anyone the "equal protection of the laws" (as guaranteed by the Constitution), since these restrictions apply equally to every individual.

Some people may wish to do away with one or more of these longstanding restrictions upon one's choice of marital partner. However, the fact that a tiny but vocal minority of Americans desire to have someone of the same sex as a partner does not mean that they have a "right" to do so, any more than the desires of other tiny (but less vocal) minorities of Americans give them a "right" to choose a child, their own brother or sister, or a group of two or more as their marital partners.

Isn't Prohibiting Homosexual "Marriage" Just as Discriminatory as Prohibiting Interracial Marriage, Like Some States Used to Do?

This analogy is not valid at all. Bridging the divide of the sexes by uniting men and women is both a worthy goal and a part of the fundamental purpose of marriage, common to all human civilizations.

Laws against interracial marriage, on the other hand, served only the purpose of preserving a social system of racial segregation. This was both an unworthy goal and one utterly irrelevant to the fundamental nature of marriage.

Allowing a black woman to marry a white man does not change the definition of marriage, which requires one man and one woman. Allowing two men or two women to marry would change that fundamental definition. Banning the "marriage" of same-sex couples is therefore essential to preserve the nature and purpose of marriage itself. . . .

How Would Allowing Same-Sex Couples to Marry Change Society's Concept of Marriage?

As an example, marriage will open wide the door to homosexual adoption, which will simply lead to more children suffering the negative consequences of growing up without both a mother and a father.

Among homosexual men in particular, casual sex, rather than committed relationships, is the rule and not the exception. And even when they do enter into a more committed relationship, it is usually of relatively short duration. For example, a study of homosexual men in the Netherlands (the first country in the world to legalize "marriage" for same-sex couples), published in the journal *AIDS* in 2003, found that the average length of "steady partnerships" was not more than 2 < years (Maria Xiridou et al., in *AIDS* 2003, 17:1029–1038).

In addition, studies have shown that even homosexual men who are in "committed" relationships are not sexually faithful to each other. While infidelity among heterosexuals is much too common, it does not begin to compare to the rates among homosexual men. The 1994 National Health and Social Life Survey, which remains the most comprehensive study of Americans' sexual practices ever undertaken, found that 75 percent of married men and 90 percent of married women had been sexually faithful to their spouse. On the other hand, a major study of homosexual men in "committed" relationships found that only seven out of 156 had been sexually faithful, or 4.5 percent. The Dutch study cited above found that even homosexual men in "steady partnerships" had an average of eight "casual" sex partners per year.

So if same-sex relationships are legally recognized as "marriage," the idea of marriage as a sexually exclusive and faithful relationship will be dealt a serious blow. Adding monogamy and faithfulness to the other pillars of marriage that have already fallen will have overwhelmingly negative consequences for Americans' physical and mental health. . . .

Don't Homosexuals Need Marriage Rights so That They Will Be Able to Visit Their Partners in the Hospital?

The idea that homosexuals are routinely denied the right to visit their partners in the hospital is nonsense. When this issue was raised during debate over the Defense of Marriage Act in 1996, the Family Research Council did an informal survey of nine hospitals in four states and the District of Columbia. None of the administrators surveyed could recall a single case in which a visitor was barred because of their homosexuality, and they were incredulous that this would even be considered an issue.

Except when a doctor limits visitation for medical reasons, final authority over who may visit an adult patient rests with that patient. This is and should be the case regardless of the sexual orientation or marital status of the patient or the visitor.

The only situation in which there would be a possibility that the blood relatives of a patient might attempt to exclude the patient's homosexual partner is if the patient is unable to express his or her wishes due to unconsciousness or mental incapacity. Homosexual partners concerned about this (remote) possibility can effectively preclude it by granting to one another a health care proxy (the legal right to make medical decisions for the patient) and a power of attorney (the right to make all legal decisions for another person). Marriage is not necessary for this. It is inconceivable that a hospital would exclude someone who holds the health care proxy and power of attorney for a patient from visiting that patient, except for medical reasons.

The hypothetical "hospital visitation hardship" is nothing but an emotional smokescreen to distract people from the more serious implications of radically redefining marriage.

Don't Homosexuals Need the Right to Marry Each Other in Order to Ensure That They Will Be Able to Leave Their Estates to Their Partner when They Die?

As with the hospital visitation issue, the concern over inheritance rights is something that simply does not require marriage to resolve it. Nothing in current law prevents homosexual partners from being joint owners of property such as a home or a car, in which case the survivor would automatically become the owner if the partner dies.

An individual may leave the remainder of his estate to whomever he wishes—again, without regard to sexual orientation or marital status—simply by writing a will. As with the hospital visitation issue, blood relatives would only be able to overrule the surviving homosexual partner in the event that the deceased had failed to record his wishes in a common, inexpensive legal document. Changing the definition of a fundamental social institution like marriage is a rather extreme way of addressing this issue. Preparing a will is a much simpler solution.

Don't Homosexuals Need Marriage Rights so That They Can Get Social Security Survivor Benefits when a Partner Dies?

. . . Social Security survivor benefits were designed to recognize the non-monetary contribution made to a family by the homemaking and child-rearing activities of a wife and mother, and to ensure that a woman and her children would not become destitute if the husband and father were to die.

The Supreme Court ruled in the 1970s that such benefits must be gender-neutral. However, they still are largely based on the premise of a division of roles within a couple between a breadwinner who works to raise money and a homemaker who stays home to raise children.

Very few homosexual couples organize their lives along the lines of such a "traditional" division of labor and roles. They are far more likely to consist of two earners, each of whom can be supported in old age by their own personal Social Security pension.

Furthermore, far fewer homosexual couples than heterosexual ones are raising children at all, for the obvious reason that they are incapable of natural reproduction with each other. This, too, reduces the likelihood of a traditional division of labor among them.

Survivor benefits for the legal (biological or adopted) *children* of homosexual parents (as opposed to their partners) are already available under current law, so "marriage" rights for homosexual couples are unnecessary to protect the interests of these children themselves. . . .

Even if "Marriage" Itself Is Uniquely Heterosexual, Doesn't Fairness Require That the Legal and Financial Benefits of Marriage Be Granted to Same-Sex Couples—Perhaps Through "Civil Unions" or "Domestic Partnerships"?

No. The legal and financial benefits of marriage are not an entitlement to be distributed equally to all (if they were, single people would have as much reason to consider them "discriminatory" as same-sex couples). Society grants benefits to marriage because marriage has benefits for society—including, but not limited to, the reproduction of the species in households with the optimal household structure (i.e., the presence of both a mother and a father).

Homosexual relationships, on the other hand, have no comparable benefit for society, and in fact impose substantial costs on society. The fact that

AIDS is at least ten times more common among men who have sex with men than among the general population is but one example. . . .

What about the Argument That Homosexual Relations Are Harmful? What Do You Mean by That?

Homosexual men experience higher rates of many diseases, including:

- Human Papillomavirus (HPV), which causes most cases of cervical cancer in women and anal cancer in men
- Hepatitis A, B, and C
- Gonorrhea
- Syphilis
- "Gay Bowel Syndrome," a set of sexually transmitted gastrointestinal problems such as proctitis, proctocolitis, and enteritis
- HIV/AIDS (One Canadian study found that as a result of HIV alone, "life expectancy for gay and bisexual men is eight to twenty years less than for all men.")

Lesbian women, meanwhile, have a higher prevalence of:

- Bacterial vaginosis
- Hepatitis C
- HIV risk behaviors
- Cancer risk factors such as smoking, alcohol use, poor diet, and being overweight . . .

Do Homosexuals Have More Mental Health Problems as Well?

Yes. Various research studies have found that homosexuals have higher rates of:

- Alcohol abuse
- Drug abuse
- Nicotine dependence
- Depression
- Suicide

Isn't It Possible That These Problems Result from Society's "Discrimination" Against Homosexuals?

This is the argument usually put forward by pro-homosexual activists. However, there is a simple way to test this hypothesis. If "discrimination" were the cause of homosexuals' mental health problems, then one would expect those problems to be much less common in cities or countries, like San Francisco or the Netherlands, where homosexuality has achieved the highest levels of acceptance.

In fact, the opposite is the case. In places where homosexuality is widely accepted, the physical and mental health problems of homosexuals are greater, not less. This suggests that the real problem lies in the homosexual lifestyle itself, not in society's response to it. In fact, it suggests that increasing the level of social support *for* homosexual behavior (by, for instance, allowing same-sex couples to "marry") would only increase these problems, not reduce them. . . .

Haven't Studies Shown That Children Raised by Homosexual
Parents Are No Different from Other Children?
No. This claim is often put forward, even by professional organizations. The truth is that most research on "homosexual parents" thus far has been marred by serious methodological problems. However, even pro-homosexual sociologists Judith Stacey and Timothy Biblarz report that the actual data from key studies show the "no differences" claim to be false.

Surveying the research (primarily regarding lesbians) in an *American Sociological Review* article in 2001, they found that:

- Children of lesbians are less likely to conform to traditional gender norms.
- Children of lesbians are more likely to engage in homosexual behavior.
- Daughters of lesbians are "more sexually adventurous and less chaste."
- Lesbian "co-parent relationships" are more likely to end than heterosexual ones.

A 1996 study by an Australian sociologist compared children raised by heterosexual married couples, heterosexual cohabiting couples, and homosexual cohabiting couples. It found that the children of heterosexual married couples did the best, and children of homosexual couples the worst, in nine of the thirteen academic and social categories measured. . . .

Do the American People Want to See "Marriages" Between
Same-Sex Couples Recognized by Law?
No—and in the wake of the June 2003 court decisions to legalize such "marriages" in the Canadian province of Ontario and to legalize homosexual sodomy in the United States, the nation's opposition to such a radical social experiment has actually grown.

Five separate national opinion polls taken between June 24 and July 27, 2003 showed opponents of civil "marriage" for same-sex couples outnumbering supporters by not less than fifteen percentage points in every poll. The wording of poll questions can make a significant difference, and in this case, the poll with the most straightforward language (a Harris/CNN/Time poll asking "Do you think marriages between homosexual men or homosexual women should be recognized as legal by the law?") resulted in the strongest opposition, with 60 percent saying "No" and only 33 percent saying "Yes."

EXPLORING THE ISSUE

Should Same-Sex Marriages Be Legally Recognized?

Critical Thinking and Reflection

1. What is your theory about homosexuality? Do you think it is a choice or is there a biological basis for it? Can homosexuals be repro-grammed to be heterosexuals? (The research is not decisive on this point. No gene for homosexuality has been discovered yet, but peo-ple do vary considerably in their levels of various hormones.)
2. Does your theory influence your opinion on the debate issue?
3. Can the civil rights of homosexuals on the issue of unions be pro-tected in any other way than by same-sex marriages?
4. No proposed law would require religious leaders to perform same-sex marriages. Do you think this largely nullifies the religious objection to same-sex marriage?
5. Has the legalization of same-sex marriages in several states and for-eign countries produced problems that provide grounds for opposing same-sex marriages in the United States?
6. Evaluate the argument that homosexual marriage is a threat to het-erosexual marriage. Has it had negative effects on heterosexual mar-riages so far as you can tell?

Is There Common Ground?

The issue of the rights of homosexuals creates a social dilemma. Most people would agree that all members of society should have equal rights. However, the majority may disapprove of the lifestyles of a minority group and pass laws against some of their behaviors. The question is, when do these laws violate civil rights? Are laws against same-sex marriage such a violation? Another common set of values is the right to life, liberty, and the pursuit of happiness. Life is not threat-ened in this issue but liberty and happiness are. Thus, the liberty and happiness of homosexuals should be promoted unless that would harm heterosexuals. We must ask, therefore, who is hurt by same-sex marriages? Are heterosexuals being hurt? As far as I know, I have not been hurt as a heterosexual. I know some people who are upset by same-sex marriage laws, but I know more who are upset by the lack of such laws. Do these feelings have any standing in the moral argument?

Additional Resources

There is a considerable literature on homosexuality and the social and legal status of homosexuals. Recent works on gay marriage include Craig A. Rim-merman and Clyde Wilcox, eds., *The Politics of Same-Sex Marriage* (University of

Chicago Press, 2007); Daniel R. Pinello, *America's Struggle for Same-Sex Marriage* (Cambridge University Press, 2006); Donald J. Cantor et al., *Same-Sex Marriage: The Legal and Psychological Evolution in America* (Wesleyan University Press, 2006); R. Claire Snyder, *Gay Marriage and Democracy Equality for All* (Rowman & Littlefield, 2006); David Moats, *Civil Wars: A Battle for Gay Marriage* (Harcourt, 2004); Evan Gerstmann, *Same-Sex Marriage and the Constitution* (Cambridge University Press, 2004); Jonathan Rauch, *Gay Marriage: Why It Is Good for Gays, Good for Straights, and Good for America* (Times Books, 2004); Lynn D. Wordle et al., eds., *Marriage and Same-Sex Unions: A Debate* (Praeger, 2003); Martin Dupuis, *Same-Sex Marriage, Legal Mobilization, and the Politics of Rights* (Peter Lang, 2002); Kevin Bourassa, *Just Married: Gay Marriage and the Expansion of Human Rights* (University of Wisconsin Press, 2002); and a four-volume set: *Defending Same-Sex Marriage*, vol. 1; *"Separate But Equal" No More: A Guide to the Legal Status of Same-Sex Marriage, Civil Unions, and Other Partnerships*, vol. 2, edited by Mark Strasser; *Our Family Values: Same-Sex Marriage and Religion*, vol. 3, edited by Traci C. West; *The Freedom-to-Marry Movement: Education, Advocacy, Culture, and the Media*, vol. 4, edited by Martin Dupuis and William A. Thompson (Praeger, 2007). Most works are pro gay rights. For opposition to same-sex marriage, see Jaye Cee Whitehead, *The Nuptial Deal: Same-Sex Marriage and Neo-Liberal Governance* (University of Chicago Press, 2012). Recent works on the history of the gay rights movement include Dudley Clendinen and Adam Nagourney, *Out for Good: The Struggle to Build a Gay Rights Movement in America* (Simon & Schuster, 1999); Ronald J. Hunt, *Historical Dictionary of the Gay Liberation Movement* (Scarecrow Press, 1999); JoAnne Myers, *Historical Dictionary of the Lesbian Liberation Movement: Still the Rage* (Scarecrow Press, 2003); and John Loughery, *The Other Side of Silence: Men's Lives and Gay Identities: A Twentieth-Century History* (Henry Holt, 1998). For broad academic works on homosexuality, see Kath Weston, *Long Slow Burn: Sexuality and Social Science* (Routledge, 1998), and Michael Ruse, *Homosexuality: A Philosophical Inquiry* (Blackwell, 1998). Recent works that focus on homosexual rights include David A. J. Richards, *Identity and the Case for Gay Rights* (University of Chicago Press, 1999); Daniel R. Pinello, *Gay Rights and American Law* (Cambridge University Press, 2003); Carlos A. Ball, *The Morality of Gay Rights: An Exploration in Political Philosophy* (Routledge, 2003); Brette McWhorter Sember, *Gay and Lesbian Rights: A Guide for GLBT Singles, Couples, and Families* (Sphinx, 2003); and Nan D. Hunter, *The Rights of Lesbians, Gay Men, Bisexuals, and Transgender People: The Authoritative ACLU Guide to a Lesbian, Gay, Bisexual, or Transgender Person's Rights*, 4th ed. (Southern Illinois University Press, 2004).

Internet References . . .

Statistical Resources on the Web: Sociology

This Statistical Resources on the website provides links to data on poverty in the United States. Included is a link that contains both current and historical poverty data.

www.lib.umich.edu/government-documents-center/explore

Institute for Research on Poverty (IRP)

The Institute for Research on Poverty researches the causes and consequences of social inequality and poverty in the United States. This website includes frequently asked questions about poverty and links to other Internet resources on the subject.

www.ssc.wisc.edu/irp/

About.com: Affirmative Action

About.com's website on affirmative action contains information about resources and organizations that focus on affirmative action policies and current events. This site also enables you to search other topics related to race relations.

www.racerelations.about.com/
cs/affirmativeaction

Stratification and Inequality

*W*hy is there so much poverty in a society as rich as ours? Why has there been such a noticeable increase in inequality over the past quarter century? Although the ideal of equal opportunity for all is strong in the United States, many charge that the American political and economic system is unfair. Does extensive poverty demonstrate that policymakers have failed to live up to U.S. egalitarian principles? Are American institutions deeply flawed in that they provide fabulous opportunities for the educated and rich and meager opportunities for the uneducated and poor? Is the American stratification system at fault or are the poor themselves at fault? And what about the racial gap? The civil rights movement and the Civil Rights Act have made America more fair than it was, so why does a sizable racial gap remain? Various affirmative action programs have been implemented to remedy unequal opportunities, but some argue that this is discrimination in reverse. In fact, California passed a referendum banning affirmative action. Where should America go from here? Social scientists debate these questions in this part.

- Is Increasing Economic Inequality a Serious Problem?

- Is America Close to Being a Post-Racial Society?

- Has Feminism Benefited American Society?

- Is the Gender Wage Gap Justified?

ISSUE 6

Is Increasing Economic Inequality a Serious Problem?

YES: James Kurth, from "The Rich Get Richer," *The American Conservative* (September 25, 2006)

NO: Gary S. Becker and Kevin M. Murphy, from "The Upside of Income Inequality," *The American* (May/June 2007)

Learning Outcomes

After reading this issue, you should be able to:

- Know the basic facts about the level of income inequality in America and how it compares with the degree of income inequality in other developed countries.
- Explain the high levels of inequality in America and predict whether those same forces will increase inequality in the future.
- Identify what commentators claim are the benefits of income inequality and what are the adverse effects.
- Present the pros and cons of the trickle-down theory.
- Understand what policies, institutions, or technologies can increase or decrease income inequality in America.
- Critique the thesis that the poor are to be blamed for their poverty.

ISSUE SUMMARY

YES: James Kurth, Claude Smith Professor of Political Science at Swarthmore College, warns of very negative consequences for America of the growing income inequality from a conservative perspective. He also mentions the liberal criticisms of inequality but downplays their importance, because America has institutions that mitigate them.

NO: Gary S. Becker and Kevin M. Murphy, both economists teaching at the University of Chicago and senior fellows at the Hoover Institution, swim upstream on this issue by pointing out the positive consequences of the growing income inequality. The main reason for the increasing inequality is the increasing returns to education, which, in turn, inspire greater efforts by young people to increase their social capital.

T he cover of the January 29, 1996, issue of *Time* magazine bears a picture of 1996 Republican presidential candidate Steve Forbes and large letters reading: "DOES A FLAT TAX MAKE SENSE?" During his campaign, Forbes expressed his willingness to spend $25 million of his own wealth in pursuit of the presidency, with the major focus of his presidential campaign being a flat tax that would reduce taxes substantially for the rich. It seems reasonable to say that if the rich pay less in taxes, others would have to pay more. Is it acceptable for the tax burden to be shifted away from the rich in America? Forbes believed that the flat tax would benefit the poor as well as the rich. He theorized that the economy would surge ahead because investors would shift their money from relatively nonproductive, but tax-exempt, investments to productive investments. Although Forbes has disappeared from the political scene, his basic argument still thrives today. It is an example of the trickle-down theory, which states that helping the rich stimulates the economy, which in turn helps the poor. In fact, the trickle-down theory is the major rationalization for the view that great economic inequality benefits all of society.

Inequality is not a simple subject. For example, America is commonly viewed as having more social equality than do the more hierarchical societies of Europe and Japan, but America has more income inequality than almost all other industrial societies. This apparent contradiction is explained when one recognizes that American equality is not in income, but in the opportunity to obtain higher incomes. The issue of economic inequality is further complicated by other categories of equality/inequality, which include political power, social status, and legal rights.

Americans believe that everyone should have an equal opportunity to compete for jobs and rewards. This belief is backed up by free public school education, which provides poor children with a ladder to success, and by laws that forbid discrimination. Americans, however, do not agree on many specific issues regarding opportunities or rights. For example, should society compensate for handicaps such as disadvantaged family backgrounds or the legacy of past discrimination? This issue has divided the country. Americans do not agree on programs such as income-based scholarships, quotas, affirmative action, or the Head Start compensatory education program for poor preschoolers.

America's commitment to political equality is strong in principle, although less strong in practice. Everyone over 18 years old gets one vote, and all votes are counted equally. However, the political system tilts in the direction of special interest groups; those who do not belong to such groups are seldom heard. Furthermore, as in the case of Forbes, money plays an increasingly important role in political campaigns.

The final dimension of equality/inequality is status. Inequality of status involves differences in prestige, and it cannot be eliminated by legislation. Ideally, the people who contribute the most to society are the most highly esteemed. To what extent does this principle hold true in the United States? The Declaration of Independence proclaims that "all men are created equal," and the Founding Fathers who wrote the Declaration of Independence went on to base the laws of the land on the principle of equality. The equality they were referring to was equality of opportunity and legal and political rights for white, property-owning males. In the two centuries following the signing of the Declaration, nonwhites and women struggled for and won considerable equality of opportunity and rights. Meanwhile, income gaps in the United States have been widening.

In the readings that follow, James Kurth mentions the danger of ever greater concentration of market power but thinks that antitrust laws and global competition will keep this problem in check. Other economic problems are also manageable. He is most concerned about the numerous political consequences of inequality, which include increased terrorist threats. Gary S. Becker and Kevin M. Murphy focus on the increased value of higher education that is at the root of the increasing inequality. The main consequence of increasing inequality, therefore, is the substantial increase in college attendance by all groups in society.

YES

James Kurth

The Rich Get Richer

In 1914, Henry Ford paid his factory workers $5 a day, twice the going rate, with the aim of creating a broad middle class able to buy the cars they were building. Today, that project isn't faring so well: *The Economist* reports that in the U.S. "the gap between rich and poor is bigger than in any other advanced country." And it's growing. According to the Congressional Budget Office, from 1979 to 2001, the after-tax income of the top 1 percent of U.S. households soared 139 percent, while the income of the middle fifth rose only 17 percent and the income of the poorest fifth climbed just 9 percent. Last year American CEOs earned 262 times the average wage of their workers—up tenfold from 1970.

This widening gap can be seen virtually everywhere we look—in America; within other countries, even those hitherto distinguished by a high degree of equality (in particular, Japan, South Korea, and China); and between rich and poor countries in the world at large. This pervasive reality has been explored ably and comprehensively in recent books by the popular and learned conservative writer Kevin Phillips. But it has also been recognized by professional analysts at the very heart of the capitalist system: a recent study by Citigroup Global Markets entitled "Plutonomy: Buying Luxury, Explaining Global Imbalances" suggested investment strategy on the basis of these trends.

Since most of the writing on inequality is done by economists, it is natural that they focus on the fiscal consequences. But in this essay, our focus will be on the ramifications for politics and culture, both within America and within the world more generally.

As Phillips documents, there have been several previous eras in American history that were characterized by growing economic inequality. They include not only the famous (and infamous) Gilded Age of the 1880s but also the 1830s and the 1920s. These previous eras and their eventual end may provide some prototypes for our own. But as we shall see, there are certain unique features of our era of growing inequality that make it something new under the sun.

It would be one thing, and bad enough, if great personal wealth were simply expended on more goods, in order to engage in conspicuous consumption. The consequences for society would include ever greater public displays of materialistic values. But this phenomenon seems to be as old as recorded history, and it is hard for a conservative to get really angry about something that has so much tradition behind it.

From *The American Conservative*, September 25, 2006, pp. 6–11. Copyright © 2006 by The American Conservative. Reprinted by permission.

It would be another thing, and even worse, if great personal wealth were simply translated into more great wealth—if capital were invested in capital in order to get even more capital. The consequences for society would include ever greater concentration of market power. But in the United States, this phenomenon has been around for more than a century, and we have dealt with it by permitting more competition, not only by antitrust legislation but also by opening the American economy to similar goods imported from abroad and, even more effectively, to entirely new goods and services that have resulted from technological innovation. It is difficult to get anxious about a problem that has been so readily and so often solved in the past.

A more serious problem results because the rich also like to buy people—personal servants who work in their homes and grounds as maids, cooks, nannies, painters, and gardeners. Nowadays, this largely means Mexican and Central American immigrants—and illegal ones at that. Of course, U.S. agricultural and manufacturing businesses want to hire illegal immigrants, too. However, the really animated core of the political lobby that supports illegal immigration—its mass base, so to speak—is composed of rich homeowners, who desperately want someone to do their dirty work and to do it cheaply. Although they are the largest beneficiaries of the American way of life, including the rule of law, when it comes to the issue of illegal immigration, the rich do everything they can to undermine the American way for the vast majority of other Americans. There is nothing conservative about these actions by the rich; rather, the true conservatives are the less well-off who oppose illegal immigration and who are trying to preserve (and conserve) what was once an established and respected order.

But immigration policy is only one example of the most serious problem with increasing economic inequality: the holders of great wealth—especially if they are organized into a political lobby of similar holders of great wealth—can buy not only more goods, more capital, and more people. They can also buy (through the vehicle of campaign contributions) more important people: politicians and other public officials and therefore public policies.

Some of these bought policies may be for the purpose of making the rich even richer, most obviously the current regressive tax policies of the Bush administration. The wealth of the very rich is never the product of free enterprise and the free market alone but comes by operating within and exploiting a network of government supports, such as licenses, regulations, subsidies, and contracts. It is the product of a sort of giveaway. Consequently, to reduce the taxes on wealth (estate taxes) or on the income from wealth (capital-gains taxes), when that wealth has been acquired with one or another kind of government support, is in effect to give the wealth holder an additional giveaway. Again, there is nothing authentically conservative about this process.

Having even more wealth than they had before, the very rich can thus buy even more government supports and giveaways and acquire even more wealth, enabling them to buy even more government supports and giveaways. And so on. The result of great wealth buying public policies is a positive feedback loop, or perhaps a vicious cycle, which transfers ever greater wealth and power to the very rich and away from everyone else.

What is to prevent this cycle from going on forever? Historically, there have been two major constraining (or reversing) processes: one derives from macroeconomics, and the other derives from mass politics. Both constraints were once very powerful but neither are really operating today.

If the rich are getting richer, and the poor, if they are not getting poorer in real terms are not seeing their fortunes rise at comparable rates, this would seem to mean that the increasingly opulent consumption by the rich will have as its counterpart the increasingly austere consumption by the poor, and even by the now shrinking middle class. Eventually, the newly poor will not be able to earn enough to maintain their previous levels of consumption. Consequently, some goods produced will not be consumed, thus there will be fewer goods produced, there will be fewer producers or workers, there will be fewer goods consumed, and so on. We have yet another kind of cycle. It is exactly this process that has long been identified (by John Maynard Keynes, among others) as one of the classical explanations of how the growing inequality of the 1920s led to a crisis of underconsumption and overproduction and then to the Great Depression of the 1930s. A similar cycle had occurred earlier, when the growing inequality of the 1880s had issued in the depression of the 1890s (which, at that time, had also been called the Great Depression).

Given this simple model and given the recent pattern of growing economic inequality, one would have expected that the American economy would already be in a new Great Depression. What element has been added that has suspended, perhaps only temporarily, the execution of this macroeconomic iron law? The answer, of course, is consumer credit and record levels of consumer debt. Over one billion credit cards are in circulation in the U.S.—four for every man, woman, and child—and with 40 percent of families spending more than they earn, this keeps consumption rising, even as income may be declining.

In addition, some of the American consumption is also financed, albeit in an indirect and complex way, through the credit extended to the U.S. government and to U.S. lending institutions by the producers (or more precisely, by their governments) of many of the very goods that Americans are consuming—those of China, Japan, and South Korea. On the one hand, these foreign creditors have enabled the United States to avoid another Great Depression. On the other, this has come at the cost of a growing Great Dependence: the proportion of foreign-held debt is half what we owe as a nation and interest alone totals nearly $100 billion per year. That dependence is more immediate and obvious with respect to the U.S. government than it is for the American consumer. It does mean, however, that our government will have to tax American citizens more in order to finance its debt. With the tax policies of the Bush administration, this will in turn add to the growing inequality. It also means that the U.S. government may come to be more constrained in confronting the creditor governments on a variety of foreign-policy issues.

It strains credulity to believe that this cycle of increasing credit—be its sources domestic or foreign—can go on forever. When it ends, the old macroeconomic iron law will impose its penalties.

When we turn from economic responses to growing inequality to political ones, we quickly recall a dramatic parade of social—and socialist—movements

marching across the historical landscape, from the beginning of the Industrial Revolution to the end of the Cold War. In America, these included the
Jacksonian movement of the 1830s; the Populist movement of the 1880s–1890s;
and the New Deal, along with a variety of Marxist movements, in the 1930s.
Each of these represented a popular, even mass, reaction to growing economic
inequality.

In Europe, of course, these social movements were more massive and
more radical. They included the Labour Party in Britain in its early decades;
Marxist parties in most nations on the Continent; anarchist movements in
Southern Europe; and of course a successful Communist revolution in Russia.
Each of these also represented a mass reaction to growing inequality. Communist movements and parties also spread to Asia, where they represented
not only the class conflict between rich and poor within countries but also
the international conflict between rich and poor countries within the world
at large, with these Communist movements becoming anti-colonialist and
nationalist ones as well (as in China and Indochina). Marxist movements
also spread to Latin America, but there the reaction against growing inequality more often took the form of populist ones (the most familiar case being
Peronism in Argentina).

Wherever their locale, most of these mass social movement were eventually
able to impose some kind of constraint upon, or even reversal of, the growing
inequality within their countries (but not, however, upon the inequality between
countries). Sometimes the constraint was imposed by democratic elections and
egalitarian legislation as with the American New Deal, the British Labour Party,
and the Scandinavian social democratic parties. Sometimes an electoral triumph
by socialist parties was followed by a repressive reaction imposed by parties
of the Right as in much of Continental Europe during the 1920s–1930s. And
on a few occasions, a Communist party succeeded in making a revolution and
imposing a reversal of inequality that was ruthless and terrible indeed as in
Russia, China, and Indochina.

But of course, this long historical parade of mass social movements effectively came to an end with the end of the Cold War and with the discrediting
and collapse of Communism and of much of Marxism more generally. With the
end of the Marxist version of mass social movements, it is not surprising that
the past 15 years have been a period of growing economic inequality that is now
almost completely unconstrained.

Given the extensive historical record of equalitarian social movements
and the recent pattern of growing economic inequality, however, one might
have expected that some such movement would have already arisen. If we
look around the world, perhaps we will be able to see it before our very eyes.
Indeed, when we eventually turn our attention to particular poor countries or
regions, this will be the case.

In regard to contemporary America, however, there is no evidence of
any social movement at all. Has a new element been added to American politics that has suspended, perhaps only temporarily, operation of the social-
movement constraint in our own time? Actually, we can identify three such
new elements.

First, there has been a change in the nature of the working population, which always constitutes a good part of the poor or increasingly poor within a society. The conditions of the working class, including the conditions conducive to political organization, are one thing in an industrial economy and a very different thing in a post-industrial, or information, economy such as our own. Sociologists have long observed and specified the many reasons it is much more difficult to politically organize workers who perform clerical, technical, or professional tasks in offices than workers who perform industrial or manufacturing tasks in factories. In any event, there are very few labor unions that are composed of clerical, technical, or professional employees. When we remember that unions of industrial workers were a fundamental and major pillar of the Democratic Party in America, the Labour Party in Britain, and the socialist and Marxist parties in continental Europe, we can see how, by itself, the shift to an information economy has removed the most powerful political constraint on growing economic inequality.

Second, there has also been a change in the economic self-identification of the general population. The way people define themselves is different in a consumer society, with a total focus upon individual self-gratification, than it is in a producer society, with an emphasis on the social consequences and connections of one's work. It is obviously much more difficult to politically organize masses of people if they all think of themselves as individual consumers or as expressive individualists, each freely choosing his own unique (even if vapid and banal) lifestyle, than to organize masses of people who think of themselves as members of working classes or local communities, who share in common most of the important conditions of their lives.

Third, and a variation on the consumer mentality, there has been a change in the non-working or leisure activities—the preoccupations and not just the occupations—of much of the population. For many Americans today, especially those in what was once the working class, there is indeed a kind of mass activity, but it is not mass political or social activism. Rather, it involves spectator entertainment, especially sports. For them, there is no participation in anything involving real interaction with other human beings, be it political parties, labor unions, community associations, fraternal societies, or, if they have become adults, even in participatory team sports themselves. It is the poorer classes, in contrast to the richer ones, that spend most of their free time with spectator entertainment. As more and more people become poor or poorer and lose any reasonable hope of improving their economic status, either by their own economic efforts or by anything like political activism, it is not surprising that they would seek to fill their bleak hours and vent their sullen frustrations with escapist (and violent) entertainment. What would have been seen as juvenile and abnormal preoccupations in the society of half a century or more ago have become normal ones in the society of our own time.

The same three shifts that have essentially demolished the social-movement constraint on growing inequality in America have also gone far toward doing so in other Western countries as well and even in Japan. All of these have now followed America far along the path of becoming information economies, consumer societies, and spectator cultures. . . .

What happens when we turn our attention from America and the West to the world at large? Of course, due to the promotion of globalization by successive U.S. governments and by American elites, the United States is now very much in that world—and in its face.

As it happens, globalization adds to the processes producing a widening gap between rich and poor. First, as is well known, in any country that is immersed and enmeshed in globalization, it has resulted in both winners (those who already have international connections, English-language proficiency, or information-age skills) and losers (those engaged in traditional agricultural, industrial, and cultural occupations). Those who are already rich tend to benefit from globalization, and many of those who are already poor tend to be hurt by it. It is no accident that the era of globalization—which has largely been the era since the end of the Cold War—has also been an era of a widening gap between rich and poor. Anyone who claims that globalization is a conservative process is either a liar or a fool.

What has been true within countries has been true between countries as well. Over the past 15 years or so, globalization has generally increased the GNP per capita of the countries that were already rich—the United States, Europe, and Japan—although of course even in these countries there are some sectors and groups that have been hurt by it. More momentously, globalization has also increased the GNP per capita of some countries that were once poor or near-poor, particularly many countries in Asia and including such immense ones as China and India. This is a very impressive result indeed, although again, even in these countries there are very large sectors and groups in the traditional economy that have been hurt by globalization.

However, there are three big regions where a very large majority of the people have lost out from globalization, or are at least convinced that they have: Africa, Latin America, and most consequentially, the Middle East and more generally the Muslim world. The increasing economic inequality within the countries of these regions combined with the increasing economic inequality between these regions and the rest of the world has generated vast reservoirs of resentment toward the globalization process, toward the West, and especially toward that arch-promoter of globalization, the United States. And starting in the early 2000s, that popular resentment has developed into actual resistance movements, which bear some resemblance to the egalitarian movements of earlier eras.

The resistance to globalization has developed least in Africa, which in any case is the least developed—the poorest and the most anarchic—region of the world. In Latin America, however, populist—and anti-globalization and anti-American—movements have surged in the past few years. Radical versions have been voted into power in Venezuela and Bolivia; more moderate versions have been successful in Argentina, Chile, and Uruguay; and populist candidates have come close to electoral victory in Mexico and Peru. In many ways, these contemporary populist movements and leaders are reminiscent of earlier ones in Latin America history. If the United States were not now bogged down in the quagmire of Iraq, the attention of the U.S. government and the American media would be fixated upon what they would perceive as a dangerous populist threat sweeping Latin America.

But the really serious resistance movement to globalization, the West, and the United States has arisen within the Muslim world. This is Islamism, which is also often called political Islam. When we in America consider Islamism, we do not think of it as an egalitarian social movement. However, the theology (more accurately, ideology) of political Islam is permeated with egalitarian norms and sentiments, and Islamists are often animated by egalitarian resentments and anger as well. Islamists speak frequently about the injustices and exploitation inflicted by the rich upon the poor, and by the rich West upon the poor Muslim world. "Social justice" is a central concept in most Islamist programs. They have their own way of claiming, as the Communists claimed in an earlier era, to speak for "the wretched of the earth." . . .

Perhaps the most interesting place where the Islamist ideology of social justice will resonate is that part of the Muslim world within the West itself: Western Europe's communities of Muslim immigrants and their European-born children and descendents. By now several major European countries—Spain, Britain, France, and the Netherlands—have suffered either Islamist terrorist attacks or Muslim youth riots and violence, and there will doubtless be more of this in the future.

Indeed, many Western European countries are becoming two nations. The first is the original, ethnic-European nation; it is now largely secular or even pagan, rich, and aging. And because of its extraordinarily low birth rates, it is shrinking in numbers. The second is the immigrant, non-European nation, the Muslim nation or *umma*; it is substantially religious or even Islamist, poor, and young. And because of its high birth rate, it will continue to grow in numbers.

The two nations are coming to view each other with mutual contempt, but in the new Muslim nation there is a growing rage, and in the old, ethnic-European nation there is a growing fear. This will provide the perfect conditions for a widespread Islamist sense of social injustice, a deep Islamist hatred of what are perceived as rich Europeans, and as a natural consequence, an endemic threat of Islamist violence. . . .

And finally, of course, Islamist terrorists may soon acquire weapons of mass destruction, something that only states have possessed up to now. States, being established, hierarchical institutions, have not really wanted to put their WMD at the service of egalitarian projects. With Islamist transnational networks, however, there is no obvious reason why they would not be willing, even eager, to use WMD to bring the rich and the powerful, and rich and powerful states, crashing down. Although Islamist terrorist networks are not really very good examples of mass social movements, they will be very good at achieving mass social destruction. And, brimming over with egalitarian envy and self-righteous wrath, they will delight in doing so.

And so, what will be the eventual fate of the current drive toward greater economic inequality, in America and around the world? Within America and the other rich countries (or rather, the countries with a lot of rich), there do not now seem to be any internal forces that will arrest this drive. As for external forces, only Islamism is now beginning to mount a serious threat to the security of the rich, and that threat is also directed at all the other groups and peoples that the Islamists despise as well. Still, whoever might be the specific target of a particular Islamist attack with a weapon of truly mass destruction, it will take a lot of the rich along with it. Furthermore, by exploding established expectations about the future of economic and financial assets, and therefore by reducing the value of those assets, it will take a lot of their wealth too.

In the course of the 20th century, there were several years of growing economic inequality. On a few occasions, they came to an end in a relatively gentle way, with democratic elections and more egalitarian legislation. More often, however, they were ended by a catastrophe, such as the Great Depression, a violent social revolution, or a world war. When the rich went out, it seems, they normally did so with a bang, and not with a whimper. The way things are now going, it is likely to be so in the future.

Gary S. Becker and
Kevin M. Murphy

 **NO**

The Upside of Income Inequality

Income inequality in China substantially widened, particularly between households in the city and the countryside, after China began its rapid rate of economic development around 1980. The average urban resident now makes 3.2 times as much as the average rural resident, and among city dwellers alone, the top 10 percent makes 9.2 times as much as the bottom 10 percent. But at the same time that inequality rose, the number of Chinese who live in poverty fell—from 260 million in 1978 to 42 million in 1998. Despite the widening gap in incomes, rapid economic development dramatically improved the lives of China's poor.

Politicians and many others in the United States have recently grown concerned that earnings inequality has increased among Americans. But as the example of China—or India, for that matter—illustrates, the rise in inequality does not occur in a vacuum. In the case of China and India, the rise in inequality came along with an acceleration of economic growth that raised the standard of living for both the rich and the poor. In the United States, the rise in inequality accompanied a rise in the payoff to education and other skills. We believe that the rise in returns on investments in human capital is beneficial and desirable, and policies designed to deal with inequality must take account of its cause.

To show the importance to inequality of the increased return to human capital, consider Figure 1 . . . , which shows the link between earnings and education by displaying the wage premium received by college-educated workers compared with high school graduates. In 1980, an American with a college degree earned about 30 percent more than an American who stopped education at high school. But, in recent years, a person with a college education earned roughly 70 percent more. Meanwhile, the premium for having a graduate degree increased from roughly 50 percent in 1980 to well over 100 percent today. The labor market is placing a greater emphasis on education, dispensing rapidly rising rewards to those who stay in school the longest.

This trend has contributed significantly to the growth in overall earnings inequality in the United States. And just as in China and India, this growing inequality gap is associated with growing opportunity—in this case, the opportunity to advance through education. The upward trend in the returns to education is not limited to one segment of the population. Education premiums for women and African Americans have increased as much as, or more than, the premiums for all workers.

From *The American*, May/June 2007, pp. 20–23. Copyright © 2007 by American Enterprise Institute. Reprinted by permission via Copyright Clearance Center.

Figure 1

Percentage by which the wage of workers with college and graduate school educations exceeds that of workers with high school only.

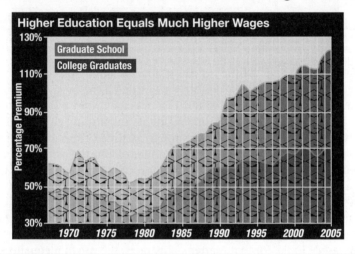

Source: Current Population Survey, U.S. Bureau of Labor Statistics.

Figure 2 shows that the growth in returns to education for women has paralleled that for men over the past 25 years, but has remained at a somewhat higher level. Figure 3 shows that returns for blacks have increased as much

Figure 2

Percentage by which the wages of college-educated men and women exceed those of men and women with high school only.

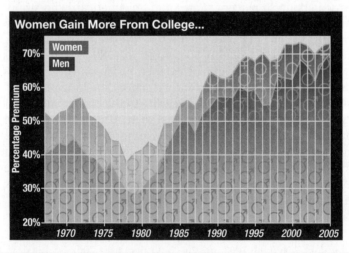

Source: Current Population Survey, U.S. Bureau of Labor Statistics.

Figure 3

Percentage by which the wages of blacks and whites with college educations exceed those of both races with high school only.

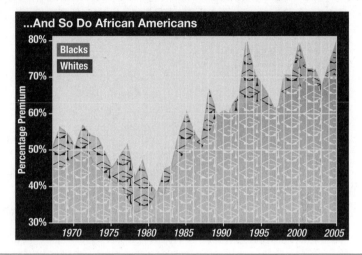

Source: Current Population Survey, U.S. Bureau of Labor Statistics.

as those for whites. As these two figures show, the potential to improve one's labor-market prospects through higher education is greater now than at any time in the recent past, and this potential extends across gender and racial lines.

The growth in returns to college has generated a predictable response: as the education earnings gap increased, a larger fraction of high school graduates went on to college. As Figure 4 shows, the proportion of men and women ages 20 to 25 who attended college jumped by about half over the past 40 years, tracking the rise in the wage premium. When returns fell in the 1970s, the fraction going on to college declined. The rise in returns since 1980 has been accompanied by a significant rise in the fraction going on to college.

This increase in the proportion of persons going on to higher education is found among all racial and ethnic groups, but it is particularly important for women, who, in 2004, outnumbered men as students in degree-granting institutions of higher education by 33 percent.

Women have also shifted toward higher-earnings fields, such as business, law, and medicine: the number of women in graduate schools rose 66 percent between 1994 and 2004, while the number of men rose just 25 percent. And the greater education achievement of women compared to men is particularly prominent among blacks and Latinos: the proportion of black women who attend colleges and universities jumped from 24 percent to 43 percent between 1974 and 2003, while the proportion of white men rose only from 41 percent to 49 percent.

The potential generated by higher returns to education extends from individuals to the economy as a whole. Growth in the education level of the population has been a significant source of rising wages, productivity,

Figure 4

The proportion of Americans going to college roughly tracks the rising economic premium that college offers.

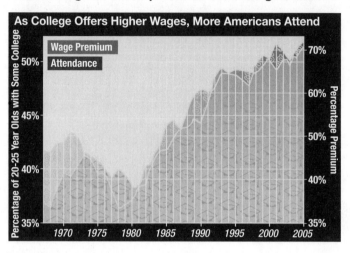

Source: Current Population Survey, U.S. Bureau of Labor Statistics.

and living standards over the past century. Higher returns to education will accelerate growth in living standards as existing investments have a higher return, and additional investments in education will be made in response to the higher returns. Gains from the higher returns will not be limited to GDP and other measures of economic activity; education provides a wide range of benefits not captured in GDP, and these will grow more rapidly as well due to the additional investments in schooling.

Why is the earnings gap widening? Because the demand for educated and other skilled persons is growing. That is hardly surprising, given developments in computers and the Internet, advances in biotechnology, and a general shift in economic activity to more education-intensive sectors, such as finance and professional services. Also, globalization has encouraged the importing of products using relatively low-skilled labor from abroad. At the same time, world demand has risen for the kinds of products and services that are provided by high-skilled employees.

When calculating the returns to education, we look at the *costs* of education as well. And even accounting for the rise in university tuition (it more than doubled, on average, in constant dollars between 1980 and 2005), overall returns to college and graduate study have increased substantially. Indeed, it appears that the increases in tuition were partly induced by the greater return to college education. Pablo Peña, in a Ph.D. dissertation in progress at the University of Chicago, argues convincingly that tuition rose in part because students want to invest more in the quality of their education, and increased spending per student by colleges is partly financed by higher tuition levels. More investment in the quality and quantity of schooling will benefit both individuals and society.

This brings us to our punch line. Should an increase in earnings inequality due primarily to higher rates of return on education and other skills be considered a favorable rather than an unfavorable development? We think so. Higher rates of return on capital are a sign of greater productivity in the economy, and that inference is fully applicable to human capital as well as to physical capital. The initial impact of higher returns to human capital is wider inequality in earnings (the same as the initial effect of higher returns on physical capital), but that impact becomes more muted and may be reversed over time as young men and women invest more in their human capital.

We conclude that the forces raising earnings inequality in the United States are beneficial to the extent that they reflect higher returns to investments in education and other human capital. Yet this conclusion should not produce complacency, for the response so far to these higher returns has been disturbingly limited. For example, why haven't more high school graduates gone on to a college education when the benefits are so apparent? Why don't more of those who go to college finish a four-year degree? (Only about half do so.) And why has the proportion of American youth who drop out of high school, especially African-American and Hispanic males, remained fairly constant?

The answers to these and related questions lie partly in the breakdown of the American family, and the resulting low skill levels acquired by many children in elementary and secondary school—particularly individuals from broken households. Cognitive skills tend to get developed at very early ages while, as our colleague James Heckman has shown, noncognitive skills—such as study habits, getting to appointments on time, and attitudes toward work—get fixed at later, although still relatively young, ages. Most high school dropouts certainly appear to be seriously deficient in the noncognitive skills that would enable them to take advantage of the higher rates of return to education and other human capital.

So instead of lamenting the increased earnings gap caused by education, policy makers and the public should focus attention on how to raise the fraction of American youth who complete high school and then go on for a college education. Solutions are not cheap or easy. But it will be a disaster if the focus remains so much on the earnings inequality itself that Congress tries to interfere directly with this inequality rather than trying to raise the education levels of those who are now being left behind.

For many, the solution to an increase in inequality is to make the tax structure more progressive—raise taxes on high-income households and reduce taxes on low-income households. While this may sound sensible, it is not. Would these same individuals advocate a tax on going to college and a subsidy for dropping out of high school in response to the increased importance of education? We think not. Yet shifting the tax structure has exactly this effect.

A more sensible policy is to try to take greater advantage of the opportunities afforded by the higher returns to human capital and encourage more human capital investment. Attempts to raise taxes and impose other penalties on the higher earnings that come from greater skills could greatly reduce the productivity of the world's leading economy by discouraging investments in its most productive and precious form of capital—human capital.

EXPLORING THE ISSUE

Is Increasing Economic Inequality a Serious Problem?

Critical Thinking and Reflection

1. How did a country with such a strong commitment to equality come to have such a high level of inequality?
2. What are the arguments for the trickle-down theory and what are the arguments against it?
3. How does the growing inequality in America affect the functioning of democracy? Does it further corrupt the election processes? Does it directly affect the legislative and administrative processes? If so, how?
4. How can the adverse effects of inequality be mitigated by policies or regulations?
5. Currently many activists are claiming that the 1 percent is screwing the 99 percent. What evidence supports this claim and what evidence contradicts it?
6. What should be done about the growing inequality, or should nothing be done?

Is There Common Ground?

The list of negative consequences mentioned by James Kurth is quite long and varied. It includes conspicuous consumption, corporate concentration, biased immigration policies, regressive tax policies, many subsidies for the well off, limitations on many policies benefitting lower groups, the coming of a crisis of overproduction and under consumption and thus a bad recession, excessive debt, trade imbalances, and even greater danger from terrorism. Can anything good be said about the growing inequality?

According to Gary S. Becker and Kevin M. Murphy, the inequality is making America much stronger. Inequality puts a high premium on higher education. While education drives the gap, it also allows Americans to better themselves.

Both sides want America to be prosperous, and that includes a prosperous lower class. The debate is about the best way to achieve these goals. The problematic issue, therefore, becomes what should be done for the lower class? How much and what kind of assistance should they receive? All agree that they should get educational assistance. Do free public schools accomplish that? Some European countries make education free through college. Should America do the same? Are food stamps, free school lunches, Head Start, and welfare for the needy enough at their current levels to enable the poor young people to climb the ladder of success? Everyone recognizes that there is a danger that help can create dependency, so how much is enough and not too much?

Additional Resources

Inequality, stratification, and social mobility are central concerns of sociology, and they are addressed by a large body of literature. Important discussions of income inequality include Rebecca M. Blank, *Changing Inequality* (University of California Press, 2011); Nathan J. Kelly, *The Politics of Income Inequality in the United States* (Cambridge University Press, 2009); Robert H. Frank, *Falling Behind: How Rising Inequality Harms the Middle Class* (University of California Press, 2007); Thom Hartmann, *Screwed: The Undeclared War on the Middle Class— And What We Can Do about It* (Berrett-Koehler Publishers, 2006); Lou Dobbs, *War on the Middle Class: How the Government, Big Business, and Special Interest Groups Are Waging War on the American Dream and How to Fight Back* (Viking, 2006); Allan C. Ornstein, *Class Counts: Education, Inequality, and the Shrinking Middle Class* (Rowman & Littlefield, 2007); John Hively, *The Rigged Game: Corporate America and a People Betrayed* (Black Rose Books, 2006); Barry Bluestone and Bennett Harrison, *Growing Prosperity: The Battle for Growth with Equity in the Twenty-First Century* (Houghton Mifflin, 2000); Richard B. Freeman, *When Earnings Diverge: Causes, Consequences, and Cures for the New Inequality in the U.S.* (National Policy Association, 1997); Andrew Hacker, *Money: Who Has How Much and Why* (Scribner's Reference, 1997); Chuck Collins and Felice Yeskel, *Economic Apartheid in America* (New Press, 2005); Paul Ryscavage, *Rethinking the Income Gap* (Transaction Publishers, 2009); Edward N. Wolff, *Top Heavy: The Increasing Inequality of Wealth in America and What Can Be Done about It* (New Press, 2002); Finis Welch (ed.), *The Causes and Consequences of Increasing Inequality* (University of Chicago Press, 2001); James Tardner and David Smith (eds.), *Inequality Matters: The Growing Economic Divide in America and Its Poisonous Consequences* (New Press, 2005); and Samuel Bowles et al. (eds.) *Unequal Chances* (Princeton University Press, 2005). The survey coverage of the inequality is covered by Benjamin I. Page in *Class War?: What Americans Really Think about Economic Inequality* (University of Chicago Press, 2009). A big part of the inequality picture is the condition of the working poor, which is analyzed by Lawrence Mishel et al., *The State of Working America, 2002–2003* (Cornell University Press, 2003); Eileen Appelbaum et al. (eds.), *Low-Wage America: How Employers Are Reshaping Opportunity in the Workplace* (Russell Sage Foundation, 2003); and David K. Shipler, *The Working Poor: Invisible in America* (Knopf, 2004). For a poignant ethnographic study of the poor and their disadvantages, see Elliot Liebow, *Tell Them Who I Am: The Lives of Homeless Women* (Free Press, 1993).

ISSUE 7

Is America Close to Being a Post-Racial Society?

YES: **Alvin Poussaint**, from "Obama, Cosby, King and the Mountaintop," *CNN.com* (November 13, 2008)

NO: **Lawrence D. Bobo**, from "Somewhere Between Jim Crow and Post-Racialism: Reflections on the Racial Divide in America Today," *Daedalus* (Spring 2011)

Learning Outcomes

After reading this issue, you should be able to:

- Apprehend the changes in the civil rights of blacks in America in the past half century.
- Evaluate the discrimination, biases, prejudices, stereotypes, and values that still hold blacks back.
- Know basic facts about current racial inequalities and a sense of the extent of change since the 1950s.
- Understand how change is resisted.
- Understand how public figures affect children's perceptions and thereby their lives.
- Discern what can be accomplished by new policies and what cannot be accomplished by them.
- Understand indirect victimization and judge its importance in current racial inequality.

ISSUE SUMMARY

YES: Alvin Poussaint is a professor of psychiatry at the Harvard Medical School with a focus on child psychiatry. He argues that the election of Barack Obama may indicate that America is approaching the mountaintop that King preached about.

NO: Lawrence D. Bobo, the W. E. B. Du Bois Professor of the Social Sciences at Harvard University, provides a scholarly analysis of racial inequalities. He explains how inequalities in America are constantly being recreated. Change occurs and is much celebrated, but change is successfully resisted in many subtle ways.

This debate analyzes interracial (and interethnic) relations, but our focus will be on black–white relations. Our starting point is the question, "What does the election of Barack Obama indicate about race relations in America today?" A black was elected to the highest position in America. This was impossible to imagine 50 years ago. Clearly America has changed. There were important precursors to the Obama presidency such as very popular Oprah Winfrey and many other popular black entertainers. Blacks have also become prominent political leaders such as Colin Powell and Condoleezza Rice. The public image of blacks has greatly improved. *The Cosby Show* had something to do with this. As a viewer I identified with Dr. Huckstable and his family as well as many other black actors and actresses in movies and TV shows over the years. The images that young people see are quite different from what I saw when I was growing up. The first movie that I saw about interracial marriage was *Guess Who's Coming to Dinner* with Spencer Tracy, Katherine Hepburn, and Sidney Poitier. It came out in 1967, and was a bombshell at the time—very tense. Many people could not handle it.

Today the situation is totally different. Interracial and interethnic marriages are more common and thus more normal, and this reflects changes in interracial attitudes and laws. Interracial marriages were illegal in many states until the Supreme Court declared these laws unconstitutional in 1967. Change in interracial marriages has been slow, however, since only 2.9 percent of the population were interracial in 2010. On the other hand, 5.6 percent of the population under age 18 are interracial. According to the 2010 census, 8.5 percent of married black men and 3.9 percent of married black women had a white spouse. According to the 2008 Pew Research Center Report based on the Census Bureau's 2008 American Community Survey:

> Among all newlyweds in 2008, 9% of whites, 16% of blacks, 26% of Hispanics and 31% of Asians married someone whose race or ethnicity was different from their own. . . . Among all newlyweds in 2008, inter-married pairings were primarily White-Hispanic (41%) as compared to White-Asian (15%), White-Black (11%), and Other Combinations (33%). . . . Rates of intermarriages among newlyweds in the U.S. more than doubled between 1980 (6.7%) and 2008 (14.6%). . . . Most Americans say they approve of racial or ethnic intermarriage—not just in the abstract, but in their own families. More than six-in-ten say it would be fine with them if a family member told them they were going to marry someone from any of three major race/ethnic groups other than their own. More than a third of adults (35%) say they have a family member who is married to someone of a different race. Blacks say this at higher rates than do whites; younger adults at higher rates than older adults; and Westerners at higher rates than people living in other regions of the country.

These statistics demonstrate that considerable change has occurred, and also show that there is room for a great deal more change. The United States is moving toward a post-racial society, but it is debatable whether it is moving enough to get there this century.

Alvin Poussaint, an African American child psychiatrist, predicts that Barack Obama's election will have a major impact on race perceptions, especially of children. Black children will feel less like outsiders and more like full members of society. White children will also have different perceptions of blacks than their parents did. The overall impact will be much greater if Obama wins reelection and is widely judged to have been successful. A lot is riding on the next 4 years. Lawrence D. Bobo focuses more on the resistance to change than the progress that appears on the surface. Discrimination and bias are subtle and often unseen. Whites are unaware of the extent of their advantages and are likely to assume that people get what they deserve. Bobo skillfully reveals the true story.

YES

Alvin Poussaint

Obama, Cosby, King and the Mountaintop

(**C**NN)—Rev. Martin Luther King Jr. told followers the night before he was killed that he had been "to the mountaintop" and seen the promised land of racial equality. Last week's election of Barack Obama was the equivalent of taking all African-Americans to that peak, says Dr. Alvin Poussaint.

In his view, Obama's victory last week wasn't just a political triumph. It was a seismic event in the history of black America.

Poussaint has made it his life's work to study how African-Americans see themselves and how the larger society sees them.

From the days of the civil rights movement through the 1980s, when he was a script consultant on "The Cosby Show," to today, he has been a leader in assessing how images of black people in the media shape perceptions. Poussaint, who is 74, is professor of psychiatry at Judge Baker Children's Center in Boston and at Harvard Medical School.

At a key point in the civil rights movement, Poussaint moved to Mississippi and worked for the Medical Committee for Human Rights, in Jackson, from 1965 to 1967, helping care for civil rights workers and aiding the desegregation of hospitals and other health care institutions.

Poussaint met Bill Cosby in the 1970s and has worked with him on a variety of books and shows, most recently co-authoring a book with Cosby. He was interviewed by CNN on Wednesday.

CNN: What do you think is the long-term impact of the election of Barack Obama as a symbol and a message to the black community in America?

Dr. Alvin Poussaint: We're going to have a generation of children—if he's in there for eight years—being born in 2009, looking at television and images, hearing before they can talk, absorbing it in their brain and being wired to see the visual images of a black man being president of the United States and understanding very early that that's the highest position in the United States.

So I think that's going to be very powerful in its visual imagery . . . and they're going to see these images constantly on television, probably offsetting a lot of the negative imagery that they may see in shows and videos and sometimes in stereotypic comedy.

These images will also make black parents proud. Although there are many barriers to this, it might put back on the table the importance of the two-parent family. . . . Maybe it will do something for couples and bring black men and black women closer together.

The sense of pride may carry over into family life, the same way it is being carried over now into the life of the church already. At black churches this past Sunday, all of them were talking about Obama and being ambassadors for Obama—in other words, suggesting that now that he's president, that black people should take the high road.

The big problem with all of this is that if there's high expectations that somehow the social ills that the black community faces will suddenly evaporate, they're going to be disappointed—because the economy, the economic crisis is a major issue that's going to affect the black community, making things worse. . . . So there's going to be more unemployment, more poor people, more black homeless and more poverty. . . .

Obama's also going to have a positive effect on the white community. Way back in the 1960s, I used to go to Atlanta when it was segregated and even after it started desegregating. When you went downtown to restaurants, you would walk in as a black person and they would kind of act like, "What are you doing here?" You weren't welcome, you know, you just felt it.

And Maynard Jackson became the first black mayor, and I felt a whole change in the tone of the city. You went places and when you walked in, people had to consider: "Is this someone who knows the mayor, this black person?" And so I think they began to treat all black people better because black people were now in power. . . . This may help to eradicate stereotypes that they hold. . . .

So this may have a spinoff effect . . . maybe more blacks will break through the glass ceiling in corporations, more blacks may, because of their newfound confidence, become more civically engaged, run for office.

CNN: What if he had lost, what would the impact have been then?

Poussaint: A lot of black people would have concluded that he lost because of his race, and the black people who had no faith in the system in the first place would have continued to feel that way, maybe even more strongly, and maybe even have more anger at the institutions that have authority over them and that they see as white-controlled.

CNN: Obama is taking over at a time of tremendous international and national challenges. Every president has setbacks. What would be the impact of setbacks on a political level?

Poussaint: Nearly everybody that you hear talk about it realizes that he's inheriting a horrible situation. In fact one of the black leaders joked about how, as soon as things are falling apart in the country, that they hand it over to a black person—"Here, you take it."

People are saying that he's just been dealt a terrible hand and is going to have to work very hard to be successful and they're rooting for him and hoping. There's a mindset right now of "What can we do to help Obama?"

And I don't think it's just black people saying it, it's all the people who voted for him, young people and women, the workers, the unions—"What can we do to help him be successful, and undo the mess that we're in?"

CNN: What do you make of the idea that "The Cosby Show" made America more ready to vote for a black man to be president?

Poussaint: I don't know, you can't study this stuff scientifically. The intent when the Cosby show came on . . . was to present a black family that was not the old stereotypical family that white people laughed at in a sitcom. And we wanted the show to have a universality, in terms of a mother, a father, wonderful children, a lot of love being shown, an emphasis on education.

Today if you have 12 or 15 million viewers of a show a week, it's number one. Well, Cosby was bringing in about 60 million people a week. So this had a deep effect on white children, Latino children, and even many adults, what their images of black people were.

So that's why Karl Rove reached into the hat the other day and said this was the beginning of the post-racial era, because it made white people embrace this black family like a family of their own and fall in love with it.

It probably played some role at chipping away at those negative images, which made white people . . . more ready to embrace a lot of things, including Tiger Woods and Oprah Winfrey and Denzel Washington and Will Smith. Certainly when Obama gets on the scene, people don't say, "What kind of black family is that? We haven't seen any black family like that."

Because that's what they said about the Cosby show, . . . that this doesn't represent a black family, this is fantasy. And it wasn't fantasy, because there were black families like that in 1984, and there are many more black families like that in the middle class and upper-middle class today.

CNN: You were a consultant on the Cosby show. How did that come about?

Poussaint: I knew him and his wife. When the show was coming on, he called me and said he wanted me to . . . be a production consultant to keep this a positive show without stereotyping: "I want you to read and critique every single script before it goes into production, anything you want to say to make this family psychologically believable, living in reality." He wanted the story lines to have a plot that made sense. . . . He told me to weed out what he called put-down humor, which he felt was too prevalent, particularly on a lot of black shows where you make fun of people.

I was allowed to comment on anything, from the clothes to some of the people they were casting, to making sure there was a wide range of colors on the show in terms of complexion, what's on the reading table, what cultural activities the kids are going to, what colleges they're applying to. . . .

CNN: You co-authored a book with Bill Cosby. What's the message of that book?

Poussaint: It's called, "Come on People: On the Road from Victims to Victors." The message is, don't be helpless and hopeless and see yourself as a victim and wallow in failing and think that's your lot in life. What you have to do is take the high road and you have to work hard to try to achieve against the odds. . . .

Most of the black people are where they are today because we succeeded against the odds, we didn't allow the racism out there to totally squelch us. And we feel that spirit is being lost, particularly in low-income communities and sometimes among middle-income people too. And we felt they had to adopt more of an attitude of being victors.

And victors are active, they try to do their best, they take education very seriously. And Obama's a good example—if he took a victim's attitude and said, "Well, a black man could never get elected president of the United States," which a lot of us felt like, he wouldn't have run for the presidency. So he adopted what we call a victor's attitude—"I'm going to go for it, it may be a longshot, but it's possible."

CNN: What do you compare the Obama victory to in terms of significance?

Poussaint: The civil rights movement's success in getting the civil rights bill of '64 and the Voting Rights Act of '65, that opened things mightily for the black communities all over the country. Obviously getting those bills and those accomplishments—forget about The Cosby Show—the voting rights bill played a significant role in Obama's victory.

CNN: Does Obama's victory as a historical moment equal those?

Poussaint: It equals those but it has a more powerful visual symbolism. It's like people are going from [Martin Luther] King, who was moving us toward the mountaintop . . . to Obama, people saying [we're] getting to the mountaintop and now being able to gaze down. So it's the fruition of a movement beginning in slavery. . . . We were in slavery for 250 years, and then Jim Crow segregation for another 100, and we've been struggling for freedom. Obama represents us winning our freedom—like "free at last, free at last, free at last."

But it's not really true. We still have racial discrimination in the country, we're still going to have racial injustice.

Lawrence D. Bobo  **NO**

Somewhere Between Jim Crow and Post-Racialism: Reflections on the Racial Divide in America Today

> In assessing the results of the Negro revolution so far, it can be concluded that Negroes have established a foothold, no more. We have written a Declaration of Independence, itself an accomplishment, but the effort to transform the words into a life experience still lies ahead.
>
> —Martin Luther King, Jr., *Where Do We Go from Here?* (1968)

> By the middle of the twentieth century, the color line was as well defined and as firmly entrenched as any institution in the land. After all, it was older than most institutions, including the federal government itself. More important, it informed the content and shaped the lives of those institutions and the people who lived under them.
>
> —John Hope Franklin, *The Color Line* (1993)

> This is where we are right now. It's a racial stalemate we've been stuck in for years. Contrary to the claims of some of my critics, black and white, I have never been so naive as to believe that we can get beyond our racial divisions in a single election cycle, or with a single candidacy— particularly a candidacy as imperfect as my own.
>
> —Barack H. Obama, "A More Perfect Union" (May 18, 2008)

The year 1965 marked an important inflection point in the struggle for racial justice in the United States, underscoring two fundamental points about race in America. First, that racial inequality and division were not only Southern problems attached to Jim Crow segregation. Second, that the nature of those inequalities and divisions was a matter not merely of formal civil status and law, but also of deeply etched economic arrangements, social and political conditions, and cultural outlooks and practices. Viewed in full, the racial divide was a challenge of truly national reach, multilayered in its complexity and depth. Therefore, the achievement of basic citizenship rights in the South was a pivotal but far from exhaustive stage of the struggle.

The positive trend of the times revolved around the achievement of voting rights. March 7, 1965, now known as Bloody Sunday, saw police and state troopers attack several hundred peaceful civil rights protestors at the Edmund Pettus Bridge in Selma, Alabama. The subsequent march from Selma to Montgomery, participated in by tens of thousands, along with other protest actions, provided the pressure that finally compelled Congress to pass the Voting Rights Act of 1965. A triumphant Reverend Martin Luther King, Jr., and other activists attended the signing in Washington, D.C., on August 6, 1965. It was a moment of great triumph for civil rights.

The long march to freedom seemed to be at its apex, inspiring talk of an era of "Second Reconstruction." A decade earlier, in the historic *Brown v. Board of Education* decision of 1954, the U.S. Supreme Court repudiated the "separate but equal" doctrine. Subsequently, a major civil rights movement victory was achieved with the passage of the Civil Rights Act of 1964, which forbade discrimination in employment and in most public places. With voting rights now protected as well, and the federal government authorized to intervene directly to assure those rights, one might have expected 1965 to stand as a moment of shimmering and untarnished civil rights progress. Yet the mood of optimism and triumph did not last for long.

The negative trend of the times was epitomized by deep and explosive inequalities and resentments of race smoldering in many Northern, urban ghettos. The extent to which the "race problem" was not just a Southern problem of civil rights, but a national problem of inequality woven deep into our economic and cultural fabric, would quickly be laid bare following passage of the Voting Rights Act. Scarcely five days after then-President Johnson signed the bill into law, the Los Angeles community of Watts erupted into flames. Quelling the disorder, which raged for roughly six days, required the mobilization of the National Guard and nearly fifteen thousand troops. When disorder finally subsided, thirty-four people had died, more than one thousand had been injured, well over three thousand were arrested, and approximately $35 million in property damage had been done. Subsequent studies and reports revealed patterns of police abuse, political marginalization, intense poverty, and myriad forms of economic, housing, and social discrimination as contributing to the mix of conditions that led to the riots.

It was thus more than fitting that in 1965, *Daedalus* committed two issues to examining the conditions of "The Negro American. . . ." Some critical observations stand out from two of those earlier essays, which have been amplified and made centerpieces of much subsequent social science scholarship. Sociologist and anthropologist St. Clair Drake drew a distinction between what he termed primary victimization and indirect victimization. Primary victimization involved overt discrimination in the labor market that imposed a job ceiling on the economic opportunities available to blacks alongside housing discrimination and segregation that relegated blacks to racially distinct urban ghettos. Indirect or secondary victimization involved the multidimensional and cumulative disadvantages resulting from primary victimization. These consequences included poorer schooling, poor health, and greater exposure to disorder and crime. In a related vein, sociologist Daniel Patrick Moynihan stressed the central importance of employment prospects in the wake of the civil rights victories that secured the basic citizenship rights of African Americans. Both Drake and Moynihan expressed concern about a black class structure marked by signs of a large and growing economically marginalized segment of the black community. Drake went so far as to declare, "If Negroes are not to become a permanent lumpen-proletariat within American society as a result of social forces already at work and increased automation, deliberate planning by governmental and private agencies will be necessary." Striking a similar chord, Moynihan asserted: "[T]here would also seem to be no question that opportunities for a large mass of Negro workers in the lower ranges of training and education have not been improving, that in many ways the circumstances of these workers relative to the white work force have grown worse." This marginalized economic status, both scholars suggested, would have ramifying effects, including weakening family structures in ways likely to worsen the challenges faced by black communities.

If the scholarly assessments of 1965 occurred against a backdrop of powerful and transformative mass-based movement for civil rights and an inchoate sense of deep but imminent change, the backdrop for most scholarly assessments today is the election of Barack Obama as president of the United States, the rise of a potent narrative of post-racialism, and a sense of stalemate or stagnation in racial change. Many meanings or interpretations can be attached to the term post-racial. In its simplest and least controversial form, the term is intended merely to signal a hopeful trajectory for events and social trends, not an accomplished fact of social life. It is something toward which we as a nation still strive and remain guardedly hopeful about fully achieving. Three other meanings of post-racialism are filled with more grounds for dispute and controversy. One of these meanings attaches to the waning salience of what some have portrayed as a "black victimology" narrative. From this perspective, black complaints and grievances about inequality and discrimination are well-worn tales, at least passé if not now pointedly false assessments of the main challenges facing blacks in a world largely free of the dismal burdens of overt racial divisions and oppression.

A second and no less controversial view of post-racialism takes the position that the level and pace of change in the demographic makeup and the identity choices and politics of Americans are rendering the traditional black–white divide irrelevant. Accordingly, Americans increasingly revere mixture and hybridity and are rushing to embrace a decidedly "beige" view of themselves and what is good for the body politic. Old-fashioned racial dichotomies pale against the surge toward flexible, deracialized, and mixed ethnoracial identities and outlooks.

A third, and perhaps the most controversial, view of post-racialism has the most in common with the well-rehearsed rhetoric of color blindness. To wit, American society, or at least a large and steadily growing fraction of it, has genuinely moved beyond race—so much so that we as a nation are now ready to transcend the disabling racial divisions of the past. From this perspective, nothing symbolizes better the moment of transcendence than Obama's election as president. This transcendence is said to be especially true of a younger generation, what *New Yorker* editor David Remnick has referred to as "the Joshua Generation." More than any other, this generation is ready to cross the great river of racial identity, division, and acrimony that has for so long defined American culture and politics.

It is in this context of the first African American president of the United States and the rise to prominence of the narrative of post-racialism that a group of social scientists were asked to examine, from many different disciplinary and intellectual vantage points, changes in the racial divide since the time of the *Daedalus* issues focusing on race in 1965 and 1966.

The context today has points of great discontinuity and of great similarity to that mid-1960s inflection point. From the viewpoint of 1965, the election of Obama as the first African American president of the United States, as well as the expansion and the cultural prominence and success of the black middle class of which Obama is a member, speak to the enormous and enduring successes of the civil rights era. Yet also from the standpoint of 1965, the persistence of deep poverty and joblessness for a large fraction of the black population, slowly changing rates of residential segregation by race, continued evidence of antiblack discrimination in many domains of life, and historically high rates of black incarceration signal a journey toward racial justice that remains, even by superficial accounting, seriously incomplete.

In order to set a context for the essays contained in this volume, I address three key questions in this introduction. The first concerns racial boundaries. In an era of widespread talk of having achieved the post-racial society, do we have real evidence that attention to and the meaning of basic race categories are fundamentally breaking down? The second set of questions concerns the extent of economic inequality along the racial divide. Has racial economic inequality narrowed to a point where we need no longer think or talk of black disadvantage? Or have the bases of race-linked economic inequality changed so much that, at the least, the dynamics of discrimination and prejudice no longer need concern us? The third question is, how have racial attitudes changed in the period since the mid-1960s *Daedalus* issues?

To foreshadow a bit, I will show that basic racial boundaries are not quickly and inevitably collapsing, though they are changing and under great pressure. Racial economic inequality is less extreme today, there is a substantial black middle class, and inequality within the black population itself has probably never been greater. Yet there remain large and durable patterns of black–white economic inequality as well, patterns that are not overcome or eliminated even for the middle class and that still rest to a significant degree on discriminatory social processes. In addition, I maintain that we continue to witness the erosion and decline of Jim Crow racist attitudes in the United States. However, in their place has emerged a new pattern of attitudes and beliefs, variously labeled symbolic racism, modern racism, color-blind racism, or as I prefer it, laissez-faire racism. The new form of racism is a more covert, sophisticated, culture-centered, and subtle racist ideology, qualitatively less extreme and more socially permeable than Jim Crow racism with its attendant biological foundations and calls for overt discrimination. But this new racism yields a powerful influence in our culture and politics.

Consider first the matter of group boundaries. The 2000 Census broke new ground by allowing individuals to mark more than one box in designating racial background. Nearly seven million people exercised that option in 2000. . . . Despite Obama's electoral success and the press attention given to the phenomenon, some will no doubt find it surprising that the overwhelming majority of Americans identify with only one race. . . . Less than 2 percent of the population marked more than one box on the 2000 Census in designating their racial background. Fully 98 percent marked just one. I claim no deep-rootedness or profound personal salience for these identities. Rather, my point is that we should be mindful that the level of "discussion" and contention around mixture is far out of proportion to the extent to which most Americans actually designate and see themselves in these terms.

Moreover, even if we restrict attention to just those who marked more than one box, two-thirds of these respondents designated two groups other than blacks (namely, Hispanic-white, Asian-white, or Hispanic and Asian mixtures). . . . Some degree of mixture with black constituted just under a third of mixed race identifiers in 2000. Given the historic size of the black population and the extended length of contact with white Americans, this remarkable result says something powerful about the potency and durability of the historic black–white divide.

It is worth recalling that sexual relations and childbearing across the racial divide are not recent phenomena. The 1890 U.S. Census contained categories for not only "Negro" but also "Mulatto," "Quadroon," and even "Octoroon"; these were clear signs of the extent of "mixing" that had taken place in the United States. Indeed, well over one million individuals fell into one of the mixed race categories at that time. In order to protect the institution of slavery and to prevent the offspring of white slave masters and exploited black slave women from having a claim on freedom as well as on the property of the master, slave status, as defined by law, followed the mother's status, not the father's. For most of its history, the United States legally barred or discouraged racial mixing and intermarriage. At the time of the *Loving v. Virginia* case in 1967, seventeen states still banned racial intermarriage.

Formal, legal definitions of who was black, and especially the development of rules of "hypodescent," or the one drop rule, have a further implication that is often lost in discussions of race: these practices tended to fuse together race and class, in effect making blackness synonymous with the very bottom of the class structure. As historian David Hollinger explains: The combination of hypodescent with the denial to blacks residing in many states with large black populations of any opportunity for legal marriage to whites ensured that the color line would long remain to a very large extent a property line. Hence, the dynamics of race formation and the dynamics of class formation were, in this most crucial of all American cases, largely the same. This is one of the most important truths about the history of the United States brought into sharper focus when that history is viewed through the lens of the question of ethnoracial mixture.

Still, we know that today the ethnoracial landscape in the United States is changing. As of the 2000 Census, whites constituted just 69 percent of the U.S. population, with Hispanics and blacks each around 12 percent. This distribution represents a substantial decline in the percentage of whites from twenty or, even more so, forty years ago.

With continued immigration, differential group fertility patterns, and the continued degree of intermarriage and mixing, these patterns will not remain stable. . . . Forecasts predict that somewhere between 2040 and 2045, whites will cease to be a numerical majority of the population. (This change could possibly happen much sooner than that.) The relative size of the Hispanic population is expected to grow substantially, with the black, Asian, Native Hawaiian and other Pacific Islander, American Indian, and Alaska Native groups remaining relatively constant. [This] strongly implies that pressure to transform our understanding of racial categories will continue.

Does that pressure for change foretell the ultimate undoing of the black–white divide? At least three lines of research raise doubts about such a forecast. First, studies of the perceptions of and identities among those of mixed racial backgrounds point to strong evidence of the cultural persistence of the one-drop rule. Systematic experiments by sociologists and social psychologists are intriguing in this regard. For example, sociologist Melissa Herman's recent research concluded that "others' perceptions shape a person's identity and social understandings of race. My study found that part black multiracial youth are more likely to be seen as black by observers and to define themselves as black when forced to choose one race."

Second, studies of patterns in racial intermarriage point to a highly durable if somewhat less extreme black–white divide today. A careful assessment of racial intermarriage patterns in 1990 by demographer Vincent Kang Fu found that "one key feature of the data is overwhelming endogamy for blacks and whites. At least 92 percent of white men, white women, black women and black men are married to members of their own group. . . ."

Third, some key synthetic works argue for an evolving racial scheme in the United States, but a scheme that nonetheless preserves a heavily stigmatized black category. A decade ago, sociologist Herbert Gans offered the provocative but well-grounded speculation that the United States would witness a transition from a society defined by a great white–nonwhite divide to one increasingly defined by a black–non-black fissure, with an in-between or residual category for those granted provisional or "honorary white" status. . . .

If basic racial categories and identities are not soon to dissolve, then let me now address that second set of questions, concerning the degree of racial economic inequality. I should begin by noting that there has been considerable expansion in the size, security, and, arguably, salience and influence of the black middle class.

Turning to the question of income, we find a similar trend. . . . At the very bottom are those who the Census would designate as the "very poor": that is, having a family income that is 50 percent or less of the poverty level. At the very top are those in the "comfortable" category, having family incomes that are five times or more the poverty level. The proportion of whites in this upper category exceeded 10 percent in 1960 and rose to nearly 30 percent by 2008. For blacks, the proportion was less than 5 percent in 1968 but about 12 percent in 2008. Likewise, the fraction in the middle class (those with family incomes more than twice the poverty level) grows for both groups. But crucially, the proportion of blacks in the "poor" (at the poverty line) or "very poor" categories remains large, at a combined figure of nearly 40 percent in 2008. This contrasts with the roughly 20 percent of whites in those same categories.

The official black poverty rate has fluctuated between two to three times the poverty rate for whites. Recent trend analyses suggest that this disparity declined during the economic boom years of the 1990s but remained substantial. As public policy analyst Michael Stoll explains: "Among all black families, the poverty rate declined from a 20 year high of about 40 percent in 1982 and 1993 to 25 percent in 2000. During this period, the poverty rate for white families remained fairly constant, at about 10 percent." That figure of 25 percent remains true through more recent estimates. In addition, the Great Recession has taken a particularly heavy toll on minority communities, African Americans perhaps most of all. As the Center for American Progress declared in a recent report: "Economic security and losses during the recession and recovery exacerbated the already weak situation for African Americans. They experienced declining employment rates, rising poverty rates, falling home ownership rates, decreasing health insurance and retirement coverage during the last business cycle from 2001 to 2007. The recession that followed made a bad situation much worse."

Overall trends in poverty, however, do not fully capture the cumulative and multidimensional nature of black economic disadvantage. Sociologist William Julius Wilson stresses how circumstances of persistently weak employment prospects and joblessness, particularly for low-skilled black men, weaken the formation of stable two-parent households and undermine other community structures. Persistent economic hardship and weakened social institutions then create circumstances that lead to rising rates of single-parent households, out-of-wedlock childbearing, welfare dependency, and greater risk of juvenile delinquency and involvement in crime. Harvard sociologist Robert Sampson points to an extraordinary circumstance of exposure to living in deeply disadvantaged communities for large segments of the African American population. This disadvantage involves living in conditions that expose residents to high surrounding rates of unemployment, family breakup, individuals and families reliant on welfare, poor-performing schools, juvenile delinquency, and crime. As Sampson explains:

> [A]lthough we knew that the average national rate of family disruption and poverty among blacks was two to four times higher than among whites, the number of distinct ecological contexts in which blacks achieve equality to whites is striking. In not one city of 100,000 or more in the United States do blacks live in ecological equality with whites when it comes to these basic features of economic and family organization. Accordingly, racial differences in poverty and family disruption are so strong that the "worst" urban contexts in which whites reside are considerably better than the average context of black communities.

Recent work published by sociologist Patrick Sharkey assesses race differences in the chances of mobility out of impoverished neighborhoods. The result is a very depressing one. He finds evidence of little upward social mobility for disadvantaged blacks and a fragile capacity to maintain advantaged status among even the most well-off African Americans. He writes: "[M]ore than 70% of black children who are raised in the poorest quarter of American neighborhoods will continue to live in the poorest quarter of neighborhoods as adults. Since the 1970s, more than half of black families have lived in the poorest quarter of neighborhoods in consecutive generations, compared to just 7% of white families. "Discussing the upper end, Sharkey writes: "Among the small number of black families who live in the top quartile, only 35% remain there in the second generation. . . . "White families exhibit a high rate of mobility out of the poor neighborhoods and a low rate of moving out of the most affluent neighborhoods, and the opposite is true among black families."

The general labor market prospects of Americans have undergone key changes in the last several decades. Three loom large. There is far more internal differentiation and inequality within the black population than was true at close of World War II. . . . The fortunes of men and women have recently diverged within the black community. Black women have considerably narrowed the gap between themselves and white women in terms of educational attainment, major occupational categories, and earnings. Black men have faced a growing problem of economic marginalization. Importantly, this is contingent on levels of education; education has become a far sharper dividing line, shaping life chances more heavily than ever before in the black community.

Several other dimensions of socioeconomic status bear mentioning. Even by conservative estimates, the high school dropout rate among blacks is twice that of whites, at 20 percent versus 11 percent. Blacks also have much lower college completion rates (17 percent versus 30 percent) and lower advanced degree completion rates (6 percent versus 11 percent). These differences are enormously consequential. . . . [E]ducational attainment and achievement increasingly define access to the good life, broadly defined.

One of the major social trends affecting African Americans over the past several decades has been the sharply punitive and incarceration-focused turn in the American criminal justice system. Between 1980 and 2000, the rate of black incarceration nearly tripled. The black-to-white incarceration ratio increased to above eight to one during this time period. . . . The reach of mass incarceration has risen to such levels that some analysts view it as altering normative life-course experiences for blacks in low-income neighborhoods. Indeed, the fabric of social life changes in heavily policed, low income urban communities.

Processes of racial residential segregation are a key factor in contemporary racial inequality. Despite important declines in overall rates of segregation over the past three decades and blacks' increasing suburbanization, blacks remain highly segregated from whites. Some have suggested that active self-segregation on the part of blacks is now a major factor sustaining residential segregation. A number of careful investigations of preferences for neighborhood characteristics and makeup and of the housing search process strongly challenge such claims. Instead, there is substantial evidence that, particularly among white Americans, neighborhoods and social spaces are strongly racially coded, with negative racial stereotypes playing a powerful role in shaping the degree of willingness to enter (or remain) in racially integrated living spaces. Moreover, careful auditing studies continue to show lower, but still significant, rates of antiblack discrimination on the part of real estate agents, homeowners, and landlords.

Lastly, I want to stress that wealth inequality between blacks and whites remains enormous. Recent scholarship has convincingly argued that wealth (or accumulated assets) is a crucial determinant of quality of life. Blacks at all levels of the class hierarchy typically possess far less wealth than otherwise comparable whites. Moreover, the composition of black wealth is more heavily based in homes and automobiles as compared to white wealth, which includes a more even spread across savings, stocks and bonds, business ownership, and other more readily liquidated assets. Whereas approximately 75 percent of whites own their homes, only 47 percent of blacks do. Looking beyond home ownership to the full range of financial assets, analyses from sociologists Melvin Oliver and Tom Shapiro put the black-to-white wealth gap ratio in the range of ten or eleven to one. . . .

What do we know about changes in racial attitudes in the United States? The first and most consistent finding of the major national studies of racial attitudes in the United States has been a steady repudiation of the outlooks that supported the Jim Crow social order. Jim Crow racism once reigned in American society, particularly in the South. Accordingly, blacks were understood as inherently inferior to whites, both intellectually and temperamentally. As a result, society was to be expressly ordered in terms of white privilege, with blacks relegated to secondary status in education, access to jobs, and in civic status such as the right to vote. Above all, racial mixture was to be avoided; hence, society needed to be segregated. The best survey data on American public opinion suggest that this set of ideas has been in steady retreat since the 1940s.

This picture of the repudiation of Jim Crow is complicated somewhat by evidence of significant social distance preferences. To be sure, low and typically declining percentages of whites objected when asked about entering into integrated social settings—neighborhoods or schools—where one or just a small number of blacks might be present. But as the number of blacks involved increased, and as one shifts from more impersonal and public domains of life (workplaces, schools, neighborhoods) to more intimate and personal domains (intermarriage), expressed levels of white resistance rise and the degree of positive change is not as great.

There is low and decreasing support among whites for the overtly racist belief that blacks have less inborn ability. The most widely endorsed account among whites points to a lack of motivation or willpower on the part of blacks as a key factor in racial inequality, though this attribution declines over time. . . . Blacks are generally far more likely than whites to endorse structural accounts of racial inequality, particularly the strongest attribution of discrimination. However, like their white counterparts, a declining number of blacks point to discrimination as the key factor, and there is actually a rise in the percentage of African Americans attributing racial inequality to a lack of motivation or willpower on the part of blacks themselves. . . .

To the extent that unfavorable beliefs about the behavioral characteristics of blacks have a bearing on levels of support for policies designed to benefit blacks, these data imply, and much evidence confirms, that negative beliefs about blacks' abilities and behavioral choices contribute to low levels of white support for significant social policy interventions to ameliorate racial inequality.

Judged by the trends considered here. . . , declarations of having arrived at the post-racial moment are premature. Much has changed—and unequivocally for the better—in light of where the United States stood in 1965. Indeed, I will speculate that none of the contributors to the 1965/1966 *Daedalus* volumes would have considered likely changes that have now, a mere four or so decades later, been realized, including the election of an African American President of the United States, the appointment of the first black Chair of the Joint Chiefs of Staff, and the appointment of two different African American Secretaries of State. Similarly, the size and reach of today's black middle class were not easy to forecast from the scholarly perch of mid-1960s data and understandings. At the same time, troublingly entrenched patterns of poverty, segregation, gaps in educational attainment and achievement, racial identity formation, and disparaging racial stereotypes all endure into the present, even if in somewhat less extreme forms. And the scandalous rise in what is now termed racialized mass incarceration was not foreseen but now adds a new measure of urgency to these concerns. . . .

These results underscore why discussions of race so easily and quickly become polarized and fractious along racial lines. The central tendencies of public opinion on these issues, despite real increasing overlap, remain enormously far apart between black and white Americans. When such differences in perception and belief are grounded in, or at least reinforced by, wide economic inequality, persistent residential segregation, largely racially homogeneous family units and close friendship networks, and a popular culture still suffused with negative ideas and images about African Americans, then there should be little surprise that we still find it enormously difficult to have sustained civil discussions about race and racial matters. Despite growing much closer together in recent decades, the gaps in perspective between blacks and whites are still sizable.

EXPLORING THE ISSUE

Is America Close to Being a Post-Racial Society?

Critical Thinking and Reflection

1. What criteria should a scholar use to judge a social movement's success?
2. What are the advantages and disadvantages of movement leaders setting movement goals higher than it is possible to achieve?
3. Can civil rights equity be legislated? Can integration be legislated? If integration can be legislated in the economy, can it also be legislated in the churches?
4. Does complete integration require that intermarriages become as common as intramarriages?
5. Are black self-images on a par with white self-images? If not, why not?
6. Consider the power of symbols in national life.
7. The election of Obama had the potential to unite our country racially and ethnically. Why are we more divided than ever?

Is There Common Ground?

Both authors agree that much progress has been made in the civil rights of blacks. The main difference in their opinions regards how far this country has come and how far it has yet to go. According to Lawrence D. Bobo's title, America is somewhere between Jim Crow and post-racialism. According to Alvin Poussaint, America is closer to King's mountaintop than Jim Crow. It comes down to what you emphasize: half empty or half full. I went to Princeton University in 1953 and there was only one black in my class. In fact the first African American undergraduate to enter Princeton during peacetime arrived only 6 years earlier. According to an article in the *Princeton Alumni Weekly* in 2010, "The percentage of minority students—defined by Princeton University as Asian-Americans, African-Americans, Hispanics, Native Americans, and those who self-identify as multiracial—make up 37 percent of students in the Class of 2013. Asian-American students are the largest ethnic minority in the freshman class (17.7 percent), followed by African-Americans (7.3 percent), Hispanics (6.8 percent), and Native Americans (0.5 percent). In recent years, the University has allowed students to identify themselves as multiracial, and more than 5 percent of freshmen do so." Check the history of your college or employer and you will see a dramatic story. The story of your neighborhood will probably also involve racial changes but in several different directions. The story of your church or other religious body will probably show the least change, and that is a story in itself. From what has happened around you, how much do you think America has moved toward a post-racial society?

Additional Resources

The following books bitterly proclaim that the treatment of blacks is definitely unfair: Gregory S. Parks and Matthew W. Hughey, eds., *12 Angry Men: True Stories of Being a Black Man in America Today* (New Press, 2010); Molefi K. Asante, *Erasing Racism: The Survival of the American Nation* (Prometheus Books, 2009); Michael C. Dawson, *Not in Our Lifetimes: The Future of Black Politics* (University of Chicago Press, 2011); Joe R. Feagan, *Racist America: Roots, Current Realities, and Future Reparations* (Routledge, 2010); John Hartigan, *What Can You Say?: America's National Conversation on Race* (Stanford University Press, 2010); Roy H. Kaplan, *The Myth of Post-Racial America: Searching for Equality in the Age of Materialism* (Rowman & Littlefield Education, 2011); Robert E. Pierre, *A Day Late and a Dollar Short: High Hopes and Deferred Dreams in Obama's "Postracial" America* (Wiley, 2010); and Tim J. Wise, *Colorblind: The Rise of Post-Racial Politics and the Retreat from Equity* (City Lights Books, 2010). The historical perspective is presented in Greta De Jong, *Invisible Enemy: The African American Freedom Struggle After 1965* (Wiley-Blackwell, 2010); Cynthia Griggs Fleming, *Yes We Did?: From King's Dream to Obama's Promise* (University of Kentucky Press, 2009); and Emilye Crosby, ed., *Civil Rights History from the Ground Up: Local Struggles, a National Movement* (University of Georgia Press, 2011). *The Obamas and a (Post) Racial America?* edited by Gregory S. Parks and Matthew W. Highey (Oxford University Press, 2011) focuses on the role of the Obamas in altering racial relations.

This debate connects strongly with black politics, which is the focus of several books including Manning Marable, *Beyond Black and White: Transforming African-American Politics* (Verso, 2009); Desmond S. King, *Still a House Divided: Race and Politics in Obama's America* (Princeton University Press, 2011); Gwen Ifill, *The Breakthrough: Politics and Race in the Age of Obama* (Doubleday, 2009); Theodore James Davis, *Black Politics Today: The Era of Socioeconomic Transition* (Routledge, 2012); and Manning Marable and Kristen Clarke, eds., *Barack Obama and African American Empowerment: The Rise of Black America's New Leadership* (Palgrave Macmillan, 2009). The broader issue of racism is analyzed in George Lipsitz, *How Racism Takes Place* (Temple University Press, 2011) and Roy L. Brooks, *Racial Justice in the Age of Obama* (Princeton University Press, 2009).

ISSUE 8

Has Feminism Benefited American Society?

YES: Barbara Epstein, from "The Successes and Failures of Feminism," *Journal of Women's History* (Summer 2002)

NO: Kate O'Beirne, from *Women Who Make the World Worse* (Sentinel, 2006)

Learning Outcomes
After reading this issue, you should be able to:
• Understand the gender inequalities before the feminist movement in the 1960s and compare them to today.
• Assess the role of feminism in the changes in gender inequalities with time. Assess the positive and negative impacts of the identified changes.
• Identify the gender inequality issues that remain, and identify the obstacles to making changes to achieve equity.
• Assess the extent to which the feminist movement has created structural disadvantages for men.
• Estimate the extent to which society has benefited from the feminist movement.

ISSUE SUMMARY

YES: History Professor Barbara Epstein argues that the feminist movement has been highly successful in changing the consciousness of Americans to "an awareness of the inequality of women and a determination to resist it." She explains how feminists succeeded at the consciousness level but have declined as a movement for social change.

NO: Journalist Kate O'Beirne argues that feminism is unpopular with women and is pushing an agenda that most women do not support. She claims that most women have concluded "that the feminist movement is both socially destructive and personally disappointing."

The publication of Betty Friedan's *The Feminine Mystique* (W. W. Norton, 1963) is generally thought of as the beginning of the modern women's movement, and since that time significant changes have occurred in American society. Data on advanced degrees and on income mark the profound changes. In 1960, only 35 percent of BAs were awarded to women, but in 2003 that percentage had increased to 57 percent. The comparable figures for MAs were 32 percent in 1960 and 59 percent in 2003, for PhDs were 11 percent in 1960 and 48 percent in 2003, and for law degrees were 2.5 percent in 1960 and 48 percent in 2003. The number of women in Congress in 1960 was 20 and in 2002 was 73. In 1963, the average full-time adult woman worker earned 58 percent of what the average adult male worker earned, while in 2009 they earned 80 percent. Many other changes marking women's progress are readily available. Occupations and professions, schools, clubs, associations, and governmental positions that were by tradition or law previously reserved for men only are now open to women. Women are found in increasing numbers among lawyers, judges, physicians, and elected officials. In 1981, President Ronald Reagan appointed the first woman, Sandra Day O'Connor, to the Supreme Court. In 1983, the first American woman astronaut, Sally Ride, was included in the crew of a space shuttle, and recently women have been on many of the space shuttle missions. The service academies have accepted women since 1976, and women in the military participated in the U.S. invasion of Panama in December 1989, the Persian Gulf War in 1990–1991, and the war to liberate Iraq in 2003. Elizabeth Watson became the first woman to head a big-city police department when the mayor of Houston appointed her chief of police in January 1990. New breakthroughs for women are now common, and a woman president may not be far off.

Surprisingly, America is no longer the leading nation in gender equity. According to the multivariable measure of gender equity used by the World Economic Forum, the United States ranks 19th in terms of achieving gender equity. The Forum explains, "In the U.S., women are more likely than men to live in poverty, earn less money for the same work, are more likely to be victims of intimate partner violence and rape, and have less of a political voice."

These sorts of changes—quantifiable and highly publicized—signal a change in women's roles in the direction that feminists have championed. But more than three decades after Friedan's book, there are still many inequalities that favor men, including income and poverty indicators. Much change toward greater equality has also occurred in the cultural area, but full parity has not yet been achieved. Femininity and femaleness are not valued as high as maleness and masculinity. Housework and childrearing are not shared equally in dual career families, although substantial progress has been made. Women are still adapting to a man's world.

Feminism—an ideology that, in its most basic form, directly opposes sexism by supporting gender equality and portraying women and men as essentially equals—has been a driving force in shaping the modern women's movement. The final legal victory of the women's movement was supposed to be the passage of the Equal Rights Amendment (ERA) to the Constitution, which would have made a person's sex an irrelevant distinction under the law. The ERA passed both houses of Congress by overwhelming margins in 1972, but it failed to win ratification from the required three-fourths of the state legislatures. The amendment was not ratified in part due to the efforts of a coalition of groups, composed overwhelmingly of women, who went to battle against it. Obviously, the women's movement did not represent the views of all women; many continued to believe in traditional gender roles. This pattern continues to today. Some of the prominent opponents against today's feminism are women.

In the readings that follow, a favorable view of feminism is presented by Barbara Epstein. The strongest arguments for feminism are the intolerable inequities that existed before the women's movement and the accomplishments of feminists since then, as Epstein demonstrates. In contrast, Kate O'Beirne argues that feminists falsely reconstruct gender realities to portray men as exploiters and women as victims and to blame women's unhappiness on being chained to child-raising and homemaking. Her main criticism is that feminism attacks the family and seeks policies that run counter to natural differences between the sexes. She concludes that the feminist program of action will have largely adverse impacts such as undermining the family, encouraging divorce, and harming children.

YES

Barbara Epstein

The Successes and Failures of Feminism

I have been trying to figure out for several years how feminism should go forward. This seems to me to be the perfect audience to present these ideas to, and get reactions from, so I am going to try out some of my thoughts on you. I want to talk about what the achievements of the women's movement have been and what remains undone—what the strengths were and what some of the weaknesses are.

Leaving aside the antiwar movement of the 1960s, which I think played an important role in bringing the war to an end, the women's movement was the most successful movement of the 1960s and 1970s. The idea that women should enjoy full equality with men was a startlingly radical idea then. That idea has been widely accepted. It seems clear that women in the United States think differently about themselves now than they did 30 years ago because of the women's movement. There have been advances in opportunities for women, especially in the professions, also to, I think, a lesser degree in working-class jobs. Such issues as child care, violence against women, and reproductive rights have been placed on the public agenda as legitimate issues—dramatically different from the political agenda of the 1950s and through the 1960s. There have also been some actual advances in other areas, around such issues as women's health and violence against women, though, given the rightward drift of politics in the United States generally over the last several decades, the record on these concerns has been somewhat mixed. But on a rhetorical level at least, women's equality has been accepted as a goal by mainstream society. The gap between rhetoric and reality remains, but the fact that women's equality has been accepted as a legitimate goal creates an opportunity for changing the reality. It seems to me that probably the most important contribution of the women's movement of the 1960s and 1970s was that it gave women a sense of their collective power. And I think it is useful to look at the difference between second-wave feminism and first-wave feminism in relation to this sort of issue. Women who participated in the women's movement of the late nineteenth and early twentieth centuries also learned this lesson, but the lesson had a narrower impact. First of all, that movement, particularly in the latter part of the nineteenth and early twentieth centuries, was largely confined to middle-class and upper-middle-class, overwhelmingly white women. Working-class women also participated, but they constituted

From *Journal of Women's History,* vol. 4, no. 2 (2002), pp. 118–125. Copyright © Journal of Women's History. Reprinted by permission.

quite a small element of the movement and the memory of that movement was quite effectively obliterated during the 1940s and 1950s, such that feminism in a sense had to be reinvented in the 1960s. The impact of the second wave of feminism has been broader and deeper and the obliteration of that lesson is not going to happen. So that's a very major accomplishment.

The second wave of feminism was successful not only because it led to changes in the lives of huge numbers of women, but also because the movement evolved over time. And I think in many ways, the movement evolved in positive directions. When the women's movement first emerged in the mid 1960s, it was largely confined to university students, other young people of more or less the same class and a slightly older group of women professionals. There were women of color and working-class women in these movements, but they tended to enter the movements through the same routes that everybody else did, namely the fact that they were in college or in the professions despite unusual origins. Their presence in the movement in the late 1960s did not mean that feminism was being adopted within working-class communities or within communities of color. In those years, there was a wide gap between the feminist claim to speak for all women and the reality, which had to do with the specific class and social origins of the women making up the movement. Most of them were from the middle class or the upper middle class, and I suspect actually that most of them were from the suburbs. In the 1970s and into the 1980s, women of color began to articulate their own versions of feminism, and working women, who had not been part of feminism's earlier university student cohort, began to organize around demands of equal treatment in the workplace and other issues working-class women faced. If one were to contrast the women's movement of the 1960s and beyond with the women's movement of the nineteenth and early twentieth centuries, I think one might say that while the first movement narrowed over time, in terms of its constituency and its class perspective, the latter movement—our movement—widened over time. Another way of putting this is to remember that the nineteenth-century women's movement emerged out of an alliance between white women and African Americans in the struggle for abolitionism. But after the Civil War, in the context of a white middle class shifting toward the political right in the late nineteenth century, the women's movement shifted away from earlier alliances. By the early twentieth century, the activists were arguing for women's suffrage on racist and anti-immigrant grounds. So there was a shift away from the alliance with black people specifically, and with a broader, progressive agenda, more generally. I do not think the women's movement of our era has ever been racist in that sense, but I also think it has improved over time. In the mid-1960s, the movement was largely composed of white women who were often blind to the fact that they could not actually speak for all women, but by the 1970s and certainly by the 1980s, there was a much greater awareness of the need to recognize difference within the women's movement, and a much greater awareness of the need to build alliances with other progressive constituencies, particularly groups of color.

Over the 1980s and 1990s, feminism as a perspective or as an identity spread widely and a kind of diffuse feminist consciousness has become a mass phenomenon. There are enormous numbers of women who identify as feminists or who think about women's issues in a different way as a result of feminism. There are also now countless projects, groups, and organizations that are, in one way or another, infused by a feminist perspective. But it is also the case that the main organizations of the women's movement, the most visible organizations such as the National Organization for Women and others, have narrowed in their perspective and are no longer mass-based. They are no longer connected to mass movements, and they have become organizations that are run by staffs rather than on the basis of membership engagement. These organizations have become more cautious in their approach than was the case with even the liberal wing of the women's movement in the late 1960s and 1970s, and they have become more identified with professional, middle-class women and their perspectives. This is not true of the whole women's movement, and actually this conference represents other strands within the movement. There are many organizations that rest on grassroots organizing among women, such as the National Congress of Neighborhood Women. There are many local groups focused on women of color and working women's concerns. There are many such groups in California, including the Mothers of East Los Angeles and the Women's Action for New Directions. While there are many grassroots-based women's organizations with broad social concerns, these do not make up the most visible wing of the women's movement. Despite a great deal of grassroots organizing, there is a way in which the women's movement has lost a sense of coherent direction and urgency. The wind has gone out of the sails. And I would like to address why.

The wind has gone out of the sails, not only of the women's movement but also of the progressive movement as a whole in the United States generally. There are hopeful signs. Among these is the struggle against globalization and corporate control that emerged in Seattle, and in which feminism has been a major component. Though it has not yet congealed into a movement, it holds out the possibility of something new and exciting. There are probably more people involved in grassroots organizing around progressive issues in the United States now than there were in the 1960s and 1970s. But despite these positive signs, the progressive movement as a whole has become institutionalized. It has become an arena in which many of us live and find consensus on many issues. But this progressive sector is not having much effect on the political direction of the country as a whole. Why is that? What has happened?

Part of the answer is that feminism has become more an idea than a movement. And even as a movement, it lacks some of the impetus that it once had. I think that in the case of the women's movement, the gap between the breadth of the original vision and the current state of activism comes from the gap between the feminism's broad and radical vision and the much narrower character of its actual tangible accomplishments—something Linda Gordon alluded to in her contribution to this conference when she said that the inspiration within the feminist movement came very largely from women's liberation in the 1960s and 1970s, but the liberal wing of feminism accomplished the concrete victories. I would go a little bit further and say that not only was it liberal feminists that were able to accomplish those victories, but that their victories were narrower than the intentions of the larger movement. There are many historical cases of popular movements that made broad and radical demands which then became winnowed down such that the final achievement was the least threatening element of the original set of demands. So it is not a big surprise that this should happen to the women's movement as it has happened to other movements, but it is worth looking at the fact that it did happen, and what the consequences have been.

Linda Gordon also mentioned that there were the two wings of the women's movement. People have categorized these differently. On the one hand, there was liberal feminism; on the other hand, there was women's liberation. People also sometimes talked about that wing as comprised of radical feminism and socialist feminism, with radical feminists regarding women's oppression as the root of all oppression, and socialist feminists placing women's oppression within the context of other forms of oppression, particularly race and class. But if one contrasts radical feminism with the liberal wing, you could say that the main goal of the liberal wing of the movement was to win equal access for women to the public sphere on equal terms with men, particularly to the sphere of work. While women's liberation or radical feminism supported that goal, it also aimed for two broader visions. One was that women's liberation insisted that the subordination of women in the public realm could not be separated from the subordination of women in the private realm—both had to be addressed simultaneously. Radical feminists also insisted that it was not possible to win equality for women without winning equality in society across the board. In other words, women could not be equals in a society deeply stratified by race and class.

In the 1960s and 1970s, there was actually a lot of overlap between women's liberation or radical feminism, and liberal feminism. I think the influence tended to go from the radical sphere towards the liberal sphere; that liberal feminists were pushed by radical activists. Many liberals adopted radical ideas. Another element, particularly in the 1970s, was that people from women's liberation participated in an enormous amount of organizing around feminist issues among working-class women. Working-class women's caucuses demanded affirmative action to help themselves and others like them. So in a certain sense, it's not accurate to divide the women's movement up into different spheres because they overlapped, and because the goal of affirmative action—which is usually, and I think appropriately, associated with liberal feminism—also contained a very important working-class element.[1] However, despite the sort of ferment and intersection of liberal and radical demands that took place in the 1960s and 1970s, the fact of the matter is that demands and results are not always the same thing. Affirmative action campaigns in the end were more effective in the professions than elsewhere, and educated and overwhelmingly white women took the greatest advantage of these opportunities. I think that these gains in affirmative action, combined with the growing gap between the lower and higher rungs of the economy (which continued to increase divisions among women despite the gains of affirmative action), pushed the women's movement as a whole away from the radical demands of the 1960s and 1970s.

Meanwhile, radical feminism itself became stalled in the 1970s. It was torn apart by two things. The first was the kind of factionalism, ideological conflicts, and internal struggles that Linda Gordon addressed, which led to the decline of radical feminism and the emergence of a much less political version of feminism that we called cultural feminism by the end of the decade.[2] Such sectarianism is ordinarily associated with movements that are in decline, but feminism at the time was strong and growing. My analysis of why this happened is that the radical wing of the women's movement became a bit crazed in the late 1960s and early 1970s, for the same reason that radicalism in the United States as a whole was becoming a bit crazed (and I speak as someone who was part of this movement). Radicals not only adopted revolution as their aim, but also thought that revolution was within reach. Now there were many versions of revolution—feminist, Marxist/Leninist, Black, and so on. But everybody thought revolution was a good idea, and virtually everybody thought it was around the corner. In my view at least, there was nothing wrong with the commitment to revolution; I wish we had more of it now. But there was something unrealistic about the view that if we did just the right thing, it would happen.

At bottom, the war in Vietnam produced a major crisis in U.S. society. Protest against the war combined with protests against racism and sexism made it seem possible to create a new society. But the fact of the matter was that once the war was over, the major basis for protest evaporated. And those of us who thought that protest would go on to become a revolutionary movement in the United States turned out to be wrong. In fact, what happened was that when the war came to an end, the largest sector of the movement evaporated, and the radical core of the various movements began to find itself isolated. I think it took longer for this to happen in the case of radical feminism than it did in the case of other sectors of the radical movement simply because the mainstream feminist movement was strong and growing, and within the feminist movement, there were many people who were quite open to radical ideas. But nevertheless, the trajectory of American society as a whole was toward the right, and the idea that revolution would happen tomorrow if you did just the right thing was clearly not accurate. By the 1980s, radical feminism too had been pushed to the margins and it was no longer a central current within American politics.

So I am arguing that two things happened more or less simultaneously. First, affirmative action was more or less accomplished, but in a form that was relatively conservative. At the same time, the radical sector of the movement more or less evaporated—or more accurately, it moved into academia. While most radicals did not become academics, enough people did that there was a sort of a critical mass of radicals in academia. Because it was a safe space for radicals and because of access to publishing and whatnot, the university became one of the spaces where feminism was defined. At the same time, academic feminism was gradually losing its ties to activism outside the academy.

This did not happen to all academics, of course, and this conference is in a certain sense about the people who took a different path. I am very pleased that this conference and the collections have highlighted the work of Frances Fox Piven, for example, who is a model in continuing to construct that bridge between activism and academia. Academic feminism, by and large, took a different path.

I suggested earlier that the politics and constituency of first-wave feminism narrowed and that was not the case with our feminist movement. But I think I was careful to say that there were also some problems. Even though I think our movement has not narrowed, particularly in relation to race, I think there is another respect in which the current women's movement has rather unconsciously narrowed its politics, which mirrors what happened in the nineteenth century. As the women's movement aged, so to speak, it became vulnerable to absorbing trends within its own class. And I think that is what has happened to the most visible and prominent aspects of our women's movement.

The women's movement of the 1960s and 1970s, especially the radical core of that movement, demanded not only equality for women, but also equality across the board. Feminists sought an egalitarian society governed by humane values. But since the early 1970s, economic inequalities have steadily widened in the United States. Most people now work longer hours at less secure jobs. Often these jobs are associated with increasing stress. Many people have spoken of work having become a religion in the United States. I think it might be more accurate to say that for many people, work has become the only meaningful source of identity. In a broader sense, the United States is becoming an increasingly individualistic, cold, and selfish society. It seems to me that we now live in a society in which people's concern for other people is becoming a kind of quaint, archaic value. People seem to assume that you should really be mostly concerned with yourself and maybe for other members of your nuclear family, if you happen to have one, but beyond that, it is a sort of silliness to be concerned with anybody else. Many progressives seem to have absorbed these ideas too. And I think the ways we have absorbed them has been by throwing ourselves into work and adopting or absorbing the view into the way we value ourselves. I know that this is true of me. I have the sense that it is also true of other people in our general community. I cannot really speak for the United States as a whole, but I am struck, even in visiting other countries, with the reigning individualism in the United States, which seems to be much further advanced than it is elsewhere in the world—even though I also think that individualism is a kind of global tendency.

Feminism is not marking a noticeable challenge to this cultural shift. In fact, I think that the version of feminism that was formed through the demand for women's equality in the workplace, and then, in practice, became focused around the success of the demand for affirmative action for professional women, has blindly absorbed many of the dominant cultural values of the middle class. In the 1970s, many feminists thought that if only we could get enough women into academic jobs, academia would change. It would become a less elitist, more humane place, concerned with social good. Well, a fair number of women are in the academy and I do not think that the academy has changed in those directions. Instead, I think the academy has gone in the opposite direction. This is not women's fault; it is because we are caught up in a wildly accelerating global version of capitalism that is drawing everything, including the universities, into its vortex and bringing market values to every area of life. Simply having more women in the academy does nothing to oppose this. As more people are in institutions that are adopting greater market values, the greater the pressures are for those people to adopt those values. We need a movement that explicitly and overtly criticizes this shift and the values associated with it.

I am suggesting here—and this is all completely impressionistic—that although the values of individualism, market values, and so forth, have taken on increased importance throughout the United States as a whole, there is a way in which the professional middle class has been the carrier of these values. We live in a society that is rapidly dividing between those who make it to the top and those who fall to the bottom, and generally speaking, people in the professional middle class would much rather rise than fall. There is a kind of scramble going on, and we are in the sector of society that is engaged in that scramble rather than critical of it. The media image of feminists as careerists was not entirely invented by a hostile press but feminists are no more careerists than other members of the same class. If this is true, then we are admitting that we have lost a grip on the social vision that feminism originally embraced. So I am calling for a return to a sort of revised version of radical feminism. It seems to me that we have to place feminism within the demand for an egalitarian society and a demand for a society that respects human connection and respects communities and promotes them rather than destroying them. And I do think we can look back to the legacy of women's liberation for at least some very good hints about how to do this.

Notes

1. I learned about this from Nancy Maclean, whose very important article on the use of affirmative action by working-class women appeared in a recent issue of *Feminist Studies*.

2. These developments are wonderfully described by Alice Echols in her book *Daring to Be Bad: Radical Feminism in America, 1967–1975*, and also by Ruth Rosen in her recent book *The World Split Open: How the Modern Women's Movement Changed America*. What is striking about both these books is that they are written from a perspective which is deeply feminist and deeply respectful of the women's movement, but also very clear-eyed about its problems.

 **NO**

Women Who Make the World Worse

How Radical Feminists Have Weakened the Family

The traditional family boosts the health, happiness, and wealth of husbands, wives, and children and raises the blood pressure of a certain kind of woman. Betty Friedan's 1963 *The Feminine Mystique* is typically included on lists of the one hundred most influential books of the last century. In a chapter entitled "The Comfortable Concentration Camp," she likened the passivity and hopelessness of American POWs in Korea to American women trapped at home with children in the suburbs. She later wrote, "For fear of being alone, I almost lost my own self-respect trying to hold on to a marriage that was based no longer on love but on dependent hate. It was easier for me to start the women's movement which was needed to change society than to change my own personal life."

Friedan got a divorce in 1969, but unfortunately not before she expounded on the merits of Marxist economics, persuaded far too many women that a selfless devotion to their families was a recipe for misery, helped to create the National Organization for Women (NOW), and destructively politicized relations between the sexes. Over the next decades, Friedan's fans moved beyond her criticisms of mothers at home and launched a hostile assault on marriage and family life.

The radical demand for androgyny and personal autonomy is irreconcilable with the need for different sex roles and mutual self-sacrifice between parents raising their offspring. Influential feminists see two major problems with the family that inhibit women's equality—husbands and fathers. Their advocacy and propaganda have eroded support for the family as an indispensable institution for both individuals and society.

Marriage Under Assault

In 1969, Marlene Dixon, a sociology professor at the University of Chicago, wrote, "The institution of marriage is the chief vehicle for the perpetuation of the oppression of women; it is through the role of wife that the subjugation of women is maintained. In a very real way the role of wife has been the genesis of women's rebellion throughout history."

That same year, Kate Millett's *Sexual Politics* was published. What began as a thesis for the Columbia University doctoral candidate became a celebrated call for the end of a patriarchal Institution that treated women like chattel. In 1970, Robin Morgan, a founder of *Ms.* magazine, was calling marriage "a slavery-like practice," and arguing, "We can't destroy the inequities between men and women until we destroy marriage." The following year, Australian feminist Germaine Greer's *The Female Eunuch* argued that married women had to save themselves by fleeing from their marriages in favor of "rambling organic structures."

By 1972, the angry screeds against marriage were being dressed up with academic adornments. In her influential book *The Future of Marriage*, Pennsylvania State University sociologist Jessie Bernard claimed that the "destructive nature" of marriage harmed women's mental and emotional health. In short, according to Bernard, "Being a housewife makes women sick." The fact that married women regularly reported that they were happier than unmarried women was dismissed as a symptom of this marital illness. "To be happy in a relationship which imposes so many impediments on her, as traditional marriage does, women must be slightly mentally ill." It was their oppression speaking when wives reported satisfaction with their lives. "Women accustomed to expressing themselves freely could not be happy in such a relationship."

Although the late Professor Bernard's pronouncements were those of a left-wing ideologue with a radical agenda, she was considered one of the top women sociologists in the world, and according to *The Boston Globe*, her twenty-three books established her as "the preeminent scholar of the women's movement." She held visiting professorships at Princeton and at the University of California. In *The Future of Motherhood* she argued that being a mother was also hazardous to women's health. She saw the desire for children as a sexist social construction and believed that many women preferred celibacy to "the degradation of most male-female sexual relationships." Professor Bernard sounded a warning about what truly liberated women could expect: "Men will resist and punish them; unliberated women, brainwashed not only to accept their slavery in marriage but also to love it, will resist them." The Center for Women's Policy Studies established a Jessie Bernard Wise Women award to recognize similar worthy insights.

Many establishment figures share Bernard's views. Laura Singer, who was president of the American Association for Marriage and Family Therapy in the 1970s, has explained, "I wouldn't say that marriage and self-actualization are *necessarily* mutually exclusive, but they are difficult to achieve together."

If these attacks on marriage strike you as extreme, you have some surprising company. Twenty years after she helped launch the modern women's movement, even Betty Friedan was criticizing her feminist sisters for their hostility to family life. In her 1981 book *The Second Stage*, she wrote: "The women's movement is being blamed, above all, for the destruction of the family." She cited the increase in divorces, in single-parent households, and in the number of women living alone and asked, "Can we keep on shrugging all this off as enemy propaganda—'their problem, not ours'? I think we must at least admit and begin openly to discuss feminist denial of the importance of family, of women's own needs to give and get love and nurture, tender loving care."

This time Betty Friedan's appeals fell on deaf feminist ears. The scholarship and sentiment that sounded dire warnings about marriage's harmful effects on women's well-being and ambitions had found an enthusiastic audience in women's studies programs and was popularized by journalists like Barbara Ehrenreich, a former columnist for *Time* magazine.

Writing from that powerful perch, Ehrenreich repeatedly denigrated marriage and family life. She advocated that the government concentrate on promoting "good divorces" rather than attempt to strengthen marriages and argued that the only problem with single-parent households was the lack of sufficient government support. She used the Menendez brothers and O.J. Simpson cases as an opportunity to share her opinion about the malevolent forces afoot in American families. The murders should prompt us to think "that the family may not be the ideal and perfect living arrangement after all—that it can be a nest of pathology and a cradle of gruesome violence." She asserted that "millions flock to therapy groups" and "we are all, it is often said, 'in recovery.' And from what? Our families, in most cases." She cited the "long and honorable tradition of 'anti-family' thought" and quoted Edmund Leach, the renowned British anthropologist, stating that "far from being the basis of a good society, the family, with its narrow privacy and tawdry secrets, is the source of all discontents."

Marlo Thomas and her pals, including Lily Tomlin, Bea Arthur, and Whoopi Goldberg, literally sang the praises of never-formed or broken families. Thomas's earlier *Free to Be . . . You and Me* attempted to overcome nasty sex stereotypes and create a more welcoming world for boys who played with dolls. In her *Free to Be . . . a Family,* any arrangement at all was promoted as just fine for raising children. The book and album wanted to teach children that "if the people whom you live with are happy to see your face, that's a family." The stories, songs and poems were "really about the family as it exists today, not the family as a storybook idea."

During the 2004 campaign, Teresa Heinz Kerry reflected a casual contempt for the role of wife and mother when she proclaimed that Laura Bush hadn't worked at a "real job . . . since she's been grown up." Laura Bush worked as a teacher and librarian for ten years, before giving up her career in education to raise her twin daughters. Most people, who haven't inherited a condiments empire and the resources to allow them to keep busy handing out fat foundation grants, think being a wife and mother is a "real job" for a "grown-up."

Before long, the antipathy to marriage infected the academy and was reflected in social science textbooks. When a nonpartisan group studied twenty textbooks used in eight thousand college courses in the mid-nineties, they found, "These books repeatedly suggest that marriage is more a problem than a solution. The potential costs of marriage to adults, particularly women, often receive exaggerated treatment, while the benefits of marriage, both to individuals and society, are frequently downplayed or ignored."

In *Changing Families*, Judy Root Aulette, a sociology professor at the University of North Carolina at Charlotte, didn't mention a single beneficial effect of marriage in the three chapters she devoted to the subject (one of which was titled "Battering and Marital Rape"). She did find room to approvingly cite Friedrich Engels stating that marriage was "created for a particular purpose: to control women and children."

While Professor Aulette had a lot to learn about the institution of marriage, she was well schooled in the politics of phony grievances. She accused the report's author of trying "to get rid of my voice, and my right to be in a classroom and present a feminist point of view."

In her textbook, Marine Baca Zinn proved herself worthy of a Jessie Bernard Wise Women award when she wrote, "If marriage is so difficult for wives, why do the majority surveyed judge themselves as happy? . . . [The reason] is that happiness is interpreted by wives in terms of conformity. Since they are conforming to society's expectations, this must be happiness."

The study's author, Professor Norval Glenn of the University of Texas, explained that the textbooks studied represented "the distilled essence of the current conventional wisdom" and were used to train the next generation of counselors, social workers, therapists, and teachers. He illustrated the conventional wisdom by contrasting the number of pages in each book focusing on the benefits of marriage for adults—less than one—with the pages per book devoted to domestic violence—twelve.

Marriage Benefits Men and Women

Professor Linda Waite of the University of Chicago filled a well-researched book with the good news about marriage. In *The Case for Marriage: Why Married People Are Happier, Healthier, and Better Off Financially*, Waite, a self-described liberal Democrat, and her conservative co-author, Maggie Gallagher, detailed the research findings that thoroughly refute Jessie Bernard and her acolytes' case against marriage. Linda Waite saw the notion that marriage was a much better deal for men than women as "the most powerful and persuasive" of the modern myths about marriage. She thought it was important for young women to be well-informed before they make their choices. "If we pretend that women are not advantaged by being married, we are doing them a great disservice."

Among Waite and Gallagher's findings: Because wives influence husbands to take better care of themselves, men do get more health benefits from marriage than women, but both married men and women express "very high and very similar levels of satisfaction with their marriages" and are similarly committed to their spouses. Women gain more financially from marriage than men do, and while both sexes are winners in sexual satisfaction, women gain even more owing to the sense of commitment that improves their sex life. And, when a wide range of disorders is considered, both sexes enjoy a boost in mental health. In fact, married women are generally less depressed than *Sex and the City*'s Carrie Bradshaw and her single sisters.

A well-respected study found that similar percentages of married women and men (41 percent and 38 percent) report they are "very happy," rates that are far higher than for those who have never married or are divorced. Social psychologist David G. Myers, author of *The Pursuit of Happiness*, strongly endorses Waite and Gallagher's conclusions. "The idea that women are happier if they are unmarried and men happier if they are married is blatantly untrue. The evidence is mountainous in the other direction."

Unlike other liberal women engaged in research on family issues, Dr. Waite had no preconceived notions or ideological axes to grind when she began to look at the data on marital status and mortality ten years ago. She was aware of other researchers looking at earnings data and health issues, but no one had put together the big picture. Waite recognized, "There's a general pattern here that nobody's noticed. All of the big things in life—good outcomes for children, health, long life—depend on marriage." This insight became the subject of a speech she delivered to the Population Association of America as its president in 1995.

Divorce Hurts

Professor Waite and her colleagues have more recently published a study on divorce that showed that unhappily married people were no happier after their marriages ended. They analyzed data from a national survey on families and households and found, "When the adults who said they were unhappily married in the late 1980s were interviewed again five years later, those who had divorced were on average still unhappy or even less happy, while those who stayed in their marriages on average had moved past the bad times and were at a happier stage."

Waite, who has been married for over thirty years, has a married daughter and a daughter with cerebral palsy who lives at home. She was married as an undergraduate and divorced from her first husband after four years with no children. She explains that her case against divorce is less applicable to the kind of short, early union she had. "It's very different. You're not leaving somebody who's financially dependent, you haven't built years of friendships, you don't have kids, you're not as much a working single unit as people who are married for a long time."

Waite explains that once children are present, the case against divorce becomes stronger. Professor Waite and Maggie Gallagher looked at the effect of divorce on children in their book and concluded that children were usually not better off when their parents split up. They pointed out that divorce might end marital conflict for parents, but it doesn't end "what really bothers kids: parental conflict." Their research indicates, "Children of divorce also have less money, live in poorer neighborhoods, go to poorer schools, and do worse in school than children of married parents—even if those marriages have a high degree of conflict."

In their book *Generation at Risk*, two liberal social scientists estimated that only about a third of divorces with children involved are so troubled that children are likely to benefit from the break-up. The remaining 70 percent of divorces involve low-conflict marriages where children are less harmed than they would be if their parents separated.

Fractured Families and Disposable Dads

In the past, the majority of Americans believed that unhappily married couples should stay together for the sake of their children. Now, only 15 percent agree that "when there are children in the family, parents should stay together even if they don't get along." When the traditional virtues of self-sacrifice and duty lose in a conflict with the feminist doctrine of self-fulfillment and personal autonomy, children pay a very steep price.

In an ominous sign that the well-being of children is unlikely to take precedence over the desires of adults any time soon, among young people there is little appreciation for the benefits of marriage and widespread support for "alternative lifestyles" as perfectly suitable for raising children. A national survey of high school seniors found that although a large majority of these teenagers expect to marry, less than a third of girls and only slightly more than a third of boys believe "that most people will have fuller and happier lives if they choose legal marriage rather than staying single or just living with someone." More than half of both boys and girls think out-of-wedlock childbearing is a "worthwhile lifestyle."

In 1988, among never-married people between the ages of eighteen and thirty-four, 64 percent of males and 56 percent of females thought "those who want children should get married." In 2002, only 51 percent of males and 42 percent of females in this age group thought having children and being married shouldn't be separate pursuits.

While the pathetic plight of wives and mothers was being peddled by women like Bernard, Aulette, and Zinn, others were making the case that dads are dispensable.

Male lions roar to protect their young from threatening predators, penguin pops balance fragile eggs on their feet in frigid temperatures, while adult male elephants temper the delinquent behavior of the young bulls. When the National Fatherhood Initiative used these arresting thirty-second images from the animal kingdom to depict the importance of fathers in their "Nature of Fatherhood" ad campaign, they drove some feminists wild. NOW raised an alarm about the "dangerous policy" of paternal responsibility being promoted by the initiative, which hoped to encourage fathers to commit to marriage and parenting.

An article that argued "neither mothers nor fathers are unique or essential" was promoted to bolster the case that "NOW Knows Best." In "Deconstructing the Essential Father," published in the influential *American Psychologist* in 1999, the authors maintained that children are perfectly fine as long as they have "parenting figures" of either sex, who need not be biologically related. Predicatably, the authors favored policies that support the legitimacy of "diverse family structures" rather than "privileging the two-parent, heterosexual, married family." Fatherhood is a retrograde gender role and therefore verboten.

The academics did not just dismiss the unique contributions of fathers as unimportant. It was argued that a father's presence in the home extracts an overlooked cost because "some fathers' consumption of family resources in terms of gambling, purchasing alcohol, cigarettes, or other nonessential commodities, actually increases women's workload and stress level." So, message to moms: Throw the bums out.

Professor Louise B. Silverstein, a Yeshiva University psychology professor and family therapist, co-authored the study that sought "to create an ideology that defines the father-child bond as independent of the father-mother relationship." Professor Silverstein is a past president of the American Psychological Association's Division of Family Psychology and chairman (a title that could put her in therapy) of the Feminist Family Therapy Task Force within the APA Division of the Psychology of Women. Her 1999 article making the case for throwaway dads won the Association for Women in Psychology's Distinguished Publication Award.

From the indispensable Maggie Gallagher it won condemnation. Gallagher graduated from Yale University in 1982. Married with two sons, this Portland, Oregon, native lives in New York and is a syndicated columnist and president of the Institute for Marriage and Public Policy. The author of three books, she has been an editor of *National Review* and a senior editor of the Manhattan Institute's *City Journal*. George Gilder called her first book, *Enemies of Eros: How the Sexual Revolution Is Killing Family, Marriage, and Sex, and What We Can Do About It*, published in 1989, "the best book ever written on men, women and marriage."

Maggie Gallagher has mastered the social science research on marriage, the family, and child well-being to become a leading authority on the most personal public-policy questions we face. She devotes her formidable skills to debunking clichés and conventional wisdom about love, marriage, and children and has the fortitude to challenge a culture more interested in self-gratification to confront the consequences of our failure to keep our commitments.

After having some fun with Dr. Silverstein's conclusion that "both men and women have the same biological potential for nurturing" based on her examination of the behavior of marmoset fathers, Gallagher deconstructs Silverstein's deconstruction handiwork. "Our new desire to strengthen marriage is in their view just a scary attempt to reassert 'the cultural hegemony of traditional values, such as heterocentrism, Judeo-Christian marriage, and male power and privilege.' It leads to horrible, unrealistic policies—like giving job help to low-income married fathers (and not just welfare mothers), or a more marriage-friendly tax code. Instead, these hard-headed professors urge more practical solutions, like reconstructing traditional masculine ideology so men care for infants as much as women."

Maggie Gallagher incisively confronts the fundamental questions that Silverstein ignores. "Under what conditions are children likely to fare best? And, are adults obligated to provide, if they can, the best situation for their kids?" Answers: Living with their married biological parents, and Yes.

Louise Silverstein is the glorified guru of gender warriors, but Comell University professor Urie Bronfenbrenner, who was widely regarded as one of the world's leading scholars in developmental psychology, child-rearing, and human ecology—the interdisciplinary field he created—strongly disagreed with her Dispensable Dad thesis. "Controlling for factors such as low income, children growing up in father-absent households are at a greater risk for experiencing a variety of behavioral and educational problems, including extremes of hyperactivity and withdrawal; lack of attentiveness in the classroom; difficulty in deferring gratification; impaired academic achievement; school misbehavior; absenteeism; dropping out; involvement in socially alienated peer groups; and the so-called 'teen-age syndrome' of behaviors that tend to hang together—smoking, drinking, early and frequent sexual experience, and in the more extreme cases, drugs, suicide, vandalism, violence and criminal acts."

In his defense of responsible fatherhood, Karl Zinsmeister counters Marlo Thomas's dismissal of the traditional family as a "storybook idea" by reminding us of its indispensability for men, women, and children. "It's when a culture stops upholding the paternal rituals, rules, and rewards that fathering withers. . . . Some people have actually convinced themselves families can do fine without fathers. They're wrong. Wherever men are not lured or corralled into concerning themselves with their children and mates, decent human society fades . . . the magic ingredients needed to tie men to their children are the ancient ones: Sexual restraint and enduring marriage." When men are committed to protecting and providing for their families, wives and children benefit and so too do husbands.

Studies show that men become more economically productive after they marry, with married men earning between 10 and 40 percent more than single men with similar education and job experience. Marriage also increases median family income, which more than doubled between 1947 and 1977. Over the past twenty years, the growth in median family income has slowed, increasing by just 9.6 percent, in large part because married couples, who do better economically, make up a decreasing proportion of all families.

In Britain, 49 percent of all births are illegitimate. In a sign that the British public has had its fill with the social and financial costs of unwed child-bearing, three unmarried sisters and their babies recently made front-page news. MUM AT 12, MUM AT 16, MUM AT 14, the headlines blared. The father of the sixteen-year-old's baby is a thirty-eight-year-old man in a "long-term relationship" with her; he lives with his parents. Their divorced mother had been married twice, but never to the fathers of her daughters. She became a grandmother three times in a year.

While most of the commentary criticized the intergenerational illegitimacy and complained that taxpayers had to pick up the considerable tab, Germaine Greer surfaced to celebrate the self-actualization of young girls doing their own thing. "Social historians will tell you that illegitimacy is highly hereditary. There have always been women like Yeats' Crazy Jane whose gardens grow 'nothing but babies and washing.' They live in an alternative society that is matrilineal, matrifocal, and matrilocal, a society that the patriarchy has always feared and hated." The "alternative society" Greer celebrates is on the brink of representing a majority of British births.

In 1960, only 9 percent of all children lived in single-parent households. Presently in the United States, almost one-third of children are born to single mothers. A large number of children will see their parents divorced before their eighteenth birthday. Two-thirds of black children are born out of wedlock. Over half of American children will spend all or part of their childhood without their father in the home.

According to my former colleague, the Heritage Foundation's poverty guru Robert Rector, "The collapse of marriage is the principal cause of child poverty and a host of other social ills. A child raised by a never-married mother is seven times more likely to live in poverty than a child raised by his biological parents in an intact marriage." Nearly two-thirds of poor children live in single-parent homes, and an additional 1.3 million children are born out of wedlock every year. We have never experienced so many children growing up without knowing what it means to live with the daily support and attention of their fathers.

Half of children living without their fathers have never been in their father's home, and one study found that only 27 percent of children over age four saw their father at least once a week, while 31 percent had no contact at all in the previous year.

In *The Abolition of Marriage*, Maggie Gallagher reminds us, "When we tell our girls that becoming a single mother—through divorce or failure to marry—is a perfectly acceptable lifestyle choice, we forget that our boys are listening too. And this is what they hear: Men aren't necessary. Women can do it alone. Women and children are usually better off without men. Breadwinning oppresses women and children. Marriage and breadwinning can be hard. Why do it, if you are only oppressing the ones you love?"

Barbara Dafoe Whitehead is co-director of the National Marriage Project at Rutgers University. She famously concluded in *Atlantic Monthly* article that "Dan Quayle Was Right" following the feminist fits over the vice president's *Murphy Brown* comments. Dr. Whitehead recently reported, "According to some researchers, growing up with both married parents in a low-conflict marriage is so important to child well-being that it is replacing race, class, and neighborhood as the greatest source of difference in child outcomes."

According to the National Marriage Project, men today are increasingly staying single longer, fathering more illegitimate children, cohabiting rather than marrying, and divorcing in large numbers. In 1970, only 7 percent of men between the ages thirty-five and forty-four had never married, compared with 18 percent today.

The National Fatherhood Initiative that NOW's feminists rail against as a patriarchal plot offers some inescapable "Father Facts." The rate of child abuse in single-parent households is nearly twice the rate of child abuse in two-parent families. Even after controlling for factors like family background and neighborhood variables, boys who grew up outside of intact marriages were, on average, more than twice as likely to end up in jail as other boys, and twice as likely to use illegal drugs.

Intact families are a far more effective "program" than are most government schemes to reduce poverty, child abuse, crime, and drug abuse, or to boost educational outcomes.

Although costly to men, women, children, and taxpayers, opposition to the traditional family is growing. The influential American Law Institute (ALI) recently released a report arguing that family law should be reformed so that marriage and cohabitation are treated equally and that marriage should be redefined as a gender-neutral arrangement in order to accommodate same-sex couples. These lawyers want to wipe out biology as a basis for parenthood in order to ensure "family diversity."

Professor Katharine Bartlett, a feminist scholar and dean of Duke University's law school, is one of the principal authors of the ALI report. She explains that her passion is "the value I place on family diversity and on the freedom of individuals to choose from a variety of family forms. This same value leads me to be generally opposed to efforts to standardize families into a certain type of nuclear family because a majority may believe this is the best kind of family or because it is the most deeply rooted ideologically in our traditions." Ignoring the overwhelming evidence about the benefits to family members and society from traditional marriage, Professor Bartlett attributes its support to either ignorant belief or blind ideology, befitting her status as a celebrated feminist scholar.

EXPLORING THE ISSUE

Has Feminism Benefited American Society?

Critical Thinking and Reflection

1. What changes have occurred concerning women in the labor force in the past half century?
2. To what extent do you think these changes have resulted from feminists' actions?
3. What other changes have feminists help bring about?
4. In what ways are women still not equal to men? Why is this so?
5. According to O'Beirne, how has the feminist movement harmed women?
6. Do you think that women are now advantaged relative to males? If so, in what ways?

Is There Common Ground?

The most convincing arguments of the antifeminists are made against extremist positions, which "reasonable feminists" might not hold. For example, one can be a feminist and still love a husband, desire to mother children, and even leave the labor force in order to raise them. Certainly most current feminists do not want to destroy marriage, stifle her mothering instincts, or sacrifice family to her career. They seek a balanced life which is radically different than the traditional housewife role of the 1950s, but is relatively normal in today's culture. In fact, antifeminists may be more at variance with today's culture than the feminists. Nonetheless, there are legitimate issues in the debate about feminism. Does their demand for truly equal opportunity and affirmative action require the premise that men and women are essentially the same? Does feminist activism cultivate an antipathy to men as their oppressors? Has the feminist program adversely affected the family and gender relations? Do feminists deny that nondiscriminatory bases exist for many inequalities between men and women?

Additional Resources

Over the past 40 years, there has been a deluge of books, articles, and periodicals devoted to expounding feminist positions. Among the earliest feminist publications was Betty Friedan's book *The Feminine Mystique* (W. W. Norton, 1963). Friedan later wrote *The Second Stage* (Summit Books, 1981), which was less antagonistic to men and more accepting of motherhood and traditional women's roles. In her latest book, *Life So Far* (Simon & Schuster, 2000), she presents her memoirs, which largely cover the women's movement that she helped start. Important statements by other past feminist leaders are Gloria Steinem, *Outrageous Acts and Everyday Rebellions*, 2nd ed. (Henry Holt, 1995) and "Revving Up for the Next 25 Years," *Ms.* (September/October, 1997); Patricia Ireland, *What Women Want* (Penguin, 1996); and Susan Brownmiller, *In Our Time: Memoir of a Revolution* (Dial Press, 1999). For recent appraisals of the effects of feminism, see Lynne P. Cook, *Gender-Class Equality in Political Economies* (Routledge, 2011); Cecilia L. Ridgeway, *Framed by Gender: How Gender Inequality Persists in the Modern World* (Oxford University Press, 2011); Sheryl J. Grana, *Women and Justice* (Rowman & Littlefield, 2010); Jeffery Klaehn, ed., *Roadblocks to Equality: Women Challenging Boundaries* (Black Rose Books, 2009); Angela McRobbie, *The Aftermath of Feminism: Gender, Culture and Social Change* (Sage, 2009). Molly Dragiewicz provides an academic treatment of the backlash to feminism in *Equality with a Vengeance: Men's Rights Groups, Battered Women, and Antifeminist Backlash* (Northwestern University Press, 2011). For an attack on the attackers and misrepresenters of the women's movement, see Susan Faludi's *Backlash: The Undeclared War on American Women* (Crown Publishing, 1991). For histories of the women's movement, see Kathleen C. Berkeley, *The Women's Movement in America* (Greenwood Press, 1999); Dorothy Sue Cobble, *The Other Women's Movement: Workplace Justice and Social Rights in Modern America* (Princeton University Press, 2004); Barbara J. Love, ed., *Feminists Who Changed America, 1963–1975* (University of Illinois Press, 2006); and Judith M. Bennett, *History Matters: Patriarchy and the Challenge of Feminism* (University of Pennsylvania Press, 2006). For discussions of the current state of feminism, see Catherine Redfern, *Reclaiming the F Word: The New Feminist Movement* (Zed, 2010); Sylvia Walby, *The Future of Feminism* (Polity Press, 2011); Shelley Budgeon, *Third-Wave Feminism and the Politics of Gender in Late Modernity* (Palgrave, 2011); Ruth Abbey, *The Return of Feminist Liberalism* (McGill-Queen's University Press, 2011); Kristin Rowe-Finkbeiner, *The F-Word: Feminism in Jeopardy: Women, Politics, and the Future* (Seal Press, 2004); Judith Lorber, *Breaking the Bowls: Degendering and Feminist Change* (W. W. Norton, 2005); Maureen Dowd, *Are Men Necessary?* (G. P. Putnam's Sons, 2005); Phyllis Chesler, *The Death of Feminism: What's Next in the Struggle for Women's Freedom* (Palgrave Macmillan, 2005); Naomi Zack, *Inclusive Feminism: A Third Wave Theory of Women's Commonality* (Rowman & Littlefield, 2005); Stacy Gillis, Gillian Howie, and Rebbeca Munford, eds., *Third Wave Feminism* (Palgrave Macmillan, 2004). A superb analysis of the full range of gender issues is found in *Paradoxes of Gender* by Judith Lorber (Yale University Press, 1994). For radical feminist views, see Catharine A. MacKinnon's *Feminism Unmodified* (Harvard University Press, 1987); Marilyn French's *Beyond Power* (Summit Books, 1985); and Margaret Randall's *Gathering Rage: The Failure of Twentieth-Century Revolutions to Develop a Feminist Agenda* (Monthly Review Press, 1992). For a radical feminist analysis of the oppression of women, see Marilyn French, *The War Against Women* (Summit Books, 1992). For an insightful analysis of how ideology has been used by men to mute the rebellion of women against exploitative and subordinate relations, see Mary R. Jackman, *The Velvet Glove: Paternalism and Conflict in Gender, Class, and Race Relations* (University of California Press, 1994). A rich analysis of gender inequality and its social and psychological roots is provided by Sandra Lipsitz Bem in *The Lenses of Gender: Transforming the Debate on Sexual Inequality* (Yale University Press, 1994). For discussions of feminism around the world, see Myra Marx Ferree and Aili Marl Tripp, eds., *Global Feminism: Transnational Women's Activism, Organizing, and Human Rights* (New York University Press, 2006); Mary E. Hawkesworth, *Globalization and Feminist Activism* (Rowan & Littlefield, 2006); Valentine M. Moghadam, *Globalizing Women: Transnational Feminist Network* (Johns Hopkins University Press, 2005); Shamillah Wilson, Anasuya Sengupta, and Kristy Evans, eds., *Defending Our Dreams: Global Feminist Voices for a New Generation* (Zed Books, 2005); Peggy Antrobus, *The Global Women's Movement* (Zed, 2004); Trudie M. Eklund, *Sisters Around the World: The Global Struggle for Female Equality* (Hamilton Books, 2004). For a discussion of women's rights, see Catharine A. MacKinnon, *Are Women Human?* (Belknap Press, 2006), and *Women's Lives, Men's Laws* (Belknap Press); and Linda M. G. Zerilli, *Feminism and the Abyss of Freedom* (University of Chicago Press, 2005).

Antifeminist works are rarer. One antifeminist, Nicholas Davidson, charges that it is "extremely difficult to find a publisher for a work critical of feminism." See Davidson's *The Failure of Feminism* (Prometheus Books, 1988). Other antifeminist arguments may be found in Elizabeth Powers' "A Farewell to Feminism," *Commentary* (January 1997); Ellen R. Klein, *Feminism Under Fire* (Prometheus, 1996), and *Undressing Feminism: A Philosophical Exposé* (Paragon House, 2002); Ariel Levy, *Female Chauvinist Pigs: Women and the Rise of Raunch Culture* (Free Press, 2005); and Neil Boyd, *Big Sister: How Extreme Feminism Has Betrayed the Fight for Sexual Equality* (Greystone Press, 2004). Some, like Christine Hoff Sommers, in *Who Stole Feminism: How Women Have Betrayed Women* (Simon & Schuster, 1994), advocate equity (liberal) feminism while criticizing feminist extremists and sloppy research.

For a defense of men against the accusations of feminists, see Warren Farrell, *The Myth of Male Power* (Simon & Schuster, 1993), and David Thomas, *Not Guilty: The Case in Defense of Men* (William Morrow, 1993). For a profeminist male viewpoint, see Steven P. Schacht and Doris W. Ewing, *Feminism with Men: Bridging the Gender Gap* (Rowan & Littlefield, 2004).

ISSUE 9

Is the Gender Wage Gap Justified?

YES: J. R. Shackleton, from "Explaining the Overall Pay Gap" in *Should We Mind the Gap? Gender Pay Differentials and Public Policy* (Institute of Economic Affairs, 2008)

NO: Hilary M. Lips, from "The Gender Wage Gap: Debunking the Rationalizations" and "Blaming Women's Choices for the Gender Pay Gap," *Expert Advice for Working Women*, www.womensmedia.com (2009)

Learning Outcomes

After reading this issue, you should be able to:

- Explain why women earn less money than men, or at least know the main theories that explain these differences.
- Understand the various possible meanings of "equal pay" and understand the difficulties of legislating equal pay for comparable work.
- Understand the motives that underlie women's work/family choices.
- Have insights into the consequences for society of women's work/family choices.
- Debate the pros and cons of women's work/family choices.

ISSUE SUMMARY

YES: J. R. Shackleton, a professor of economics and dean of the Royal Docks Business School at the University of East London, argues that the gender wage gap is not largely due to discrimination. It is largely due to the differential value of male and female workers in the employment market. Employers want profits, so they pay differently for different skills, commitment, and performance, and women choose less profitable training and limit their commitment.

NO: Hilary M. Lips, professor and chair of psychology and director of the Center for Gender Studies at Radford University, documents the continuing gender gap in wages and blames it largely on discrimination based on stereotypes and prejudice.

According to the 2012 *Statistical Abstract*, the median income of full-time women workers was 71.8 percent of median income of full-time men workers. This is a troubling fact that needs to be explained. It calls into question the success of the feminist movement. It calls into question the effectiveness of the antidiscrimination laws and their enforcement. It may not be the result of discrimination but may indicate that women are choosing to limit their participation in the labor force to less demanding and less stressful jobs. It may be driven by the same forces that lead to the "opting out" phenomena debated in Issue 4. Another possibility is that the discrimination against women that still exists makes women want to reduce their participation in the labor force.

Most commentators approach this issue in agreement on several basic issues. First, discrimination is wrong. Equal pay for equal work has been a feminist demand from the beginning and very few would argue against this principle today. Second, both work and family are important to most adults. Third, most married persons experience tension between work and family. Fourth, the "traditional" family value system resulted in less tension between work and family than today's value system. Traditionally, the husband was the provider and the wife was the homemaker. Today, both tend to be providers and active parents. In spite of these agreements, commentators today provide very different judgments about the gender wage gap. The argument starts with the meaning of equal work. Feminists argue that it should include equal pay for comparable work, but many object to this standard. Many argue that the market should determine what different occupations should be paid. The Equal Pay Act states, "Employers may not pay unequal wages to men and women who perform jobs that require substantially equal skill, effort, and responsibility, and that are performed under similar working conditions within the same establishment." It therefore proposes the comparable work rule. It also states, "Pay differentials are permitted when they are based on seniority, merit, quantity or quality of production, or a factor other than sex." This provision provides the grounds for more definitional debates. Another issue is how willing should the employer be to facilitate various special considerations that wives might need to accommodate her family role such as a greater use of sick days or unavailability for out-of-town travel? So what is fair? This is a matter of values, not science.

One side argues that the wage gap is justified because it is the outcome of women's free choices to work at less demanding jobs. The other side argues that it is not justified because the wage gap largely results from discrimination, prejudice, and stereotypes. J. R. Shackleton presents the first view and Hilary L. Lips presents the second view.

YES

J. R. Shackleton

Explaining the Overall Pay Gap

In this chapter various possible explanations for the differences in male and female earnings are examined.

We should begin by asking what determines pay, in general terms, in a competitive market. In such a market we would not expect everybody to earn the same. In the short run, wages are determined simply by supply and demand. If there is a sudden increase in the demand for construction workers because a new underground line is being built, and a limited supply of those with the necessary skills, wages will rise. But in the longer term, more workers will be attracted into construction, perhaps from abroad, or workers in other occupations will retrain. Longer term, it is possible that big pay differentials can persist if people possess unique skills or talents in high demand. . . .

Compensating Differentials

Even where people are free to enter a well-paid field of employment, however, they may not choose to do so. Long ago Adam Smith, in his *Wealth of Nations,* spelled out several reasons why some workers consistently earn more than others. His reasoning forms the basis for the modern idea of "compensating differentials"—where jobs that are unattractive may have to be rewarded with higher pay if they are to attract sufficient workers.

One factor is what Smith called "the difficulty and expense" of learning a job. Some forms of employment require years of training, education, and work experience—generically classed as human capital. The acquisition of human capital typically involves some cost to the trainee in terms of time and forgone earnings, even if the direct costs are paid by the state or the employer, and the worker will expect to be compensated by higher pay. This is clearly relevant to discussion of the gender pay gap, because women are likely to differ from men in relation to their human capital.

Note, however, that the amount of extra pay required will vary, Smith argues, with the "agreeableness or disagreeableness" of the job. Apparently an academic job in a high-ranking research department at Oxford carries sufficient kudos to offset the higher salary obtainable in other universities. By contrast, a cook on a North Sea oil rig, for example, will normally be paid more than a similarly skilled cook working in a city. But whether a premium is paid, and its size, will depend on the tastes and preferences of individuals. If, over

From *Should We Mind the Gap? Gender Pay Differentials and Public Policy,* Institute of Economic Affairs, 2008, pp. 45–66. Copyright © 2008 by Institute of Economic Affairs. Reprinted by permission.

time, Oxford becomes overcrowded and less attractive as a city, the university will have to pay more to attract the best academics. If lots of cooks develop a taste for working at sea, their premium will diminish or disappear. This is pertinent to discussion of the pay gap, for women's preferences in relation to jobs may differ systematically from those of men, as we shall see.

It is rarely discussed in the debate over the pay gap, but part of the explanation for men's higher average pay could well be that there is a compensating differential for less attractive working conditions. Men are more likely to work outside in all weathers. They are more likely to work unsocial hours. Thirty-six percent of male managers work more than 48 hours a week; the figure for women managers is only 18 percent. Men suffer much higher rates of industrial injury.

Looking at the economy as a whole, we see that women's jobs are less at risk: in the three months from November 2007 to January 2008, there were 3.4 redundancies per thousand female employees; the figure for men was 5.3. Women are more likely to get employer-provided training: 13.6 percent of females had received job-related training in the last four weeks in the third quarter of 2007, as against 11.3 percent of males. They have a shorter commuting time to work and take more time off work. No wonder, perhaps, that they report greater job satisfaction than men.

The implication of this is that the "true" gender pay gap may be less than the measured one, as male pay may include an element of compensation for less attractive working conditions. This is ignored in many empirical studies, and it is a serious omission.

Discrimination

Discrimination is often seen as an important explanation of the gender pay gap. The concept needs some clarification before we assess this belief.

Discrimination is a word that has changed its common meaning. Whereas once it was seen as something worthy of praise—as in somebody displaying "a fine discrimination" between paintings or pieces of music—it now usually means something unfair, unacceptable, and, in an increasing number of cases, illegal.

Economic analysis of the subject effectively began with the work of Gary Becker in the 1950s. In Becker's analysis, employers, fellow employees, and governments may engage in discrimination, which he interprets as an economically unjustified preference for one group over another, such that members of the favoured group would be more likely to be given a job, to be paid more, or otherwise treated better than another group or groups. Becker's particular insight was that this preference, this "taste for discrimination," could be seen as an end in itself, something that therefore entailed a "cost" to the discriminator. For example, employers might prefer to hire male rather than female workers even if this were more expensive. In this respect Becker differed fundamentally from Marxists and other critics of capitalism who saw discrimination as a means of exploiting subordinate groups to the benefit of the discriminator.

If this taste for discrimination exists, it *may* be manifested in the existence of a pay gap. This is not necessarily the case, however. If rigorous laws prevent women being paid less than men, discriminating firms may simply hire fewer women, but they will be paid the same as men. So Becker's analysis supports the point made earlier in relation to Italy and Spain: the size of the pay gap in itself does not say very much about the extent of discrimination.

From Becker's analysis, originally applied to racial differences, it followed that discriminating firms would hire white workers, or pay them a higher wage, rather than black workers of identical or superior productivity characteristics. But, he reasoned, this behaviour would raise costs. If other employers who were "colour-blind" entered the market, they would be able to undercut the discriminators and gain a competitive edge.

From this, Becker argued that, in a competitive market where non-discriminators were free to enter, discrimination would be unlikely to persist for long. It could be found where firms had monopsony power;[1] it could also be found where trade unions exercised power to protect white workers against blacks, or, in our context, men against women. But Becker, as a Chicago economist, argued that market power to sustain discrimination is unlikely to persist for any extended period if free entry of firms is allowed and union power is limited. Therefore any sustained discriminatory power is to be attributed to government interference in the free market. Apartheid South Africa is an obvious example. And in the USA, the so-called "Jim Crow" laws in the South sustained labour market discrimination for many years: when they were abolished there was a big increase in the relative pay of black workers—the reduction in the white/black pay gap since then has been relatively modest.

In our current context, it should be remembered that government discrimination against women was often quite explicit in the UK until the mid-twentieth century, with different pay rates for men and women civil servants and teachers, requirements to resign on marriage, and prohibitions on working at all in certain jobs.

A quite different approach to the economics of discrimination was taken by Arrow and Phelps. In their view, employer discrimination was not the result of "tastes" or simple prejudice. Rather, it was a rational response to imperfect knowledge about the characteristics of individual job applicants. This led risk-averse employers to operate with stereotypes, which might be accurate or inaccurate, of common group characteristics. Suppose—and this is true, whatever its cause—that women on average take more time off work than men for sickness, employers might hold this against a female job applicant even if, unknown to the employer, she as an individual had a low sickness risk. Such "statistical discrimination" would be economically rational even if unfair to individuals in particular cases.

As in Becker's reasoning, however, free competition ought to reduce discrimination. Some firms might find it easier than others to acquire more information about individuals, or would be prepared to take a chance on them, because they faced different cost and demand conditions. Not all firms, therefore, will behave in the same way. Furthermore, individuals are not passive. They can signal more information about themselves and market themselves more effectively to potential employers. One way they could in principle do this is to offer to work for less pay during a trial period. In most developed countries, however, such trial arrangements are difficult if not impossible because of legislation on equal pay, minimum wages, and employment protection. Again, governments may be part of the problem.

Some support is given to the common Becker and Arrow/Phelps thesis that free competition tends to eliminate discrimination, while some forms of government intervention assist it, countries with greater economic competition, as measured by the Economic Freedom Index, display lower gender pay gaps. The OECD has recently reached similar conclusions, with the added insight that product market regulation may be an important factor, by protecting disproportionately male "insiders" from new entrants. It finds that "regulatory barriers to competition explain between 20% and 40% of the cross country/time series variation in the gender wage gap."

As overt discrimination is now illegal, direct evidence of its existence is hard to come by. Some studies have used "correspondence tests," where there is some limited evidence that matched job applications from females and males elicit more interview offers for males. Another example is that of "blind" musical auditions which suggest women do better if only their playing is heard. And careful documentation of practices in, for instance, construction indicates prejudice against female employees. But this sort of evidence is sparse.

Those seeking evidence of discrimination might also point to the large number of employment tribunal cases over sex discrimination and equal pay issues as evidence of the problem. It is certainly true that the number of such cases has risen recently: between 2004/05 and 2006/07, the number of sex discrimination cases accepted by tribunals rose from 11,726 to 28,153, while equal pay cases rose from 8,229 to a massive 44,013. There has been little detailed analysis of the growth of these cases, but it is known that there were special factors associated with changes in the law, and with the advent of "no-win, no-fee" lawyers. It is interesting, incidentally, that a disproportionate number of these cases are against public sector employers, although as we have seen, the gender pay gap is much smaller in the public sector. The majority of these claims were multiple claims brought against local authorities and the NHS, paradoxically as a result of the introduction of Job Evaluation Schemes aimed at closing the pay gap.

Looking at the private sector, though, it is clear that only a small proportion of equal pay and sex discrimination claims succeed. The Women and Work Commission examined all private sector equal pay claims from 2000 to 2004 and found that only 25 reached the decision stage, with applicants winning in only five cases.

Despite their growing numbers, tribunal cases are brought by only a tiny proportion of the workforce and cannot really do much to explain the aggregate phenomenon of the overall gender pay gap. They often concern procedural issues rather than more fundamental matters: in the case of sex discrimination tribunal claims, they are often about issues such as sexual harassment, bullying, and other offences rather than issues directly related to pay.

Econometric Analysis of the Pay Gap

Given the limited evidence of direct discrimination, in trying to analyse pay inequality researchers have increasingly concentrated on econometric work.[2] A substantial literature is concerned with separating out that part of the overall gender pay gap that can be accounted for by relevant economic characteristics and that residual part which could possibly be attributable to discrimination—defined as paying different amounts to men and women for identical skills and abilities, and usually seen as conscious or unconscious behaviour by misguided employers.

The large number of studies that have been made of pay gaps in many different countries vary considerably in methodology and conclusions, but there are some common threads. Most studies use a statistical technique first developed more or less simultaneously by Oaxaca and Blinder. This decomposes the gender pay gap into two parts. The first component is the difference in pay associated with differences in observable characteristics such as experience and education. The second is the "residual," which may partly result from discrimination.

The procedure involves first estimating a wage equation, which relates the logarithm of wages to years of education, work experience, and a range of other productivity-related characteristics that are available in the particular dataset the researcher is using. . . .

Variations in rates of return might reflect discrimination or the systematic undervaluing of the jobs of graduates in areas where women dominate. But there are some obvious structural factors at work. One is the sector in which different types of graduates are likely to work. Over a quarter of all women in higher education are studying nursing or education. The vast majority of graduates in these areas will work in the public sector: there are relatively few highly paid jobs in government employment.

Lifestyles, Preferences, Attitudes, Expectations

After allowing for these factors, is that part of the pay gap left unexplained attributable to discrimination, as many claim? Well, possibly, but in addition to [various] factors [such as amount of full-time experience; interruption in employment; education; years of part-time experience, etc.] there is also what econometricians call "unobservable heterogeneity." Here this means differences in attitudes, preferences, and expectations which can cause apparently similarly qualified and experienced individuals to behave very differently.

Catherine Hakim, a sociologist whose work on "preference theory" has created some controversy, claims that, in countries such as the UK, women now have a wide range of lifestyle options and that they can be classified into three relatively distinct groups by their preferences—those who are home-centred, those who are work-centred, and those who are "adaptive."

The first group, which she estimates to be approximately 20 percent of UK women, prioritise family life and children, and prefer not to work in the labour market (though they do so, they are not career-driven). Work-centred women, again about 20 percent, are likely to be childless, committed to their careers, and with a high level of investment in qualifications and training. The largest group, the "adaptives," around 60 percent of UK women, want to work, but they also want families. Their careers tend to be more erratic.

Hakim carried out a national survey which indicated that women's expressed preferences were good predictors of their employment status, whereas, perhaps surprisingly, their educational qualifications were not: some well-qualified women were in the "home-centred" camp. She argues that her preference theory "explains continuing sex differentials in labour market behaviour (workrates, labour turnover, the choice of job etc) and hence also in the pay gap." . . .

[Another study] includes information on the values that graduates attach to jobs and their career expectations. Men and women differ significantly with regard to these characteristics: men are more likely to state that career development and financial rewards are very important, and are much more likely to define themselves as very ambitious, while women emphasise job satisfaction, being valued by employers and doing a socially useful job. Two-thirds of women in this sample expect to take career breaks for family reasons; 40 percent of men expect their partners to do this, but only 12 percent expect to do it themselves.

When these attitudinal variables are added to the specification, the result is that 84 percent of the wage gap can now be explained. This suggests that many of the models that generate large "unexplained" wage gaps, and from which non-specialists frequently infer a significant element of employer discrimination, are simply misspecified. They just don't incorporate sufficient explanatory variables for a satisfactory analysis of the causes of the gender pay differential. . . .

So the conclusion we can draw from empirical analysis of the full-time pay gap is that a high proportion of this gap can be accounted for, given sufficient information on individual and job characteristics and the attitudes and expectations of employees. Males and females make different choices in the labour market, in terms of the trade-off between pay and other job characteristics, choice of education, choice of occupation, and attitudes to work. These strongly influence earnings. Employer attitudes and discrimination seem not to be nearly as important as politicians and lobbyists have suggested.

Summary

There is a sizeable gap between the average hourly earnings of UK men and women working full time: this is the gender pay gap. The gap has, however, declined over time and is expected to decline further given demographic trends and changes in women's qualifications. It could even go into reverse.

The view that the UK has a particularly large gender pay gap by international standards is misleading. The gap is anyway only one indicator of women's economic status. Its size is not necessarily related to other indicators of sex discrimination and it can increase or decrease for reasons that have nothing to do with employers' behaviour.

The pay gap may partly reflect compensating differentials: men's jobs may typically have disadvantages that are reflected in higher pay. Women report greater job satisfaction than men.

There is little evidence of direct discrimination by employers against women. Discrimination is often inferred from the unexplained residual in econometric analyses of the causes of the gender pay gap.

When attitudes and preferences, as well as objective characteristics such as work experience and qualifications, are brought into the picture, however, most of the pay gap can be explained without reference to discrimination.

Notes

1. Where a firm is the dominant employer in an area, it may be able to segment the job market and pay different rates to different groups of workers without being undercut by other firms. Such a situation could also arise if gender segregation occurred as a result of employee job choice.
2. Econometrics uses statistical methods to analyse and test relationships between economic variables.

Hilary M. Lips    NO

The Gender Wage Gap: Debunking the Rationalizations

Last year, a labor economist from the Economic Policy Institute made the widely-quoted estimate that the gender pay gap would be closed within 30 years. Other commentators state confidently that the gap does not reflect discrimination, but other factors, such as the high wages of a few white men, and gendered patterns of occupational and educational choice and work experience. The effect of such assertions is to make women feel complacent about the wage gap—and perhaps to feel that they can avoid its impact by making the right educational, occupational, and negotiation-related choices. Such complacency is unwarranted.

The Wage Gap Exists within Racial/Ethnic Groups

White men are not the only group that out-earns women, although the wage gap is largest between white men and white women. Within other groups, such as African Americans, Latinos, and Asian/Pacific Islanders, men earn more than women (Source: U.S. Census Bureau).

What Difference Does Education Make?

Higher levels of education increase women's earnings, just as they do for men. However, there is no evidence that the gender gap in wages closes at higher levels of education. If anything, the reverse is true: at the very highest levels of education, the gap is at its largest.

The Wage Gap Exists within Occupations

Some people think that if women move into male-dominated occupations in larger numbers, the wage gap will close. However, there appears to be a gender-related wage gap in virtually every occupational category. In researching this issue at the Center for Gender Studies, we found only four occupational categories for which comparison data were available in which women earned even a little more than men: special education teachers, order clerks, electrical and electronic engineers, and miscellaneous food preparation occupations (Source: Bureau of Labor Statistics).

The movement of women into higher paid occupations, whether male-dominated or not, may not have the impact of narrowing the earnings gap. Social psychologists have demonstrated repeatedly that occupations associated with women or requiring stereotypically feminine skills are rated as less prestigious and deserving of less pay than occupations associated with men and masculine skills. Thus, as more and more women enter an occupation, there may be a tendency to value (and reward) that occupation less and less.

Do Women Earn Less Because They Work Less?

Women are more likely than men to work part-time. However, most gender wage comparisons leave out part-time workers and focus only on full-time, year-round workers. A close look at the earnings of women and men who work 40 hours or more per week reveals that the wage gap may actually widen as the number of hours worked increases. Women working 41 to 44 hours per week earn 84.6% of what men working similar hours earn; women working more than 60 hours per week earn only 78.3% of what men in the same time category earn (Source: Bureau of Labor Statistics). Furthermore, women may work longer to receive the promotions that provide access to higher pay. For example, among school principals, women have an average of 3 years longer as teachers than men do (Source: National Center for Education Statistics). So it is hard to argue that women's lower earnings are simply a result of women putting in fewer hours per week, or even fewer years than men.

Is the Wage Gap Closing?

The U.S. Census Bureau has made available statistics on women's and men's earnings for several decades. By examining this time series of data, it is possible to get a feel for the changes and trends in earnings. One thing revealed by a simple visual examination of the series since 1960 is how closely the shapes of the two lines parallel each other. The dips and bumps in women's and men's earnings seem to move in tandem. Clearly, similar economic and social forces are at work in influencing the rise and fall of earnings for both sexes. Men's earnings do not stand still and wait for women's to catch up.

Another thing that is apparent is that there is some minor fluctuation in the size of the wage gap. For example, the gap widened in the 1960s, closed a little in the 1980s, and widened slightly in the late 1990s. Thus, depending on which chunk of years one examines, it may be possible to conclude that the gap is either widening or narrowing. The only way to get a clear picture of what is happening is to examine the whole series rather than a few years at a time.

The series of data points from 1960 onward provides a basis for a forecast of the future, although such forecasts are always estimates rather than hard certainties. When we used forecasting analyses to project the earnings of women and men into the future, to the year 2010, we found no evidence on which we could base a prediction for a closing (or widening) wage gap. The forecast was, in essence, for the two lines to remain parallel, although the 90% confidence intervals (the range within which we are 90% certain the actual future earnings will fall) do overlap a little.

A Question of Value

As women and men left their jobs this spring because they were called up for military duty, employers scrambled to make sure that these workers did not suffer losses of salary and benefits. In a number of cases, organizations made up the difference between their employees' military pay and their normal pay, held jobs open, and made sure that benefits continued during workers' absence. At the same time, the media made a hero out of a father who chose to ship out with his military unit rather than stay home with his infant son who was awaiting a heart transplant. The message about what we as a society consider important is clear:

- When something perceived as very important needs to be done outside of the workplace, employers feel obligated to provide support for their employees to go and do it.
- In the eyes of society, or at least many employers, family concerns and the care of children do not fall into the category of "very important"—certainly not as important as military duty.

Are these the values we want to live by? If women and men continue to accept the notion that the domestic and caretaking work traditionally classified as "women's work" is not important enough for employers to accommodate, the gender gap in wages will never close. A few individual women may be able to evade the gap by choosing to be childfree, being fortunate enough to have a supportive spouse, and carefully following a model of career advancement that was developed to fit men's needs. However, to make the wage gap disappear will require that we stop buying into the idea that the rules are gender-neutral and that men just follow them better than women do. One by one, employers must be convinced to re-examine assumptions that unwittingly place higher value on the type of work men do than on the type of work women do. The most important step in closing the wage gap is for all of us to give up the notion that, to be paid fairly, a woman must "make it in a man's world."

Blaming Women's Choices for the Gender Pay Gap

A 2006 article in the *New York Times* cited Labor Department statistics that, for college-educated women in middle adulthood, the gender pay gap had widened during the previous decade. The phenomenon was attributed partly to discrimination, but also to "women's own choices. The number of women staying home with young children has risen . . . especially among highly educated mothers, who might otherwise be earning high salaries."

A 2007 report from the American Association of University Women sounded the alarm about a continuing wage gap that is evident even in the first year after college graduation. The authors noted, however, that individual choices with respect to college major, occupation, and parenthood have a strong impact on the gap. Accepting the idea that much of the pay gap can be accounted for by such neutral factors as experience and training, they concluded that, in the first year after college graduation, about 5 percent of the pay gap is unexplained by such factors—and it is that 5 percent that represents the impact of discrimination.

The language attributing women's lower pay to their own lifestyle choices is seductive—in an era when women are widely believed to have overcome the most serious forms of discrimination and in a society in which we are fond of emphasizing individual responsibility for life outcomes. Indeed, it is possible to point to a variety of ways in which women's work lives differ from men's in ways that might justify gender differences in earnings. Women work in lower-paid occupations; on average they work fewer paid hours per week and fewer paid weeks per year than men do; their employment is more likely than men's to be discontinuous. As many economists with a predilection for the "human capital model" would argue, women as a group make lower investments in their working lives, so they logically reap fewer rewards.

At first blush, this argument sounds reasonable. However, a closer look reveals that the language of "choice" obscures larger social forces that maintain the wage gap and the very real constraints under which women labor. The impact of discrimination, far from being limited to the portion of the wage gap that cannot be accounted for by women's choices, is actually deeply embedded in and constrains these choices.

Do Women Choose Lower-Paid Occupations?

Women continue to be clustered in low-paid occupational categories: office and administrative support and various service jobs. While they now make up a majority of university students, they are concentrated in academic specialties that lead to lower paid occupations: education rather than engineering, for example. If women persist in choosing work that is poorly paid, shouldn't the responsibility for the wage gap be laid squarely at their own doorstep?

Actually, within groups graduating with particular academic majors, women earn less than men, as illustrated in the AAUW report cited above. And within occupational categories, women earn less than their male counterparts, as revealed in this chart.

Furthermore, there is a catch-22 embedded in women's occupational choices: the migration of women into an occupation is associated with a lowering of its status and salary, and defining an occupation as requiring stereotypically masculine skills is associated with higher prestige, salary, and discrimination in favor of male job applicants. So convincing women in large numbers to shift their occupational choices is unlikely to obliterate the earnings gap.

As well, using the language of choice to refer to women's career outcomes tacitly ignores the many subtle constraints on such decisions. From childhood

U.S. Women's Earnings as a Percent of Men's*
within Occupational Categories: 2005[1]

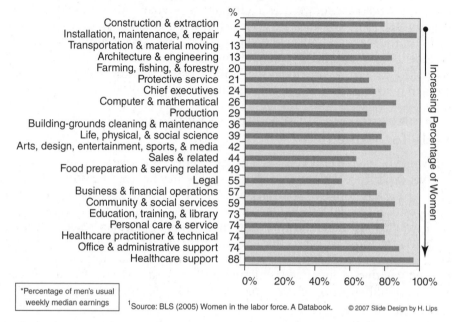

	%
Construction & extraction	2
Installation, maintenance, & repair	4
Transportation & material moving	13
Architecture & engineering	13
Farming, fishing, & forestry	20
Protective service	21
Chief executives	24
Computer & mathematical	26
Production	29
Building-grounds cleaning & maintenance	36
Life, physical, & social science	39
Arts, design, entertainment, sports, & media	42
Sales & related	44
Food preparation & serving related	49
Legal	55
Business & financial operations	57
Community & social services	59
Education, training, & library	73
Personal care & service	74
Healthcare practitioner & technical	74
Office & administrative support	74
Healthcare support	88

0%   20%   40%   60%   80%   100%

Increasing Percentage of Women

*Percentage of men's usual weekly median earnings

[1]Source: BLS (2005) Women in the labor force. A Databook.   © 2007 Slide Design by H. Lips

onward, we view media that consistently portray men more often than women in professional occupations and in masculine-stereotyped jobs. Not surprisingly, researchers find that the more TV children watch, the more accepting they are of occupational gender stereotypes. Why does the acceptance of gender stereotypes matter? Gender-stereotyped messages about particular skills (e.g., "males are generally better at this than females") lower women's beliefs in their competence—even when they perform at exactly the same level as their male counterparts. In such situations, women's lower confidence in their abilities translates into a reluctance to pursue career paths that require such abilities.

So, there are many problems with treating women's occupational choices as based purely on individual temperament and as occurring within a static occupational system that is unaffected by such choices. Women's employment choices are systematically channeled and constrained—and when women elude the constraints and flow into previously male-dominated jobs, the system apparently adapts to keep those jobs low-paid.

If Women Chose to Work More Hours, Would They Close the Gap?

Women work fewer paid hours per week than men do, but among workers who labor more than 40 hours per week, women earn less than men. Indeed, among workers working 60 hours or more per week at their primary job, women earned only 82% of men's median weekly earnings in 2006. Furthermore, women do not necessarily choose to work fewer hours than men do.

One researcher found that 58% of workers want to change their work hours in some way—and that 19% of women report they want the opportunity to work more hours. Also, women have recently brought lawsuits against corporations such as Boeing and CBS claiming discrimination in access to overtime. Thus, in the realm of hours worked for pay, it is probably a mistake to use the number of hours worked as a simple indicator of women's (or men's) choices. As in the case of occupational segregation by gender, the number of hours worked reflects some systematic constraints.

Choosing Parenthood Means Lower Wages Only for Women

For women, having children has a negative effect on wages, even when labor market experience is taken into account. This may be due to mothers' temporary separation from the workforce and/or the loss of the benefits of seniority and position-specific training, experience, and contacts. Among married persons working full-time, the ratio of women's to men's median weekly earnings is 76.4% for those with no children under the age of 18, but only 73.6% for those with children. And when women and men of all marital statuses are considered together, women with children under 18 earn 97.1% of what women without children earn, whereas men with children under 18 earn 122% of what men without children earn.

So, the choice to have children is associated with very different earnings-related outcomes for women and men. In terms of children, it is not that women and men are making different choices, but that the same choices have very different consequences for the two groups. Those consequences reflect society's failure to value the work of parenting. Yet, if most women decided to forego motherhood, the declining birthrate already causing concern in some parts of the developed world would soon become catastrophic.

Women's Choices Are Not the Problem

Individual women can sometimes evade the effects of the gender pay gap by making certain kinds of choices, such as selecting male-dominated occupations, working more hours, avoiding parenthood. However, these choices occur in an environment suffused with subtle sexism and discrimination: there are more barriers for women than for men to making certain choices, and the consequences of some choices are starkly different for women and men.

Moreover, these individual solutions are not effective on a societal level; they work only if the women enacting them remain in a minority. For example, if most women moved into jobs that are now male-dominated, signs are that the salaries associated with those jobs would likely drop. But, by making it difficult to go against the tide, the forces of discrimination ensure that most women don't move into such jobs. And as long as a few women get past the barriers, the illusion persists that any woman could do it if she wanted to—it's a matter of free choice. However, women's choices will not be free until their abilities and their work are valued equally with men's, and until women and men reap equivalent consequences for their choices in the realm of work and family.

EXPLORING THE ISSUE

Is the Gender Wage Gap Justified?

Critical Thinking and Reflection

1. How can any inequality be justified? Does the gender wage gap fit under one of these justifications of inequality?
2. Why are current values about gender roles better than traditional values which were more patriarchial?
3. Are values entirely relative or are there logical standards that can justify some values and actions and condemn other values and actions. God can make some values absolute but can secular reasoning also make some values superior to others?
4. What obligations do women have? What obligations do men have? Why do women have more obligations to childrearing and housework than men? Do men have more obligations to work outside the home than women, and if so, why?
5. What work/family arrangements best serve the general good (good of society)?

Is There Common Ground?

Equality is a commonly held value in America. Very few would argue against different groups getting equal pay for equal work. That agreement breaks down when the equality formula is equal pay for comparable work. Many think that "comparable" is used politically and often is unfair. There is also general agreement that disadvantaged people should be given some assistance such as Head Start to make their competition with advantaged people more fair. There is vehement disagreement, however, over how much assistance is fair. The assistance principle is the basis for affirmative action programs that had more support in the past because many whites now claim that affirmative action has gone too far and are putting whites at too great a disadvantage. This may be true in specific cases but on the whole, I as a white would not want to trade all the advantages whites currently have for the supposed advantages that blacks have.

Another area of agreement in America is that women are on a par with men as having moral value. In some societies, women are the property of their husband or father and have very few rights. Here they have rights and supposedly equal value. Nevertheless, in the 1950s, they did not have equal rights in the workplace and few paid attention. As women went to college in large numbers and young people spoke out against the war, traditions, authorities, and injustices in the 1960s, a new women's movement developed that changed the political landscape. Equal treatment in the workplace became a hot issue with no strong moral arguments against it. The progress of women has been impressive except for the "glass ceiling" that limited women's promotions at the highest levels. Now this is part of the present debate about the justice or injustice of the gender wage gap.

Additional Resources

Gender discrimination has been greatly reduced in the last several decades, but it still remains. Several works that research this problem include Barbara A. Gutek and M. S. Stockdale, "Sex Discrimination in Employment," in F. Landy, ed., *Employment Discrimination Litigation: Behavioral, Quantitative, and Legal Perspectives* (Jossey-Bass, 2005); Cecilia L. Ridgeway, *Framed by Gender: How Gender Inequality Persists in the Modern World* (Oxford University Press, 2011); Robert L. Kaufman, *Race, Gender, and the Labor Market: Inequalities at Work* (Lynne Rienner Publishers, 2010); Louise Marie Roth, *Selling Women Short: Gender Inequality on Wall Street* (Princeton University Press, 2006); and Lis W. Wiehl, *The 51% Minority: How Women Still Are Not Equal and What You Can Do about It* (Ballantine Books, 2007). Robert L. Nelson focuses on the legal aspects of this issue in *Legalizing Gender Inequality: Courts, Markets, and Unequal Pay for Women in America* (Cambridge University Press, 1999). Two books look at a number of issues in addition to pay inequality: International Labor Office, *Gender Equality and Decent Work: Good Practices at the Workplace* (Brookings Institution Press, 2005), and Jeanette N. Cleveland, Kevin R. Murphy, and Margaret Stockdale, eds., *Women and Men in Organizations: Sex and Gender Issues at Work* (Lawrence Erlbaum Associates, 2001). Two works that focus on gender inequality at the manager level are Kjell Erik Lommerud and Steinar Vagstad, *Mommy Tracks and Public Policy: On Self-Fulfilling Prophecies and Gender Gaps in Promotion* (Centre for Economic Policy Research, 2000), and Linda Wirth, *Breaking Through the Glass Ceiling: Women in Management* (International Labour Organization, 2001). Works that examine theoretical and historical aspects of the gender pay gap include Sonya O. Rose, *What Is Gender History?* (Polity, 2010), and Joan Huber, *On the Origins of Gender Inequality* (Paradigm Publishers, 2007).

Internet References . . .

Economic Report of the President

The Economic Report of the President website includes current and anticipated trends in the United States and annual numerical goals concerning topics such as employment, production, real income, and federal budget outlays. The database notes employment objectives for significant groups of the labor force, annual numeric goals, and a plan for carrying out program objectives.

www.gpoaccess.gov/eop/index.html

National Center for Policy Analysis

Through the National Center for Policy Analysis site you can read discussions that are of major interest in the study of American politics and government from a sociological perspective.

www.ncpa.org/

Speakout.com

The Speakout.com website contains a library of online information and links related to public policy issues, primarily those in the United States. The issues are organized into topics and subtopics for easy searching.

www.speakout.com/activism/issues/

Policy.com

Visit Policy.com, the site of the "policy community," to examine major issues related to social welfare, welfare reform, social work, and many other topics. The site includes substantial resources for researching issues online.

www.policy.com

Political Economy and Institutions

*W*hat is the proper role of government in the economy? Some believe that the government must correct for the many failures of the market, while others think that the government usually complicates the workings of the free market and reduces its effectiveness. The next debate concerns public policy: What is the impact of the end of the federal AFDC program? The fifth issue examines alternative educational policies for significantly improving public education. Finally, the last issue in this part looks at the use of biotechnology to alter and enhance humans.

- Is Government Dominated by Big Business?
- Does Capitalism Undermine Democracy?
- Should Government Intervene in a Capitalist Economy?
- Was the Welfare Reform the Right Approach to Poverty?
- Is No Child Left Behind Irretrievably Flawed?
- Should Biotechnology Be Used to Alter and Enhance Humans?

ISSUE 10

Is Government Dominated by Big Business?

YES: G. William Domhoff, from *Who Rules America? Power, Politics, and Social Change,* 5th ed. (McGraw-Hill, 2006)

NO: Sheldon Kamieniecki, from *Corporate America and Environmental Policy: How Often Does Business Get Its Way?* (Stanford Law and Politics 2006)

Learning Outcomes
After reading this issue, you should be able to: • Know which groups have been identified as the ones with the greatest influence over the U.S. government and the main evidence supporting the thesis of their inordinate influence. • Understand the tactics that are used to influence government policies and the administration of these policies. • Understand the concept of negative power and use it to explain how minority groups can stop policies that are perceived as likely to adversely affect them. • Identify the limits to the power of big corporations in influencing government policies. • Analyze the recent bank bailout and its aftermath on the one hand and the stimulus package to generate jobs on the other. Comment on the rebound of the stock market (although still fragile) and the continued high unemployment. • Analyze the consequences of the current structure of power in America.

ISSUE SUMMARY

YES: Political sociologist G. William Domhoff argues that the "owners and top-level managers in large income-producing properties are far and away the dominant power figures in the United States" and that they have inordinate influence in the federal government.

NO: Political scientist Sheldon Kamieniecki's research finds that business interests do not participate at a high rate in policy issues that affect them, "and when they do, they have mixed success in influencing policy outcomes." In fact, environmental and other groups often have considerable influence vis-à-vis business interests.

Since the framing of the U.S. Constitution in 1787, there have been periodic charges that America is unduly influenced by wealthy financial interests. Richard Henry Lee, a signer of the Declaration of Independence, spoke for many Anti-Federalists (those who opposed ratification of the Constitution) when he warned that the proposed charter shifted power away from the people and into the hands of the "aristocrats" and "moneyites."

Before the Civil War, Jacksonian Democrats denounced the eastern merchants and bankers who, they charged, were usurping the power of the people. After the Civil War, a number of radical parties and movements revived this theme of antielitism. The ferment—which was brought about by the rise of industrial monopolies, government corruption, and economic hardship for Western farmers—culminated in the founding of the People's Party at the beginning of the 1890s. The Populists, as they were more commonly called, wanted economic and political reforms aimed at transferring power away from the rich and back to "the plain people."

By the early 1900s, the People's Party had disintegrated, but many writers and activists have continued to echo the Populists' central thesis: that the U.S. democratic political system is in fact dominated by business elites. Yet the thesis has not gone unchallenged. During the 1950s and the early 1960s, many social scientists subscribed to the pluralist view of America.

Pluralists argue that because there are many influential elites in America, each group is limited to some extent by the others. There are some groups, like the business elites, that are more powerful than their opponents, but even the more powerful groups are denied their objectives at times. Labor groups are often opposed to business groups; conservative interests challenge liberal interests, and vice versa; and organized civil libertarians sometimes fight with groups that seek government-imposed bans on pornography or groups that demand tougher criminal laws. No single group, the pluralists argue, can dominate the political system.

Pluralists readily acknowledge that American government is not democratic in the full sense of the word; it is not driven by the majority. But neither, they insist, is it run by a conspiratorial "power elite." In the pluralist view, the closest description of the American form of government would be neither majority rule nor minority rule but minorities rule. (Note that in this context, "minorities" does not necessarily refer to race or ethnicity but to any organized group of people with something in common—including race, religion, or economic interests—not constituting a majority of the population.) Each organized minority enjoys some degree of power in the making of public policy. In extreme cases, when a minority feels threatened, its power may take a negative form: the power to derail policy. When the majority—or, more accurately, a coalition of other minorities—attempts to pass a measure that threatens the vital interests of an organized minority, that group may use its power to obstruct their efforts. (Often cited in this connection is the use of the Senate filibuster, which is the practice of using tactics during the legislative process that cause extreme delays or prevent action, thus enabling a group to "talk to death" a bill that threatens its vital interests.) But in the pluralist view, negative power is not the only driving force: When minorities work together and reach consensus on certain issues, they can institute new laws and policy initiatives that enjoy broad public support. Pluralism, although capable of producing temporary gridlock, ultimately leads to compromise, consensus, and moderation.

Critics of pluralism argue that pluralism is an idealized depiction of a political system that is in the grip of powerful elite groups. Critics fault pluralist theory for failing to recognize the extent to which big business dominates the policy-making process. In the selections that follow, G. William Domhoff supports this view, identifies the groups that compose the power elite, and details the way they control or support social, political, and knowledge-producing associations and organizations that advance their interests. Sheldon Kamieniecki, in opposition, argues that, thanks to new consumer, environmental, and other citizen groups, big business has a much more limited influence on Washington policymakers than Domhoff claims.

YES

G. William Domhoff

Who Rules America?
Power, Politics, and Social Change

Introduction

Using a wide range of systematic empirical findings, this book shows how the owners and top-level managers in large companies work together to maintain themselves as the core of the dominant power group. Their corporations, banks, and agribusinesses form a *corporate community* that shapes the federal government on the policy issues of interest to it, issues that have a major impact on the income, job security, and well-being of most other Americans. At the same time, there is competition within the corporate community for profit opportunities, which can lead to highly visible policy conflicts among rival corporate leaders that are sometimes fought out in Congress. Yet the corporate community is cohesive on the policy issues that affect its general welfare, which is often at stake when political challenges are made by organized workers, liberals, or strong environmentalists. The book therefore deals with another seeming paradox: How can a highly competitive group of corporate leaders cooperate enough to work their common will in the political and policy arenas?

Partly because the owners and high-level managers within the corporate community share great wealth and common economic interests, but also due to political opposition to their interests, they band together to develop their own social institutions—gated neighborhoods, private schools, exclusive social clubs, debutante balls, and secluded summer resorts. These social institutions create social cohesion and a sense of group belonging, a "we" feeling, and thereby mold wealthy people into a *social upper class*. In addition, the owners and managers supplement their small numbers by financing and directing a wide variety of nonprofit organizations—e.g., tax-free foundations, think tanks, and policy-discussion groups—to aid them in developing policy alternatives that serve their interests. The highest-ranking employees in these nonprofit organizations become part of a general leadership group for the corporate community and the upper class, called the *power elite*.

Corporate owners and their top executives enter into the electoral arena as the leaders of a *corporate-conservative coalition,* which they shape through large campaign contributions, the advocacy of policy options developed by their hired experts, and easy access to the mass media. They are aided by a

From *Who Rules America? Power, Politics, and Social Change* by G. William Domhoff (Mayfield, 2002), pp. xi–xv, 15–16, 161, 165, 173–175, 199–201. Copyright © 1998, 2002, 2006, 2010 by the McGraw-Hill Companies, Inc. Reprinted by permission.

wide variety of middle-class patriotic, antitax, and single-issue organizations that celebrate the status quo and warn against "big government." These opinion-shaping organizations are funded in good part by the corporate community, but they have some degree of independence due to direct-mail appeals and modest donations by a large number of middle-class conservatives. The corporate leaders play a large role in both of the major political parties at the presidential level and succeeded in electing a pro-corporate majority to Congress throughout the twentieth century. Historically, this majority in Congress consisted of Northern Republicans and Southern Democrats, but that arrangement changed gradually after the Voting Rights Act of 1965 made it possible for a coalition of African-Americans and white liberals to push the most conservative Southern Democrats into the Republican Party.

Since the last quarter of the twentieth century, the corporate-conservative coalition has been joined by the Christian Right, which consists of a wide range of middle-class religious groups concerned with a variety of social issues, including abortion, prayer in schools, teenage sexual behavior, homosexuality, gay marriage, and pornography. The alliance is sometimes an uneasy one because the corporate community and the Christian Right do not have quite the same priorities, yet they work together because of their common mistrust of government power.

The corporate community's ability to transform its economic power into policy influence and political access, along with its capacity to enter into a coalition with middle-class social and religious conservatives, makes it the most important influence in the federal government. Its key leaders are appointed to top positions in the executive branch and the policy recommendations of its experts are listened to carefully by its allies in Congress. This combination of economic power, policy expertise, and continuing political success makes the corporate owners and executives a *dominant class*, not in the sense of complete and absolute power, but in the sense that they have the power to shape the economic and political frameworks within which other groups and classes must operate. They therefore win far more often than they lose on the issues of concern to them.

Who Wins?

There are many issues over which the corporate-conservative and liberal-labor coalitions disagree, including taxation, unionization, business regulation, foreign trade, the outsourcing of jobs, and the funding of Social Security. Power can be inferred on the basis of these issue conflicts by determining who successfully initiates, modifies, or vetoes policy alternatives. This indicator, by focusing on relationships between the two rival coalitions, comes closest to approximating the process of power contained in the formal definition. It is the indicator preferred by most social scientists. For many reasons, however, it is also the most difficult to use in an accurate way. Aspects of a decision process may remain hidden, some informants may exaggerate or downplay their roles, and people's memories about who did what often become cloudy shortly after the event. Worse, the key concerns of the corporate community may never arise as issues for public discussion because it has the power to keep them off the agenda through a variety of means that are explained throughout later chapters.

Despite the difficulties in using the *Who wins?* indicator of power, it is possible to provide a theoretical framework for analyzing governmental decision-making that mitigates many of them. This framework encompasses the various means by which the corporate community attempts to influence both the government and the general population in a conscious and planned manner, thereby making it possible to assess its degree of success very directly. More specifically, there are four relatively distinct, but overlapping processes (discovered by means of membership network analysis) through which the corporate community controls the public agenda and then wins on most issues that appear on it. These four power networks, which are discussed in detail in later chapters, are as follows:

1. The *special-interest process* deals with the narrow and short-run policy concerns of wealthy families, specific corporations, and specific business sectors. It operates primarily through lobbyists, company lawyers, and trade associations, with a focus on congressional committees, departments of the executive branch, and regulatory agencies.
2. The *policy-planning process* formulates the general interests of the corporate community. It operates through a policy-planning network of foundations, think tanks, and policy-discussion groups, with a focus on the White House, relevant congressional committees, and the high-status newspapers and opinion magazines published in New York and Washington.
3. The *candidate-selection process* is concerned with the election of candidates who are sympathetic to the agenda put forth in the special-interest and policy-planning processes. It operates through large campaign donations and hired political consultants, with a focus on the presidential campaigns of both major political parties and the congressional campaigns of the Republican Party.
4. The *opinion-shaping process* attempts to influence public opinion and keep some issues off the public agenda. Often drawing on policy positions, rationales, and statements developed within the policy-planning process, it operates through the public relations departments of large corporations, general public relations firms, and many small opinion-shaping organizations, with a focus on middle-class voluntary organizations, educational institutions, and the mass media.

Taken together, the people and organizations that operate in these four networks constitute the political-action arm of the corporate community and upper class.

How the Power Elite Dominate Government

The power elite build on their structural economic power, their storehouse of policy expertise, and their success in the electoral arena to dominate the federal government on the issues about which they care. Lobbyists from corporations, law firms, and trade associations play a key role in shaping government on narrow issues of concern to specific corporations or business sectors, and the policy-planning network supplies new policy directions on major issues, along with top-level governmental appointees to implement those policies.

However, victories within government are far from automatic. As is the case in the competition for public opinion and electoral success, the power elite face opposition from a minority of elected officials and their supporters in labor unions and liberal advocacy groups. These liberal opponents are sometimes successful in blocking the social initiatives put forth by the Christian Right, but the corporate-conservative coalition itself seldom loses when it is united.

Appointees to Government

The first way to see how the power elite shapes the federal government is to look at the social and occupational backgrounds of the people who are appointed to manage the major departments of the executive branch, such as state, treasury, defense, and justice. If the power elite are as important as this book claims, they should come disproportionately from the upper class, the corporate community, and the policy-planning network.

There have been numerous studies of major governmental appointees under both Republican and Democratic administrations, usually focusing on the top appointees in the departments that are represented in the president's cabinet. These studies are unanimous in their conclusion that most top appointees in both Republican and Democratic administrations are corporate executives and corporate lawyers, and hence members of the power elite. Moreover, they are often part of the policy-planning network as well, supporting the claim that the network plays a central role in preparing members of the power elite for government service.

The Special-Interest Process

The special-interest process consists of the many and varied means by which specific corporations and business sectors gain the favors, tax breaks, regulatory rulings, and other governmental assistance they need to realize their narrow and short-run interests. The process is carried out by people with a wide range of experiences: former elected officials, experts who once served on congressional staffs or in regulatory agencies, employees of trade associations, corporate executives whose explicit function is government liaison, and an assortment of lawyers and public-relations specialists. The process is based on a great amount of personal contact, but its most important ingredients are the information and financial support that the lobbyists have to offer. Much of the time this information comes from grassroots pressure generated by the lobbyists to show that voting for a given measure will or will not hurt a particular politician.

Corporations spend far more money on lobbying than their officers give to PACs, by a margin of ten to one. In 2000, for example, the tobacco industry, facing lawsuits and regulatory threats, spent $44 million on lobbyists and

$17 million on the Tobacco Institute, an industry public relations arm, but gave only $8.4 million to political campaigns through PACs. More generally, a study of the top 20 defense contractors showed that they spent $400 million on lobbying between 1997 and 2003, but only $46 million on campaign contributions.

The trend toward increasingly large tax breaks continued from 2001 to 2003, with the effective tax rate on corporations declining from 21.7 percent during the last years of the Clinton Administration to 17.2 percent in 2003. Forty-six of 275 major companies studied for 2003 paid no federal income taxes, a considerable increase from a similar study in the late 1990s. A new tax bill in October 2004 added another $137 billion in tax breaks for manufacturing and energy companies, with General Electric, which spent $17 million in lobbying fees in 2003, once again the biggest beneficiary. At the same time, other legal loopholes have allowed multinational corporations to increase the sheltering of profits in foreign tax havens by tens of billions of dollars.

Special interests also work through Congress to try to hamstring regulatory agencies or reverse military purchasing decisions they do not like. When the Federal Communications Commission tried to issue licenses for over 1,000 low-power FM stations for schools and community groups, Congress blocked the initiative at the behest of big broadcasting companies, setting standards that will restrict new licenses to a small number of stations in the least populated parts of the country. When the Food and Drug Administration tried to regulate tobacco, Congress refused authorization in 2000 in deference to the tobacco industry. The FDA is now so lax with pharmaceutical companies that one-third of its scientific employees have less than full confidence that it tests new drugs adequately, and two-thirds expressed a lack of complete confidence in its monitoring of the safety of drugs once they are on the market.

The special-interest process often is used to create loopholes in legislation that is accepted by the corporate community in principle. "I spent the last seven years fighting the Clean Air Act," said a corporate lobbyist in charge of PAC donations, who then went on to explain why he gave money to elected officials even though they voted for the strengthening of the Clean Air Act in 1990:

> How a person votes on the final piece of legislation is not representative of what they have done. Somebody will do a lot of things during the process. How many guys voted against the Clean Air Act? But during the process some of them were very sympathetic to some of our concerns.

Translated, this means there are forty pages of exceptions, extensions, and other loopholes in the 1990 version of the act after a thirteen-year standoff between the Business Roundtable's Clean Air Working Group and the liberal-labor coalition's National Clean Air Coalition. For example, the steel industry has thirty years to bring twenty-six large coke ovens into compliance with the new standards. Once the bill passed, lobbyists went to work on the Environmental Protection Agency to win the most lax regulations possible for implementing the legislation. As of 1998, after twenty-eight years of argument and delay, the agency had been able to issue standards for less than ten of the many hazardous chemicals emitted into the air.

The Big Picture

This book began with two seeming paradoxes. How can the owners and managers of highly competitive corporations develop the policy unity to shape government policies? How can large corporations have such great power in a democratic country? The step-by-step argument and evidence presented in previous chapters provide the foundation for a theory that can explain these paradoxes—a *class-domination theory of power* in the United States.

Domination means that the commands of a group or class are carried out with relatively little resistance, which is possible because that group or class has been able to establish the rules and customs through which everyday life is conducted. Domination, in other words, is the institutionalized outcome of great distributive power. The upper class of owners and high-level executives, based in the corporate community, is a dominant class in terms of this defini- tion because the cumulative effect of its various distributive powers leads to a situation where its policies are generally accepted by most Americans. The routinized ways of acting in the United States follow from the rules and regu- lations needed by the corporate community to continue to grow and make profits.

The overall distributive power of the dominant class is first of all based in its structural economic power, which falls to it by virtue of its members being owners and high-level executives in corporations that sell goods and services for a profit in a market economy. The power to invest or not invest, and to hire and fire employees, leads to a political context where elected officials try to do as much as they can to create a favorable investment climate to avoid being voted out of office in the event of an economic downturn. This structural power is augmented by the ability to create new policies through a complex policy- planning network, which the upper class has been able to institutional- ize because common economic interests and social cohesion have given the corporate community enough unity to sustain such an endeavor over many decades.

But even these powers might not have been enough to generate a system of extreme class domination if the bargains and compromises embodied in the Constitution had not led unexpectedly to a two-party system in which one party was controlled by the Northern rich and the other by the Southern rich. This in turn created a personality-oriented candidate-selection process that is heavily dependent on large campaign donations—now and in the past as well. The system of party primaries is the one adaptation to this constrictive two-party system that has provided some openings for insurgent liberals and trade unionists.

Structural economic power and control of the two parties, along with the elaboration of an opinion-shaping network, results in a polity where there is little or no organized public opinion independent of the limits set by debates within the power elite itself. There is no organizational base from which to construct an alternative public opinion, and there have been until recently no openings within the political system that could carry an alternative message to government.

Finally, the fragmented and constrained system of government carefully crafted by the Founding Fathers led to a relatively small federal government that is easily entered and influenced by wealthy and well-organized private citizens, whether through Congress, the separate departments of the executive branch, or a myriad of regulatory agencies. The net result is that the owners and managers of large income-producing properties score very high on all three power indicators: who benefits, who governs, and who wins. They have a greater proportion of wealth and income than their counterparts in any other capitalist democracy, and through the power elite they are vastly overrepresented in key government positions and decision-making groups. They win far more often than they lose on those issues that make it to the government for legislative consideration, although their lack of unity in the face of worker militancy in the 1930s made it possible for organized workers to have far more independence, income, and power than they ever had in the past.

Many Americans feel a sense of empowerment because they have religious freedom, free speech, and a belief that they can strike it rich or rise in the system if they try hard enough. Those with educational credentials and/or secure employment experience a degree of dignity and respect because there is no tradition of public degradation for those of average or low incomes. Liberals and leftists can retain hope because in recent decades they have had success in helping to expand individual rights and freedom—for women, for people of color, and most recently for gays and lesbians. But individual rights and freedoms do not necessarily add up to distributive power. In the same time period, when individual rights and freedoms expanded, corporate power also became greater because unions were decimated and the liberal-labor coalition splintered. This analysis suggests there is class domination in spite of a widening of individual freedoms and an expansion of the right to vote.

Sheldon Kamieniecki  **NO**

Corporate America and Environmental Policy: How Often Does Business Get Its Way?

The findings reported in this study directly challenge prevailing assumptions both in- and outside the scholarly community about the regularity of business involvement in agenda building and policymaking as well as the ability of business to influence government decisions concerning pollution control and natural resource management. This outcome was unexpected. When I first began working on this book more than three years ago, I anticipated finding that American corporations are regularly involved in environmental agenda building and policymaking and that they exert a great deal of influence over government decision making. Like many, I accepted the conventional wisdom that business frequently opposes proposals that will improve environmental quality in order to protect its profits. After all, reports in the media nearly always place the blame for the defeat of environmental initiatives on the undue influence of business. As an environmentalist myself, I have been quite disappointed in the lack of progress the United States has made, especially recently, in the areas of pollution control and natural resource conservation. Most policy analysts attribute this lack of progress to the ability of corporate America to block or dilute critical federal legislation and to the inability of environmental groups to compete in the policymaking process. . . .

I was determined to . . . conduct a fair and balanced assessment of the role of business interests in environmental and natural resource policymaking.

As the data show, business interests do not participate in environmental policy debates at a high rate, and when they do, they have mixed success in influencing policy outcomes. These results generally hold when one examines agenda building in Congress, agency rulemaking, and, to some extent, the courts. Analyses of salient conflicts involving pollution control and natural resources also tend to bear this out. Business interests, instead, appear to select strategically the controversies in which they become involved and how much money they spend on lobbying activities of various kinds. A major conclusion of my work is that agenda building within the environmental policy domain is a highly complex process and cannot be explained by a single theory. This and other surprising related findings are the subject of this book. . . .

From *Corporate America and Environmental Policy,* by Sheldon Kamieniecki (Stanford Law and Politics, 2006), excerpts from Preface, Chapters 1 and 2, and Conclusion. Copyright © 2006 by the Board of Trustees of Leland Stanford Jr. University. Reprinted by permission of Stanford University Press. www.sup.org

The central question of the book is, how often does business get its way on environmental issues? Do corporations, given the immense wealth and resources they command, exert an unequal and unfair influence over American government whereby they are able to compel elected representatives and agency officials to reject or compromise substantially appropriate and necessary environmental rules and regulations? A related concern, often ignored in the interest group literature, is the frequency with which firms are able to prevent environmental and natural resource policy proposals from even reaching the government agenda. Although recent research suggests that firms do not possess the amount of influence necessary to shape or block public policymaking on a consistent basis more generally, few studies have critically analyzed their ability to affect agenda setting specifically within the environmental policy sphere. This investigation addresses this issue by empirically assessing the ability of companies to affect legislative, administrative, and judicial decision making and mold the government's environmental and natural resource policy agenda since the beginning of the environmental movement. . . .

In particular, the size and wealth of business lobbying organizations have grown dramatically since World War Two, prompting some observers to argue that they are now too powerful and are undermining democracy and threatening the well-being of society. The weakening of the political parties, the rising costs of media advertising and election campaigns, and the increasing contributions by Political Action Committees (PACs) to candidates and parties have led to calls for reform in the way American elections are financed. Business interests, among others, are key targets of critics who demand the enactment of meaningful campaign finance reform at the federal level. The campaign finance reform legislation enacted in 2002 bans "soft money," among other things, and is a significant attempt to level the playing field. Loopholes in the act exist, however, and it will be necessary to adopt additional regulations in the future in order to correct inequities in the financing of campaigns. Thus, despite Madison's assurances, the question of how we allow business and other interest groups to form and participate but control their influence remains a dilemma in modern times. . . .

Corporate America and Environmental Policy: Opposing Views

The influence of business over environmental policy is often used as an example of the substantial and unfair leverage certain interest groups have over government actions, especially when compared to the level of influence of average citizens. Many believe that the power business wields in American politics threatens democracy and, among other things, undermines the nation's efforts to control pollution and conserve natural resources. Environmentalists assert that "big business" has continuously been an impediment to the formulation and implementation of clean air and water quality standards. Ranchers and land developers, they argue, have successfully fought endangered species protection;

oil, coal, and natural gas companies have opposed strict energy-conservation measures and have lobbied against the adoption of renewable sources of energy; mining companies have thwarted the revision of mining laws and regulations; and chemical companies have fought legislation intended to control pesticides, promote the safe disposal of hazardous waste, and abate old, abandoned toxic waste sites. . . .

Many critics maintain that interest groups subvert democracy, in part by pressing Congress to pass too much "special-interest" legislation that benefits the few at the expense of the majority and in part by blocking legislative initiatives they oppose even when those measures are favored by, or would benefit, the broad public. In addition, critics contend that campaign contributions by interest groups undermine democratic government and degrade the American electoral system. In contrast, Berry rejects these arguments, saying that interest groups help to link citizens to government: "They empower people by organizing those citizens with similar interests and expressing those interests to policymakers. In this regard, the growth of citizen groups reflects an expansion of organizing around interests that have too often received too little attention in Washington." Berry carefully avoids saying that business interests are no longer a force in American politics, but he does argue that their influence has significantly declined. . . .

Interestingly, Berry's findings and conclusions are a throwback to some of the positions of the early pluralists, namely that interest group politics is equitable and fair. For this reason, Berry and his contemporaries, such as Baumgartner and Leech who also share this view, are referred to as *neopluralists* in this volume. Specifically, neopluralists argue that the increasing number and size of citizen groups has furthered democracy and the public good by involving a broad range of interests in policymaking and by substantially countering the influence of business in the political system. The neopluralists, like the early pluralists, point to the positive aspects of group pressures on politics and government. Scholars who believe that public opinion also provides a check on the power of business are considered neopluralists as well. The degree to which environmental groups and public opinion mitigate business influence in environmental policymaking is examined in the present study. . . .

The Business Advantage?

Mark Smith's provocative investigation explores the widely held assumption that business dominates the policymaking process when it is unified on specific policy issues, thereby undermining democracy. Using the policy positions of the U.S. Chamber of Commerce as a guide, he identifies 2,364 unifying issues that were considered by Congress between 1953 and 1996. His list of unifying issues encompasses a wide range of policy areas including employment policy, labor-management relations, and clean air regulation. Agenda building in Congress over time is his dependent variable. Among the independent variables he analyzes are "public mood," public attitudes toward corporations, partisan composition of Congress, "presidential leadership opening" (that is, when partisan turnover in Congress runs in the president's favor), corporate PAC funding, and the state of the economy. Mark Smith finds that

> unity does not increase the direct influence of business and reduce democratic control by the citizenry. Instead, unity coincides with the opposite results. Issues marked by a common business position are precisely those for which government decisions are affected most strongly by election outcomes and the responsiveness of officeholders to their constituents. Policies match the collective desires of business only when citizens, through their policy preferences and voting choices, embrace ideas and candidates supportive of what business wants. To bolster its odds of winning in politics, business needs to seek backing from the broad public.

According to Mark Smith, therefore, only when the public supports the unified positions of business on policy issues does business achieve its legislative goals. When the public opposes the positions of business, however, Congress tends to follow the public will even though business is unified. Since all unifying policy issues are highly ideological, partisan, and salient, Congress nearly always follows the public on these issues. He concludes by stating, "The long-standing debates over unity among pluralists, elite theorists, and ruling class theorists have focused our attention in the wrong place. Widespread scholarly concerns about business unity are misplaced, for unifying issues are marked by the highest, rather than the lowest, degree of democratic control by the citizenry." Smith's interpretation of his findings places him in the neopluralist camp along with Baumgartner and Leech and Berry. . . .

Baumgartner and Jones report significant changes in the environmental interest group sphere and show dramatic growth in the numbers of environmental groups and the resources available to them. Based on their analysis, the number of environmental organizations nearly tripled from 1960 to 1990, and the combined staff reported by those groups increased nearly ten times. This surge in environmental group membership is one of the most important reasons for the enactment of so many major environmental laws during the 1970s and 1980s, often over the protests of powerful business lobbyists. . . .

This book provided a comprehensive investigation of how much corporate America has influenced agenda building and environmental policymaking since 1970. The study began by charting the development of business interests since the founding of the nation and by raising important issues about democratic theory and the role of business in American politics. A review of the literature on interest groups addressed collective-action issues and the emergence of citizen groups in the agenda-setting process. Research by the neopluralists suggests that public opinion and citizen groups have tempered the influence of business interests in social policymaking. Based on their findings, one would expect this to be the case in environmental and natural resource policy. Theories addressing certain political and economic variables, issue definition, framing processes, and agenda building were introduced and applied in the analysis of the role of business in Congress, at the EPA and natural resource agencies, in federal court, and in environmental and natural resource disputes. . . .

Major Findings

This book reports a number of major findings. In sharp contrast to the conventional wisdom that business interests actively oppose environmental and natural resource protection on a continuous basis, the data presented [clearly shows that] corporations do not take a position on proposed legislation in Congress about four-fifths of the time. The widely held belief that business frequently opposes environmental regulation and natural resource conservation is also not true. Regardless of how companies align (that is, unified or particularized), they tend to support environmental legislation more often than not. . . .

The study also reports several important findings concerning the influence of business over federal agencies and the courts. As the data indicate, the number of public comments on proposed environmental and natural resource rules and which segments of the population participate in the rule-making process varies depending on the saliency and nature of the policy issue involved. As Golden discovers, a large percentage of those who submit comments are located outside Washington DC. The exceptionally large number of comments submitted by citizen groups on the natural resource rules examined in this research supports the position by the neopluralists that the dramatic rise in the number and size of such groups is effectively competing against the lobbying activities of business interests. Comments by corporations were generally hostile toward the EPA's efforts to promulgate new environmental regulations. Overall, public comments on proposed rules by EPA, the Forest Service, and the FWS have no or very little effect on the composition of final rules. Comments that contain new facts and information normally receive the closest attention by agency officials. Thus, as Golden finds, business does not exercise an undue influence over rulemaking involving environmental and natural resource issues. Instead, what kinds of rules are proposed to begin with is most important. This is determined by who occupies the White House and who the president appoints to senior positions in the environmental protection and natural resource agencies. . . .

The findings from the analyses of business influence in government institutions provide compelling reasons for investigating the influence of corporate interests within specific contexts involving disputes over environmental regulation and the use of natural resources. As this study indicated, in the end GE did not get its way in its fight to block the EPA's order that it clean up the PCBs it had dumped in the Hudson River. Likewise, the coal companies and utilities were unable to persuade Congress to exclude controls on sulfur dioxide emissions to reduce acid rain from the clean Air Act Amendments of 1990. In both cases, the scientific evidence concerning the negative impact of PCBs and SO_2 emissions on the environment and public health was overwhelming and undercut opposing political and economic forces in the debate over policy. Public concern was also high, prompting the FPA and Congress, respectively, to take action against the wishes of powerful economic interests.

The battle over controlling GHG emissions and climate change, however, presents a very different story. Extremely influential energy producers and consumers have teamed up to prevent the U.S. government from ratifying the Kyoto agreement and from taking a leadership role at the international level to address the climate change issue. The ratification of the Kyoto treaty by Russia represents a significant step forward to resolving the global climate change problem. Nonetheless, the global effort is considerably weakened without the participation of large CO_2 emitters such as the United States and Australia. It is unlikely that U.S. policy on climate change will reverse course during President Bush's second term.

In addition, the study explored the influence of business in three controversies concerning natural resource issues. Despite calls for reform, mining interests have successfully beaten back attempts to revise the General Mining Law of 1872. Sugarcane growers and development forces were able to thwart efforts to restore the Florida Everglades until scientists and environmentalists banded together and persuaded the federal government, particularly the U.S. Army Corps of Engineers and Congress, to take action. The state government, which has been continuously pressured from all sides, has waffled in its intentions to improve the wetlands ecosystem in South Florida. Environmentalists have been successful in attracting media attention, expanding the scope of conflict beyond the region and the state, and using the courts to protect the northern spotted owl and old-growth forests in the Pacific Northwest. The ESA continues to provide a strong pillar in the debate over logging old-growth trees on public lands. Revision of the ESA by the Republican-controlled White House and Congress in the coming years could place economic interests ahead of habitat protection and eventually spell the demise of the northern spotted owl and other endangered species across the country. . . .

Implications of the Study's Findings

This study's findings have a number of implications for the way analysts view the role of business in environmental and natural resource policymaking. At the aggregate level it is clear that business interests selectively choose which bills to oppose or support in Congress, and they do not, as environmentalists, media commentators, and some scholars assume, continuously and unrelentingly pressure legislators for favorable treatment. They are most likely to become active in critical and salient policy debates. Although their participation in the legislative process is far less than expected, the controversies in which they decide to become involved tend to be ones where there is much at stake for them *and* the environment. In this sense, the lobbying activities of business can have an enormous impact on the nation's effort to protect the environment and natural resources.

When business does choose to lobby Congress on environmental legislation, it more often supports rather than opposes such legislation. This result probably indicates that the views of business interests are often conveyed and considered during the initial writing of bills. The multiple indicators approach used by Mark Smith and employed in this research unfortunately does not include this somewhat hidden but critical facet of the agenda-building process in Congress. Of course, business interests will actively oppose legislation when their views are not reflected in legislative proposals and when there is much at stake. Such legislation is adopted when pressure from environmental groups and public opinion requires congressional representatives to take immediate action to address urgent pollution or natural resource problems. Congress is unable to always act according to the desires of the business community because of the existence of previous, and oftentimes landmark, law. In such cases corporations seldom get their way. . . .

Analysis of the six case studies, however, offers more support for the position of the neopluralists. Generally, when much is at stake, environmental groups tend to mobilize and provide an effective check on the influence of business interests. This is evident in the conflicts involving GE and the dumping of PCBs in the Hudson River, the promulgation of acid rain regulations, the restoration of the Everglades, and protection of the northern spotted owl and old-growth forests. Public opinion was a factor in all these controversies, though to varying degrees. Therefore, when conflicts are salient, environmental groups and public opinion tend to present an important, countervailing force to business interests. Mancur Olson would not have predicted this finding.

Finally, the overall results of the investigation have important implications for the influence of business in environmental and natural resource policymaking in particular, and democratic theory in general. Corporations strategically select which legislative debates to enter, and they take positions on environmental and natural resource legislation only a small percentage of the time. Furthermore, business interests do not exert an undue influence in the rulemaking process. Yet, they tend to win as many cases as they lose in the federal court of appeals. Overall, however, business does not get what it wants from government institutions a majority of the time, as some argue. This study's findings suggest that the influence of business in environmental and natural resource policymaking is modest at best.

The examination of the case studies presents a similar picture. Although business interests experienced early success in conflicts over the contamination of the Hudson River. SO_2 emissions, the pollution of the Everglades, and the logging of old-growth forests, they eventually were forced to bow to the demands of federal officials. This is not the situation, of course, in disputes over hardrock mining and climate change. In these instances, corporations have thus far been able to defeat efforts to reform the General Mining Act of 1872 and reduce GHG emissions. Based on the overall analysis of the environmental regulatory and the natural resource case studies, however, business interests do not often get their way. As this study shows, they tend to have a mixed rate of success in influencing the outcomes of salient policy controversies.

In addition to environmental groups and public opinion, other factors also mitigate the influence of business in agenda building and policymaking. Competing elites in the media and scientific community, for example, can point out differences between what corporations are claiming and the actual evidence. As this study revealed, the media played a central role in the controversy over the northern spotted owl and old-growth forests. What started out as a regional (Pacific Northwest) issue quickly expanded to the national level as a result of extensive media coverage of the plight of the owl and its habitat. The timber industry was thus forced to reduce logging on public land considerably. Likewise, scientists brought to light the negative impacts of PCB contamination of the Hudson River, SO_2 emissions on aquatic bodies and forests, and agricultural runoff in the Everglades. In each case business groups were forced to moderate significantly their stands. Federal district trial court judges, too, placed controls on pollution of the Everglades and logging in old-growth forests. This was only possible because of the existence of groundbreaking federal laws governing environmental and natural resource protection (for example, the Clean Water Act and the ESA). As James Madison suggested would generally happen in *Federalist Paper Number 10,* the environmental policy arena is characterized by a healthy balance between competing interests and stakeholders. The system of checks and balances between the three branches of government and the protection of individual rights allow business interests to pursue aggressively their aims but at the same time prevent them from completely destroying the environment and severely harming public health.

EXPLORING THE ISSUE

Is Government Dominated by Big Business?

Critical Thinking and Reflection

1. Give an example of corporations influencing the federal government to pass or repeal policies they favored or opposed.
2. Can you identify policies that were passed against the opposition of the corporate sector? Can you identify what made that action possible?
3. What regulations or other policies have been used to limit the power of corporations to control or influence the federal government? How effective have they been? What more could be done?
4. What do recent elections reveal about the influence of big business over the government? The Koch brothers' money has been a major support for the Tea Party. What is the difference between the political support by big business and the support by wealthy individuals?
5. How is political influence exercised?
6. Discuss and critique the theory of political power that underlies the "occupy" movement and the conflict between the 99 percent and the 1 percent.

Is There Common Ground?

No one denies that big business has a lot of power and can get their way in many areas including their influence over government. There is agreement that the political system is not a level playing field. The key issue in this debate is the extent of the influence of corporate power over the making and administering of government policies on issues that concern them. The dominant view is that neither the public nor mobilized noncorporate interests can effectively counterpose corporate interests. But EPA was created in 1970 to regulate business and other sources of pollution. NEPA was passed over the objections of business. Wall Street opposed the reforms recently imposed upon them. So everyone agrees that big business has too much power but does not have absolute power. Those are broad boundaries, so there is much room to debate how much power big business has over the federal government.

Additional Resources

Two political scientists who argue that big business dominates America in a lifetime of publications are G. William Domhoff and Thomas R. Dye. Domhoff's article in this debate contains selections from the fifth edition of his book *Who Rules America?* (McGraw-Hill, 2006). In an earlier book, *Changing the Powers That Be: How the Left Can Stop Losing and Win* (Rowman & Littlefield, 2003), he focused on how to fight this corporate power. Three of Dye's recent books are *Politics in America*, 7th ed. (Pearson Prentice Hall, 2007), *Who's Running America? The Bush Restoration* (Prentice Hall, 2003), and *Top Down Policymaking* (Chatham House, 2001). Other works supporting this view are Michael Parenti, *Democracy for the Few* (Thomson-Wadsworth, 2008); Melissa L. Rossi, *What Every American Should Know about Who's Really Running America* (Plume Books, 2007); Lou Dobbs, *War on the Middle Class: How Government, Big Business, and Special Interest Groups Are Waging War on the American Dream and How to Fight Back* (Viking, 2006); Charles Perrow, *Organizing America: Wealth, Power, and the Origins of Corporate America* (Princeton University Press, 2002); Peter Kobrak, *Cozy Politics: Political Parties, Campaign Finance, and Compromised Governance* (Lynne Rienner, 2002); Arianna Stassinopoulos Huffington, *Pigs at the Trough: How Corporate Greed and Political Corruption Are Undermining America* (Crown, 2003); Ted Nace, *Gangs of America: The Rise of Corporate Power and the Disabling of Democracy* (Berrett-Koehler, 2003); Dan Clawson et al., *Dollars and Votes: How Business Campaign Contributions Subvert Democracy* (Temple University Press, 1998); John B. Parrott, *Being Like God: How American Elites Abuse Politics and Power* (University Press of America, 2003); Russell Mokhiber and Robert Weissman, *On the Rampage: Corporate Predators and the Destruction of Democracy* (Common Courage Press, 2005); Paul Kivel, *You Call This Democracy? Who Benefits, Who Pays and Who Really Decides?* (Apex Press, 2004); and Charles Derber, *Hidden Power: What You Need to Know to Save Our Democracy* (Berrett-Koehler, 2005).

Several authors advance the thesis that American corporations also seek to some degree to rule the world, including David C. Korten, *When Corporations Rule the World*, 2nd ed. (Kumarian Press, 2001); and Peter Alexis Gourevich and James J. Shinn, *Political Power and Corporate Control: The New Global Politics of Corporate Governance* (Princeton University Press, 2005).

For some pluralist arguments, see Stephen E. Frantzich, *Citizen Democracy: Political Activists in a Cynical Age*, 3rd ed. (Rowman & Littlefield, 2008); Feliz Kolb, *Protest and Opportunities: The Political Outcomes of Social Movements* (Campus Verlag, 2007); Michael Rabinder James, *Deliberative Democracy and the Plural Polity* (University Press of Kansas, 2004); Kevin Danaher, *Insurrection: Citizen Challenges to Corporate Power* (Routledge, 2003); David S. Meyers et al., eds., *Routing the Opposition: Social Movements, Public Policy, and Democracy* (University of Minnesota Press, 2005); Jeffrey M. Berry, *The New Liberalism: The Rising Power of Citizen Groups* (Brookings Institution, 1999); and *Battling Big Business: Countering Greenwash, Infiltration, and Other Forms of Corporate Bullying* (Common Courage Press, 2002). Recently, the pluralist view is being reworked into political process theory; see Andrew S. McFarland, *Neopluralism: The Evolution of Political Process Theory* (University Press of Kansas, 2004).

ISSUE 11

Does Capitalism Undermine Democracy?

YES: **Robert B. Reich,** from "How Capitalism Is Killing Democracy," *Foreign Policy* (September/October 2007)

NO: **Anthony B. Kim,** from "Economic Freedom Underpins Human Rights and Democratic Governance," *Heritage Foundation Web Memo* (March 18, 2008)

Learning Outcomes

After reading this issue, you should be able to:

- Learn how scholars deal with extremely broad and complex phenomena such as "capitalism" and "democracy" and how the actors in these systems impact each other.
- Learn how scholars use historical cases to support very general hypotheses. Understand the resulting imprecision and thus the likelihood of disagreement over the interpretations of the results.
- Understand that a variable or factor can have one set of consequences in one period of time and another set of consequences in another period of time because many conditions have changed.
- Understand that the meaning of concepts can change over time. Democracy when most politics were local is different from democracy in massive federal regimes. Capitalism was small scale in the nineteenth century except for railroads and steel, but is very large scale today. The two forms of capitalism behave very differently.
- Discern differences between the interests of various sectors of corporate America and understand the processes that coordinate their political actions. (Direct collusion is illegal.)

ISSUE SUMMARY

YES: Robert B. Reich, professor of public policy at the University of California, Berkeley, and former U.S. Secretary of Labor, accuses capitalism of undermining democratic governments' ability to serve the public good and advance the general welfare. The political power of the corporations exceeds that of the people, so many nations with democratic elections do not function as democracies.

NO: Anthony B. Kim, a policy analyst at the Heritage Foundation's Center for International Trade and Economics, contends that economic progress through advancing economic freedom has allowed more people to discuss and adopt different views more candidly, ultimately leading societies to be more open, inclusive, and democratic.

Ｏne of the long-standing findings of the social sciences is the connection between economic development and democracy. Economic growth creates the need for skilled and professional workers and thus the expansion of education and the growth of the middle class. Over time the educated and the middle class pressure for rights and eventually the right to participate in the selection of leaders and to influence government policies. Economic growth over the long run also tends to create government support for freer markets and individual and organizational initiatives, which can eventually increase opposition to despots. Indirectly, therefore, economic growth is a major cause of democracy.

But is this how economic growth impacts modern developed nations today? Economic growth also has produced powerful multinational corporations with concentrated economic power, and these powerful corporations are a threat to democracy. Corporations finance politicians' campaigns, lobby Congress, arrange to participate in the writing of legislation, and use their resources in many legal and even illegal ways to influence government to serve their interests or to oppose actions that would hurt their interests. The social sciences are united in this view of the alignment of power in America and many other nations. There is a debate, however, about whether this situation is a case of corporate control or only corporate influence. The latter allows other interests, including the public good, to also have influence over the government and thus make it more democratic, that is, rule by the people. The thesis of corporate control versus corporate influence is debated in Issue 10. Issue 11 examines whether capitalism, the driver of economic growth, is good or bad for democracy.

According to Reich, "Conventional wisdom holds that where either capitalism or democracy flourishes, the other must soon follow. Yet today, their fortunes are beginning to diverge." His thesis, as stated in his title, is that capitalism is killing democracy. It is undermining "the government's capacity to respond to citizens' concerns." His article was written before the current recession, which has revealed the chasm between the interests of the corporations and the people. Hundreds of billions of dollars have been spent by the federal government to bail out corporations. This helps to save some jobs, free up credit, minimize the losses suffered by pensions, and turn around the recession. Thus, individuals have been helped, but little has been spent directly for individuals except "cash for clunkers." The American public sees the American government as serving corporations first and individuals last. Anthony B. Kim is a salesman for capitalism. After all, he works for the American Enterprise Institute. But he backs up his argument that free enterprise spawns and strengthens democracy with solid data.

YES

Robert B. Reich

How Capitalism Is Killing Democracy

It was supposed to be a match made in heaven. Capitalism and democracy, we've long been told, are the twin ideological pillars capable of bringing unprecedented prosperity and freedom to the world. In recent decades, the duo has shared a common ascent. By almost any measure, global capitalism is triumphant. Most nations around the world are today part of a single, integrated, and turbocharged global market. Democracy has enjoyed a similar renaissance. Three decades ago, a third of the world's nations held free elections; today, nearly two thirds do.

Conventional wisdom holds that where either capitalism or democracy flourishes, the other must soon follow. Yet today, their fortunes are beginning to diverge. Capitalism, long sold as the yin to democracy's yang, is thriving, while democracy is struggling to keep up. China, poised to become the world's third largest capitalist nation this year after the United States and Japan, has embraced market freedom, but not political freedom. Many economically successful nations—from Russia to Mexico—are democracies in name only. They are encumbered by the same problems that have hobbled American democracy in recent years, allowing corporations and elites buoyed by run-away economic success to undermine the government's capacity to respond to citizens' concerns.

Of course, democracy means much more than the process of free and fair elections. It is a system for accomplishing what can only be achieved by citizens joining together to further the common good. But though free markets have brought unprecedented prosperity to many, they have been accompanied by widening inequalities of income and wealth, heightened job insecurity, and environmental hazards such as global warming. Democracy is designed to allow citizens to address these very issues in constructive ways. And yet a sense of political powerlessness is on the rise among citizens in Europe, Japan, and the United States, even as consumers and investors feel more empowered. In short, no democratic nation is effectively coping with capitalism's negative side effects.

This fact is not, however, a failing of capitalism. As these two forces have spread around the world, we have blurred their responsibilities, to the detriment of our democratic duties. Capitalism's role is to increase the economic pie, nothing more. And while capitalism has become remarkably responsive

Reprinted in entirety by McGraw-Hill with permission from *Foreign Policy*, September/October 2007, pp. 38–42. www.foreignpolicy.com. Copyright © 2007 Washingtonpost.Newsweek Interactive, LLC.

to what people want as individual consumers, democracies have struggled to perform their own basic functions: to articulate and act upon the common good, and to help societies achieve both growth and equity. Democracy, at its best, enables citizens to debate collectively how the slices of the pie should be divided and to determine which rules apply to private goods and which to public goods. Today, those tasks are increasingly being left to the market. What is desperately needed is a clear delineation of the boundary between global capitalism and democracy—between the economic game, on the one hand, and how its rules are set, on the other. If the purpose of capitalism is to allow corporations to play the market as aggressively as possible, the challenge for citizens is to stop these economic entities from being the authors of the rules by which we live.

The Cost of Doing Business

Most people are of two minds: As consumers and investors, we want the bargains and high returns that the global economy provides. As citizens, we don't like many of the social consequences that flow from these transactions. We like to blame corporations for the ills that follow, but in truth we've made this compact with ourselves. After all, we know the roots of the great economic deals we're getting. They come from workers forced to settle for lower wages and benefits. They come from companies that shed their loyalties to communities and morph into global supply chains. They come from CEOs who take home exorbitant paychecks. And they come from industries that often wreak havoc on the environment.

Unfortunately, in the United States, the debate about economic change tends to occur between two extremist camps: those who want the market to rule unimpeded, and those who want to protect jobs and preserve communities as they are. Instead of finding ways to soften the blows of globalization, compensate the losers, or slow the pace of change, we go to battle. Consumers and investors nearly always win the day, but citizens lash out occasionally in symbolic fashion, by attempting to block a new trade agreement or protesting the sale of U.S. companies to foreign firms. It is a sign of the inner conflict Americans feel—between the consumer in us and the citizen in us—that the reactions are often so schizophrenic.

Such conflicting sentiments are hardly limited to the United States. The recent wave of corporate restructurings in Europe has shaken the continent's typical commitment to job security and social welfare. It's leaving Europeans at odds as to whether they prefer the private benefits of global capitalism in the face of increasing social costs at home and abroad. Take, for instance, the auto industry. In 2001, DaimlerChrysler faced mounting financial losses as European car buyers abandoned the company in favor of cheaper competitors. So, CEO Dieter Zetsche cut 26,000 jobs from his global workforce and closed six factories. Even profitable companies are feeling the pressure to become ever more efficient. In 2005, Deutsche Bank simultaneously announced an 87 percent increase in net profits and a plan to cut 6,400 jobs, nearly half of them in Germany and Britain. Twelve-hundred of the jobs were then moved to low-wage nations. Today, European consumers and investors are doing better than ever, but job insecurity and inequality are rising, even in social democracies that were established to counter the injustices of the market. In the face of such change, Europe's democracies have shown themselves to be so paralyzed that the only way citizens routinely express opposition is through massive boycotts and strikes.

In Japan, many companies have abandoned lifetime employment, cut workforces, and closed down unprofitable lines. Just months after Howard Stringer was named Sony's first non-Japanese CEO, he announced the company would trim 10,000 employees, about 7 percent of its workforce. Surely some Japanese consumers and investors benefit from such corporate downsizing: By 2006, the Japanese stock market had reached a 14-year high. But many Japanese workers have been left behind. A nation that once prided itself on being an "all middle-class society" is beginning to show sharp disparities in income and wealth. Between 1999 and 2005, the share of Japanese households without savings doubled, from 12 percent to 24 percent. And citizens there routinely express a sense of powerlessness. Like many free countries around the world, Japan is embracing global capitalism with a democracy too enfeebled to face the free market's many social penalties.

On the other end of the political spectrum sits China, which is surging toward capitalism without democracy at all. That's good news for people who invest in China, but the social consequences for the country's citizens are mounting. Income inequality has widened enormously. China's new business elites live in McMansions inside gated suburban communities and send their children to study overseas. At the same time, China's cities are bursting with peasants from the countryside who have sunk into urban poverty and unemployment. And those who are affected most have little political recourse to change the situation, beyond riots that are routinely put down by force.

But citizens living in democratic nations aren't similarly constrained. They have the ability to alter the rules of the game so that the cost to society need not be so great. And yet, we've increasingly left those responsibilities to the private sector—to the companies themselves and their squadrons of lobbyists and public-relations experts—pretending as if some inherent morality or corporate good citizenship will compel them to look out for the greater good. But they have no responsibility to address inequality or protect the environment on their own. We forget that they are simply duty bound to protect the bottom line.

The Rules of the Game

Why has capitalism succeeded while democracy has steadily weakened? Democracy has become enfeebled largely because companies, in intensifying competition for global consumers and investors, have invested ever greater sums in lobbying, public relations, and even bribes and kickbacks, seeking laws that give them a competitive advantage over their rivals. The result is an arms race for political influence that is drowning out the voices of average citizens. In the United States, for example, the fights that preoccupy Congress, those that consume weeks or months of congressional staff time, are typically contests between competing companies or industries.

While corporations are increasingly writing their own rules, they are also being entrusted with a kind of social responsibility or morality. Politicians praise companies for acting "responsibly" or condemn them for not doing so. Yet the purpose of capitalism is to get great deals for consumers and investors. Corporate executives are not authorized by anyone—least of all by their investors—to balance profits against the public good. Nor do they have any expertise in making such moral calculations. Democracy is supposed to represent the public in drawing such lines. And the message that companies are moral beings with social responsibilities diverts public attention from the task of establishing such laws and rules in the first place.

It is much the same with what passes for corporate charity. Under today's intensely competitive form of global capitalism, companies donate money to good causes only to the extent the donation has public-relations value, thereby boosting the bottom line. But shareholders do not invest in firms expecting the money to be used for charitable purposes. They invest to earn high returns. Shareholders who wish to be charitable would, presumably, make donations to charities of their own choosing in amounts they decide for themselves. The larger danger is that these conspicuous displays of corporate beneficence hoodwink the public into believing corporations have charitable impulses that can be relied on in a pinch.

By pretending that the economic success corporations enjoy saddles them with particular social duties only serves to distract the public from democracy's responsibility to set the rules of the game and thereby protect the common good. The only way for the citizens in us to trump the consumers in us is through laws and rules that make our purchases and investments social choices as well as personal ones. A change in labor laws making it easier for employees to organize and negotiate better terms, for example, might increase the price of products and services. My inner consumer won't like that very much, but the citizen in me might think it a fair price to pay. A small transfer tax on sales of stock, to slow the movement of capital ever so slightly, might give communities a bit more time to adapt to changing circumstances. The return on my retirement fund might go down by a small fraction, but the citizen in me thinks it worth the price. Extended unemployment insurance combined with wage insurance and job training could ease the pain for workers caught in the downdrafts of globalization.

Let us be clear: The purpose of democracy is to accomplish ends we cannot achieve as individuals. But democracy cannot fulfill this role when companies use politics to advance or maintain their competitive standing, or when they appear to take on social responsibilities that they have no real capacity or authority to fulfill. That leaves societies unable to address the trade-offs between economic growth and social problems such as job insecurity, widening inequality, and climate change. As a result, consumer and investor interests almost invariably trump common concerns.

The vast majority of us are global consumers and, at least indirectly, global investors. In these roles we should strive for the best deals possible. That is how we participate in the global market economy. But those private benefits usually have social costs. And for those of us living in democracies, it is imperative to remember that we are also citizens who have it in our power to reduce these social costs, making the true price of the goods and services we purchase as low as possible. We can accomplish this larger feat only if we take our roles as citizens seriously. The first step, which is often the hardest, is to get our thinking straight.

Want to Know More?

Robert B. Reich argues that the effectiveness of democracy has waned in the face of the modern global market in *Supercapitalism: The Transformation of Business, Democracy, and Everyday Life* (New York: Alfred A. Knopf, 2007). He blogs regularly about global economics and politics at robertreich.blogspot.com.

Milton Friedman's classic *Capitalism and Freedom* (Chicago: University of Chicago Press, 1962) established economic freedom as a key precondition for political freedom. In *The Great Risk Shift: The Assault on American Jobs, Families, Health Care and Retirement—And How You Can Fight Back* (New York: Oxford University Press, 2006), Jacob S. Hacker examines a prosperous United States where citizens increasingly feel politically powerless. Martin Wolf refutes the allegation that the global economy undermines democracy in *The Morality of the Market* (Foreign Policy, September/October 2003).

For links to relevant Web sites, access to the *FP* Archive, and a comprehensive index of related *Foreign Policy* articles, go to www.ForeignPolicy.com.

Anthony B. Kim  **NO**

Economic Freedom Underpins Human Rights and Democratic Governance

In her preface to the Department of State's recently published *Country Reports on Human Rights Practices for 2007,* Secretary of State Condoleezza Rice wrote: "These values [liberty, dignity, and rights] are the basic endowments of all human beings, and the surest way to protect and preserve them is through effective, lawful, democratic governance."[1] There is no distinct formula through which to guarantee this process, but an unequivocal linkage to ensuring this progression lies in economic freedom. As a fundamental element of enhancing human rights, economic freedom is an indispensable means toward promoting effective, lawful, and democratic governance.

A Valuable End in Itself

Economic freedom is a part of human liberty that is concerned with the material autonomy of the individual in relation to the government and other organized groups. As Friedrich Hayek once observed, "To be controlled in our economic pursuits means to be controlled in everything."[2] Hayek's observation on economic freedom is based on the truth that each person is a free and responsible being with an inalienable dignity and fundamental human rights that should come first in any political system.

It is not surprising to see that seven of the 10 countries identified as "the most systematic human rights violators"[3] (North Korea, Burma, Iran, Syria, Zimbabwe, Cuba, and Belarus) by the State Department's human rights report are "repressed" economies according to the *Index of Economic Freedom,* an annual publication by The Heritage Foundation and *The Wall Street Journal* that measures economic freedom around the world.[4] Government leaders in these countries put their own tyrannical political systems ahead of the people's economic freedoms. The concentration of power and wealth in the hands of unaccountable and autocratic political elites results in erosion and nullification of basic social and economic rights such as the rights to health, food, water, and education.

As the *Index* defines it, "the highest form of economic freedom provides an absolute absence of coercion or constraint of economic liberty beyond the

From *Heritage Foundation Web Memo,* #1861, March 18, 2008. Copyright © 2008 by Heritage Foundation. Reprinted by permission.

extent necessary for citizens to protect and maintain liberty itself."[5] In other words, economic freedom is about individuals' basic economic rights to work, produce, save, and consume without the state's intimidation and infringement. It encompasses the freedom to engage in entrepreneurial activities, having choices in education and health care, fair taxation, and just treatment by the courts under the rule of law.

Greater economic freedom generates opportunities for people and creates sustainable wealth and respect for human rights. By reducing barriers to economic activities, economic freedom helps to create a framework in which people fulfill their dreams of success. This is well-documented in the *Index,* which identifies strong synergies among the 10 key ingredients of economic freedom, among which are openness to the world, transparency, and the rule of law.

Empirical findings confirm that greater economic freedom empowers people and improves their quality of life by unleashing opportunities and innovative ideas. As Chart 1 demonstrates, there is a strong positive relationship between economic freedom and prosperity. People in countries with greater economic freedom enjoy higher standards of living than people in countries with less economic freedom.

More important, there is another noticeable dimension to the relationship between economic freedom and prosperity; one that involves the evolution of economic freedom and standard of living over time. Table 1 shows

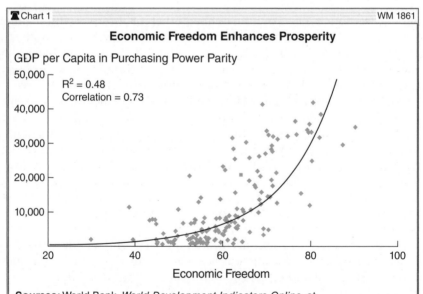

Chart 1   WM 1861

Economic Freedom Enhances Prosperity

GDP per Capita in Purchasing Power Parity

$R^2 = 0.48$
Correlation = 0.73

Economic Freedom

Sources: World Bank, *World Development Indicators Online,* at *publications.worldbank.org/subscriptions/WDI* (September 5, 2007; subscription required); Central Intelligence Agency, The World Factbook 2007 (September 5, 2007); International Monetary Fund, World Economic Outlook database, April 2007 (September 5, 2007); and Kim R. Holmes, Edwin J. Feulner, and Mary Anastasia O'Grady, *2008 Index of Economic Freedom* (Washington, D.C.: The Heritage Foundation and Dow Jones & Company, Inc., 2008).

☎ Table I   WM 1861

Change in Economic Freedom Score and GDP per Capita Growth

Change in Economic Freedom (%) (1998 Index–2008 Index)	Average GDP per Capita Growth (%) (1996–2006)
Over 2 (20 Countries)	5.50
Between 1 and 2 (25 Countries)	2.73
Between 0 and 1 (53 Countries)	2.55
Between –1 and 0 (36 Countries)	2.38
Below –1 (13 Countries)	1.68

Sources: International Monetary Fund, World Economic Outlook database, October 2007; Kim R. Holmes, Edwin J. Feulner, and Mary Anastasia O'Grady, *2008 Index of Economic Freedom* (Washington, D.C.: The Heritage Foundation and Dow Jones & Company, Inc., 2008).

that, measured by 10-year compound averages, countries' improvements in their *Index* scores and their growth rates of per capita GDP are positively related to each other with the simple correlation of 0.44. In other words, countries moving toward greater economic freedom tend to achieve higher growth rates of per capita GDP over time.[6]

Promoting and preserving human rights cannot be seen in isolation from economic freedom. When living standards are low and poverty persists, violence often replaces peace, and basic human rights are easily violated. Sustainable economic development backed by economic freedom thereby plays a vital role in supporting the expansion and protection of human rights.

A Vital Means to Democratic Governance

Greater economic freedom can also provide more fertile ground for effective and democratic governance. It empowers people to exercise greater control over their daily decision-making processes. In doing so, economic freedom ultimately nurtures political reform as well. Economic freedom makes it possible for independent sources of wealth to counterbalance political power and encourages the cultivation of a pluralistic society.

Debate over the direction of causality between economic freedom and democracy has been somewhat controversial due to the complex interplay between the two freedoms. However, the positive relationship is undeniable. Chart 2 shows the relationship between economic freedom and democratic governance measured by the Economist Intelligence Unit's democracy index.[7] They are clearly interrelated and together form a coherent whole.

It is undeniable that freedom has reached every area of the world over the past century. Economic freedom is a powerful building block for advancing effective and democratic governance. Yet the world needs to be mobilized behind that cause more effectively, and it needs to confront those who advocate ideologies of repression and extremism.

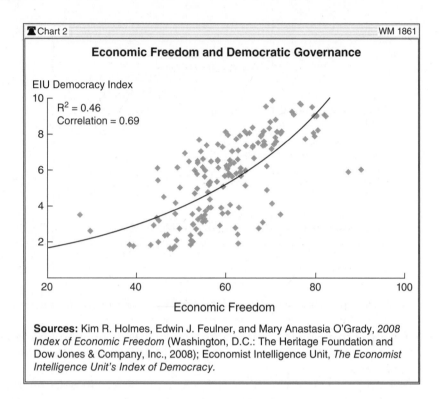

Chart 2   WM 1861

Economic Freedom and Democratic Governance

EIU Democracy Index

$R^2 = 0.46$
Correlation = 0.69

Economic Freedom

Sources: Kim R. Holmes, Edwin J. Feulner, and Mary Anastasia O'Grady, *2008 Index of Economic Freedom* (Washington, D.C.: The Heritage Foundation and Dow Jones & Company, Inc., 2008); Economist Intelligence Unit, *The Economist Intelligence Unit's Index of Democracy.*

In his recent book, *Liberty's Best Hope: American Leadership for the 21st Century,* Heritage Foundation Vice President Kim Holmes highlights the need to build coalitions of freedom-loving countries around the world. He suggests inviting countries to join a common alliance of liberty through a "Global Economic Freedom Forum" and a "Liberty Forum for Human Rights" that would enshrine the powerful interplay of economic freedom, human rights, and political freedom.[8]

Conclusion

As President George W. Bush once noted, "Freedom can be resisted, and freedom can be delayed, but freedom cannot be denied."[9] This is why the United States should continue to stress freedom as a liberating moral force and the foundation of America's leadership for the future. It is the compelling force of economic freedom that empowers people, unleashes powerful forces of choice and opportunity, and nourishes other liberties. As the 21st century progresses, freedom's champions must join to advance their common cause of freedom, peace, and prosperity.

Notes

1. U.S. Department of State, *Country Reports on Human Rights Practices for 2007.*

2. Friedrich Hayek, *The Road to Serfdom* (Chicago, Ill.: The University of Chicago Press, 1944).

3. Jonathan Farrar, Acting Assistant Secretary, Bureau of Democracy, Human Rights, and Labor, "Remarks on the State Department's 2007 Country Reports on Human Rights Practices," March 11, 2008.

4. Kim R. Holmes, Edwin J. Feulner, and Mary Anastasia O'Grady, *2008 Index of Economic Freedom* (Washington, D.C.: The Heritage Foundation and Dow Jones & Company, Inc., 2008).

5. Ibid.

6. Countries are grouped by their *Index* score changes based on 10-year compound average growth rate. As shown in the number of countries in each group in the table, the countries are divided under a normal distribution curve.

7. Covering 192 countries, the EIU Democracy Index is based on five categories: electoral process and pluralism; civil liberties; the functioning of government; political participation; and political culture. The Index classifies: full democracy: scores of 8 to 10; flawed democracy: scores of 6 to 7.9; hybrid regimes: scores of 4 to 5.9; authoritarian regimes: scores below 4.

8. Kim R. Holmes, *Liberty's Best Hope: American Leadership for the 21st Century* (Washington, D.C.: The Heritage Foundation, 2008).

9. President George W. Bush, speech given in Prague, Czech Republic, June 2007.

EXPLORING THE ISSUE

Does Capitalism Undermine Democracy?

Critical Thinking and Reflection

1. Provide a definition of capitalism that distinguishes it from socialism, communism, collectivism, and a mixed economy. What aspects of the economy are capitalistic and what aspects are socialistic? (Remember that I teach at the University of Maryland, which is socialism because the public owns the means of production. Good socialism, I would argue.)
2. How does capitalism supposedly undermine democracy? How does it supposedly help create democracies?
3. Why does capitalism need to be restrained by the government or is it better for capitalism to not be regulated?
4. If the corporations run the country, they have to be organized. How are they organized? Many corporations have contrary interests. How and when do they push in unison? Some benefit from free trade and some benefit from unfree trade. Why do we assume that they stand united?
5. What are some cases where big business does not get what it wants? How do you explain those cases?
6. Consider tax breaks and subsidies which help corporations. If they do not also serve the public good, they are likely the result of corporate influence. What other benefits do the corporations get?
7. Do organizations that oppose corporate interests feel that they succeed sometimes against the corporations? If they do, how do you explain this?
8. What happens when the corporate sector makes compromises with opposing groups? If they have almost all the power, they do not have to make compromises. Why do they?

Is There Common Ground?

The foremost issue in understanding our society is the structure of power. Both Issues 10 and 11 address this phenomena. Issue 10 debates the power elite thesis, and Issue 11 debates the impact of capitalism on democracy. On both issues, there is common agreement that power is unevenly distributed in America and this power inequality has been increasing over time. When that inequality gets too large, it effectively destroys democracy because the votes of the people do not really count. The candidates are selected (funded) by the capitalist class that also controls them when in office. The debate is over whether the inequality in America has reached that point or not. The other half of the issue is the relative power of opposing groups, and whether they are able to win some notable issues against the powerful corporations.

Additional Resources

In 1962, Milton Friedman convincingly demonstrated that economic freedom is a key precondition for political freedom in his classic book *Capitalism and Freedom* (University of Chicago Press). His thesis became the common wisdom to which Reich referred to and which he sought to refute. Other works that support Freeman's and Kim's view include Azar Gat, *Victorious and Vulnerable: Why Democracy Won in the 20th Century and How It Is Still Imperiled* (Rowman & Littlefield, 2010); Alasdair Roberts, *The Logic of Discipline: Global Capitalism and the Architecture of Government* (Oxford University Press, 2010); Colin Cremin, *Capitalism's New Clothes: Enterprise, Ethics and Enjoyment in Times of Crisis* (Pluto Press, 2011); Peter L. Berger, *The Capitalist Revolution: Fifty Propositions about Prosperity, Equality, and Liberty* [a classic] (Basic Books, 1986); Andrew Bernstein, *The Capitalist Manifesto: The Historic, Economic and Philosophic Case for Laissez-Faire* (University Press of America, 2005); Dhanjoo N. Ghista, *Socio-Economic Democracy and the World Government: Collective Capitalism, Depovertization, Human Rights, Template for Sustainable Peace* (World Scientific, 2004); Michael G. Heller, *Capitalism, Institutions, and Economic Development* (Routledge, 2009); Dennis C. Mueller, *Capitalism and Democracy: Challenges and Responses in an Increasingly Interdependent World* (Edward Elgar Publishing, 2003); Arthur Seldon, ed., *The Virtues of Capitalism* (Liberty Fund, 2004); and Edward W. Younkins, *Champions of a Free Society: Ideas of Capitalism's Philosophers and Economists* (Lexington Books, 2008).

The works that are critical of capitalism's impact on democracy include Henry A. Giroux, *Zombie Politics and Culture in the Age of Casino Capitalism* (Peter Lang, 2011); Brian C. Anderson, *Democratic Capitalism and Its Discontents* (ISI Books, 2007); Yves Smith, *ECONned: How Unenlightened Self Interest Undermined Democracy and Corrupted Capitalism* (Palgrave Macmillan, 2010); Noreena Hertz, *The Silent Takeover: Global Capitalism and the Death of Democracy* (Heinemann, 2001); Michael Parenti, *Democracy for the Few* (Thompson-Wadsworth, 2008); Alex Callinicos, *An Anti-Capitalist Manifesto* (Polity Press, 2003); Mark A. Martinez, *The Myth of the Free Market: The Role of the State in a Capitalist Economy* (Kumarian Press, 2009); and Reich's own *Super-Capitalism: The Transformation of Business, Democracy, and Everyday Life* (Alfred A. Knopf, 2007). Jacob S. Hacker examines a prosperous United States where citizens increasingly feel politically powerless in *Great Risk Shift: The Assault on American Jobs, Families, Health Care and Retirement—And How You Can Fight Back* (Oxford University Press, 2006).

A major response to the above critics of capitalism is Martin Wolf's "The Morality of the Market," *Foreign Policy* (September/October 2003), in which he tries to refute the allegation that the global economy undermines democracy. Three works that study the connection of capitalism and democracy more neutrally are Tony Porter and Karsten Ronit, eds., *The Challenges of Global Business Authority: Democratic Renewal, Stalemate, or Decay?* (State

University of New York Press, 2010); Amiya Kumar Bagchi, *Perilous Passage: Mankind and the Global Ascendancy of Capital* (Rowman & Littlefield, 2005), and Peter Nolan, *Capitalism and Freedom: The Contradictory Character of Globalisation* (Anthem Press, 2007). Two works that see very positive effects of capitalism if it were modified in certain ways are Sandra A. Waddock, *See Change: Making the Transition to a Sustainable Enterprise Economy* (Greenleaf Publishing, 2011) and R. P. Bootle, *The Trouble with Markets: Saving Capitalism from Itself* (Nicholas Brealey Publishing, 2011). Several authors propose alternative economic systems to capitalism which will better support democracy, including Allen Engler, *Economic Democracy: The Working-Class Alternative to Capitalism* (Fernwood Publishing, 2010); Chris Wyatt, *The Defetishized Society: New Economic Democracy as a Libertarian Alternative to Capitalism* (Continuum, 2011); Peer Hull Kristensen and Kari Lilja, eds., *Nordic Capitalisms and Globalization: New Forms of Economic Organization and Welfare Institutions* (Oxford University Press, 2011); and Costas Panayotakis, *Remaking Scarcity: From Capitalist Inefficiency to Economic Democracy* (Pluto, 2011).

ISSUE 12

Should Government Intervene in a Capitalist Economy?

YES: Joseph E. Stiglitz, from "Government Failure vs. Market Failure: Principles of Regulation," paper prepared for the conference "Government and Markets: Toward a New Theory of Regulation," February 1–3, 2008, Yulee, Florida (2009)

NO: Walter Williams, from "Future Prospects for Economic Liberty," *Imprimis* (September 2009)

Learning Outcomes

After reading this issue, you should be able to:

- Understand why many believe that intervention is necessary to address many problems and why many others believe that almost always the government will cause more harm than good.

- Identify a number of specific problems that seem to require government interventions.

- Identify a number of specific adverse consequences that government interventions could cause.

- Conduct a simple qualitative risk assessment of government interventions in a capitalist economy. This method would list possible positive and negative consequences of a specific potential government intervention and estimate whether each of the possible consequences are very likely, likely, 50/50, unlikely, or very unlikely. On the basis of the results, draw your conclusion of whether the government should intervene or not in the case that you were considering. Perhaps this method would allow you to tentatively identify when government intervention would be good and when it would be bad.

- Evaluate the type and strength of the support that is provided for each side of this debate. Is the argument based mainly on a few stories, on ideology, on theories, on carefully selected cases, or on a large number of cases.

- Figure out how you or your family have been hurt or helped by government intervention in the economy.

YES: Joseph E. Stiglitz, University Professor at Columbia University, argues that the government plays an essential role in enabling the market to work properly. Capitalism runs amok if it is not regulated to protect against abuse and ensure fairness.

NO: Walter Williams, professor of economics at George Mason University, argues that the founders defined a small role for government in the Constitution and protected the freedom of individuals. Now the role of government is increasing and individual freedoms are declining. The free market has achieved great prosperity for America and the intervention of government has had net negative impacts.

The expression "That government is best which governs least" sums up a deeply rooted attitude of many Americans. From early presidents Thomas Jefferson and Andrew Jackson to America's most recent leaders, Ronald Reagan, George Bush, Bill Clinton, and George W. Bush, American politicians have often echoed the popular view that there are certain areas of life best left to the private actions of citizens.

One such area is the economic sphere, where people make their living by buying, selling, and producing goods and services. The tendency of most Americans is to regard direct government involvement in the economic sphere as both unnecessary and dangerous. The purest expression of this view is the economic theory of laissez-faire, a French term meaning "let be" or "let alone."

The seminal formulation of laissez-faire theory was the work of eighteenth-century Scottish philosopher Adam Smith, whose treatise *The Wealth of Nations* appeared in 1776. Smith's thesis was that each individual, pursuing his or her own selfish interests in a competitive market, will be "led by an invisible hand to promote an end which was no part of his intention." In other words, when people single-mindedly seek profit, they actually serve the community, because sellers must keep prices down and quality up if they are to meet the competition of other sellers.

Laissez-faire economics was much honored (in theory, if not always in practice) during the nineteenth and early twentieth centuries. But as the nineteenth century drew to a close, the Populist Party sprang up. The Populists denounced eastern bankers, Wall Street stock manipulators, and rich "money-eyed interests," and they called for government ownership of railroads, a progressive income tax, and other forms of state intervention. The Populist Party died out early in the twentieth century, but the Populist message was not forgotten. In fact, it was given new life after 1929, when the stock market collapsed and the United States was plunged into the worst economic depression in its history.

By 1932, a quarter of the nation's workforce was unemployed, and most Americans were finding it hard to believe that the "invisible hand" would set things right. Some Americans totally repudiated the idea of a free market and embraced socialism, the belief that the state (or "the community") should run all major industries. Most stopped short of supporting socialism, but they were now prepared to welcome some forms of state intervention in the economy. President Franklin D. Roosevelt, elected in 1932, spoke to this mood when he pledged a "New Deal" to the American people. "New Deal" has come to stand for a variety of programs that were enacted during the first eight years of Roosevelt's presidency, including business and banking regulations, government pension programs, federal aid to the disabled, unemployment compensation, and government-sponsored work programs. Side by side with the "invisible hand" of the marketplace was now the very visible hand of an activist government.

Government intervention in the economic sphere increased during World War II as the government fixed prices, rationed goods, and put millions to work in government-subsidized war industries. After the war the government's role in the economy declined dramatically, but the government continued to be fairly active during the 1950s. During the late 1960s and early 1970s, however, the role of the government in the economy increased greatly. It launched a variety of new welfare and regulatory programs: the multibillion-dollar War on Poverty; new civil rights and affirmative action mandates; and new laws protecting consumers, workers, disabled people, and the environment. These, in turn, led to a proliferation of new government agencies and bureaus, as well as shelves and shelves of published regulations. Proponents of the new activism like Stiglitz conceded that it was expensive, but they insisted that activist government was necessary to protect Americans against pollution, discrimination, dangerous products, and other effects of the modern marketplace. Critics of government involvement like Williams called attention not only to its direct costs but also to its effect on business activity and individual freedom.

Government Failure vs. Market Failure: Principles of Regulation

The subject of regulation has been one of the most contentious, with critics arguing that regulations interfere with the efficiency of the market, and advocates arguing that well-designed regulations not only make markets more efficient but also help ensure that market outcomes are more equitable. Interestingly, as the economy plunges into a slowdown, if not a recession, with more than 2 million Americans expected to lose their homes (unless the government intervenes), there is a growing consensus: there was a need for more government regulation. Responding to these calls—as if to close the barn door after all the horses have gotten out—the Federal Reserve has tightened some regulations. If it is the case that better regulations could have prevented, or even mitigated, the downturn, the country, and the world, will be paying a heavy price for the failure to regulate adequately. And the social costs are no less grave—as hundreds of thousands of Americans will not only have lost their homes but their lifetime savings. Home ownership has long been thought of as contributing to the strength of communities; with the share of home ownership falling, communities too will be weaker. The foreclosures will exacerbate the decline in housing prices, and property tax bases will erode—a further knock on effect of inadequate regulation.

When Upton Sinclair's novel *The Jungle* depicted the terrible sanitary conditions in America's stock yards, Americans turned away from meat; and the meat packing industry asked for government food safety regulation to restore confidence. When the Enron/WorldCom scandal eroded confidence in America's financial markets and accounting firms, there was again a demand for stronger regulation to restore confidence. Whether Sarbanes-Oxley went too far or not far enough may be debated; but what is not debatable is that such regulations were viewed, at least by many Americans, as essential for restoring confidence in America's markets, where scandal had touched every accounting firm, most of the major investment banks, and many of its leading corporations.

Today, America's air and water is cleaner—and Americans are living longer—because of environmental regulations. No one can imagine a world today without food, safety, and environmental regulations. The debate is only whether we have gone too far, and whether we could have gotten the desired results at lower costs.

The General Theory of Regulation

The general theory of regulation begins with a simple question: Why is regulation needed? [The answer is] . . . market failures. Adam Smith (it is widely believed) argued that markets by themselves are efficient. Arrow and Debreu established the sense in which that was true (Pareto efficiency, i.e., no one could be made better off without making someone else worse off), and the conditions under which it was true (perfect competition, no externalities, no public goods). Subsequently, Greenwald and Stiglitz showed that whenever information is imperfect or markets incomplete—that is, always—there is a presumption that markets are not (constrained) Pareto efficient. Thus, the notion that markets, by themselves, lead to efficient outcomes has, today, no theoretical justification: no one believes that the conditions under which that statement is true are satisfied.

Some advocates of free markets take it as a matter of faith that the magnitude of the inefficiencies are small (though no one has suggested how one might prove that); but more commonly advocates of free markets take it as a matter of faith that government attempts to correct market failures by and large make things worse. To be sure, there are examples of badly designed government regulations, but the disasters associated with unfettered markets at least provide a prima facie case for the desirability of *some* regulation.

Regulations can thus play an important role in addressing market failures. There are several particular categories of market failures to which I want to call attention. We have regulations designed to mitigate the extent of *externalities*. These include, for instance, zoning restrictions and environmental regulations. We have regulations designed to maintain competition (restrictions on anti-competitive practices), and to ensure that natural monopolies do not abuse their monopoly position (utilities regulations). We have a large set of regulations aimed at protecting consumers (ensuring that the banks where they deposit their money are sufficiently sound, that food and products are safe, or that they are not taken advantage of by unscrupulous merchants, advertising, or lenders). In several of these cases, as we shall note, disclosure is important; but the regulations go well beyond disclosure, for reasons which I explain below.

There are two further categories on which I want to comment, both related to *information problems*. The first concerns insurance. Private sector contractual arrangements often have what would appear to be "regulatory" structures. A fire insurance firm requires that the insured install sprinklers. Sometimes, insurance companies use the price system, i.e., they give a discount if sprinklers are installed. But sometimes they simply will not write the insurance policy if sprinklers are not installed. Many government regulations are similarly motivated: government absorbs risk, and to reduce its risk exposure, imposes constraints; it provides flood and earthquake insurance (explicitly in some cases and implicitly in others—if an earthquake occurs, it knows that it cannot deny assistance to anyone) and demands that houses be constructed so as to reduce the risk of loss. Because of moral hazard—or even because of a failure to perceive accurately the magnitude of the risk—individuals will take insufficient care.

The second category concerns what might be called certification. The meatpackers wanted certification that their products were produced in a safe and humane manner. They also knew that the only credible source of such certification was the government—if the meatpackers paid the certifiers directly, there would be a conflict of interest.

Recent troubles in accounting and rating agencies highlight the problems of private certification. The Enron scandal highlighted that the accounting firms' incentives were distorted; and while Sarbanes-Oxley improved matters, it did not fully resolve them. Similarly, with the rating agencies being paid by the financial firms to rate the complex products they were creating, it is perhaps no surprise that they gave AAA ratings to highly risky products.

Information is a public good. All individuals want to be assured that if they put money in a bank, the bank will be there when it comes time to withdraw the money. Government bank regulation is in part certification: it sets certain standards that a bank must satisfy—and inspects that it fulfills those standards. It could, of course, stop there, allowing individuals to deposit their money in "uncertified" banks (and in a sense, it does that—there are many non-certified financial institutions). But it goes beyond that: it does not allow banks to operate unless they satisfy certain conditions. And that, in part, is because it knows that if a bank fails, it may have to be bailed out. As one astute observer put it: there are two kinds of governments—those who provide deposit insurance and know it; and those who do so and don't know it. This in turn means that in order to mitigate the moral hazard problem, restrictions on banks have to be imposed.

Irrationality

The market failure approach growing out of an analysis of the standard assumptions required to establish the Pareto efficiency of the economy (the First Fundamental Theorem) is, however, only one of at least three strands of analysis underlying the demand for regulation. A second focuses on *market irrationality*. The standard competitive equilibrium model assumed that all individuals were rational; it explained why rational individuals (households) interacting with profit (or value) maximizing firms in a competitive marketplace might not result in Pareto efficient allocations. But individuals may not be rational and may deviate from rationality in systematic ways. Individuals (and even more so societies) have to be saved from themselves. Markets suffer from irrational exuberance and irrational pessimism. Individuals may not save adequately for their retirement.

Until the recent work on behavioral economics, economists typically looked askance at such paternalistic arguments for government intervention. Why, it was argued, should there be any presumption that governments are more rational or better informed than individuals? Who are we to impose our beliefs of what is rational on others? Part of the answer was provided by the classic theory of market failure: one might argue that so long as the individual only harms himself, there is no reason for government intervention. But individual actions may adversely affect others (there are, in effect, externalities). Regulation may reduce the likelihood of these adverse effects occurring and their impacts when they do. There is a special category of externalities that arises in democratic societies. Society cannot stand idly by when it sees someone starving—even if it is a result of the individual's own mistakes, say, not saving enough. Society will bail out the individual (or a bank which is too big to fail). Knowing that, individuals have an incentive to save too little (or banks to take too much risk). Knowing that, government should impose regulations to ensure that individuals do save enough (or banks do not undertake excessive risk).

But the new behavioral economics puts a new perspective on these issues: individuals may, in some sense, be better off if they are compelled to undertake some actions or are circumscribed from undertaking others. A potential alcoholic or drug addict may realize that he may be tempted to consume these toxic products and then become addicted. He knows *before he becomes addicted* that he will regret getting the addiction, but once he is addicted, will not be able to change his behavior. He therefore wants the government (or someone else) to make it impossible, or at least more difficult, to become addicted. (Matters are made worse by the fact that there are firms, such as those in the tobacco industry, who profit by taking advantage of addiction. By increasing the addictive properties of their products, they reduce the elasticity of demand and increase profitability.)

Similarly, individuals may know that they can easily be induced to save very little or a great deal, simply on the basis of the default set by the employer in choosing the fraction of income to put into a savings account. Accordingly, they might want the government to force the firm to undertake a kind of analysis that sets the default rate in ways which enable the individual to have a reasonably comfortable retirement, without sacrificing excessively current levels of consumption.

A formal welfare analysis of such regulations within the traditional welfare economics paradigm is, of course, difficult: Do we evaluate the impacts of the policy intervention using individuals' *ex ante* expected utility (their incorrect beliefs, for instance, about the consequences of their actions), or using *ex post* realized (average) utility?

Distributive Justice

There is a third category of rationale for government interventions: the best that can be said for the market economy is that it produces *efficient* outcomes; there is no presumption that it produces outcomes that are viewed as socially just. Regulations may be an important instrument for achieving distributive objectives, especially when governments face tight budgetary constraints (or other administrative constraints). CRA (Community

Reinvestment Act) lending requirements or health insurance mandates may be an effective way of helping poor individuals when the government cannot afford other ways of helping them.

Some advocates of free markets appeal to Coase's conjecture (sometimes called Coase's theorem) that, even in the presence of externalities, individuals can bargain themselves to an efficient outcome, so long as there are clearly defined property rights. But such claims cannot be supported so long as there is imperfect information (e.g., concerning individuals' valuation of the external costs) or transactions costs, as there always are. Indeed, one of the standard arguments for regulation is that it economizes on transactions costs.

A variant of Coase's argument is that those injured should (be entitled to) sue those who are doing the injury. With a good tort legal system (including class action suits), individuals will have appropriate incentives. Interestingly, conservatives (like those in the Bush Administration) argue both for less regulation and reduced capacity to recover damages. They sometimes have a valid argument against the legal system: as currently constituted, in many areas it provides "excessive" recovery—providing excessive incentives for care—at the same time that in other areas it provides insufficient incentives (without class actions, the transactions costs are so large that recovery of damages is impossible).

More generally, sums required to compensate for damage done to individuals may not provide appropriate incentives; by linking the two together, incentives are not in general optimized. Moreover, in many cases, there is no adequate monetary incentive: someone whose child has died as a result of lead poisoning can never really be adequately compensated. *Ex post* compensation is not enough. We have to stop the bad behavior *ex ante*, if we can.

Other forms of market mechanisms, it is now realized, also are insufficient—reputation mechanisms help but do not ensure efficiency.

Regulations vs. Other Forms of Intervention

Critics of regulation argue the objectives of regulation can be achieved better at lower costs by using "market based" interventions, i.e., taxes and subsidies. If smoking gives rise to an externality, tax smoking. If greenhouse gases give rise to global warming, tax greenhouse gas emissions. Price interventions have much to commend them: they are general, simple, and often have low transaction costs. But research over the last quarter century has clarified an important set of limitations. Indeed, the very conditions (such as imperfect and asymmetric information) that imply that markets by themselves do not in general lead to (constrained) Pareto efficient outcomes also imply that price interventions by themselves will not suffice.

i. Imperfect information and incomplete contracting

Most importantly, in the presence of imperfect information and incomplete contracting, optimal incentive schemes typically are highly non-linear (they do not take the form of a price intervention) and may even impose constraints (like rationing and terminations). In a sense, most regulations can be recast as (typically simple) forms of non-linear price schedules; but few price schedules, used in the private or public sector, are in fact anywhere near the complexities of those that emerge from optimal incentive schemes. Whether a particular regulatory structure is better or worse than a particular simplified non-linear price system may be hard to ascertain; and in any case, viewed through lens, the distinction between regulatory systems and (non-linear) price systems is more a matter of semantics than anything else.

There is, of course, a literature contrasting polar forms: a pure price system or a pure quantity (regulatory) system. But there is seldom reason to resort to such extremes, and in many cases, the standard formulation is simply not relevant.

Prices vs. Quantities

Nonetheless, much of the literature has been couched in exactly these extremes. It has been argued, for instance, that, depending on the nature of the shocks (to the demand and supply curves), quantity interventions (regulations) may lead to a higher level of expected utility than price interventions. Consider, for instance, the problem of greenhouse gases. Some have suggested that this is a classic case where quantity regulation is to be preferred. With price interventions, the level of greenhouse gas emissions is uncertain; a change in the demand or supply curve will mean that we will have less or more emissions than is desirable.

But the argument is hardly persuasive: global warming is related to the level of concentration of greenhouse gases in the atmosphere, and what matters for this is not the level of emissions in any particular year. There is, in fact, even some uncertainty about the relationship between emission levels and changes in concentration levels and about the relationship between the level of concentration of greenhouse gases and the (precise) change in climate. There will have to be, in any case, adjustments to the allowable levels of emissions over time. Using prices (emission taxes), there will have to be adjustments too, with one additional factor of uncertainty: the relationship between taxes and emissions. But provided that adjustments are made in a relatively timely way, there is little additional risk in the variables of concern, the level of concentration of greenhouse gases, and climate change.

But there are contexts in which regulations may be better than price interventions. If import supply functions are highly variable but domestic demand and supply conditions do not vary, then setting a tariff leads to high variability in price, domestic output, and production; setting a quota eliminates this costly source of "imported" risk. Tariffication (shifting from quotas to tariffs) may, accordingly, not be welfare enhancing. In general, with imperfect information (and incomplete contracting) it is optimal to use a complex set of "controls" which entail both (generalized) incentives and constraints.

Walter Williams  **NO**

Future Prospects for Economic Liberty

One of the justifications for the massive growth of government in the 20th and now the 21st centuries, far beyond the narrow limits envisioned by the founders of our nation, is the need to promote what the government defines as fair and just. But this begs the prior and more fundamental question: What is the legitimate role of government in a free society? To understand how America's Founders answered this question, we have only to look at the rule book they gave us—the Constitution. Most of what they understood as legitimate powers of the federal government are enumerated in Article 1, Section 8. Congress is authorized there to do 21 things, and as much as three-quarters of what Congress taxes us and spends our money for today is nowhere to be found on that list. To cite just a few examples, there is no constitutional authority for Congress to subsidize farms, bail out banks, or manage car companies. In this sense, I think we can safely say that America has departed from the constitutional principle of limited government that made us great and prosperous.

On the other side of the coin from limited government is individual liberty. The Founders understood private property as the bulwark of freedom for all Americans, rich and poor alike. But following a series of successful attacks on private property and free enterprise—beginning in the early 20th century and picking up steam during the New Deal, the Great Society, and then again recently—the government designed by our Founders and outlined in the Constitution has all but disappeared. Thomas Jefferson anticipated this when he said, "The natural progress of things is for liberty to yield and government to gain ground."

To see the extent to which liberty is yielding and government is gaining ground, one need simply look at what has happened to taxes and spending. A tax, of course, represents a government claim on private property. Every tax confiscates private property that could otherwise be freely spent or freely invested. At the same time, every additional dollar of government spending demands another tax dollar, whether now or in the future. With this in mind, consider that the average American now works from January 1 until May 5 to pay the federal, state, and local taxes required for current government spending levels. Thus the fruits of more than one-third of our labor are used in ways decided upon by others. The Founders favored the free market because

Reprinted by permission from *Imprimis,* a publication of Hillsdale College.

it maximizes the freedom of all citizens and teaches respect for the rights of others. Expansive government, by contrast, contracts individual freedom and teaches disrespect for the rights of others. Thus clearly we are on what Friedrich Hayek called the road to serfdom, or what I prefer to call the road to tyranny.

As I said, the Constitution restricts the federal government to certain functions. What are they? The most fundamental one is the protection of citizens' lives. Therefore, the first legitimate function of the government is to provide for national defense against foreign enemies and for protection against criminals here at home. These and other legitimate public goods (as we economists call them) obviously require that each citizen pay his share in taxes. But along with people's lives, it is a vital function of the government to protect people's liberty as well—including economic liberty or property rights. So while I am not saying that we should pay no taxes, I am saying that they should be much lower—as they would be, if the government abided by the Constitution and allowed the free market system to flourish.

And it is important to remember what makes the free market work. Is it a desire we all have to do good for others? Do people in New York enjoy fresh steak for dinner at their favorite restaurant because cattle ranchers in Texas love to make New Yorkers happy? Of course not. It is in the interest of Texas ranchers to provide the steak. They benefit themselves and their families by doing so. This is the kind of enlightened self-interest discussed by Adam Smith in his *Wealth of Nations*, in which he argues that the social good is best served by pursuing private interests. The same principle explains why I take better care of my property than the government would. It explains as well why a large transfer or estate tax weakens the incentive a property owner has to care for his property and pass it along to his children in the best possible condition. It explains, in general, why free enterprise leads to prosperity.

Ironically, the free market system is threatened today not because of its failure, but because of its success. Capitalism has done so well in eliminating the traditional problems of mankind—disease, pestilence, gross hunger, and poverty—that other human problems seem to us unacceptable. So in the name of equalizing income, achieving sex and race balance, guaranteeing housing and medical care, protecting consumers, and conserving energy—just to name a few prominent causes of liberal government these days—individual liberty has become of secondary or tertiary concern.

Imagine what would happen if I wrote a letter to Congress and informed its members that, because I am fully capable of taking care of my own retirement needs, I respectfully request that they stop taking money out of my paycheck for Social Security. Such a letter would be greeted with contempt. But is there any difference between being forced to save for retirement and being forced to save for housing or for my child's education or for any other perceived good? None whatsoever. Yet for government to force us to do such things is to treat us as children rather than as rational citizens in possession of equal and inalienable natural rights.

We do not yet live under a tyranny, of course. Nor is one imminent. But a series of steps, whether small or large, tending toward a certain destination will eventually take us there. The philosopher David Hume observed that liberty is seldom lost all at once, but rather bit by bit. Or as my late colleague Leonard Read used to put it, taking liberty from Americans is like cooking a frog: It can't be done quickly because the frog will feel the heat and escape. But put a frog in cold water and heat it slowly, and by the time the frog grasps the danger, it's too late.

Again, the primary justification for increasing the size and scale of government at the expense of liberty is that government can achieve what it perceives as good. But government has no resources of its own with which to do so. Congressmen and senators don't reach into their own pockets to pay for a government program. They reach into yours and mine. Absent Santa Claus or the tooth fairy, the only way government can give one American a dollar in the name of this or that good thing is by taking it from some other American by force. If a private person did the same thing, no matter how admirable the motive, he would be arrested and tried as a thief. That is why I like to call what Congress does, more often than not, "legal theft." The question we have to ask ourselves is whether there is a moral basis for forcibly taking the rightful property of one person and giving it to another to whom it does not belong. I cannot think of one. Charity is noble and good when it involves reaching into your own pocket. But reaching into someone else's pocket is wrong.

In a free society, we want the great majority, if not all, of our relationships to be voluntary. I like to explain a voluntary exchange as a kind of non-amorous seduction. Both parties to the exchange feel good in an economic sense. Economists call this a positive sum gain. For example, if I offer my local grocer three dollars for a gallon of milk, implicit in the offer is that we will both be winners. The grocer is better off because he values the three dollars more than the milk, and I am better off because I value the milk more than the three dollars. That is a positive sum gain. Involuntary exchange, by contrast, means that one party gains and the other loses. If I use a gun to steal a gallon of milk, I win and the grocer loses. Economists call this a zero sum gain. And we are like that grocer in most of what Congress does these days.

Some will respond that big government is what the majority of voters want, and that in a democracy the majority rules. But America's Founders didn't found a democracy, they founded a republic. The authors of *The Federalist Papers*, arguing for ratification of the Constitution, showed how pure democracy has led historically to tyranny. Instead, they set up a limited government, with checks and balances, to help ensure that the reason of the people, rather than the selfish passions of a majority, would hold sway. Unaware of the distinction between a democracy and a republic, many today believe that a majority consensus establishes morality. Nothing could be further from the truth.

Another common argument is that we need big government to protect the little guy from corporate giants. But a corporation can't pick a consumer's pocket. The consumer must voluntarily pay money for the corporation's product. It is big government, not corporations, that have the power to take our money by force. I should also point out that private business *can* force us to pay them by employing government. To see this happening, just look at the automobile industry or at most corporate farmers today. If General Motors or a corporate farm is having trouble, they can ask me for help, and I may or may not choose to help. But if they ask government to help and an IRS agent shows up at my door demanding money, I have no choice but to hand it over. It is big government that the little guy needs protection against, not big business. And the only protection available is in the Constitution and the ballot box.

Speaking of the ballot box, we can blame politicians to some extent for the trampling of our liberty. But the bulk of the blame lies with us voters, because politicians are often doing what we elect them to do. The sad truth is that we elect them for the specific purpose of taking the property of other Americans and giving it to us. Many manufacturers think that the government owes them a protective tariff to keep out foreign goods, resulting in artificially higher prices for consumers. Many farmers think the government owes them a crop subsidy, which raises the price of food. Organized labor thinks government should protect their jobs from non-union competition. And so on. We could even consider many college professors, who love to secure government grants to study poverty and then meet at hotels in Miami during the winter to talk about poor people. All of these—and hundreds of other similar demands on government that I could cite—represent involuntary exchanges and diminish our freedom.

This reminds me of a lunch I had a number of years ago with my friend Jesse Helms, the late Senator from North Carolina. He knew that I was critical of farm subsidies, and he said he agreed with me 100 percent. But he wondered how a Senator from North Carolina could possibly vote against them. If he did so, his fellow North Carolinians would dump him and elect somebody worse in his place. And I remember wondering at the time if it is reasonable to ask a politician to commit political suicide for the sake of principle. The fact is that it's unreasonable of us to expect even principled politicians to vote against things like crop subsidies and stand up for the Constitution. This presents us with a challenge. It's up to us to ensure that it's in our representatives' interest to stand up for constitutional government.

Americans have never done the wrong thing for a long time, but if we're not going to go down the tubes as a great nation, we must get about changing things while we still have the liberty to do so.

EXPLORING THE ISSUE

Should Government Intervene in a Capitalist Economy?

Critical Thinking and Reflection

1. What role does the government already play in the economy and how successful has it been?
2. Would you say that the removal or weakening of government regulations was a primary cause of the recent financial crisis?
3. Are American businesses at a disadvantage compared to European businesses and if so, why?
4. Could regulations have prevented the depression and other failures of the market?
5. Have regulations noticeably slowed economic growth in the United States? Have they hindered American businesses in their competition with international companies?
6. If American businesses have the dominant influence over the government, they would have the regulations that would help them and not have the regulations that would hinder them. Is that the way things are? If not, why?
7. In 2011 a GOP candidate publicly declared that he would eliminate three departments if elected president because that would appeal to many voters. Can you explain this appeal?

Is There Common Ground?

As with most good debates, the issue of the rightness of government intervention is difficult to decide. Part of the difficulty is that it involves the trade-off of values that are in conflict in real situations, and part of the difficulty is that it involves uncertain estimations of the future consequences of policy changes. Both experts and interested parties can differ greatly on value trade-offs and estimations of impacts. Government regulations and other interventions cost money for both administration and compliance. Nevertheless, Stiglitz argues that certain government actions will provide benefits that greatly exceed the costs, and Williams argues the contrary view, that the costs will be far greater than Stiglitz expects and probably will have net negative results. Part of the strength of Williams's argument is that regulations often fail to do what they are designed to do. Part of the strength of Stiglitz's argument is that there are many observable problems that need to be addressed, and for some of these government action seems to be the only viable option. Possibly the best solution is to intervene as little as possible. This avoids the extreme positions that all interventions are bad or that beneficial interventions can address almost all problems of the market. Of course, the debate would continue over where the tipping point is between good and bad interventions.

Additional Resources

One aspect of the issue is the morality of businesses. Most commentators have a low opinion of business ethics and the way corporations use their power, and point to the recent corporate scandals as confirmation. Many works criticize capitalism for a variety of reasons and these criticisms support the idea that corporations need to be regulated. Since they will not do what is right, they must be made to do what is right. For support of this view, see Frank Partnoy, *Infectious Greed: How Deceit and Risk Corrupted the Financial Markets* (PublicAffairs, 2009); Matthew Robinson and Daniel Murphy, *Greed Is Good: Maximization and Elite Deviance in America* (Rowman & Littlefield, 2009); Paul Mattick, *Business as Usual: The Economic Crisis and the Failure of Capitalism* (Reaktion Books, 2011); Robert H. Parks, *The End of Capitalism: Destructive Forces of an Economy Out of Control* (Prometheus Books, 2011); R. P. Bootle, *The Trouble with Markets: Saving Capitalism from Itself* (Nicholas Brealey Publishing, 2011); Joel Bakan, *The Corporation: The Pathological Pursuit of Profit and Power* (Free Press, 2004); Claude V. Chang, *Aggressive Capitalism: The Overleveraging of America's Wealth, Integrity, and Dollar* (University Press of America, 2010); Ha-Joon Chang, *23 Things They Don't Tell You about Capitalism* (Bloomsbury Press, 2010); John Bellamy Foster, *The Ecological Rift: Capitalism's War on the Earth* (Monthly Review Press, 2010); Chris Harman, *Zombie Capitalism: Global Crisis and the Relevance of Marx* (Bookmarks, 2009); John Weeks, *Capital, Exploitation, and Economic Crisis* (Routledge, 2010); David McNally, *Monsters of the Market: Zombies, Vampires, and Global Capitalism* (Brill, 2011); George Liodakis, *Totalitarian Capitalism and Beyond* (Ashgate, 2010); Justin O'Brien, *Wall Street on Trial: A Corrupted State?* (Wiley, 2003); Steve Tombs and Dave Whyte, *Unmasking the Crimes of the Powerful: Scrutinizing States and Corporations* (P. Lang, 2003); Jamie Court, *Corporateering: How Corporate Power Steals Your Personal Freedom—And What You Can Do about It* (Jeremy P. Tarcher/Putnam, 2003); Kenneth R. Gray et al., *Corporate Scandals: The Many Faces of Greed: The Great Heist, Financial Bubbles, and the Absence of Virtue* (Paragon House, 2005); and Victor Perlo, *Superprofits and Crisis: Modern U.S. Capitalism* (International Publishers, 1988).

Some commentators, however, defend businesses in a competitive capitalistic market. Philosopher Michael Novak contends that the ethos of capitalism transcends mere moneymaking and is (or can be made) compatible with Judeo-Christian morality. See *The Spirit of Democratic Capitalism* (Madison Books, 1991) and *The Catholic Ethic and the Spirit of Capitalism* (Free Press, 1993). Two other defenses of capitalism on moral grounds are Peter Wehner and Arthur C. Brooks, *Wealth and Justice: The Morality of Democratic Capitalism* (AEI Press, 2011), and Andrew Bernstein, *Capitalism Unbound: The Incontestable Moral Case for Individual Rights* (University Press of America, 2010). Another broad-based defense of capitalism is Peter L. Berger's *The Capitalist Revolution: Fifty Propositions about Prosperity, Equality and Liberty* (Basic Books, 1988). For a feminist critique of capitalism, see J. K. Gibson-Graham, *The End of Capitalism (As We Know It): A Feminist Critique of Political Economy* (Blackwell, 1996). Two works that want to save capitalism through reforms are Roger P., *The Trouble with Markets: Saving Capitalism from Itself* (Nicholas Brealey Publishing, 2011), and Matthew Bishop and Michael Green, *The Road from Ruin: How to Revive Capitalism and Put America Back on Top* (Crown Business, 2010). Howard K. Bloom argues that one of the positive features of capitalism is that it constantly revises itself in *The Genius of the Beast: A Radical Re-Vision of Capitalism* (Prometheus books, 2010). For a mixed view of capitalism, see Ann E. Cudd and Nancy Holmstrom, *Capitalism For and Against: A Feminist Debate* (Cambridge University Press, 2010), and Charles Wolf Jr., *Markets or Governments: Choosing Between Imperfect Alternatives* (MIT Press, 1993). A strong attack on government interventions in the market is Jonathan Rauch, *Demosclerosis: The Silent Killer of American Government* (Times Books, 1994). For an in-depth understanding of the way that markets work and the role that institutions maintained by the state, including property rights, function to maintain markets, see Neil Fligstein, *The Architecture of Markets: An Economic Sociology of Twenty-First Century Capitalist Societies* (Princeton University Press, 2001). An interesting role of government is its bailing out failed corporations. See *Too Big to Fail: Policies and Practices in Government Bailouts* edited by Benton E. Gup (Praeger, 2004), and David G. Mayes et al., *Who Pays for Bank Insolvency?* (Palgrave Macmillan, 2004). Often self-regulation is better than government regulation. See Virgina Haufler, *A Public Role for the Private Sector: Industry Self-Regulation in a Global Economy* (Carnegie Endowment for International Peace, 2001).

ISSUE 13

Was the Welfare Reform the Right Approach to Poverty?

YES: David Coates, from "Cutting 'Welfare' to Help the Poor," *A Liberal Toolkit: Progressive Responses to Conservative Arguments* (Praeger, 2007)

NO: Stephanie Mencimer, from "Brave New Welfare," *Mother Jones* (January/February 2009)

Learning Outcomes

After reading this issue, you should be able to:

- Understand labor force changes since the 1950s and the changing role of welfare (Aid to Families with Dependent Children (AFDC)) up to the Welfare Reform Act in 1996.
- Understand the basic changes that the new welfare law made. Know the main differences between AFDC and TANF (Temporary Assistance for Needy Families).
- Understand what was wrong with AFDC which made both Republicans and Democrats want to abolish it and replace it with a very different welfare system.
- Evaluate how successful the new welfare bill was in creating widespread welfare-to-work transitions.
- Understand the problems that are occurring in administering the new welfare law and assess how it needs to be improved.

ISSUE SUMMARY

YES: David Coates presents the argument for welfare reform, which is that most poverty is self-induced; the previous welfare program created poverty and many other problems; and the reform reduces poverty, improves the lives of the people who left welfare, and solves other problems.

NO: Stephanie Mencimer, staff reporter for *Mother Jones*, does not denigrate the current welfare law but documents the horrible way welfare is administered in many states. Many welfare workers deny many benefits to many people who qualify for welfare. Thus, many welfare benefits do not reach the poor.

In his 1984 book *Losing Ground: American Social Policy, 1950–1980* (Basic Books), policy analyst Charles Murray recommended abolishing Aid to Families with Dependent Children (AFDC), the program at the heart of the welfare debate. At the time of the book's publication, this suggestion struck many as simply a dramatic way for Murray to make some of his anti-welfare points. However, 14 years later this idea became the dominant idea in Congress. In 1996, President Bill Clinton signed into law the Work Opportunity Reconciliation Act and fulfilled his 1992 campaign pledge to "end welfare as we know it." Murray's thesis that welfare hurt the poor had become widely accepted. In "What to Do about Welfare," *Commentary* (December 1994), Murray argues that welfare contributes to dependency, illegitimacy, and the number of absent fathers, which in turn can have terrible effects on the children involved. He states that workfare, enforced child support, and the abolition of welfare would greatly reduce these problems. One reason why Congress ended AFDC was the emergence of a widespread backlash against welfare recipients. Much of the backlash, however, was misguided. It often rested on the assumptions that welfare is generous and that most people on welfare are professional loafers. In fact, over the previous two decades, payments to families with dependent children eroded considerably relative to the cost of living. Average monthly benefits went from $238 in 1978 to $154 in 2006. Furthermore, most women with dependent children on welfare had intermittent periods of work, were elderly, or were disabled. Petty fraud may be common because welfare payments are insufficient to live on in many cities, but "welfare queens" who cheat the system for spectacular sums are so rare that they should not be part of any serious debate on welfare issues. The majority of people on welfare are those whose condition would become desperate if payments were cut off. Although many believe that women on welfare commonly bear children in order to increase their benefits, there is no conclusive evidence to support this idea.

Not all objections to AFDC can be easily dismissed, however. There does seem to be evidence that in some cases AFDC reduces work incentives and increases the likelihood of family breakups. But there is also a positive side to AFDC—it helped many needy people get back on their feet. When all things are considered together, therefore, it is not clear that welfare, meaning AFDC, was bad enough to be abolished. But it was abolished on July 1, 1997, when the Work Opportunity Reconciliation Act went into effect. Now the question is whether the new policy is better than the old policy.

It is too soon to obtain an accurate assessment of the long-term impacts of the Act. Nevertheless, AFDC rolls have declined since the Act was passed, so many conclude that it is a success rather than a failure. Of course, the early leavers are the ones with the best prospects of succeeding in the work world; the welfare-to-work transition gets harder as the program works with the more difficult cases. The crucial question is whether the reform will benefit those it affects. Already, many working former welfare recipients are better off. But what about the average or more vulnerable recipient?

In the readings that follow, David Coates presents a fair summary of the case for the benefits of welfare reform. Stephanie Mencimer tells the unseemly story of how many states seek to keep welfare payment to a minimum, and therefore cheat many people who need and deserve welfare.

YES

David Coates

Cutting "Welfare" to Help the Poor

Welfare states in the modern world aren't very old—60 or 70 years at most. Some parts are older—the German social insurance system started with Bismarck—but in general the provision of government help to the poor, the sick, the disabled, and the elderly is a recent phenomenon. Not all governments make that provision even now, but most do. Certainly in recent times, all governments in the advanced democracies have taken on a major welfare role, and that includes federal and state authorities here in the United States.

Yet in this, as in so much else, the United States has proved to be unique. Unique in coverage: No universal system of health care, free at the point of use, emerged here in the late 1940s as it did in much of Western Europe. Unique in delivery system: From the early 1950s, pensions and health care were tied directly to wage settlements here, in wage-and-benefit packages with few foreign parallels. Unique in timing: The United States set the pace in the 1930s with the New Deal, and again in the late 1960s with its own War on Poverty. Unique in vocabulary: The U.S. state pension system is known as *social security* and the term *welfare* is restricted to payments to the poor, giving it a stigma it lacks in much of Western Europe. And unique in fragility: The United States is the only major industrial democracy formally committed to the "ending of welfare as we know it," through the 1996 Personal Responsibility and Work Opportunity Reconciliation Act.

The result has been the consolidation in the United States of a publicly financed welfare system, which, in comparative terms, is now both residual and modest. It's residual in that it leaves the bulk of provision for the sick and the old to the private sector. It's modest in that the public provision made available (pensions apart) is less generous than that now commonplace in Western Europe and Japan. For many American liberals, there's something profoundly embarrassing about the richest country on earth getting by with the most limited welfare system in the advanced industrial world. But that's not how the Conservative Right sees it. On the contrary, having a residual and modest welfare state is, for them, one of the key reasons why the United States is the richest country on earth. Protecting that economic success then requires U.S. welfare provision to be made ever more residual and modest over time. In a manner and scale without precedence elsewhere, *cutting welfare*—either to the bone, or away completely—is regularly and seriously canvassed by conservative forces in the United States as the best way to help the poor. . . .

⊷⟨⟩⟶

A Liberal Response

Oh, if it was only that simple. But, for the following reasons at least, it's not. . . .

There's More Poverty Out There Than You Might Think

12.7 percent of all Americans now live on incomes that fall at or below the official poverty lines. Even worse, of the 37 million people living in officially defined poverty in 2004, 13 million were children. That's equivalent to the entire populations of Sweden and Norway. The poverty rate for very young children in the United States in the first half-decade of the twenty-first century was slightly over 20 percent: That's one preschool child in every five. And around them are what the Economic Policy Institute (EPI) calls "the twice-poor," that is, Americans living on or below incomes that are only twice the officially defined level for their family size. Amazingly, more than 89 million Americans fell into that broader category in 2003—all close to poverty and all accordingly obliged to watch every penny. Collectively, the poor and the twice-poor now constitute 31 percent of the population—that's 3 in every 10 Americans. That's a lot of people in or near the poverty margin, no matter what Congress is or isn't being told by the people in suits.

What they experience is real poverty, in both the absolute and relative senses of the term. Currently, 39 million Americans are classified as "food insecure" and 40 percent of all those using food banks live in families in which at least one adult is working. . . . It doesn't help them—or indeed us—to be told that most of them have cars. Of course they do. Given the absence of adequate systems of public transport in vast swathes of the United States, how else are they meant to get to shops or to the food bank? A car in the United States isn't a luxury. It's a necessity; an extra financial burden that can't be avoided if doing the ordinary things of life is not to become nearly impossible. The Western European poor don't need cars to anything like the same degree, because the scale of public provision—the size of the social wage that everyone enjoys regardless of income—is so much larger in those countries.

That's one reason why it's simply untrue to claim that the American poor are better off than most ordinary Europeans and better off than the entirety of the Western European poor. Sadly, they're not. On the contrary, the child poverty rate in the United States is currently *four* times that of northern Europe.

There are *only three* Western European countries whose poor children have a lower living standard than do poor children in the United States. . . .

If All This Poverty Is Self-Inflicted, Then Masochism in the United States Is Amazingly Rife

This is why there's something particularly offensive about the speed and ease with which so many commentators on the American Right, instead of probing beneath the surface for the underlying causes of the "pathologies" of poverty they so dislike, move instead to demonize the poor, endlessly blaming them for making "bad choices" as though good ones were plentiful and immediately at hand. Telling young black women to marry the fathers of their children, for example, carries with it the premise that the men are there to be married. Yet "twelve percent of all black men between eighteen and thirty-four are [currently] in jail," a bigger proportion of "men away" than the United States as a whole experienced during the entirety of World War II. Unemployment rates among young black men are double those among their white contemporaries. "The problem is not that the nation's poorest women have systematically passed up good jobs and good marriage partners. The problem is that there are significant economic and cultural inadequacies in the choices available to them. They, like the rest of America, value children; but unlike the rest of America, they cannot easily support them." . . .

Given a Chance, Welfare Works Better Than Is Claimed

The payment of welfare stands accused by many on the American Right of creating poverty and damaging those to whom it is given. With one important caveat—welfare traps—to which we will come later, the claim is literally ludicrous. Welfare did not create poverty in America. Poverty was here long before the New Deal and long before Johnson's "war." Neither set of welfare initiatives created their clienteles. They simply responded to their prior existence. The poverty of the 1930s was of a mass kind, the product of a general economic collapse that was rectified not by welfare programs but by the United States' mobilization for war. Within it, however, were categories of the poor that had existed before 1929 and that continued to exist after 1941—the temporarily unemployed, the genetically infirm, widows, and the elderly. By the 1960s, those categories of the poor had been joined by another, one explicitly excluded from the coverage of the original New Deal. To get any sort of legislative package through a Congress whose committees were dominated by southern Democrats, Roosevelt had excluded black workers in the south. Servants and agricultural workers gained no benefits from the core programs of the New Deal. They survived instead in the invisible southern poverty, poverty which—as prosperity returned with the war—then drew them out of the south into the cities and industries of the northeast and the midwest. In the first half of the postwar period, African Americans increasingly exchanged *invisible* southern rural poverty for its *visible* urban northern equivalent. It was an exchange to which the welfare programs of the 1960s were a belated response.

So it was a case of poverty first, and welfare second, and not the other way around. It was also a case of a welfare response that, when properly funded, took the rate of poverty *down* not up: a response that over time definitely improved the lives of many categories of the American poor. The official poverty rate in 1959—the first year in the United States that it was taken—was 22.4 percent: By 1973, with the War on Poverty at its height, that rate had halved. Then, as programs were cut back in the 1970s and 1980s, the rate grew again. It was back to 14.5 percent by 1992, although it's slightly lower now, as we've seen. . . .

The Charity Illusion

Unless, of course, as the Cato people would have it, private charity would have stepped into the breach and done a better job. But there's just no evidence to sustain that claim. There's certainly no evidence that private charity could, or did, scratch more than the surface of the poverty experienced by the old, the infirm, and the widowed before the New Deal. And of the nature of things, no evidence can sustain the claim that if welfare were entirely removed (and tax levels cut accordingly), those benefiting from the tax cuts would then redirect all or most of their extra income into charitable endeavors. American altruism—although impressive by international standards—is not without limit, and because it isn't, the private sector can't be treated as a reliable and problem-free alternative to existing welfare programs. Charity-based welfare contains no mechanisms to guard against unevenness of provision, moralizing in the terms set for aid given, or the onset of "gift exhaustion" over time. The gathering of funds by private charities is in any case always time-consuming, intrusive, and administratively inefficient; and the distribution of funds as private handouts only serves to reinforce—for those who receive them—the very sense of dependency and impotence that conservatives are apparently so keen to avoid. . . .

The Fallacy of the Incompetent State

In any event, in making the pitch for the full privatization of welfare, the Charles Murrays and Michael Tanners of this world are not comparing like with like. They're also generalizing from an extraordinarily parochial base. They advocate the replacement of the American welfare system by an idealized and untested network of private charities, using as their evidence inadequacies in American public welfare policy since the 1970s. With few exceptions, they don't appear to have looked in any systematic way at Western Europe, where states have run welfare systems successfully for years. Nor have they engaged with—indeed have they even read—the fabulous and extensive scholarly literature on comparative welfare systems. If they had, they'd quickly have come to see that the great tragedy of Lyndon Johnson's War on Poverty was not that poverty won, but that the war itself was not pursued with sufficient consistency and zeal.

All governments—European and American alike—distribute income and dispense welfare. They're all, in James Galbraith's telling term, "transfer states," and inequality always shows what he called "the fingerprints of state policy." The War on Poverty required those fingerprints to distribute income downward, and initially it did. General poverty levels fell. But command of the war then shifted. Under Reagan and the two Bush administrations, the fingerprints were deployed differently. Income was consciously moved upward. Welfare systems can always be made to fail, if inadequately financed and led. An agency such as Federal Emergency Management Agency (FEMA) will always fail if it's led by cronies and managed by fools. But by the same token, welfare systems can always be made to work well if supplied with sufficient funds and commitment. Indeed, take a welfare system up to about 40 percent of gross domestic product (GDP)—when it's servicing the entire community and not just the poor—and popular support for it will rise, not fall. That's been the universal Western European experience. . . .

The Limits of Welfare-to-Work Programs in a World of Low Pay

The 1996 Act is the Republicans' ace card in their attempt to roll back the American welfare state, and they have one huge piece of evidence going in their favor: the dramatic fall in the number of people—especially young single mothers—in receipt of welfare since its passing. But the figures on caseload reduction, although real, are also deceptive, and we need to say so. They're deceptive in a *causal* sense: in that the full implementation of the Act coincided with a significant period of job growth in the American economy. When that growth stalled, so too did the rate of job take-up by single mothers. The figures on caseload reduction are deceptive, too, in a *social* sense. People came off welfare, but then ran into a whole series of new problems that the figures don't catch. Women fleeing domestic violence lost a vital source of autonomy from the men who had violated them. Young women with small children lost a significant percentage of their new wages on child care and transport costs; and the children themselves—whose enhanced well-being was, after all, a key aim of the new legislation—often found themselves in inadequate child care, looked after by undertrained and underpaid female staff. Women didn't stop providing child care. They simply stopped providing their own. And, overwhelmingly, the figures on caseload reduction are deceptive in an *economic* sense. Going off welfare, although it reduced the numbers, did not reduce the scale and rate of poverty among those who previously had been in receipt of aid. The Cato Institute's Michael Tanner has conceded as much, noting that "self-sufficiency appears to be eluding the grasp of many, if not most, former recipients." And of course it is, because (quite predictably) the vast majority of the jobs into which former welfare recipients were moved turned out to be *low-paid* jobs. Welfare-to-work moved people from government-sponsored poverty to private sector-based poverty, adding to their transport and child care costs as it did so. Workfare changed the source of poverty; but not the poverty itself. . . .

The "Welfare Poor" and the "Working Poor" Are on the Same Side

Republicans like to present themselves as champions of the working poor against the welfare poor, implying that the interests of the two groups are in tension and painting the Democratic Party into a "tax-and-spend" corner as they do so. But the argument is false in both of its premises: The interests of the two are not in tension and the Republicans are not the defenders of the real interests of the working poor.

The existence of a large group of full-time workers—paid so little that they themselves are on the margin of poverty—actually traps the welfare poor a second time. If you're on welfare, you're poor. If you get out of welfare and into work, you'll still be poor, because the move will only take you into the bottom tier of the poorly paid. If the people in that low-pay group are then financially pressed—and they definitely are—it's not because of the weight of any welfare taxation that they carry. It's because their wages are low. It's not taxes that make them poor, but the lack of income growth. What really hurts the low paid is not the poverty of the people below them but the greed of the people above. As we read in Chapter 3, the truly unique feature of the recent American income story is the proportion of total income growth taken by the ultrarich. You remember, 24 percent of all income growth in the U.S. economy between 1997 and 2001 was taken by just 1 percent of the population, and it was taken at the end of a quarter-century in which wages remained flat for the majority of working Americans. What the working poor need is not welfare retrenchment but higher wages. They *and* the welfare poor need the creation of a high-wage, high-growth economy to ease the burden of poverty on them both. They both need full employment and rising wages in an economy in which there is a fair distribution of rewards. That's the kind of economy that the Republicans always promise in the run-up to elections, but it's also the kind of economy that after the elections, for 80 million Americans at least, the party regularly fails to deliver. . . .

Welfare Doesn't Trap the Poor in an Underclass—We Do

Welfare critics are right on at least this: There is a welfare trap, work disincentive issue in any welfare system. As people come off welfare and lose benefits, the effective tax rate on their own earnings can be extraordinarily high. Depending on the rules, in the move from welfare to work you might lose 60 cents of welfare provision for every dollar you earn, and effectively be only 40 cents better off—a rate of taxation against which the rich regularly howl when experiencing it themselves. So there is a problem of "disincentives to work" associated with welfare, one on which the Right regularly latch. But it's not the only, or indeed the main, problem currently facing young mothers in search of good jobs in America's inner cities. Good jobs are scarce because the middle-class workers have left those cities, taking the jobs with them. Available child care is poor because the programs have been cut. Young men are scarce because incarceration rates have been systematically ratcheted up. Suburban flight, welfare retrenchment, drugs, and the rise of a prison economy are the real villains here. As Barack Obama said, "the people of New Orleans weren't just abandoned during the hurricane. They were abandoned long ago—to murder and mayhem in the streets, to sub-standard schools, to dilapidated housing, to inadequate health care, to a pervasive sense of hopelessness." Underclasses don't create themselves. They're created. You can't be trapped unless somebody does the trapping.

The great thing about traps, however, is that they can be sprung. The solution to the disincentive effect of welfare payments is to phase in benefit reductions slowly—allowing people to earn and receive benefits in parallel until their incomes reach a tolerable level. . . .

Poverty Is a Matter of Choice—It's Just Not a Choice Made by the Poor

The ultimate irony here is that poverty, as the Republican Right regularly claims, is indeed a matter of choice. It's just not a choice that the poor themselves are called on to make. It's a choice made by the rest of us. In the main, for most of us, by how we vote, and for those who govern us, by how they legislate. They and us, not the poor, have the power to choose. We can choose, as an economy and a society, to meet the arrival of intensified global competition by outsourcing production, lowering American wages, and increasing income inequality. Or we can choose to reset the way we organize the economy and regulate trade to pull jobs back to the United States and to improve the quality of work and levels of remuneration attached to them. There is a choice to be made. If we take the first route, we'll create new sources of poverty for those low-skilled American workers currently in employment and extra barriers for those trying to move into work from welfare dependency. If we take the second, we'll have to dismantle much of the hidden welfare state now going to the rich, and perhaps not just to them. A proper system of rent subsidy for people on low incomes, for example, may have to be financed by phasing out the enormous tax subsidy currently provided to those of us fortunate enough to be buying rather than renting our houses. But at least the more affluent among us have a choice. The poor do not. Or perhaps more accurately, the affluent have the choice of making a big difference by making a small sacrifice. The poor, by contrast, have to labor mightily just to change their individual circumstances by merely an inch.

"Poor people and investment bankers have one thing in common. They both spend considerable energy thinking about money." Which is why, on this topic at least, the Republicans are both right and wrong. They're right: When discussing poverty, policy is ultimately a matter of making right choices. But they're also wrong. Over and over again, the choices they make are the wrong ones—and we need to say so.

Brave New Welfare

Georgia officials lied to Gabby's mom to keep her from getting a $100 monthly check. From red tape to dirty tricks and outright abuse, here's what awaits if your luck runs out.

In 2006, Letorrea Clark was 22 years old, unemployed, and living with her boyfriend in Homerville, a tiny town near the Okefenokee Swamp in southern Georgia, when she discovered she was pregnant. The timing wasn't ideal. Her boyfriend's job at the local can-manufacturing plant supported them both, but his largesse came at a price. The man was controlling, unfaithful, and jealous, a problem only enhanced by the wide array of drugs that filled his freezer. Clark had hit the stash, too, but the pregnancy pushed her to get clean and get out. She slept on a park bench until a friend helped her secure a place to stay.

Two-year-old Gabby and her mother are among thousands eligible for welfare who have been denied benefits as states push to trim the rolls.

Desperate, with her due date fast approaching, Clark decided to apply for Temporary Assistance for Needy Families (TANF), better known as welfare. But when she went to the local Division of Family and Children Services office, a caseworker told her—wrongly—that she couldn't apply until after the baby was born. "They basically said, 'Go get a job,'" says Clark. "I was eight months pregnant."

Gabby arrived by C-section a month later, and Clark brought the chubby newborn home to a sweltering trailer with a busted fridge, no air conditioning, and no running water. (Her ex had reneged on promises to get the water turned on.) Clark got by with help from her church and her landlord, who let her stay for free until she was able to move. Later, she found a job in a day care. But the center docked her paycheck for Gabby's care, an expense the state would have picked up had she been able to get on TANF. Sometimes she'd go home with just $20 at the end of the week.

Clark patched things together with food stamps and $256 a month in child support. But after nine months, Gabby's father stopped paying just long enough for Clark to get evicted. She went back to the welfare office, where caseworkers turned her away, saying—falsely again—that because she'd been getting child support she was ineligible for TANF.

What Clark didn't know was that Georgia, like many other states, was in the midst of an aggressive push to get thousands of eligible mothers like her off TANF, often by duplicitous means, to use the savings elsewhere in the state budget. Fewer than 2,500 Georgia adults now receive benefits, down from 28,000 in 2004—a 90 percent decline. Louisiana, Texas, and Illinois have each dropped 80 percent of adult recipients since January 2001. Nationally, the number of TANF recipients fell more than 40 percent between then and June 2008, the most recent month for which data are available. In Georgia last year, only 18 percent of children living below 50 percent of the poverty line—that is, on less than $733 a month for a family of three—were receiving TANF.

Plunging welfare rolls were big news in the wake of Bill Clinton's 1996 welfare reform, which limited benefits and required recipients to engage in "work related" activities. Those declines coincided with record numbers of poor single mothers heading into the workplace and a significant drop in child poverty—proof, supporters said, that the new policy was a success. But the reform took effect at a time when unemployment was at a historic low—there were actually jobs for welfare moms to go to. In recent years, by contrast, TANF caseloads have been falling even as unemployment has soared and other poverty programs have experienced explosive growth. (Nearly 11 million more people received food stamps last year than did in 2000.) With the economy settling into a prolonged slump, this trend could be devastating.

Welfare is the only cash safety-net program for single moms and their kids, notes Rebecca Blank, an economist at the Brookings Institution and one of the nation's leading experts on poverty. "One has to worry, with a recession, about the number of women who, if they get unemployed, are not going to have anywhere to turn."

No longer the polarizing, racially tinged political issue it was when Ronald Reagan attacked "welfare queens," the welfare system today is dying a quiet death, neatly chronicled in the pages of academic and policy journals, largely unnoticed by the rest of us. Yet its demise carries significant implications. Among the most serious: the rise of what academics call the "disconnected," people who live well below the poverty line and are neither working nor receiving cash benefits like Social Security disability or TANF. Estimates put this group at roughly 2 million women caring for 4 million children, many dealing with a host of challenges from mental illness to domestic violence. "We don't really know how they survive," says Blank.

Women turned away from TANF lose more than a check. TANF is a gateway to education, drug rehab or mental health care, child care, even transportation and disability benefits—tools for upward mobility. Without those options, some women are driven to more desperate measures. In one of the towns in Georgia where I traveled to research this story, arrests of women for prostitution and petty crime went up as more and more families were pushed off welfare. And women are increasingly vulnerable to sexual assault and exploitation—sometimes, as I discovered, from the very officials or caseworkers who are supposed to help them. In the worst cases, they are losing custody of their children, precisely what TANF was designed to prevent. "I worry a lot about the kids in these families," Blank says. "We don't know where the kids are going."

One good thing did come from Letorrea Clark's final attempt to get on TANF. Federal law requires caseworkers to ask applicants about domestic violence, and when Clark mentioned that Gabby's father was stalking her, a concerned caseworker sent her to a shelter in another city. When the ex found

Clark there, she was transferred to a shelter an hour away in Albany, a midsize town nestled among some of the nation's most impoverished rural counties.

The shelter staff did for Clark what the TANF office would not: extended her a lifeline. With their help, Clark and Gabby moved to a dingy one-room apartment in a low-slung brick complex filled with ex-cons and drug addicts, clients of the nonprofit group that runs the building. This is where I found them during several visits over the summer. Mother and daughter slept on a donated mattress; crates set inside an oversize, listing four-poster frame served as the box spring. Free rent made the roaches tolerable, but there were other liabilities. Upon Clark's arrival, the nonprofit group's caseworker asked her for sex. "He said, 'You ain't got nothing; you might as well,'" she said.

As we spoke in July, Clark sat in an overstuffed chair holding Gabby, a vivacious toddler whose head sprouted with braids. Clark was worried. She needed to get a job so she could keep food in the house; she was haunted by the possibility of losing Gabby if she didn't. But there were serious obstacles. She's been diagnosed with bipolar disorder and ADHD; "I don't like to be around a lot of people," she said. She can't drive and fears the bus because "I suffer from paranoia. I always think I'm going to fall off those seats."

Born in Hattiesburg, Mississippi, one of six children, Clark barely knows her father. She suspects both her mother and grandmother suffer from mental illness. One day when she was five, she told me, her mother whipped her back with an extension cord and then made her stand in a corner all night long. In kindergarten the next day, a concerned teacher lifted up her shirt and fell to her knees at the sight of so much blood. Social workers investigated but didn't take Clark away from her mother for another six years of crushing abuse.

In school, she languished in special education classes; her behavior turned violent. At 11, the state finally put her into foster care, and later, when foster families wouldn't have her, a mental hospital. Eventually she was returned to her mother, who coveted her monthly disability check. "When I turned 18, my mom wanted me to stay home to live off my tit," she says. Instead, "I saw an ad on TV for Job Corps and thought that was my ticket out." After she got her GED and became certified as a nursing assistant, Job Corps helped her find work in a nursing home, but the death of a woman she cared for left her rattled. She quit and was soon homeless. Somewhere along the way, she lost the disability benefits she'd received since she was a child. After she was raped in a crack house, Clark sought refuge in the only safe place she could think of: jail. "I hadn't ate in like two weeks," she says, so she went to Wal-Mart and started taking things off the shelves—a sandwich, soda, candy. "I knew I was going to get caught, but I just kept eating. I kept thinking that if I went to jail I could sleep."

After her sojourn in lockup, she met Gabby's father and moved in with him. While her pregnancy was unplanned, Clark believes that Gabby saved her life. "If I didn't have her, I'd have probably lost my mind," says Clark. "She's my pride and joy."

In his 1903 book *The Souls of Black Folk,* W.E.B. Du Bois described Albany as the capital of Georgia's "Black Belt." At the time, the area was home to 2,000 white people and 10,000 blacks; the cotton trade had collapsed, and Albany was a landscape of decaying one-room slave cabins occupied by tenant farmers eking out a meager existence from the depleted soil.

Things have improved since then, but only slightly. Despite the addition of an aquarium and civic center, the downtown looks much as it must have when Martin Luther King Jr. was jailed here after a civil rights protest in 1961. The main drags offer gas stations, dollar stores, and an outfit advertising $99 headstones. More than one-fifth of Albany families live below the poverty line—nearly twice the national average. About one in three adults is illiterate. Nearly 16 percent are unemployed. Eighty percent of children born here in 2007 had single mothers, many of them teenagers.

Despite those dismal demographics, in July 2006, only 143 adults in the 14 surrounding counties—some of whose demographics make Albany look downright prosperous—were receiving TANF benefits. The number had fallen 96 percent from 2002, according to the Georgia Budget and Policy Institute, though not because poverty was on the retreat: During the same period, unemployment in the area shot up 15 percent and food stamp use increased 24 percent.

After interviewing dozens of clients of Liberty House, the Albany domestic violence shelter where Clark sought refuge, I discovered that getting TANF in Albany is virtually impossible. While most of the women were eligible for benefits under state rules, many had been turned away for some reason or another. A caseworker incorrectly told one woman that she didn't qualify because her three kids—all under 15—were too old. Another, a 30-year-old with six kids between the ages of 2 and 12, had been in the shelter for a month after the district attorney from her hometown drove her there from the hospital. ("The guy that I was dating tried to kill me," she explained matter-of-factly.) She'd applied for TANF to get subsidized child care and go back to work. But a four-hour visit to the welfare office produced nothing but a promise that she'd receive a letter with an appointment date. A month later, she still hadn't gotten the letter. She says the county offered her three weeks of child care with the warning—false— that if she didn't find a job during that time, she wouldn't be eligible for TANF. "But if I find a job, I don't need TANF," she said with a laugh.

In 2006, the Georgia Coalition Against Domestic Violence conducted a survey to figure out why so many women were suddenly failing to get TANF benefits. They discovered that caseworkers were actively talking women out of applying, often using inaccurate information. (Lying to applicants to deny them benefits is a violation of federal law, but the 1996 welfare reform legislation largely stripped the Department of Health and Human Services of its power to punish states for doing it. Meanwhile, county officials have tried to head off lawyers who might take up the issue by pressing applicants to sign waivers saying they voluntarily turned down benefits.) Allison Smith, the economic justice coordinator at the coalition, says the group has gotten reports of caseworkers telling TANF applicants they have to be surgically sterilized before they can apply. Disabled women have been told they can't apply because they can't meet the work requirement. Others have been warned that the state could take their children if they get benefits. Makita Perry, a 23-year-old mother of four who did manage to get on TANF for a year, told me caseworkers "ask you all sorts of personal questions, like when the last time you had sex was and with who." Elsewhere, women are being told to get a letter proving they've visited a family-planning doctor.

Simply landing an appointment with a caseworker is an ordeal that can take 45 days, according to some of the women I interviewed—and applicants must clear numerous other hurdles, including conducting a job search, before being approved. Few complete the process. One study found that in April 2006, caseworkers in Georgia green-lighted only 20 percent of TANF applications, down from 40 percent in 2004. The lucky few who are accepted must often work full time in "volunteer" jobs in exchange for their benefits, which max out at $280 a month for a family of three.

Even as it blocks potential applicants, Georgia is also pushing current TANF recipients off the rolls at a rapid clip. Sandy Bamford runs a federally funded family literacy program in Albany where single mothers can get their GEDs. TANF allows recipients to attend school, but Bamford says officials routinely tell her clients otherwise: In a single month, one caseworker informed three of her students (incorrectly) that because they had turned 20, they could no longer receive benefits while completing their degrees. One was about to become the first in her family to graduate from high school. She quit and took a job as a dishwasher. Students as young as 16 have been told they must go to work full time or lose benefits. The employee who threatened to drop the students, says Bamford, became "caseworker of the month" for getting so many people off TANF.

As welfare officials go, B.J. Walker is something of a rock star. Appointed commissioner of Georgia's Department of Human Resources in 2004, Walker quickly became famous for her push to get virtually every adult off the state's public assistance rolls. By 2006, the state claimed Walker's agency had produced an astounding increase in the work participation rate of its TANF recipients, which in four years had jumped from 8 percent to nearly 70 percent.

Those numbers caught the attention of the Bush administration, which was in the midst of writing strict new regulations to require states to put 50 percent of their TANF caseloads into work activities, a target that only a handful of states had ever met. To unveil the new regs, administration officials brought Walker to Washington for a photo op and declared Georgia a model for other states.

To researchers, though, Georgia's rosy statistics looked too good to be true—especially given that Walker's own agency had found that the collapse of Georgia's textile industry and other manufacturing sectors left former TANF clients with far fewer job opportunities. In fact, even as the number of TANF recipients fell nearly 90 percent between January 2002 and November 2007, unemployment jumped 30 percent.

So how did Georgia put all those welfare moms to work? It didn't. As the Center on Budget and Policy Priorities' Liz Schott explained in a 2007 paper, "the increased work participation rate is primarily a factor of fewer families receiving assistance."

As for that "work participation," Stacy Haire, an outreach worker at Liberty House, says it's unlikely to help recipients find actual jobs. "They will put you at a police department. You'll be cleaning up behind toilets, picking up trash," she says. The TANF office once sent a client of hers to see a local government official about a job. The official told her he'd be glad to help out if she'd have sex with him. The woman filed a police report, but the man was never prosecuted. "That's what they can do in these towns," Haire says. "I see some sickening stuff."

Georgia isn't the only state that's found that dropping people from TANF is the easiest and cheapest way to meet federal work requirements. Texas reduced its caseloads by outsourcing applications to a call center, which wrongfully denied some families and lost others' applications altogether. In Florida, one innovative region started requiring TANF applicants to attend 40 hours of classes before they could even apply. Clients trying to restore lost benefits had once been able to straighten out paperwork with the help of caseworkers. In 2005, officials assigned all such work to a single employee, available two hours a week. The area's TANF caseload fell by half in a year.

Walker admits that Georgia has actively discouraged people from getting on TANF, primarily by emphasizing how meager the benefits are. "Two hundred eighty dollars a month does not make for a very good life," she told me. "This is really in the best interest of the children."

Walker acknowledges that some people struggle. "A lot of the people we see on TANF have made a mistake in choosing to have children," she offers. "We meet them at the front door and try to make sure that from day one they're engaged in some sort of productive activity." As for people like Clark who can't seem to get and keep a full-time job, Walker responds simply, "Can't? Won't."

Whatever their philosophical convictions, officials have another incentive for paring the TANF rolls: money. That's because the Clinton-era welfare reform turned what had been an entitlement program like Social Security—the more people needed help, the more money was spent—into a block grant, a fixed amount of money given to the states, regardless of need. The money, $16.5 billion a year, came mostly unencumbered by regulation. States could divert the funds to any program vaguely related to serving the needy.

Not only did the block grant doom the program to a slow death by inflation (by 2010, it will have lost 27 percent of its value), it also encouraged states to deny benefits to families, since they'd get the same amount of federal funds regardless of how many people received assistance. Georgia's share of the federal grant is nearly $370 million a year. "Even if caseloads go to zero, they get the same amount of money," notes Robert Welsh of the Georgia Budget and Policy Institute.

Some states have used surplus TANF money to expand child care, job training, and transportation to help recipients find jobs. But Georgia didn't use the bulk of its money for those programs—instead, it cut spending on child care and put the money into child protective services in the wake of a lawsuit against the state over the mistreatment of children in foster care. "The Feds are just fine with that," Walker insists. "We use our block grant to support other vulnerable families. That was the intent of the block grant."

Georgia is not alone in shifting its TANF money to other areas. The Government Accountability Office found in 2006 that many states were moving federal welfare funds away from cash assistance to the poor, or even "work supports" like child care, to plug holes in state budgets. Yet over the past

12 years, federal regulators have cited states only 11 times for misusing their TANF block grant, and only two suffered any financial penalty, according to Ken Wolfe, a spokesman for the Administration for Children and Families, which oversees the program. "As far as the federal government's concerned, it's not a big problem," he says.

On the run from an abusive boyfriend, Letorrea Clark struggles to keep food in the house for her daughter.

Terrell County, population 10,260, covers a rural corner of southwest Georgia not far from Jimmy Carter's boyhood peanut farm. Forty percent of the children here live below the poverty line; since the civil rights era the place has been known as "Terrible Terrell" because of the racial violence that erupted in the area. When I visited the Martin Luther King Jr. public housing project in the town of Dawson, a cluster of postwar-era brick buildings in the shadow of the Golden Peanut factory, three women sat in folding chairs, drinking Miller Lites under a big oak tree, bird-dogging the gaggle of children darting through the shirts flapping on laundry lines. One of them was a sturdy 30-year-old in a yellow T-shirt with three children, 13, 11, and 10, no husband, and no job.

The woman, who did not want her name used, had her first baby at 17, dropped out, and moved into the three-bedroom apartment where she's been ever since. For a decade, she had help from her children's father, who worked at the peanut factory. But three years ago they broke up, and he hasn't been heard from since. Not long ago, she got a letter from the state saying it had seized $900 from his tax refund for child support, but rather than sending it to his kids, the state would keep it as "back pay" for TANF checks she received years ago. She long ago exhausted her TANF benefits, which Georgia limits to 48 months over the course of a lifetime. She and the kids get $542 a month in food stamps; her electric bill alone runs $265 a month when the air conditioning's on.

So, as some women have always done in desperate times, she gets help from men. "Shit like that happens," she says. "If it was me, I probably wouldn't do stuff like that, but I got three babies to care for." She has held down jobs in the past, at Dawson Manufacturing, which made auto parts, and the Tyson chicken plant. But Dawson closed in 2007. Tyson won't rehire her because she had too many write-ups on the job. The only other major employer in town is Golden Peanut, right next door, but applying requires a trip to a temp agency in Sylvester, 45 miles away with no bus connection, which might as well be outer Mongolia for someone with no car and no money for gas. "I get on my knees and pray to that man above to make things change," she says.

In the meantime, she's getting by with help from her mom, and the man who slips in and out of her house when the kids aren't home. "I keep it on the down low from them," she explains. When she has bills due, her friend will give her $200 or $250, just about what she used to get in TANF benefits. "If he wants some and I need some money to keep the lights on, he hands out a pretty good penny," she says with a laugh.

Her experience isn't especially unusual. Toni Grebel, a relief worker at the Lord's Pantry, an Albany food bank, says she's heard many similar stories from her clients, who, at one time, were virtually all receiving TANF. Stacy Haire, the domestic violence outreach worker, says, "A lot of my clients, they're resorting to favors from men to get money." Albany police data show a sharp jump in arrests for prostitution and other crimes committed by women in 2005—shortly after the state began dumping its TANF caseloads.

Other women are turning to various illicit schemes: trading food stamps for cash to buy diapers; selling their kids' Social Security numbers to people with jobs, who use them to collect the Earned Income Tax Credit. One woman told me she got $800 each for her children's Social Security numbers, which she used to buy her kids summer clothes and new beds. "That money comes in handy. If you're not using it, why not help someone else?" she said.

One afternoon last fall, Letorrea Clark's caseworker from Liberty House, Ellen Folmar, stopped in to give her a ride to the post office. For a while, Clark had landed a job as a nanny, but that ended when school started. A Legal Aid lawyer helped her try to regain her lost disability benefits, but the appeal had recently been denied. Now, she'd lost her food stamp card. For the past few weeks, Gabby had subsisted on little but eggs and rice, and Clark was frantic.

Clark's life is a string of these sorts of crises. Mental illness wreaks havoc with her organizational skills. Medicaid doesn't pay for all her drugs, so when her child support money runs out, she doesn't always take the medication that keeps her stable. Finding no food stamp card at the post office, Clark fell apart. She was such a pathetic sight that a woman handed her $40. A weepy Clark got back in the van, consoled only after Folmar rounded up some emergency food from the shelter to tide the family over. "I got gravy!" Clark exclaimed with delight as she examined her bounty.

Back home later that week, Clark was happily entertaining a fellow Jehovah's Witness, who had a daughter Gabby's age. Gabby danced around the tiny space in her princess nightgown while Clark made the girls a brunch of eggs, bologna slices, tortilla chips, and apple juice cut with water to make it last longer. She put the paper plates on a plastic crate serving as a table. Clark was hoping her friend would get a job so that she could babysit her daughter. "Even in high school I worked with kids. That's my niche," she said. "That's the only thing that makes me happy. If it paid better, I'd be real happy."

As she talked, Clark stuck some donated chicken nuggets into the oven. She joked that her ADD was showing as she burned the first batch. As she started over, the two women swapped stories about ringing doorbells for the Lord. "I get a better response rate with Gabby," Clark said with a laugh. The Witnesses' generosity was on display in her apartment—a donated microwave, the TV, curtains, toys. Clark had piles of religious tracts in the apartment, some in Spanish, a language she was trying to learn from CDs, "so I can find me a Spanish husband," she joked.

The happy scene was but a temporary respite. Gabby's father had found Clark again. Two weeks later, her nonprofit landlord would tell her she had to move, citing budget woes. Shelter workers would search frantically to find her somewhere else to go. (They eventually found a place in yet another town.) Right now, though, Clark was focused on the chicken nuggets, and on Gabby, who climbed up, kissed her mother, and erupted into giggles. "I'm doing a good job with her," Clark said.

EXPLORING THE ISSUE

Was the Welfare Reform the Right Approach to Poverty?

Critical Thinking and Reflection

1. How can welfare actually hurt the people than it helps?
2. How has the bill that abolished AFDC created a program that avoids the problems and failures of its predecessor?
3. Is there a legitimate place for the old style of welfare?
4. A welfare hand up can make the recipient dependent but can also help him or her to become independent. What factors make the difference?
5. To what extent is the welfare problem a cultural or values problem?
6. Does our country provide the opportunities that encourage and enable the poor to get out of their poverty?

Is There Common Ground?

There was considerable national agreement that the old welfare system had to be changed so that it would encourage people to find jobs and achieve self-sufficiency. Much success has been gained regarding this goal so far, but some analysts point out that numerous problems still remain. Coates focuses on the positive results of the new system and Mencimer focuses on shortcomings of the administration of the welfare. One of the reforms under this act was the welfare-to-work initiative, which required work of at least 20 hours per week in exchange for time-limited financial assistance. It also listed 12 authorized activities that could meet this requirement. According to reports, within 3 years millions of Americans had moved from being dependent on welfare to being self-sufficient. At the same time welfare rolls declined significantly. In 2003, welfare was reformed again with the goal of protecting children and strengthening families as well as providing assistance to individuals and families in achieving financial independence from the government.

Additional Resources

Michael B. Katz, in *The Undeserving Poor: From the War on Poverty to the War on Welfare* (Pantheon Books, 1989), traces the evolution of welfare policies in the United States from the 1960s through the 1980s. Charles Noble, in *Welfare as We Knew It: A Political History of the American Welfare State* (Oxford University Press, 1997), traces the evolution of welfare policies into the late 1990s and argues that the structure of the political economy has greatly limited the welfare state. Joel F. Handler, in *Blame Welfare, Ignore Poverty and Inequality* (Cambridge University Press, 2007), carries the historical analysis of welfare in the United States close to the present. Bruce S. Johnson, in *The Sixteen-Trillion-Dollar Mistake: How the U.S. Bungled Its National Priorities from the New Deal to the Present* (Columbia University Press, 2001), criticizes welfare policies in the United States since the 1930s. For discussions of welfare reform, see Jeff Grogger and Lynn A. Karoly, *Welfare Reform: Effects of a Decade of Change* (Harvard University Press, 2005); Ron Haskins, *Work Over Welfare: The Inside Story of the 1996 Welfare Reform Law* (Brookings Institution Press, 2006); Mary Reintsma, *The Political Economy of Welfare Reform in the United States* (Edward Elgar, 2007); Harrell R. Rodgers Jr., *American Poverty in a New Era of Reform* (M. E. Sharpe, 2006); Sharon Hayes, *Flat Broke with Children: Women in the Age of Welfare Reform* (Oxford University Press, 2003); Scott W. Allard, *Out of Reach: Place, Poverty, and the New American Welfare State* (Yale University Press, 2009); Frank Ridzi, *Selling Welfare Reform: Work-First and the New Common Sense of Employment* (New York University Press, 2009); and Frances Fox Piven et al., eds., *Work, Welfare and Politics: Confronting Poverty in the Wake of Welfare* (University of Oregon Press, 2002). Four works that suggest how welfare should be handled under current conditions are David Snow, *What's Wrong with Benevolence: Happiness, Private Property, and the Limits of Enlightenment* (Encounter Books, 2011); Lawrence M. Mead, *From Prophecy to Charity: How to Help the Poor* (AEI Press, 2011); Andrew R. Feldman, *What Works in Work-First Welfare: Designing and Managing Employment Programs in New York City* (W. E. Upjohn Institute for Employment Research, 2011); and Matthew D. Adler, *Well-Being and Fair Distribution: Beyond Cost-Benefit Analysis* (Oxford University Press, 2011). A great deal of information can be obtained from the reauthorization hearings in the House Committee on Education and the Workforce, *Welfare Reform: Reauthorization of Work and Child Care* (March 15, 2005). A new emphasis in current welfare policy involves faith-based programs, which are discussed in Mary Jo Bane and Lawrence M. Mead, *Lifting Up the Poor: A Dialogue on Religion, Poverty, and Welfare Reform* (Brookings Institution Press, 2003), and John P. Bartkowski, *Charitable Choices: Religion, Race, and Poverty in the Post-Welfare Era* (New York University Press, 2003).

Most assessments of the 1996 welfare reform are positive. Two works that explore the negative consequences of this bill are Jane Henrici, ed., *Doing Without: Women and Work after Welfare Reform* (University of Arizona Press, 2006), and Kathleen M. Shaw et al., *Putting Poor People to Work: How the Work-First Idea Eroded College Access for the Poor* (Russell Sage Foundation, 2006). Many recognize that the key to reducing welfare rolls is to make work profitable. To understand welfare from this perspective, see Robert Kuttner, ed., *Making Work Pay: America after Welfare: A Reader* (New York Press, 2002), and Dave Hage, *Reforming Welfare by Rewarding Work: One State's Successful Experiment* (University of Minnesota Press, 2004). Two books that offer explanations as to why welfare provision is so minimal in the United States are Frank Stricker, *Why America Lost the War on Poverty—And How to Win It* (University of North Carolina Press, 2007), and Linda Gordon, *Pitied but Not Entitled: Single Mothers and the History of Welfare* (Free Press, 1994).

ISSUE 14

Is No Child Left Behind Irretrievably Flawed?

YES: **Sharon L. Nichols and David C. Berliner**, from "Testing the Joy Out of Learning," *Educational Leadership* (March 2008)

NO: **Dianne Piché**, from "Basically a Good Model," *Education Next* (Fall 2007)

Learning Outcomes

After reading this issue, you should be able to:

- Know the main provisions of the No Child Left Behind (NCLB) Act and what they have accomplished so far.
- Know and evaluate the main criticisms of NCLB.
- Understand what changes were made in the reauthorization of NCLB in 2007 and what shortcomings were being addressed.
- Understand the need for measurements (testing) and incentives including shutting schools that failed for 5 or more years.

ISSUE SUMMARY

YES: Education professors Sharon Nichols and David Berliner provide evidence that the test-dominated schooling of No Child Left Behind (NCLB) has negative effects.

NO: Dianne Piché, executive director of the Citizens' Commission on Civil Rights, supports NCLB, contending that the annual testing for progress will measure and reward improvements. The poor and minorities have a lot to gain in this system.

T he quality of American public schooling has been criticized for several decades. Secretary of Education Richard Riley said in 1994 that some American schools are so bad that they "should never be called schools at all." The average school year in the United States is 180 days, whereas Japanese children attend school 240 days of the year. American schoolchildren score lower than the children of many other Western countries on certain standardized achievement tests. In 1983, the National Commission on Excellence in Education published *A Nation at Risk,* which argued that American education was a failure. Critics of *A Nation at Risk* maintain that the report produced very little evidence to support its thesis, but the public accepted it anyway. Currently, much of the public still thinks that the American school system is failing and needs to be fixed. The solution that the Bush administration instituted in 2002 with overwhelming bipartisan support in Congress was the No Child Left Behind Act (NCLB).

The main feature of NCLB is standards-based education. High standards and measurable goals are set and monitored by the states. All government-run schools receiving federal funding administer a state-wide standardized test. The students' scores determine the performance score of the schools and progress is expected annually. If schools fall below their goals then increasingly radical steps are taken to fix the problems. Five failing years results in plans to restructure the entire school. Common options include closing the school, turning the school into a charter school, hiring a private company to run the school, or asking the state office of education to run the school directly. This is a tough standard and drew much criticism for being unreasonable. More than 4,500 schools serving over 2 million students failed to meet annual progress goals for 4 years or more. Wade A. Carpenter, in "The Other Side of No Child Left Behind," *Educational Horizons* (Fall 2006), states that he does not blame the Bush administration for its goals but blames it for its method, namely "test-driven minimalism, with the slower and resistant kids monopolizing the time of frustrated and surly teachers and the brighter kids sitting quietly, bored stupid."

The main points of dispute, as outlined in the *American School Board Journal* of January 2007, are the adequacy of federal funding, the mode of measuring yearly progress, the facilitation of school transfers (an option now taken by a very small percentage of parents of eligible students), the act of providing tutorial services, the recruitment of highly qualified teachers, and the problem of flexibility in dealing with special education students and English language learners. Supporters of NCLB argue that the law's core provisions are sound and point to significant gains in math and reading scores and new levels of achievement by minority students, as reported in the *Congressional Digest* of May 2008. In addition, a "blueprint" for strengthening the reform has been issued by the administration, emphasizing more rigorous coursework, new tools for chronically underperforming schools, and more options for families. Representative George Miller, a co-author of the law, has put forth some key changes, among them giving credit to schools that make progress, bringing employers and colleges together as stakeholders, and increasing attention to middle and secondary schools. U.S. Department of Education Secretary Margaret Spellings has stated that after decades of doling out federal dollars and hoping for the best, we are now expecting and getting results.

A 2007 report by Jennifer McMurrer of the Center on Education Policy, "Choices, Changes, and Challenges," recommends staggering testing requirements to include tests in other academic subjects, encouraging states to give adequate emphasis to art and music, and requiring states to arrange for an independent review of standards and assessments at least once every 3 years. Other constructive appraisals of NCLB can be found in "Ten Big Effects of the No Child Left Behind Act on Public Schools" by Jack Jennings and Diane Stark Rentner in *Phi Delta Kappan* (October 2006) and in a forum of articles in the Fall 2007 edition of *Education Next*.

Under NCLB, the federal government has taken an increasingly active role in steering the public schools, perhaps more than at any time in the nation's history. Some see this as a federal takeover, a usurpation of local control.

Stephen J. Caldas and Carl L. Bankston III, in "Federal Involvement in Local School Districts," *Society* (May/June 2005), state, "If districts are in accord with the goals of NCLB, then perhaps following the federal guidelines is not viewed as sacrificing local initiative for federal money. The sad truth is, however, that most districts cannot even imagine existence without the huge amount of federal aid they receive. Thus, they are rarely in a position to even ask themselves the hard question of whether or not following federal stipulations is what is best for their students or their communities." This problem is explored in depth by Phillip C. Schlechty in "No Community Left Behind," *Phi Delta Kappan* (April 2008). He contends that the most fundamental flaw in NCLB is that decisions regarding what the young should know and be able to do are removed from the hands of parents and local community leaders, and turned over to officials and experts located far from the schoolhouse door.

This, Schlechty feels, "destroys one of the greatest resources the nation has in the struggle to maintain a sense of community in an increasingly globalized and impersonal world."

In the following selections, Nichols and Berliner argue that the high-stakes test emphasis of NCLB exacerbates the problems of reluctant learners, making the law untenable, while Dianne Piché defends NCLB as a boon to students historically shortchanged in our public schools.

YES

**Sharon L. Nichols and
David C. Berliner**

Testing the Joy Out of Learning

Since the passage of No Child Left Behind (NCLB), students have been exposed to an unprecedented number of tests. Every year in grades 3–8 and at least once in high school, virtually all public school students take tests in math and reading (and soon science). Students also take regular benchmark tests—supposedly to predict performance on the mandated tests—and district assessments throughout the school year. The time spent talking about, preparing for, and taking tests has increased exponentially.

What has all this testing achieved? Five years after NCLB was enacted, there is no convincing evidence that student learning has increased in any significant way on tests other than the states' own tests. On measures such as the National Assessment of Educational Progress (NAEP), no reliable increases in scores have occurred, nor have achievement gaps between students of higher and lower socioeconomic classes narrowed.

In contrast, a wealth of documentation indicates that the unintended and largely negative effects of high-stakes testing are pervasive and a cause for concern. In our own research, we have documented hundreds of cases in which high-stakes testing has harmed teaching and learning. For example, high-stakes testing has been associated with suspicious forms of data manipulation, as well as outright cheating. The tests undermine teacher–student relationships, lead to a narrowing of the curriculum, demoralize teachers, and bore students.

Research has not fully examined the impact of this test-dominated school environment on students' attitudes and dispositions toward learning. But we suspect that for most students, schooling is less joyful than it was; and for reluctant learners, schooling is worse than ever.

Overvaluing Testing, Undervaluing Learning

From the motivation literature, we know that learners are more likely to enjoy learning when activities are meaningful, fun, or interesting. Yet, again and again, high-stakes testing diminishes the fun and meaning of learning. Under pressure to prepare students to perform well in math and reading, teachers engage in repetitive instruction that boils down content to isolated bits of information, leaving little time to engage in creative interdisciplinary activities or project-based inquiry. One Colorado teacher reports,

> Our district told us to focus on reading, writing, and mathematics. . . . In the past I had hatched out baby chicks in the classroom as part of the science unit. I don't have time to do that. . . . We don't do community outreach like we used to, like visiting the nursing home or cleaning up the park that we had adopted.

We also know that students are more hardworking and persistent when they perceive the purpose of learning as self-improvement or achievement of personal goals. Yet a high-stakes testing climate sends a message that the primary purpose of learning is to score well on the test. Sometimes teaching to the test is blatant, as when teachers assign daily worksheets taken from released older versions of the test. Sometimes it is less obvious, as when instruction is based on the specific information that will be on the test. One teacher explains,

> I'm teaching more test-taking skills and how to use your time wisely. Also what to look for in a piece of literature and how to underline important details. There is a lot more time spent on teaching those kinds of skills. . . . Read questions, restate the question in your answer, write so the person grading the test can read it, etc.

As a result of the overvaluing of test results, the curriculum has narrowed. All across the United States, the time devoted to untested subjects like art, music, and social studies has been reduced or eliminated completely so that schools can teach more math, reading, writing, and now science. For example, in Kansas in 2006, high school freshmen were required to "double dose" their English classes instead of participating in electives. In a California middle school, students were required to take two periods of all core subjects and funding was dropped for music, Spanish, art, and classes in the trades and industrial design.

In 2006, the Bill and Melinda Gates Foundation released a report on the reasons students drop out of school. In this small survey of students who had already dropped out, 47 percent reported that school was "uninteresting." About 70 percent commented that they didn't feel "inspired" at school. For such reluctant learners, the increased test preparation and narrower curriculum resulting from high-stakes testing exacerbates the problem. Faced with an increasingly disjointed, decontextualized curriculum, many become actively disengaged; others simply leave.

I Pledge Allegiance to the Test

A disturbing phenomenon popping up in more and more U.S. schools is the prevalence of schoolwide pep rallies, ice cream socials, and other peculiar events meant to "motivate" students to do well on the state-mandated test. For example, one Texas high school held a rally for parents, teachers, and students during which the principal informed parents of the importance of the Texas

Assessment of Knowledge and Skills (TAKS) and compared it to a marathon, in which "students need endurance." He was not subtle when he said, "This is the test of your lives!" This speech was followed by a class pledge in which students promised to "pass the test and take Parker High School to the top and lead us to exemplary."

This is not an isolated incident. In one New York school, every spring just before test time, the principal brings students together to sing songs that will "inspire" them before and during the test. Some songs included "I'm a Believer" and "I've Been Working on My Writing."

Bulletin boards, posters, and daily mantras constitute additional forms of explicit emphasis on the importance of tests. Clichéd slogans often appear on posters and banners throughout the school. Messages like "Take Us to Exemplary" are pervasive in many Texas schools.

When teachers report that most of their time is spent preparing for the test, when we go into schools and find hundreds of posters related to the upcoming test, when we hear of schools with daily announcements about the "test standard of the day," and when students tell us that not a day goes by without mention of the test, we can be pretty sure that the test has become the primary focus for learning.

Marginalizing Youth

High-stakes testing encourages teachers to view students not in terms of their potential, or what unique or new qualities they bring to the learning environment, but rather as test-score increasers or suppressors. Students quickly pick this up and realize they are defined as winners or losers on the basis of their test scores.

Test-score suppressors receive the clear message that they are not valued as highly as their better-performing peers. Sadly, some teachers and principals have done all sorts of unprofessional things to ensure that test-score suppressors either pass (because of rigorous test-prep activities or even more questionable means) or are dropped from testing altogether. For example, more than 500 low-scoring students in Birmingham, Alabama, were administratively "dropped" from school just days before state testing. Scores rose, principals received substantial bonuses, and hundreds of students had their lives made infinitely more difficult in the process. Such actions help to transform slow learners into reluctant learners, compounding their problems in school.

Issues associated with test score suppressors are exacerbated in states where high school students have to pass a test to receive a diploma. Hundreds of students are dropping out or opting to take the GED route, mainly because passing the test has become an insurmountable obstacle to them. This is especially true for special education students and English language learners (ELLs). Thousands try as hard as they can but cannot pass the test despite meeting all other graduation requirements. Chronic failure is demeaning, causing many otherwise highly engaged students to give up, drop out, or become increasingly cynical about schooling. The high-stakes testing culture communicates to students that their other abilities are of no value. Outstanding talent in dance, welding, art, knowledge of the U.S. Civil War, computer programming, consensus building in small groups, foreign languages, acting, and so forth count for little.

Even students who score high may become less motivated as a result of the high-stakes testing culture. These test-score increasers often feel "used"— for example, when they are pressured to take the test even when they are sick. As a result, they may adopt cynical attitudes about the purpose of being in school. As one student points out,

> The TAKS is a big joke. . . . *This is the easiest test you could ever take.* . . . I mean, forget logarithms and algebra, forget knowing about government and the Bill of Rights. Instead, we read a two-page story and then answer 11 short questions about it such as, "What was the meaning of the word *futile* in paragraph two? A: generous, B: deceptive, C: useless, and D: applesauce."

Learners Weigh In

When many students see education as punitive and uninteresting, and when they have their abilities narrowly defined by a single test score, the potential for irreparable and damaging consequences is high. For students who struggle academically, high-stakes testing can diminish their sense of self worth, leading to decreased motivation to do well in school. And for students who see the tests as an easy rite of passage, a school culture formed around high-stakes testing is boring and unconnected. Thus, high-stakes testing cultures build reluctant learners out of even these academically talented students.

How do we know this? The voices of youth are pretty clear. They understand the exaggerated importance of tests in their lives, and it frustrates them. A 12th grader writes,

> Students (teachers as well) focus on only the TAKS. It's almost as if they have been given an ultimatum: Either pass the test and get the ticket out of there, or pass the test months later and live with the disappointment all your life. It's not fair.

Others find the tests dehumanizing and feel angry about the narrow curriculum being forced on them. They worry that their schooling ignores other aspects of their lives. An 11th grade student writes,

> In Texas many public school districts have found raising their standardized testing averages to be the No. 1 goal of classroom curriculum. Consequently, school is no longer a forum where students can discuss the effects of alcohol, or the best method to achieve a life filled with value and pleasure, or the simple antics of their daily life.

The pressure to achieve is highest in high-poverty schools because they are most likely to be shut down or reconsolidated under NCLB. There, the score suppressors are often force-fed a daily curriculum that includes bits of information devoid of any connection to their real lives. Foster, talking with Latino students attending a high-poverty high school heard, "We learn in isolation. We learn one skill one day or in a week and then we never see it again until test time." Another Latino student in the same school commented,

> I was written up and sent to the office because I didn't want to do a TAKS assignment. I was told in the office that I had to do it because it was important that I pass this test. I am tired of doing TAKS, TAKS, TAKS. I am not learning anything.

Especially revealing are the following excerpts from a transcript of one teacher's attempt to motivate her 16 Latino 11th graders. The teacher had just handed out an essay similar to those that would be on the upcoming state test. Her goal was to motivate and inspire students to perform well on the test. But students were savvy about what was happening.

Teacher: OK, this is last-minute work for TAKS. You can pass the test. You don't want to take it again, right?

Students: *No response.*

Teacher: Please say yes.

Students: *No response.*

Teacher: You are brilliant. . . . The test is not hard. Take your time; in fact take all the time you need.

Students: *No response.*

Teacher: OK, there will be three types of open-ended questions and three types of literary selections. What does "literary" mean?

Students: *No response.*

Teacher: Is it fiction, nonfiction, or biography?

Students: *No response.*

Teacher: Are you going to talk to me or you don't know?

Students: *No response.*

Teacher: (*in an angry voice*) It's fiction, you all. (*pause*) First thing you do is answer the question. It must be insightful and thoughtful. Do not restate the question. You have five lines to fill in. Then you have to support a response. If you summarize in an open-ended question you get a zero. But if you use support for the passage, you get points. Look at this essay. Do you see how this student used textual support?

Students: *No response.*

Teacher: (*in an angry voice*) Come on!

Students: *No response*

And on it goes. Another exciting day at school marked only by passive resistance to what students accurately perceive to be an inferior (and boring) education.

What Can We Do?

High-stakes tests are not likely to go away, but schools can and should try to minimize their harmful effects. Schools should at least refrain from engaging in test-prep rallies, ice cream socials, or social events that focus specifically on the test. Such activities only reinforce the impression that the test is the primary goal of schooling. If schools want to hold such events to create a sense of community, they might simply rename the events to emphasize learning, not testing (for example, a Rally for Learning). Of course, the learning celebrated has to be genuine: completing outstanding science fair projects; presenting classroom projects to the town council; writing poetry, essays, or a play; and so forth. Schools need to reward demonstrations of learning in all its varieties.

Administrators and teachers should work together to reframe the purposes of learning in their school. As a start, eliminate the word "test" from any banner, poster, or encouraging slogan. Instead, use language that focuses on mastering knowledge, improving individual performance, or seeing the value of schooling for enhancing one's future.

In addition, teachers and administrators should strive to create a climate of caring and cooperation, instead of competition. We know that students are more likely to attend school and excel when they feel they belong. Feelings of connection lead to greater effort, greater persistence, and positive attitudes. Feelings of rejection have the opposite effects.

Significant changes in NCLB are unlikely to occur soon. This law has not only exacerbated the problems of reluctant learners already in our schools, but also manufactured additional reluctant learners for the schools to deal with. It is up to administrators and teachers to mitigate the damaging effects of this untenable law on many of our students by proactively working to diminish the importance of high-stakes testing in schools.

Dianne Piché  **NO**

Basically a Good Model

No Child Left Behind (NCLB) may be the most vilified act of Congress in modern times. Just about anybody can find something in the law to get worked up over: the testing rules, "highly qualified teachers," funding shortfalls and so on. It's great fodder for presidential candidates, too, one of whom recently went so far as to blame the childhood obesity problem on NCLB and to equate companies providing tutoring to low-income students to Halliburton. Funny thing is NCLB is actually doing some good things for real people, many of them students who historically have been shortchanged in our public schools.

I was an early, proud supporter of the law, and I still am. My civil rights colleagues and I fought for some of its tougher provisions, like accountability for subgroups of students, the 2014 proficiency deadline, requiring states to submit plans for the equitable assignment of teachers, and providing a way out for kids trapped in failing schools. By now, most of the criticism of NCLB—some legitimate but some ginned up by special interests opposed to real accountability—seems pretty old and tiresome.

Let's examine some of the grenades most commonly lobbed at NCLB. First, there is the oft-heard complaint that the measurement system for accountability is all wrong. Why? Because NCLB doesn't call for measuring students' growth from year to year. Instead, the measurement system in the law compares the proficiency levels of this year's 3rd graders to last year's 3rd graders. This is also called the "status model."

Suggesting that NCLB 1.0 is flawed because it did not explicitly provide, back in 2001, for "growth models" is like saying my 2001 desktop was a bad buy because in 2007 it can't run Windows Vista or streaming video. Virtually none of the states had the technology and other capacity to design and implement growth-measurement systems in the early years of this authorization. The fact that Education Secretary Margaret Spellings has approved only seven to date is not because she's not eager to see many states move in this direction. There simply aren't, even today, many states ready, willing, and able to carry out a credible, statistically sound growth-based accountability system.

Since 1994 the "status model" has been the accountability paradigm embedded in Title I, and in many state accountability systems as well. It was based, in part, on public health models that aspire, for example, to increase numbers of annual healthy births and immunized kindergarteners and decrease things like malnutrition, disease, and teen pregnancy. Significantly, it was not until sometime after NCLB's final passage that the noise level about the "status" model and the plea for growth measures became audible. And this was not because states suddenly had vast new capacity to measure growth. They didn't. Instead, increasingly, leaders of the education establishment (i.e., school boards, administrators, and the teacher unions) were doing their Adequate Yearly Progress (AYP) math in the context of the 2014 deadline. They rightly feared that, unlike the Clinton administration, the Bush administration was determined to enforce the law, particularly with regard to assessment and accountability. Simply put, they hoped that with a growth model, they might get credit for *some* amount of improvement in test scores, even if the requisite numbers of students were not actually proficient.

This political background is important context for the debate taking place in Congress. Virtually nobody disputes the merits of allowing states to base their accountability systems on the value a school or teacher adds to a student's knowledge and skills. But when it comes time for Congress to get down to actual legislative language, members will have to choose whether to open the door to all comers, including states with pitifully low standards (compared to those of the National Assessment of Educational Progress), deficient data and student-tracking systems, and a poor track record on including English language learners and students with disabilities. Or they can take the more prudent course, accede to the secretary's good judgment, and limit the "growth" option to those states that can demonstrate both the capacity and the rigor required to bring students to proficiency within a specified period. Thus, simply arguing "growth measures good, current law bad" may in the end not be very helpful to the deliberations on Capitol Hill and could well undermine the efforts of those who favor only those growth systems that can meet tough standards for rigor, reliability, and inclusion of all students.

Then there's the suggestion that the 2014 proficiency deadline is crazy. Says who? Certainly not the parents whose children attend persistently low-performing schools and for whom even one school year is too much time to lose.

Increasingly we are seeing high-poverty, high-minority schools across the country that are achieving outstanding academic success. In high-achieving schools, proficiency for all students is possible *this year*. Let's do what we can with NCLB to drive the dollars and incentives to the schools that are replicating the no-excuses approach to teaching the children of the poor.

Common Ground?

Perhaps surprisingly, my fellow forum authors and I agree on the importance of NCLB's core aspirations:

- Transparency and public reporting of student achievement data
- The need for high standards pegged to postsecondary education and careers
- Regular assessment in reading and math
- Accountability based on assessment results
- Options for parents.

We even agree on some of the more nuanced, yet potentially powerful, improvements Congress and states could enact to strengthen education reform:

- Differentiated consequences
- Continued efforts to measure growth from year to year
- Measuring effectiveness and attaching rewards/consequences for administrators and teachers.

Finally, we may actually agree on the most radical proposal from the standpoint of the more than 40-year history of the Elementary and Secondary Education Act (ESEA): Congress should not continue to subsidize failure after providing years of assistance and the opportunity to improve. There are a variety of ways to remove funding from chronically low-performing schools and transfer it to better schools (including moving the dollars in the figurative "backpacks" of the students) that merit serious consideration.

Our disagreements reflect our fundamentally different beliefs about the role of the federal government itself, particularly with respect to advancing the interests of the poor and minorities. Since when has leaving it all up to the states helped the poor and minorities achieve equality of opportunity? Not when it came to voting rules. Not when it came to public accommodations. Not when it came to desegregating schools in the aftermath of *Brown v. Board of Education*. And certainly not now, when the achievement gaps based on race and class are as virulent as ever, with only modest signs of abatement.

Of course, not everything is working perfectly yet. School choice and supplemental educational services were not high on the political priority list under the first Bush administration, but it does not follow that these two vital provisions for parents cannot be made to work. It often takes a period of years (sometimes even a complete authorization cycle) for a controversial new provision to take root. For example, most states did not pay much attention to the "accountability lite" provisions in the Clinton-era Improving America's Schools Act (IASA), nor did that administration do much to signal to states that it would enforce IASA's requirements for "corrective action" and school improvement. It took another authorization and a clear signal from the Bush administration that the federal government was serious about accountability in order for the states to come up with plans to hold their own schools and districts accountable.

Moreover, there are encouraging signs of bipartisan support for proposals to add some real teeth to the public school transfer options in NCLB. Currently, parents may choose a better school when their child's school fails to make AYP, but as the Lawyers' Committee for Civil Rights Under Law has called it, the choice option is "a right without a remedy." School districts implement the provision only halfheartedly and many argue a lack of space in successful schools. The interdistrict provisions in the law are weak, and charter options are not meaningful in states with arbitrary limits on new charter schools.

The Citizens' Commission on Civil Rights, along with the Aspen Institute's NCLB Commission and other proponents, have proposed tough new measures to guarantee public school choice to children who attend persistently low-performing schools. One proposal would deny states that do not provide parents and children with demonstrably better choices their Title I money. States would have the obligation to create and offer those children in the worst schools seats in better-performing schools. To increase seats, states could lift caps on the number of charter schools, expand successful schools, or provide for interdistrict transfers. A second proposal would require an "audit" to determine whether capacity in better schools actually exists and, if so, where. Finally, the Aspen Institute and a number of civil rights organizations favor enabling parents to take legal action when rights conferred under NCLB, like the right to place their child in a better-performing school, are violated. Congress should consider how best to target funding to the schools, leaders, and models that have the best record of success in high-poverty communities. But the bottom line is that unless and until the money is used to leverage dramatic change, there is unlikely to be any marked change. And without dramatic change, achievement gaps are unlikely to close any time soon. The status quo is a powerful player to be reckoned with in the struggle for educational equity.

The Pace of Reform

NCLB is in many respects the latest in a long line of efforts in the policy and legal arenas to promote equity and opportunity in the public schools, including desegregation cases, the Civil Rights Act of 1964, the original ESEA, and school finance and adequacy cases in the states.

How long does it take a cutting-edge civil rights law to "work"? Could a credible argument have been made in 1969, five years after passage of the Civil Rights Act, that the ambitious law was "not working" and therefore ought to be abandoned?

This particular legislation needs to be strengthened by ensuring high state standards, reliable assessments, realistic school-improvement measures, an equitable distribution of effective teachers, and real parental choice. Those of us—on the left, right, and middle—who believe in the transformative power of education need to draw more from the work of the increasing numbers of urban schools that are demonstrating *how* to succeed with large numbers of poor and minority students despite the odds. We need to learn from the contagious successes of outstanding public schools and choice programs like the Amistad Academy in Connecticut, the Green Dot schools in California, and the voluntary interdistrict transfer program in St. Louis.

Abandoning NCLB now would be the height of cynicism. Instead, like the civil rights movement itself, the education reform movement is in dire need of creative thinking, committed education leaders, and informed, involved parents—all united in our belief in the worth and value of every young life and each child's potential to learn and do great things.

EXPLORING THE ISSUE

Is No Child Left Behind Irretrievably Flawed?

Critical Thinking and Reflection

1. Why are there constant, frequent, and fervent cries for school reforms and yet it always seems to need to be reformed again? Why do the reforms not work most of the time?
2. Do you see a way to improve NCLB or should it be abandoned?
3. What are the impacts of attaching rewards and sanctions to the type of testing promoted in NCLB?
4. Even with NCLB enforced in schools since 2002, American students' scores in comparable international tests are below almost all European nations. Why?
5. Are public school teachers bad teachers relative to private schools in America or public schools in Europe? Why?
6. How much of a problem are the teachers' unions?
7. Is the problem of poor average test scores largely a problem of inadequate funds for schools?

Is There Common Ground?

As I read the provisions of the NCLB, I noted how much hard work and intelligence went into this bill. The authors strongly sought to push school systems to improve and do it with a complex set of rewards and sanctions. The problem is that new policies have multiple consequences and some of the unintended consequences are quite negative. NCLB has improved many schools, as demonstrated by improving test scores. Others, a minority, have failed. But even in successful schools teaching to the test is a problem, as is the shift in teachers' attention from the poorer students to the neglect of the better students. No one wants these and other negative impacts but they seem to be unavoidable. However, we must continue to try to correct them. Experts at least agree that something needs to be done.

Additional Resources

"NCLB is influenced deeply by the market-based philosophies of its prime, neoconservative movers. Markets inherently create winners and losers. The rhetoric of leaving NCLB is belied by a system geared to a narrow standardization of goals that results in a diminished realm of opportunity to demonstrate accomplishment and achievement." These thoughts from Margaret McKenna and David Haselkorn, in "NCLB and the Lessons of Columbine," *USA Today*

(May 2005), certainly run counter to the assessment offered by Dianne Piché. McKenna and Haselkorn believe that our national education policies are seriously misguided, based as they are on a long-discredited behaviorist view of human development prompted by extrinsic rewards and consequences rather than intrinsic motivation.

Another critic, Richard Rothstein, in "The Corruption of School Accountability," *The School Administrator* (June 2008), agrees with Nichols and Berliner that under NCLB reliance solely on flawed numerical measures to evaluate performance has corrupted schooling, causing an emphasis on drill, teaching to the test, and manipulating data. Similarly, W. James Popham, in *America's Failing Schools: How Parents and Teachers Can Cope with "No Child Left Behind"* (Routledge, 2004), argues that the prescribed achievement goals are altogether unrealistic, that "the establishment of expectations that are unattainable will rarely spur people to perform at new levels of excellence." Other interesting articles on testing and accountability include Mark F. Goldberg, "The Test Mess," *Phi Delta Kappan* (January 2004) and "Test Mess 2: Are We Doing Better a Year Later?" *Phi Delta Kappan* (January 2005); Thomas Toch, "Turmoil in the Testing Industry," *Educational Leadership* (November 2006); Lawrence A. Uzzell, "Cheat Sheets: No Child Left Behind Has Taught Our Nation's Schools One Thing— How to Lie," *The American Spectator* (September 2005); and Richard Rothstein, "The Limits of Testing," *American School Board Journal* (February 2005). Important books on NCLB include Joanne M. Carris, *Ghosts of No Child Left Behind* (P. Lang, 2011); John E. Chubb, *Learning from No Child Left Behind: How and Why the Nation's Most Important but Controversial Education Law Should Be Renewed* (Hover Institution Press, 2009); Todd Alan Price and Elizabeth Peterson, eds., *The Myth and Reality of No Child Left Behind: Public Education and High Stakes Assessment* (University Press of America, 2009); Brian M. Stecher et al., *Pain and Gain: Implementing No Child Left Behind in Three States, 2004–2006* (Rand Corporation, 2008); William Hayes, *No Child Left Behind: Past, Present, and Future* (Rowman & Littlefield Education, 2008); and Michael A. Rebell and Jessica R. Wolff, eds., *NCLB at the Crossroads: Reexamining the Federal Effort to Close the Achievement Gap* (Teachers College, Columbia University, 2009). For the history of education reform, see William J. Reese, *America's Public Schools: From the Common School to "No Child Left Behind"* (Johns Hopkins University Press, 2011). For more general treatments of accountability in education, see Kathryn A. McDermott, *High-Stakes Reform: The Politics of Educational Accountability* (Georgetown University Press, 2011); Keven Carey and Mark Schneider, eds., *Accountability in American Higher Education* (Palgrave Macmillan, 2010); Theodore Hershberg and Claire Robertson-Kraft, eds., *A Grand Bargain for Education Reform: New Rewards and Supports for New Accountability* (Harvard University Press, 2009); and Sherman Dorn, *Accountability Frankenstein: Understanding and Taming the Monster* (Information Age Publishing, 2007). Covering some other crucial related issues are these recommended articles: David Mathews, "The Public and the Public Schools: The Coproduction of Education," *Phi Delta Kappan* (April 2008); Paul D. Houston, "The Seven Deadly Sins of No Child Left Behind," *Phi Delta Kappan* (June 2007); and John Chubb and Diane Ravitch, "The Future of No Child Left Behind: End It? Or Mend It?" *Education Next* (Summer 2009).

ISSUE 15

Should Biotechnology Be Used to Alter and Enhance Humans?

YES: President's Council on Bioethics, from *Beyond Therapy: Biotechnology and the Pursuit of Happiness* (October 2003)

NO: Michael J. Sandel, from "The Case Against Perfection: Ethics in the Age of Genetic Engineering," *The Atlantic Monthly* (April 2004)

Learning Outcomes

After reading this issue, you should be able to:

- Have a general understanding of where genetic research stands today and what it has accomplished up to now.
- Have a general understanding of what research will achieve in the future and what possibilities could take place.
- Know what choices individuals are making that involve genetic modification.
- Know the potential dangers of genetic engineering and, where possible, have a sense of their likelihood.
- Know the potential achievements that genetic engineering could make possible.
- Understand the moral debates about genetic engineering. Know especially the moral issues concerning genetically engineered babies.

ISSUE SUMMARY

YES: The President's Council on Bioethics was commissioned by George Bush to report to him their findings about the ethical issues involved in the uses of biotechnology. Included in this selection are the expected positive benefits from the biotechnologies that are on the horizon.

NO: Political science professor Michael J. Sandel was on the President's Council on Bioethics but presents his private view in this selection, which is very cautionary on the use of biotechnology to alter and enhance humans. Many other uses of biotechnology he praises, but he condemns using biotechnology to alter and enhance humans. In these activities, humans play God and attempt inappropriate remaking of nature.

As a sociologist I feel that I am on relatively firm ground discussing the 21 other issues in this book. I am not on firm ground discussing the issue of how biotechnology should or should not be used. And I am not alone. The nation does not know what to think about this issue, at least not in a coherent way. But the discussion must begin because the issue is coming at us like a tornado. Already America is debating the use of drugs to enhance athletic performance. Athletes and body builders want to use them to build muscle, strength, and/or endurance, but much of the public do not approve. They have been outlawed for competitive sports, and users have been publicly discredited. Soon, however, parents will be able to pay for genetic engineering to make their children good athletes and perhaps even great athletes. Will that also be illegal? This is only the tip of the iceberg. Thousands of difficult questions will arise as the technology for designing babies will become more and more powerful. Stem cell research is currently a divisive issue. Are we blocking the development of technologies that can save thousands of lives by severely limiting stem cell research? The classic expression of this issue is in the stories and legends of a very learned sixteenth-century German doctor named Faust. According to legend, he sold his soul to the devil in exchange for knowledge and magical power. The first printed version of the legend was by Johann Spiess, which was later used by Christopher Marlow as the basis for his famous play, *Dr. Faustus* (1593). Spiess and Marlow presented Faust as a scoundrel who deserved damnation. Some of the other representations of Faust made him a heroic figure who strived for knowledge and power for good. This theme was continued by the most famous Faust legend of all, written by Johann Wolfgang von Goethe in both a poem and a play. In the beginning, Faust's bargain with the devil was for a moment of perfect happiness or contentment. The devil, however, could not deliver this to Faust. More elements are added to the story, including women's love. In the end, Faust finds a moment of perfect contentment and happiness in helping others and dies because of the wager. But Goethe gives the story a Hollywood ending and Faust, the hero, goes to heaven.

Many of the issues in the biotechnology debate are found in the Faust legends. Both are focused on the search for knowledge and its use. Is the knowledge-seeking Faust a scoundrel or a saint? Will his knowledge be used for selfish or altruistic purposes? Is mankind better off with it or without it? If powerful new biotechnologies are able to make our babies safe from diseases and defects, certainly we should use them. By the same logic, we should also use them when they can enhance our children's physical and mental powers. Continuing this line of reasoning, we should also use them to enhance our physical and mental powers as adults. Sooner or later, however, we must face the Faustian myth, which suggests that at some point mankind's reach for knowledge may transcend man's proper role in the universe and be devilish. But this question takes us into realms where I get quickly lost. How do I discuss mankind's proper role in the universe? The wise thing for me to do is not to try, but to leave it to you and the readings.

The President's Council on Bioethics presents the reasons for using biotechnology to alter and enhance humans. They are simply the many benefits that biotechnology can produce. The Council also presented the case against using biotechnology for altering and enhancing humans. It is a very evenhanded report. But I have not used that part of the report. Instead I have selected Michael J. Sandel to present the arguments against using biotechnology for altering and enhancing humans. Sandel is not evenhanded. He is passionately against going down this road.

Beyond Therapy: Biotechnology and the Pursuit of Happiness

Chapter Five

Who has not wanted to escape the clutches of oppressive and punishing memories? Or to calm the burdensome feelings of anxiety, disappointment, and regret? Or to achieve a psychic state of pure and undivided pleasure and joy? The satisfaction of such desires seems inseparable from our happiness, which we pursue by right and with passion.

. . .

In these efforts at peace of mind, human beings have from time immemorial sought help from doctors and drugs. In a famous literary instance, Shakespeare's Macbeth entreats his doctor to free Lady Macbeth from the haunting memory of her own guilty acts:

> *Macbeth.* Canst thou not minister to a mind diseas'd,
> Pluck from the memory a rooted sorrow,
> Raze out the written troubles of the brain,
> And with some sweet oblivious antidote
> Cleanse the stuff'd bosom of that perilous stuff
> Which weighs upon the heart?
>
> *Doctor.* Therein the patient
> Must minister to himself.

Ministering to oneself, however, is easier said than done, and many people have found themselves unequal to the task without some outside assistance. For centuries, they have made use of external agents to drown their sorrows or lift their spirits.

. . .

The burgeoning field of neuroscience is providing new, more specific, and safer agents to help us combat all sorts of psychic distress. Soon, doctors may have just the "sweet oblivious antidote" that Macbeth so desired: drugs (such as beta-adrenergic blockers) that numb the emotional sting typically associated with our intensely bad memories.

. . .

From the President's Council on Bioethics, October 2003.

To be sure, these agents—and their better versions, yet to come—are, for now at least, being developed not as means for drug-induced happiness but rather as agents for combating major depression or preventing post-traumatic stress disorder (PTSD). Yet once available for those purposes, they could also be used to ease the soul and enhance the mood of nearly anyone.

. . .

By using drugs to satisfy more easily the enduring aspirations to forget what torments us and approach the world with greater peace of mind, what deeper human aspirations might we occlude or frustrate? What qualities of character may become less necessary and, with diminished use, atrophy or become extinct, as we increasingly depend on drugs to cope with misfortune? How will we experience our incompleteness or understand our mortality as our ability grows to medically dissolve all sorts of anxiety? Will the availability of drug-induced conditions of ecstatic pleasure estrange us from the forms of pleasure that depend upon discipline and devotion? And, going beyond the implications for individuals, what kind of a society are we likely to have when the powers to control memory, mood, and mental life through drugs reach their full maturity and are widely used?

. . .

I. What Are "Happy Souls"?

. . .

Because the happiness we seek we seek for *ourselves*—for *our* self, not for someone else's, and for our *self* or embodied soul, not for our bodies as material stuff—our happiness is bound up with our personhood and our identity. We would not want to attain happiness (or any other object of our desires) if the condition for attaining it required that we become someone else, that we lose our identity in the process.

The importance of identity for happiness implies necessarily the importance of memory. If experiencing our happiness depends upon experiencing a stable identity, then our happiness depends also on our memory, on knowing who we are in relation to who we have been.

. . .

But if enfeebled memory can cripple identity, selectively altered memory can distort it. Changing the content of our memories or altering their emotional tonalities, however desirable to alleviate guilty or painful consciousness, could subtly reshape who we are, at least to ourselves. With altered memories we might feel better about ourselves, but it is not clear that the better-feeling "we" remains the same as before. Lady Macbeth, cured of her guilty torment, would remain the murderess she was, but not the conscience-stricken being even she could not help but be.

. . .

[A]n unchecked power to erase memories, brighten moods, and alter our emotional dispositions could imperil our capacity to form a strong and coherent personal identity. To the extent that our inner life ceases to reflect the ups and downs of daily existence and instead operates independently of them, we dissipate our identity, which is formed through engagement with others and through immersion in the mix of routine and unpredictable events that constitute our lives.

. . .

II. Memory and Happiness

. . .

Our identity or sense of self emerges, grows, and changes. Yet, despite all the changes, thanks to the integrating powers of memory, our identity also, remarkably, persists *as ours*.

. . .

We especially want our memories to be not simply a sequence of disconnected experiences, but a narrative that seems to contain some unfolding purpose, some larger point from beginning to end, some aspiration discovered, pursued, and at least partially fulfilled.

Memory is central to human flourishing, in other words, precisely because we pursue happiness in time, as time-bound beings. We have a past and a future as well as a present, and being happy through time requires that these be connected in a meaningful way. If we are to flourish as ourselves, we must do so without abandoning or forgetting who we are or once were. Yet because our lives are time-bound, our happiness is always incomplete—always not-yet and on-the-way, always here but slipping away, but also always possible again and in the future. Our happiest experiences can be revivified. And, as we reminisce from greater distance and with more experience, even our painful experiences can often acquire for us a meaning not in evidence when they occurred.

The place of memory in the pursuit of happiness also suggests something essential about human identity, a theme raised in various places and in different ways throughout this report: namely, our identities are formed both by what we do and by what we undergo or suffer. We actively choose paths and do deeds fit to be remembered. But we also live through memorable experiences that we would never have chosen—experiences we often wish never happened at all. To some extent, these unchosen memories constrain us; though we may regret the shadows they cast over our pursuit of happiness, we cannot simply escape them while remaining who we really are. And yet, through the act of remembering— the act of discerning and giving meaning to the past as it really was—we can shape, to some degree, the meaning of our memories, both good and bad.

. . .

The capacity to alter or numb our remembrance of things past cuts to the heart of what it means to remember in a human way, and it is this biotechnical possibility that we focus on here. Deciding when or whether to use such biotechnical power will require that we think long and hard about what it means to remember truthfully, to live in time, and to seek happiness without losing or abandoning our identity. The rest of this discussion of "memory and happiness" is an invitation to such reflection.

A. Good Memories and Bad

. . .

[T]he significance of past events often becomes clear to us only after much rumination in light of later experience, and what seems trivial at one time may appear crucial at another. Neither can an excellent memory be one that remembers only what we *want* to remember: sometimes our most valuable memories are of events that were painful when they occurred, but that on reflection teach us vital lessons.

. . .

B. Biotechnology and Memory Alteration

It is a commonplace observation that, while some events fade quickly from the mind, emotionally intense experiences form memories that are peculiarly vivid and long-lasting. Not only do we recall such events long after they happened, but the recollection is often accompanied, in some measure, by a recurrence of the emotions aroused during the original experience.

. . .

When a person experiences especially shocking or violent events (such as a plane crash or bloody combat), the release of stress hormones may be so intense that the memory-encoding system is over-activated. The result is a consolidation of memories both far stronger and more persistent than normal and also more apt, upon recollection, to call forth the intense emotional response of the original experience. In such cases, each time the person relives the traumatic memory, a new flood of stress hormones is released, and the experience may be so emotionally intense as to be encoded as a new experience. With time, the memories grow more recurrent and intrusive, and the response—fear, helplessness, horror—more incapacitating. As we shall see, drugs that might prevent or alleviate the symptoms of PTSD are among the chief medical benefits that scientists expect from recent research in the neurochemistry of memory formation.

In fact, the discovery of hormonal regulation of memory formation was quickly followed up by clinical studies on human subjects demonstrating that memory of emotional experiences can be altered pharmacologically. In one particularly interesting series of experiments, Larry Cahill and his colleagues showed that injections of beta-blockers can, by inhibiting the action of stress hormones, suppress the memory-enhancing effects of strong emotional arousal.

. . .

[T]aking propranolol appears to have little or no effect on how we remember everyday or emotionally neutral information. But when taken at the time of highly emotional experiences, propranolol appears to suppress the normal memory-enhancing effects of emotional arousal—while leaving the immediate emotional response unaffected. These results suggested the possibility of using beta-blockers to help survivors of traumatic events to reduce their intrusive—and in some cases crippling—memories of those events.

. . .

"[A]lthough the pharmacology of memory alteration is a science still in its infancy, the significance of this potential new power—to separate the subjective experience of memory from the truth of the experience that is remembered—should not be underestimated. It surely returns us to the large ethical and anthropological questions with which we began—about memory's role in shaping personal identity and the character of human life, and about the meaning of remembering things that we would rather forget and of forgetting things that we perhaps ought to remember.

C. Memory-Blunting: Ethical Analysis

If we had the power, by promptly taking a memory-altering drug, to dull the emotional impact of what could become very painful memories, when might we be tempted to use it? And for what reasons should we yield to or resist the temptation?

At first glance, such a drug would seem ideally suited for the prevention of PTSD, the complex of debilitating symptoms that sometimes afflict those who have experienced severe trauma. These symptoms—which include persistent re-experiencing of the traumatic event and avoidance of every person, place, or thing that might stimulate the horrid memory's return[1]—can so burden mental life as to make normal everyday living extremely difficult, if not impossible.[2] For those suffering these disturbing symptoms, a drug that could separate a painful memory from its powerful emotional component would appear very welcome indeed.

Yet the prospect of preventing (even) PTSD with beta-blockers or other memory-blunting agents seems to be, for several reasons, problematic. First of all, the drugs in question appear to be effective only when administered during or shortly after a traumatic event—and thus well before any symptoms of PTSD would be manifested. How then could we make, and make on the spot, the *prospective* judgment that a particular event is sufficiently terrible to warrant preemptive memory-blunting? Second, how shall we judge *which* participants in the event merit such treatment? After all, not everyone who suffers through painful experiences is destined to have pathological memory effects. Should the drugs in question be given to everyone or only to those with an observed susceptibility to PTSD, and, if the latter, how will we know who these are? Finally, in some cases merely witnessing a disturbing event (for example, a murder, rape, or terrorist attack) is sufficient to cause PTSD-like symptoms long afterwards. Should we then, as soon as disaster strikes, consider giving memory-altering drugs to all the witnesses, in addition to those directly involved?

. . .

If the apparent powers of memory-blunting drugs are confirmed, some might be inclined to prescribe them liberally to all who are involved in a sufficiently terrible event. After all, even those not destined to come down with full-blown PTSD are likely to suffer painful recurrent memories of an airplane crash, an incident of terrorism, or a violent combat operation. In the aftermath of such shocking incidents, why not give everyone the chance to remember these events without the added burden of painful emotions? This line of reasoning might, in fact, tempt us to give beta-blockers liberally to soldiers on the eve of combat, to emergency workers en route to a disaster site, or even to individuals requesting prophylaxis against the shame or guilt they might incur from future misdeeds—in general, to anyone facing an experience that is likely to leave lasting intrusive memories.

Yet on further reflection it seems clear that not every intrusive memory is a suitable candidate for prospective pharmacological blunting. As Daniel Schacter has observed, "attempts to avoid traumatic memories often backfire."

Intrusive memories need to be acknowledged, confronted, and worked through, in order to set them to rest for the long term. Unwelcome memories of trauma are symptoms of a disrupted psyche that requires attention before it can resume healthy functioning. Beta-blockers might make it easier for trauma survivors to face and incorporate traumatic recollections, and in that sense could facilitate long-term adaptation. Yet it is also possible that beta-blockers would work against the normal process of recovery: traumatic memories would not spring to mind with the kind of psychological force that demands attention and perhaps intervention. Prescription of beta-blockers could bring about an effective trade-off between short-term reductions in the sting of traumatic memories and long-term increases in persistence of related symptoms of a trauma that has not been adequately confronted.[3]

The point can be generalized: in the immediate aftermath of a painful experience, we simply cannot know either the full meaning of the experience in question or the ultimate character and future prospects of the individual who experiences it. We cannot know how this experience will change this person at this time and over time. Will he be cursed forever by unbearable memories that, in retrospect, clearly should have been blunted medically? Or will he succeed, over time, in "redeeming" those painful memories by actively integrating them into the narrative of his life? By "rewriting" memories pharmacologically we might succeed in easing real suffering at the risk of falsifying our perception of the world and undermining our true identity.

Finally, the decision whether or not to use memory-blunting drugs must be made in the absence of clearly diagnosable disease. The drug must be taken right after a traumatic experience has occurred, and thus before the different ways that different individuals handle the same experience has become clear. In some cases, these interventions will turn out to have been preventive medicine, intervening to ward off the onset of PTSD before it arrives—though it is worth noting that we would lack even post hoc knowledge of whether any particular now-unaffected individual, in the absence of using the drug, would have become symptomatic.[4] In other cases, the interventions would not be medicine at all: altering the memory of individuals who could have lived well, even with severely painful memories, without pharmacologically dulling the pain. Worse, in still other cases, the use of such drugs would inoculate individuals in advance against the psychic pain that *should* accompany their commission of cruel, brutal, or shameful deeds. But in all cases, from the defensible to the dubious, the use of such powers changes the character of human memory, by intervening directly in the way individuals "encode," and thus the way they understand, the happenings of their own lives and the realities of the world around them.

. . .

1. Remembering Fitly and Truly.

Altering the formation of emotionally powerful memories risks severing what we remember from how we remember it and distorting the link between our perception of significant human events and the significance of the events themselves. It risks, in a word, falsifying our perception and understanding of the world. It risks making shameful acts seem less shameful, or terrible acts less terrible, than they really are.

Imagine the experience of a person who witnesses a shocking murder. Fearing that he will be haunted by images of this event, he immediately takes propranolol (or its more potent successor) to render his memory of the murder less painful and intrusive. Thanks to the drug, his memory of the murder gets encoded as a garden-variety, emotionally neutral experience. But in manipulating his memory in this way, he risks coming to think about the murder as more tolerable than it really is, as an event that should not sting those who witness it. For our opinions about the meaning of our experiences are shaped partly by the feelings evoked when we remember them. If, psychologically, the murder is transformed into an event our witness can recall without pain—or without *any* particular emotion—perhaps its moral significance will also fade from consciousness. If so, he would in a sense have ceased to be a genuine witness of the murder. When asked about it, he might say, "Yes, I was there. But it wasn't so terrible."

This points us to a deeper set of questions about bad memories: Would dulling our memory of terrible things make us too comfortable with the world, unmoved by suffering, wrongdoing, or cruelty? Does not the experience of hard truths—of the unchosen, the inexplicable, the tragic—remind us that we can never be fully at home in the world, especially if we are to take seriously the reality of human evil? Further, by blunting our experience and awareness of shameful, fearful, and hateful things, might we not also risk deadening our response to what is admirable, inspiring, and lovable? Can we become numb to life's sharpest sorrows without also becoming numb to its greatest joys?

. . .

There seems to be little doubt that some bitter memories are so painful and intrusive as to ruin the possibility for normal experience of much of life and the world. In such cases the impulse to relieve a crushing burden and restore lost innocence is fully understandable: If there are some things that it is better never to have experienced at all—things we would avoid if we possibly could—why not erase them from the memory of those unfortunate enough to have suffered them? If there are some things it is better never to have known or seen, why not use our power over memory to restore a witness's shattered peace of mind? There is great force in this argument, perhaps especially in cases where children lose prematurely that innocence that is rightfully theirs.

And yet, there may be a great cost to acting compassionately for those who suffer bad memories, if we do so by compromising the truthfulness of how they remember. We risk having them live falsely in order simply to cope, to survive by whatever means possible.

. . .

2. The Obligation to Remember.

Having truthful memories is not simply a personal matter. Strange to say, our own memory is not merely our own; it is part of the fabric of the society in which we live. Consider the case of a person who has suffered or witnessed atrocities that occasion unbearable memories: for example, those with firsthand experience of the Holocaust. The life of that individual might well be served by dulling such bitter memories,[5] but such a humanitarian intervention, if widely practiced, would seem deeply troubling: Would the community as a whole—would the human race—be served by such a mass numbing of this terrible but indispensable memory? Do those who suffer evil have a duty to remember and bear witness, lest we all forget the very horrors that haunt them?

. . .

Surely, we cannot and should not force those who live through great trauma to endure its painful memory *for the benefit of the rest of us*. But as a community, there are certain events that we have an obligation to remember—an obligation that falls disproportionately, one might even say unfairly, on those who experience such events most directly.[6] What kind of people would we be if we did not "want" to remember the Holocaust, if we sought to make the anguish it caused simply go away? And yet, what kind of people are we, especially those who face such horrors firsthand, that we can endure such awful memories?

The answer, in part, is that those who suffer terrible things cannot or should not have to endure their own bad memories alone. If, as a people, we have an obligation to remember certain terrible events truthfully, surely we ought to help those who suffered through those events to come to terms with their worst memories. Of course, one might see the new biotechnical powers, developed precisely to ease the psychic pain of bad memories, as the mark of such solidarity: perhaps it is our new way of meeting the obligation to aid those who remember the hardest things, those who bear witness to us and for us. But such solidarity may, in the end, prove false: for it exempts us from the duty to suffer-with (literally, to feel *com*-passion for) those who remember; it does not demand that we preserve the truth of their memories; it attempts instead to make the problem go away, and with it the truth of the experience in question.

4. The Soul of Memory, The Remembering Soul.

. . .

[W]e might often be tempted to sacrifice the accuracy of our memories for the sake of easing our pain or expanding our control over our own psychic lives. But doing so means, ultimately, severing ourselves from reality and leaving our own identity behind; it risks making us false, small, or capable of great illusions, and thus capable of great decadence or great evil, or perhaps simply willing to accept a phony contentment. We might be tempted to alter our memories to preserve an open future—to live the life we wanted to live before a particular experience happened to us. But in another sense, such interventions assume that our own future is not open—that we cannot and could never redeem the unwanted memory over time, that we cannot and could never integrate the remembered experience with our own truthful pursuit of happiness.

. . .

To have only happy memories would be a blessing—and a curse. Nothing would trouble us, but we would probably be shallow people, never falling to the depths of despair because we have little interest in the heights of human happiness or in the complicated lives of those around us. In the end, to have only happy memories is not to be happy in a truly human way. It is simply to be free of misery—an understandable desire given the many troubles of life, but a low aspiration for those who seek a truly human happiness.

Footnotes

1. There is no definitive diagnostic criterion for PTSD, but the core symptoms are thought to include persistent re-experiencing of the traumatic event, avoidance of associated stimuli, and hyperarousal. See *Diagnostic and Statistical Manual of Mental Disorders, Fourth Edition,* text revision, Washington, D.C.: American Psychiatric Association, 2000, pp. 463–486.

2. These symptoms are observed especially among combat veterans; indeed, PTSD is the modern name for what used to be called "shell shock" or "combat neurosis." Among veterans, PTSD is frequently associated with recurrent nightmares, substance abuse, and delusional outbursts of violence. There is controversy about the prevalence of PTSD, with some studies finding that up to 8 percent of adult Americans have suffered the disorder, as well as a third of all veterans of the Vietnam War. See Kessler, R. C., et al., "Post-Traumatic Stress Disorder in the National Comorbidity Survey," *Archives of General Psychiatry* 52(12): 1048–1060, 1995; Kulka, R. A., et al., *Trauma and the Vietnam War Generation: Report of Findings from the National Vietnam Veterans Readjustment Study,* New York: Brunner/Mazel, 1990.

3. Schacter, D., *The Seven Sins of Memory: How the Mind Forgets and Remembers,* New York: Houghton Mifflin, 2001, p. 183.

4. There is already ongoing controversy about excessive diagnosis of PTSD. Many psychotherapists believe that a patient's psychic troubles are generally based on some earlier (now repressed) traumatic experience which must be unearthed and dealt with if relief is to be found. True PTSD is, however, generally transient, and the search for treatment is directed against the symptoms of its initial (worst) phase—the sleeplessness, the nightmares, the excessive jitteriness.

5. Of course, many Holocaust survivors managed, without pharmacological assistance, to live fulfilling lives while never forgetting what they lived through. At the same time, many survivors would almost certainly have benefited from pharmacological treatment.

6. For a discussion of memory-altering drugs and the meaning of "bearing witness," see the essay by Cohen, E., "Our Psychotropic Memory," *SEED*, no. 8, Fall 2003, p. 42.

Michael J. Sandel  **NO**

The Case Against Perfection: Ethics in the Age of Genetic Engineering

The Ethics of Enhancement

A few years ago, a couple decided they wanted to have a child, preferably a deaf one. Both partners were deaf, and proudly so. Like others in the deaf-pride community, Sharon Duchesneau and Candy McCullough considered deafness a cultural identity, not a disability to be cured. "Being deaf is just a way of life," said Duchesneau. "We feel whole as deaf people and we want to share the wonderful aspects of our deaf community—a sense of belonging and connectedness—with children. We truly feel we live rich lives as deaf people."

In hopes of conceiving a deaf child, they sought out a sperm donor with five generations of deafness in his family. And they succeeded. Their son Gauvin was born deaf.

The new parents were surprised when their story, which was reported in the *Washington Post,* brought widespread condemnation. Most of the outrage focused on the charge that they had deliberately inflicted a disability on their child. Duchesneau and McCullough (who are lesbian partners) denied that deafness is a disability and argued that they had simply wanted a child like themselves. "We do not view what we did as very different from what many straight couples do when they have children," said Duchesneau.

Is it wrong to make a child deaf by design? If so, what makes it wrong—the deafness or the design? Suppose, for the sake of argument, that deafness is not a disability but a distinctive identity. Is there still something wrong with the idea of parents picking and choosing the kind of child they will have? Or do parents do that all the time, in their choice of mate and, these days, in their use of new reproductive technologies? . . .

Articulating Our Unease

Breakthroughs in genetics present us with a promise and a predicament. The promise is that we may soon be able to treat and prevent a host of debilitating diseases. The predicament is that our new-found genetic knowledge may also enable us to manipulate our own nature—to enhance our muscles, memories, and moods; to choose the sex, height, and other genetic traits of our children; to improve our physical and cognitive capacities; to make ourselves "better

From *The Atlantic Monthly,* April 2004. pp. 50–62. Copyright © 2004 by Michael J. Sandel, Ph.D. Reprinted by permission of the author.

than well." Most people find at least some forms of genetic engineering dis-
quieting. But it is not easy to articulate the source of our unease. The familiar
terms of moral and political discourse make it difficult to say what is wrong
with reengineering our nature. . . .

When science moves faster than moral understanding, as it does today,
men and women struggle to articulate their unease. In liberal societies, they
reach first for the language of autonomy, fairness, and individual rights.
But this part of our moral vocabulary does not equip us to address the hardest
questions posed by cloning, designer children, and genetic engineering. That
is why the genomic revolution has induced a kind of moral vertigo. To grapple
with the ethics of enhancement, we need to confront questions largely lost
from view in the modern world—questions about the moral status of nature,
and about the proper stance of human beings toward the given world. Since
these questions verge on theology, modern philosophers and political theorists tend to shrink from them. But our new powers of biotechnology make
them unavoidable.

Genetic Engineering

To see how this is so, consider four examples of bioengineering already on the
horizon: muscle enhancement, memory enhancement, height enhancement,
and sex selection. In each case, what began as an attempt to treat a disease or
prevent a genetic disorder now beckons as an instrument of improvement and
consumer choice.

Muscles

Everyone would welcome a gene therapy to alleviate muscular dystrophy and
to reverse the debilitating muscle loss that comes with old age. But what if the
same therapy were used to produce genetically altered athletes? Researchers
have developed a synthetic gene that, when injected into the muscle cells of
mice, makes muscles grow and prevents them from deteriorating with age. The
success bodes well for human applications. Dr. H. Lee Sweeney, who leads the
research, hopes his discovery will cure the immobility that afflicts the elderly.
But Dr. Sweeney's bulked-up mice have already attracted the attention of athletes seeking a competitive edge. The gene not only repairs injured muscles
but also strengthens healthy ones. Although the therapy is not yet approved
for human use, the prospect of genetically enhanced weight lifters, home-run
sluggers, linebackers, and sprinters is easy to imagine. The widespread use of
steroids and other performance-enhancing drugs in professional sports suggests that many athletes will be eager to avail themselves of genetic enhancement. The International Olympic Committee has already begun to worry
about the fact that, unlike drugs, altered genes cannot be detected in urine or
blood tests.

The prospect of genetically altered athletes offers a good illustration of
the ethical quandaries surrounding enhancement. Should the IOC and professional sports leagues ban genetically enhanced athletes, and if so, on what

grounds? The two most obvious reasons for banning drugs in sports are safety and fairness: Steroids have harmful side effects, and to allow some to boost their performance by incurring serious health risks would put their competitors at an unfair disadvantage. But suppose, for the sake of argument, that muscle-enhancing gene therapy turned out to be safe, or at least no riskier than a rigorous weight-training regime. Would there still be a reason to ban its use in sports? There is something unsettling about the specter of genetically altered athletes lifting SUVs or hitting 650-foot home runs or running a three-minute mile. But what exactly is troubling about these scenarios? Is it simply that we find such superhuman spectacles too bizarre to contemplate, or does our unease point to something of ethical significance? . . .

Designer Children, Designing Parents

The ethic of giftedness, under siege in sports, persists in the practice of parenting. But here, too, bioengineering and genetic enhancement threaten to dislodge it. To appreciate children as gifts is to accept them as they come, not as objects of our design, or products of our will, or instruments of our ambition. Parental love is not contingent on the talents and attributes the child happens to have. We choose our friends and spouses at least partly on the basis of qualities we find attractive. But we do not choose our children. Their qualities are unpredictable, and even the most conscientious parents cannot be held wholly responsible for the kind of child they have. That is why parenthood, more than other human relationships, teaches what the theologian William F. May calls an "openness to the unbidden."

Molding and Beholding

May's resonant phrase describes a quality of character and heart that restrains the impulse to mastery and control and prompts a sense of life as gift. It helps us see that the deepest moral objection to enhancement lies less in the perfection it seeks than in the human disposition it expresses and promotes. The problem is not that the parents usurp the autonomy of the child they design. (It is not as if the child could otherwise choose her genetic traits for herself.) The problem lies in the hubris of the designing parents, in their drive to master the mystery of birth. Even if this disposition does not make parents tyrants to their children, it disfigures the relation between parent and child, and deprives the parent of the humility and enlarged human sympathies that an openness to the unbidden can cultivate.

To appreciate children as gifts or blessings is not to be passive in the face of illness or disease. Healing a sick or injured child does not override her natural capacities but permits them to flourish. Although medical treatment intervenes in nature, it does so for the sake of health, and so does not represent a boundless bid for mastery and dominion. Even strenuous attempts to treat or cure disease do not constitute a Promethean assault on the given. The reason is that medicine is governed, or at least guided, by the norm of restoring and preserving the natural human functions that constitute health.

Medicine, like sports, is a practice with a purpose, a telos, that orients and constrains it. Of course what counts as good health or normal human functioning is open to argument; it is not only a biological question. People disagree, for example, about whether deafness is a disability to be cured or a form of community and identity to be cherished. But even the disagreement proceeds from the assumption that the point of medicine is to promote health and cure disease.

Some people argue that a parent's obligation to heal a sick child implies an obligation to enhance a healthy one, to maximize his or her potential for success in life. But this is true only if one accepts the utilitarian idea that health is not a distinctive human good, but simply a means of maximizing happiness or well-being. Bioethicist Julian Savulescu argues, for example, that "health is not intrinsically valuable," only "instrumentally valuable," a "resource" that allows us to do what we want. This way of thinking about health rejects the distinction between healing and enhancing. According to Savulescu, parents not only have a duty to promote their children's health; they are also "morally obliged to genetically modify their children." Parents should use technology to manipulate their children's "memory, temperament, patience, empathy, sense of humor, optimism," and other characteristics in order to give them "the best opportunity of the best life."

But it is a mistake to think of health in wholly instrumental terms, as a way of maximizing something else. Good health, like good character, is a constitutive element of human flourishing. Although more health is better than less, at least within a certain range, it is not the kind of good that can be maximized. No one aspires to be a virtuoso at health (except, perhaps, a hypochondriac). During the 1920s, eugenicists held health contests at state fairs and awarded prizes to the "fittest families." But this bizarre practice illustrates the folly of conceiving health in instrumental terms, or as a good to be maximized. Unlike the talents and traits that bring success in a competitive society, health is a bounded good; parents can seek it for their children without risk of being drawn into an ever-escalating arms race.

In caring for the health of their children, parents do not cast themselves as designers or convert their children into products of their will or instruments of their ambition. The same cannot be said of parents who pay large sums to select the sex of their child (for nonmedical reasons) or who aspire to bioengineer their child's intellectual endowments or athletic prowess. Like all distinctions, the line between therapy and enhancement blurs at the edges. (What about orthodontics, for example, or growth hormone for very short kids?) But this does not obscure the reason the distinction matters: parents bent on enhancing their children are more likely to overreach, to express and entrench attitudes at odds with the norm of unconditional love.

Of course, unconditional love does not require that parents refrain from shaping and directing the development of their child. To the contrary, parents have an obligation to cultivate their children, to help them discover and develop their talents and gifts. As May points out, parental love has two aspects: accepting love and transforming love. Accepting love affirms the being of the child, whereas transforming love seeks the well-being of the child. Each side of parental love corrects the excesses of the other: "Attachment becomes too quietistic if it slackens into mere acceptance of the child as he is." Parents have a duty to promote their child's excellence.

These days, however, overly ambitious parents are prone to get carried away with transforming love—promoting and demanding all manner of accomplishments from their children, seeking perfection. "Parents find it difficult to maintain an equilibrium between the two sides of love," May observes. "Accepting love, without transforming love, slides into indulgence and finally neglect. Transforming love, without accepting love, badgers and finally rejects." May finds in these competing impulses a parallel with modern science; it, too, engages us in beholding the given world, studying and savoring it, and also in molding the world, transforming and perfecting it.

The mandate to mold our children, to cultivate and improve them, complicates the case against enhancement. We admire parents who seek the best for their children, who spare no effort to help them achieve happiness and success. What, then, is the difference between providing such help through education and training and providing it by means of genetic enhancement? Some parents confer advantages on their children by enrolling them in expensive schools, hiring private tutors, sending them to tennis camp, providing them with piano lessons, ballet lessons, swimming lessons, SAT prep courses, and so on. If it is permissible, even admirable, for parents to help their children in these ways, why isn't it equally admirable for parents to use whatever genetic technologies may emerge (provided they are safe) to enhance their child's intelligence, musical ability, or athletic skill?

Defenders of enhancement argue that there is no difference, in principle, between improving children through education and improving them through bioengineering. Critics of enhancement insist there is all the difference in the world. They argue that trying to improve children by manipulating their genetic makeup is reminiscent of eugenics, the discredited movement of the past century to improve the human race through policies (including forced sterilization and other odious measures) aimed at improving the gene pool. These competing analogies help clarify the moral status of genetic enhancement. Is the attempt of parents to enhance their children through genetic engineering more like education and training (a presumably good thing) or more like eugenics (a presumably bad thing)?

The defenders of enhancement are right to this extent: Improving children through genetic engineering is similar in spirit to the heavily managed, high-pressure child-rearing practices that have become common these days. But this similarity does not vindicate genetic enhancement. On the contrary, it highlights a problem with the trend toward hyperparenting. . . .

The Pressure to Perform

Grubman's willingness to move heaven and earth, and even the market, to get his two-year-olds into a fancy nursery school is a sign of the times. It tells of mounting pressures in American life that are changing the expectations parents have for their children and increasing the demands placed on children to perform. When preschoolers apply to private kindergartens and elementary schools, their fate depends on favorable letters of recommendation and a standardized test intended to measure their intelligence and development. Some parents have their four-year-olds coached to prepare for the test. . . .

Some see a bright line between genetic enhancement and other ways that people seek improvement in their children and themselves. Genetic manipulation seems somehow worse—more intrusive, more sinister—than other ways of enhancing performance and seeking success. But morally speaking, the difference is less significant than it seems.

Those who argue that bioengineering is similar in spirit to other ways ambitious parents shape and mold their children have a point. But this similarity does not give us reason to embrace the genetic manipulation of children. Instead, it gives us reason to question the low-tech, high-pressure child-rearing practices we commonly accept. The hyperparenting familiar in our time represents an anxious excess of mastery and dominion that misses the sense of life as gift. This draws it disturbingly close to eugenics. . . .

Although liberal eugenics finds support among many Anglo-American moral and political philosophers, Jürgen Habermas, Germany's most prominent political philosopher, opposes it. Acutely aware of Germany's dark eugenic past, Habermas argues against the use of embryo screening and genetic manipulation for nonmedical enhancement. His case against liberal eugenics is especially intriguing because he believes it rests wholly on liberal premises and need not invoke spiritual or theological notions. His critique of genetic engineering "does not relinquish the premises of postmeta-physical thinking," by which he means it does not depend on any particular conception of the good life. Habermas agrees with John Rawls that, since people in modern pluralist societies disagree about morality and religion, a just society should not take sides in such disputes but should instead accord each person the freedom to choose and pursue his or her own conception of the good life.

Genetic intervention to select or improve children is objectionable, Habermas argues, because it violates the liberal principles of autonomy and equality. It violates autonomy because genetically programmed persons cannot regard themselves as "the sole authors of their own life history." And it undermines equality by destroying "the essentially symmetrical relations between free and equal human beings" across generations. One measure of this asymmetry is that, once parents become the designers of their children, they inevitably incur a responsibility for their children's lives that cannot possibly be reciprocal.

Habermas is right to oppose eugenic parenting, but wrong to think that the case against it can rest on liberal terms alone. The defenders of liberal eugenics have a point when they argue that designer children are no less autonomous with respect to their genetic traits that children born the natural way. It is not as if, absent eugenic manipulation, we can choose our genetic inheritance for ourselves. As for Habermas's worry about equality and reciprocity between the generations, defenders of liberal eugenics can reply that this worry, though legitimate, does not apply uniquely to genetic manipulation. The parent who forces her child to practice the piano incessantly from the age of three, or to hit tennis balls from dawn to dusk, also exerts a kind of control over the child's life that cannot possibly be reciprocal. The question, liberals insist, is whether the parental intervention, be it eugenic or environmental, undermines the child's freedom to choose her own life plan.

An ethic of autonomy and equality cannot explain what is wrong with eugenics. But Habermas has a further argument that cuts deeper, even as it points beyond the limits of liberal, or "postmeta-physical" considerations. This is the idea that "we experience our own freedom with reference to something which, by its very nature, is not at our disposal." To think of ourselves as free, we must be able to ascribe our origins "to a beginning which eludes human disposal," a beginning that arises from "something—like God or nature—that is not at the disposal of some *other* person." Habermas goes on to suggest that birth, "being a natural fact, meets the conceptual requirement of constituting a beginning we cannot control. Philosophy has but rarely addressed this matter." An exception, he observes, is found in the work of Hannah Arendt, who sees "natality," the fact that human beings are born not made, as a condition of their capacity to initiate action.

Habermas is onto something important, I think, when he asserts a "connection between the contingency of a life's beginning that is not at our disposal and the freedom to give one's life an ethical shape." For him, this connection matters because it explains why a genetically designed child is beholden and subordinate to another person (the designing parent) in a way that a child born of a contingent, impersonal beginning is not. But the notion that our freedom is bound up with "a beginning we cannot control" also carries a broader significance: Whatever its effect on the autonomy of the child, the drive to banish contingency and to master the mystery of birth diminishes the designing parent and corrupts parenting as a social practice governed by norms of unconditional love.

This takes us back to the notion of giftedness. Even if it does not harm the child or impair its autonomy, eugenic parenting is objectionable because it expresses and entrenches a certain stance toward the world—a stance of mastery and dominion that fails to appreciate the gifted character of human powers and achievements, and misses the part of freedom that consists in a persisting negotiation with the given.

Mastery and Gift

The problem with eugenics and genetic engineering is that they represent the one-sided triumph of willfulness over giftedness, of dominion over reverence, of molding over beholding. But why, we may wonder, should we worry about this triumph? Why not shake off our unease with enhancement as so much superstition? What would be lost if biotechnology dissolved our sense of giftedness?

Humility, Responsibility, and Solidarity

From the standpoint of religion, the answer is clear: To believe that our talents and powers are wholly our own doing is to misunderstand our place in creation, to confuse our role with God's. But religion is not the only source of reasons to care about giftedness. The moral stakes can also be described in secular terms. If the genetic revolution erodes our appreciation for the gifted character of human powers and achievements, it will transform three key features of our moral landscape—humility, responsibility, and solidarity.

In a social world that prizes mastery and control, parenthood is a school for humility. That we care deeply about our children, and yet cannot choose the kind we want, teaches parents to be open to the unbidden. Such openness is a disposition worth affirming, not only within families but in the wider world as well. It invites us to abide the unexpected, to live with dissonance, to reign in the impulse to control. A *Gattaca*-like world, in which parents became accustomed to specifying the sex and genetic traits of their children, would be a world inhospitable to the unbidden, a gated community writ large. . . .

It is sometimes thought that genetic enhancement erodes human responsibility by overriding effort and striving. But the real problem is the explosion, not the erosion, of responsibility. As humility gives way, responsibility expands to daunting proportions. We attribute less to chance and more to choice. Parents become responsible for choosing, or failing to choose, the right traits for their children. Athletes become responsible for acquiring, or failing to acquire, the talents that will help their team win.

One of the blessings of seeing ourselves as creatures of nature, God, or fortune is that we are not wholly responsible for the way we are. The more we become masters of our genetic endowments, the greater the burden we bear for the talents we have and the way we perform. Today when a basketball player misses a rebound, his coach can blame him for being out of position. Tomorrow the coach may blame him for being too short.

Even now, the growing use of performance-enhancing drugs in professional sports is subtly transforming the expectations players have for one another. In the past when a starting pitcher's team scored too few runs to win, he could only curse his bad luck and take it in stride. These days, the use of amphetamines and other stimulants is so wide-spread that players who take the field without them are criticized for "playing naked." A recently retired major league outfielder told *Sports Illustrated* that some pitchers blame teammates who play unenhanced: "If the starting pitcher knows that you're going out there naked, he's upset that you're not giving him [everything] you can. The big-time pitcher wants to make sure you're beaning up before the game." . . .

The Promethean impulse is contagious. In parenting as in sports, it unsettles and erodes the gifted dimension of human experience. When performance-enhancing drugs become commonplace, unenhanced ballplayers find themselves "playing naked." When genetic screening becomes a routine part of pregnancy, parents who eschew it are regarded as "flying blind" and are held responsible for whatever genetic defect befalls their child. . . .

If genetic engineering enabled us to override the results of the genetic lottery, to replace chance with choice, the gifted character of human powers and achievements would recede, and with it, perhaps, our capacity to see ourselves as sharing a common fate. The successful would become even more likely than they are now to view themselves as self-made and self-sufficient, and hence wholly responsible for their success. Those at the bottom of society would be viewed not as disadvantaged, and so worthy of a measure of compensation, but as simply unfit, and so worthy of eugenic repair. The meritocracy, less chastened by chance, would become harder, less forgiving. As perfect genetic knowledge would end the simulacrum of solidarity in insurance markets, perfect genetic control would erode the actual solidarity that arises when men and women reflect on the contingency of their talents and fortunes. . . .

There is something appealing, even intoxicating, about a vision of human freedom unfettered by the given. It may even be the case that the allure of that vision played a part in summoning the genomic age into being. It is often assumed that the powers of enhancement we now possess arose as an inadvertent by-product of biomedical progress—the genetic revolution came, so to speak, to cure disease, but stayed to tempt us with the prospect of enhancing our performance, designing our children, and perfecting our nature. But that may have the story backward. It is also possible to view genetic engineering as the ultimate expression of our resolve to see ourselves astride the world, the masters of our nature. But that vision of freedom is flawed. It threatens to banish our appreciation of life as a gift, and to leave us with nothing to affirm or behold outside our own will. . . .

EXPLORING THE ISSUE

Should Biotechnology Be Used to Alter and Enhance Humans?

Critical Thinking and Reflection

1. What are the potential benefits of biotechnologies for enhancing humans?
2. If babies can be genetically engineered to be relatively disease free or resistant and also intellectually and physically improved, why not do it?
3. What moral values would oppose gains from genetic engineering that would be safe?
4. Who would make the decisions about bioengineering? Should it be left to the parents for bioengineering babies? What should the role of society via government be? Should religions have a say or even a final say?
5. Enhancement drugs are regulated in sports. Should they be regulated outside of sports if they are not harmful?
6. Do you trust people to make good decisions about their own health and drug-induced changes? How much should they be guided or even regulated?

Is There Common Ground?

The most often cited arguments in favor of using biotechnologies for altering and enhancing humans are the benefits of protecting children from diseases, preventing handicaps and deficiencies, and enhancing physical and mental abilities. The main arguments against using biotechnology include the moral arguments against playing God and too mightily interfering in nature. But what about the possibility of making people more moral in the sense of more caring, compassionate, cooperative, trusting, and helpful and less uncooperative, unsympathetic, and easily irritated? A number of scientists believe that these characteristics are fairly closely related to genes, so the moral improvement of the human race could be assisted by bioengineering. Furthermore, chemical treatments could help adults become less selfish and aggressive and become more altruistic and cooperative. In sum, bioengineering could produce many benefits, but society should proceed cautiously because risks and unintended consequences are associated with these life-changing technologies.

Additional Resources

Thus, the moral argument can be used in favor of biotechnologies. In some sense, this is an old debate, as the Faust legend indicates. Nevertheless, it is only recently that science has brought us to the doorstep of the bioengineering of humans. Two books from the mid-1980s serve as classics in this field.

Jeremy Rivkin and Nicanor Perlas warn against bioengineering in *Algeny* (Penguin Books, 1984). They argue that biotechnology's destructive power far exceeds its potential benefits. Jonathan Glover reverses the weights for benefits and costs and champions bioengineering in *What Sort of People Should There Be?* (Penguin Books, 1984). Other works that are opposed to bioengineering include Marcus Wohlsen, *Biopunk: DIY Scientists Hack the Software of Life* (Current, 2011); Craig Holdrege, *Beyond Biotechnology: The Barren Promise of Genetic Engineering* (University of Kentucky Press, 2010); Jeremy Rivkin, *The Biotech Century* (Tarcher/Putnam, 1998); Francis Fukuyama, *Our Posthuman Future* (Farrar, Strauss, and Giroux, 2002); and Bill McKibben, *Enough* (Henry Holt, 2003). More positive views of genetic engineering are found in the following: Eric S. Grace, *Biotechnology Unzipped: Promises and Realities* (Joseph Henry Press, 2006); Ramex Naam, *More Than Human: Embracing the Promise of Biological Enhancement* (Broadway Books, 2005); Gregory Stock, *Redesigning Humans: Our Inevitable Genetic Future* (Houghton Mifflin Harcourt, 2002); Allan Buchanan et al., *From Chance to Choice: Genetics and Justice* (Cambridge University Press, 2000); and Emirates Center for Strategic Studies and Research, *Biotechnology and the Future of Society: Challenges and Opportunities* (Emirates Center for Strategic Studies and Research, 2004). For works that present multiple views, see Allen E. Buchanan, *Better Than Human: The Promise and Perils of Enhancing Ourselves* (Oxford University Press, 2011); Robert H. Carlson, *Biology Is Technology: The Promise, Peril, and New Business of Engineering Life* (Harvard University Press, 2010); Linda L. McCabe, *DNA: Promise and Peril* (University of California Press, 2008); Bernard E. Rollin, *Science and Ethics* (Cambridge University Press, 2006); Lori P. Knowles and Gregory E. Kaebnick, eds., *Reprogenetics: Law, Policy, and Ethical Issues* (Johns Hopkins University Press, 2007); Rose M. Morgan, *The Genetics Revolution: History, Fears, and Future of a Life-Altering Science* (Greenwood Press, 2006); Pete Shanks, *Human Genetic Engineering: A Guide for Activists, Skeptics, and the Very Perplexed* (Nation Books, 2005); Gerald Magill, ed., *Genetics and Ethics: An Interdisciplinary Study* (Saint Louis University Press, 2004); Audrey R. Chapman and Mark S. Frankel, eds., *Designing Our Descendants: The Promises and Perils of Genetic Modifications* (Johns Hopkins University Press, 2003); Scott Gilbert et al., *Bioethics and the New Embryology: Springboards for Debate* (W. H. Freeman, 2005); Howard W. Baillie and Timothy K. Casey, eds., *Is Human Nature Obsolete? Genetics, Bioengineering, and the Future of the Human Condition* (MIT Press, 2005); and Rose M. Morgan, *The Genetic Revolution: History, Fears, and Future of a Life-Altering Science* (Greenwood Press, 2006). For discussions of human cloning, see Martha C. Nussbaum and Cass R. Sunstein, eds., *Clones and Clones: Facts and Fantasies about Human Cloning* (W. W. Norton, 1998); and President's Council on Bioethics, *Human Cloning and Human Dignity: An Ethical Inquiry* (Government Printing Office, 2002).

Obviously, this issue is at rock bottom an ethical issue and a confusing one at that. It does not line up highly ethical thinkers on one side and ethical relativist on the other. The following books discuss the ethical issues from a variety of points of views: Sheila Jasanoff, ed., *Reframing Rights: Bioconstitutionalism in the Genetic Age* (MIT Press, 2011); Lawrence E. Johnson, *A Life-Centered Approach to Biocentric Ethics* (Cambridge University Press, 2011); Neil Messer,

Respecting Life: Theology and Bioethics (SCM Press, 2011); Richard Scherlock, *Nature's End: The Theological Meaning of the New Genetics* (ISI Books, 2010); Alexandra Plows, *Debating Human Genetics: Contemporary Issues in Public Policy and Ethics* (Routledge, 2011); and Ronald Michael Green, *Babies by Design: The Ethics of Genetic Choice* (Yale University Press, 2007).

We leave to Colin Tudge ("The Future of Humanity," *New Statesman*, April 8, 2002) the final word on this subject. "On present knowledge, or even with what we are likely to know in the next two centuries, it would be as presumptuous to try to improve on the genes of a healthy human baby as it would be to edit sacred verse in medieval Chinese if all we had to go on was a bad dictionary. So all in all, human beings are likely to remain as they are, genetically speaking . . . and there doesn't seem to be much that meddling human beings can do about it. This, surely, is a mercy. We may have been shaped blindly by evolution. We may have been guided on our way by God. Whichever it was, or both, the job has been done a million times better than we are ever likely to do. Natural selection is far more subtle than human invention. 'What a piece of work is a man!' said Hamlet. 'How beauteous mankind is!' said Miranda. Both of them were absolutely right."

Internet References . . .

American Society of Criminology

The American Society of Criminology website (style sheet) is an excellent starting point for studying all aspects of criminology and criminal justice. This page provides links to sites on criminal justice in general, international criminal justice, juvenile justice, courts, the police, and the government.

www.asc41.com/

Crime Times

This *Crime Times* site lists research reviews and other information regarding the causes of criminal and violent behavior. It is provided by the nonprofit Wacker Foundation, publishers of *Crime Times.*

www.crimetimes.org/

Justice Information Center (JIC)

Provided by the National Criminal Justice Reference Service, the Justice Information Center (JIC) site connects to information about corrections, courts, crime prevention, criminal justice, statistics, drugs and crime, law enforcement, and victims, among other topics.

www.ncjrs.gov/

Crime and Social Control

*A*ll societies label certain hurtful actions as crimes and punish those who commit them. Other harmful actions, however, are not defined as crimes, and the perpetrators are not punished. Today the definition of crime and the appropriate treatment of criminals is widely debated. Some of the major questions are: Does street crime pose more of a threat to the public's well-being than white-collar crime? Billions of dollars have been spent on the "war on drugs," but who is winning? Would legalizing some drugs free up money that could be directed to other types of social welfare programs, such as the rehabilitation of addicts? Is the threat of nuclear terrorism legitimate or overstated?

- Is Street Crime More Harmful Than White-Collar Crime?
- Should Laws Against Drug Use Remain Restrictive?
- Are We Headed Toward a Nuclear 9/11?
- Is Torture Ever Justified?

ISSUE 16

Is Street Crime More Harmful Than White-Collar Crime?

YES: David A. Anderson, from "The Aggregate Burden of Crime,"
Journal of Law and Economics (vol. XLII, no. 2, October 1999)

NO: Jeffrey Reiman, from *The Rich Get Richer and the Poor Get Prison:
Ideology, Class, and Criminal Justice,* 5th ed. (Allyn & Bacon, 1998)

Learning Outcomes

After reading this issue, you should be able to:

- Understand the many costs of various crimes including law
  enforcement, security costs, health and death costs, fear and
  deprivation, lost work time, and the value of stolen goods.
- Know that the costs of crime exceed $1 trillion a year and that
  most of the public is largely unaware of many of these costs.
- Know the relative costs in all of its dimensions of street crime
  versus white-collar crime and make a judgment of which set
  of crimes is worse according to your values.
- Know that corporations are responsible for more deaths than
  are murders.
- Analyze where guilt lies when decisions made in board rooms
  end up causing deaths through a long causal chain.

ISSUE SUMMARY

YES: David A. Anderson estimates the total annual cost of crime
including law enforcement and security services. The costs exceed
$1 trillion, with fraud (mostly white-collar crime) causing about
one-fifth of the total. His calculations of the full costs of the loss of
life and injury comes to about half of the total costs. It is right, therefore, to view personal and violent crime as the big crime problem.

NO: Professor of philosophy Jeffrey Reiman argues that the dangers
posed by negligent corporations and white-collar criminals are a
greater menace to society than are the activities of typical street
criminals.

T he word *crime* entered the English language (from the Old French) around A.D. 1250, when it was identified with "sinfulness." Later, the meaning of the word was modified: Crime became the kind of sinfulness that was rightly punishable by law. Even medieval writers, who did not distinguish very sharply between church and state, recognized that there were some sins for which punishment was best left to God; the laws should punish only those that cause harm to the community. Of course, their concept of harm was a very broad one, embracing such offenses as witchcraft and blasphemy. Modern jurists, even those who deplore such practices, would say that the state has no business punishing the perpetrators of these types of offenses.

What, then, should the laws punish? The answer depends in part on our notion of harm. We usually limit the term to the kind of harm that is tangible and obvious: taking a life, causing bodily injury or psychological trauma, and destroying property. For most Americans today, particularly those who live in cities, the word *crime* is practically synonymous with street crime. Anyone who has ever been robbed or beaten by street criminals will never forget the experience. The harm that these criminals cause is tangible, and the connection between the harm and the perpetrator is very direct.

But suppose the connection is not so direct. Suppose, for example, that A hires B to shoot C. Is that any less a crime? B is the actual shooter, but is A any less guilty? Of course not, we say; he may even be more guilty because he is the ultimate mover behind the crime. A would be guilty even if the chain of command were much longer, involving A's orders to B, and B's to C, then on to D, E, and F to kill G. Organized crime kingpins go to jail even when they are far removed from the people who carry out their orders. High officials of the Nixon administration, even though they were not directly involved in the burglary attempt at the Democratic National Committee headquarters at the Watergate Hotel complex in 1972, were imprisoned.

This brings us to the topic of white-collar crime. The burglars at the Watergate Hotel were acting on orders that trickled down from the highest reaches of political power in the United States. Other white-collar criminals are as varied as the occupations from which they come. They include stock brokers who make millions through insider trading, as Ivan Boesky did; members of Congress who take payoffs; and people who cheat on their income taxes, like hotel owner and billionaire Leona Helmsley. Some, like Helmsley, get stiff prison sentences when convicted, although many others (like most of the officials in the Watergate scandal) do little or no time in prison. Do they deserve stiffer punishment, or are their crimes less harmful than the crimes of street criminals?

Although white-collar criminals do not directly cause physical harm or relieve people of their wallets, they can still end up doing considerable harm. The harm done by Nixon's aides threatened the integrity of the U.S. electoral system. Every embezzler, corrupt politician, and tax cheat exacts a toll on our society. Individuals can be hurt in more tangible ways by decisions made in corporate boardrooms: Auto executives, for example, have approved design features that have caused fatalities. Managers of chemical companies have allowed practices that have polluted the environment with cancer-causing agents. And heads of corporations have presided over industries wherein workers have been needlessly killed or maimed.

Whether these decisions should be considered crimes is debatable. A crime must always involve "malicious intent," or what the legal system calls *mens rea*. This certainly applies to street crime—the mugger obviously has sinister designs—but does it apply to every decision made in a boardroom that ends up causing harm? And does that harm match or exceed the harm caused by street criminals? In the following selections, David A. Anderson tries to calculate all the costs of all crimes. His message is that crime costs society far more than we realize. But for the debate on the relative costs of street vs. white-collar crime, his study shows that street crime costs society more than white-collar crime. According to Jeffrey Reiman, white-collar crime does more harm than is commonly recognized. By his count, white-collar crime causes far more deaths, injuries, illnesses, and financial loss than street crime. In light of this, he argues, we must redefine our ideas about what crime is and who the criminals are.

YES

David A. Anderson

The Aggregate Burden of Crime

Introduction

Distinct from previous studies that have focused on selected crimes, regions, or outcomes, this study attempts an exhaustively broad estimation of the crime burden. . . .

Overt annual expenditures on crime in the United States include $47 billion for police protection, $36 billion for corrections, and $19 billion for the legal and judicial costs of state and local criminal cases. (Unless otherwise noted, all figures are adjusted to reflect 1997 dollars using the Consumer Price Index.) Crime victims suffer $876 million worth of lost workdays, and guns cost society $25 billion in medical bills and lost productivity in a typical year. Beyond the costs of the legal system, victim losses, and crime prevention agencies, the crime burden includes the costs of deterrence (locks, safety lighting and fencing, alarm systems and munitions), the costs of compliance enforcement (non-gendarme inspectors and regulators), implicit psychic and health costs (fear, agony, and the inability to behave as desired), and the opportunity costs of time spent preventing, carrying out, and serving prison terms for criminal activity.

This study estimates the impact of crime, taking a comprehensive list of the repercussions of aberrant behavior into account. While the standard measures of criminal activity count crimes and direct costs, this study measures the impact of crimes and includes indirect costs as well. Further, the available data on which crime cost figures are typically based is imprecise. Problems with crime figures stem from the prevalence of unreported crimes, inconsistencies in recording procedures among law enforcement agencies, policies of recording only the most serious crime in events with multiple offenses, and a lack of distinction between attempted and completed crimes. This research does not eliminate these problems, but it includes critical crime-prevention and opportunity costs that are measured with relative precision, and thus places less emphasis on the imprecise figures used in most other measures of the impact of crime. . . .

Previous Studies

Several studies have estimated the impact of crime; however, none has been thorough in its assessment of the substantial indirect costs of crime and the crucial consideration of private crime prevention expenditures. The FBI Crime

From *Journal of Law and Economics*, vol. XLII, October 1999, pp. 611–642. Copyright © 1999 by David A. Anderson. Reprinted by permission of the author.

Table 1

Previous Study	Focus	Not Included	$ (billions)
Colins (1994)	General	Opportunity Costs, Miscellaneous Indirect Components	728
Cohen, Miller, and Wiersema (1995)	Victim Costs of Violent and Property Crimes	Prevention, Opportunity, and Indirect Costs	472
U.S. News (1974)	General	Opportunity Costs, Miscellaneous Indirect Components	288
Cohen, Miller, Rossman (1994)	Cost of Rape, Robbery, and Assault	Prevention, Opportunity, and Indirect Costs	183
Zedlewski (1985)	Firearms, Guard Dogs, Victim Losses, Commercial Security	Residential Security, Opportunity Costs, Indirect Costs	160
Cohen (1990)	Cost of Personal and Household Crime to Victims	Prevention, Opportunity, and Indirect Costs	113
President's Commission on Law Enforcement (1967)	General	Opportunity Costs, Miscellaneous Indirect Components	107
Klaus (1994)	National Crime and Victimization Survey Crimes	Prevention, Opportunity, and Indirect Costs	19

Index provides a measure of the level of crime by counting the acts of murder, rape, robbery, aggravated assault, burglary, larceny, motor vehicle theft, and arson each year. The FBI Index is purely a count of crimes and does not attempt to place weights on various criminal acts based on their severity. If the number of acts of burglary, larceny, motor vehicle theft, or arson decreases, society might be better off, but with no measure of the severity of the crimes, such a conclusion is necessarily tentative. From a societal standpoint what matters is the extent of damage inflicted by these crimes, which the FBI Index does not measure.

Over the past three decades, studies of the cost of crime have reported increasing crime burdens, perhaps more as a result of improved understanding and accounting for the broad repercussions of crime than due to the increase in the burden itself. Table 1 summarizes the findings of eight previous studies. . . .

The Effects of Crime

The effects of crime fall into several categories depending on whether they constitute the allocation of resources due to crime that could otherwise be used more productively, the production of ill-favored commodities, transfers from victims to criminals, opportunity costs, or implicit costs associated with risks to life and health. This section examines the meaning and ramifications of each of these categories of crime costs.

Crime-Induced Production

Crime can result in the allocation of resources towards products and activities that do not contribute to society except in their association with crime. Examples include the production of personal protection devices, the trafficking of drugs, and the operation of correctional facilities. In the absence of crime, the time, money, and material resources absorbed by the provision of these goods and services could be used for the creation of benefits rather than the avoidance of harm. The foregone benefits from these alternatives represent a real cost of crime to society. (Twenty dollars spent on a door lock is twenty dollars that cannot be spent on groceries.) Thus, expenditures on crime-related products are treated as a loss to society.

Crimes against property also create unnecessary production due to the destruction and expenditure of resources, and crimes against persons necessitate the use of medical and psychological care resources. In each of these cases, crime-related purchases bid-up prices for the associated items, resulting in higher prices for all consumers of the goods. In the absence of crime, the dollars currently spent to remedy and recover from crime would largely be spent in pursuit of other goals, bidding-up the prices of alternative categories of goods. For this reason, the *net* impact of price effects is assumed to be zero in the present research.

Opportunity Costs

As the number of incarcerated individuals increases steadily, society faces the large and growing loss of these potential workers' productivity. . . . Criminals are risk takers and instigators—characteristics that could make them contributors to society if their entrepreneurial talents were not misguided. Crimes also take time to conceive and carry out, and thus involve the opportunity cost of the criminals' time regardless of detection and incarceration. For many, crime is a full-time occupation. Society is deprived of the goods and services a criminal would have produced in the time consumed by crime and the production of "bads" if he or she were on the level. Additional opportunity costs arise due to victims' lost workdays, and time spent securing assets, looking for keys, purchasing and installing crime prevention devices, and patrolling neighborhood-watch areas.

The Value of Risks to Life and Health

The implicit costs of violent crime include the fear of being injured or killed, the anger associated with the inability to behave as desired, and the agony of being a crime victim. Costs associated with life and health risks are perhaps the most difficult to ascertain, although a considerable literature is devoted to their estimation. The implicit values of lost life and injury are included in the list of crime costs below; those not wishing to consider them can simply subtract these estimates from the aggregate figure.

Transfers

One result of fraud and theft is a transfer of assets from victim to criminal. . . .

Numerical Findings

Crime-Induced Production

... Crime-induced production accounts for about $400 billion in expenditures annually. Table 2 presents the costs of goods and services that would not have to be produced in the absence of crime. Drug trafficking accounts for an estimated $161 billion in expenditure. With the $28 billion cost of prenatal drug exposure and almost $11 billion worth of federal, state, and local drug control efforts (including drug treatment, education, interdiction, research, and intelligence), the combined cost of drug-related activities is about $200 billion. Findings that over half of the arrestees in 24 cities tested positive for recent drug use and about one-third of offenders reported being under the influence of drugs at the time of their offense suggest that significant portions of the other crime-cost categories may result indirectly from drug use.

About 682,000 police and 17,000 federal, state, special (park, transit, or county) and local police agencies account for $47 billion in expenditures

Table 2

Crime-Induced Production	$ (millions)
Drug Trafficking	160,584
Police Protection	47,129
Corrections	35,879
Prenatal Exposure to Cocaine and Heroin	28,156
Federal Agencies	23,381
Judicial and Legal Services—State & Local	18,901
Guards	17,917
Drug Control	10,951
DUI Costs to Driver	10,302
Medical Care for Victims	8,990
Computer Viruses and Security	8,000
Alarm Systems	6,478
Passes for Business Access	4,659
Locks, Sales, and Vaults	4,359
Vandalism (except arson)	2,317
Small Arms and Small Arms Ammunition	2,252
Replacements Due to Arson	1,902
Surveillance Cameras	1,471
Safety Lighting	1,466
Protective Fences and Gates	1,159
Airport Security	448
Nonlethal Weaponary, e.g., Mace	324
Elec. Retail Article Surveillance	149
Theft Insurance (less indemnity)	96
Guard Dogs	49
Mothers Against Drunk Driving	49
Library Theft Detection	28
Total	**397,395**

annually. Thirty-six billion dollars is dedicated each year to the 895 federal and state prisons, 3,019 jails, and 1,091 state, county, and local juvenile detention centers. Aside from guards in correctional institutions, private expenditure on guards amounts to more than $18 billion annually. Security guard agencies employ 55 percent of the 867,000 guards in the U.S.; the remainder are employed in-house. While guards are expected and identifiable at banks and military complexes, they have a less conspicuous presence at railroads, ports, golf courses, laboratories, factories, hospitals, retail stores, and other places of business. The figures in this paper do not include receptionists, who often play a dual role of monitoring unlawful entry into a building and providing information and assistance. . . .

Opportunity Costs

In their study of the costs of murder, rape, robbery, and aggravated assault, Cohen, Miller, and Rossman estimate that the average incarcerated offender costs society $5,700 in lost productivity per year. Their estimate was based on the observation that many prisoners did not work in the legal market prior to their offense, and the opportunity cost of those prisoners' time can be considered to be zero. The current study uses a higher estimate of the opportunity cost of incarceration because unlike previous studies, it examines the relative savings from a *crime-free* society. It is likely that in the absence of crime including drug use, some criminals who are not presently employed in the legal workforce would be willing and able to find gainful employment. This assumption is supported by the fact that many criminals are, in a way, motivated entrepreneurs whose energy has taken an unfortunate focus. In the absence of more enticing underground activities, some of the same individuals could apply these skills successfully in the legal sector. . . .

The Value of Risks to Life and Health

Table 3 presents estimates of the implicit costs of violent crime. The value of life and injury estimates used here reflect the amounts individuals are willing to accept to enter a work environment in which their health state might change. The labor market estimates do not include losses covered by workers' compensation, namely health care costs (usually provided without dollar or time limits) and lost earnings (within modest bounds, victims or their spouses typically receive about two-thirds of lost earnings for life or the duration of the injury). The values do capture perceived risks of pain, suffering, and mental

Table 3

The Value of Risks to Life and Health	$ (millions)
Value of Lost Life	439,880
Value of Injuries	134,515
Total	**574,395**

distress associated with the health losses. If the risk of involvement in violent crime evokes more mental distress than the risk of occupational injuries and fatalities, the labor market values represent conservative estimates of the corresponding costs of crime. Similar estimates have been used in previous studies of crime costs. . . .

The average of 27 previous estimates of the implicit value of human life as reported by W. Kip Viscusi is 7.1 million. Removing two outlying estimates of just under $20 million about which the authors express reservation, the average of the remaining studies is $6.1 million. Viscusi points out that the majority of the estimates fall between $3.7 and $8.6 million ($3 and $7 million in 1990 dollars), the average of which is again $6.1 million. The $6.1 million figure was multiplied by the 72,111 crime-related deaths to obtain the $440 billion estimate of the value of lives lost to crime. Similarly, the average of 15 studies of the implicit value of non-fatal injuries, $52,637, was multiplied by the 2,555,520 reported injuries resulting from drunk driving and boating, arson, rape, robbery, and assaults to find the $135 billion estimate for the implicit cost of crime-related injuries.

Transfers

More than $603 billion worth of transfers result from crime. After the $204 billion lost to occupational fraud and the $123 billion in unpaid taxes, the $109 billion lost to health insurance fraud represents the greatest transfer by more than a factor of two, and the associated costs amount to almost ten percent of the nation's health care expenditures. Robberies, perhaps the classic crime, ironically generate a smaller volume of transfers ($775 million) than any other category of crime. The transfers of goods and money resulting from fraud and theft do not necessarily impose a net burden on society, and may in fact increase social welfare to the extent that those on the receiving end value the goods more than those losing them. Nonetheless, as Table 4 illustrates, those on the losing side bear a $603 billion annual burden. . . .

There are additional cost categories that are not included here, largely because measures that are included absorb much of their impact. Nonetheless, several are worth noting. Thaler, Hellman and Naroff, and Rizzo estimate the erosion of property values per crime. An average of their figures, $2,024, can be multiplied by the total number of crimes reported in 1994, 13,992, to estimate an aggregate housing devaluation of $28 billion. Although this figure should reflect the inability to behave as desired in the presence of crime, it also includes psychic and monetary costs imposed by criminal behavior that are already included in this [article].

Julie Berry Cullen and Stephen D. Levitt discuss urban flight resulting from crime. They report a nearly one-to-one relationship between serious crimes and individuals parting from major cities. The cost component of this is difficult to assess because higher commuting costs must be measured against lower property costs in rural areas, and the conveniences of city living must be compared with the amenities of suburbia. Several other categories of crime costs receive incomplete representation due to insufficient data, and therefore

Table 4

Transfers	$ (millions)
Occupational Fraud	203,952
Unpaid Taxes	123,108
Health Insurance Fraud	108,610
Financial Institution Fraud	52,901
Mail Fraud	35,986
Property/Casualty Insurance Fraud	20,527
Telemarketing Fraud	16,609
Business Burglary	13,229
Motor Vehicle Theft	8,913
Shoplifting	7,185
Household Burglary	4,527
Personal Theft	3,909
Household Larceny	1,996
Coupon Fraud	912
Robbery	775
Total	**603,140**

make the estimates here conservative. These include the costs of unreported crimes (although the National Crime Victimization Survey provides information beyond that reported to the police), lost taxes due to the underground economy, and restrictions of behavior due to crime.

When criminals' costs are estimated implicitly as the value of the assets they receive through crime, the gross cost of crime (including transfers) is estimated to exceed $2,269 billion each year, and the net cost is an estimated $1,666 billion. When criminals' costs are assumed to equal the value of time spent planning and committing crimes and in prison, the estimated annual gross and net costs of crime are $1,705 and $1,102 billion respectively. Table 5 presents the aggregate costs of crime based on the more conservative, time-based estimation method. The disaggregation of this and the previous tables facilitates the creation of customized estimates based on the reader's preferred assumptions. Each of the general studies summarized in Table 1 included transfers, so the appropriate comparison is to the gross cost estimate in the current

Table 5

The Aggregate Burden of Crime	$ (billions)
Crime-Induced Production	397
Opportunity Costs	130
Risks to Life and Health	574
Transfers	603
Gross Burden	**$1,705**
Net of Transfers	**$1,102**
Per Capita (in dollars)	**$4,118**

study. As the result of a more comprehensive treatment of repercussions, the cost of crime is now seen to be more than twice as large as previously recognized.

Conclusion

Previous studies of the burden of crime have counted crimes or concentrated on direct crime costs. This paper calculates the aggregate burden of crime rather than absolute numbers, includes indirect costs, and recognizes that transfers resulting from theft should not be included in the net burden of crime to society. The accuracy of society's perspective on crime costs will improve with the understanding that these costs extend beyond victims' losses and the cost of law enforcement to include the opportunity costs of criminals' and prisoners' time, our inability to behave as desired, and the private costs of crime deterrence.

As criminals acquire an estimated $603 billion dollars worth of assets from their victims, they generate an additional $1,102 billion worth of lost productivity, crime-related expenses, and diminished quality of life. The net losses represent an annual per capita burden of $4,118. Including transfers, the aggregate burden of crime is $1,705 billion. In the United States, this is of the same order of magnitude as life insurance purchases ($1,680 billion), the outstanding mortgage debt to commercial banks and savings institutions ($1,853 billion), and annual expenditures on health ($1,038 billion).

As the enormity of this negative-sum game comes to light, so, too, will the need for countervailing efforts to redefine legal policy and forge new ethical standards. Periodic estimates of the full cost of crime could speak to the success of national strategies to encourage decorum, including increased expenditures on law enforcement, new community strategic approaches, technological innovations, legal reform, education, and the development of ethics curricula. Economic theory dictates that resources should be devoted to moral enhancement until the benefits from marginal efforts are surpassed by their costs. Programs that decrease the burden of crime by more than the cost of implementation should be continued, while those associated with negligible or positive net increments in the cost of crime should be altered to better serve societal goals.

Jeffrey Reiman  **NO**

The Rich Get Richer and the Poor Get Prison: Ideology, Class, and Criminal Justice

If one individual inflicts a bodily injury upon another which leads to the death of the person attacked we call it manslaughter; on the other hand, if the attacker knows beforehand that the blow will be fatal we call it murder. Murder has also been committed if society places hundreds of workers in such a position that they inevitably come to premature and unnatural ends. Their death is as violent as if they had been stabbed or shot. . . . Murder has been committed if society knows perfectly well that thousands of workers cannot avoid being sacrificed so long as these conditions are allowed to continue. Murder of this sort is just as culpable as the murder committed by an individual.

—Frederick Engels
The Condition of the Working Class in England

What's in a Name?

If it takes you an hour to read this chapter, by the time you reach the last page, three of your fellow citizens will have been murdered. *During that same time, at least four Americans will die as a result of unhealthy or unsafe conditions in the workplace!* Although these work-related deaths could have been prevented, they are not called murders. Why not? Doesn't crime by any other name still cause misery and suffering? What's in a name?

The fact is that the label "crime" is not used in America to name all or the worst of the actions that cause misery and suffering to Americans. It is primarily reserved for the dangerous actions of the poor.

In the February 21, 1993, edition of the *New York Times*, an article appears with the headline: "Company in Mine Deaths Set to Pay Big Fine." It describes an agreement by the owners of a Kentucky mine to pay a fine for safety misconduct that may have led to "the worst American mining accident in nearly a decade." Ten workers died in a methane explosion, and the company pleaded guilty to "a pattern of safety misconduct" that included falsifying reports of methane levels and requiring miners to work under unsupported roofs. The company was fined $3.75 million. The acting foreman at the mine was the only individual charged by the federal government, and for his cooperation with the investigation, prosecutors were recommending that he receive the minimum sentence: probation to six months in prison. The company's president expressed regret for the tragedy that occurred. And the U.S. attorney said he hoped the case "sent a clear message that violations of Federal safety and health regulations that endanger the lives of our citizens will not be tolerated."

Compare this with the story of Colin Ferguson, who prompted an editorial in the *New York Times* of December 10, 1993, with the headline: "Mass Murder on the 5:33." A few days earlier, Colin had boarded a commuter train in Garden City, Long Island, and methodically shot passengers with a 9-millimeter pistol, killing 5 and wounding 18. Colin Ferguson was surely a murderer, maybe a mass murderer. My question is, Why wasn't the death of the miners also murder? Why weren't those responsible for subjecting ten miners to deadly conditions also "mass murderers"?

Why do ten dead miners amount to an "accident," a "tragedy," and five dead commuters a "mass murder"? "Murder" suggests a murderer, whereas "accident" and "tragedy" suggest the work of impersonal forces. But the charge against the company that owned the mine said that they "repeatedly exposed the mine's work crews to danger and that such conditions were frequently concealed from Federal inspectors responsible for enforcing the mine safety act." And the acting foreman admitted to falsifying records of methane levels only two months before the fatal blast. Someone was responsible for the conditions that led to the death of ten miners. Is that person not a murderer, perhaps even a *mass murderer*?

These questions are at this point rhetorical. My aim is not to discuss this case but rather to point to the blinders we wear when we look at such an "accident." There was an investigation. One person, the acting foreman, was held responsible for falsifying records. He is to be sentenced to six months in prison (at most). The company was fined. But no one will be tried for *murder*. No one will be thought of as a murderer. *Why not?. . .*

Didn't those miners have a right to protection from the violence that took their lives? *And if not, why not?*

Once we are ready to ask this question seriously, we are in a position to see that the reality of crime—that is, the acts we label crime, the acts we think of as crime, the actors and actions we treat as criminal—is *created*: It is an image shaped by decisions as to *what* will be called crime and *who* will be treated as a criminal.

The Carnival Mirror

. . . The American criminal justice system is a mirror that shows a distorted image of the dangers that threaten us—an image created more by the shape of the mirror than by the reality reflected. What do we see when we look in the criminal justice mirror? . . .

He is, first of all, a *he*. Out of 2,012,906 persons arrested for FBI Index crimes [which are criminal homicide, forcible rape, robbery, aggravated assault, burglary, larceny, and motor vehicle theft] in 1991, 1,572,591, or 78 percent, were males. Second, he is a *youth*. . . . Third, he is predominantly *urban*. . . . Fourth, he is disproportionately *black*—blacks are arrested for Index crimes at a rate three times that of their percentage in the national population. . . . Finally, he is *poor*: Among state prisoners in 1991, 33 percent were unemployed prior to being arrested—a rate nearly four times that of males in the general population. . . .

This is the Typical Criminal feared by most law-abiding Americans. Poor, young, urban, (disproportionately) black males make up the core of the enemy forces in the war against crime. They are the heart of a vicious, unorganized guerrilla army, threatening the lives, limbs, and possessions of the law-abiding members of society—necessitating recourse to the ultimate weapons of force and detention in our common defense.

. . . The acts of the Typical Criminal are not the only acts that endanger us, nor are they the acts that endanger us the most. As I shall show . . . , we have as great or sometimes even a greater chance of being killed or disabled by an occupational injury or disease, by unnecessary surgery, or by shoddy emergency medical services than by aggravated assault or even homicide! Yet even though these threats to our well-being are graver than those posed by our poor young criminals, they do not show up in the FBI's Index of serious crimes. The individuals responsible for them do not turn up in arrest records or prison statistics. *They never become part of the reality reflected in the criminal justice mirror, although the danger they pose is at least as great and often greater than the danger posed by those who do!*

Similarly, the general public loses more money . . . from price-fixing and monopolistic practices and from consumer deception and embezzlement than from all the property crimes in the FBI's Index combined. Yet these far more costly acts are either not criminal, or if technically criminal, not prosecuted, or if prosecuted, not punished, or if punished, only mildly. . . . *Their faces rarely appear in the criminal justice mirror, although the danger they pose is at least as great and often greater than that of those who do.* . . .

The criminal justice system is like a mirror in which society can see the face of the evil in its midst. Because the system deals with some evil and not with others, because it treats small evils as the gravest and treats some of the gravest evils as minor, the image it throws back is distorted like the image in a carnival mirror. Thus, the image cast back is false not because it is invented out of thin air but because the proportions of the real are distorted. . . .

If criminal justice really gives us a carnival-mirror of "crime," we are doubly deceived. First, we are led to believe that the criminal justice system is protecting us against the gravest threats to our well-being when, in fact, the system is protecting us against only some threats and not necessarily the gravest ones. We are deceived about how much protection we are receiving and thus left vulnerable. The second deception is just the other side of this one. If people believe that the carnival mirror is a true mirror—that is, if they believe the criminal justice system simply *reacts* to the gravest threats to their well-being—they come to believe that whatever is the target of the criminal justice system must be the greatest threat to their well-being. . . .

A Crime by Any Other Name . . .

Think of a crime, any crime. Picture the first "crime" that comes into your mind. What do you see? The odds are you are not imagining a mining company executive sitting at his desk, calculating the costs of proper safety precautions and deciding not to invest in them. Probably what you do see with your mind's eye is one person physically attacking another or robbing something from another via the threat of physical attack. Look more closely. What does the attacker look like? It's a safe bet he (and it is a *he*, of course) is not wearing a suit and tie. In fact, my hunch is that you—like me, like almost anyone else in America—picture a young, tough lower-class male when the thought of crime first pops into your head. You (we) picture someone like the Typical Criminal described above. The crime itself is one in which the Typical Criminal sets out to attack or rob some specific person.

It is important to identify this model of the Typical Crime because it functions like a set of blinders. It keeps us from calling a mine disaster a mass murder even if ten men are killed, even if someone is responsible for the unsafe conditions in which they worked and died. I contend that this particular piece of mental furniture so blocks our view that it keeps us from using the criminal justice system to protect ourselves from the greatest threats to our persons and possessions.

What keeps a mine disaster from being a mass murder in our eyes is that it is not a one-on-one harm. What is important in one-on-one harm is not the numbers but the *desire of someone (or ones) to harm someone (or ones) else.* An attack by a gang on one or more persons or an attack by one individual on several fits the model of one-on-one harm; that is, for each person harmed there is at least one individual who wanted to harm that person. Once he selects his victim, the rapist, the mugger, the murderer all want this person they have selected to suffer. A mine executive, on the other hand, does not want his employees to be harmed. He would truly prefer that there be no accident, no injured or dead miners. What he does want is something legitimate. It is what he has been hired to get: maximum profits at minimum costs. If he cuts corners to save a buck, he is just doing his job. If ten men die because he cut corners on safety, we may think him crude or callous but not a murderer. He is, at most, responsible for an *indirect harm*, not a one-on-one harm. For this, he may even be criminally indictable for violating safety regulations—but not for murder. The ten men are dead as an unwanted consequence of his (perhaps overzealous or undercautious) pursuit of a legitimate goal. So, unlike the Typical Criminal, he has not committed the Typical Crime—or so we generally believe. As a result, ten men are dead who might be alive now if cutting corners of the kind that leads to loss of life, whether suffering is specifically aimed at or not, were treated as murder.

This is my point. Because we accept the belief . . . that the model for crime is one person specifically trying to harm another, we accept a legal system that leaves us unprotected against much greater dangers to our lives and well-being than those threatened by the Typical Criminal. . . .

According to the FBI's *Uniform Crime Reports,* in 1991, there were 24,703 murders and nonnegligent manslaughters, and 1,092,739 aggravated assaults.

In 1992, there were 23,760 murders and nonnegligent manslaughters, and 1,126,970 aggravated assaults. . . . Thus, as a measure of the physical harm done by crime in the beginning of the 1990s, we can say that reported crimes lead to roughly 24,000 deaths and 1,000,000 instances of serious bodily injury short of death a year. As a measure of monetary loss due to property crime, we can use $15.1 billion—the total estimated dollar losses due to property crime in 1992 according to the UCR. Whatever the shortcomings of these reported crime statistics, they are the statistics upon which public policy has traditionally been based. Thus, I will consider any actions that lead to loss of life, physical harm, and property loss comparable to the figures in the UCR as actions that pose grave dangers to the community comparable to the threats posed by crimes. . . .

In testimony before the Senate Committee on Labor and Human Resources, Dr. Philip Landrigan, director of the Division of Environmental and Occupational Medicine at the Mount Sinai School of Medicine in New York City, stated that

> [I]t may be calculated that occupational disease is responsible each year in the United States for 50,000 to 70,000 deaths, and for approximately 350,000 new cases of illness.

. . . The BLS estimate of 330,000 job-related illnesses for 1990 roughly matches Dr. Landrigan's estimates. For 1991, BLS estimates 368,000 job-related illnesses. These illnesses are of varying severity. . . . Because I want to compare these occupational harms with those resulting from aggravated assault, I shall stay on the conservative side here too, as with deaths from occupational diseases, and say that there are annually in the United States approximately 150,000 job-related serious illnesses. Taken together with 25,000 deaths from occupational diseases, how does this compare with the threat posed by crime?

Before jumping to any conclusions, note that the risk of occupational disease and death falls only on members of the labor force, whereas the risk of crime falls on the whole population, from infants to the elderly. Because the labor force is about half the total population (124,810,000 in 1990, out of a total population of 249,900,000), to get a true picture of the *relative* threat posed by occupational diseases compared with that posed by crimes, we should *halve* the crime statistics when comparing them with the figures for industrial disease and death. Using the crime figures for the first years of the 1990s, . . . we note that the *comparable* figures would be

	Occupational Hazard	Crime (halved)
Death	25,000	12,000
Other physical harm	150,000	500,000

. . . Note . . . that the estimates in the last chart are *only* for occupational *diseases* and deaths from those diseases. They do not include death and disability from work-related injuries. Here, too, the statistics are gruesome. The National Safety Council reported that in 1991, work-related accidents caused

9,600 deaths and 1.7 million disabling work injuries, a total cost to the economy of $63.3 billion. This brings the number of occupation-related deaths to 34,600 a year and other physical harms to 1,850,000. If, on the basis of these additional figures, we recalculated our chart comparing occupational harms from both disease and accident with criminal harms, it would look like this:

	Occupational Hazard	Crime (halved)
Death	34,600	12,000
Other physical harm	1,850,000	500,000

Can there be any doubt that workers are more likely to stay alive and healthy in the face of the danger from the underworld than in the workworld? . . .

To say that some of these workers died from accidents due to their own carelessness is about as helpful as saying that some of those who died at the hands of murderers asked for it. It overlooks the fact that where workers are careless, it is not because they love to live dangerously. They have production quotas to meet, quotas that they themselves do not set. If quotas were set with an eye to keeping work at a safe pace rather than to keeping the production-to-wages ratio as high as possible, it might be more reasonable to expect workers to take the time to be careful. Beyond this, we should bear in mind that the vast majority of occupational deaths result from disease, not accident, and disease is generally a function of conditions outside a worker's control. Examples of such conditions are the level of coal dust in the air ("260,000 miners receive benefits for [black lung] disease, and perhaps as many as 4,000 retired miners die from the illness or its complications each year"; about 10,000 currently working miners "have X-ray evidence of the beginnings of the crippling and often fatal disease") or textile dust . . . or asbestos fibers . . . or coal tars . . . ; (coke oven workers develop cancer of the scrotum at a rate five times that of the general population). Also, some 800,000 people suffer from occupationally related skin disease each year. . . .

To blame the workers for occupational disease and deaths is to ignore the history of governmental attempts to compel industrial firms to meet safety standards that would keep dangers (such as chemicals or fibers or dust particles in the air) that are outside the worker's control down to a safe level. This has been a continual struggle, with firms using everything from their own "independent" research institutes to more direct and often questionable forms of political pressure to influence government in the direction of loose standards and lax enforcement. So far, industry has been winning because OSHA [Occupational Safety and Health Administration] has been given neither the personnel nor the mandate to fulfill its purpose. It is so understaffed that, in 1973, when 1,500 federal sky marshals guarded the nation's airplanes from hijackers, only 500 OSHA inspectors toured the nation's workplaces. By 1980, OSHA employed 1,581 compliance safety and health officers, but this still enabled inspection of only roughly 2 percent of the 2.5 million establishments covered by OSHA. The *New York Times* reports that in 1987 the number of OSHA inspectors was down to 1,044. As might be expected, the agency performs fewer inspections that it did a dozen years ago. . . .

According to a report issued by the AFL-CIO [American Federation of Labor and Congress of Industrial Organizations] in 1992, "The median penalty paid by an employer during the years 1972–1990 following an incident resulting in death or serious injury of a worker was just $480." The same report claims that the federal government spends $1.1 billion a year to protect fish and wildlife and only $300 million a year to protect workers from health and safety hazards on the job. . . .

Is a person who kills another in a bar brawl a greater threat to society than a business executive who refuses to cut into his profits to make his plant a safe place to work? By any measure of death and suffering the latter is by far a greater danger than the former. Because he wishes his workers no harm, because he is only indirectly responsible for death and disability while pursuing legitimate economic goals, his acts are not called "crimes." Once we free our imagination from the blinders of the one-on-one model of crime, can there be any doubt that the criminal justice system does *not* protect us from the gravest threats to life and limb? It seeks to protect us when danger comes from a young, lower-class male in the inner city. When a threat comes from an upper-class business executive in an office, the criminal justice system looks the other way. This is in the face of growing evidence that for every three American citizens murdered by thugs, at least four American workers are killed by the recklessness of their bosses and the indifference of their government.

Health Care May Be Dangerous to Your Health

. . . On July 15, 1975, Dr. Sidney Wolfe of Ralph Nader's Public Interest Health Research Group testified before the House Commerce Oversight and Investigations Subcommittee that there "were 3.2 million cases of unnecessary surgery performed each year in the United States." These unneeded operations, Wolfe added, "cost close to $5 billion a year and kill as many as 16,000 Americans.". . .

In an article on an experimental program by Blue Cross and Blue Shield aimed at curbing unnecessary surgery, *Newsweek* reports that

> a Congressional committee earlier this year [1976] estimated that more than 2 million of the elective operations performed in 1974 were not only unnecessary—but also killed about 12,000 patients and cost nearly $4 billion.

Because the number of surgical operations performed in the United States rose from 16.7 million in 1975 to 22.4 million in 1991, there is reason to believe that at least somewhere between . . . 12,000 and . . . 16,000 people a year still die from unnecessary surgery. In 1991, the FBI reported that 3,405 murders were committed by a "cutting or stabbing instrument." Obviously, the FBI does not include the scalpel as a cutting or stabbing instrument. If they did, they would have had to report that between 15,405 and 19,405 persons were killed by "cutting or stabbing" in 1991. . . . No matter how you slice it, the scalpel may be more dangerous than the switchblade. . . .

Waging Chemical Warfare Against America

One in 4 Americans can expect to contract cancer during their lifetimes. The American Cancer Society estimated that 420,000 Americans would die of cancer in 1981. The National Cancer Institute's estimate for 1993 is 526,000 deaths from cancer. "A 1978 report issued by the President's Council on Environmental Quality (CEQ) unequivocally states that 'most researchers agree that 70 to 90 percent of cancers are caused by environmental influences and are hence theoretically preventable.'" This means that a concerted national effort could result in saving 350,000 or more lives a year and reducing each individual's chances of getting cancer in his or her lifetime from 1 in 4 to 1 in 12 or fewer. If you think this would require a massive effort in terms of money and personnel, you are right. How much of an effort, though, would the nation make to stop a foreign invader who was killing a thousand people and bent on capturing one-quarter of the present population?

In face of this "invasion" that is already under way, the U.S. government has allocated $1.9 billion to the National Cancer Institute (NCI) for fiscal year 1992, and NCI has allocated $219 million to the study of the physical and chemical (i.e., environmental) causes of cancer. Compare this with the (at least) $45 billion spent to fight the Persian Gulf War. The simple truth is that the government that strove so mightily to protect the borders of a small, undemocratic nation 7,000 miles away is doing next to nothing to protect us against the chemical war in our midst. This war is being waged against us on three fronts:

- Pollution
- Cigarette smoking
- Food additives

. . . The evidence linking *air pollution* and cancer, as well as other serious and often fatal diseases, has been rapidly accumulating in recent years. In 1993, the *Journal of the American Medical Association* reported on research that found "'robust' associations between premature mortality and air pollution levels." They estimate that pollutants cause about 2 percent of all cancer deaths (at least 10,000 a year). . . .

A . . . recent study . . . concluded that air pollution at 1988 levels was responsible for 60,000 deaths a year. The Natural Resources Defense Council sued the EPA [Environmental Protection Agency] for its foot-dragging in implementation of the Clean Air Act, charging that "One hundred million people live in areas of unhealthy air."

This chemical war is not limited to the air. The National Cancer Institute has identified as carcinogens or suspected carcinogens 23 of the chemicals commonly found in our drinking water. Moreover, according to one observer, we are now facing a "new plague—toxic exposure." . . .

The evidence linking *cigarette smoking* and cancer is overwhelming and need not be repeated here. The Centers for Disease Control estimates that cigarettes cause 87 percent of lung cancers—approximately 146,000 in 1992. Tobacco continues to kill an estimated 400,000 Americans a year. Cigarettes are widely estimated to cause 30 percent of all cancer deaths. . . .

This is enough to expose the hypocrisy of running a full-scale war against heroin (which produces no degenerative disease) while allowing cigarette sales and advertising to flourish. It also should be enough to underscore the point that once again there are threats to our lives much greater than criminal homicide. The legal order does not protect us against them. Indeed, not only does our government fail to protect us against this threat, it promotes it! . . .

Based on the knowledge we have, there can be no doubt that air pollution, tobacco, and food additives amount to a chemical war that makes the crime wave look like a football scrimmage. Even with the most conservative estimates, it is clear that *the death toll in this war is far higher than the number of people killed by criminal homicide!*

Summary

Once again, our investigations lead to the same result. The criminal justice system does not protect us against the gravest threats to life, limb, or possessions. Its definitions of crime are not simply a reflection of the objective dangers that threaten us. The workplace, the medical profession, the air we breathe, and the poverty we refuse to rectify lead to far more human suffering, far more death and disability, and take far more dollars from our pockets than the murders, aggravated assaults, and thefts reported annually by the FBI. What is more, this human suffering is preventable. A government really intent on protecting our well-being could enforce work safety regulations, police the medical profession, require that clean air standards be met, and funnel sufficient money to the poor to alleviate the major disabilities of poverty—but it does not. Instead we hear a lot of cant about law and order and a lot of rant about crime in the streets. It is as if our leaders were not only refusing to protect us from the major threats to our well-being but trying to cover up this refusal by diverting our attention to crime—as if this were the only real threat.

EXPLORING THE ISSUE

Is Street Crime More Harmful Than White-Collar Crime?

Critical Thinking and Reflection

1. People fear street crime more than white-collar crime, but which causes more harm to the public and which costs more money when all costs are counted?
2. Why are the punishments for street crimes so much greater than for white-collar crime?
3. Many white-collar criminals are highly respected persons. Often they continue to be respected even when sentenced to prison as in the case of Martha Stewart. Can you explain this?
4. The most famous statement about crime is "Crime does not pay." Is this a defensible statement today?
5. Sociologists point out that crime is a skill that has to be learned just like other skills. Where and how are street crime skills learned and where and how are white-collar crime skills learned?

Is There Common Ground?

It is important to consider both the suffering and the wider ramifications caused by crimes. Anderson captures many of these dimensions and gives a full account of the harms of street crime. Today the public is very concerned about street crime, especially wanton violence. However, it seems relatively unconcerned about white-collar crime. Reiman tries to change that perception. By defining many harmful actions by managers and professionals as crimes, he argues that white-collar crime is worse than street crime. He says that more people are killed and injured by "occupational injury or disease, by unnecessary surgery, and by shoddy emergency medical services than by aggravated assault or even homicide!" But are shoddy medical services a crime? In the end, the questions remain: What is a crime? Who are the criminals?

Additional Resources

Readings that support Reiman's viewpoint include Roger J. Berger, *White-Collar Crime: The Abuse of Corporate and Government Power* (Lynne Rienner Publishers, 2011); Nicholas Ryder, *Financial Crime in the 21st Century: Law and Polity* (Edward Elgar, 2011); Loretta Napoleoni, *Rogue Economics: Capitalism's New Reality* (Seven Stories Press, 2009); Michael L. Benson and Sally S. Simpson, *White-Collar Crime: An Opportunity Perspective* (Routledge, 2009); Matthew Robinson, *Greed Is Good: Maximization and Elite Deviance in America* (Rowman & Littlefield, 2009); Peter

Gottschalk, *White-Collar Criminals: Theoretical and Managerial Perspectives of Financial Crime* (Nova Science, 2010); Peter Fleming, *Charting Corporate Corruption: Agency, Structure, and Escalation* (Edward Elgar, 2009); Scott B. MacDonald, *Separating Fools from Their Money: A History of American Financial Scandals* (Transaction Publishers, 2007); David O. Friedrichs, *Trusted Criminals: White Collar Crime in Contemporary Society* (Thomson Higher Education, 2007); Stuart L. Hills, ed., *Corporate Violence: Injury and Death for Profit* (Rowman & Littlefield, 1987); Steve Tombs and Dave Whyte, eds., *Unmasking the Crimes of the Powerful: Scrutinizing States and Corporations* (P. Lang, 2003); Joel Bakan, *The Corporation: The Pathological Pursuit of Profit and Power* (Free Press, 2004); Stephen M. Rosoff et al., *Looting America: Greed, Corruption, Villains, and Victims* (Prentice Hall, 2003). Most works on crime deal mainly with theft, drugs, and violence, and the injury and fear that they cause, including Danielle Lively Neal, *Social Capital and Urban Crime* (LFB Scholarly Publishing, 2011); Marcus Felson and Rachel L. Boba, *Crime and Everyday Life* (Sage, 2010); Elizabeth Kandel Englander, *Understanding Violence* (Lawrence Erlbaum Associates, 2007); Leslie Williams Reid, *Crime in the City: A Political and Economic Analysis of Urban Crime* (LFB Scholarly Publishing, 2003); Walter S. DeKeseredy, *Under Siege: Poverty and Crime in a Public Housing Community* (Lexington Books, 2003); Alex Alverez and Ronet Bachman, *Murder American Style* (Wadsworth, 2003); Claire Valier, *Crime and Punishment in Contemporary Culture* (Routledge, 2004); Matthew B. Robinson, *Why Crime? An Integrated Systems Theory of Antisocial Behavior* (Pearson, 2004); Ronald B. Flowers, *Male Crime and Deviance: Exploring Its Causes, Dynamics, and Nature* (C. C. Thomas, 2003); and Meda Chesney-Lind and Lisa Pasko, *The Female Offender: Girls, Women, and Crime*, 2nd ed. (Sage, 2004). Five works on gangs, which are often connected with violent street crime, are William J. Mitchell, ed., *Code of the Street: Violent Youths and Gangs* (Nova Science, 2011); Robert J. Franzese, Herbert C. Covey, and Scott Menard, *Youth Gangs* (Charles C. Thomas, 2006); Jay T. Soordhas, ed., *Gangs: Violence, Crime and Antigang Initiatives* (Nova Science, 2009); Martin Sanchez Jankowski, *Islands in the Street: Gangs and American Urban Society* (University of California Press, 1991), and Felix M. Padilla, *The Gang as an American Enterprise* (Rutgers University Press, 1992). William J. Bennett, John J. DiIulio, and John P. Walters, in *Body Count: Moral Poverty—And How to Win America's War Against Crime and Drugs* (Simon & Schuster, 1996), argue that moral poverty is the root cause of crime (meaning street crime). How applicable is this thesis to white-collar crime? One interesting aspect of many corporate, or white-collar, crimes is that they involve crimes of obedience, as discussed in Herman C. Kelman and V. Lee Hamilton, *Crimes of Obedience: Toward a Social Psychology of Authority and Responsibility* (Yale University Press, 1989). For recent effort to calculate the costs of crime and law enforcement, see Jacek Czabanski, *Estimates of Cost of Crime: History, Methodologies, and Implications* (Springer, 2008) and Mark A. Cohen, *The Costs of Crime and Justice* (Routledge, 2005). Finally, there is a new type of crime that is increasingly troublesome: digital crime and terrorism. This is thoroughly examined by Robert W. Taylor, et al., in *Digital Crime and Digital Terrorism* (Pearson/Prentice Hall, 2006).

ISSUE 17

Should Laws Against Drug Use Remain Restrictive?

YES: Herbert Kleber and Joseph A. Califano Jr., from "Legalization: Panacea or Pandora's Box?" *The National Center on Addiction and Substance Abuse at Columbia University* (January 2006)

NO: Peter Gorman, from "Veteran Cops Against the Drug War," *The World & I Online* (January 2006)

Learning Outcomes

After reading this issue, you should be able to:

- Understand that government laws that outlaw behavior that citizens do not think are wrong have a legitimacy problem. Laws against prostitution, alcohol, smoking, business on Sundays, pornography, kissing in public, etc. will lack moral authority for many and perhaps for the majority and will be ignored by many if they can get away with it. In the long run, these laws are likely to be repealed or ignored.

- Understand how moralists can get public support for these types of laws including drug laws and put people who oppose such laws in a bad light. They do it to protect drug users from themselves. Seldom are these laws the result of scientific studies. They generally result from emotional responses to stories about the evil that happens to the "victims."

- Sort out how much factual support there is for the main arguments on both sides of this debate.

- Estimate the extent of corruption of the police force which results from the drug laws.

- Know that the proportion of arrests, convictions, prison time, and prisoners are due to drug enforcement.

- Identify the options for policies dealing with recreational drugs.

ISSUE SUMMARY

YES: Herbert Kleber, the executive vice president of the Center on Addiction and Substance Abuse (CASA), and Joseph Califano, founder of CASA, maintain that drug laws should remain restrictive because legalization would result in increased use, especially by children. Kleber and Califano contend that drug legalization would not eliminate drug-related violence and harm caused by drugs.

NO: Author Peter Gorman states that restrictive drug laws have been ineffective. He notes that drug use and drug addiction have increased since drug laws became more stringent. Despite the crackdown on drug use, the availability of drugs has increased while the cost of drugs has decreased. In addition, restrictive drug laws, says Gorman, are racist and endanger civil liberties.

In 2008, the federal government allocated nearly $13 billion to control drug use and to enforce laws that are designed to protect society from the perils created by drug use. Some people believe that the government's war on drugs could be more effective but that governmental agencies and communities are not fighting hard enough to stop drug use. They also hold that laws to halt drug use are too few and too lenient. Others contend that the war against drugs is unnecessary, that, in fact, society has already lost the war on drugs. These individuals feel that the best way to remedy drug problems is to end the fight altogether by ending the current restrictive policies regarding drug use.

There are conflicting views among both liberals and conservatives on whether legislation has had the intended result of curtailing the problems of drug use. Many argue that legislation and the criminalization of drugs have been counterproductive in controlling drug problems. Some suggest that the criminalization of drugs has actually contributed to and worsened the social ills associated with drugs. Proponents of drug legalization maintain that the war on drugs, not drugs themselves, is damaging to American society. They do not advocate drug use; they argue only that laws against drugs exacerbate problems related to drugs.

Proponents of drug decriminalization argue that the strict enforcement of drug laws damages American society because it drives people to violence and crime and that the drug laws have a racist element associated with them. People arrested for drug offenses overburden the court system, thus rendering it ineffective. Moreover, proponents contend that the criminalization of drugs fuels organized crime, allows children to be pulled into the drug business, and makes illegal drugs more dangerous because they are manufactured without government standards or regulations. Hence, drugs may be adulterated or of unidentified potency. Decriminalization advocates also argue that decriminalization would take the profits out of drug sales, thereby decreasing the value of and demand for drugs. In addition, the costs resulting from law enforcement are far greater to society than the benefits of criminalization.

Some decriminalization advocates argue that the federal government's prohibition stance on drugs is an immoral and impossible objective. To achieve a "drug-free society" is self-defeating and a misnomer because drugs have always been a part of human culture. Furthermore, prohibition efforts indicate a disregard for the private freedom of individuals because they assume that individuals are incapable of making their own choices. Drug proponents assert that their personal sovereignty should be respected over any government agenda, including the war on drugs. Less restrictive laws, they argue, would take the emphasis off of law enforcement policies and allow more effort to be put toward education, prevention, and treatment. Also, it is felt that most of the negative implications of drug prohibition would disappear.

Opponents of this view maintain that less restrictive drug laws are not the solution to drug problems and that it is a very dangerous idea. Less restrictive laws, they assert, will drastically increase drug use. This upsurge in drug use will come at an incredibly high price: American society will be overrun with drug-related accidents, lost worker productivity, and hospital emergency rooms filled with drug-related emergencies. Drug treatment efforts would be futile because users would have no legal incentive to stop taking drugs. Also, users may prefer drugs rather than rehabilitation, and education programs may be ineffective in dissuading children from using drugs.

Advocates of less restrictive laws maintain that drug abuse is a "victimless crime" in which the only person being hurt is the drug user. Opponents argue that this notion is ludicrous and dangerous because drug use has dire repercussions for all of society. Drugs can destroy the minds and bodies of many people. Also, regulations to control drug use have a legitimate social aim to protect society and its citizens from the harm of drugs.

In the following selections, Herbert Kleber and Joseph Califano Jr. explain why they feel drugs should remain illegal, whereas Peter Gorman describes the detrimental effects that he believes occur as a result of the restrictive laws associated with drugs.

YES

Herbert Kleber and
Joseph A. Califano Jr.

Legalization:
Panacea or Pandora's Box?

Introduction

Legalization of drugs has recently received some attention as a policy option for the United States. Proponents of such a radical change in policy argue that the "war on drugs" has been lost; drug prohibition, as opposed to illegal drugs themselves, spawns increasing violence and crime; drugs are available to anyone who wants them, even under present restrictions; drug abuse and addiction would not increase after legalization; individuals have a right to use whatever drugs they wish; and foreign experiments with legalization work and should be adopted in the United States.

In this, its first White Paper, the Center on Addiction and Substance Abuse at Columbia University (CASA) examines these propositions; recent trends in drug use; the probable consequences of legalization for children and drug-related violence; lessons to be learned from America's legal drugs, alcohol and tobacco; the question of civil liberties; and the experiences of foreign countries. On the basis of its review, CASA concludes that while legalization might temporarily take some burden off the criminal justice system, such a policy would impose heavy additional costs on the health care system, schools, and workplace, severely impair the ability of millions of young Americans to develop their talents, and in the long term overburden the criminal justice system.

Drugs like heroin and cocaine are not dangerous because they are illegal; they are illegal because they are dangerous. Such drugs are not a threat to American society because they are illegal; they are illegal because they are a threat to American society.

Any relaxation in standards of illegality poses a clear and present danger to the nation's children and their ability to learn and grow into productive citizens. Individuals who reach age 21 without using illegal drugs are virtually certain never to do so. Viewed from this perspective, substance abuse and addiction is a disease acquired during childhood and adolescence. Thus, legalization of drugs such as heroin, cocaine, and marijuana would threaten a pediatric pandemic in the United States.

While current prohibitions on the import, manufacture, distribution, and possession of marijuana, cocaine, heroin, and other drugs should remain,

America's drug policies do need a fix. More resources and energy should be devoted to prevention and treatment, and each citizen and institution should take responsibility to combat drug abuse and addiction in America. . . .

Legalization, Decriminalization, Medicalization, Harm Reduction: What's the Difference?

The term "legalization" encompasses a wide variety of policy options from the legal use of marijuana in private to free markets for all drugs. Four terms are commonly used: legalization, decriminalization, medicalization, and harm reduction—with much variation in each.

Legalization usually implies the most radical departure from current policy. Legalization proposals vary from making marijuana cigarettes as available as tobacco cigarettes to establishing an open and free market for drugs. Variations on legalization include: making drugs legal for the adult population, but illegal for minors; having only the government produce and sell drugs; and/or allowing a private market in drugs, but with restrictions on advertising, dosage, and place of consumption. Few proponents put forth detailed visions of a legalized market.

Decriminalization proposals retain most drug laws that forbid manufacture, importation, and sale of illegal drugs, but remove criminal sanctions for possession of small amounts of drugs for personal use. Such proposals suggest that possession of drugs for personal use be legal or subject only to civil penalties such as fines. Decriminalization is most commonly advocated for marijuana.

Medicalization refers to the prescription of currently illegal drugs by physicians to addicts already dependent on such drugs. The most frequently mentioned variation is heroin maintenance. Proponents argue that providing addicts with drugs prevents them from having to commit crimes to finance their habit and insures that drugs they ingest are pure.

Harm reduction generally implies that government policies should concentrate on lowering the harm associated with drugs both for users and society, rather than on eradicating drug use and imprisoning users. Beginning with the proposition that drug use is inevitable, harm reduction proposals can include the prescription of heroin and other drugs to addicts; removal of penalties for personal use of marijuana; needle-exchange programs for injection drug users to prevent the spread of AIDS and other diseases that result from needle sharing among addicts; and making drugs available at low or no cost to eliminate the harm caused by users who commit crimes to support a drug habit.

Variations on these options are infinite. Some do not require any change in the illegal status of drugs. The government could, for instance, allow needle exchanges while maintaining current laws banning heroin, the most commonly injected drug. Others, however, represent a major shift from the current role of government and the goal of its policies with regard to drug use and availability. Some advocates use the term "harm reduction" as a politically attractive cover for legalization.

Where We Are

Most arguments for legalization in all its different forms start with the contention that the "war on drugs" has been lost and that prevailing criminal justice and social policies with respect to drug use have been a failure. To support the claim that current drug policies have failed, legalization advocates point to the 80 million Americans who have tried drugs during their lifetime. Since so many individuals have broken drug laws, these advocates argue, the laws are futile and lead to widespread disrespect for the law. A liberal democracy, they contend, should not ban what so many people do.[1]

The 80 million Americans include everyone who has ever smoked even a single joint. The majority of these individuals have used only marijuana, and for many their use was brief experimentation. In fact, the size of this number reflects the large number of young people who tried marijuana and hallucinogenic drugs during the late 1960s and the 1970s when drug use was widely tolerated. During this time, drug use was so commonly accepted that the 1972 Shafer Commission, established during the Nixon Administration, and later, President Jimmy Carter called for decriminalization of marijuana.[2]

Since then, concerned public health and government leaders have mounted energetic efforts to de-normalize drug use, including First Lady Nancy Reagan's "Just Say No" campaign. As a result, current* users of any illicit drugs, as measured by the National Household Survey on Drug Abuse, decreased from 24.8 million in 1979 to 13 million in 1994, a nearly 50 percent drop. Over the same time period, current marijuana users dropped from 23 million to 10 million and cocaine users from 4.4 million to 1.4 million.[3] The drug-using segment of the population is also aging. In 1979, 10 percent of current drug users were older than 34; today almost 30 percent are.[4]

With these results and only 6 percent of the population over age 12 currently using drugs,[5] it is difficult to say that drug reduction efforts have failed. This sharp decline in drug use occurred during a period of strict drug laws, societal disapproval, and increasing knowledge and awareness of the dangers and costs of illegal drug use.

Several factors, however, lead many to conclude that we have not made progress against drugs. This feeling of despair stems from the uneven nature of the success. While casual drug use and experimentation have declined substantially, certain neighborhoods and areas of the country remain infested with drugs and drug-related crime, and these continuing trouble spots draw media attention. At the same time, the number of drug addicts has not dropped significantly and the spread of HIV among addicts has added a deadly new dimension to the problem. The number of hardcore** cocaine users (as estimated by the Office of National Drug Control Policy based on a number of surveys including the Household Survey, Drug Use Forecasting, and Drug

---

*Throughout this paper, "current" drug users refers to individuals who have used drugs within the past month, the definition used in most drug use surveys.

**Throughout this paper, "hardcore" users refers to individuals who use drugs at least weekly.

Abuse Warning Network) has remained steady at roughly 2 million.[6] The overall number of illicit drug addicts has hovered around 6 million, a situation that many experts attribute both to a lack of treatment facilities[7] and the large numbers of drug-using individuals already in the pipeline to addiction, even though overall casual use has dropped.

Teenage drug use has been creeping up in the past three years. In the face of the enormous decline in the number of users, however, it is difficult to conclude that current policies have so failed that a change as radical as legalization is warranted. While strict drug laws and criminal sanctions are not likely to deter hardcore addicts, increased resources can be dedicated to treatment without legalizing drugs. Indeed, the criminal justice system can be used to place addicted offenders into treatment. In short, though substantial problems remain, we have made significant progress in our struggle against drug abuse.

Will Legalization Increase Drug Use?

Proponents of drug legalization claim that making drugs legally available would not increase the number of addicts. They argue that drugs are already available to those who want them and that a policy of legalization could be combined with education and prevention programs to discourage drug use.[8] Some contend that legalization might even reduce the number of users, arguing that there would be no pushers to lure new users and drugs would lose the "forbidden fruit" allure of illegality, which can be seductive to children.[9] Proponents of legalization also play down the consequences of drug use, saying that most drug users can function normally.[10] Some legalization advocates assert that a certain level of drug addiction is inevitable and will not vary, regardless of government policies; thus, they claim, even if legalization increased the number of users, it would have little effect on the numbers of users who become addicts.[11]

The effects of legalization on the numbers of users and addicts is an important question because the answer in large part determines whether legalization will reduce crime, improve public health, and lower economic, social, and health care costs. The presumed benefits of legalization evaporate if the number of users and addicts, particularly among children, increases significantly.

Availability

An examination of this question begins with the issue of availability, which has three components:

- **Physical,** how convenient is access to drugs.
- **Psychological,** the moral and social acceptability and perceived consequences of drug use.
- **Economic,** the affordability of drugs.

Physical
Despite assertions to the contrary, the evidence indicates that presently drugs are not accessible to all. Fewer than 50 percent of high school seniors and young adults under 22 believed they could obtain cocaine "fairly easily" or

"very easily."[12] Only 39 percent of the adult population reported they could get cocaine; and only 25 percent reported that they could obtain heroin, PCP, and LSD.[13] Thus, only one-quarter to one-half of people can easily get illegal drugs (other than marijuana). After legalization, drugs would be more widely and easily available. Currently, only 11 percent of individuals reported seeing drugs available in the area where they lived;[14] after legalization, there could be a place to purchase drugs in every neighborhood. Under such circumstances, it is logical to conclude that more individuals would use drugs.

Psychological

In arguing that legalization would not result in increased use, proponents of legalization often cite public opinion polls, which indicate that the vast majority of Americans would not try drugs even if they were legally available.[15] They fail to take into account, however, that this strong public antagonism towards drugs has been formed during a period of strict prohibition when government and institutions at every level have made clear the health and criminal justice consequences of drug use. Furthermore, even if only 15 percent of population would use drugs after legalization, this would be triple the current level of 5.6 percent.

Laws define what is acceptable conduct in a society, express the will of its citizens, and represent a commitment on the part of the Congress, the President, state legislatures, and governors. Drug laws not only create a criminal sanction, they also serve as educational and normative statements that shape public attitudes.[16] Criminal laws constitute a far stronger statement than civil laws, but even the latter can discourage individual consumption. Laws regulating smoking in public and workplaces, prohibiting certain types of tobacco advertising, and mandating warning labels are in part responsible for the decline in smoking prevalence among adults.

The challenge of reducing drug abuse and addiction would be decidedly more difficult if society passed laws indicating that these substances are not sufficiently harmful to prohibit their use. Any move toward legalization would decrease the perception of risks and costs of drug use, which would lead to wider use.[17] During the late 1960s and the 1970s, as society, laws, and law enforcement became more permissive about drug use, the number of individuals smoking marijuana and using heroin, hallucinogens, and other drugs rose sharply. During the 1980s, as society's attitude became more restrictive and anti-drug laws stricter and more vigorously enforced, the perceived harmfulness of marijuana and other illicit drugs increased and use decreased.

Some legalization advocates point to the campaign against smoking as proof that reducing use is possible while substances are legally available.[18] But it has taken smoking more than 30 years to decline as much as illegal drug use did in 10.[19] Moreover, reducing use of legal drugs among the young has proven especially difficult. While use of illegal drugs by high school seniors dropped 50 percent from 1979 to 1993, tobacco use remained virtually constant.[20]

Economic

By all of the laws of economics, reducing the price of drugs will increase consumption.[21] Though interdiction and law enforcement have had limited success in reducing supply (seizing only 25 percent to 30 percent of cocaine imports, for example)[22] the illegality of drugs has increased their price.[23] Prices of illegal drugs are roughly 10 times what they would cost to produce legally. Cocaine, for example, sells at $80 a gram today, but would cost only $10 a gram legally to produce and distribute. That would set the price of a dose at 50 cents, well within the reach of a school child's lunch money.[24]

Until the mid-1980s, cocaine was the drug of the middle and upper classes. Regular use was limited to those who had the money to purchase it or got the money through white collar crime or selling such assets as their car, house, or children's college funds. In the mid-1980s, the $5 crack cocaine vial made the drug inexpensive and available to all regardless of income. Use spread. Cocaine-exposed babies began to fill hospital neonatal wards, cocaine-related emergency room visits increased sharply, and cocaine-related crime and violence jumped.[25]

Efforts to increase the price of legal drugs by taxing them heavily in order to discourage consumption, if successful, would encourage the black market, crime, violence, and corruption associated with the illegal drug trade. Heroin addicts, who gradually build a tolerance to the drug, and cocaine addicts, who crave more of the drug as soon as its effects subside, would turn to a black market if an affordable and rising level of drugs were not made available to them legally.

Children

Drug use among children is of particular concern since almost all individuals who use drugs begin before they are 21. Furthermore, adolescents rate drugs as the number one problem they face.[26] Since we have been unable to keep legal drugs, like tobacco and alcohol, out of the hands of children, legalization of illegal drugs could cause a pediatric pandemic of drug abuse and addiction.

Most advocates of legalization support a regulated system in which access to presently illicit drugs would be illegal for minors.[27] Such regulations would retain for children the "forbidden fruit" allure that many argue legalization would eliminate. Furthermore any such distinction between adults and minors could make drugs, like beer and cigarettes today, an attractive badge of adulthood.

The American experience with laws restricting access by children and adolescents to tobacco and alcohol makes it clear that keeping legal drugs away from minors would be a formidable, probably impossible, task. Today, 62 percent of high school seniors have smoked, 30 percent in the past month.[28] Three million adolescents smoke cigarettes, an average of one-half a pack per day, a $1 billion a year market.[29] Twelve million underage Americans drink beer and other alcohol, a market approaching $10 billion a year. Although alcohol use is illegal for all those under the age of 21, 87 percent of high school seniors report using alcohol, more than half in the past month.[30] These rates of use persist despite school, community, and media activities that inform youths about the dangers of smoking and drinking and despite increasing public awareness of these risks. This record indicates that efforts to ban drug use among minors while allowing it for adults would face enormous difficulty.

Moreover, in contrast to these high rates of alcohol and tobacco use, only 18 percent of seniors use illicit drugs, which are illegal for the entire society.[31] It is no accident that those substances which are mostly easily obtainable— alcohol, tobacco, and inhalants such as those found in household cleaning fluids—are those most widely used by the youngest students.[32]

Supporters and opponents of legalization generally agree that education and prevention programs are an integral part of efforts to reduce drug use by children and adolescents. School programs, media campaigns such as those of the Partnership for a Drug-Free America (PDFA), and news reports on the dangers of illegal drugs have helped reduce use by changing attitudes towards drugs. In 1992, New York City school children were surveyed on their perceptions of illegal drugs before and after a PDFA campaign of anti-drug messages on television, in newspapers, and on billboards. The second survey showed that the percentage of children who said they might want to try drugs fell 29 points and those who said drugs would make them "cool" fell 17 points.[33] Another study found that 75 percent of students who saw anti-drug advertisements reported that the ads had a deterrent effect on their own actual or intended use.[34]

Along with such educational programs, however, the stigma of illegality is especially important in preventing use among adolescents. From 1978 to 1993, current marijuana use among high school seniors dropped twice as fast as alcohol use.[35] California started a $600 million anti-smoking campaign in 1989, and by 1995, the overall smoking rate had dropped 30 percent. But among teenagers, the smoking rate remained constant—even though almost one-quarter of the campaign targeted them.[36]

In separate studies, 60 to 70 percent of New Jersey and California students reported that fear of getting in trouble with the authorities was a major reason why they did not use drugs.[37] Another study found that the greater the perceived likelihood of apprehension and swift punishment for using marijuana, the less likely adolescents are to smoke it.[38] Because a legalized system would remove much, if not all of this deterrent, drug use among teenagers could be expected to rise. Since most teens begin using drugs because their peers do[39]—not because of pressure from pushers[40]—and most drugs users initially exhibit few ill effects, more teenagers would be likely to try drugs.[41]

As a result, legalization of marijuana, cocaine, and heroin for adults would mean that increased numbers of teenagers would smoke, snort, and inject these substances at a time when habits are formed and the social, academic, and physical skills needed for a satisfying and independent life are acquired.

Hardcore Addiction

A review of addiction in the past shows that the number of alcohol, heroin, and cocaine addicts, even when adjusted for changes in population, fluctuates widely over time, in response to changes in access, price, societal attitudes, and legal consequences. The fact that alcohol and tobacco, the most accepted and available legal drugs, are the most widely abused, demonstrates that behavior is influenced by opportunity, stigma, and price. Many soldiers who were regular heroin users in Vietnam stopped once they returned to the United States where heroin was much more difficult and dangerous to get.[42] Studies have shown that even among chronic alcoholics, alcohol taxes lower consumption.[43]

Dr. Jack Homer of the University of Southern California and a founding member of the International System Dynamics Society estimates that without retail-level drug arrests and seizures—which reduce availability, increase the danger of arrest for the drug user, and stigmatize use—the number of compulsive cocaine users would rise to between 10 and 32 million, a level 5 to 16 times the present one.[44]

Not all new users become addicts. But few individuals foresee their addiction when they start using; most think they can control their consumption.[45] Among the new users created by legalization, many, including children, would find themselves unable to live without the drug, no longer able to work, go to school, or maintain personal relationships. In fact, as University of California at Los Angeles criminologist James Q. Wilson points out with regard to cocaine,[46] the percentage of drug triers who become abusers when the drugs are illegal, socially unacceptable, and generally hard to get, may be only a fraction of the users who become addicts when drugs are legal and easily available—physically, psychologically, and economically.

Harming Thy Neighbor and Thyself: Addiction and Casual Drug Use

To offset any increased use as a result of legalization, many proponents contend that money presently spent on criminal justice and law enforcement could be used for treatment of addicts and prevention.[47] In 1995, the federal government is spending $13.2 billion to fight drug abuse, nearly two-thirds of that amount on law enforcement; state and local governments are spending at least another $16 billion on drug control efforts, largely on law enforcement.[48] Legalization proponents argue that most of this money could be used to fund treatment on demand for all addicts who want it and extensive public health campaigns to discourage new use.

With legalization, the number of prisoners would initially decrease because many are currently there for drug law violations. But to the extent that legalization increases drug use, we can expect to see more of its familiar consequences. Costs would quickly rise in health care, schools, and businesses. In the long term, wider use and addiction would increase criminal activity related to the psychological and physical effects of drug use and criminal justice costs would rise again. The higher number of casual users and addicts would reduce worker productivity and students' ability and motivation to learn, cause more highway accidents and fatalities, and fill hospital beds with individuals suffering from ailments and injuries caused or aggravated by drug abuse.

Costs

It is doubtful whether legalization would produce any cost savings, over time even in the area of law enforcement. Indeed, the legal availability of alcohol has not eliminated law enforcement costs due to alcohol-related violence. A third of state prison inmates committed their crimes while under the influence of alcohol.[49] Despite intense educational campaigns, the highest number of arrests in 1993—1.5 million—was for driving while intoxicated.[50] Even if, as some legalization proponents propose, drug sales were taxed, revenues raised would be more than offset by erosion of the general tax base as abuse and addiction limited the ability of individuals to work.

Like advocates of legalization today, opponents of alcohol prohibition claimed that taxes on the legal sale of alcohol would dramatically increase revenues and even help erase the federal deficit.[51] The real-world result has been quite different. The approximately $20 billion in state and federal revenues from alcohol taxes in 1995[52] pay for only half the $40 billion that alcohol abuse imposes in direct health care costs,[53] much less the costs laid on federal entitlement programs and the legal and criminal justice systems, to say nothing of lost economic productivity. The nearly $13 billion in federal and state cigarette tax revenue[54] is one-sixth of the $75 billion in direct health care costs attributable to tobacco,[55] to say nothing of the other costs such as the $4.6 billion in social security disability payments to individuals disabled by cancer, heart disease, and respiratory ailments caused by smoking.[56]

Health care costs directly attributable to illegal drugs exceed $30 billion,[57] an amount that would increase significantly if use spread after legalization. Experience renders it unrealistic to expect that taxes could be imposed on newly legalized drugs sufficient to cover the costs of increased use and abuse.

Public Health

Legalization proponents contend that prohibition has negative public health consequences such as the spread of HIV from addicts who share dirty needles, accidental poisoning, and overdoses from impure drugs of variable potency. In 1994, more than one-third of new AIDS cases were among injection drug users who shared needles, cookers, cottons, rinse water, and other paraphernalia; many other individuals contracted AIDS by having sex, often while high, with infected injection drug users.[58]

Advocates of medicalization argue that while illicit drugs should not be freely available to all, doctors should be allowed to prescribe them (particularly heroin, but also cocaine) to addicts. They contend that giving addicts drugs assures purity and eliminates the need for addicts to steal in order to buy them.[59]

Giving addicts drugs like heroin, however, poses many problems. Providing them by prescription raises the danger of diversion for sale on the black market. The alternative—insisting that addicts take drugs on the prescriber's premises—entails at least two visits a day, thus interfering with the stated goal of many maintenance programs to enable addicts to hold jobs.

Heroin addicts require two to four shots each day in increasing doses as they build tolerance to its euphoric effect. On the other hand, methadone can be given at a constant dose since euphoria is not the objective. Addicts maintained on methadone need only a single dose each day and take it orally, eliminating the need for injection.[60] Because cocaine produces an intense, but short euphoria and an immediate desire for more,[61] addicts would have to be given the drug even more often than heroin in order to satisfy their craving sufficiently to prevent them from seeking additional cocaine on the street.

Other less radical harm reduction proposals also have serious flaws. Distributing free needles, for example, does not guarantee that addicts desperate for a high would refuse to share them. But to the extent that needle exchange programs are effective in reducing the spread of the AIDS virus and other diseases without increasing drug use, they can be adopted without legalizing drugs. Studies of whether needle exchange programs increase drug use have generally focused on periods of no longer than 12 months.[62] While use does not seem to increase in this period, data is lacking on the long-term effects of such programs and whether they prompt attitude shifts that in turn lead to increased drug use.

Some individuals do die as a result of drug impurities. But while drug purity could be assured in a government-regulated system (though not for those drugs sold on the black market), careful use could not. The increased numbers of users would probably produce a rising number of overdose deaths, similar to those caused by alcohol poisoning today.

The deaths and costs due to unregulated drug quality pale in comparison to the negative impact that legalization would have on drug users, their families, and society. Casual drug use is dangerous, not simply because it can lead to addiction or accidental overdoses, but because it is harmful per se, producing worker accidents, highway fatalities, and children born with physical and mental handicaps. Each year, roughly 500,000 newborns are exposed to illegal drugs in the womb; many others are never born because of drug-induced spontaneous abortions.[63] Newborns already exposed to drugs are far more likely to need intensive care and suffer the physical and mental consequences of low birth weight and premature birth, including early death.[64] The additional costs just to raise drug-exposed babies would outweigh any potential savings of legalization in criminal justice expenditures.[65]

Substance abuse aggravates medical conditions. Medicaid patients with a secondary diagnosis of substance abuse remain in hospitals twice as long as patients with the same primary diagnosis but with no substance abuse problems. Girls and boys under age 15 remain in the hospital three and four times as long, respectively, when they have a secondary diagnosis of substance abuse.[66] One-third to one-half of individuals with psychiatric problems are also substance abusers.[67] Young people who use drugs are at higher risk of mental health problems, including depression, suicide, and personality disorders.[68] Teenagers who use illegal drugs are more likely to have sex[69] and are less likely to use a condom than those who do not use drugs.[70] Such sexual behavior exposes these teens to increased risk of pregnancy as well as AIDS and other sexually transmitted diseases.

In schools and families, drug abuse is devastating. Students who use drugs not only limit their own ability to learn, they also disrupt classrooms, interfering with the education of other students. Drug users tear apart families by failing to provide economic support, spending money on drugs, neglecting the emotional support of the spouse and guidance of children, and putting their children at greater risk of becoming substance abusers themselves.[71] With the advent of crack cocaine in the mid-1980s, foster care cases soared over 50 percent nationwide in five years; more than 70 percent of these cases involved families in which at least one parent abused drugs.[72]

Decreased coordination and impaired motor skills that result from drug use are dangerous. A recent study in Tennessee found that 59 percent of reckless drivers who, having been stopped by the police, test negative for alcohol on the breathalyzer, test positive for marijuana and/or cocaine.[73] Twenty percent of New York City drivers who die in automobile accidents test positive for cocaine use.[74] The extent of driving while high on marijuana and other illegal drugs is still not well-known because usually the police do not have the same capability for roadside drug testing as they do for alcohol testing. . . .

Crime and Violence

Legalization advocates contend that *drug-related* violence is really *drug-trade-related* violence. They argue that what we have today is not a drug problem but a drug prohibition problem, that anti-drug laws spawn more violence and crime than the drugs themselves. Because illegality creates high prices for drugs and huge profits for dealers, advocates of legalization point out that users commit crimes to support their habit; drug pushers fight over turf; gangs and organized crime thrive; and users become criminals by coming into contact with the underworld.[75]

Legalization proponents argue that repeal of current laws, which criminalize drug use and sales, and wider availability of drugs at lower prices will end this black market and thus reduce the violence, crime, and incarceration associated with drugs.

Researchers divide drug-related violence into three types: systemic, economically compulsive, and psychopharmacological:[76]

- **Systemic violence** is that intrinsic to involvement with illegal drugs, including murders over drug turf, retribution for selling "bad" drugs, and fighting among users over drugs or drug paraphernalia.
- **Economically compulsive violence** results from addicts who engage in violent crime in order to support their addiction.
- **Psychopharmacological violence** is caused by the short or long-term use of certain drugs which lead to excitability, irrationality and violence, such as a brutal murder committed under the influence of cocaine.

Legalization of the drug trade and lower prices might decrease the first two types of violence, but higher use and abuse would increase the third. Dr. Mitchell Rosenthal, President of the Phoenix House treatment centers, warns, "What I and many other treatment professionals would expect to see in a drug-legalized America is a sharp rise in the amount of drug-related crime that is *not* committed for gain—homicide, assault, rape, and child abuse. Along with this, an increase in social disorder, due to rising levels of drug consumption and a growing number of drug abusers."[77]

In a study of 130 drug-related homicides, 60 percent resulted from the psychopharmacological effects of the drug; only 20 percent were found to be related to the drug trade; 3.1 percent were committed for economic reasons. (The remaining 17 percent either fell into more than one of these categories or were categorized as "other.")[78] U.S. Department of Justice statistics reveal that six times as many homicides, four times as many assaults, and almost one and a half times as many robberies are committed under the influence of drugs as are committed in order to get money to buy drugs.[79] Given these facts, any decreases in violent acts committed because of the current high cost of drugs would be more than offset by increases in psychopharmacological violence, such as that caused by cocaine psychosis.

The threat of rising violence is particularly serious in the case of cocaine, crack, methamphetamine, and PCP—drugs closely associated with violent behavior. Unlike marijuana or heroin, which depress activity, these drugs cause irritability and physical aggression. For instance, past increases in the New York City homicide rate have been tied to increases in cocaine use.[80]

Repeal of drug laws would not affect all addicts in the same way. Addicts engage in criminal behavior for different reasons. A small proportion of addicts is responsible for a disproportionately high number of drug-related crimes and arrests. Virtually all of these addicts committed crimes before abusing drugs and use crime to support themselves as well as their habits. Their criminal activity and drug use are symptomatic of chronic antisocial behavior and attitudes. Legally available drugs at lower prices would do little to discourage crime by this group. For a second group, criminal activity is associated with the high cost of illegal drugs. For these addicts, lower prices would decrease drug-related crimes. For a third group, legally available drugs would mean an opportunity to create illegal diversion markets, as some addicts currently do with methadone.[81]

Legalization advocates point to the exploding prison population and the failure of strict drug laws to lower crime rates.[82] Arrests for drug offenses doubled from 470,000 in 1980 to 1 million in 1993.[83] Some 60 percent of the 95,000 federal inmates are incarcerated for drug-law violations.[84]

Rising prison populations are generated in large part by stricter laws, tough enforcement, and mandatory minimum sentencing laws—policy choices of the public and Congress. But the growing number of prisoners is also a product of the high rate of recidivism—a phenomenon tied in good measure to the lack of treatment facilities, particularly in prison. Eighty percent of prisoners have prior convictions and 60 percent have served time before.[85] Despite the fact that more than 60 percent of all state inmates have used illegal drugs regularly and 30 percent were under the influence of drugs at the time they committed the crime for which they were incarcerated,[86] fewer than 20 percent of inmates with drug problems receive any treatment.[87] Many of these inmates also abuse alcohol, but there is little alcoholism treatment either for them or for those prisoners dependent only on alcohol.[88]

While strict laws and enforcement do not deter addicts from using drugs, the criminal justice system can be used to get them in treatment. Because of the nature of addiction, most drug abusers do not seek treatment voluntarily, but many respond to outside pressures including the threat of incarceration.[89]

Where the criminal justice system is used to encourage participation in treatment, addicts are more likely to complete treatment and stay off drugs. . . .[90]

Notes

1. Kurt Schmoke, "Decriminalizing Drugs: It Just Might Work—And Nothing Else Does," in *Drug Legalization: For and Against,* ed. Rod Evans and Irwin Berent (Lasalle: Open Court Press, 1992), p. 216; Merrill Smith, "The Drug Problem: Is There an Answer?" in Evans and Berent, eds., p. 84; Steven Wisotsky, "Statement Before the Select Committee on Narcotics Abuse and Control," in Evans and Berent, eds., p. 189.

2. National Commission on Marijuana and Drug Abuse, *Marijuana: Signal of Misunderstanding* (Washington, DC: GPO, 1972); Musto, p. 267.

3. U.S. Department of Health and Human Services, *Preliminary Estimates from the 1994 National Household Survey on Drug Abuse* (September 1995), pp. 2, 58.

4. Dept. of Health and Human Services (1995), p. 11.

5. Dept. of Health and Human Services (1995), p. 2.

6. Office of National Drug Control Policy (ONDCP), *National Drug Control Strategy: Strengthening Communities' Response to Drugs and Crime* (February 1995), p. 139.

7. ONDCP, *Breaking the Cycle of Drug Abuse* (September 1993), pp. 6–9.

8. Todd Austin Brenner, "The Legalization of Drugs: Why Prolong the Inevitable," in Evans and Berent, eds., p. 173; Schmoke, in Evans and Berent, eds., p. 218; Smith, in Evans and Berent, eds., p. 85.

9. Smith, in Evans and Berent, eds., pp. 83–86; Kevin Zeese, "Drug War Forever?" in *Searching for Alternatives: Drug-Control Policy in the United States,* eds. Melvyn Krauss and Edward Lazear (Stanford: Hoover Institute Press, 1992), p. 265.

10. Ethan Nadelmann, "The Case for Legalization," in *The Drug Legalization Debate,* ed. James Inciardi (Newbury Park: Sage Publications, 1991), pp. 39–40.

11. Michael Gazzaniga, "The Opium of the People: Crack in Perspective," in Evans and Berent, eds., p. 236.

12. Lloyd Johnston, Patrick O'Malley, and Jerald Bachman, *National Survey Results on Drug Use from the Monitoring the Future Study, 1975–1993* (Rockville: 1994), Vol. 1, p. 191 and Vol. 2, p. 144; Center on Addiction and Substance Abuse at Columbia University, *National Survey of American Attitudes on Substance Abuse* (July 1995).

13. Dept. of Health and Human Services *Preliminary Estimates from the 1993 National Household Survey: Press Release* (July 1994), p. 4.

14. Dept. of Health and Human Services (July 1994), p. 4.

15. See for example, Lester Grinspoon and James Bakalar, "The War on Drugs—A Peace Proposal," *The New England Journal of Medicine,* 330(5) 1994, pp. 357–60; Arnold Trebach, "For Legalization of Drugs" in *Legalize It? Debating American Drug Policy,* Arnold Trebach and James Inciardi, eds., (Washington: American University Press, 1993), p. 108.

16. Mark Moore, "Drugs: Getting a Fix on the Problem and the Solution," in Evans and Berent, eds., p. 152.

17. Johnston, O'Malley and Bachman, Vol. 1, p. 206.

18. Schmoke, in Evans and Berent, eds., p. 218; Brenner, in Evans and Berent, eds., p. 171; Wisotsky in Evans and Berent, eds., p. 210.

19. ONDCP (1995), p. 139; Centers for Disease Control, *Morbidity and Mortality Weekly Report,* 34(SS-3) 1994, p. 8.

20. Johnston, O'Malley and Bachman, Vol. 1, p. 79.

21. Moore in Evans and Berent, eds., p. 148; and Mark Moore, "Supply Reduction and Law Enforcement" in *Drugs and Crime,* Michael Tonry and James Wilson, eds., *Crime and Justice: A Review of Research,* Volume 13 (Chicago: University of Chicago Press, 1990), pp. 109–158; Michael Grossman, Gary Becker and Kevin Murphy, "Rational Addiction and the Effect of Price on Consumption," in Krauss and Lazear, eds., p. 83.

22. ONDCP (1995), p. 146.

23. Michael Farrell, John Strang and Peter Reuter, "The Non-Case for Legalization" in *Winning the War on Drugs: To Legalize or Not* (Institute of Economic Affairs: London, 1994).

24. Herbert Kleber, "Our Current Approach to Drug Abuse—Progress, Problems, Proposals," *The New England Journal of Medicine* 330(5), 1994, pp. 362–363; for higher estimates of the differences between illegal and legal costs see Moore, in Evans and Berent, eds., p. 148 and Wisotsky, in Evans and Berent, eds., p. 190.

25. Moore, in Evans and Berent, eds., pp. 129–130.

26. Center on Addiction and Substance Abuse at Columbia University, *National Survey of American Attitudes on Substance Abuse* (July 1995).

27. See for example, Wisotsky, in Evans and Berent, eds., p. 204.

28. Johnston, O'Malley and Bachman, Vol. 1, pp. 76–79.

29. K. Michael Cummings, Terry Pechacek and Donald Shopland, "The Illegal Sale of Cigarettes to US Minors: Estimates by State," *American Journal of Public Health,* 84(2) 1994, pp. 300–302.

30. Johnston, O'Malley and Bachman, Vol. 1, pp. 76–79.

31. Johnston, O'Malley and Bachman, Vol. 1, p. 79.

32. Lloyd Johnston, "A Synopsis of the Key Points in the 1994 Monitoring the Future Results" (December 1994), Table 1; Johnston, O'Malley and Bachman, Vol. 1, pp. 136–137.

33. Drug Strategies, *Keeping Score* (Washington, DC: 1995), p. 11.

34. Evelyn Cohen Reis et al., "The Impact of Anti-Drug Advertising: Perceptions of Middle and High School Students," *Archives of Pediatric and Adolescent Medicine,* 148, December 1994, pp. 1262–1268.

35. Johnston, O'Malley and Bachman, Vol. 1, p. 79.

36. "Hooked on Tobacco: The Teen Epidemic," *Consumer Reports,* March 1995, pp. 142–148.

37. Rodney Skager and Gregory Austin, *Fourth Biennial Statewide Survey of Drug and Alcohol Use Among California Students in Grades 7, 9, and 11,* Office

of the Attorney General, June 1993; Wayne Fisher, *Drug and Alcohol Use Among New Jersey High School Students,* New Jersey Department of Law and Public Safety, 1993.

38. David Peck, "Legal and Social Factors in the Deterrence of Adolescent Marijuana Use," *Journal of Alcohol and Drug Education,* 28(3) 1983, pp. 58–74.

39. Diedre Dupre, "Initiation and Progression of Alcohol, Marijuana and Cocaine Use Among Adolescent Abusers," *The American Journal on Addiction,* 4, 1995, pp. 43–48.

40. Ronald Simmons, Rand Conger and Leslie Whitbeck, "A Multistage Learning Model of the Influences of Family and Peers Upon Adolescent Substance Abuse," *Journal of Drug Issues* 18(3) 1988, pp. 293–315.

41. Simmons, Conger and Whitbeck, p. 304; Mark Moore, "Drugs: Getting a Fix on the Problem and the Solution," in Evans and Berent, eds., p. 143.

42. Musto, pp. 258–259.

43. Philip Cook, "The Effect of Liquor Taxes on Drinking, Cirrhosis, and Auto Accidents" in *Alcohol and Public Policy: Beyond the Shadow of Prohibition,* Mark Moore and Dean Gerstein, eds. (Washington, DC: National Academy Press, 1981), p. 256.

44. Jack Homer, "Projecting the Impact of Law Enforcement on Cocaine Prevalence: A System Dynamics Approach," *Journal of Drug Issues* 23(2) 1993, pp. 281–295.

45. Kleber, p. 361.

46. James Q. Wilson, "Against the Legalization of Drugs," *Commentary* (February 1990), pp. 21–28.

47. See for example, Schmoke in Evans and Berent, eds., p. 218.

48. ONDCP (1995), p. 138.

49. Bureau of Justice Statistics, *Survey of State Prison Inmates, 1991* (Washington, DC: 1993), p. 26.

50. Bureau of Justice Statistics, *Prisoners in 1994* (Washington, DC: 1995), p. 13.

51. Paul Aaron and David Musto, "Temperance and Prohibition in America: A Historical Overview," in Moore and Gerstein, eds., p. 172.

52. Drug Enforcement Administration (DEA), *How to Hold Your Own in a Drug Legalization Debate* (Washington, DC, 1994), p. 26, adjusted to 1995.

53. Center on Addiction and Substance Abuse at Columbia University (CASA), *The Cost of Substance Abuse to America's Health Care System, Final Report* (To be issued, 1995).

54. The Tobacco Institute (1994), adjusted to 1995.

55. CASA (To be issued, 1995).

56. Center on Addiction and Substance Abuse at Columbia University, *Substance Abuse and Federal Entitlement Programs* (February 1995).

57. CASA (To be issued, 1995).

58. Centers for Disease Control, National AIDS Clearinghouse (1994).

59. See for example, "Prescribing to Addicts Appears to Work in Britain: Interview with Dr. John Marks," *Psychiatric News,* December 17, 1993, pp. 8, 14.

60. Joyce Lowinson et al., "Methadone Maintenance," pp. 550–561; Jerome Jaffe, "Opiates: Clinical Aspects," pp. 186–194; and Eric Simon, "Opiates: Neurobiology," pp. 195–204 in *Substance Abuse: A Comprehensive Textbook,* 2nd ed., Joyce Lowinson, Pedro Ruiz and Robert Millman, eds. (Baltimore: Williams and Wilkins, 1992).

61. Mark Gold, "Cocaine (and Crack): Clinical Aspects," in Lowinson, Ruiz and Millman, eds., pp. 205–221.

62. Peter Lurie, Arthur Reingold et al., *The Public Health Impact of Needle Exchange Programs in the United States and Abroad,* 2 vols. (University of California, 1993).

63. Dept. of Justice (1992), p. 12; Paul Taubman, "Externalities and Decriminalization of Drugs," in Krauss and Lazear, eds., p. 99.

64. Dept. of Justice (1992), p. 12; Joel Hay, "The Harm They Do to Others," in Krauss and Lazear, eds., pp. 204–213.

65. Hay, in Krauss and Lazear, eds., p. 208.

66. Center on Addiction and Substance Abuse at Columbia University (CASA), *The Cost of Substance Abuse to America's Health Care System, Report 1: Medicaid Hospital Costs,* (July 1993), pp. 38–46.

67. Ronald Kessler et al., "Lifetime and 12-month prevalence of DSM-III-R psychiatric disorders in the United States: Results from the National Comorbidity Study," *Archives of General Psychiatry,* 51(1) 1994, pp. 8–19.

68. Dept. of Justice (1992), p. 11.

69. Centers for Disease Control, "Youth Risk Behavior Survey, 1991."

70. M. Lynne Cooper, Robert Pierce, and Rebecca Farmer Huselid, "Substance Abuse and Sexual Risk Taking Among Black Adolescents and White Adolescents," *Health Psychology* 13(3) 1994, pp. 251–262.

71. Dept. of Justice (1992), p. 9.

72. General Accounting Office, *Foster Care: Parental Drug Abuse Has Alarming Impact on Young Children* (Washington, DC: 1994).

73. Daniel Brookoff et al., "Testing Reckless Drivers for Cocaine and Marijuana," *The New England Journal of Medicine* 331(8) 1994, pp. 518–522.

74. Peter Marzuk, Kenneth Tardiff, et al., "Prevalence of Recent Cocaine Use among Motor Vehicle Fatalities in New York City," *Journal of the American Medical Association* 1990; 263, pp. 250–256.

75. See for example, Nadelmann, in Inciardi (1991), ed., pp. 31–32; Brenner, in Evans and Berent, eds., p. 174; Ira Glasser, "Drug Prohibition: An Engine for Crime," in Krauss and Lazear, eds., pp. 271–283; Milton Friedman, "The War We Are Losing," in Krauss and Lazear, eds., pp. 53–57.

76. Paul J. Goldstein, "The Drugs/Violence Nexus: A Tripartite Conceptual Framework," *Journal of Drug Issues* (Fall 1985), pp. 493–516.

77. Mitchell Rosenthal, "Panacea or Chaos: The Legalization of Drugs in America," *Journal of Substance Abuse Treatment* 11(1) 1994, pp. 3–7.

78. Henry Brownstein and Paul J. Goldstein, "A Typology of Drug-Related Homicides" in *Drugs, Crime and the Criminal Justice System,* Ralph Weisheit, ed. (Cincinnati, OH: Anderson Publishing Co., 1990), pp. 171–191.

79. Bureau of Justice Statistics (1993), p. 22.

80. Kenneth Tardiff et al., "Homicide in New York City: Cocaine Use and Firearms," *Journal of the American Medical Association* 272(1) 1994, pp. 43–46.

81. Jon Chaiken and Marcia Chaiken, "Varieties of Criminal Behavior," (Santa Monica: Rand, 1982); HK Wexler and George De Leon, "Criminals as Drug Abusers and Drug Abusers Who Are Criminals," Paper presented to the Annual Convention of the American Psychological Association, Washington, DC, 1980; cited in George De Leon, "Some Problems with the Anti-Prohibitionist Position on Legalization of Drugs," *Journal of Addictive Diseases* 13(2) 1994, p. 38.

82. See for example, New York City Bar Association, "A Wiser Course: Ending Drug Prohibition," *The Record* 49(5) 1994, pp. 525–534.

83. Bureau of Justice Statistics (1995), p. 13.

84. Bureau of Justice Statistics (1995), pp. 1, 10.

85. Bureau of Justice Statistics (1993), p. 11.

86. Bureau of Justice Statistics (1993), p. 21.

87. General Accounting Office, *Drug Treatment: State Prisons Face Challenges in Providing Services* (Washington, DC: 1991).

88. Bureau of Justice Statistics (1993), p. 26.

89. De Leon, p. 38.

90. M. Douglas Anglin. "The Efficacy of Civil Commitment in Treating Narcotic Addiction" in *Compulsory Treatment of Drug Abuse: Research and Clinical Practice,* NIDA Research Monograph 86, 1988, pp. 8–34; Robert Hubbard et al., *Drug Abuse Treatment: A National Study of Effectiveness* (Chapel Hill: University of North Carolina Press, 1989).

Peter Gorman    **NO**

Veteran Cops Against the Drug War

Howard Woolridge is outside of Utica, New York, heading east on horseback on a beautiful late summer day. He's wearing a T-shirt with the slogan "Cops Say Legalize Drugs. Ask Me Why." For the last 3,000 miles, he's been switching off between his two horses, Misty and Sam. But the T-shirt slogan has stayed the same.

The rangy, good-looking guy is also talking on the cell phone to a reporter back in North Texas. But he interrupts that conversation to speak to someone who pulls up next to him in a car. "That's right—cops say legalize," he tells the newcomer in a deep voice. "Why? Because if we do, we just might be able to keep drugs out of the hands of your 14-year-old."

"Right on!" the motorist shouts, and drives off.

Woolridge is not a lunatic and he's not been out in the sun too long, even if he did cross the United States on horseback in the summer heat. He's a retired law enforcement officer with 18 years on the job who finally decided that the war on drugs was more of a problem than the illicit drugs it was purporting to fight.

He's also a serious long-distance horseman, on the road this time since March 4, when he left Los Angeles for the 3,400-mile ride to New York Harbor. It's the second time Woolridge has crossed the United States to publicize the campaign to repeal most of the drug laws in this country. In 2003 he rode from Georgia to Oregon. When he finished this trip on October 5, looking out at the Statue of Liberty, he was honored by the Long Riders' Guild as only the second person known to have ridden horseback all the way across the country in both directions. And he'll still be wearing one of his "Ask Me Why" T-shirts, the same shirts he's been wearing for six years.

"When I first started wearing it," he says, "people in Texas thought I was crazy. They thought my idea would destroy Texas and America. They believed the government propaganda that millions of people would pick up heroin or methamphetamines and become junkies overnight if you legalized it." But in the last two to three years, he's seen a sea change in the attitude of the American public regarding the war on drugs.

Jailed over Medicinal Marijuana

"At any given Arby's, McDonald's, Rotary Club or veterans hall," he says, "people are overwhelmingly in favor of calling a halt to drug prohibition. Overwhelmingly."

From *The World & I Online*, January 2006. Copyright © 2006 by The World & I Online. Reprinted by permission. www.Worldandl.com

Many of the houses Woolridge is riding past carry plaques attesting to the Utica area's involvement in the Underground Railroad that once funneled runaway slaves from the south up to Canada. It makes him think about Bernie Ellis, a fellow soldier in the war against the drug war, who has lost his own freedom.

"For 10 years he provided free medical marijuana to three oncologists in the Nashville, Tennessee, area for their patients undergoing chemotherapy. He never once met the doctors, of course; it was all cloak-and-dagger. He'd bring the marijuana to an office worker who'd get it to the patient.

"Well, he finally got busted last year. Now he's looking at five years mandatory federal prison time, though that might go up to 10 because he had a shotgun on his farm when he got busted. And of course his million-dollar farm has been forfeited because he grew the medical marijuana there."

The phone goes quiet for a minute, and there's the sound of a strangled sob. "Sorry. Got a little choked up for a second," he says. He pauses to explain his T-shirt to a motorist, then he's back on the phone talking about Bernie. "This is a guy who broke the law to help people and is now facing the consequences of that. Poor son of a bitch. Next time I see him he'll be in prison."

Woolridge is not a lone ranger in the fight to legalize drugs. He's a founding member of an organization called Law Enforcement Against Prohibition or LEAP, an organization made up entirely of current or former members of law enforcement who feel the drug war's a failure and believe legalization and regulation are preferable to the incarceration of drug users and control of the drug market by organized crime.

Founded in March 2002 by five police officers, LEAP now counts about 3,000 members, from the ranks of policemen, prison guards, Drug Enforcement Administration (DEA) agents, judges and even prosecutors in 48 states and 45 foreign countries. The idea behind LEAP is that, as with the Vietnam Veterans Against the War, the call for an end to the drug war carries more weight when it comes from folks who were in the trenches.

"We're the ones who fought the war," said Jack Cole, LEAP's executive director, who retired from the New Jersey state police as a detective lieutenant after 26 years, including 14 in their Narcotics Bureau, mostly undercover. "And I bear witness to the abject failure of the U.S. war on drugs and to the horrors these prohibitionist policies have produced."

The LEAP Web site provides the statistical backup for that argument. "After nearly four decades of fueling the U.S. policy of a war on drugs with over half a trillion tax dollars and increasingly punitive policies, our confined population has quadrupled," it says. "More than 2.2 million of our citizens are currently incarcerated and every year we arrest an additional 1.6 million for nonviolent drug offenses—more per capita than any country in the world. . . . Meanwhile, people continue dying in our streets while drug barons and terrorists continue to grow richer."

To get that message out, LEAP members have given nearly 1,500 speeches since 2003. And they don't preach to the choir. "We don't do hemp rallies or Million Man Marijuana Marches," said Woolridge. "We do Kiwanis Clubs and PTA meetings and cop conventions. That's where the people we've got to reach go."

To parents and teachers and Rotarians and other cops, LEAP members tell their own stories, about their work and about how they came to feel the drug war was not the answer.

Woolridge, for instance, was a street cop in Michigan for 15 of his 18 years of service, before moving up to the rank of detective. "I didn't work directly with the drug war, in that I wasn't in narcotics," he said. "Still, as a detective I was constantly working with felonies that touched on the drug war. Eight of 10 burglary suspects I dealt with were on crack at the time. They were stealing for drug money."

The burglary victims "were all in real pain," he said. "And I got so fed up with it I began saying, 'Why not let these guys have all the crack they want until they die?' Now I'd say, 'Have all you want for a dollar.' That makes it their choice to live or die. Either way, you don't have people breaking into houses for drug money anymore."

"Dehumanizing" Drug Users

To Cole, who did work directly in narcotics, the whole concept of the war on drugs is wrong. "You declare war, you need soldiers. You have soldiers, they need an enemy. So we've effectively taken a peacekeeping force—the police—and turned them into soldiers whose enemies are the 110 million people who have tried illegal substances in the U.S."

To be an effective soldier, you've got to dehumanize your enemy. "When I started out in narcotics I believed everything they told me," said Cole, a no-BS kind of guy. "Drugs were bad. The people who did them were less than human. I was all for locking them up."

Worse, he said, he and others often applied what they called a little "street justice" to the people they were arresting. "In our training we were taught to believe that drug users were the worst people in the world and whatever we did to them to try to stop their drug use was justified."

What they did was kick in home or apartment doors and have every man woman and child inside lie on the floor. If people didn't cooperate immediately, they were thrown to the floor. Then the place was ransacked. "When we searched for drugs we pretty much did as much damage as possible. We'd break bureaus, turn over beds, smash mirrors, throw things on the floor. Didn't matter, because the people there weren't humans, right? And then, if we did find any drugs, we'd arrest everyone in the house: parents, sisters, brothers. And since we'd already kicked the door down when we came in, it would be left open and anyone who wanted to enter could steal what they wanted. We never cared about that."

Street justice didn't stop there, said Cole. In court, he said officers routinely changed testimony to insure convictions—times, locations, amounts of drug, "anything that couldn't be checked to catch the officer in a lie."

It didn't take long for Cole to reach the conclusion that the drug war and its street justice weren't for him. He was mostly going after small-timers, and his job, he came to feel, was to insert himself into voluntary, private business transactions. "To do that, I had to become someone's confidant, their best friend. And once I was, I would bust them."

But he, too, got hooked—on the adrenaline high of the game. "By the time I came to my senses, I was working on big-timers, and pitting your mind against theirs was a great rush," he said. "Also, it was hard to quit because we were considered by the public and our peers as heroes. And then, given that I'd worked with a lot of cops who applied bad street justice, I let myself believe that at least if I was the one catching [the dopers] they'd be legally caught, and I'd tell the truth and justice would prevail."

He laughed. "Know what was the worst? When I realized that I liked and respected a lot of the bad guys much more than I liked or respected the guys I was working with."

Prohibition: Has It Worked by Its Own Standards?

The stated goals of the war on drugs are to lower drug consumption, reduce addiction and dependence, and decrease the quality and quantity of illegal drugs available on American streets. Those have been the goals since President Richard Nixon first declared the war as part of his attempt to look tough on crime during the presidential election in 1968.

Since then, the strategy of prohibition has been ramped up by every succeeding administration. Few people in this country—or anywhere—have escaped the effects of the U.S. drug war, from the toll of burglaries and car thefts committed to pay for drugs, to the tax bills for prisons to hold the increasing percentages of citizens locked up for nonviolent drug-related crimes, to the millions of kids who've grown up without one or both parents as a result of drug convictions and drug addictions. Drug-related murders reach into the tens of thousands in this country, and the toll is much higher in drug-producing and-shipping nations, from Colombia to Afghanistan to Jamaica. Thousands of peace officers have died fighting the drug war. Whole countries have found themselves under the boot of the illegal drug industry, their governments controlled or intimidated by drug cartels, their politicians and police forces infiltrated, and honest public servants assassinated.

The assumption in American drug policy has always been that those are the impacts of illegal drugs themselves. But LEAP members have come to believe those are the wages not of drugs, but of the war on drugs. And they want the rest of the country to look closely at the costs of that strategy and what they see as its failures.

Despite the billions of dollars spent on the fight in nearly 40 years, LEAP members point out, the drug war has failed on every one of its own stated goals.

Drug consumption, for instance, shows little sign of dropping. Whereas in 1965, according to the Drug Enforcement Administration, fewer than 4 million Americans had ever tried an illegal drug, the figure is now more than 110 million. In 2000, the federal government estimated that there were about 33 million people in this country who had used cocaine at least once—a more than 700 percent increase over the total number of people 35 years before who had used any illegal drug.

Dependence and addiction? According to the Office of National Drug Control Policy (ONDCP), the federal agency that sets and administers U.S. drug policy, in 2002 more than 7 million Americans were either dependent on or abusing illegal substances—nearly double the number of people who had even tried such drugs when Nixon declared his war. Heroin addicts have jumped from a few hundred thousand in the 1960s to between 750,000 and one million today according to the ONDCP.

Attempts to decrease the quality of available drugs also have failed. In 1970, average street heroin in this country had a potency of 1 to 2 percent. In 2000, according to the DEA, that purity figure was 36.8 percent—although U.S. drug czar John Walters did praise anti-drug forces recently for reducing the strength of street heroin coming from South America to 32.1 percent. Similarly, street cocaine was roughly 2 to 4 percent pure in 1968—and a whopping 56 percent in 2001, according to the ONDCP. The average strength of the active ingredient (THC) in marijuana sold in this country more than doubled between the late 1970s and 2001.

Nor is there much good news on drug quantities and availability, at least not judging by the numbers of users and the prices on the street. The ONDCP estimates that Americans' use of cocaine and crack has dropped from 447 tons in 1990 to 259 tons in 2000. But the price of cocaine has dropped from $100 per gram in 1970 to $25 to $50 per gram in 2002—for cocaine that was many times stronger. At the wholesale level, a kilogram of cocaine (2.2 pounds at roughly 25 percent purity) cost $45,000 in New York City in 1970. Today, in any large city in the U.S., it costs less than $15,000 and it's about 65 percent pure.

Only marijuana showed a price increase. In 1970, a bag of Mexican ditchweed (roughly an ounce) cost $20. In 2005, that same bag costs nearly $50. But most Americans who can afford it don't smoke Mexican ditchweed. They smoke U.S.-grown sinsemilla, which runs up to $400 per ounce.

With availability, price, and quality making drugs as attractive as ever, the only other barometer of the success of the drug war might be if it's stopped anyone from trying drugs—an area where programs like DARE, a huge effort targeted at schoolkids—have had a noted lack of success. "It didn't stop George Bush, Bill Clinton, Al Gore or me from smoking pot," said Woolridge. "I don't think it probably ever stopped anyone."

Collateral Damage

The cops and prosecutors and judges who belong to LEAP think the bad results of the drug war go beyond its policy failures, even beyond the lives lost to drug violence and incarceration.

"Let's be honest," Cole said. "The war on drugs has taken an incredible toll in terms of the loss of our civil liberties, particularly in terms of the Fourth Amendment, from property forfeiture laws that fund law enforcement agencies to warrantless searches. It's promoted institutionalized racism, and it's created a systemic level of corruption among law enforcement unheard of prior to its initiation."

Law enforcement veterans like Cole and Woolridge believe the increase in institutional racism is one of the deepest wounds. They point out, for instance, that crack users (generally inner-city blacks) are subject to mandatory minimum sentences of five years for possession of five grams of crack, while powder cocaine users (generally middle-class whites) have to be caught with 500 grams to get the same mandatory sentence.

While ONDCP statistics show that whites use more than 70 percent of all illegal drugs, blacks are sentenced to prison for drug crimes seven times more often than whites.

"Imagine," said Cole, "one of the most racist places in the world: South Africa, 1993. At that time, the South African government was incarcerating black males at the rate of 859 per 100,000 population." And yet in 2004 in the United States—with more people and a higher percent of its population in prison than any country in the world—the incarceration rate for black males was 4,919 per 100,000 (compared to 726 overall).

He pointed to an FBI estimate that one in three black male babies born in the U.S. in 2004 have an expectation of going to prison during their lifetime. "That just blows my mind," he said.

LEAP members believe that a large percentage of the corruption found in U.S. police agencies is tied to drugs. In Texas, recent drug-related scandals included the Dallas fake-drugs operation, in which a snitch was paid more than $200,000 over a two-year period to provide local cops with drug dealers. The "dealers" turned out to be nearly all illegal immigrants; their "drugs" turned out to be crushed sheetrock and pool chalk.

And then there was Tulia, in the Texas Panhandle, in which a multi-county drug task force hired a corrupt deputy sheriff to rid the town of its drug problem; when it turned out there wasn't one, the deputy created one, and more than 40 people wound up arrested.

LEAP spokesmen see both of those high-profile Texas drug corruption cases as indicative of a much wider problem: officers cutting corners to get the arrest numbers that will keep the fuel line of federal and state anti-drug funding open. And those scandals don't begin to touch on the border patrol agents, police, and other law enforcement officials who have been corrupted because the drug money is so available.

More Law-Enforcement Corruption

Rusty White, another LEAP member, is a self-described redneck who grew up hard in east Texas and now, after many stops in other states and countries, lives just north of Fort Worth. At 13, he saw a friend shoot up black-tar heroin and decided he didn't like hard drugs. By 16, he'd been to juvenile detention five times and gotten kicked out of his high school "because I was traveling with an older crowd of bad-ass kids that I was trying to live up to."

In quick succession, he married, became a father, joined the Army and got divorced. After a second tour with the Army, he ended up in Florence, Arizona, where he went to work at the state penitentiary, which, he said, was "one of the most violent prisons in the United States at that time."

From 1973 to 1978, he worked as a guard on maximum security, death row, and administrative segregation cellblocks, dealing with horrors daily. "Life meant very little to those inside the walls," he said, noting that two prison guards were killed and mutilated by inmates in 1973. "And drugs were one of the biggest problems we had. They were the cause of most of the deaths and power struggles." And most of the drugs were brought in by family members of prison workers. "I got fed up with the corruption and left to go into the oil-drilling business in 1979," he said.

After working overseas for several years, White moved to Oklahoma. And there, he said, he got to see the war on drugs from a very different vantage point. "The county I lived in had a sheriff who controlled the drug market. And he did so with force. It was common knowledge that if you crossed him he could be—and had been—deadly."

But the same sheriff regularly flew around the county in National Guard helicopters, providing photo ops for news crews to show how tough he was on drugs. "The only thing he was getting rid of was the competition," said White disgustedly.

His only personal encounter with the sheriff and his machine occurred when White's brother-in-law, a small-time pot dealer, was busted. "He was poor, didn't have a car that ran, and was living off [government] commodities. Yet he was going to be played by the sheriff as a drug-dealing kingpin," the former prison guard said.

"Anyway, he's the father of three little ones, all younger than six, and when the police arrived, he offered to go with them willingly. But he asked that his kids be allowed to stay with an uncle who was there rather than dragging them down to the station. Well, you know how people feel about 'drug dealers.' The police said no, the kids were coming to the station to watch their father get busted, and then they'd be released to the uncle."

When the man's trial came up, White said, it turned out the district attorney didn't have any evidence against him as a big-time dealer. Nonetheless, he was offered a plea deal: Admit to being a big dealer and get a one- to three-year sentence. If he took it to trial, however, the prosecutor promised he'd ask for a full 10 years.

"He copped to the plea. But to see him struggle with having to lie in front of his kids and admit to something he hadn't done—well, I sort of snapped and screamed at the prosecutor and asked him if he'd thought he'd earned his money that day and why he was playing God, and he looked at me and answered, 'Because in this county, I am God.'"

A couple of years later, White said, the DA went back into private practice and shortly thereafter was arrested and convicted for dealing methamphetamines. "How the sheriff escaped that net, I don't know," White said. "But the thing to remember is that . . . this sort of thing is happening every day in the war on drugs, all over the country. And that abuse of trust and power is far more harmful to Americans than drugs could ever be."

No Place for "Anyone with a Conscience"

Shortly after his brother-in-law's conviction, White went back to work in the prison system, and became a drug-dog trainer and handler. It was the sort of work White said he was meant to do. "I tracked several escapees from the prison and even some cop killers using my track K-9s. We helped departments all over the state. I'd be sent to prisons to look for drugs—I had no problem with that. But the more we were used with other police organizations the more my conscience started to become a problem."

Two incidents stick in White's mind. Once while his partner was helping another officer, part of a joint was discovered in the ashtray of an old pickup belonging to an elderly man. The dogs were brought in, and in the camper shell on the back of the truck in which the old man lived the dogs sniffed out a brief-case with more than $9,000 in it. Because it was a drug dog that had alerted on it, the money was confiscated. "And they just stood around laughing as the old man begged them not to take his life savings. It just made me sick and ashamed. Heck, it's common knowledge that over 90 percent of the paper money in this country is tainted with a drug scent a dog can find. But using that to rob our people disgusts me. Heck, if you walk any K-9 into a bank vault the dog will mark on that money, too. How come that money isn't confiscated?"

The second incident occurred one night when White and his drug dog were called to help a local police department search a house for drugs. When he pulled up to the house, he asked to see the warrant. The officer told him it wasn't there yet but to go ahead and start the search, and it would be there shortly. "I told him that's just not how it works. I needed the warrant for the search to be legal. So I put my K-9 back into the truck and brought him back to the kennel. And then I got called on the carpet for refusing to assist."

White thought getting into trouble for following the law he'd sworn to uphold was just too much, so he quit. "Heck, there was so much corruption, even among K-9 handlers. If they didn't want someone with drugs caught they'd say the dog didn't mark. If they did, well, we heard of cases where guys went so far as to 'salt' the areas their dogs were searching to make sure some-one got busted. It was so bad that, being honest, you couldn't do it. . . . I don't think anyone with a conscience can be part of law enforcement anymore."

Richard Watkins saw the same corruption inside prison that White did, but from a unique perspective. A decorated Vietnam veteran with a Ph.D. in education, Watkins worked at Texas' Huntsville prison for 20 years; the last several as warden of Holiday Unit, a 2,100-bed facility housing a range of crim-inals from nonviolent to violent/maximum security.

He was originally hired to revamp and professionalize the correctional officers training program—something the prison system was forced to do by federal mandate, and which Watkins said was badly needed. "It was just hor-rible. Corrupt, bad, just plain horrible," he said.

Watkins had always had reservations about the war on drugs. He figured the drug dealers wouldn't go away as long as there was a market. And looking at this country's experience with Prohibition, "and how that created mobsters and criminal gangs," he figured that legalizing drugs made more sense. When selling and drinking booze became legal in this country again, he said, "you had so much more control of it. You had supporting laws that managed the use of alcohol."

Watkins was first exposed to drugs in Vietnam. He didn't use them—he preferred alcohol—but he saw a lot of other guys getting high on marijuana and other drugs. Many of those men wound up in prison when they came home with addiction problems. "And in prison, you could always get whatever drugs you wanted. Heck, we arrested a mom one time who was putting a lip-lock on her son to pass him a balloon full of heroin. But most of the drugs came in through the guards. Drugs are packaged so small, it's almost impossible to keep them out. Think about that: If you can't keep drugs out of a maximum-security prison, you can't keep them out of schools or anywhere else."

Once drugs land someone in prison in Texas, he said, life's prospects get a lot dimmer. "We've got these minor players put in with professional criminals. If they weren't criminals going in they damn sure are when they get out. Imagine a system where we put people into a society that's really a training ground for criminals, then don't provide them with either schooling or treatment, then put them back on the streets where they came from. Do you really expect them to be reformed? Life doesn't work that way."

He wishes people wouldn't make the decision to use drugs. "But if they did use them, I wouldn't put them in prison. I'd rather see the money we spend on prisons going to give these kids the tools they need to make better choices."

Voices Opposing LEAP's Perspective

You might imagine that it would be easy to find law enforcement agencies and personnel who oppose LEAP's call for legalization and regulation as an alternative to the war on drugs. But neither the FBI nor the DEA would discuss the subject.

"Our job is to stop the flow of illegal drugs both at home and abroad, as well as to stop our citizens from wanting to use them, through education and prevention methods," said an ONDCP representative. "We will not discuss legalization or any organization which thinks that would be a solution."

Jack Cole wasn't surprised. "They're good soldiers," he said. "They're not allowed to question their commands. Our job is to simply have their commanders change their marching orders."

Mike Smithson, who runs LEAP's speakers bureau, said he's made more than 100 attempts to get law enforcement and drug policy officials to come out and debate LEAP, "and we've only been taken up on it five times. Policymakers generally say that debating us will lend us credence. We think they're just afraid. How can they defend a policy that is already being defended by every major drug dealer, cartel and drug-producing government worldwide?"

Woolridge says that on his entire ride from Los Angeles he's talked to only two officers who disagreed with LEAP's point of view. "One guy thought we'd destroy America if we legalized drugs. He was so angry when he couldn't find anything to write me a ticket for that he gave me the finger as he drove away. And there was a state trooper with 22 years on the job who told me to take off my shirt because it said 'Cops say legalize drugs,' and he didn't agree with that. I told him go make up his own shirt."

One person did agree to discuss his opposition to LEAP's stand was Sheriff John Cooke of Wells County in Colorado. Cooke is a member of a Rotary Club at which Howard Woolridge spoke. He was so taken aback by the idea of legalizing drugs that he demanded equal time and recently spoke to the Rotary Club himself.

"In my opinion, there are several reasons not to legalize drugs," Cooke told Fort Worth Weekly. First of all, when people say you're going to eliminate the black market, does that mean you're going to sell drugs to 12- and 15-year olds? Because if you don't, someone will. Law enforcement surely hasn't done a good job at keeping alcohol and cigarettes out of the hands of kids, so what makes them think they'll do any better with drugs? And if you don't sell drugs to them, there will be a black market created to sell to them. So I don't buy the end of the black market theory.

"Secondly, we already have social ills from the legal use of alcohol and tobacco. Why on earth would we want to turn other addictive substances loose on the public?

"Thirdly, these LEAP folks want to throw in the towel, say we've lost the drug war. But the thing is that I think we're winning the war on drugs. I think drug use is down. I think if we keep at it, we will win.

"Then there's the question of use. Right now, I believe that the threat of the hammer of law enforcement is keeping a great many people from doing drugs. The threat of prison time is a big hammer. I think if we legalized you'd see the number of people doing drugs in this country skyrocket. I believe we'd have a drug-dependent society . . . and I don't want to see America as a drug-dependent country."

Michael Gilbert, director of the Department of Criminal Justice at the University of Texas at San Antonio, said he doubted that there would be any sizeable black market aimed at teens if drugs were legalized. Gilbert is a LEAP member who worked in prisons—including Leavenworth—and with Justice Department agencies for more than 20 years.

"The reason there's so much money in the black market is not because of the small portion of destabilized street addicts we have, or even kids experimenting with drugs. It's because you have long-time productive millions [of people] who regularly purchase small quantities of the drugs of their choice but they don't use them in a way that becomes destructive to their lives," he said. "They're working, paying their taxes and so forth. The real money is from the enormous number of middle-class people who use drugs. So while you might still have a small market of teens purchasing drugs, it wouldn't be large enough to fund criminal enterprises as it does today."

While few policy makers will discuss the benefits of drug prohibition, several well-known former policy makers have come out against it. Among them are Nobel Prize-winning economist Milton Friedman, a former member of President Reagan's Economic Advisory Board; former Secretary of State (under Ronald Reagan) George P. Shultz; former governor of New Mexico Gary Johnson; former Baltimore Mayor Kurt Schmoke; and U.S. Rep. Dennis Kucinich of Ohio, a former presidential candidate.

Benefits of the LEAP Solution

None of the LEAP members interviewed for this article believes abusing drugs is a good choice. But that's different, they say, from the legal system further ruining people's lives because of that bad choice. They also figure that, like tattoos, hair color decisions, and bad marriages, drug use is a poor choice that society should only care about when it hurts other people. In town, running around in your yard naked and screaming at 4 a.m. breaks the social contract. On a ranch where no one else can see or hear, few people would care about it. Likewise, LEAP members figure, if you can do drugs and not break the social contract, go ahead. And in fact, the federal government figures that 72 percent of chronic drug users continue to function well in society, without harming others.

Even considering the harm that drugs can cause, however, LEAP members believe that the war on drugs is even more harmful. Legalizing drugs, on the other hand, would take profits out of the hands of criminals and hugely reduce the need for people to commit crime to pay for drugs, they say. Regulation would take drug manufacture out of the hands of bathtub chemists and put it into the hands of real chemists, eliminating many of the deaths from bad drugs—much like the end of Prohibition did for deaths from homemade booze. HIV and hepatitis C, rampant among needle-sharing junkies, could be significantly reduced with the availability of clean needles, reducing a major health-care burden for the country.

"Don't forget my favorite," Woolridge said. "If as Bush said, drug money funds terrorists, [then] legalizing drugs would take half a billion dollars a day out of Afghanistan alone, much of which is going to al Qaeda to buy weapons to be used to kill our boys. We could eliminate that overnight."

Legalization, in fact, would probably not increase drug use long-term, many believe—especially since nearly half the population has already tried it. "In all likelihood," Watkins said, "you would see a spike in use as we did with the end of alcohol prohibition. But that normalized pretty quickly, and would probably be the same with drugs. There would be a period of experimentation that would level out, and we'd be left with all the benefits and none of the negatives."

It was Sunday afternoon and Howard Woolridge and Misty were still in upstate New York, having made it from Utica to a ghetto in Schenectady. Woolridge was back on the phone again, when a woman approached him.

"What do you mean cops say legalize drugs?" she could be heard asking.

"Just that. Let's legalize drugs, take them off the street corner."

"What kind of drugs?"

"Heroin, crack, methamphetamine, anything you can think of."

"Are you crazy? I don't want my kids doing those drugs!"

"Neither do I," he told her. "They're no good. But that doesn't keep them from being sold on the corner in this very neighborhood, does it? I'd legalize them and get them into pharmacies. Keep your kids from being shot while walking down the street."

There was a pause and then she laughed. "I never thought of it that way before. You're making me think now."

EXPLORING THE ISSUE

Should Laws Against Drug Use Remain Restrictive?

Critical Thinking and Reflection

1. Should individuals (adults) or governments decide what drugs they can take?
2. What would happen if drugs were legalized?
3. What are all the consequences of America's drug laws?
4. In your estimate, do the benefits of America's drug laws outweigh the costs?
5. How could drug laws banning drugs be modified to greatly reduce their costs?
6. Would legalizing only marijuana use be a good policy? Why?
7. Can a society maintain its moral integrity and authority when it is lax on these types of laws?

Is There Common Ground?

Everyone agrees that America has a drug problem. Drugs have ruined many lives. Everyone agrees that something should be done about it. But what? The answer is easy, outlaw drug use. So we did that. Everyone agrees the result was not what we were hoping for. Now we are not sure whether outlawing drugs was the right action to take, but other options also have bad consequences. Kleber and Califano assert that utilizing the criminal justice system to maintain the illegal nature of drugs is necessary to keep society free of the detrimental effects of drugs. Loosening drug laws is unwise and dangerous. They argue that international control efforts, interdiction, and domestic law enforcement are effective and that many problems associated with drug use are mitigated by drug regulation policies. They maintain that restrictive drug laws are a feasible and desirable means of dealing with the drug crisis.

Gorman charges that restrictive drug laws are highly destructive and discriminatory. He professes that if drug laws remain stringent, the result would be more drug users in prison and that drug abusers and addicts would engage in more criminal activity. Also, there is the possibility that more drug-related social problems would occur. Gorman concludes that society cannot afford to retain its intransigent position on drug legalization. The potential risks of the current federal policies on drug criminalization outweigh any potential benefits. Society suffers from harsh drug laws, says Gorman, by losing many of its civil liberties.

Proponents of less restrictive drug laws argue that such laws have not worked and that the drug battle has been lost. They believe that drug-related problems would diminish if more tolerant policies were implemented. Citing the legal drugs alcohol and tobacco as examples, legalization opponents argue that less restrictive drug laws would not decrease profits from the sale of drugs (the profits from cigarettes and alcohol are incredibly high). Moreover, opponents argue, relaxing drug laws does not make problems associated with drugs disappear (alcohol and tobacco have extremely high addiction rates as well as a myriad of other problems associated with their use).

Many European countries, such as the Netherlands and Switzerland, have a system of legalized drugs, and most have far lower addiction rates and lower incidences of drug-related violence and crime than the United States. These countries make a distinction between soft drugs (those identified as less harmful) and hard drugs (those with serious consequences). However, would the outcomes of less restrictive laws in the United States be the same as in Europe? Relaxed drug laws in the United States could still be a tremendous risk because its drug problems could escalate and reimposing strict drug laws would be difficult. This was the case with Prohibition in the 1920s, which, in changing the status of alcohol from legal to illegal, produced numerous crime- and alcohol-related problems.

Additional Resources

Many good articles debate the pros and cons of this issue. These include "Who's Using and Who's Doing Time: Incarceration, the War on Drugs, and Public Health," by Lisa Moore and Amy Elkavich (*American Journal of Public Health*, September 2008); "Too Dangerous Not to Regulate," by Peter Moskos (*U.S. News and World Report*, August 4, 2008); "Reorienting U.S. Drug Policy," by Jonathan Caulkins and Peter Reuter (*Issues in Science and Technology*, Fall 2006); "No Surrender: The Drug War Saves Lives," by John Walters (*National Review*, September 27, 2004), the current director of the Office of National Drug Control Policy; "Lighting Up in Amsterdam," by John Tierney (*The New York Times*, August 26, 2006); "What Drug Policies Cost: Estimating Government Drug Policy Expenditures," by Peter Reuter (*Addiction*, March 2006); "An Effective Drug Policy to Protect America's Youth and Communities," by Asa Hutchinson (*Fordham Urban Law Journal*, January 2003); and "The War at Home: Our Jails Overflow with Nonviolent Drug Offenders. Have We Reached the Point Where the Drug War Causes More Harm Than the Drugs Themselves?" by Sanho Tree (*Sojourners*, May–June 2003).

Recent books that deal with drugs, drug policies and laws, and the consequences of drugs include Richard E. Isralowitz and Peter L. Myers, *Illicit Drugs* (Greenwood, 2011); J. Bryan Page and Merrill Singer, *Comprehending Drug Use: Ethnographic Research at the Social Margins* (Rutgers University Press, 2010); Alex Stevens, *Drugs, Crime and Public Health: The Political Economy of Drug Policy* (Routledge, 2011); Thomas Babor et al., *Drug Policy and the Public Good* (Oxford University Press, 2010); Damon Barrett, ed., *Children of the Drug War: Perspectives on the Impact of Drug Policies on Young People* (International

Debate Education Association, 2011); Paul Manning, ed., *Drugs and Popular Culture: Drugs, Media and Identity in Contemporary Society* (Willan Publishing, 2007); William L. Marcy, *the Politics of Cocaine: How U.S. Policy Has Created a Thriving Drug Industry in Central and South America* (Lawrence Hill Books, 2010); and World Health Organization, *Ensuring Balance in National Policies on Controlled Substances* (World Health Organization, 2011). Marina Barnard covers the effect of drugs on families in *Drug Addiction and Families* (Jessica Kingsley Publishers, 2007). Some excellent work on drugs and drug policies examine the drug situation in Great Britain, including Martin Plant et al., *Drug Nation: Patterns, Problems, Panics, and Policies* (Oxford University Press, 2011); Philip Bean, *Legalizing Drugs: Debates and Dilemmas* (Policy, 2010); and Trevor Bennett, *Drug-Crime Connections* (Cambridge University Press, 2007).

ISSUE 18

Are We Headed Toward a Nuclear 9/11?

YES: **Brian Michael Jenkins**, from "Terrorists Can Think Strategically: Lessons Learned from the Mumbai Attacks," *Testimony Series* (Rand Corporation, January 2009)

NO: **Graham Allison**, from "Time to Bury a Dangerous Legacy—Part I," *YaleGlobal Online* (March 14, 2008)

Learning Outcomes

After reading this issue, you should be able to:

- Understand the reasons why a nuclear terrorist act in the United States is a likely event.
- Understand the reasons why others believe that a nuclear terrorist event in the United States is unlikely.
- Identify important factors that you should examine more closely to gain more confidence in your judgment about the likelihood of a nuclear terrorist event. For example, you might examine further how easy it is for terrorists to obtain nuclear materials.
- Identify the actions that America can take to reduce the likelihood of a nuclear terrorist event.
- Attempt to figure out how what you learned should affect your life.

ISSUE SUMMARY

YES: Brian Michael Jenkins, senior advisor to the president of the Rand Corporation, in testimony before the U.S. Senate Committee on Homeland Security and Governmental Affairs, posited that a team of terrorists could be inserted into the United States and carry out a Mumbai-style attack, as terrorism has "increasingly become an effective strategic weapon."

NO: Graham Allison, Harvard professor and director of the Belfer Center for Science and International Affairs, affirms that we are not likely to experience a nuclear 9/11 because "nuclear terrorism is preventable by a feasible, affordable agenda of actions that . . . would shrink the risk of nuclear terrorism to nearly zero."

Since the terrorist attacks of September 11, 2001, much has been written about the specter of nuclear terrorism and the releasing of a dirty bomb (one loaded with radioactive material) in an urban/civilian setting. The events of September 11 have all but ensured the world's preoccupation with such an event for the foreseeable future. Indeed, the arrest of a U.S. man that was suspected of having dirty bomb materials indicates that such plans may indeed be in the works between Al-Qaeda and other terrorist cells. When this horror is combined with the availability of elements of nuclear-related material in places like the states of the former Soviet Union, Pakistan, India, Iraq, Iran, North Korea, and many other states, one can envision a variety of sobering scenarios.

Hollywood feeds these views with such films as *The Sum of All Fears* and *The Peacemaker,* in which nuclear terrorism is portrayed as all too easy to carry out and likely to occur. It is difficult in such environments to separate fact from fiction and to ascertain objectively the probabilities of such events. So many factors go into a successful initiative in this area. One must find a committed cadre of terrorists, sufficient financial backing, technological know-how, intense security and secrecy, the means of delivery, and many other variables, including luck. In truth, such acts may have already been advanced and thwarted by governments, security services, or terrorist mistakes and incompetence. We do not know, and we may never know.

Regional and ethnic conflicts of a particularly savage nature in places like Chechnya, Kashmir, Colombia, and Afghanistan help to fuel fears that adequately financed zealots will see in nuclear weapons a swift and catastrophic answer to their demands and angers. Osama bin Laden's contribution to worldwide terrorism has been the success of money over security and the realization that particularly destructive acts with high levels of coordination can be "successful." This will undoubtedly encourage others with similar ambitions against real or perceived enemies.

Conversely, many argue that fear of the terrorist threat has left us imagining that which is not likely. They point to a myriad of roadblocks to terrorist groups' obtaining all of the elements necessary for a nuclear or dirty bomb. They cite technological impediments, monetary issues, lack of sophistication, and inability to deliver. They also cite governments' universal desire to prevent such actions. Even critics of former Iraqi leader Saddam Hussein have argued that were he to develop such weapons, he would not deliver them to terrorist groups, nor would he use them except in the most dire of circumstances, such as his own regime's survival. They argue that the threat is overblown and, in some cases, merely used to justify increased security and the restriction of civil liberties.

The following selections reflect the debate about a nuclear 9/11. Jenkins focuses on the ability and resourcefulness of the terrorists and argues that recent events indicate a real ability to carry out such an attack. Allison focuses on the targets, the United States and the West, and insists that a coordinated strategy can stop such an event.

YES

Brian Michael Jenkins

Terrorists Can Think Strategically: Lessons Learned from the Mumbai Attacks

Mr. Chairman and Members of the Committee, it is an honor to appear before you today. The Mumbai attack was still ongoing when RAND initiated an analysis to determine what lessons might be learned from it. This analysis, part of RAND's continuing research on terrorism and homeland security, was documented in a report I co-authored along with other RAND analysts. Specifically, I contributed the sections on the terrorists' strategic motives and the execution of the attack.

We relied on both informed official sources and media reporting. My analysis benefited greatly from the detailed descriptions of the attack provided by officers from the New York Police Department, who were on the scene and whose reports were shared with law enforcement and others in the United States.

Copies of our report have been made available to members of the Committee. Additional copies are available here, and the report is also on RAND's website. For convenience, I have appended the key findings to my testimony. The following observations derive from this report and other relevant research.

Terrorism has increasingly become an effective strategic weapon. Earlier generations of terrorists seldom thought beyond the barrels of their guns. In contrast, the masterminds of the Mumbai terrorist attacks displayed sophisticated strategic thinking in their choice of targets and their efforts to achieve multiple objectives. They were able to capture and hold international attention. They sought to exacerbate communal tensions in India and provoke a crisis between India and Pakistan, thereby persuading Pakistan to redeploy troops to its frontier with India, which in turn would take pressure off of the Taliban, al Qaeda, and other groups operating along the Afghan frontier. All terrorist attacks are recruiting posters. The Mumbai attackers established their terrorist credentials and now rival al Qaeda in reputation.

Al Qaeda is not the only galaxy in the jihadist universe—new contenders have signed on to al Qaeda's ideology of global terror. Even as we have degraded al Qaeda's operational capabilities, the idea of a violent global jihad has spread from North Africa to South Asia. The Mumbai attack foreshadows

From *Testimony Series*, January 2009, pp. 1–4. Copyright © 2009 by Rand Corporation. Reprinted by permission via Copyright Clearance Center.

a continuing terrorist campaign in India. More broadly, it suggests that the global struggle against the jihadists is far from over.

Terrorists can innovate tactically to obviate existing security measures and confuse authorities.   Authorities are obliged to prevent the recurrence of the most recent attack, while knowing that other terrorists will analyze the security in place, devise new tactics, and do the unexpected. The Mumbai attackers did not plant bombs in crowded train coaches, as in the 2006 Mumbai terrorist attack. Instead, gunmen attacked the train station. They did not detonate car bombs as in the 1993 Mumbai attacks or the more recent terrorist attacks on hotels in Indonesia, Egypt, Jordan and Pakistan. They seized control of hotels where they started fires. Multiple attacks at different locations prevented authorities from developing an overall assessment of the situation.

Once again, terrorists have demonstrated that with simple tactics and low-tech weapons, they can produce vastly disproportionate results.   The Mumbai attack was sequential, highly mobile, and a departure from the now common suicide bombings, but the tactics were simple—armed assaults, carjackings, drive-by shootings, building takeovers, barricade and hostage situations. The attack was carried out by ten men armed with easily obtained assault weapons, semi-automatic pistols, hand grenades, and simple improvised explosive devices—little more than the arsenal of an infantryman in the 1940s—along with 21st century cell phones, BlackBerries, and GPS locators.

Terrorists will continue to focus on soft targets that offer high body counts and that have iconic value.   Nationally and internationally recognized venues that offer ease of access, certainty of tactical success, and the opportunity to kill in quantity will guide target selection. Public spaces are inherently difficult to protect. Major investments in target hardening make sense for government only when these provide a net security benefit, that is, when they do not merely displace the risk to another equally lucrative and accessible target.

Terrorists view public surface transportation as a killing field.   One of the two-man terrorist teams went to Mumbai's main train station and opened fire on commuters. While the attacks on the other targets were theoretically aimed at killing foreigners, the attack at the train station was aimed solely at slaughter. It accounted for more than a third of the total deaths.

This underscores a trend that should be a priority issue in the United States. Public surface transportation offers terrorists easily accessible, dense populations in confined environments—ideal killing zones for gunmen or improvised explosive devices, which remain the most common form of attack. According to analysis by the Mineta Transportation Institute's National Transportation Security Center, two-thirds of all terrorist attacks on surface transportation were intended to kill; 37 percent resulted in fatalities (compared with between 20 and 25 percent of terrorist attacks overall); 75 percent of the fatal attacks involved multiple fatalities; and 28 percent of those involved 10 or more fatalities.

Terrorist attacks on flagship hotels are increasing in number, in total casualties, and in casualties per incident.   This trend places increasing demands on hotel security. However, while terrorist attacks are spectacular, they are statistically rare in comparison to ordinary violent crime. In the past forty years, fewer than five hundred hotel guests in the entire world have been killed by terrorists, out of a total global hotel guest population at any time of nearly ten million.

Pakistan's principal defense against external pressure is not its nuclear arsenal, but its own political fragility—its government's less-than-full cooperation is preferable to the country's collapse and descent into chaos.   Pakistan continues to play a prominent and problematic role in the overlapping armed conflicts and terrorist campaigns in India, Afghanistan, and Pakistan itself. Al Qaeda, the Taliban, Lashkar-e-Taiba and other insurgent and terrorist groups find sanctuary in Pakistan's turbulent tribal areas. Historically, some of them have drawn on support from the Pakistan government itself. While the Government of Pakistan has been helpful in capturing some key terrorist operatives, Pakistan is accused of protecting others. And it has been understandably reluctant to use military force against its own citizens in the remote tribal areas where these groups reside. When it has used military force, government forces have not fared well. Public sentiment imposes further constraints. Many Pakistanis regard India and the United States, not al Qaeda or the Taliban, as greater threats to Pakistan's national security. This was perceived as an obstacle to U.S. counterterrorist efforts even before 9/11.

The success of the Mumbai attackers in paralyzing a large city and commanding the attention of the world's news media for nearly three days will encourage similar operations in the future.   Terrorists will continue to effectively embed themselves among civilians, taking hostages and using them as human shields to impede responders and maximize collateral casualties. We should expect to see more of this tactic.

Could a Mumbai-style attack happen in the United States?   It could. The difference lies in planning and scale. Assembling and training a ten-man team of suicidal attackers seems far beyond the capabilities of the conspirators identified in any of the local terrorist plots discovered in this country since 9/11. We have no evidence of that level of dedication or planning skills.

However, we have seen lone gunmen and pairs of shooters, motivated by mental illness or political cause, run amok, determined to kill in quantity. The Long Island Railroad, Empire State Building, LAX, Virginia Tech, and Columbine cases come to mind. In 1955, four Puerto Rican separatists opened fire in a then unguarded Capitol Building, wounding five members of Congress. Firearms are readily available in the United States. And some of the perpetrators of the attacks mentioned above planned for their attacks for months, while building their arsenals. Therefore, an attack on the ground, carried out by a small number of self-radicalized, homegrown terrorists armed with readily available weapons, perhaps causing scores of casualties, while still far beyond what we have seen in the terrorist plots uncovered thus far, is not inconceivable.

Could a team of terrorists, recruited and trained abroad as the Mumbai attackers were, be inserted into the United States, perhaps on a U.S.-registered fishing vessel or pleasure boat, to carry out a Mumbai-style attack? Although our intelligence has greatly improved, the answer again must be a qualified yes. It could conceivably happen here, although I would expect our police response to be much swifter and more effective than we saw in Mumbai.

Time to Bury a Dangerous Legacy—Part I

One month after the terrorist assault on the World Trade Center and the Pentagon, on October 11, 2001, President George W. Bush faced a more terrifying prospect. At that morning's presidential daily intelligence briefing, George Tenet, the director of central intelligence, informed the president that a CIA agent codenamed "Dragonfire" had reported that Al Qaeda terrorists possessed a 10-kiloton nuclear bomb, evidently stolen from the Russian arsenal. According to Dragonfire, this nuclear weapon was in New York City.

The government dispatched a top-secret nuclear emergency support team to the city. Under a cloak of secrecy that excluded even Mayor Rudolph Giuliani, these nuclear ninjas searched for the bomb. On a normal workday, half a million people crowd the area within a half-mile radius of Times Square. A noon detonation in Midtown Manhattan would kill them all instantly. Hundreds of thousands of others would die from collapsing buildings, fire and fallout in the hours thereafter. The electromagnetic pulse generated by the blast would fry cell phones and other electronic communication. The wounded would overwhelm hospitals and emergency services. Firemen would fight an uncontrolled ring of fires for days afterward.

In the hours that followed, Condoleezza Rice, then national security adviser, analyzed what strategists call the "problem from hell." Unlike the Cold War, when the US and the Soviet Union knew that an attack against the other would elicit a retaliatory strike or greater measure, Al Qaeda—with no return address—had no such fear of reprisal. Even if the president were prepared to negotiate, Al Qaeda has no phone number to call.

Concerned that Al Qaeda could have smuggled a nuclear weapon into Washington as well, the president ordered Vice President Dick Cheney to leave the capital for an "undisclosed location," where he would remain for weeks to follow—standard procedure to ensure "continuity of government" in case of a decapitation strike against US political leadership. Several hundred federal employees from more than a dozen government agencies joined the vice president at this secret site, the core of an alternative government that would seek to cope in the aftermath of a nuclear explosion that destroyed Washington.

Six months earlier the CIA's Counterterrorism Center had picked up chatter in Al Qaeda channels about an "American Hiroshima." The CIA knew that Osama bin Laden's fascination with nuclear weapons went back at least to

1992, when he attempted to buy highly enriched uranium from South Africa. Al Qaeda operatives were alleged to have negotiated with Chechen separatists in Russia to buy a nuclear warhead, which the Chechen warlord Shamil Basayev claimed to have acquired from Russian arsenals. The CIA's special task force on Al Qaeda had noted the terrorist group's emphasis on thorough planning, intensive training and repetition of successful tactics. The task force highlighted Al Qaeda's preference for symbolic targets and spectacular attacks.

As CIA analysts examined Dragonfire's report and compared it with other bits of information, they noted that the September attack on the World Trade Center had set the bar higher for future terrorist attacks. Psychologically, a nuclear attack would stagger the world's imagination. New York was, in the jargon of national-security experts, "target rich."

As it turned out, Dragonfire's report proved to be a false alarm. But the central takeaway from the case is this: The US government had no grounds in science or logic to dismiss this possibility, nor could it do so today.

There's no established methodology for assessing the probability of an unprecedented event that could have such catastrophic consequences. Nonetheless, in "Nuclear Terrorism" I state my considered judgment that if the US and other governments just keep doing what they are doing today, a nuclear terrorist attack in a major city is more likely than not by 2014.

Richard Garwin, a designer of the hydrogen bomb, whom Enrico Fermi once called, "the only true genius I had ever met," told Congress in March 2007 that he estimated a "20 percent per year probability of a nuclear explosion with American cities and European cities included." My Harvard colleague Matthew Bunn has created a model that estimates the probability of a nuclear terrorist attack over a 10-year period to be 29 percent—identical to the average estimate from a poll of security experts commissioned by Senator Richard Lugar in 2005.

Former Secretary of Defense William Perry has expressed his own view that my work may underestimate the risk. Warren Buffett, the world's most successful investor and legendary odds-maker in pricing insurance policies for unlikely but catastrophic events, concluded that nuclear terrorism is "inevitable." As he has stated: "I don't see any way that it won't happen."

The good news is that nuclear terrorism is preventable by a feasible, affordable agenda of actions that, if taken, would shrink the risk of nuclear terrorism to nearly zero. A global strategy to prevent this ultimate catastrophe can be organized under a Doctrine of Three No's: No loose nukes, no new nascent nukes, no new nuclear weapons. The first requires securing all nuclear weapons and weapons-usable material, on the fastest possible timetable, to a new "gold standard." The second does not allow for any new national capabilities to enrich uranium or reprocess plutonium. The third draws a line under the current eight and a half nuclear powers—the five members of the Security Council and India, Israel, Pakistan and North Korea—and says unambiguously: "Stop. No More."

The US cannot unilaterally sustain a successful strategy to prevent nuclear terrorism. Nor can the necessary actions simply be commanded, compelled or coerced. Instead, they require deep and steady international cooperation rooted in the recognition that nations share a common threat that requires a common strategy. A Global Alliance Against Nuclear Terrorism is therefore in order. The mission of this alliance should be to minimize the risk of nuclear terrorism by taking every action physically, technically and diplomatically possible to prevent nuclear weapons or materials from falling into the hands of terrorists.

Constructing such an alliance will require the US and other nuclear-weapons states to confront the question of a "fourth no": no nuclear weapons. While US or Russian possession of nuclear arsenals is not a major driver of Iran's nuclear ambitions, and while Osama bin Laden would not be less interested in acquiring a nuclear weapon if the US eliminated its current arsenals, the proposition that nuclear weapons are necessary for the security of US and Russia but intolerably dangerous if acquired by Iran or South Africa is difficult to sell to nuclear have-nots.

The question of a categorical "fourth no" has come to the fore with the January 2007 opinion piece in the *Wall Street Journal* by George P. Shultz, William J. Perry, Henry A. Kissinger and Sam Nunn, calling upon the US and other states to act to realize their Non-Proliferation Treaty commitment and President Reagan's vision of "a world free of nuclear weapons." Towards that goal, the immediate agenda should be to devalue nuclear weapons and minimize their role in international affairs. This should begin with nuclear-weapons states pledging to the following principles: no new national enrichment, no nuclear tests, no first use of a nuclear bomb and no new nuclear weapons.

Faced with the possibility of an American Hiroshima, many are paralyzed by a combination of denial and fatalism. This is unwarranted. Through a combination of imagination, a clear agenda for action and fierce determination to pursue it, the countdown to a nuclear 9/11 can be stopped.

EXPLORING THE ISSUE

Are We Headed Toward a Nuclear 9/11?

Critical Thinking and Reflection

1. Why would anyone want to nuclear bomb America?
2. What can be done to minimize the desire of people to terrorize us?
3. How much expansion of police powers should we accept to increase our security? How much more should we bar people from entering the United States to increase our security?
4. What more can we do to protect ourselves?

Is There Common Ground?

There are many arguments to support the contention that nuclear and dirty bombs are hard to obtain, difficult to move and assemble, and even harder to deliver. There is also ample evidence to suggest that most, if not all, of the U.S. government's work is in one way or another designed to thwart such actions because of the enormous consequences were such acts to be carried out. These facts should make Americans rest easier and allay fears if only for reasons of probability.

However, Allison's contention that failure to assume the worst may prevent the thwarting of such terrorist designs is persuasive. Since September 11, it is clear that the world has entered a new phase of terrorist action and a new level of funding, sophistication, and motivation. It is dangerous for a nation to believe that because something is difficult it is unlikely to take place. The collapse of the USSR has unleashed a variety of forces, some positive and some more sinister and secretive. The enormous prices that radioactive material and nuclear devices can command on the black market make the likelihood of temptation strong and possibly irresistible.

What everyone agrees on is that terrorism and especially nuclear terrorism is a major concern for this country, and that almost everything possible should be done to prevent such an attack. Also, most people agree that if states are to err, perhaps they should err on the side of caution and preventive action rather than on reliance on the statistical probability that nuclear terrorism is unlikely. We may never see a nuclear terrorist act in this century, but it is statistically likely that the reason for this will not be lack of effort on the part of motivated terrorist groups. Most people also agree that we must not panic. However, when the time comes we probably will panic. Extraordinary leadership may lead us to a different response, but I would not bet on it.

Additional Resources

Some important research and commentary on nuclear terrorism can be found in Benjamin Cole, *The Changing Face of Terrorism: How Real Is the Threat from Biological, Chemical and Nuclear Weapons?* (I. B. Tauris, 2011); Brian Michael Jenkins, *Will Terrorists Go Nuclear?* (Prometheus Books, 2008); Todd Masse, *Nuclear Jihad: A Clear and Present Danger?* (Potomac Books, 2011); Jack Caravelli, *Nuclear Insecurity: Understanding the Threat from Rogue Nations and Terrorists* (Praeger Security International, 2008); John E. Mueller, *Atomic Obsession: Nuclear Alarmism from Hiroshima to al-Qaeda* (Oxford University Press, 2010); Michael A. Levi, *On Nuclear Terrorism* (Harvard University Press, 2007); Elaine Landau, *Osama bin Laden: A War Against the West* (Twenty-First Century Books, 2002); Jan Lodal, *The Price of Dominance: The New Weapons of Mass Destruction and Their Challenge to American Leadership* (Council on Foreign Relations Press, 2001); Jessica Stern, *The Ultimate Terrorists* (Harvard University Press, 1999); Graham Allison, *Nuclear Terrorism: The Ultimate Preventable Catastrophe* (Times Books, 2004); Gavin Cameron, *Nuclear Terrorism: A Threat Assessment for the 21st Century* (St. Martin's Press, 1999); Charles D. Ferguson and William C. Potter, with Amy Sands et al., *The Four Faces of Nuclear Terrorism* (Routledge, 2005); Robin M. Frost, *Nuclear Terrorism After 9/11* (Routledge (for the International Institute for Strategic Studies), 2005); and Zbigniew Brzezinski, *The Choice: Global Domination or Global Leadership* (Basic Books, 2005).

Some recent general works on terrorism include Jonathan Barker, *The No-Nonsense Guide to Global Terrorism,* 2nd ed. (New Internationalist, 2008); Cornelia Beyer, *Violent Globalisms: Conflict in Response to Empire* (Ashgate, 2008); Michael Chandler and Rohan Gunaratna, *Countering Terrorism: Can We Meet the Threat of Global Violence?* (Reaktion, 2007); Peter R. Neumann, *Old and New Terrorism: Late Modernity, Globalization and the Transformation of Political Violence* (Polity, 2009); John Robb, *Brave New War: The Next Stage of Terrorism and the End of Globalization* (John Wiley & Sons, 2007); Paul J. Smith, *The Terrorism Ahead: Confronting Transnational Violence in the Twenty-First Century* (M. E. Sharpe, 2008); and Ian Bellany, *Terrorism and Weapons of Mass Destruction: Responding to the Challenge* (Routledge, 2007). For information on how to respond to a nuclear terrorist event, see *Responding to a Radiological or Nuclear Terrorism Incident: A Guide for Decision Makers* (National Council on Radiation Protection and Measurements, 2010).

ISSUE 19

Is Torture Ever Justified?

YES: Mirko Bagaric and Julie Clarke, from "Not Enough Official Torture in the World? The Circumstances in Which Torture Is Morally Justifiable," *University of San Francisco Law Review* (Spring 2005)

NO: Philip E. Devine, from "What's Wrong with Torture?" *International Philosophical Quarterly* (vol. 49, September 2009)

Learning Outcomes

After reading this issue, you should be able to:

- Observe that both the argument for torture and the argument against torture are based on high moral viewpoints. This debate is not between good guys and bad guys but between guys seeking the good.
- Understand that sometimes a good argument can be made that achieving good ends may require bad means.
- Think knowledgeably about the conflict between absolute versus relativistic value systems.
- Understand that those who advocate torture hate torture (except for sadists).
- Understand that terrorism forces America to face the issue of torture and have an explicit policy about it.
- Understand that both a torture policy and an anti-torture policy will have many unintended and unknown consequences because they will impact what other nations and peoples think of us and how they will act toward us.
- Recognize that the morality of the torture debate involves the premise that hurting "them" to save "us" is legitimate. Us–them thinking is basic to many questionable moral arguments.

ISSUE SUMMARY

YES: Bagaric and Clarke remind us, first of all, that torture, although prohibited by international law, is nevertheless widely practiced. A rational examination of torture and a consideration of hypothetical (but realistic) cases show that torture is justifiable in order to prevent great harm. Torture should be regulated and carefully practiced as an information-gathering technique in extreme cases.

NO: Philosopher Philip E. Devine argues for an absolute (or virtually absolute) position against torture. Devine suggests that the wrongness of torture and the repugnance that we feel toward it ultimately go beyond any moral theory. In addition, the examination of extreme cases should not inform our general thought about these and other matters.

T his is a question that might not even have arisen in a serious way if it were not for current events and the war on terrorism. Actually, philosophers had been talking about questions like this before 9/11, but only in a purely hypothetical way. No one anticipated that seemingly crazy ideas about buildings being blown up in New York and thousands of people being killed would actually become a reality. But times have changed. And the question is now asked as a reflection of the times. Yet to ask the question does not mean that one is considering torture as a possibility. For some of those who address this very question—Philip Devine, for example—would insist that the answer is no and would further insist that in this day of terrorism one of the important values that distinguishes us from the terrorists is that our answer should be that torture is absolutely out of the question. We should not try to imagine situations or conditions under which we torture people. So, on this view, we should not try to "draw a line," for one side of the line will be the side where torture is justified. But, in order to stay faithful to a negative answer to the issue question, we should not define any such area. Opponents of the view that torture is never justified might construct various scenarios. Suppose, for example, that there was a ticking bomb that was hidden in a secret location and was set to go off at a certain time and would be sure to kill hundreds or thousands of innocent people. And suppose that the authorities had in their custody an individual who had detailed information about the bomb, including its location and the time it was set to go off. If this person were unwilling to disclose the information voluntarily, would torture be justified? After all, so much is at stake. If that one person were tortured, the very lives of a great many innocent people lie in the balance. How, it might be asked, could his well-being outweigh theirs?

The opponents of torture would probably respond that the question of torturing the person does not really have to do with his well-being at all, but rather with our own actions. The imagined scenario seems to suggest that so much is (potentially) at stake that we must be prepared to torture people. If so, we can't lay claim to ideas about human rights, the sacredness of life, etc. For example, if we really are going to be prepared to torture people, we have to have trained torturers who know how to do their job well. Even in the imagined "ticking bomb" scenario, the innocent people wouldn't be saved if we used an incompetent torturer who bungled the job and did something that resulted in the person's death—in which case we'd never find out any information about the ticking bomb. But the torturer has to cause some serious pain nevertheless. Proponents of torture seem to need someone who is a trained torturer, someone who is not doing this for the first time. So one question is whether we should initiate action now to produce such people in case they might be used. In the first reading, Bagaric and Clarke argue that torture is already being practiced widely—although unmonitored and "underground." Their idea is to acknowledge it, endorse it to some extent, but draw lines. In the second reading, Philip Devine does not wish to condone torture at all. On his view, our attitude toward torture as something repugnant is not an attitude that we should change.

YES

**Mirko Bagaric
and Julie Clarke**

Not Enough Official Torture in the World? The Circumstances in Which Torture Is Morally Justifiable

Recent events stemming from the "war on terrorism" have highlighted the prevalence of torture, both as an interrogation technique and as a punitive measure. Torture is almost universally deplored. It is prohibited by international law and is not officially sanctioned by the domestic laws of any state. The formal prohibition against torture is absolute—there are no exceptions to it. This is not only pragmatically unrealistic, but unsound at a normative level. Despite the absolute ban on torture, it is widely used. Contrary to common belief, torture is not the preserve of despot military regimes in third world nations. For example, there are serious concerns regarding the treatment by the United States of senior Al Qaeda leader Khalid Shaikh Mohammad. There is also irrefutable evidence that the United States tortured large numbers of Iraqi prisoners, as well as strong evidence that it tortured prisoners at Guantanamo Bay prison in Cuba, where suspected Al Qaeda terrorists are held. More generally Professor Alan Dershowitz has noted, "[C]ountries all over the world violate the Geneva Accords [prohibiting torture]. They do it secretly and hypothetically, the way the French did it in Algeria."

Dershowitz has also recently argued that torture should be made lawful. His argument is based on a harm minimization rationale from the perspective of victims of torture. He said, "Of course it would be best if we didn't use torture at all, but if the United States is going to continue to torture people, we need to make the process legal and accountable." Our argument goes one step beyond this. We argue that torture is indeed morally defensible, not just pragmatically desirable. The harm minimization rationale is used to supplement our argument.

While a "civilized" community does not typically condone such conduct, this Article contends that torture is morally defensible in certain circumstances, mainly when more grave harm can be avoided by using torture as an interrogation device. The pejorative connotation associated with torture should be abolished. A dispassionate analysis of the propriety of torture indicates that it is morally justifiable. At the outset of this analytical discussion, this Article requires readers to move from the question of whether torture is *ever* defensible to the issue of the circumstances in which it is morally permissible.

From *University of San Francisco Law Review,* vol. 39, Spring 2005, pp. 581–616. Copyright © 2005 by University of San Francisco Law Review. Reprinted by permission.

Consider the following example: A terrorist network has activated a large bomb on one of hundreds of commercial planes carrying over three hundred passengers that is flying somewhere in the world at any point in time. The bomb is set to explode in thirty minutes. The leader of the terrorist organization announces this intent via a statement on the Internet. He states that the bomb was planted by one of his colleagues at one of the major airports in the world in the past few hours. No details are provided regarding the location of the plane where the bomb is located. Unbeknown to him, he was under police surveillance and is immediately apprehended by police. The terrorist leader refuses to answer any questions of the police, declaring that the passengers must die and will do so shortly.

Who in the world would deny that all possible means should be used to extract the details of the plane and the location of the bomb? The answer is not many. The passengers, their relatives and friends, and many in society would expect that all means should be used to extract the information, even if the pain and suffering imposed on the terrorist resulted in his death.

Although the above example is hypothetical and is not one that has occurred in the real world, the force of the argument cannot be dismissed on that basis. As C.L. Ten notes, "fantastic examples" that raise fundamental issues for consideration, such as whether it is proper to torture wrongdoers, play an important role in the evaluation of moral principles and theories. These examples sharpen contrasts and illuminate the logical conclusions of the respective principles to test the true strength of our commitment to the principles. Thus, fantastic examples cannot be dismissed summarily merely because they are "simply" hypothetical.

Real life is, of course, rarely this clear cut, but there are certainly scenarios approaching this degree of desperation, which raise for discussion whether it is justifiable to inflict harm on one person to reduce a greater level of harm occurring to a large number of blameless people. Ultimately, torture is simply the sharp end of conduct whereby the interests of one agent are sacrificed for the greater good. As a community, we are willing to accept this principle. Thus, although differing in degree, torture is no different in nature from conduct that we sanction in other circumstances. It should be viewed in this light.

Given this, it is illogical to insist on a blanket prohibition against torture. Therefore, the debate must turn to the circumstances when torture is morally appropriate. This is the topic of this Article.

International law defines torture as severe pain and suffering, generally used as an interrogation device or as a punitive measure. This Article focuses on the use of torture as an interrogation device and poses that the device is only permissible to prevent significant harm to others. In these circumstances, there are five variables relevant in determining whether torture is permissible and the degree of torture that is appropriate. The variables are (1) the number of lives at risk; (2) the immediacy of the harm; (3) the availability of other means to acquire the information; (4) the level of wrongdoing of the agent; and (5) the likelihood that the agent actually does possess the relevant information.

This Article analyzes the meaning of torture and the nature and scope of the legal prohibition against torture [and] examines whether torture is morally defensible. It is argued that torture is no different than other forms of morally permissible behavior and is justifiable on a utilitarian ethic. It is also argued that, on close reflection, torture is also justifiable against a backdrop of a non-consequentialist rights-based ethic, which is widely regarded as prohibiting torture in all circumstances. Thus, the Article concludes that torture is morally justifiable in rare circumstances, irrespective of which normative theory one adopts. [We] examine the circumstances in which torture is justifiable. Finally, [we] debunk the argument that torture should not be legalized because it will open the floodgates to more torture.

Torture: Reality and Legal Position

The Law on Torture

Pursuant to international law, "torture" is defined as:

> Any act by which severe pain or suffering, whether physical or mental, is intentionally inflicted on a person for such purposes as obtaining from him or a third person information or a confession, punishing him for an act he or a third person has committed or is suspected of having committed, or intimidating or coercing him or a third person, or for any reason based on discrimination of any kind, when such pain or suffering is inflicted by or at the instigation of or with the consent or acquiescence of a public official or other person acting in an official capacity. It does not include pain or suffering arising only from, inherent in or incidental to lawful sanctions.

Torture is prohibited by a number of international documents. It is also considered to carry a special status in customary international law, that of *jus cogens*, which is a "peremptory norm" of customary international law. The significance of this is that customary international law is binding on all states, even if they have not ratified a particular treaty. At the treaty level, there are both general treaties that proscribe torture and specific treaties banning the practice. . . .

The rigidity of the rule against torture is exemplified by the fact that it has a non-derogable status in human rights law. That is, there are no circumstances in which torture is permissible. This prohibition is made clear in Article 2(2) of the U.N. Convention Against Torture, which states, "No exceptional circumstances whatsoever, whether a state of war or a threat of war, internal political instability or any other public emergency, may be invoked as a justification of torture." Thus, the right not to be tortured is absolute. . . . [According to Amnesty International] "It cannot be denied to anyone in any circumstances." . . .

The Reality of Torture

As with many legal precepts, the black letter law must be considered against the context of reality. As this part shows, various forms of torture are used despite the legal prohibition of it.

1. Forms of Torture

As is noted by Dershowitz, torture comes in many different forms and intensities:

> Torture is a continuum and the two extremes are on the one hand torturing someone to death—that is torturing an enemy to death so that others will know that if you are caught, you will be caused excruciating pain—that's torture as a deterrent. . . . At the other extreme, there's non-lethal torture which leaves only psychological scars. The perfect example of this is a sterilised needle inserted under the fingernail, causing unbearable pain but no possible long-term damage. These are very different phenomena. What they have in common of course is that they allow the government physically to come into contact with you in order to produce pain.

Various methods of torture have and continue to be applied in a multitude of countries. The most common methods are beating, electric shock, rape and sexual abuse, mock execution or threat of death, and prolonged solitary confinement. Other common methods include sleep and sensory deprivation, suspension of the body, "shackling interrogees in contorted painful positions" or in "painful stretching positions," and applying pressure to sensitive areas, such as the "neck, throat, genitals, chest and head."

2. The Benefits of Torture: An Effective Information Gathering Device

The main benefit of torture is that it is an excellent means of gathering information. Humans have an intense desire to avoid pain, no matter how short term, and most will comply with the demands of a torturer to avoid the pain. Often even the threat of torture alone will evoke cooperation. To this end, Dershowitz cites a recent kidnapping case in Germany in which the son of a distinguished banker was kidnapped. The eleven-year-old boy had been missing for three days. The police had in their custody a man they were convinced had perpetrated the kidnapping. The man was taken into custody after being seen collecting a ransom that was paid by the boy's family. During seven hours of interrogation the man "toyed" with police, leading them to one false location after another. After exhausting all lawful means of interrogation, the deputy commissioner of the Frankfurt police instructed his officers, in writing, that they could try to extract information "by means of the infliction of pain, under medical supervision and subject to prior warning." Ten minutes after the warning was given the suspect told the police where the boy was; unfortunately the boy was already dead, having been killed shortly after the kidnapping.

3. The Widespread Use of Torture

a. Torture Around the World   Despite the contemporary abhorrence against it, dozens of countries continue to use torture. A study of 195 countries and territories by Amnesty International between 1997 and mid-2000 found reports of torture or ill-treatment by state officials in more than 150 countries and in more than seventy countries that torture or ill-treatment was reported as "widespread or persistent." It is also clear that torture is not limited to military regimes in third world nations. Amnesty International recently reported that in 2003 it had received reports of torture and ill-treatment from 132 countries, including the United States, Canada, Japan, France, Italy, Spain, and Germany. . . .

The Circumstances in Which Torture Is Acceptable

The only situation where torture is justifiable is where it is used as an information gathering technique to avert a grave risk. In such circumstances, there are five variables relevant in determining whether torture is permissible and the degree of torture that is appropriate. The variables are (1) the number of lives at risk; (2) the immediacy of the harm; (3) the availability of other means to acquire the information; (4) the level of wrongdoing of the agent; and (5) the likelihood that the agent actually does possess the relevant information. Where (1), (2), (4) and (5) rate highly and (3) is low, all forms of harm may be inflicted on the agent—even if this results in death.

The Harm to Be Prevented

The key consideration regarding the permissibility of torture is the magnitude of harm that is sought to be prevented. To this end, the appropriate measure is the number of lives that are likely to be lost if the threatened harm is not alleviated. Obviously, the more lives that are at stake, the more weight that is attributed to this variable.

Lesser forms of threatened harm will not justify torture. Logically, the right to life is the most basic and fundamental of all human rights—nonobservance of it would render all other human rights devoid of meaning. Every society has some prohibition against taking life, and "the intentional taking of human life is . . . the offence which society condemns most strongly.". . .

Immediacy of Harm and Other Options to Obtain Information

Torture should only be used as a last resort and hence should not be utilized where there is time to pursue other avenues of forestalling the harm. It is for this reason that torture should only be used where there is no other means to obtain the relevant information. Thus, where a terrorist has planted a bomb on a plane, torture will not be permissible where, for example, video tapes of international airports are likely to reveal the identity of the plane that has been targeted.

The Likelihood of Knowledge or Guilt

As a general rule torture should normally be confined to people that are responsible in some way for the threatened harm. This is not, however, invariably the case. People who are simply aware of the threatened harm, that is "innocent people," may in some circumstances also be subjected to torture.

Regardless of the guilt of the agent, it is most important that torture is only used against individuals who actually possess the relevant information. . . .

The Formula

Incorporating all these considerations, the strength of the case in favor of torture can be mapped as follows:

$$\frac{W + L + P}{T \times O}$$

Where:

W = whether the agent is the wrongdoer

L = the number of lives that will be lost if the information is not provided

P = the probability that the agent has the relevant knowledge

T = the time available before the disaster will occur ("immediacy of the harm")

O = the likelihood that other inquiries will forestall the risk

W is a weighting that is attributable to whether the agent has had any direct connection with the potential catastrophe. Where the person is responsible for the incident—for example, planted or organized the bomb—more emphasis should be attached. Where the agent is innocent and has simply stumbled on the relevant information—for example, she saw the bomb being planted or overheard the plan to plant the bomb—this should be reduced by a certain amount. The prohibition against inflicting harm on the innocent is certainly strong, but it is not inviolable.

Torture should be permitted where the application of the variables exceeds a threshold level. Once beyond this level, the higher the figure the more severe the forms of torture that are permissible. There is no bright line that can be drawn concerning the point at which the "torture threshold" should be set. More precision can, however, be obtained by first ascribing unit ranges to each of the above variables (depending on their relative importance), then applying the formula to a range of hypothetical situations, and then making a judgment about the numerical point at which torture is acceptable.

. . . The purpose of this Article is not to set in stone the full range of circumstances where torture is justifiable. Our aim is more modest—to convince readers that torture is justifiable in some circumstances and to set out the variables that are relevant to such an inquiry.

Regulation Better Than Prohibition

In addition to the moral argument for torture as an interrogation device, Dershowitz has argued that torture should be legalized for harm minimization reasons. Dershowitz has pushed for the introduction of "a torture warrant," which would place a "heavy burden on the government to demonstrate by factual evidence the necessity to administer this horrible, horrible technique of torture." He further adds:

I think that we're much, much better off admitting what we're doing or not doing it at all. I agree with you, it will much better if we never did it. But if we're going to do it and subcontract and find ways of circumventing, it's much better to do what Israel did. They were the only country in the world ever directly to confront the issue, and it led to a supreme court decision, as you say, outlawing torture, and yet Israel has been criticized all over the world for confronting the issue directly. Candor and accountability in a democracy is very important. Hypocrisy has no place.

The obvious counter to this is the slippery slope argument. "If you start opening the door, making a little exception here, a little exception there, you've basically sent the signal that the ends justify the means," resulting in even more torture. The slippery slope argument is often invoked in relation to acts that in themselves are justified, but which have similarities with objectionable practices, and urges that in morally appraising an action we must not only consider its intrinsic features but also the likelihood of it being used as a basis for condoning similar, but in fact relevantly different undesirable practices. The slippery slope argument in the context of torture holds that while torture might be justified in the extreme cases, legalizing it in these circumstances will invariably lead to torture in other less desperate situations.

This argument is not sound in the context of torture. First, the floodgates are already open—torture is widely used, despite the absolute legal prohibition against it. It is, in fact, arguable that it is the existence of an unrealistic absolute ban on torture that has driven torture "beneath the radar screen of accountability" and that the legalization of torture in very rare circumstances would, in fact, reduce the instances of torture because of the increased level of accountability.

Second, there is no evidence to suggest that the *lawful* violation of fundamental human interests will necessarily lead to a violation of fundamental rights where the pre-conditions for the activity are clearly delineated and controlled. Thus, in the United States the use of the death penalty has not resulted in a gradual extension of the offenses for which people may be executed or an erosion in the respect for human life. Third, promulgating the message that the "means justifies the ends [sometimes]" is not inherently undesirable. Debate can then focus on the precise means and ends that are justifiable.

Conclusion

The absolute prohibition against torture is morally unsound and pragmatically unworkable. There is a need for measured discussion regarding the merits of torture as an information gathering device. This would result in the legal use of torture in circumstances where there are a large number of lives at risk in the immediate future and there is no other means of alleviating the threat. While none of the recent high profile cases of torture appear to satisfy these criteria, it is likely that circumstances will arise in the future where torture is legitimate and desirable. A legal framework should be established to properly accommodate these situations.

Philip E. Devine
 **NO**

What's Wrong with Torture?

It is hard to believe that we are sitting here talking about torture.

—*Dana Priest*

On 8 March 2008 President Bush vetoed a bill forbidding torture by the CIA. An attempt to override his veto failed in the House of Representatives three days later. Thus a moral issue that many people thought had been settled, at last so far as public discourse is concerned, is with us, very likely for the duration.

Torture is pain or suffering inflicted for its own sake or as means to an end. Surgery without anesthetics is not torture because the pain inflicted is an unintended side effect. Corporal punishments such as caning, if they do not do permanent damage, might be morally preferable to imprisonment for long periods, and in that case I would not regard them as torture.

But torture does not only inflict pain upon its victim; it also dehumanizes him or her. On any reasonable definition, torture involves not only the infliction of pain but also of fear and bodily shame. Some forms of torture involve outrage to a person's religious or ideological identity. The reported flushing of a copy of the *Qur'an* in the presence of a pious Muslim at Guantánamo Bay (roughly comparable to the defiling of the Sacrament in the presence of a pious Catholic) is an example of this sort of torture.

Torture also dehumanizes the perpetrators. We have every reason to believe that it contributes to a downward spiral of retaliation, and therefore to the collapse of whatever vestiges of civilization may remain into utter barbarism. And the information gained by torture is not reliable since someone under torture will tell his or her tormentors whatever they want to hear. Hence, if it is not possible, in an imperfect world, to abolish torture altogether, it should be limited as much as possible, and in no case receive public approval. As Elaine Scarry puts it,

> The best way to preserve the future from "our enemies" is to reaffirm each day the blanket prohibition of torture, and to work with newspapers, human rights groups, and investigative bodies to document and hold those who torture accountable for their acts. . . .

One question that we expect a definition of "torture" to answer is how to draw the line between forms of coercive interrogation that are legitimate under extreme circumstances and torture, against which we want to maintain at least a virtually absolute prohibition. (A virtually absolute prohibition has exceptions, but these are so rare that they need and should not be mentioned in moral teaching.) The European Court on Human Rights has identified interrogation methods that, though they fall short of torture in the full sense, are nonetheless prohibited. The expression *torture lite,* which has been coined to cover such behavior, should make us shudder, but the concept still poses complex problems for moral judgment. (For the record, waterboarding is not torture lite in my view.) European courts have also held that the suffering of people on death row renders capital punishment tantamount to torture. Judge Richard Posner has concluded: "What is involved in using the word [torture] is picking out a point along a continuum where the observer's queasiness turns to revulsion." On the other hand, the reluctance of officials to admit that what they are authorizing is torture, or their insistence that it is at most torture lite, does testify to a continuing conviction that torture, real torture, is wrong.

. . .

Torture Defended

Jeremy Bentham provides a classic formulation of the "ticking bomb" argument, though his argument does not mention bombs:

> Suppose an occasion to arise, in which a suspicion is entertained . . . that at this very time a considerable number of individuals are actually suffering, by illegal violence inflictions equal in intensity to those which if inflicted by the hand of justice, would universally be spoken of under the name of torture. For the purpose of rescuing from torture these hundred innocents, should any scruple be made of applying equal or superior torture, to extract the requisite information from the mouth of one criminal, who having it in his power to make known the place where at this time the enormity was practising or about to be practised, should refuse to do so?

Michael Levin applies this argument to the contemporary situation:

> Suppose a terrorist has hidden an atomic bomb on Manhattan Island, which will detonate on July 4 unless. . . . If the only way to save [the] lives [of the people there] is to subject the terrorist to the most excruciating possible pain, what grounds can there be for not doing so? . . . Once you concede that torture is justified in extreme cases, you have admitted that the decision to use torture is a matter of balancing innocent lives against the means needed to save them. . . . The line demarcating the legitimate use of torture can be drawn. Torture only the obviously guilty, and only for the sake of saving innocents, and the line between US and THEM will remain clear.

Hence, he argues that torture of terrorists is in general legitimate, when used by an otherwise legitimate government to save innocent lives.

We have every reason to question the general form of Levin's argument. He starts with an extreme case and moves from it to a general permission. Other arguments of this form are standard in the polemical literature. . . . What makes these arguments work, despite their apparent badness, is the difficulty of maintaining a firm line between the permissible and the impermissible once a well-established prohibition has been displaced. Those who deride the slippery slope argument when used defensively find it a very useful offensive weapon.

Whatever moral rules we may accept, as individuals or as a society, there will be occasional cases where everything but the rule itself seems to speak for a violation. These cases, while they may arise in private life, are more common in politics where horrifying consequences on a large scale are a real possibility. But they are unlikely to arise for torture since there is always a palpable reason for abstaining, unless one has excluded the victim from common humanity before proceeding.

. . . My concern is what moral principles should inform our laws and public policies, including the training of our servicemen and women. As David Luban asks, "Should we create a professional cadre of trained torturers? . . . Should there be a medical sub-specialty of torture doctors, who ensure that captives do not die before they talk?" I am concerned, in short, with any policy that might normalize torture as a practice, not with the possibility of an unusual situation in which all moral bets are off. . . .

Even if torture is permissible under some circumstances, it still does not follow, contra Levin's second proposition, that the question of its legitimacy is merely one of balancing goods and evils in a quasi-utilitarian fashion. The social value of the rule, over and above the pain and suffering caused the victim of torture and his friends and family, is a vital consideration. In the words of the Israeli Supreme Court, "[t]his is the destiny of a democracy, as all means are not acceptable to it, and not all means employed by its enemies are open to it."

Levin's third proposition is the crux of his argument. Everything depends on a hardening of the "the line between *us* and *them*," in a context in which, as Levin himself admits, "'clear guilt' is difficult to define." Though not all Muslims are terrorists (or defenders of terrorism) and not all terrorists (or defenders of terrorism) are Muslim, under the pressure of politics such distinctions get lost. The West has experienced, and has every reason to fear, the sort of society that rests on a need for absolute distinctions between *them* and *us*.

The stock case for torture therefore fails. But establishing that conclusion is not the same thing as establishing, in positive terms, the wrongness of torture, or finding principles to distinguish torture from forms of rough treatment possibly legitimate in extreme circumstances.

Torture and Theory

Ethical and social theory has a limited role in the discussion of moral issues. Few people are thoroughgoing utilitarians, and even the most conventional people are not conventionalists in the sense of Bradley or of Hobbes. Moreover, the application of moral theories to real cases displays their malleability. None-theless, examining their implications may shed some light on the issue.

Conventionalism

Conventional morality is the result of a tacit agreement among its adherents and of their converging and mutually reinforcing moral emotions. Laws, cus-toms, and codes of professional ethics independent of civil law, as well as the "gut" feelings of my readers, are witnesses to conventional morality.

Torture is a violation of both American and international law—law that was supported, at least until recently, by a degree of moral consensus difficult to obtain about any other issue. The participation of doctors and nurses in torture is a violation of established principles of medical ethics. The Eighth Amendment's prohibition on cruel and unusual punishments trumps any stat-ute or executive policy to the contrary. The United Nations Convention is categorical: "No exceptional circumstances, whether in a state of war of threat of war, internal political instability or other public emergency, may be invoked as a justification of torture." Even the lenient treatment of torturers acting in good faith runs afoul of the Convention's provision that "each State Party shall make these offenses punishable by appropriate penalties that take into account their grave nature.". . .

That torture is evil is as conventional a moral judgment as one can hope to find. But conventional morality everywhere allows that acts that it finds dis-tasteful may sometimes be necessary. For if society is the author of the moral law, then the needs of society—and in particular those of the society to which the agent or evaluator belongs—take precedence over those of any individual. And the judge of those needs, both as a matter of fact and as a matter of value, is society itself through its acknowledged leaders. Moral minorities can and do attempt to pressure or persuade the majority to accept their views but cannot hold, as a matter of secular morality, that they are right even if society persis-tently rejects their arguments. Nor can one hold, in conventionalist terms, that there are things that one may not do to a person whatever the circumstances (including the judgment of one's society).

Hence, the verdict of conventional morality on torture is that of Jean Bethke Elshtain:

> Few "moral imperatives make such sense on a large scale"—referring to the prohibition against torture—"but break down so dramatically in the particular." When you put a microscope above the word "torture" and peer through it, you see a teeming mass of possibilities, prohibi-tions, complexities, legalities, and ethical perils.

Doing better than this requires going beyond convention.

Liberal Political Philosophy

. . . I here address the issue in terms of the broad liberal ideology, held by nearly everyone in America, regardless of his political persuasion otherwise.

Liberal political philosophy looks for a mean between authoritarianism and anarchism, and for that reason concentrates on limiting the power of the state. Thus it attempts to impose limits on what the majority may do to the minority, usually on strictly secular grounds. The liberal tradition is reflected in such official definitions of *torture* as the following: "any act by which severe pain or suffering, whether physical or mental, is intentionally inflicted on a person . . . when such pain or suffering is inflicted by or at the instigation of or with the acquiescence of a public official or other person acting in an official capacity." (Much, of course, depends on how we read "severe.")

. . .

Kantianism

The Kantian tradition supports a form of liberalism that holds that torture is wrong, whatever the conventions of society, because it is a violation of human dignity. . . . Kant also holds that it is wrong to treat a human being as a mere means. . . .

Utilitarianism

The most obvious objection to the torture of human beings is that it inflicts intense suffering upon its victim, including both physical pain and the "higher pains" of dread, anguish, and self-disgust, as well as many long-term disabling effects. Many torture victims report that these effects are such as to destroy any hope of communication or shared experience. For a utilitarian, however, the torture of a human being is at root no different from the torture of an animal. For most people, however, though cruelty to animals is wrong, but the rules are different from those concerning human beings.

People whom no one calls softies endorse the key premise of the utilitarian argument against interrogational torture—that the information it produces is unreliable. Hobbes writes:

> Also accusations upon torture are not to be reputed as testimonies. For torture is to be used merely as a means of conjecture and light, in the further examination and search for truth; and what in that case is confessed tendeth to the ease of him that is tortured, not to the informing of the torturers, and therefore ought not to have the credit of sufficient testimony; for whether he deliver himself by true or false accusation, he does it by the right of preserving his own life.

A retired Marine general observes that "different kinds of interrogation techniques, most specifically those that are gentle but persistent, that cause a detainee to gain confidence in his interrogator and so forth, usually produce better information." In short, there is a reputable utilitarian case against torture that may suffice for some argumentative purposes. Colonel Davis points out another consequentialist argument against torture: "During the Persian Gulf war in 1991, the Iraqi armed forces surrendered by the tens of thousands because they believed Americans would treat them humanely." . . .

Virtue Ethics

The effect of torture on the torturer and his likely behavior toward others outside official contexts are of persistent concern to opponents of the practice. Even Admiral Mayoga, a participant in Argentina's 'dirty war,' said, "The day we stop condemning torture—although we tortured—the day we become insensitive to mothers who lose their guerilla sons—even though they are guerillas—is the day we stop being human beings."

The underlying picture here is that of a normative human nature that is distorted by certain kinds of action and of "gut" responses that support this judgment even when circumstances might require us to act against it. . . .

Natural Law

Thomas Aquinas neither defended nor opposed torture, though church legislation of 1252 and 1259 authorized those forms that "did not imperil life or limb." Despite such troubling precedents, and the behavior of some priests and bishops on the ground, Roman Catholic authority now says all the right things about torture. The Second Vatican Council summarily condemns "torments inflicted on body or mind" along with a host of other contemporary practices such as abortion and euthanasia. Pope John Paul II cites this passage as establishing exceptionless prohibitions against torture, among other things, without attention to the question why these prohibitions and not others have this character. The pope holds that the existence of absolute norms, though perhaps not all the examples cited, is a deliverance of reason. The Catechism of Catholic Church adds a (not very useful) definition: "'Torture' . . . uses physical or moral violence to extract confessions, punish the guilty, frighten opponents, or satisfy hatred" and regrets the prior acceptance of such practices by church authority.

I take these judgments as results of rational reflection on shared human experience—in other words, of natural law—rather than an appeal to faith or revelation. (Religious responses to torture will depend on the particular features of the tradition in question. In the Christian case, such responses invoke the figure of the crucified Lord.) Yet the attempt to give theoretical substance to this judgment has lagged far behind the firmness with which it is asserted. One prominent and rigorous moral theologian does not even discuss torture, though he implicitly condemns those forms of it that involve mutilation or sexual assault:

Torture, besides being degrading to the torturer is an assault on the entire person of the victim, not on one or more of some list of basic goods. Torturers strip their victims of their humanity, whether because the victim is thought subhuman already, as in penal torture, or for the sake of some further end, as in interrogational torture. (In practice, these forms of assault blend.) The degradation imposed on the victims of torture has at least four aspects.

First, severe physical pain occupies the entire consciousness and blocks out the higher human capacities.

Second, sexual assault reduces a person to his or her bodily parts and functions.

Third, assaults on a person's belief system undermine the terms in which he or she defines his or her humanity: those hostile to Islam should realize that the pertinent alternative is not Christian faith or secular liberalism, but nihilism.

Finally, the aim of interrogational torture is to get its victims to betray their deeply held moral and political commitments, as well as their personal and group loyalties. Men and women who do such things become hateful in their own eyes as well as those of their former associates. . . .

Conclusion

No theoretical argument can fit the horror that torture evokes in many of us. We want to say that such behavior is not only wrong but also unthinkable. Connor Gearty's remarks that proposals to legalize torture are like "reacting to a series of police killings with proposals to reform the law of homicide as to sanction officially approved pre-trial executions."

Torture is important for social and political philosophy because its victim is a social outsider in two different ways. He or she is an outsider already, either on ethnic or ideological grounds, or because accused of a crime so reprobated by authority that, whatever contrary official professions may be in place, the maxim *guilty because accused* informs practice. A man suspected of terrorism is far more likely to be tortured if his name is "Mohammed" than if it is "Timothy." The point of declaring Afghanistan a failed state is to strip its citizens of protection under international law by rendering them stateless. "Prisoner of war" is an honorable legal status to which not all persons in captivity are entitled. . . .

EXPLORING THE ISSUE

Is Torture Ever Justified?

Critical Thinking and Reflection

1. Who should decide the American policy on torture?
2. There are many different degrees of torture. Should all torture be banned? Should only the highest level of torture be banned? Should the level of torture that is permitted be determined by the importance of the information being sought?
3. Everyone is against torture at some level. Everyone agrees that children should not torture each other to find out what the other is thinking. So when is torture not bad but the right thing to do?
4. The issue here is whether torture is justified to stop terrorism. Is it?
5. Can the good behavior of not torturing encourage our enemies to practice good behavior toward us?
6. Supposedly in World War II America did relatively little torture and Japan did relatively more torture. What difference did that make besides spoiling the reputation of the Japanese?

Is There Common Ground?

Bagaric and Clarke first remind us that torture is a widespread reality. Just because treaties are signed and international agreements are made, we should not assume that there is no torture (or that what little torture there may be is practiced only by rogue states, dictators, international pariahs, etc.). To this, however, there may be two sorts of responses. One is to seek to get a handle on torture, to regulate it in some way, so that the harm is reduced. Think of a somewhat similar response to the situation in which hard drugs are a social problem: Here a harm reduction strategy may involve the distribution of clean needles. The problem isn't solved in such a way that it no longer exists. Rather, the harm that may result—for example, the transmission of HIV—is minimized. Another type of response is to reinforce the prohibition of torture rather than regulating it. According to this view, torture is to be stopped not modulated. But this policy puts us at a disadvantage vis-à-vis our opponents. We try as hard as we can to prevent others from torturing, but we have ultimate control only over our own actions, not theirs. Our stopping torture may encourage them to stop, but it will not make them stop. They can choose the path that best serves their purposes. This raises the question of whether our leaders have acted in the best interests of our country.

We have to protect innocent people from "the bad guys." Here, we face one of the major problems in politics: how to act right in a world in which other people do not act right. For, in the end, this is the kind of world that we live in. In this world, is torture ever justified?

Additional Resources

Further resources on torture are Tobias Kelly, *This Side of Silence: Human Rights, Torture, and the Recognition of Cruelty* (University of Pennsylvania Press, 2012); Marjorie Cohn, ed., *The United States and Torture: Interrogation, Incarceration, and Abuse* (New York University Press, 2011); Frances Myrna Kamm, *Ethics for Enemies: Terror, Torture, and War* (Oxford University Press, 2011); Tracy Lightcap, *The Politics of Torture* (Palgrave Macmillan, 2011); Robert M. Pallitto, ed., *Torture and State Violence in the United States: A Short Documentary History* (Johns Hopkins Press, 2011); Tamara L. Roleff, ed., *Is Torture Ever Justified?* (Greenhaven Press, 2011); Charles and Gregory Fried, *Because It Is Wrong: Torture, Privacy and Presidential Power in the Age of Terror* (W. W. Norton, 2010); John P. Parry, *Understanding Torture: Law, Violence, and Political Identity* (University of Michigan Press, 2010); Gareth Peirce, *Dispatches from the Dark Side: On Torture and the Death of Justice* (Verso, 2010); James P. Pfiffner, *Torture as Public Policy: Restoring U.S. Credibility on the World Stage* (Paradigm Publishers, 2010); Jeremy Waldron, *Torture, Terror, and Trade-Offs: Philosophy for the White House* (Oxford University Press, 2010); J. Jeremy Wisnewski, *Understanding Torture* (Edinburgh University Press, 2010); Sanford Levinson, *Torture: A Collection* (Oxford University Press, 2006); Karen J. Greenberg, *The Torture Debate in America* (Cambridge University Press, 2005); Alfred W. McCoy, *A Question of Torture: CIA Interrogation, from the Cold War to the War on Terror* (Owl Books, reprint edition, 2007); Jennifer K. Harbury, *Truth, Torture, and the American Way: The History and Consequences of U.S. Involvement in Torture* (Beacon Press, 2005); Karen J. Greenberg and Joshua L. Dratel, eds., *The Torture Papers: The Road to Abu Ghraib* (Cambridge University Press, 2005); Darius Rejali, *Torture and Democracy* (Princeton University Press, 2007); James E. White, *Contemporary Moral Problems: War, Terrorism, and Torture,* 3rd ed. (Wadsworth Publishing, 2008); and David Cole, *Torture Memos: Rationalizing the Unthinkable* (The New Press, 2009).

Internet References . . .

United Nations Environment Program (UNEP)

The United Nations Environment Program (UNEP) website offers links to environmental topics of critical concern to sociologists. The site will direct you to useful databases and global resource information.

www.unep.ch

Worldwatch Institute Home Page

The Worldwatch Institute is dedicated to fostering the evolution of an environmentally sustainable society in which human needs are met without threatening the health of the natural environment. This site provides access to *World Watch* magazine and *State of the World 2000*.

www.worldwatch.org

William Davidson Institute

The William Davidson Institute at the University of Michigan Business School is dedicated to the understanding and promotion of economic transition. Consult this site for discussions of topics related to the changing global economy and the effects of globalization on society.

www.wdi.bus.umich.edu

World Future Society

The World Future Society is an educational and scientific organization for those interested in how social and technological developments are shaping the future.

www.wfs.org

Population Division: Department of Economic and Social Affairs

The Department of Economic and Social Affairs, Population Division, is responsible for monitoring and appraisal of the broad range of areas in the field of population.

www.un.org/esa/population/aboutpop.htm

The Future: Population/ Environment/Society

*T*he leading issues for the beginning of the twenty-first century include global warming, environmental decline, and globalization. The state of the environment and the effects of globalization produce strong arguments concerning what can be harmful or beneficial. Technology has increased enormously in the last 100 years, as have world-wide population growth, consumption, and new forms of pollution that threaten to undermine the world's fragile ecological support system. Although all nations have a stake in the health of the planet, many believe that none are doing enough to protect its health. Will technology itself be the key to controlling or accommodating the increase in population and consumption, along with the resulting increase in waste production? Perhaps so, but new policies will also be needed. Technology is driving the process of globalization, which can be seen as both good and bad. Those who support globalization theory state that globalization increases competition, production, wealth, and the peaceful integration of nations. However, not everyone agrees. This unit explores what is occurring in our environment and in our current global economy.

- Does Immigration Benefit the Economy?
- Is Humankind Dangerously Harming the Environment?
- Is Economic Globalization Good for Both Rich and Poor?

ISSUE 20

Does Immigration Benefit the Economy?

YES: **George W. Bush White House**, from "Immigration's Economic Impact," *White House Release* (June 20, 2007)

NO: **Steven A. Camarota**, from "Testimony Before the U.S. House of Representatives Committee on the Judiciary, Subcommittee on Immigration, Citizenship, Refugees, Border Security and International Law" (U.S. House of Representatives, September 30, 2010)

Learning Outcomes

After reading this issue, you should be able to:

- With effort understand the economic arguments on which the different sides are based.
- Sort out where the two articles agree and where they disagree.
- Understand how terrorism has radically changed the debate on immigration.
- Understand how the country could benefit from immigration but certain groups could lose benefits due to the immigration.
- Understand that most immigrants have mostly positive values like the importance of strong family ties, hard work, ambition to better themselves, etc.
- Know that illegal immigration raises other issues and greater public resentment.

ISSUE SUMMARY

YES: The George W. Bush White House surveys the professional literature and assesses immigration's economic impact and concludes that immigration has a positive effect on the American economy as a whole and even on the income of native-born American workers.

NO: Steven A. Camarota, director of research at the Center for Immigration Studies, argues that immigration's benefit to the economy is so tiny that it should be ignored. On the other hand, immigration reduces the income of the poor with whom many immigrants compete for jobs.

Immigrants move to the United States for various reasons: to flee tyranny and terrorism, to escape war, or to join relatives who have already settled. Above all, they immigrate because in their eyes America is an island of affluence in a global sea of poverty; here they will earn many times what they could only hope to earn in their native countries. One hotly debated question is, What will these new immigrants do to the United States—or for it?

Opposition to immigration comes from several sources. One is prejudice based on race, ethnicity, religion, or some other characteristic. Second, more legitimate in the view of many, is worry that immigrants are diluting the host country's language and other aspects of its national culture (this issue is covered in Issue 2). Security concerns are a third source of opposition to immigration. Some critics of immigration argue that crime is higher among immigrant populations, and in recent years the possibility of immigrants being terrorists has increased this worry for some. Economic concerns are a fourth source of opposition to immigrants and are the focus of this issue. One economic argument is that immigrants work for low wages, thereby undercutting the wages of native-born workers. Also, they are seen as taking jobs away from American workers. Another charge is that immigrants are an economic burden, requiring far more in terms of welfare, medical care, education, and other services than the migrants return to the economy in terms of productivity and taxes. These charges are met by counter-arguments that depict immigrants as providing needed workers and filling jobs that American workers do not want anyway. Finally, it can be argued that they give a boost to their new country's economy. In fact, several countries including the United States were largely developed by immigrants. Sometimes such influxes have gone fairly smoothly. At other times, they have met significant opposition within the country of destination. Such is the case currently, with the global tide of refugees and immigrants, both legal and illegal, facing increasing resistance. Certainly, the fact that immigrants attacked the World Trade Center and the Pentagon on September 11, 2001, made many Americans favor the reduction of immigration. But would we have a better economy if we continued to allow immigration on a generous scale?

Since 1965, the number of immigrants has changed markedly. Legal immigration has grown almost 300 percent from a yearly average of 330,000 in the 1960s to an annual average of 978,000 in the 1990s and just over 1 million during 2000–2007. Illegal (undocumented, unauthorized) immigrants probably add over 1 million to this total. Perhaps 11 million such immigrants are currently in the United States, with approximately 80 percent of them from Central America, especially Mexico. The presence of so many undocumented immigrants has become a major political issue in the United States. At one level, it is a question unto itself. It also relates to the general concerns about immigration that many Americans have regarding culture and security. Certainly, American attitudes are different for legal and illegal immigrants, but there is also an overlap, illustrated by the fact that polls find that most Americans favor decreasing immigration overall. When Americans are asked what bothers them about illegal immigration, they talk about its impacts on wages, job availability, and the cost of social and educational services. In other words, they are concerned about economic issues. Taking up this concern, George W. Bush's White House White Paper examines the economic impact of immigrants on the United States in the first reading and finds that the country benefits. Steven A. Camarota disagrees in the second reading, finding that immigration has negative economic effects.

YES

George W. Bush White House

Immigration's Economic Impact

Introduction

In 2006, foreign-born workers accounted for 15% of the U.S. labor force, and over the last decade they have accounted for about half of the growth in the labor force. That immigration has fueled U.S. macroeconomic growth is both uncontroversial and unsurprising—more total workers yield more total output. That immigrant workers benefit from working in the United States is also uncontroversial and unsurprising—few would come here otherwise.

Assessing how immigration affects the well-being of U.S. natives is more complicated. This is because immigration's economic impact is complex and may play out over generations, and because not all natives are alike in terms of their economic characteristics. Even in retrospect it is not easy to distinguish the influence of immigration from that of other economic forces at work at the same time. Nor is it easy to project costs and benefits far into the future. Nonetheless, economists and demographers have made headway on many of the measurement problems. This white paper assesses immigration's economic impact based on the professional literature and concludes that immigration has a positive effect on the American economy as a whole and on the income of native-born American workers.

Key Findings

1. On average, U.S. natives benefit from immigration. Immigrants tend to complement (not substitute for) natives, raising natives' productivity and income.
2. Careful studies of the long-run fiscal effects of immigration conclude that it is likely to have a modest, positive influence.
3. Skilled immigrants are likely to be especially beneficial to natives. In addition to contributions to innovation, they have a significant positive fiscal impact.

General Points

- Immigrants are a critical part of the U.S. workforce and contribute to productivity growth and technological advancement. They make up 15% of all workers and even larger shares of certain occupations such as construction, food services and health care. Approximately

From White House Release, June 20, 2007.

40% of Ph.D. scientists working in the United States were born abroad. (Source: Bureau of Labor Statistics; American Community Survey)

- Many immigrants are entrepreneurs. The Kauffman Foundation's index of entrepreneurial activity is nearly 40% higher for immigrants than for natives. (Source: Kauffman Foundation)
- Immigrants and their children assimilate into U.S. culture. For example, although 72% of first-generation Latino immigrants use Spanish as their predominant language, only 7% of the second generation are Spanish-dominant. (Source: Pew Hispanic Center/Kaiser Family Foundation)
- Immigrants have lower crime rates than natives. Among men aged 18 to 40, immigrants are much less likely to be incarcerated than natives. (Source: Butcher and Piehl)
- Immigrants slightly improve the solvency of pay-as-you-go entitlement programs such as Social Security and Medicare. The 2007 OASDI Trustees Report indicates that an additional 100,000 net immigrants per year would increase the long-range actuarial balance by about 0.07% of taxable payroll. (Source: Social Security Administration)
- The long-run impact of immigration on public budgets is likely to be positive. Projections of future taxes and government spending are subject to uncertainty, but a careful study published by the National Research Council estimated that immigrants and their descendants would contribute about $80,000 more in taxes (in 1996 dollars) than they would receive in public services. (Source: Smith and Edmonston)

Evaluating the Effect of Immigration on the Income of Natives

Immigrants not only change the size of the labor force, they change the relative supplies of factors such as unskilled labor, skilled labor, and capital in the economy. U.S. natives tend to benefit from immigration precisely because immigrants are not exactly like natives in terms of their productive characteristics and factor endowments. For example, . . . in contrast to their 15% share in the total labor force, foreign-born workers accounted for much higher proportions of workers without high school degrees and of those with Ph.D. degrees (especially for those working in scientific occupations). Differences between natives and immigrants lead to production complementarities that benefit natives.

Example:

- The presence of unskilled foreign-born construction laborers allows skilled U.S. craftsmen and contractors to build more homes at lower cost than otherwise—therefore the U.S. natives' productivity and income rise.
- Thus, when immigrants are added to the U.S. labor force, they increase the economy's total output, which is split between immigrants (who receive wages) and natives (who receive wages and also earn income from their ownership of physical and human capital). Natives may also gain from having a wider variety of goods and services to consume

and from lower prices for the goods and services produced by industries with high concentrations of foreign-born workers.

The "immigration surplus" is a simple and frequently cited metric of natives' total gains from immigration. The surplus accrues to native factors of production that are complemented by immigrant workers—that is, to factors whose productivity is enhanced by the presence of immigrants. In a simple model with just capital and labor (not differentiated by skill), similar in structure to that presented in the National Research Council (NRC) analysis, one can estimate this surplus as the area of a triangle defined by a downward sloping labor demand curve and the shift in labor supply attributed to immigration. Using a standard estimate of labor demand elasticity (0.3) and measures of the foreign-born share of the labor force, the current immigration surplus is about 0.28% of GDP, or roughly $37 billion per year.

Although the simplicity of the "immigration surplus" approach is attractive, the implicit assumptions are numerous, and it is well understood by economists that this is not a full reckoning of immigration's influence on the economy. For example, the approach does not differentiate between different kinds of workers (by skill, experience, or nativity) and does not allow for an endogenous and positive capital market response to the change in labor supply. Because immigration changes the mix of factors in the economy, it may influence the pattern of factor prices, which in turn may induce endogenous changes in other factor supplies. Moreover, implicit in the surplus calculation is an assumed negative effect on average wages for natives—an effect that is difficult to detect in empirical studies of the U.S. wage structure.

A more complex approach to measuring the influence of immigration on natives' income differentiates workers by skill, nativity, and experience and also allows for a capital accumulation response to changes in the supply of labor. In this scenario complementarities from immigrant workers are allowed to accrue to native workers. A recent paper by Ottaviano and Peri (2006) takes such an approach to measuring the wage effects of immigration and concludes that immigration since 1990 has boosted the average wage of natives by between 0.7% and 1.8% depending on the assessment's time frame—the effect is more positive when the capital stock has had time to adjust. Fully 90% of U.S. native-born workers are estimated to have gained from immigration. Multiplying the average percentage gains by the total wages of U.S. natives suggests that annual wage gains from immigration are between $30 billion and $80 billion.

In both approaches described above, natives benefit from immigration because the complementarities associated with immigrants outweigh any losses from added labor market competition. Rather than focusing on average effects, special attention could be paid to the well-being of the least-skilled natives. The number of natives with less than a high school degree has declined over time, which is one reason less-skilled immigrants have been drawn into the U.S. labor force to fill relatively low-paying jobs. Even so, . . . one might expect the remaining least-skilled natives to face labor market competition from immigrants. Evidence on this issue is mixed. Studies often find small negative effects of immigration on the wages of low-skilled natives, and even the comparatively large estimate reported in Borjas (2003) is under 10% for immigration over a 20-year period. The difficulties faced by high school dropouts are a serious policy concern, but it is safe to conclude that immigration is not a central cause of those difficulties, nor is reducing immigration a well-targeted way to help these low-wage natives.

- Conclusion: Immigrants increase the economy's total output, and natives share in part of that increase because of complementarities in production. Different approaches to estimating natives' total income gains from immigration yield figures over $30 billion per year. Sharply reducing immigration would be a poorly targeted and inefficient way to assist low-wage Americans.

Evaluating the Fiscal Benefits and Costs

To assess the fiscal implications of immigration, it is important to take a long-term view of the process and its interaction with projected demographic and economic trends. The National Research Council (NRC) published a landmark study of immigration in 1997, including an assessment of the overall fiscal impact (incorporating taxes and benefits at all levels of government). Although 10 years have passed since its publication, the volume's basic methodological lessons and empirical results are worth repeating.

One key point is that "snapshot" views of immigration's fiscal impact, particularly when based on analysis of households headed by immigrants, are insufficient and potentially misleading guides to immigration's long-run fiscal impact. Instead, "Only a forward-looking projection of taxes and government spending can offer an accurate picture of the long-run fiscal consequences of admitting new immigrants" (Smith and Edmonston 1997, p. 10). This approach captures the full costs and benefits of the children of immigrants. Of course, such projections must rely on assumptions about the future path of taxes and government spending as well as economic and demographic trends. From this long-run point of view, the NRC study estimated that immigrants (including their descendants) would have a positive fiscal impact—a present discounted value of $80,000 per immigrant on average in their baseline model (in 1996 dollars). The surplus is larger for high-skilled immigrants ($198,000) and slightly negative for those with less than a high school degree (−$13,000). It is worth noting that the NRC's estimated fiscal cost from less-skilled workers is far smaller than some commentators have recently suggested based on less satisfactory methods.

The long-term fiscal approach imparts four main lessons: (1) although subject to uncertainty, it appears that immigration has a slightly positive long-run fiscal impact; (2) skilled immigrants have a more positive impact than others; (3) the positive fiscal impact tends to accrue at the federal level, but net costs tend to be concentrated at the state and local level; and (4) the overall fiscal effect of immigration is not large relative to the volume of total tax revenues—immigration is unlikely to cure or cause significant fiscal imbalances.

- Conclusion: Although subject to the uncertainties inherent to long-run projections, careful forward-looking estimates of immigration's fiscal effects, accounting for all levels of government spending and tax revenue, suggest a modest positive influence on average. The fiscal impact of skilled immigrants is more strongly positive.

Immigrants in the U.S. Labor Force

From the perspective of workers in many countries today, the potential income gains from migration are large. For example, Hanson (2006) measured average wages for Mexico-born men who had recently moved to the United States and compared them to the wages of similar men who were still working in Mexico. The real wage ratios (that is, wages adjusted for international differences in prices) ranged from about 6-to-1 to 2-to-1 in favor of the U.S.-based workers, depending on the age and education group. Facing such large international wage differences, a worker might hope to move to the U.S. permanently or with the expectation of returning home after accumulating some savings. In this scenario the opportunity to work abroad temporarily can help finance large purchases or investments (like a house, car, or new business) in home countries where credit markets are underdeveloped and where wealth accumulation is difficult due to low wages. Migration might also allow households to expand and diversify their income sources, thereby serving as a lifeline to a higher and more stable income level for family members who remain based in a less-developed economy. In short, the economic gains to immigrants and their families are typically quite large.

These immigrants, like those in the past, work hard to improve their lot and that of their children. Their labor force participation rate, reflecting their concentration in prime working ages, is somewhat higher than that of natives (69% versus 66% in 2006), and conditional on being in the labor force their unemployment rate is somewhat lower than that of natives (4.0% versus 4.7% in 2006). Although their average income level is lower than natives', . . . they do fairly well in comparison with natives who have similar levels of education. Immigrants have low rates of incarceration compared to natives. And they are more likely to engage in entrepreneurial activity. Children of Latino immigrants overwhelmingly learn English. Finally, relative to natives, the children of low-education immigrants narrow much of the educational and income gap that their parents faced.

- Conclusion: As in the past, immigrants evince a strong work ethic, and the children of immigrants tend to assimilate in terms of language acquisition and educational attainment.

Steven A. Camarota

 **NO**

Testimony Before the U.S. House of Representatives Committee on the Judiciary, Subcommittee on Immigration, Citizenship, Refugees, Border Security and International Law

Introduction

In my very brief comments I will touch on several key issues surrounding immigration and the economy. My goal will be to clear up some of the confusion that often clouds the immigration debate. In particular, I will explain the difference between increasing the overall size of the U.S. economy and increasing the per-capita income of Americans. Finally, I will touch on the issue of immigration's impact on public coffers.

Immigration and the Size of the U.S. Economy

Immigration increases the overall size of the U.S. economy. Of this there is no question. In 2009 immigrants accounted for 15 percent of all workers. More workers and more people mean a bigger GDP. Immigrants are 15 percent of U.S. workers. They likely account for about 10 percent of GDP or more than a trillion dollars annually. However, this does not mean that the native-born population benefits from immigration. Basic economic theory shows that the overwhelming majority of this increase in economic activity goes to the immigrants themselves in the form of wages and other compensation. It is important to understand that the increase in the size of the economy is not, by itself, a benefit to the existing population. Moreover, immigrants who arrived in the last 10, 20, or 50 years are without question earning and living better on average than they would be had they remained in their home countries.

If the question is how much does the existing population benefit, then the key measure is the impact of immigration on per-capita GDP in the United States, particularly the per-capita GDP of the existing population. We can see the importance of per-capita GDP versus aggregate GDP by simply

U.S. House of Representatives, September 2010.

remembering that the economy of Mexico and Canada are similar in size. But this does not mean the two countries are equally rich because Mexico's population is roughly three times that of Canada's.

Benefits to Natives

There is a standard way of calculating the benefit from immigration, also referred to as the immigrant surplus, that goes to the existing population. A 1997 study by National Academy of Sciences (NAS),[1] authored by many of the top economists in the field, summarizes the formula for calculating the benefit (see pages 151–152). The NAS study updates an earlier study by the nation's top immigration economist, George Borjas of Harvard (see page 7).[2] In 2007 the President's Council of Economic Advisers (CEA) again used the same formula to estimate the benefit of immigration to Americans.[3] A blog by professor Borjas has a clear non-technical explanation of the calculation, from which I borrow heavily in this paper.[4]

The next gain from immigration can be estimated using the following formula:

Net gain from immigration as a share of GDP = −.5 × labor's share of income × wage elasticity × immigrant share of labor force squared.

"Labor share" refers to the percentage of GDP that goes to workers, which is usually thought to be 70 percent, the rest being capital. The immigrant share of the labor force is well known, and is currently 15 percent. "Wage elasticity" refers to the percentage change in wages from immigration increasing the size of the labor force by 1 percent. The size of the elasticity is a contentious issue. The NAS study assumed an elasticity of .3, and so will I in the calculation below. This means that each 1 percent increase in supply of labor caused by immigration reduces wages by 0.3 percent. Put a different way, if immigration increased the supply of workers by 10 percent, it would reduce the wages of American workers by 3 percent. Putting the values into the formula produces the following estimate:

$$0.24\% = -.50 \times .70 \times -0.3 \times (.15 \times .15)$$

Thus the net gain from immigration is 0.24 percent of GDP. (Expressed as decimal it is .0024.) If GDP is $14 trillion, then the net benefit would be $33 billion. Three important points emerge from this analysis. First, the net effect of immigration on the existing population is positive overall, though not for all workers. Second, the benefits are trivial relative to the size of the economy, less than one-quarter of 1 percent. Third, the benefit is dependent on the size of the wage losses suffered by the existing population of workers. Or put a different way, the bigger the wage loss, the bigger the net benefit. Those who contend that immigration has no impact on the wages of immigrants are also arguing, sometimes without realizing it, that there is no economic benefit from immigration.

The same model can be used to estimate the wage losses suffered [by] American workers.

> Wage loss as a fraction of GDP = −"labor's share of income" × "wage elasticity" × "immigrant share of labor force" × "native-born share of labor force."

Putting the numbers into the equation you get the following:

$$2.7\% = -0.7 \times -0.3 \times 0.15 \times 0.85$$

This is 2.7 percent of GDP, or $375 billion in wage losses suffered by American workers because of immigration. This is not trivial. There is nothing particularly controversial about this estimate and it stems from the same basic economic formula as the one above. Think of it this way: Labor is 70 percent of the economy, which is $14 trillion in total. If the elasticity is .3 and immigrants are 15 percent of the labor force, then wages will decline several percentage points (15 × .3). Thus the total wage loss must run into the hundreds of billions of dollars. If we are to accept the benefit that the model implies from immigration, then we must also accept the wage losses that the model implies.

The money that would have gone to workers as wages if there had been no immigration does not vanish into thin air. It is retained by owners of capital as higher profits or passed on to consumers in the form of lower prices. The fact that business owners lobby so hard to keep immigration levels high is an indication that much of the lost wages are likely retained by them. Also, workers who face little or no competition from immigrants will not suffer a wage loss. In fact, demand for their labor may increase and their incomes rise as a result. For example, if you are an attorney or a journalist at an English-language news outlet in the United States you face very little competition from immigrants.[5] In fact, immigration may increase your wages as demand for your occupation rises. In contrast, if you are a nanny, maid, bus boy, cook, meat packer, or construction laborer, the negative wage impact is likely to be large because immigration has increased the supply of workers in these sectors quite a bit. But overall the gain to some workers, businesses, and consumers is still slightly larger than the loss suffered by the losers; hence the tiny net benefit reported above.

Immigrant and Native Job Competition

Some may feel that there is no job competition between immigrants and native-born workers. The argument is often made, mostly by non-economists, that immigrants only do jobs Americans don't want. But analysis of all 465 occupations defined by the Department of Commerce shows that even before the current recession only four are majority immigrant. These four occupations account for less than 1 percent of the total U.S. workforce. Many jobs often thought to be overwhelmingly immigrant are, in fact, majority native-born. For example, 55 percent of maids and housekeepers are native-born, as are 58 percent of taxi drivers and chauffeurs, 63 percent of butchers and meat processors, 65 percent of construction laborers, and 75 percent of janitors. There are 93 occupations in which at least 20 percent of workers are immigrants. There are about 24 million native-born Americans in these high-immigrant occupations.[6] Thus, the argument that immigrants and natives never compete for jobs is simply incorrect. The real question is how have the poorest and the least educated American workers fared in recent decades as immigration has increased.

Deterioration at the Bottom of the Labor Market

There has been a long-term decline in wages, even before the current recession, among the less educated. Hourly wages for those who have not completed high school declined 22 percent in real terms (adjusted for inflation) from 1979 to 2007. Hourly wages for those with only a high school education declined 10 percent in real terms from 1979 to 2007.[7]

The share of less educated adults holding a job has been deteriorating for some time. This is true even before the current recession. From 2000 to 2007 the share of adult natives (ages 18 to 65) without a high school diploma holding a job fell from 54 percent to 48 percent. For those with only a high school education, the share [of] employed fell from 73 percent to 70 percent. By 2009 it was down to 43 percent for those without a high school diploma and 65 percent for those with only a high school education. There is a huge supply of less-educated people available as potential workers. In 2007, before the recession, there were more than 22 million native-born Americans (18 to 65) with no more than high school education who were not working. By 2009 that number was 26 million.[8]

If there was a tight labor market and unskilled workers really were in short supply, then we would expect that wages to rise for the less educated. We would also expect that the share of these workers holding a job would be climbing. But even before the current recession, this was not what has happening. The deterioration in wages and employment for the less educated is the kind of pattern we would expect to see as a result of immigrant competition.

Fiscal Impact of Immigration

The impact of immigration on public coffers is not directly part of a discussion on immigration and the economy. But when thinking about the overall effect of immigration on our pocketbooks, the taxes paid and services used by immigrants are important issues. It may be the most important issue. The previously mentioned National Academy of Sciences study estimated that the net fiscal drain (taxes paid minus services used) from immigrant households in 1997 was $11 to $20 billion a year. At the same time, using the same formula discussed above, the NAS study estimated a net economic benefit of $1 billion to $10 billion a year from immigration. Thus, the estimated fiscal drain was larger than the economic benefit. (Today the economic benefit and fiscal drain are larger reflecting our larger economy and government.)

It also must be remembered that there are still wage losses for less-skilled workers. The NAS study indicated that the wages of the poorest 10 percent of American workers were reduced by 5 percent as a result of immigrant-induced increases in the supply of labor.

More recent analysis indicates that the fiscal costs of immigration remain large. Census Bureau data indicate that one-third of those without health insurance in the United States are either immigrants (legal or illegal) or U.S.-born children (under 18) of immigrants. One-fourth of children living in poverty in the United States have immigrant fathers. In 2008, 53 percent of immigrant households with children used at least one major welfare program, primarily food assistance and Medicaid.[9] These fiscal costs are incurred despite immigrants' high rates of labor force participation. Their high welfare use rates and the resulting fiscal drain they create stem from the fact that a large share have relatively little education. About one-third of immigrants who arrive as adults have not graduated from high school. The modern American economy offers limited opportunities to such workers. This fact, coupled with a welfare state designed to help low-income workers with children, is the reason for the above statistics.

Conclusion

When thinking about immigration it is important to recognize that its impact on the size of the economy is not a measure of the benefit to natives. There is no question that U.S. GDP is significantly larger because of immigrant workers. However, a larger economy is entirely irrelevant to the key question of whether the per-capita GDP of natives is higher because of immigration. Efforts to measure the impact of immigration on the per-capita GDP of Americans using the standard economic model show that the benefit is trivial relative to the size of the economy. Perhaps most important, these trivial gains are the result of reduced wages for American workers in competition with immigrants. These workers tend to be the least educated and poorest already. If there is no wage reduction, then there is no economic gain. Finally, the tiny economic gain is probably entirely offset by the fiscal drain immigrants create on taxpayers.

In the end, arguments for or against immigration are as much political and moral as they are economic. The latest research indicates that we can reduce immigration without harming the economy. Doing so makes sense if we are very concerned about low-wage and less-educated workers in the United States. On the other hand, if one places a high priority on helping unskilled workers in other countries, then we should continue to allow in a large number of such workers. Of course, only an infinitesimal proportion of the world's poor could ever come to this country even under the most open immigration policy one might imagine. Those who support the current high level of immigration should at least understand that the American workers harmed by the policies they favor are already the poorest and most vulnerable.

Notes

1. Edmonston, Barry, and James Smith, Eds., *The New Americans: Economic, Demographic, and Fiscal Effects of Immigration,* Washington D.C., National Academy Press, 1997, http://books.nap.edu/openbook.php?isbn=0309063566.

2. George Borjas, "The Economic Benefits of Immigration," *Journal of Economic Perspectives* Vol. 9, No. 2, Spring 1995, www.hks.harvard.edu/fs/gborjas/Papers/Economic_Benefits.pdf.

3. "Immigration's Economic Impact," white paper, June 20, 2007, http://georgewbush-whitehouse.archives.gov/cea/cea_immigration_062007.html.

4. "No Pain No Gain," June 8, 1997, http://borjas.typepad.com/the_borjas_blog/2007/06/index.html.

5. Steven Camarota and Karen Jensenius, "Jobs Americans Won't Do? A Detailed Look at Immigrant Employment by Occupation," Center for Immigration Studies *Memorandum,* August 2009, www.cis.org/illegalimmigration-employment.

6. *Ibid.*

7. Lawrence Mishel, Jared Bernstein and Heidi Shierholz, "The State of Working America 2008/2009," Economic Policy Institute, Table 3.16, p. 166.

8. All figures for employment are based on the author's calculation of employment and labor force participation from the public-use files of the Current Population Survey in the third quarters of 2000, 2007, and 2009.

9. Figures come from the March 2009 Current Population Survey, which asks about health insurance coverage and welfare use in the prior calendar year. It also asks where respondents' parents were born. Thus, indentifying the children of immigrant parents is a simple calculation.

EXPLORING THE ISSUE

Does Immigration Benefit the Economy?

Critical Thinking and Reflection

1. The simple rule of morality is the greatest good for the greatest number (utilitarianism). Apply this rule to the issue of immigration. Do you accept the outcome or would you amend the rule?
2. Who benefits from heavy immigration and who benefits from very light immigration?
3. Why is America at an impasse on immigration legislation?
4. What are the various economic impacts of immigration and on sum does it help or harm the economy?
5. When did you or your ancestors come to America? Was that immigration good for America?
6. What should be done about "illegal" immigrants living in America? What should be done about children of illegal immigrants who were born here and are U.S. citizens?

Is There Common Ground?

This nation was built by immigration. Now most Americans want keep what we have largely to ourselves and greatly limit immigration. Now pro-immigration commentators have to justify immigration by demonstrating the benefits of immigration for America. The George W. Bush White House White Paper claims that immigration is making America stronger. Many people like Camarota disagree because they fear the consequences of today's immigration.

This issue has deeply divided the country. It seems that Congress cannot agree on immigration policy and pass meaningful immigration legislation. At the moment, there is no common ground except all sides are committed to trying to keep illegal immigrants out. Beyond that there are options but not agreement. Some want to deport the illegal immigrants in the United States. Others favor a guest-worker program that permits undocumented immigrants currently in the country to remain for several years as temporary workers but that also requires them to leave the country. Yet others support allowing unauthorized immigrants already in the country to get a work permit and eventually to apply for citizenship. A 2007 poll found 30 percent of Americans favoring the first option, 28 percent supporting the second, and 37 percent preferring the third option, with 5 percent unsure. Opinions were similarly split in the halls of Congress, so it has failed to enact a comprehensive plan.

Additional Resources

Several major works debate whether or not immigrants, on average, economically benefit America and can assimilate. Sources that argue that immigrants largely benefit America include Jason L. Riley, *Let Them In: The Case for Open Borders* (Gotham, 2008); Darrell M. West, *Brain Gain: Rethinking U.S. Immigration Policy* (Brookings Institution Press, 2010); Joseph H. Carens, *Immigrants and the Right to Stay* (MIT Press, 2010); Julian L. Simon, *The Economic Consequences of Immigration*, 2d ed. (University of Michigan Press, 1999) and *Immigration: The Demographic and Economic Facts* (Cato Institute, 1995). Sources that argue that immigrants have more negative than positive impacts include Mark Krikorian, *The New Case Against Immigration: Both Legal and Illegal* (Sentinel, 2008); Robert E. Koulish, *Immigration and American Democracy: Subverting the Rule of Law* (Routledge, 2010); George Borjas, *Heaven's Door: Immigration Policy and the American Economy* (Princeton University Press, 1999); Roy Beck, *The Case Against Immigration* (W. W. Norton, 1996); Patrick Buchanan, *The Death of the West: How Dying Populations and Immigrant Invasions Imperil Our Country and Civilization* (Thomas Dunne Books, 2002); and Otis L. Graham Jr., *Unguarded Gates: A History of America's Immigration Crisis* (Rowman & Littlefield, 2004). For a more even-handed discussion, see Sarah Spencer, *The Migration Debate* (Policy Press, 2011); Örn B. Bodvarsson, *The Economics of Immigration: Theory and Policy* (Springer, 2009); Peter Kivisto and Thomas Faist, *Beyond the Border: The Causes and Consequences of Contemporary Immigration* (Pine Forge Press, 2010); Philip L. Martin, *Importing Poverty?: Immigration and the Changing Face of Rural America* (Yale University Press, 2009); Nancy Foner, ed., *Not Just Black and White: Historical and Contemporary Perspectives on Immigration, Race, and Ethnicity in the United States* (Russell Sage Foundation, 2004); and Frank D. Bean and Gilian Stevens, eds., *America's Newcomers and the Dynamics of Diversity* (Russell Sage Foundation, 2003). On the issue of Mexican immigration, see Douglas S. Massey, Jorge Durand, and Nolan J. Malone, *Beyond Smoke and Mirrors: Mexican Immigration in an Era of Economic Integration* (Russell Sage Foundation, 2003), and Victor Davis Hanson, *Mexifornia: A State of Becoming* (Encounter Books, 2003). Works that focus on attitudes toward immigrants and their rights include Peter Schrag, *Not Fit for Our Society: Nativism and Immigration* (University of California Press, 2010); Armando Navarro, *The Immigration Crisis: Nativism, Armed Vigilantism, and the Rise of a Countervailing Movement* (AltaMira Press, 2009); Michael Sobczak, *American Attitudes Toward Immigrants and Immigration Policy* (LFB Scholarly Publishing, 2010); Dorothee Schneider, *Crossing Borders: Immigration and Citizenship in the Twentieth-Century United States* (Harvard University Press, 2011); Christian Joppke, *Citizenship and Immigration* (Polity, 2010); and Kim Voss and Irene Bloemraad, eds., *Rallying for Immigrant Rights: The Fight for Inclusion in 21st Century America* (University of California Press, 2011).

An overview of the history of U.S. immigration and policy is found in Aristide R. Zolberg, *A Nation by Design: Immigration Policy in the Fashioning of America* (Harvard University Press, 2008). A group that favors fewer immigrant is the Center for Immigration Studies at www.cis.org. Taking a positive view of immigration and immigrants is the National Immigration Forum at www.immigrationforum.org.

ISSUE 21

Is Humankind Dangerously Harming the Environment?

YES: **Lester R. Brown,** from "On the Edge," *World on the Edge: How to Prevent Environmental and Economic Collapse* (Earth Policy Institute, 2011)

NO: **Bjorn Lomborg,** from "The Truth about the Environment," *The Economist* (August 4, 2001)

Learning Outcomes

After reading this issue, you should be able to:

- Discern the trends or issues that greatly concern many environmentalists.
- Identify what has been done to address the environmental issues and estimate what still needs to be done.
- Assess the accuracy of the information on which you depend to understand environmental issues.
- Begin to explore the potential consequences of environmental problems on societies and lifestyles.
- Identify the information that you need to acquire to have a pretty good understanding of the environmental issues that are facing us today.

ISSUE SUMMARY

YES: Lester R. Brown, founder of the Worldwatch Institute and now president of the Earth Policy Institute, argues that population growth and economic development are placing increasingly harmful demands on the environment for resources and to grow food for improving diets.

NO: Bjorn Lomborg, a statistician at the University of Aarhus, Denmark, presents evidence that population growth is slowing down; natural resources are not running out; species are disappearing very slowly; the environment is improving in some ways; and assertions about environmental decline are exaggerated.

Much of the literature on socioeconomic development in the 1960s was premised on the assumption of inevitable material progress for all. It largely ignored the impacts of development on the environment and presumed that the availability of raw materials would not be a problem. The belief was that all societies would get richer because all societies were investing in new equipment and technologies that would increase productivity and wealth. Theorists recognized that some poor countries were having trouble developing, but they blamed those problems on the deficiencies of the values and attitudes of those countries and on inefficient organizations.

In the late 1960s and early 1970s, an intellectual revolution occurred. Environmentalists had criticized the growth paradigm throughout the 1960s, but they were not taken very seriously at first. By the end of the 1960s, however, marine scientist Rachel Carson's book *Silent Spring* (Alfred A. Knopf, 1962) had worked its way into the public's consciousness. Carson's book traces the noticeable loss of birds to the use of pesticides. Her book made the middle and upper classes in the United States realize that pollution affects complex ecological systems in ways that put even the wealthy at risk.

In 1968, Paul Ehrlich, a professor of population studies, published *The Population Bomb* (Ballantine Books), which states that overpopulation is the major problem facing mankind. This means that population has to be controlled or the human race might cause the collapse of the global ecosystems and the deaths of many humans. Ehrlich explained why he thought the devastation of the world was imminent:

> Because the human population of the planet is about five times too large, and we're managing to support all these people—at today's level of misery—only by spending our capital, burning our fossil fuels, dispersing our mineral resources and turning our fresh water into salt water. We have not only overpopulated but overstretched our environment. We are poisoning the ecological systems of the earth—systems upon which we are ultimately dependent for all of our food, for all of our oxygen and for all of our waste disposal.

In 1973, *The Limits to Growth* (Universe), by Donella H. Meadows et al., was published. It presents a dynamic systems computer model for world economic, demographic, and environmental trends. When the computer model projected trends into the future, it predicted that the world would experience ecological collapse and population die-off unless population growth and economic activity were greatly reduced. This study was both attacked and defended, and the debate about the health of the world has been heated ever since.

Let us examine the population growth rates for the past, present, and future. At about A.D. 1, the world had about one-quarter billion people. It took about 1,650 years to double this number to one-half billion and 200 years to double the world population again to 1 billion by 1850. The next doubling took only about 80 years, and the last doubling took about 45 years (from

2 billion in 1930 to about 4 billion in 1975). The world population may double again to 8 billion sometime between 2015 and 2025. At the same time that population is growing, people are trying to get richer, which means consuming more, polluting more, and using more resources. Are all these trends threatening the carrying capacity of the planet and jeopardizing the prospects for future generations?

In the following selections, Lester R. Brown warns that the population growth and the sevenfold expansion of the economy in the past half century is placing demands on the environment that exceed the Earth's natural capacity. As a result we face many environmental problems. The one that Brown focuses on is the difficulty of increasing food production enough to feed growing populations with better diets and with declining natural resources. Bjorn Lomborg counters that the evidence supports optimism—not environmental pessimism. He maintains that resources are becoming more abundant, food per capita is increasing, the extinction of species is at a very slow rate, and environmental problems are transient and will get better.

YES

Lester R. Brown

On the Edge

In the summer of 2010, record-high temperatures hit Moscow. At first it was just another heat wave, but the scorching heat that started in late June continued through mid-August. Western Russia was so hot and dry in early August that 300 or 400 new fires were starting every day. Millions of acres of forest burned. So did thousands of homes. Crops withered. Day after day, Moscow was bathed in seemingly endless smoke. The elderly and those with impaired respiratory systems struggled to breathe. The death rate climbed as heat stress and smoke took their toll. The average July temperature in Moscow was a scarcely believable 14 degrees Fahrenheit above the norm. Twice during the heat wave, the Moscow temperature exceeded 100 degrees Fahrenheit, a level Muscovites had never before experienced. Watching the heat wave play out over a seven-week period on the TV evening news, with the thousands of fires and the smoke everywhere, was like watching a horror film that had no end. Russia's 140 million people were in shock, traumatized by what was happening to them and their country.

The most intense heat in Russia's 130 years of record keeping was taking a heavy economic toll. The loss of standing forests and the projected cost of their restoration totaled some $300 billion. Thousands of farmers faced bankruptcy. Russia's grain harvest shrank from nearly 100 million tons to scarcely 60 million tons as crops withered. Recently the world's number three wheat exporter, Russia banned grain exports in a desperate move to rein in soaring domestic food prices. Between mid-June and mid-August, the world price of wheat climbed 60 percent. Prolonged drought and the worst heat wave in Russian history were boosting food prices worldwide.

But there was some good news coming out of Moscow. On July 30th, Russian President Dmitry Medvedev announced that in large parts of western Russia "practically everything is burning." While sweating, he went on to say, "What's happening with the planet's climate right now needs to be a wake up call to all of us." In something akin to a deathbed conversion, Russia's president was abandoning his country's position as a climate change denier and an opponent of carbon reduction initiatives.

Even before the Russian heat wave ended, there were reports in late July of torrential rains in the mountains of northern Pakistan. The Indus River, the lifeline of Pakistan, and its tributaries were overflowing. Levees that had confined the river to a narrow channel so the fertile floodplains could be farmed had failed. Eventually the raging waters covered one fifth of the country. The destruction was everywhere. Some 2 million homes were damaged or destroyed. More than 20 million people were affected by the flooding. Nearly 2,000 Pakistanis died. Some 6 million acres of crops were damaged or destroyed. Over a million livestock drowned. Roads and bridges were washed away. Although the flooding was blamed on the heavy rainfall, there were actually several trends converging to produce what was described as the largest natural disaster in Pakistan's history.

On May 26, 2010, the official temperature in Mohenjo-daro in south-central Pakistan reached 128 degrees Fahrenheit, a record for Asia. Snow and glaciers in the western Himalayas, where the tributaries of the Indus River originate, were melting fast. As Pakistani glaciologist M. Iqbal Khan noted, the glacial melt was already swelling the flow of the Indus even before the rains came.

The pressure of population on natural resources is intense. Pakistan's 185 million people are squeezed into an area 8 percent that of the United States. Ninety percent of the original forests in the Indus Basin are gone, leaving little to absorb the rainfall and reduce runoff. Beyond this, Pakistan has a livestock population of cattle, water buffalo, sheep, and goats of 149 million, well above the 103 million grazing livestock in the United States. The result is a country stripped of vegetation. When it rains, rapid runoff erodes the soil, silting up reservoirs and reducing their capacity to store flood water.

Twenty or more years ago, Pakistan chose to define security largely in military terms. When it should have been investing in reforestation, soil conservation, education, and family planning, it was shortchanging these activities to bolster its military capacity. In 1990, the military budget was 15 times that of education and a staggering 44 times that of health and family planning. As a result, Pakistan is now a poor, overpopulated, environmentally devastated nuclear power where 60 percent of women cannot read and write.

What happened to Russia and to Pakistan in the summer of 2010 are examples of what lies ahead for all of us if we continue with business as usual. The media described the heat wave in Russia and the flooding in Pakistan as natural disasters. But were they? Climate scientists have been saying for some time that rising temperatures would bring more extreme climate events. Ecologists have warned that as human pressures on ecosystems mount and as forests and grasslands are destroyed, flooding will be more severe.

The signs that our civilization is in trouble are multiplying. During most of the 6,000 years since civilization began we lived on the sustainable yield of the earth's natural systems. But in recent decades, humanity has overshot the level that those systems can sustain. We are liquidating the earth's natural assets to fuel our consumption. Half of us live in countries where water tables are falling and wells are going dry. Soil erosion exceeds soil formation on one third of the world's cropland, draining the land of its fertility. The world's ever-growing herds of cattle, sheep, and goats are converting vast stretches of grassland to desert. Forests are shrinking by 13 million acres per year as we clear land for agriculture and cut trees for lumber and paper. Four fifths of oceanic fisheries are being fished at capacity or overfished and headed for collapse. In system after system, demand is overshooting supply.

Meanwhile, with our massive burning of fossil fuels, we are overloading the atmosphere with carbon dioxide (CO_2), pushing the earth's temperature ever higher. This in turn generates more frequent and more extreme climatic events, including crop-withering heat waves, more intense droughts, more severe floods, and more destructive storms. The earth's rising temperature is also melting polar ice sheets and mountain glaciers. If the Greenland ice sheet, which is melting at an accelerating rate, were to melt entirely, it would inundate the rice-growing river deltas of Asia and many of the world's coastal cities. It is the ice melt from the mountain glaciers in the Himalayas and on the Tibetan Plateau that helps sustain the dry-season flow of the major rivers in India and China—the Ganges, Yangtze, and Yellow Rivers—and the irrigation systems that depend on them.

At some point, what had been excessive local demands on environmental systems when the economy was small became global in scope. A 2002 study by a team of scientists led by Mathis Wackernagel aggregates the use of the earth's natural assets, including CO_2 overload in the atmosphere, into a single indicator—the ecological footprint. The authors concluded that humanity's collective demands first surpassed the earth's regenerative capacity around 1980. By 1999, global demands on the earth's natural systems exceeded sustainable yields by 20 percent. Ongoing calculations show it at 50 percent in 2007. Stated otherwise, it would take 1.5 Earths to sustain our current consumption. Environmentally, the world is in overshoot mode. If we use environmental indicators to evaluate our situation, then the global decline of the economy's natural support systems—the environmental decline that will lead to economic decline and social collapse—is well under way.

No previous civilization has survived the ongoing destruction of its natural supports. Nor will ours. Yet economists look at the future through a different lens. Relying heavily on economic data to measure progress, they see the near 10-fold growth in the world economy since 1950 and the associated gains in living standards as the crowning achievement of our modern civilization. During this period, income per person worldwide climbed nearly fourfold, boosting living standards to previously unimaginable levels. A century ago, annual growth in the world economy was measured in the billions of dollars. Today, it is measured in the trillions. In the eyes of mainstream economists, the world has not only an illustrious economic past but also a promising future.

Mainstream economists see the 2008–09 global economic recession and near-collapse of the international financial system as a bump in the road, albeit an unusually big one, before a return to growth as usual. Projections of economic growth, whether by the World Bank, Goldman Sachs, or Deutsche Bank, typically show the global economy expanding by roughly 3 percent a year. At this rate the 2010 economy would easily double in size by 2035. With these projections, economic growth in the decades ahead is more or less an extrapolation of the growth of recent decades.

How did we get into this mess? Our market-based global economy as currently managed is in trouble. The market does many things well. It allocates resources with an efficiency that no central planner could even imagine, much less achieve. But as the world economy expanded some 20-fold over the last century it has revealed a flaw—a flaw so serious that if it is not corrected it will spell the end of civilization as we know it.

The market, which sets prices, is not telling us the truth. It is omitting indirect costs that in some cases now dwarf direct costs. Consider gasoline. Pumping oil, refining it into gasoline, and delivering the gas to U.S. service stations may cost, say, $3 per gallon. The indirect costs, including climate change, treatment of respiratory illnesses, oil spills, and the U.S. military presence in the Middle East to ensure access to the oil, total $12 per gallon. Similar calculations can be done for coal. We delude ourselves with our accounting system. Leaving such huge costs off the books is a formula for bankruptcy. Environmental trends are the lead indicators telling us what lies ahead for the economy and ultimately for society itself. Falling water tables today signal rising food prices tomorrow. Shrinking polar ice sheets are a prelude to falling coastal real estate values.

Beyond this, mainstream economics pays little attention to the sustainable yield thresholds of the earth's natural systems. Modern economic thinking and policymaking have created an economy that is so out of sync with the ecosystem on which it depends that it is approaching collapse. How can we assume that the growth of an economic system that is shrinking the earth's forests, eroding its soils, depleting its aquifers, collapsing its fisheries, elevating its temperature, and melting its ice sheets can simply be projected into the long-term future? What is the intellectual process underpinning these extrapolations?

We are facing a situation in economics today similar to that in astronomy when Copernicus arrived on the scene, a time when it was believed that the sun revolved around the earth. Just as Copernicus had to formulate a new astronomical worldview after several decades of celestial observations and mathematical calculations, we too must formulate a new economic worldview based on several decades of environmental observations and analyses.

The archeological record indicates that civilizational collapse does not come suddenly out of the blue. Archeologists analyzing earlier civilizations talk about a decline-and-collapse scenario. Economic and social collapse was almost always preceded by a period of environmental decline. For past civilizations it was sometimes a single environmental trend that was primarily responsible for their decline. Sometimes it was multiple trends. For Sumer, it was rising salt concentrations in the soil as a result of an environmental flaw in the design of their otherwise extraordinary irrigation system. After a point, the salts accumulating in the soil led to a decline in wheat yields. The Sumerians then shifted to barley, a more salt-tolerant crop. But eventually barley yields also began to decline. The collapse of the civilization followed. Archeologist Robert McC. Adams describes the site of the ancient Sumerian civilization on the central floodplain of the Euphrates River in what is now Iraq as an empty, desolate area now outside the frontiers of cultivation. He says, "Vegetation is sparse, and in many areas it is almost wholly absent. . . . Yet at one time, here lay the core, the heartland, the oldest urban, literate civilization in the world."

For the Mayans, it was deforestation and soil erosion. As more and more land was cleared for farming to support the expanding empire, soil erosion undermined the productivity of their tropical soils. A team of scientists from the National Aeronautics and Space Administration has noted that the extensive land clearing by the Mayans likely also altered the regional climate, reducing rainfall. In effect, the scientists suggest, it was the convergence of several environmental trends, some reinforcing others, that led to the food shortages that brought down the Mayan civilization.

Although we live in a highly urbanized, technologically advanced society, we are as dependent on the earth's natural support systems as the Sumerians and Mayans were. If we continue with business as usual, civilizational collapse is no longer a matter of whether but when. We now have an economy that is destroying its natural support systems, one that has put us on a decline and collapse path. We are dangerously close to the edge. Peter Goldmark, former Rockefeller Foundation president, puts it well: "The death of our civilization is no longer a theory or an academic possibility; it is the road we're on."

Judging by the archeological records of earlier civilizations, more often than not food shortages appear to have precipitated their decline and collapse. Given the advances of modern agriculture, I had long rejected the idea that food could be the weak link in our twenty-first century civilization. Today I think not only that it could be the weak link but that it is the weak link.

The reality of our situation may soon become clearer for mainstream economists as we begin to see some of the early economic effects of overconsuming the earth's resources, such as rising world food prices. We got a preview when, as world grain demand raced ahead and as supplies tightened in early 2007, the prices of wheat, rice, corn, and soybeans began to climb, tripling historical levels by the spring of 2008. Only the worst global economic downturn since the Great Depression, combined with a record world grain harvest in 2008, managed to check the rise in grain prices, at least for the time being. Since 2008, world market prices have receded somewhat, but as of October 2010, following the disastrous Russian grain harvest, they were still nearly double historical levels and rising.

On the social front, the most disturbing trend is spreading hunger. For the last century's closing decades, the number of chronically hungry and malnourished people worldwide was shrinking, dropping to a low of 788 million by 1996. Then it began to rise—slowly at first, and then more rapidly—as the massive diversion of grain to produce fuel for cars doubled the annual growth in grain consumption. In 2008, it passed 900 million. By 2009, there were more than a billion hungry and malnourished people. The U.N. Food and Agriculture Organization anticipated a decline in the number of hungry people in 2010, but the Russian heat wave and the subsequent climb in grain prices may have ended that hope.

This expansion in the ranks of the hungry is disturbing not only in humanitarian terms but also because spreading hunger preceded collapse for so many of the earlier civilizations whose archeological sites we now study. If we use spreading hunger as an indicator of the decline that precedes social collapse for our global civilization, then it began more than a decade ago. As environmental degradation and economic and social stresses mount, the more fragile governments are having difficulty managing them. And as rapid population growth continues, cropland becomes scarce, wells go dry, forests disappear, soils erode, unemployment rises, and hunger spreads. In this situation, weaker governments are losing their credibility and their capacity to govern. They become failing states—countries whose governments can no longer provide personal security, food security, or basic social services, such as education and health care. For example, Somalia is now only a place on the map, not a nation-state in any meaningful sense of the term.

The term "failing state" has only recently become part of our working vocabulary. Among the many weaker governments breaking down under the mounting stresses are those in Afghanistan, Haiti, Nigeria, Pakistan, and Yemen. As the list of failing states grows longer each year, it raises a disturbing question: How many states must fail before our global civilization begins to unravel? How much longer can we remain in the decline phase, whether measured in natural asset liquidation, spreading hunger, or failing states, before our global civilization begins to break down? Even as we wrestle with the issues of resource scarcity, world population is continuing to grow. Tonight there will be 219,000 people at the dinner table who were not there last night, many of them with empty plates.

If we continue with business as usual, how much time do we have before we see serious breakdowns in the global economy? The answer is, we do not know, because we have not been here before. But if we stay with business as usual, the time is more likely measured in years than in decades. We are now so close to the edge that it could come at any time. For example, what if the 2010 heat wave centered in Moscow had instead been centered in Chicago? In round numbers, the 40 percent drop from Russia's recent harvests of nearly 100 million tons cost the world 40 million tons of grain, but a 40-percent drop in the far larger U.S. grain harvest of over 400 million tons would have cost 160 million tons.

Food price stability now depends on a record or near-record world grain harvest every year. And climate change is not the only threat to food security. Spreading water shortages are also a huge, and perhaps even more imminent, threat to food security and political stability. Water-based "food bubbles" that artificially inflate grain production by depleting aquifers are starting to burst, and as they do, irrigation-based harvests are shrinking. The first food bubble to burst is in Saudi Arabia, where the depletion of its fossil aquifer is virtually eliminating its 3-million-ton wheat harvest. And there are another 17 countries with food bubbles based on overpumping. The Saudi loss of some 3 million tons of wheat is less than 1 percent of the world wheat harvest, but the potential losses in some countries are much larger. The grain produced by overpumping in India feeds 175 million Indians, according to the World Bank. For China, the comparable number is 130 million people. We don't know exactly when these water-based food bubbles will burst, but it could be any time now.

If world irrigation water use has peaked, or is about to, we are entering an era of intense competition for water resources. Expanding world food production fast enough to avoid future price rises will be much more difficult. A global civilization that adds 80 million people each year, even as its irrigation water supply is shrinking, could be in trouble.

Further complicating our future, the world may be reaching peak water at more or less the same time that it hits peak oil. Fatih Birol, chief economist with the International Energy Agency, has said, "We should leave oil before it leaves us." I agree. If we can phase out the use of oil quickly enough to stabilize climate, it will also facilitate an orderly, managed transition to a carbon-free renewable energy economy. Otherwise we face intensifying competition among countries for dwindling oil supplies and continued vulnerability to soaring oil prices. And with our recently developed capacity to convert grain into oil (that is, ethanol), the price of grain is now tied to that of oil. Rising oil prices means rising food prices. Once the world reaches peak oil and peak water, continuing population growth would mean a rapid drop in the per capita supply of both. And since both are central to food production, the effects on the food supply could leave many countries with potentially unmanageable stresses. And these are in addition to the threats posed by increasing climate volatility.

We are facing issues of near-overwhelming complexity and unprecedented urgency. Can we think systemically and fashion policies accordingly? Can we move fast enough to avoid economic decline and collapse? Can we change direction before we go over the edge? We are in a race between natural and political tipping points, but we do not know exactly where nature's tipping points are. Nature determines these. Nature is the timekeeper, but we cannot see the clock.

Since it is the destruction of the economy's natural supports and disruption of the climate system that are driving the world toward the edge, these are the trends that must be reversed. To do so requires extraordinarily demanding measures, a fast shift away from business as usual to what we at the Earth Policy Institute call Plan B. With a scale and urgency similar to the U.S. mobilization for World War II, Plan B has four components: a massive cut in global carbon emissions of 80 percent by 2020; the stabilization of world population at no more than 8 billion by 2040; the eradication of poverty; and the restoration of forests, soils, aquifers, and fisheries.

The Earth Policy Institute estimates that stabilizing population, eradicating poverty, and restoring the economy's natural support systems would cost less than $200 billion of additional expenditures a year—a mere one eighth of current world military spending. In effect, the Plan B budget encompassing the measures needed to prevent civilization collapse is the new security budget.

One thing is certain—we are facing greater change than any generation in history. What is not clear is the source of this change. Will we stay with business as usual and enter a period of economic decline and spreading chaos? Or will we quickly reorder priorities, acting at wartime speed to move the world onto an economic path that can sustain civilization?

Bjorn Lomborg

The Truth about the Environment

Ecology and economics should push in the same direction. After all, the "eco" part of each word derives from the greek word for "home", and the protagonists of both claim to have humanity's welfare as their goal. Yet environmentalists and economists are often at loggerheads. For economists, the world seems to be getting better. For many environmentalists, it seems to be getting worse.

These environmentalists, led by such veterans as Paul Ehrlich of Stanford University, and Lester Brown of the Worldwatch Institute, have developed a sort of "litany" of four big environmental fears:

- Natural resources are running out.
- The population is ever growing, leaving less and less to eat.
- Species are becoming extinct in vast numbers: forests are disappearing and fish stocks are collapsing.
- The planet's air and water are becoming ever more polluted.

Human activity is thus defiling the earth, and humanity may end up killing itself in the process.

The trouble is, the evidence does not back up this litany. First, energy and other natural resources have become more abundant, not less so since the Club of Rome published *The Limits to Growth* in 1972. Second, more food is now produced per head of the world's population than at any time in history. Fewer people are starving. Third, although species are indeed becoming extinct, only about 0.7% of them are expected to disappear in the next 50 years, not 25–50%, as has so often been predicted. And finally, most forms of environmental pollution either appear to have been exaggerated, or are transient—associated with the early phrases of industrialisation and therefore best cured not by restricting economic growth, but by accelerating it. One form of pollution—the release of greenhouse gases that causes global warming—does appear to be a long-term phenomenon, but its total impact is unlikely to pose a devastating problem for the future of humanity. A bigger problem may well turn out to be an inappropriate response to it.

Can Things Only Get Better?

Take these four points one by one. First, the exhaustion of natural resources. The early environmental movement worried that the mineral resources on which modern industry depends would run out. Clearly, there must be some

From *The Economist*, August 4, 2001, pp. 63–65. Copyright © 2001 by The Economist Newspaper Ltd. Reprinted by permission via Copyright Clearance Center.

limit to the amount of fossil fuels and metal ores that can be extracted from the earth: the planet, after all, has a finite mass. But that limit is far greater than many environmentalists would have people believe.

Reserves of natural resources have to be located, a process that costs money. That, not natural scarcity, is the main limit on their availability. However, known reserves of all fossil fuels, and of most commercially important metals, are now larger than they were when The *Limits to Growth* was published. In the case of oil, for example, reserves that could be extracted at reasonably competitive prices would keep the world economy running for about 150 years at present consumption rates. Add to that the fact that the price of solar energy has fallen by half in every decade for the past 30 years, and appears likely to continue to do so into the future, and energy shortages do not look like a serious threat either to the economy or to the environment.

The development for non-fuel resources has been similar. Cement, aluminum, iron, copper, gold, nitrogen and zinc account for more than 75% of global expenditure on raw materials. Despite an increase in consumption of these materials of between two- and ten-fold over the past 50 years, the number of years of available reserves has actually grown. Moreover, the increasing abundance is reflected in an ever-decreasing price: *The Economist*'s index of prices of industrial raw materials has dropped some 80% in inflation-adjusted terms since 1845.

Next, the population explosion is also turning out to be a bugaboo. In 1968, Dr. Ehrlich predicted in his best selling book, *The Population Bomb*, that "the battle to feed humanity is over. In the course of the 1970s the world will experience starvation of tragic proportions—hundreds of millions of people will starve to death."

That did not happen. Instead, according to the United Nations, agricultural production in the developing world has increased by 52% per person since 1961. The daily food intake in poor countries has increased from 1,932 calories, barely enough for survival, in 1961 to 2,650 calories in 1998, and is expected to rise to 3,020 by 2030. Likewise, the proportion of people in developing countries who are starving has dropped from 45% in 1949 to 18% today, and is expected to decline even further to 12% in 2010 and just 6% in 2030. Food, in other words, is becoming not scarcer but ever more abundant. This is reflected in its price. Since 1800, food prices have decreased by more than 90%, and in 2000, according to the World Bank, prices were lower than ever before.

Modern Malthus

Dr. Ehrlich's prediction echoes that made 170 years earlier by Thomas Malthus. Malthus claimed that, if unchecked, human population would expand exponentially, while food production could increase only linearly, by bringing new land into cultivation. He was wrong. Population growth has turned out to have an internal check: as people grow richer and healthier, they have smaller families. Indeed, the growth rate of the human population reached its peak, of more than 2% a year, in the early 1960s. The rate of increase has been

Figure 1

Slowing Up

World population 1750–2200*, bn

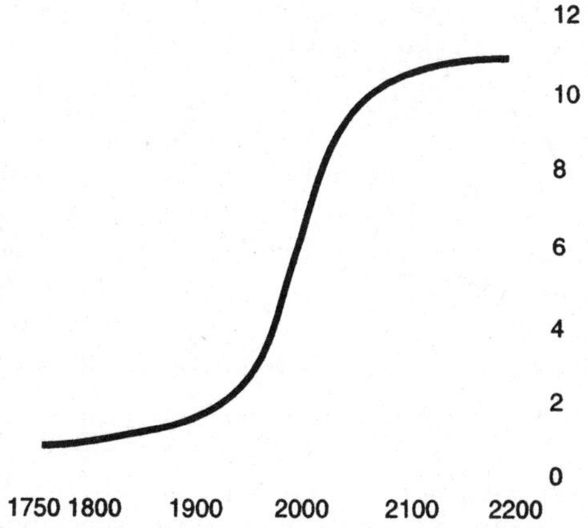

	12
	10
	8
	6
	4
	2
	0

1750 1800   1900   2000   2100   2200

*UN medium-variant forecast from 2000
Source: UNPD

declining ever since. It is now 1.26%, and is expected to fall to 0.46% in 2050. The United Nations estimates that most of the world's population growth will be over by 2100, with the population stabilising at just below 11 billion (see Figure 1).

Malthus also failed to take account of developments in agricultural technology. These have squeezed more and more food out of each hectare of land. It is this application of human ingenuity that has boosted food production, not merely in line with, but ahead of, population growth. It has also, incidentally, reduced the need to take new land into cultivation, thus reducing the pressure on biodiversity.

Third, that threat of biodiversity loss is real, but exaggerated. Most early estimates used simple island models that linked a loss in habitat with a loss of biodiversity. A rule-of-thumb indicated that loss of 90% of forest meant a 50% loss of species. As rainforests seemed to be cut at alarming rates, estimates of annual species loss of 20,000–100,000 abounded. Many people expected the number of species to fall by half globally within a generation or two.

However, the data simply do not bear out these predictions. In the eastern United States, forests were reduced over two centuries to fragments totalling just 1–2% of their original area, yet this resulted in the extinction of only one forest bird. In Puerto Rico, the primary forest area has been reduced over the past 400 years by 99%, yet "only" seven of 60 species of bird have become extinct. All but 12% of the Brazilian Atlantic rainforest was cleared in the 19th century, leaving only scattered fragments. According to the rule-of-thumb,

Figure 2

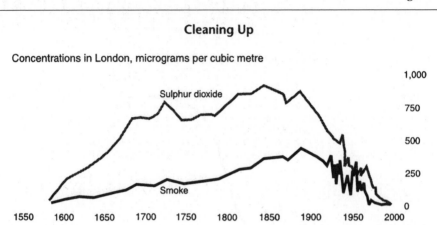

Source: B. Lomborg

half of all its species should have become extinct. Yet, when the World Conservation Union and the Brazilian Society of Zoology analysed all 291 known Atlantic forest animals, none could be declared extinct. Species, therefore, seem more resilient than expected. And tropical forests are not lost at annual rates of 2.4%, as many environmentalists have claimed: the latest UN figures indicate a loss of less than 0.5%.

Fourth, pollution is also exaggerated. Many analyses show that air pollution diminishes when a society becomes rich enough to be able to afford to be concerned about the environment. For London, the city for which the best data are available, air pollution peaked around 1890 (see Figure 2). Today, the air is cleaner than it has been since 1585. There is good reason to believe that this general picture holds true for all developed countries. And, although air pollution is increasing in many developing countries, they are merely replicating the development of the industrialised countries. When they grow sufficiently rich they, too, will start to reduce their air pollution.

All this contradicts the litany. Yet opinion polls suggest that many people, in the rich world, at least, nurture the belief that environmental standards are declining. Four factors cause this disjunction between perception and reality.

Always Look on the Dark Side of Life

One is the lopsidedness built into scientific research. Scientific funding goes mainly to areas with many problems. That may be wise policy, but it will also create an impression that many more potential problems exist than is the case.

Secondly, environmental groups need to be noticed by the mass media. They also need to keep the money rolling in. Understandably, perhaps, they sometimes exaggerate. In 1997, for example, the Worldwide Fund for Nature issued a press release entitled, "Two-thirds of the world's forests lost forever." The truth turns out to be nearer 20%.

Table 1

The Price of a Life
Cost of Saving One Year of One Person's Life – 1993$

Passing laws to make seat-belt use mandatory	69
Sickle-cell anaemia screening for black new-borns	240
Mammography for women aged 50	810
Pneumonia vaccination for people aged over 65	2,000
Giving advice on stopping smoking to people who smoke more than one packet a day	9,800
Putting men aged 30 on a low-cholesterol diet	19,000
Regular leisure-time physical activity, such as jogging for men aged 35	38,000
Making pedestrians and cyclists more visible	73,000
Installing air-bags (rather than manual lap belts) in cars	120,000
Installing arsenic emission-control at glass-manufacturing plants	51,000,000
Setting radiation emission standards for nuclear-power plants	180,000,000
Installing benzene emission control at rubber-tyre manufacturing plants	20,000,000,000

Source: T. Tengs et al, *Risk Analysis,* June 1995

Though these groups are run overwhelmingly by selfless folk, they nevertheless share many of the characteristics of other lobby groups. That would matter less if people applied the same degree of scepticism to environmental lobbying as they do to lobby groups in other fields. A trade organisation arguing for, say, weaker pollution controls is instantly seen as self-interested. Yet a green organisation opposing such a weakening is seen as altruistic, even if a dispassionate view of the controls in question might suggest they are doing more harm than good.

A third source of confusion is the attitude of the media. People are clearly more curious about bad news than good. Newspapers and broadcasters are there to provide what the public wants. That, however, can lead to significant distortions of perception. An example was America's encounter with El Niño in 1997 and 1998. This climatic phenomenon was accused of wrecking tourism, causing allergies, melting the ski-slopes and causing 22 deaths by dumping snow in Ohio.

A more balanced view comes from a recent article in the *Bulletin of the American Meteorological Society.* This tries to count up both the problems and the benefits of the 1997–98 Niño. The damage it did was estimated at $4 billion. However, the benefits amounted to some $19 billion. These came from higher winter temperatures (which saved an estimated 850 lives, reduced heating costs and diminished spring floods caused by meltwaters) and from the well-documented connection between past Niños and fewer Atlantic hurricanes. In 1998, America experienced no big Atlantic hurricanes and thus avoided huge losses. These benefits were not reported as widely as the losses.

The fourth factor is poor individual perception. People worry that the endless rise in the amount of stuff everyone throws away will cause the world to run out of places to dispose of waste. Yet, even if America's trash output continues to rise as it has done in the past, and even if the American population doubles by 2100, all the rubbish America produces through the entire 21st century will still take up only the area of a square, each of whose sides measures 28 km (18 miles). That is just one-12,000th of the area of the entire United States.

Ignorance matters only when it leads to faulty judgments. But fear of largely imaginary environmental problems can divert political energy from dealing with real ones. The table, showing the cost in the United States of various measures to save a year of a person's life, illustrates the danger. Some environmental policies, such as reducing lead in petrol and sulphur-dioxide emissions from fuel oil, are very cost-effective. But many of these are already in place. Most environmental measures are less cost-effective than interventions aimed at improving safety (such as installing air-bags in cars) and those involving medical screening and vaccination. Some are absurdly expensive.

Yet a false perception of risk may be about to lead to errors more expensive even than controlling the emission of benzene at tyre plants. Carbon-dioxide emissions are causing the planet to warm. The best estimates are that the temperature will rise by some 2°–3°C in this century, causing considerable problems, almost exclusively in the developing world, at a total cost of $5,000 billion. Getting rid of global warming would thus seem to be a good idea. The question is whether the cure will actually be more costly than ailment.

Despite the intuition that something drastic needs to be done about such a costly problem, economic analyses clearly show that it will be far more expensive to cut carbon-dioxide emissions radically than to pay the costs of adaptation to the increased temperatures. The effect of the Kyoto Protocol on the climate would be minuscule, even if it were implemented in full. A model by Tom Wigley, one of the main authors of the reports of the UN Climate Change Panel, shows how an expected temperature increase of 2.1°C in 2100 would be diminished by the treaty to an increase of 1.9°C instead. Or, to put it another way, the temperature increase that the planet would have experienced in 2094 would be postponed to 2100.

So the Kyoto agreement does not prevent global warming, but merely buys the world six years. Yet, the cost of Kyoto, for the United States alone, will be higher than the cost of solving the world's single most pressing health problems: providing universal access to clean drinking water and sanitation. Such measures would avoid 2m deaths every year, and prevent half a billion people from becoming seriously ill.

And that is the best case. If the treaty were implemented inefficiently, the cost of Kyoto could approach $1 trillion, or more than five times the cost of worldwide water and sanitation coverage. For comparison, the total global-aid budget today is about $50 billion a year.

To replace the litany with facts is crucial if people want to make the best possible decisions for the future. Of course, rational environmental management and environmental investment are good ideas—but the costs and benefits of such investments should be compared to those of similar investments in all the other important areas of human endeavour. It may be costly to be overly optimistic—but more costly still to be too pessimistic.

EXPLORING THE ISSUE

Is Humankind Dangerously Harming the Environment?

Critical Thinking and Reflection

1. What is the evidence that food production is inadequate for the current world population and probably will become even less adequate in the next two decades?
2. What current trends are worsening world agriculture's ability to keep total food production in pace with world population and increasingly rich (more meat) diets?
3. How are the world's major bio-systems declining over the past four decades: croplands, grasslands, forests, and oceans?
4. Brown writes about economic and social collapse if appropriate steps are not taken soon. On what grounds does he make such scary statements?
5. What are the likely impacts of global warming over the next half century? What are the possible but debatable impacts of global warming?
6. What factors are holding back the changes that would make us a sustainable society according to Brown?

Is There Common Ground?

There is common ground in the belief that the environment is worsening in many ways. The disagreement is about how serious these problems are and whether market responses to higher prices along with technological innovations will largely take care of them. Most environmentalists, however, cannot believe these problems can be taken care of so easily. In general, conservation actions cost three times the value of the benefits they bring. This inhibits their application if market forces determine actions. Government regulations can force actions that polluters and other environmental abusers do not want to do. But powerful people and the corporations do a good job of preventing tough regulations and policies. So far this train of thought suggests that even if solutions are available, they may be difficult to institute, so the problems are likely to worsen. If so then both the optimists and the pessimists may have good arguments. The optimists know that solutions are available and the pessimists know that too little gets done. Brown warns that the world has had 30–40 years to make the needed changes and has done little. Now it must act at wartime speed or societal collapse is possible. Lomborg calls Brown's type of thinking "crazy." After all, life is getting longer and better in many ways, so the prophets of doom must be wrong.

Additional Resources

Although a number of works (see below) support Lomborg's argument, his evidence has come under heavy attack (see Richard C. Bell, "How Did the Skeptical Environmentalist Pull the Wool Over the Eyes of So Many Editors?" *WorldWatch* (March–April 2002) and *Scientific American* (January 2002)). The issue of the state of the environment and prospects for the future has been hotly debated for over 40 years, with little chance of ending soon. Two key issues are the potential impacts of global warming and the net effects of future agricultural technologies, which will be used to feed growing populations with richer diets. On the former, for works that argue that global warming is a major world problem, see Al Gore, *An Inconvenient Truth: The Planetary Emergency of Global Warming and What We Can Do About It* (Rodale Press, 2006); William Antholis and Strobe Talbott, *Fast Forward: Ethics and Politics in the Age of Global Warming* (Brookings Institution Press, 2010); Mark Hertsgaard, *Hot: Living Through the Next Fifty Years on Earth* (Houghton Mifflin Harcourt, 2011); Brian M. Fagan, *The Great Warming: Climate Change and the Rise and Fall of Civilizations* (Bloomsbury Press, 2008); David Archer, *The Long Thaw: How Humans Are Changing the Next 100,000 Years of Earth's Climate* (Princeton University Press, 2009); Mark Lynas, *Six Degrees: Our Future on a Hotter Planet* (National Geographic, 2008); Tim F. Flannery, *Now or Never: Why We Must Act Now to End Climate Change and Create a Sustainable Future* (Atlantic Monthly Press, 2009); Charles Derber, *Greed to Green: Solving Climate Change and Remaking the Economy* (Paradigm Publishers, 2010); and Gabrielle Walker and Sir David King, *The Hot Topic: What We Can Do about Global Warming* (Harcourt, 2008).

Antagonists to the global warming thesis that human activities are a major cause of global warming include S. Fred Singer and Dennis T. Avery, *Unstoppable Global Warming: Every 1,500 Years* (Rowman & Littlefield, 2007); Roy W. Spencer, *The Great Global Warming Blunder: How Mother Nature Fooled the World's Top Climate Scientists* (Encounter Books, 2010); Ian R. Plimer, *Heaven and Earth: Global Warming, the Missing Science* (Taylor Trade, 2009); Patrick J. Michaels and Robert C. Balling Jr., *Climate of Extremes: Global Warming Science They Don't Want You to Know* (Cato Institute, 2009); Christopher Booker, *The Real Global Warming Disaster: Is the Obsession with Climate Change Turning Out to Be the Most Costly Scientific Blunder in History?* (Continuum, 2009); Garth W. Paltridge, *The Climate Caper: Facts and Fallacies of Global Warming* (Quartet Books, 2009); and Ronald Bailey, ed., *Global Warming and Other Eco-Myths: How the Environmental Movement Uses False Science to Scare Us to Death* (Prima, 2002). Lomborg's contribution to the global warming literature is *Cool It: The Skeptical Environmentalist's Guide to Global Warming* (Alfred A. Knopf, 2007). For the political side of the global warming issue, see Raymond S. Bradley, *Global Warming and Political Intimidation: How Politicians Cracked Down on Scientists as the Earth Heated Up* (University of Massachusetts Press, 2011). Two works that focus on what to do about global warming are Robert K. Musil, *Hope for a Heated Planet: How Americans Are Fighting Global Warming and Building a Better Future* (Rutgers University Press, 2009) and William D. Nordhaus, *A Question of Balance: Weighing the Options on Global Warming Policies* (Yale University Press, 2008).

On food production issues and agriculture technologies, see Lester R. Brown, *On the Edge: How to Prevent Environmental and Economic Collapse* (Earth Policy Institute, 2011) and *Plan B 4.0: Mobilizing to Save Civilization* (W. W. Norton, 2009); and Bread for the World Institute, *Are We on Track to End Hunger? 14th Annual Report on the State of World Hunger* (Bread for the World Institute, 2004). On agricultural technologies, see Vaclav Smil, *Feeding the World: A Challenge for the Twenty-First Century* (MIT Press, 2000).

Publications that are optimistic about the health of the environment and the availability of resources include Bjorn Lomborg, *The Skeptical Environmentalist: Measuring the Real State of the World* (Cambridge University Press, 2001); Ronald Bailey, ed., *The True State of the Planet* (Free Press, 1995); and Gregg Easterbrook, *A Moment on the Earth: The Coming Age of Environmental Optimism* (Viking, 1995). Publications by some who believe that population growth and human interventions in the environment have dangerous consequences for the future of mankind include Richard Krooth, *Gaia and the Fate of Midas: Wrenching Planet Earth* (University Press of America, 2009); Richard A. Matthew, ed., *Global Environmental Change and Human Society* (MIT Press, 2010); Hans Gunter Brauch et al., *Facing Global Environmental Change: Environmental, Human, Energy, Food, Health and Water Security Concepts* (Springer, 2009); Tim Jackson, *Prosperity Without Growth: Economics for a Finite Planet* (Earthscan, 2009); Joseph Wayne Smith, Graham Lyons, and Gary Sauer-Thompson, *Healing a Wounded World* (Praeger, 1997); Douglas E. Booth, *The Environmental Consequences of Growth* (Routledge, 1998); Kirill Kondratyev et al., *Stability of Life on Earth: Principal Subject of Scientific Research in the 21st Century* (Springer 2004); and James Gustive Speth, *Red Sky at Morning: America and the Crisis of the Global Environment* (Yale University Press, 2004).

Several works relate environmental problems to very severe political, social, and economic problems, including Joseph Wayne Smith and Sandro Positano, *The Self-Destructive Affluence of the First World: The Coming Crisis of Global Poverty and Ecological Collapse* (Edwin Mellen Press, 2010); Joel Kovel, *The Enemy of Nature: The End of Capitalism or the End of the World?* (Zed Books, 2007); Michael Renner, *Fighting for Survival* (W. W. Norton, 1996); Michael N. Dobkowski and Isidor Wallimann, eds., *The Coming Age of Scarcity: Preventing Mass Death and Genocide in the Twenty-First Century* (Syracuse University Press, 1998) and *On the Edge of Scarcity: Environment, Resources, Population, Sustainability, and Conflict* (Syracuse University Press, 2002); and one with a long time frame, Sing C. Chew, *World Ecological Degradation: Accumulation, Urbanization, and Deforestation, 3000 B.C.–A.D. 2000* (Roman & Littlefield, 2001). Since environmental changes could have such devastating effects, many have proposed solutions to these problems. The broadest term for these changes is sustainability. The following works suggests paths to sustainability, most of which require dramatic changes: Eric F. Lambin, *The Middle Path: Avoiding Environmental Catastrophe* (University of Chicago Press, 2007); James Gustave Speth, *The Bridge at the Edge of the World: Capitalism, the Environment, and Crossing from Crisis to Sustainability* (Yale University Press, 2008); Charles J. Kibert et al., *Working Toward Sustainability: Ethical Decision Making in a Technological World* (Wiley, 2012); Russ Beaton and Chris Maser, *Economics and Ecology:*

United for a Sustainable World (CRC Press, 2012); Robin Hahnel, *Green Economics: Confronting the Ecological Crisis* (M. E. Sharpe, 2011); Ian Chambers and John Humble, *Developing a Plan for the Planet: A Business Plan for Sustainable Living* (Gower Publishing, 2011); Jennifer Clapp and Peter Dauvergne, *Paths to a Green World: The Political Economy of the Global Environment* (MIT Press, 2011); Costas Panayotakis, *Remaking Scarcity: From Capitalist Inefficiency to Economic Democracy* (Fernwood, 2011); and Milissa Leach et al., *Dynamic Sustainabilities: Technology, Environment, Social Justice* (Earthscan, 2010).

Worldwatch Institute publishes an important series on environmental problems, which includes two annuals: *State of the World* and *Vital Signs*.

ISSUE 22

Is Economic Globalization Good for Both Rich and Poor?

YES: IMF Staff, from "Globalization: A Brief Overview," *International Monetary Fund* (May 2008)

NO: Ravinder Rena, from "Globalization Still Hurting Poor Nations," *Africa Economic Analysis* (January 2008)

Learning Outcomes

After reading this issue, you should be able to:

- Identify as complete a list as possible of the positive and negative impacts of globalization. Also identify what groups get the benefits and what groups get the harms.

- Understand the arguments that maintain that the majority of the benefits accrue to the developed nations and the majority of the harms accrue to the less developed nations. Also understand the arguments that maintain that the less developed nations obtain more benefits from globalization than harms.

- Ascertain what aspects of international relations are included in the concept of globalization. Do commentators on different sides of this debate use different dimensions of globalization and how does that affect their arguments?

- Determine what are the advantages for less developed nations to invite foreign corporate investments into their country and what are the disadvantages.

- Identify the differences between the forms of globalization today compared to several decades ago.

- Deduce the main reasons why many people have protested globalization and evaluate how factual their perspective is.

ISSUE SUMMARY

YES: IMF (International Monetary Fund) Staff examine both positive and negative effects of globalization and conclude that economic globalization contributes greatly to world prosperity.

NO: Ravinder Rena, an associate professor of economics at the Eritrea Institute of Technology, argues that globalization produces many benefits but also produces many negative impacts. The poor and poorer countries are the most harmed by globalization.

A really big issue of today is globalization, which stands for worldwide processes, activities, and institutions. It involves world markets, world finance, world communications, world media, world religions, world popular culture, world rights movements, world drug trade, etc. The focus of most commentators is on the world economy, which today spreads financial crisis from the United States to the rest of the world. Many believe, however, that globalization promises strong growth in world wealth in the long run. Critics focus on the world economy's negative impacts on workers' wages, environmental protections and regulations, national and local cultures, and vulnerability to economic crises. One thing everyone agrees on is that the impacts of globalization are gigantic. The statistics are mind boggling. Global trade has grown over 2,000 percent since 1950 and now is over $15 trillion annually. Total international investment exceeds $25 trillion. Multinational corporations dominate global commerce and the 500 largest corporations account for annual sales of over $15 trillion. Another fact that all agree on is that America and its businesses, media, and culture are at the center of the globalized world. This normally ensures that America gains more than its proportional share of the benefits. But the real debate is whether or not globalization benefits all mankind. When the whole world is considered, there may be far more minuses to be weighed against the pluses. It is hard to settle this debate because so many different and incomparable dimensions must be included in the calculation of the costs relative to benefits.

Let's identify some benefits that people around the world seem to enjoy. People are communicating by cell phones and the Internet around the world. TV and the Web bring events from all corners of the world into our living rooms or on our iPods. As a result we feel much more interconnected. Furthermore, we have an abundance of goods at low prices. So each of us personally enjoy many benefits. On the other hand, workers lose jobs to cheap foreign workers as companies relocate or invest abroad. World interconnectedness makes us feel more vulnerable to foreign enemies. I have several times had foreigners try to scam money from me. My telephone number has been used for fraudulent international calls. Businesses and government agencies are terrified about the potential damage that hackers can cause. Terrorism experts now believe that cyber attacks could be far more dangerous to us than attacks with weapons of mass destruction, and cyber attacks can be launched from anywhere in the world. Many other problems seem to have their roots in globalization. Therefore, we are both thankful for and fearful of globalization.

The lists of benefits and costs could go on for many pages. I have no idea how to sum all of them up into a net score. Instead I will turn that task over to the two readings presented below. In the following selections, staff members of IMF argue that the benefits far exceed the costs, even for the poor. IMF is well positioned to know what is happening and it has conducted high-quality research on this issue. They conclude that as nations globalize, their citizens benefit because they gain "access to a wider variety of goods and services, lower prices, more and more better-paying jobs, improved health, and higher overall living standards." These benefits, however, are very unevenly distributed both within and between nations. This problem is the backbone of Ravinder Rena's argument against globalization. He criticizes globalization for increasing the gap between rich and poor.

YES

IMF Staff

Globalization: A Brief Overview

A perennial challenge facing all of the world's countries, regardless of their level of economic development, is achieving financial stability, economic growth, and higher living standards. There are many different paths that can be taken to achieve these objectives, and every country's path will be different given the distinctive nature of national economies and political systems. The ingredients contributing to China's high growth rate over the past two decades have, for example, been very different from those that have contributed to high growth in countries as varied as Malaysia and Malta.

Yet, based on experiences throughout the world, several basic principles seem to underpin greater prosperity. These include investment (particularly foreign direct investment) [owning foreign companies or real estate], the spread of technology, strong institutions, sound macroeconomic policies, an educated workforce, and the existence of a market economy. Furthermore, a common denominator which appears to link nearly all high-growth countries together is their participation in, and integration with, the global economy.

There is substantial evidence, from countries of different sizes and different regions, that as countries "globalize" their citizens benefit, in the form of access to a wider variety of goods and services, lower prices, more and better-paying jobs, improved health, and higher overall living standards. It is probably no mere coincidence that over the past 20 years, as a number of countries have become more open to global economic forces, the percentage of the developing world living in extreme poverty—defined as living on less than $1 per day—has been cut in half.

As much as has been achieved in connection with globalization, there is much more to be done. Regional disparities persist: while poverty fell in East and South Asia, it actually rose in sub-Saharan Africa. The UN's Human Development Report notes there are still around 1 billion people surviving on less than $1 per day—with 2.6 billion living on less than $2 per day. Proponents of globalization argue that this is not because of too much globalization, but rather too little. And the biggest threat to continuing to raise living standards throughout the world is not that globalization will succeed but that it will fail. It is the people of developing economies who have the greatest need for globalization, as it provides them with the opportunities that come with being part of the world economy.

These opportunities are not without risks—such as those arising from volatile capital movements. The International Monetary Fund works to help economies manage or reduce these risks, through economic analysis and policy advice and through technical assistance in areas such as macroeconomic policy, financial sector sustainability, and the exchange-rate system.

The risks are not a reason to reverse direction, but for all concerned—in developing and advanced countries, among both investors and recipients—to embrace policy changes to build strong economies and a stronger world financial system that will produce more rapid growth and ensure that poverty is reduced.

The following is a brief overview to help guide anyone interested in gaining a better understanding of the many issues associated with globalization.

What Is Globalization?

Economic "globalization" is a historical process, the result of human innovation and technological progress. It refers to the increasing integration of economies around the world, particularly through the movement of goods, services, and capital across borders. The term sometimes also refers to the movement of people (labor) and knowledge (technology) across international borders. There are also broader cultural, political, and environmental dimensions of globalization.

The term "globalization" began to be used more commonly in the 1980s, reflecting technological advances that made it easier and quicker to complete international transactions—both trade and financial flows. It refers to an extension beyond national borders of the same market forces that have operated for centuries at all levels of human economic activity—village markets, urban industries, or financial centers.

There are countless indicators that illustrate how goods, capital, and people have become more globalized.

- The value of trade (goods and services) as a percentage of world GDP [gross domestic product: the value of all goods and services produced within an economic unit] increased from 42.1 percent in 1980 to 62.1 percent in 2007.
- Foreign direct investment increased from 6.5 percent of world GDP in 1980 to 31.8 percent in 2006.
- The stock of international claims (primarily bank loans), as a percentage of world GDP, increased from roughly 10 percent in 1980 to 48 percent in 2006.
- The number of minutes spent on cross-border telephone calls, on a per-capita basis, increased from 7.3 in 1991 to 28.8 in 2006.
- The number of foreign workers has increased from 78 million people (2.4 percent of the world population) in 1965 to 191 million people (3.0 percent of the world population) in 2005.

The growth in global markets has helped to promote efficiency through competition and the division of labor—the specialization that allows people and economies to focus on what they do best. Global markets also offer greater opportunity for people to tap into more diversified and larger markets around the world. It means that they can have access to more capital, technology, cheaper imports, and larger export markets. But markets do not necessarily ensure that the benefits of increased efficiency are shared by all. Countries must be prepared to embrace the policies needed, and, in the case of the poorest countries, may need the support of the international community as they do so. The broad reach of globalization easily extends to daily choices of personal, economic, and political life. For example, greater access to modern technologies, in the world of health care, could make the difference between life and death. In the world of communications, it would facilitate commerce and education, and allow access to independent media. Globalization can also create a framework for cooperation among nations on a range of non-economic issues that have cross-border implications, such as immigration, the environment, and legal issues. At the same time, the influx of foreign goods, services, and capital into a country can create incentives and demands for strengthening the education system, as a country's citizens recognize the competitive challenge before them.

Perhaps more importantly, globalization implies that information and knowledge get dispersed and shared.

Innovators—be they in business or government—can draw on ideas that have been successfully implemented in one jurisdiction and tailor them to suit their own jurisdiction. Just as important, they can avoid the ideas that have a clear track record of failure. Joseph Stiglitz, a Nobel laureate and frequent critic of globalization, has nonetheless observed that globalization "has reduced the sense of isolation felt in much of the developing world and has given many people in the developing world access to knowledge well beyond the reach of even the wealthiest in any country a century ago."

International Trade

A core element of globalization is the expansion of world trade through the elimination or reduction of trade barriers, such as import tariffs. Greater imports offer consumers a wider variety of goods at lower prices, while providing strong incentives for domestic industries to remain competitive. Exports, often a source of economic growth for developing nations, stimulate job creation as industries sell beyond their borders. More generally, trade enhances national competitiveness by driving workers to focus on those vocations where they, and their country, have a competitive advantage. Trade promotes economic resilience and flexibility, as higher imports help to offset adverse domestic supply shocks. Greater openness can also stimulate foreign investment, which would be a source of employment for the local workforce and could bring along new technologies—thus promoting higher productivity.

Restricting international trade—that is, engaging in protectionism— generates adverse consequences for a country that undertakes such a policy. For example, tariffs raise the prices of imported goods, harming consumers, many of which may be poor. Protectionism also tends to reward concentrated, well-organized and politically-connected groups, at the expense of those whose interests may be more diffuse (such as consumers). It also reduces the variety of goods available and generates inefficiency by reducing competition and encouraging resources to flow into protected sectors.

Developing countries can benefit from an expansion in international trade. Ernesto Zedillo, the former president of Mexico, has observed that, "In every case where a poor nation has significantly overcome its poverty, this has been achieved while engaging in production for export markets and opening itself to the influx of foreign goods, investment, and technology."

And the trend is clear. In the late 1980s, many developing countries began to dismantle their barriers to international trade, as a result of poor economic performance under protectionist polices and various economic crises. In the 1990s, many former Eastern bloc countries integrated into the global trading system and developing Asia—one of the most closed regions to trade in 1980—progressively dismantled barriers to trade. Overall, while the average tariff rate applied by developing countries is higher than that applied by advanced countries, it has declined significantly over the last several decades.

The Implications of Globalized Financial Markets

The world's financial markets have experienced a dramatic increase in globalization in recent years. Global capital flows fluctuated between 2 and 6 percent of world GDP during the period 1980–95, but since then they have risen to 14.8 percent of GDP, and in 2006 they totaled $7.2 trillion, more than tripling since 1995. The most rapid increase has been experienced by advanced economies, but emerging markets and developing countries have also become more financially integrated. As countries have strengthened their capital markets they have attracted more investment capital, which can enable a broader entrepreneurial class to develop, facilitate a more efficient allocation of capital, encourage international risk sharing, and foster economic growth. Yet there is an energetic debate underway, among leading academics and policy experts, on the precise impact of financial globalization. Some see it as a catalyst for economic growth and stability. Others see it as injecting dangerous—and often costly—volatility into the economies of growing middle-income countries.

A recent paper by the IMF's Research Department takes stock of what is known about the effects of financial globalization. The analysis of the past 30 years of data reveals two main lessons for countries to consider.

First, the findings support the view that countries must carefully weigh the risks and benefits of unfettered capital flows. The evidence points to largely unambiguous gains from financial integration for advanced economies. In emerging and developing countries, certain factors are likely to influence the effect of financial globalization on economic volatility and growth: countries with well-developed financial sectors, strong institutions, sound macroeconomic policies, and substantial trade openness are more likely to gain from financial liberalization and less likely to risk increased macroeconomic volatility and to experience financial crises. For example, well-developed financial markets help moderate boom-bust cycles that can be triggered by surges and sudden stops in international capital flows, while strong domestic institutions and sound macroeconomic policies help attract "good" capital, such as portfolio equity flows and FDI.

The second lesson to be drawn from the study is that there are also costs associated with being overly cautious about opening to capital flows. These costs include lower international trade, higher investment costs for firms, poorer economic incentives, and additional administrative/monitoring costs. Opening up to foreign investment may encourage changes in the domestic economy that eliminate these distortions and help foster growth.

Looking forward, the main policy lesson that can be drawn from these results is that capital account liberalization should be pursued as part of a broader reform package encompassing a country's macroeconomic policy framework, domestic financial system, and prudential regulation. Moreover, long-term, non-debt-creating flows, such as FDI, should be liberalized before short-term, debt-creating inflows. Countries should still weigh the possible risks involved in opening up to capital flows against the efficiency costs associated with controls, but under certain conditions (such as good institutions, sound domestic and foreign policies, and developed financial markets) the benefits from financial globalization are likely to outweigh the risks.

Globalization, Income Inequality, and Poverty

As some countries have embraced globalization, and experienced significant income increases, other countries that have rejected globalization, or embraced it only tepidly, have fallen behind. A similar phenomenon is at work within countries—some people have, inevitably, been bigger beneficiaries of globalization than others.

Over the past two decades, income inequality has risen in most regions and countries. At the same time, per capita incomes have risen across virtually all regions for even the poorest segments of populations, indicating that the poor are better off in an absolute sense during this phase of globalization, although incomes for the relatively well off have increased at a faster pace. Consumption data from groups of developing countries reveal the striking inequality that exists between the richest and the poorest in populations across different regions.

As discussed in the October 2007 issue of the *World Economic Outlook*, one must keep in mind that there are many sources of inequality. Contrary to popular belief, increased trade globalization is associated with a decline in inequality. The spread of technological advances and increased financial globalization—and foreign direct investment in particular—have instead contributed more to the recent rise in inequality by raising the demand for skilled labor and increasing the returns to skills in both developed and developing countries. Hence, while everyone benefits, those with skills benefit more.

It is important to ensure that the gains from globalization are more broadly shared across the population. To this effect, reforms to strengthen education and training would help ensure that workers have the appropriate skills for the evolving global economy. Policies that broaden the access of finance to the poor would also help, as would further trade liberalization that boosts agricultural exports from developing countries. Additional programs may include providing adequate income support to cushion, but not obstruct, the process of change, and also making health care less dependent on continued employment and increasing the portability of pension benefits in some countries.

Equally important, globalization should not be rejected because its impact has left some people unemployed. The dislocation may be a function of forces that have little to do with globalization and more to do with inevitable technological progress. And, the number of people who "lose" under globalization is likely to be outweighed by the number of people who "win."

Martin Wolf, the *Financial Times* columnist, highlights one of the fundamental contradictions inherent in those who bemoan inequality, pointing out that this charge amounts to arguing "that it would be better for everybody to be equally poor than for some to become significantly better off, even if, in the long run, this will almost certainly lead to advances for everybody."

Indeed, globalization has helped to deliver extraordinary progress for people living in developing nations. One of the most authoritative studies of the subject has been carried out by World Bank economists David Dollar and Aart Kraay. They concluded that since 1980, globalization has contributed to a reduction in poverty as well as a reduction in global income inequality. They found that in "globalizing" countries in the developing world, income per person grew three-and-a-half times faster than in "non-globalizing" countries, during the 1990s. In general, they noted, "higher growth rates in globalizing developing countries have translated into higher incomes for the poor." Dollar and Kraay also found that in virtually all events in which a country experienced growth at a rate of two percent or more, the income of the poor rose.

Critics point to those parts of the world that have achieved few gains during this period and highlight it as a failure of globalization. But that is to misdiagnose the problem. While serving as Secretary-General of the United Nations, Kofi Annan pointed out that "the main losers in today's very unequal world are not those who are too much exposed to globalization. They are those who have been left out." . . .

Myths about Globalization

No discussion of globalization would be complete without dispelling some of the myths that have been built up around it.

Downward pressure on wages: Globalization is rarely the primary factor that fosters wage moderation in low-skilled work conducted in developed countries. As discussed in a recent issue of the *World Economic Outlook,* a more significant factor is technology. As more work can be mechanized, and as fewer people are needed to do a given job than in the past, the demand for that labor will fall, and as a result the prevailing wages for that labor will be affected as well.

The "race to the bottom": Globalization has not caused the world's multinational corporations to simply scour the globe in search of the lowest-paid laborers. There are numerous factors that enter into corporate decisions on where to source products, including the supply of skilled labor, economic and political stability, the local infrastructure, the quality of institutions, and the overall business climate. In an open global market, while jurisdictions do compete with each other to attract investment, this competition incorporates factors well beyond just the hourly wage rate.

According to the UN Information Service, the developed world hosts two-thirds of the world's inward foreign direct investment. The 49 least developed countries—the poorest of the developing countries—account for around 2 percent of the total inward FDI stock of developing countries. Nor is it true that multinational corporations make a consistent practice of operating sweatshops in low-wage countries, with poor working conditions and substandard wages. While isolated examples of this can surely be uncovered, it is well established that multinationals, on average, pay higher wages than what is standard in developing nations, and offer higher labor standards. . . .

The shrinking state: Technologies that facilitate communication and commerce have curbed the power of some despots throughout the world, but in a globalized world governments take on new importance in one critical respect, namely, setting, and enforcing, rules with respect to contracts and property rights. The potential of globalization can never be realized unless there are rules and regulations in place, and individuals to enforce them. This gives economic actors confidence to engage in business transactions. Further undermining the idea of globalization shrinking states is that states are not, in fact, shrinking. Public expenditures are, on average, as high or higher today as they have been at any point in recent memory. And among OECD [Organization of Economic Cooperation and Development is composed of 30 mostly high-income countries] countries, government tax revenue as a percentage of GDP increased from 25.5 percent in 1965 to 36.6 percent in 2006.

The Future of Globalization

Like a snowball rolling down a steep mountain, globalization seems to be gathering more and more momentum. And the question frequently asked about globalization is not whether it will continue, but at what pace.

A disparate set of factors will dictate the future direction of globalization, but one important entity—sovereign governments—should not be overlooked. They still have the power to erect significant obstacles to globalization, ranging from tariffs to immigration restrictions to military hostilities.

Nearly a century ago, the global economy operated in a very open environment, with goods, services, and people able to move across borders with little if any difficulty. That openness began to wither away with the onset of World War I in 1914, and recovering what was lost is a process that is still underway. Along the process, governments recognized the importance of international cooperation and coordination, which led to the emergence of numerous international organizations and financial institutions (among which the IMF and the World Bank, in 1944).

Indeed, the lessons included avoiding fragmentation and the breakdown of cooperation among nations. The world is still made up of nation states and a global marketplace. We need to get the right rules in place so the global system is more resilient, more beneficial, and more legitimate. International institutions have a difficult but indispensable role in helping to bring more of globalization's benefits to more people throughout the world. By helping to break down barriers—ranging from the regulatory to the cultural—more countries can be integrated into the global economy, and more people can seize more of the benefits of globalization.

Ravinder Rena  **NO**

Globalization Still Hurting
Poor Nations

Globalization is a buzzword gaining increasing importance all over the world. Today, the world appears radically altered. A very significant feature of the global economy is the integration of the emerging economies in world markets and the expansion of economic activities across state borders. Other dimensions include the international movement of ideas, information, legal systems, organizations, people, popular globetrotting cuisine, cultural exchanges, and so forth.

However, the movement of people, even in this post-1970s era of globalization, is restricted and strictly regulated in the aftermath of the 9/11 attacks. More countries are now integrated into a global economic system in which trade and capital flow across borders with unprecedented energy. Nonetheless, globalization has become painful, rather than controversial, to the developing world. It has produced increasing global economic interdependence through the growing volume and variety of cross-border flows of finance, investment, goods, and services, and the rapid and widespread diffusion of technology.

A World Bank study, "Global Economic Prospects: Managing the Next Wave of Globalization," succinctly discusses the advantages of globalization. Driven by 1974-onward globalization, exports have doubled, as a proportion of world economic output, to over 25 percent, and, based on existing trends, will rise to 34 percent by 2030.

World income has doubled since 1980, and almost half-a-billion people have climbed out of poverty since 1990. According to current trends, the number of people living on less than 1-purchasing power-dollar-a-day will halve from today's 1 billion by 2030. This will take place as a result of growth in Southeast Asia, whose share of the poor will halve from 60 percent, while Africa's will rise from 30 percent to 55 percent.

The scale, benefits, and criticism of globalization are often exaggerated. On the contrary, compared to the immediate post-war period, the average rate of growth has steadily slowed during the age of globalization, from 3.5 percent per annum in the 1960s to 2.1 percent, 1.3 percent, and 1.0 percent in the 1970s, 1980s, and 1990s, respectively.

The growing economic interdependence is highly asymmetrical. The benefits of linking and the costs of de-linking are not equally distributed.

Industrialized countries—the European Union, Japan, and the United States—are genuinely and highly interdependent in their relations with one another. The developing countries, on the other hand, are largely independent from one another in terms of economic relations, while being highly dependent on industrialized countries. Indeed, globalization creates losers as well as winners, and entails risks as well as opportunities. An International Labor Organization blue-ribbon panel noted in 2005 that the problems lie not in globalization per se but in the deficiencies in its governance.

Some globalization nay-sayers have vouched that there has been a growing divergence, not convergence, in income levels, both between countries and peoples. Inequality among, and within, nations has widened. Assets and incomes are more concentrated. Wage shares have fallen while profit shares have risen. Capital mobility alongside labor immobility has reduced the bargaining power of organized labor. The rise in unemployment and the accompanying "casualization" of the workforce, with more and more people working in the informal sector, have generated an excess supply of labor and depressed real wages.

Globalization has spurred inequality—both in the wealthiest countries as well as the developing world. China and India compete globally, yet only a fraction of their citizens prosper. Increasing inequality between rural and urban populations, and between coastal and inland areas in China, could have disastrous consequences in the event of political transition. Forty of the poorest nations, many in Africa, have had zero growth during the past 20 years. Their governments followed advice from wealthy nations and World Bank consultants on issues ranging from privatization to development, but millions of people suffer from poverty. Ironically, the wealthiest people benefit from the source of cheap labor. Western policies reinforce the growing divide between rich and poor.

Nearly three-quarters of Africa's population live in rural areas in contrast with less-than-10-percent in the developed world. Globalization has driven a wedge between social classes in the rich countries, while among the world's poor, the main divide is between countries—those that adapted well to globalization and, in many areas, prospered, and those that maladjusted and, in many cases, collapsed.

As the Second World [the Soviet Union and the communist countries of Eastern Europe] collapsed and globalization took off, the latter rationale evaporated and a few countries, notably India and China, accelerated their growth rates significantly, enjoying the fruits of freer trade and larger capital flows. Although the two countries adapted well to globalization, there is little doubt that their newfound relative prosperity opened many new fissure lines. Inequality between coastal and inland provinces, as well as between urban and rural areas, skyrocketed in China.

Another large group of Third World countries in Latin America, Africa, and former Communist countries experienced a quarter-century of decline, or stagnation, punctuated by civil wars, international conflicts, and the onslaught of AIDS. While rich countries grew on average by almost 2 percent per capita annually from 1980 to 2002, the world's poorest 40 countries had a combined growth rate of zero. For large swaths of Africa, the income level today is less than 1-dollar-per-day.

For these latter countries, the promised benefits of globalization never arrived. Social services were often taken over by foreigners. Western experts and technocrats arrived on their jets, stayed in luxury hotels, and hailed the obvious worsening of economic and social conditions as a step toward better lives and international integration.

Indeed, for many people in Latin America and Africa, globalization was merely a new, more attractive label, for the old imperialism, or worse—for a form of re-colonization. The left-wing reaction sweeping Latin America, from Mexico to Argentina, is a direct consequence of the fault lines opened by policies designed to benefit Wall Street, not the people in the streets of Asmara [capital of Eritrea] or Kampala [capital of Uganda].

The rapid growth of global markets has not seen the parallel development of social and economic institutions to ensure their smooth and efficient functioning; labor rights have been less diligently protected than capital and property rights; and the global rules on trade and finance are unfair to the extent that they produce asymmetric effects on rich and poor countries.

The deepening of poverty and inequality has implications for the social and political stability among, and within, nations. It is in this context that the plight and hopes of developing countries have to be understood in the Doha Round of trade talks. Having commenced in 2001, the Doha Round was supposed to be about the trade-led and trade-facilitated development of the world's poor countries. After five years of negotiations, the talks collapsed because of unbridgeable differences among the EU [European Union], the US, and developing countries led by India, Brazil, and China. [The Doha Round is the latest and continuing series of negotiations under the aegis of the World Trade Organization to reduce restrictions on trade and other forms of international economic interchange. The Doha Round began in 2001 and is at a virtual standstill because of, among other things, disagreements between the wealthier and poorer countries.]

From the developing world's perspective, the problem is that the rich countries want access to poor countries' resources, markets, and labor forces at the lowest possible price. Some rich countries were open to implementing deep cuts in agricultural subsidies, but resisted opening their markets, others wanted the reverse. Developing countries like India, China, and Eritrea, among other[s], are determined to protect the livelihood of their farmers. In countries like India, farmer suicide has been a terrible human cost and a political problem for India's state and central governments for some time, as well as a threat to rural development. Protecting farmers' needs, therefore, is essential for social stability as well as the political survival of governments in the developing world.

The rich countries' pledges of flexibility failed to translate into concrete proposals during the Doha negotiations. Instead, they effectively protected the interests of tiny agricultural minorities. By contrast, in developing countries, farming accounts for 30 to 60 percent of the Gross Domestic Product [GDP] and up to 70 percent of the labor force. This is why labor rights protection is at least as critical for developing countries as intellectual property rights protection is for the rich.

Developing countries were promised a new regime that would allow them to sell their goods and trade their way out of poverty through undistorted market openness. This required generous market access by the rich for the products of the poor, and also reduction-cum-elimination of market-distorting producer and export subsidies, with the resulting dumping of the rich world's produce on world markets.

Thus, Europe launched its "Everything but Arms" initiative whereby it would open its markets to the world's poorest countries. The initiative foundered on too many non-tariff barriers, for example in the technical rules of origin. The US seemed to offer so-called EBP—Everything But what they Produce. Under its proposals, developing countries would have been free to export jet engines and supercomputers to the US, but not textiles, agricultural products, or processed foods.

Elimination of rich country production and export subsidies, and the opening of markets, while necessary, would not be sufficient for developing countries to trade their way out of underdevelopment. They also have a desperate need to institute market-friendly incentives and regulatory regimes and increase their farmers' productivity, and may require technical assistance from international donors to achieve this through investment in training, infrastructure, and research.

The failure of the Doha Round is also, finally, symptomatic of a much bigger malaise, namely the crisis of multilateral governance in security and environmental matters, as well as in trade. In agriculture, as in other sectors, problems-without-passports require solutions-without-borders.

To convince Africans about the benefits of globalization, we must take a more enlightened view of liberalizing trade, services, and labor-intensive manufacturing in which African countries are competitive. Trade is not only a means to prosperity, but also a means of peace-building. We need to devise an enlightened approach in negotiations over the reduction of harmful gas emissions, intellectual property rights, lifesaving drugs, and the transfer of technologies toward combating poverty. Ultimately, globalization broadens the gap between rich and poor. It also creates distortions in the global economy. Therefore, it is not a panacea for world economic development.

EXPLORING THE ISSUE

Is Economic Globalization Good for Both Rich and Poor?

Critical Thinking and Reflection

1. How can one compare different types of impacts? For example, how does one compare profits from corporate investments abroad to jobs lost in America for the same globalization action?
2. The communication revolution, which enables people throughout the world to communicate by phone and Internet, is bringing the world closer together. What specific benefits result from this and what specific harms result from this? What policies or changes could improve the benefits and what policies or changes could reduce the harms?
3. Have you benefited from globalization? If so, how?
4. Does globalization increase inequalities in the world? What changes might produce more equality in the world, both between countries and within countries?
5. Is there an alternative to globalization? Is it inevitable? Can globalization be significantly modified?

Is There Common Ground?

One thing that has been demonstrated by the above debate is that globalization has so many sides to it and so many impacts that any assessment of it can be easily challenged. The focus here is on economic globalization but that cannot be isolated from other aspects. In fact, many believe that economic integration will spawn greater political integration and cultural integration to the benefit of mankind. Others believe that it will destroy some of the protections that people need and undermine their value systems. There is evidence on both sides, but little can be determined now. Both sides are predicting the future state of affairs, so until the future declares one view the winner neither can be disproved. Finally, how do we predict the future when the current world economic crisis has contradicted many previous judgments about globalization?

Additional Resources

There has been an explosion of books on globalization recently. Any analysis of globalization should begin with Thomas Friedman's best selling *The Lexus and the Olive Tree* (Farrar, Straus and Giroux, 1999), which strongly advocated for globalization for the prosperity it brings. He continues his advocacy in

The World Is Flat: A Brief History of the Twenty-First Century (Picador, 2007) and *Hot, Flat and Crowded* (Farrar, Straus and Giroux, 2008). Friedman sees the United States as the nation that is best able to capitalize on that global economy, so it has the brightest future. Other notable pro-globalization books include Jagdish N. Bhagwati, *In Defense of Globalization* (Oxford University Press, 2007) and Pankaj Ghemawat, *World 3.0: Global Prosperity and How to Achieve It* (Harvard University Press, 2011).

Attacks on globalization are prolific as are the evils attributed to globalization. The attacks include William Grieder's *One World Ready or Not: The Manic Logic of Global Capitalism* (Simon & Schuster, 1997); David Korten's *When Corporations Rule the World* (Kumarian Press, 1996); Robert Went, *Globalization: Neoliberal Challenge, Radical Responses* (Pluto Press, 2000); William K. Tabb, *The Amoral Elephant: Globalization and the Struggle for Social Justice in the Twenty-First Century* (Monthly Review Press, 2001); Gary Teeple, *Globalization and the Decline of Social Reform* (Humanity Books, 2000); Noreena Hertz, *The Silent Takeover: Global Capitalism and the Death of Democracy* (Free Press, 2002); Alan Tomelson, *Race to the Bottom: Why a Worldwide Worker Surplus and Uncontrolled Free Trade Are Sinking American Living Standards* (Westview, 2000); Robert A. Isaak, *The Globalization Gap: How the Rich Get Richer and the Poor Get Left Further Behind* (Prentice-Hall, 2005); Joseph E. Stiglitz, *Making Globalization Work* (W. W. Norton, 2006); Gabor Steingart, *The War for Wealth: The True Story of Globalization or Why the Flat World Is Broken* (McGraw-Hill, 2008); and Rhoda E. Howard-Hassmann, *Can Globalization Promote Human Rights?* (Pennsylvania State University Press, 2010).

For relatively balanced discussions of globalization see Arthur P. J. Mol, *Globalization and Environmental Reform: The Ecological Modernization of the Global Economy* (MIT Press, 2001) which points to the environmental degradation that results from globalization but also actions that retard degradation and improve environmental quality; Kamal Dervis, *Better Globalization: Legitimacy, Governance and Reform* (Brookings, 2005); *Globalization and Antiglobalization: Dynamics of Change in the New World,* edited by Henry Veltmeyer (Ashgate, 2004); Dilip K. Das, *Two Faces of Globalization: Munificent and Malevolent* (Edward Elgar, 2009); and Alfred E. Eckes, *the Contemporary Global Economy: A History Since 1980* (Wiley-Blackwell, 2011).

Internet References . . .

U.S. Government Website for the American Recovery and Reinvestment Act of 2009

This website is the U.S. government's official website that provides easy access to data related to Recovery Act spending and allows for the reporting of potential fraud, waste, and abuse. Since its enactment in February 2009, $787.1 billion has been paid out: tax benefits $290.7 billion; contracts, grants, and loans $250.8 billion; and entitlements $245.6 billion.

www.recovery.gov

Paul Krugman

Paul Krugman's site provides prolific commentary on current fiscal policy in his blog, his frequent op-ed articles in *The New York Times,* and his 2013 book *End This Depression Now!*

http://krugman.blogs.nytimes.com

The following websites are for popular and informative news outlets that frequently have good articles on the economic recovery.

www.theatlantic.com; www.rooseveltinstitute.org; www.alternet.org; www.huffingtonpost.com; www.washingtonpost.com; www.nytimes.com; www.bbc.co.uk/news; www.cato.org/policy-report; www.heritage.org; www.aei.org; http://online.wsj.com/home-page

Pew Internet

PEW Internet is a project of the PEW Research Center, which produces many articles a year on the Internet and social media that deals with their use and their consequences.

www.pewinternet.org

Social Networking ProCon

This is a nonpartisan, nonprofit website that presents facts, studies, and pro and con statements on questions related to social networking. In my judgment it is the most informative website on the pros and cons of social media.

Social Networking ProCon.org

Bonus Issues—Special Topics for Today

*T*wo issues have surfaced recently that deeply affect our society and our personal lives. First our economy has been stalled for 5 years. It has improved slightly in the past few years but may go back into recession and even depression at any time. Little is being done about it, however, because political parties, political interests, and political theories disagree avidly over what should be done about the problem. The result is that little gets done. A stimulus was passed, but many think it was too small. Government spending has been cut, but many say that has held back the economy and prevented recovery. Obama has ideas but the Republicans oppose them. The Republicans have ideas but the Democrats oppose them. Issue 23 asks the students to get in on this debate. Issue 24 deals with the consequences of the social media, which has rocketed onto the scene in the last few years. It is here and it cannot be stopped, but is it good or bad or both? You students are good judges of this debate. You and most Americans have gained tremendously from social media but has it also cost you? How? People are learning to use it for their purposes both good and bad. Internet scams number in the many millions. Information and pictures about people diffuse widely for good and for bad. It is changing us in ways that we do not suspect. Issue 24 tries to put these phenomena into perspective, but it is only a beginning.

- Is Stimulus the Best Way to Get the American Economy Back on Its Feet?
- Does Social Media Have Largely Positive Impacts on Its Users?

ISSUE 23

Is Stimulus the Best Way to Get the American Economy Back on Its Feet?

YES: Joshua Holland, from "Paul Krugman: We Could End This Depression Right Now," *Alternet* (May 24, 2012)

NO: Dwight R. Lee, from "The Keynesian Path to Fiscal Irresponsibility," *Cato Journal* (vol. 32, no. 3, Fall 2012)

Learning Outcomes

After reading this issue, you should be able to:

- Understand the advantages and disadvantages of additional government spending (stimulus) in times of recession.
- Understand the theory behind the stimulus approach to recovering a nation's economy.
- Understand the theory behind the debt reduction (austerity) approach to recovering a nation's economy.
- Explain *Wall Street*'s degree of support for various policies for making the national economy strong again.
- Understand various public preferences for government policies for growing the economy.

ISSUE SUMMARY

YES: Freelance writer Joshua Holland and Paul Krugman, Nobel laureate economist and professor of economics and international affairs at the Woodrow Wilson School of Public and International Affairs at Princeton University, argue that while unemployment is high, the government must stimulate the economy to produce many more jobs and thus more earnings, which will increase spending, which will stimulate more business and jobs and more spending, and so on. When the economy has recovered, the government should institute policies to reduce the debt.

NO: Dwight R. Lee, the O'Neil Professor of Global Markets and Freedom in the Cox School of Business at Southern Methodist University, argues that the Keynesian approach of Paul Krugman and others will have disastrous results for America. The Keynesian prescriptions are reasonable in the abstract, but when filtered through the political system controlled by special interests, the results are some short-run benefits but long-run costs including relative economic stagnation.

Currently a debate that is tearing this country apart is whether to shrink government and the debt or to stimulate the economy. The current situation provides support and opposition for both theories. The current high unemployment and slow economic growth suggest the need for government spending to stimulate the economy. On the other hand, the high debt opposes the stimulus because it would increase the debt. The other side advocates cutting government spending to keep government debt small and allow the private sector to invest and innovate to grow the economy. The stimulus, or Keynesian, side thinks that cutting government spending would increase unemployment, decrease earnings, reduce consumption, reduce production, and stymie economic growth, which could put America back into a deeper recession. The austerity side, the opponents of Keynesian theory, admits that cutting government spending could cause a short-term economic decline but would greatly increase long-term growth.

Evidence for this debate is hard to come by. A $700 billion stimulus was enacted in 2009, though some experts argued it should have been $1.2 trillion. Did it work? Steve Benen wrote in *Washington Monthly* in 2011: "Was the effort successful? In so far as it prevented a calamity, of course it was—the stimulus took an economy that was shrinking and made it grow; it took an economy that was hemorrhaging jobs and created conditions in which it created jobs. There are millions of Americans working today who'd be unemployed were it not for the Recovery Act. . . . And yet, it was terribly unsuccessful insofar as the economy still stinks and the jobs crisis hasn't gone away." So the Keynesians can say that it created millions of jobs and prevented a deeper recession, but the austerity side can say that the stimulus did not do what it was supposed to do and then deny the job creation estimates because no one knows the job situation if the stimulus were not passed. The Keynesians can say the austerity policies in Europe have had much worse results than the considerably less austere American policies, but the anti-Keynesians can say the future may tell a different story and the two situations are not the same anyway.

Joshua Holland and Paul Krugman strongly advocate Keynesian policies under the current slow growth and high unemployment conditions. When unemployment and economic growth substantially improve (approaching full utilization of labor, assets, and resources), government policy should shift to address debt reduction. Krugman criticizes President Obama for showing a willingness to consider more spending cuts than are advisable in a slow growth economy. Dwight R. Lee hopes Obama does not listen to Krugman and greatly harm the American economy with stimulus policies that expand government and deficits. He fears that the political system will not produce much true stimulus but will instead produce "pork," which achieves little and creates heavy debts that will be a drag on the economy for decades.

YES

Joshua Holland

Paul Krugman: We Could End This Depression Right Now

The central message of Paul Krugman's new book, *End This Depression Now!* is simple: It doesn't have to be like this. No external dynamic is keeping unemployment at more than 8 percent and consigning a generation of young workers to an economy in which risk is plentiful and opportunities scarce. It is only a failure of political will—and an almost universal embrace of conservative voodoo economics—that is keeping us mired in this dark economic moment.

Of the 2009 stimulus, Krugman writes, "Those who had more or less the right ideas about what the economy needed, including President Obama, were timid, never willing either to acknowledge just how much action was required or to admit later on that what they did in the first round was inadequate." Instead of treating the dismal jobs picture as a crisis requiring their full attention, Washington "pivoted" to talking about the deficit—a phantom menace—at precisely the wrong time. "People with the wrong ideas," Krugman writes, "were vehement and untroubled by self-doubt."

This week, Paul Krugman appeared on the AlterNet Radio Hour to discuss his book. Below is a lightly edited transcript of the conversation.

> Joshua Holland: Let me ask you first about a somewhat provocative word in your title, the D-word. What makes this a depression rather than a so-called "Great Recession" that we've heard so much about?
>
> Paul Krugman: A recession is when things are going down, when the economy is heading down. A depression is when the economy is down, and stays down for a long time. We have the Great Depression, which was more than a decade. There were two recessions in there and there were two periods that were recoveries in the sense that things were getting better, but not much better. The whole period was a period that was really terrible for America and for the world. We're in a period like that right now. Not as bad as the Great Depression, but that's not much to recommend it. It's a sustained thing. We're now in year five of very high unemployment with terrible prospects for young people. It's a depression.
>
> JH: I wonder if it's similar to the so-called Long Depression in the late 19th century. It was kind of two recessions sandwiched around a period of growth. The reason I ask that is because median wages really

did not recover after the so-called tech bubble burst in 2000 before we hit this crash. Isn't that right?

PK: There is an argument that even the so-called "Bush boom"—that period of the middle years of the last decade—was still not very good for most Americans. There is that, but clearly things got an order of magnitude worse after 2007. That's mostly what I'm focusing on in *End This Depression Now.*

JH: I want to encourage people to read the book, but can you just give readers a sense of what you think is the most important thing policy makers should be thinking about doing right now?

PK: The moral of the book is: this doesn't have to be happening. This is essentially a technical process; it's a small thing. It's like having a dead battery in a car, and while there may be a lot wrong with the car, you can get the car going remarkably easily, if you're willing to accept that's what the problem really is.

First and foremost, what we have is an economy that just doesn't have enough spending. Consumers are hobbled by debt, corporations don't want to spend if they don't see consumer demand. Somebody has to step in and spend, and that somebody is the government. The government could—and by all means let's talk about forward-looking, big projects—right away get a big boost in the economy just by reversing the big cutbacks that have taken place in state and local governments these past three years. Get the schoolteachers rehired and get the policemen and firefighters back on the beat. Fill those potholes that have been developing in New Jersey and I believe all over America. We'd then be most of the way back to a decent economy again.

JH: It seems like we take two steps forward with private sector hiring, and then one step back as we're laying off public sector employees at the state and local levels. Do you have a sense of where the unemployment rate would be had we not been beset by this austerity madness?

PK: If we had had state and local governments expanding at the rate they normally do, which is by population—which is also by the way the rate in which it expanded in Bush's first term—then right there we'd have 1.3 million jobs more than we do right now. That's just the public sector jobs. There'd be indirect effects. People would have more spending power and there would be private sector jobs as well. That's something like 2 million jobs right there. When you put it all together my back of the envelope says if we weren't doing this austerity, GDP would be around 3 percentage points higher right now, the unemployment rate would be at least 1.5 points lower, which means we'd be at 6.5 percent unemployment. That's not great, but it's not a depression. We'd be in vastly better shape than we are right now.

JH: I have to ask if you're constantly banging your head against the table. Everything you write in the book strikes me as so much common sense, and yet even Democrats say the government has to pull in spending when families do. Isn't that the reverse of the truth? Isn't it the fact that when families are tightening their belts the government needs to loosen its belt to make up for that loss of demand?

PK: That's right. The whole mistake that people make is that we're all like a family. We're not because we're interdependent. Your spending is my income and my spending is your income. If we both tighten our belts at the same time thinking that's going to make us better off, it actually makes us worse off. This is a fundamental fallacy.

I'm not going to complain about being me. I've got a good job. I've got a solid income. It is frustrating, but it's frustrating because there are 4 million Americans who have been out of work for more than a year. There's a whole generation of students who are graduating who can't find jobs, or can't find jobs that are making use of the education that they've acquired at great expense. Those are the people to be concerned about.

JH: I find it frustrating that there is such a concerted effort to create this alternative reality where Keynesian economics has failed and giving tax cuts to the wealthy will create jobs. It's a parallel universe. Let me ask you for responses to a couple of common talking points. We hear these again and again. Speaking of wealthy people, are they job creators?

PK: No more than anyone else. In general, anyone who spends money is going to be helping to create jobs, but no more so if it's coming from a rich person. This notion that we have to have extreme income inequality in order to have a successful, growing economy requires that you forget history that's live in the minds of everybody over the age of 50. The best generation of economic growth we've ever had in America was the generation right after World War II. That was a society in which the rich were not even remotely as rich as they are now. How come we created all those jobs—all those good jobs—at a time when the top tax rate was as high sometimes as 90 percent? So no, this just flies in the face of all the experience we've had in the last half-century.

JH: It seems like humans are supposed to accumulate knowledge, but we haven't done a very good job in this respect. Is there any chance that we might come to look like Greece?

PK: It's pretty hard for us to look like Greece. The thing about Greece is that they don't have their own currency. That makes you vulnerable to a lot of stuff in a way that having your own currency insulates you. Now what we could have is political dysfunction, and we're working on that, but the people who are working on that are the ones who say because of Greece we must not only slash spending and cut social programs, but also for some reason we must slash taxes on rich and the corporations.

We are nowhere near having a Greek scenario. It's much more likely that we're going to find ourselves looking like ourselves in the

1930s or Japan. We're actually well on our way to a Japan-type long-term stagnation. Greece is the wrong country to be afraid of. They are not a model for us.

JH: It's the politics. Last year when our credit was downgraded it wasn't downgraded because of any economic reality, but because Congress couldn't get it together to lift the debt ceiling.

What about the bond markets? We're hearing again and again that they'll punish us if we don't cut Social Security or if we don't transfer healthcare costs onto elderly retirees. Have we seen any evidence for this? Is there anything behind this assertion?

PK: Gosh, if you believe the people saying that you would have lost a lot of money. I know people have lost a lot of money doing that. The bond markets are willing to lend America—the US government—long-term money at about 1.7 percent as of right now. That's ridiculously low. The index bonds that are protected from inflation actually have a negative interest rate. The bond markets are saying they're worried about economic stagnation. They're worried there aren't going to be investment opportunities because the demand is so weak. So they're going to park their money in US government debt, which is considered safe. The last thing you should be worrying about, at least according to the bond market, is those deficits. Those are not the problem right now.

JH: We're not the only ones who have been afflicted by this scourge of irrational deficit hysteria—the idea that we should cut spending when private sector demand is deep in a hole. Let's talk about Europe. Are we headed toward the end of the European economic union? Basically, as I understand it when you look at the very heavily indebted countries, they've essentially created a gold standard. They can't devalue their currencies and can't do any of the monetary tricks that one would logically pursue in these circumstances.

PK: They created something that's actually worse than the gold standard. If you're serious about economic history then you know the gold standard was a major reason that the Great Depression got as bad as it did. But at least countries had their own currencies. All they had to do was say all right, enough of this gold standard business, and they could escape. Now it's much harder.

I don't see how Greece stays in the euro. Leaving will be terrible, but staying is a no-hope situation. They will leave. Once people see that can happen, there will be in effect bank runs in Spain and Italy, which are much bigger players. That can only be contained if European elites start to behave very differently. They have to say, wait a second—punishing people for their alleged fiscal sins is not the priority now—saving the euro is. That means open-ended lending to the banks and the governments of those countries. It means having a much more expansionary and somewhat inflationary monetary policy. Maybe that will offer enough hope to save the system. It's moved pretty fast now. I think you can see that there's quite a large chance that there will be no euro a year from now.

JH: Let me turn you to another topic. We've seen stagnant middle-class wage growth for basically a generation. There are all sorts of theories popular in conservative think tanks about why this is either a myth or a really good thing. You wrote a piece recently about how income inequality is driving what one might call "political inequality"—one follows the other. Can you unpack that idea for us?

PK: First it starts with an observation. Inequality has had its ups and downs. We were a very unequal society before the Great Depression. We became a much more equal society during the 1930s and especially during the 1940s. We stayed middle-class for a while, then became unequal again. Political polarization, which you can actually measure using various statistical things on congressional voting, also has had its ups and downs. They track each other perfectly. Political polarization and income inequality march hand in hand. There's every reason to believe that relationship is not an accident.

What happens is when the wealthy are very wealthy they can in effect buy political support. The way that's worked in practice in the United States is that the Republican party moves with the interests of the super elite. Not the 1 percent, but the .01 percent. So the extraordinary explosion in incomes of the .01 percent relative to everybody else has pulled the Republican party far to the right to the point where there is no center. The center did not hold, it dissolved and turned into a chasm. That's not because Democrats moved to the left, because they didn't; they moved right. It's because the Republicans moved off into the Gamma quadrant. That is at the root of our political paralysis right now.

JH: They not only spend money directly on campaigns, but they also fund these networks of what I call alternative information infrastructure. If you look at for example billionaire Pete Peterson he's put $1 billion of his own money into a network of think tanks and media projects to help us understand that the greatest threat that we face are deficits, far-off deficits projected 30 or 40 years out.

I just want to turn quickly to trade. You won your Nobel Prize for your new trade theory. You were a vocal free trader in the 1990s. You got the *New York Times* column and I think you started to think more about politics. It's my long-held belief that the purely economic arguments about the benefits of trade are somewhat irrelevant in the real world, because when they go to negotiate these trade deals the US trade representative—like its counterparts in Europe and Japan—is heavily influenced by corporate lobbying. So while we may have a theoretical idea of the benefits of trade, when we're talking about the actual treaties being negotiated behind closed doors under a barrage of lobbying, can they actually yield those theoretical benefits?

PK: I would say that the first 50 years of post-war trade negotiations were a good thing because they produced a world with relatively low barriers, especially to exports of manufactured goods from poor countries. That's really important because you have success stories, countries that have moved their way up into becoming decent places to live through those exports, and countries that keep their heads above water through exports. If Bangladesh couldn't sell their exports of cheap clothing through the world market they would be a disaster area.

A lot of trade agreements in the last couple of decades haven't really been trade agreements. They've been agreements about protecting various kinds of interests. I teach a course on and off about this stuff. You look at something like the Central America Free Trade Agreement and that wasn't really a trade agreement. That was actually an intellectual property agreement largely about making sure our pharmaceutical companies had their monopoly power. So that's the sense in which you're right. A lot of what passes under the banner of free trade is actually something else and is often detrimental to the interests of workers both here and abroad.

JH: That was actually a trade protectionism agreement then?

PK: It was in effect. If you really look through it you found out that basically workers in those countries were gaining only a little bit more market access, but pharma companies here and in Europe were gaining a lot more in the ability to basically enforce their monopoly position.

JH: Now you have this elite discourse about the deficit and that elides the success that we've seen over generations in terms of Keynesian economics. Do you think the fact that we have a half-dozen countries in Europe have gone back into recession—and a couple more are teetering on the brink of going back in recession as a result of this austerity madness—is that changing people's minds in terms of policy makers?

PK: Well, some. Not enough, but I think we're making progress. I've been writing columns for a dozen years and my first principle is that to a first approximation nobody ever admits that they were wrong about anything. But you can see that, clearly, the tone of the discussion has changed quite a lot over the last six months—that we are moving back towards sanity. Whether it'll be time enough to avoid catastrophe I don't know. I think hammering on these points and pointing to the evidence does seem to work, which is why I published the book. It's in the hope we can get the debate to move a little bit further in the direction of doing the right thing.

JH: It's been interesting to watch your progression as a blogger. You're obviously a leading public intellectual, but you're not above posting silly cat videos, are you?

PK: Well, that's what you've got to do. That's a great medium for somebody who thinks the way I do. It's kind of a scratch pad for things that end being in columns and books. I find it an all-around fulfilling exercise, although it's taking up too much time everyday.

Dwight R. Lee    **NO**

The Keynesian Path to Fiscal Irresponsibility

T he basic idea behind Keynesian policy for achieving stable economic growth is straightforward, and superficially plausible. When the economy is in a downturn with underutilized resources, Keynesians believe the federal government should increase aggregate demand by increasing deficit spending through some combination of more spending and lower taxes. With the aid of a multiplier effect augmenting the government's increase in aggregate demand, the economy will move back toward full employment. In contrast, they believe that when aggregate demand exceeds the productive capacity of the economy, the federal government can prevent inflationary overheating by reducing demand with a budget surplus generated by some combination of less spending and higher taxes. The resulting decrease in government demand will be augmented by a reverse multiplier effect, which will reduce inflationary pressures by bringing aggregate demand back in line with the economy's productive capacity. As discussed by Keynes and his early followers, there was nothing fiscally irresponsible about such a policy. While the budget would not be balanced on a yearly basis, it would be balanced over time as budget deficits intended to moderate recessions would be offset by budget surpluses used to restrain economic exuberance.

Of course there are problems with Keynesian policy that have to do with the difficulty of forecasting economic trends and making timely fiscal adjustments. These are problems that are widely recognized as troublesome. They are not my concern, however, since I shall argue that even if Keynesian remedies could be implemented in a timely manner, there are other serious problems undermining Keynesian hopes for moderating the decline, duration, and frequency of economic downturns. The first problem is that Keynesian prescriptions are filtered through a political process being driven by many competing agendas, of which balanced economic growth is only one. The second problem is that both Keynesian economics and the political process are almost entirely focused on short-run demand-side concerns while largely ignoring the long-run importance of economic productivity. The result is a political dynamic that has increasingly turned Keynesian economics into a prescription for fiscal irresponsibility that undermines economic growth without promoting economic stability.

Lee, Dwight R. From *Cato Journal*, vol. 32, no. 3, Fall 2012, pp. 473–475, 477–479, 482–485, 487–490. Copyright © 2012 by Cato Institute. Reprinted by permission via Copyright Clearance Center.

Fiscal History before the Great Depression

From 1792 until 1930 the federal budget averaged 3.2 percent of gross domestic product. Peacetime spending (excluding the Civil War and World War I) averaged 2.7 percent of GDP. Over that 139-year period, the federal budget was roughly in balance, with federal deficits occurring in only 38 years. Those deficits occurred almost entirely because of spending increases during wartime or reduced revenues during economic downturns. The prevailing view was that such downturns would correct themselves through market adjustments, with increased government spending being neither necessary nor desirable. . . .

An important lesson from this experience, indeed from the entire U.S. experience until the early 1930s, is that while market economies suffer from occasional recessions, they recover and continue growing without the need of increased government spending and budget deficits called for by Keynesian prescriptions.

The fact that market economies self-correct from economic downturns without fiscal stimulus does not imply that federal spending was unimportant to U.S. economic success during the nation's first 140-plus years. The federal budget was spent primarily on such activities as providing national defense, infrastructure, law enforcement, and establishing standards on weights and measures. These activities create an environment that unleashes the power of private enterprise and entrepreneurship to create wealth. But as important as what the federal government did to promote economic success, what it did not do was just as important. It did little to override the decisions of consumers and producers with regulations and spending programs as they pursued their interests in response to market incentives. Government action was limited by the prevailing view that prosperity resulted from people keeping most of their earnings because it is their investments and spending choices that do the most to create productive jobs and general prosperity. The idea that the federal government could promote prosperity by spending more of the nation's wealth would have been widely dismissed as foolish.

Fiscal History in the Modern Era

A clear divide in U.S. fiscal history took place in the early 1930s. The proximate cause of this divide was the Great Depression, but it can be traced to a shift in the prevailing political ideology that began in the late 1800s with the populist and progressive movements. Those movements were rooted in a growing belief that market economies required the detailed guidance of the federal government. Beginning as a minority view, it became increasingly accepted that only through government regulation of economic decisions and the stimulus of more federal spending and transfers could economic growth be maintained and economic output be distributed fairly. By the 1930s this belief was sufficiently widespread to give political traction to the idea that more government spending (particularly deficit spending) and control over the economy could reverse the economic downturn that became the Great Depression. This view was given intellectual impetus with the 1936 publication of *The General Theory of Employment, Interest and Money* by John Maynard Keynes, which provided an argument for the use of fiscal policy by central governments to smooth out business cycles. The result was that federal spending expanded and its composition changed.

With the ideological shift, supported by the intellectual acceptance of Keynes's *General Theory,* politicians found themselves with an excuse to do what most had always wanted to do—take more money from the general public and transfer it to favored groups (or voting blocs). The benefits are invariably less than the costs, but they are visible, readily appreciated, and easily credited to politicians. Predictably, beginning in the 1930s federal spending began increasing as a share of GDP. It was about 4 percent of GDP in 1930, increased during the Great Depression and spiked to a historical high of about 47 percent during World War II. The federal government share of GDP then dropped to about 13 percent in 1948, reached a bumpy plateau in the early 1960s at slightly below to slightly above 20 percent that lasted for over 40 years, and then escalated rapidly in late 2008 to an estimated 25 percent in 2011.

It is not just the growth of total federal spending, however, that deserves attention. As the federal spending has grown, its composition experienced a fundamental change. Except for World War II, the bulk of the growth in federal spending has gone to funding transfers from those who earn it to those with the political influence to take it. Currently almost 45 percent of federal spending consists of transfer payments paid out by the big three transfer program—Social Security, Medicare, and Medicaid.

The growth in transfers seen in the post-WWII era would have been unimaginable in earlier times. It was obviously facilitated by the ideological shift begun in the Progressive Era and found expression in Keynesianism—namely, the idea that a government wise enough to manage the macroeconomy could also be trusted to promote both economic fairness and efficiency by taking from some and giving to "deserving" others. Once such transfers began growing, a reinforcing dynamic kicked in. As more groups were favored with transfers, the more other groups felt they deserved their share of the booty, and the less fair it seemed to deny them.

Chronic Peacetime Deficits

Keynes, and his early disciples, almost certainly did not imagine the chronic peacetime deficits experienced since 1960. The original Keynesian prescription called for offsetting the budget deficits during recessions with budget surpluses during economic booms, with the budget remaining at least roughly in balance over time. But given the political incentives, chronic and increasing budget deficits are inherent in the interaction between Keynesian economics and political incentives.

Political incentives, along with greater public acceptance of activist government, can explain the move to chronic deficits. But chronic deficits mean that when an economic contraction occurs it is highly likely to occur when the federal budget is already in deficit. Couple this with the Keynesian view that it is an increase in deficit spending—not the level—that is needed to stimulate economic activity. As expressed by Jared Bernstein, former economic advisor to Vice President Joe Biden, "To keep your foot where it is on the accelerator—even if it is pretty far down—doesn't add speed (or growth). To go (grow) faster, you've got to press down harder." This creates a dynamic that almost guarantees increasing deficits.

So without resistance to Keynes's orthodoxy (and there has always been scholarly resistance and some political resistance as well), the tendency is for budget deficits to become both chronic and to increase as a percentage of national income. Ultimately this does little, if anything, to reduce the likelihood of the next downturn. And, as shall be seen, when government spending and deficits increase, given their current levels, they destroy wealth by reducing the productive capacity of the economy below what it would otherwise be. So even if increasing deficit spending did impart a short-run stimulus effect, its long-run effect would still be negative since it is impossible to increase economic production beyond an economy's productive capacity. Unfortunately, this long-run cost has little effect when fiscal decisions are made in response to short-run political considerations.

Even the most enthusiastic Keynesians, if they value their reputations as economists, acknowledge that government spending and deficits can become large enough to reduce economic growth and the long-run prosperity of a nation. But even when they see the importance of restoring some semblance of fiscal responsibility, they argue that we should wait until larger deficits stimulate economic growth. For example, according to Krugman, "It's politically fashionable to rant against government spending and demand fiscal responsibility. But right now, increased government spending is just what the doctor ordered, and concerns about the budget deficit should be put on hold." This short-run view is not new.

Short-Run Politics vs. Long-Run Productivity

. . . The decline in fiscal discipline encouraged by Keynesian policy has led to expansions in federal spending that undermines the ability of Keynesian spending to stimulate even short-run economic growth. When the economy is in a recession, government spending motivated and directed primarily by short-run political concerns invariably slows up the adjustments necessary for economic recovery. Simple political calculus motivates undermining the self-correcting adjustments inherent in free markets by protecting favored groups against market discipline and distorting the information provided by market prices. For example, the recent Great Recession was largely precipitated by the government policies that motivated the excessive building of houses. Given this malinvestment, one important adjustment needed to make the best use of the existing stock of housing and redirect resources into employments more productive than adding to the housing stock is for housing prices to drop. This, of course, is a market adjustment that needed no help from government attempts to influence housing prices. And, of course, housing prices did fall. But they would have fallen faster except for the fact that the federal government spent a great deal of taxpayer money to prop them up.

The expansion in federal spending since 1930 has been accompanied by an increase in transfers as a percentage of the federal budget and of national income. Unfortunately, government transfers and spending in general damage long-run growth in several ways. First, it has been estimated by Payne that raising another dollar in taxes costs $0.65 in lost output. Second, transfers are commonly used to finance wasteful activities such as growing cotton in the desert, turning corn into ethanol, and producing so-called green energy in politically favored companies that manage to fail despite massive subsidies. Third, government transfers create opportunities for some to capture the wealth of others, which motivates political rent-seeking that replaces otherwise productive activities, not to mention the costly efforts people make to protect their wealth from political capture. Fourth, federal transfers, and the myriad regulations that invariably accompany them, commonly provide protection against market competition, and by doing so deflect, delay, or distort the investments needed to maintain, much less increase, economic productivity. In the final analysis, when a dollar is taken from Peter so it can be transferred to Paul, Peter ends up losing more than a dollar, Paul receives less than a dollar, and the economy's capacity to create more wealth is diminished. . . .

What about the Multiplier Effect?

The demand-side perspective of Keynesian economies makes it easy to overlook the importance of productivity to economic growth. This is vividly seen in the Keynesian belief that deficit spending by government to hire the unemployed is good for the economy even when they are hired to do unproductive tasks. This belief is based on the argument that the money paid to those being hired is all additional income for the economy since it didn't require reducing the income of others with a tax. Some portion of this additional income is then spent to provide a secondary increase in income to others, which continues to produce a sequence of additional income and spending which supposedly expands the economy by some multiple of the original government expenditure. This multiplier effect was famously used by Keynes to argue that using savings to hire the unemployed "to dig holes in the ground" is better than not increasing spending.

While the idea of a multiplier effect seems superficially plausible to many, it does not receive support from the historical record. If the multiplier effect were operative, the United States economy since the end of the Great Recession in 2009 would have been growing far faster than it did for over the quarter of a century after 1865 when the federal government was spending only around 3 percent of the GDP, and running budget surpluses every year except for three years when the budget was balanced. . . .

Conclusion

Keynesians commonly talk as if they seriously believe that a depressed economy can be trapped in a high-unemployment equilibrium and that stimulus from government spending—preferably deficit spending—is the only hope for returning to full employment. A casual look at the historical record is enough to dismiss that view. The self-correcting adjustments motivated by the combination of harsh realities imposed by market discipline and profitable opportunities revealed by market prices are not only enough to restore growth to a depressed economy, but the most effective way to do so. Keynesians have persistently ignored self-correcting market forces and the depressing effect on long-run economic productivity of escalating government spending and budget deficits caused by the interaction between Keynesian policies and political incentives. The result is that Keynesian attempts to increase economic growth by moderating economic downturns are counterproductive—they do little to stimulate economic activity in the short run while they reduce the growth of economic productivity in the long run.

Some will see the argument that Keynesian spending fails to stimulate economic recovery and harms long-run growth as pessimistic. I disagree. There is nothing pessimistic in recognizing that doing the most to promote long-run economic growth while moderating economic fluctuations is hardly likely to be achieved by unleashing politicians from the constraints required for fiscal responsibility. The political implications of my argument can be seen as pessimistic, however, since it implies that the failure of Keynesian attempts to stimulate the economy generate a temporal pattern of concentrated benefits and diffused costs that yield social benefit-cost ratios of less than one but political benefit-cost ratios of greater than one. Keynesian economics is another example of bad economics making for good politics.

Indeed, my argument is more pessimistic than indicated by the political popularity of Keynesian economics as an excuse for fiscal irresponsibility. Keynesian policies can trap politicians into continuing excessive spending and chronic budget deficits even though they realize that doing so does little to stimulate the economy in the short run and harms economic growth in the long run. The problem is that reducing government spending and deficits may cause decreased economic activity and increased unemployment in the short run. People will have made decisions in response to existing levels of government spending rendering them and their investments dependent on that spending. These workers and resources will be redeployed in response to market incentives into more productive employments if government budgets were reduced, but the transition would take a length of time that is politically unacceptable, even though the temporary loss would be small compared to the long-run gain.

Keynesian policies can also trap politicians into continuing those policies by creating support for the Keynesian claim that a depressed market economy cannot return to full employment on its own. As argued above, our market economy still maintains a great deal of self-correcting resiliency in recovering from downturns despite Keynesian views to the contrary. But the spending and budget deficits that are inherent in Keynesian efforts to direct economic growth are inevitably accompanied by a host of government rules, regulations, mandates, and subsidies that are undermining self-correcting market forces. The weaker these forces become, the less politically attractive relying on them will become relative to another round of spending increases funded by yet larger budget deficits as the best response to the next recession. The unfortunate dynamic here is obvious.

But the situation is not hopeless. Even politicians can learn from experience and, more critically, the prevailing political philosophy can shift back toward the healthy skepticism toward government activism that existed for the first 140-plus years of U.S. history, which will significantly alter political incentives. In the meantime, examining the implications for long-run productivity of implementing Keynesian policies in response to short-run political incentives can hardly do any harm.

EXPLORING THE ISSUE

Is Stimulus the Best Way to Get the American Economy Back on Its Feet?

Critical Thinking and Reflection

1. What are the causes of the recent recession and the current slow economic growth?
2. Evaluate the effectiveness or potential effectiveness of the policies that have been implemented or that have been proposed but not implemented.
3. What lessons do you draw from previous recessions, and how were they addressed?
4. How are Greek, European, and Asian economies affecting the American economy?
5. When is the best time to focus on debt reduction?

Is There Common Ground?

All—Holland, Krugman, and Lee—agree that a stimulus involving more spending and lower taxes is appropriate in times of economic decline and underutilized resources. Lee admits that "there was nothing fiscally irresponsible about such a policy." It should help the economy move back toward full employment. Their disagreement is about how the stimulus will actually work. Lee argues that perversions in the political system and inadequate knowledge will screw things up and produce "fiscal irresponsibility that undermines economic growth without promoting economic stability." Holland and Lee also agree that deficits must not be allowed to get too large. They disagree on when is the best time to reduce government spending and produce surpluses that reduce the debt. They both use history to support their arguments but use different portions of history.

Additional Resources

This issue of how to get the economy growing again traces back to the debate between John Maynard Keynes and Friedrich von Hayek. Keynes believed that government could stimulate growth, and Hayek believed the government probably would do more harm than good. Their debate is the subject of Nicholas Wapshott's book *Keynes Hayek: The Clash that Defined Modern Economics* (W.W. Norton, 2012). Keynes' major work is *The General Theory of Employment,*

Interest and Money (Cambridge University Press, 1936). The two views today tend to be labeled stimulus versus austerity, and Paul Krugman is the leading public exponent of the stimulus side. His major work is *End This Depression Now!* (W.W. Norton, 2013). He is a frequent contributor of op-ed articles for *The New York Times*, often promoting the stimulus view and blasting the failure of the austerity, policies, as in the following: "Austerity, Italian Style," (*The New York Times*, February 25, 2013); "Kick that Can" (*The New York Times*, February 5, 2013); "Looking for Mr. Goodpain" (*The New York Times*, February 1, 2013); "The Dwindling Deficit" (*The New York Times*, January 18, 2013); "The Terrible Trillions" (*The New York Times*, December 17, 2012). Another stimulus advocate is Ezra Klein, who provides an excellent account of the recession and the government response to it in "Financial Crisis and Stimulus: Could this Time Be Different?" (*Washington Post*, October 8, 2011). He argues against the austerity policy in "It's Not a Fiscal Cliff, It's an Austerity Crisis" (*Bloomberg View Newsletter*, November 28, 2012). Finally, Daniel W. Drezner documents how austerity policies have largely failed and fallen out of favor in "Have we reached consensus on austerity #fail?" (posted online at *Foreign Policy*, Wednesday, February 27, 2013).

The small-government spending proponents in America are in the austerity camp and against the Keynesians. Austerity is the policy in Europe and promoted by the World Bank. It currently is not doing well, and publics are increasingly protesting its policies. A major defender of the austerity approach is Britain's Chancellor of the Exchequer, George Osborne, who defended his government's austerity program against the protesters. Now the World Bank is saying that perhaps some of the countries pushing austerity should ease up. This shows that at times the austerity approach may hurt too much to be politically practical. Nevertheless, many hang on to the theory and push austerity to limit deficits. Reduced government spending has support from the Tea Party and conservatives who want government limited as much as possible so as not to encroach on personal liberties. We do not pursue this aspect of the austerity debate. A well-reasoned argument against the stimulus view is presented by Andrew T. Young in "Why in the World Are We All Keynesians Again? The Flimsy Case for Stimulus Spending" (*Policy Analysis*, February 14, 2013). Two other anti-stimulus articles are by David Malpass, "The U.S. Needs to Win the Battle to Limit Government Now" (*Forbes*, February 11, 2013), and Jeffrey Miron, "Should U.S. Fiscal Policy Address Slow Growth or the Debt? A Nondilemma" (*Cato Institute Policy Analysis*, no. 718 (January 8, 2013)). *The Cambridge Journal of Economics* is preparing a special issue on austerity, which will include both advocates and opponents.

ISSUE 24

Does Social Media Have Largely Positive Impacts on Its Users?

YES: **Aaron Smith**, from "Why Americans Use Social Media," *Pew Research Center Report* (November 14, 2011)

NO: **Janna Quitney Anderson and Lee Rainie**, from "Millennials Will Benefit *and* Suffer Due to Their Hyperconnected Lives," *Pew Research Center's Internet and American Life Project* (February 29, 2012)

Learning Outcomes

After reading this issue, you should be able to:

- Understand how multifaceted the impacts of social media on people and on society are.
- Be aware of the great variety of opinions that leading experts on social media have about its consequences.
- Understand the primary ways that people use social media.
- Be able to discern how different groups of users differ and are similar in their use of social media.
- Explain how social media affects the development of various intellectual and social skills of its users.
- Speculate on how social media might affect society in the future.

ISSUE SUMMARY

YES: Aaron Smith, senior research specialist of the Pew Research Center, presents the findings of his research project based on interviews in 2011 of 1,015 networking site users who reported on how they used social media. Their major use was for keeping in touch with family and current friends, and 87 percent also used it to connect with out-of-touch old friends.

NO: Janna Quitney Anderson of Elon University and Lee Rainie, research specialist of the Pew Research Center's Internet and

American Life Project, report the findings of an opt-in online survey in 2011 of a diverse but nonrandom sample of 2021 technology stakeholders and critics who report their expert opinion on the impacts of social media on the users. They report many positive and negative impacts.

We will briefly provide a survey of many of the positive and negative results of social media. On the positive side is the abundant use of social media to communicate with family and friends and increase connections and strengthen relationships. It facilitates face-to-face interaction. It especially helps people who are socially isolated or shy to connect with people. It helps seniors to feel more connected to society. Social networking has also increased life satisfaction and reduced health problems. Social media has become a main source of information for many people and they can get information very fast. On average its use also improves school performance though it can also be a distraction. It has been used by businesses to great effect and it can be argued that it has helped the economy with products, services, profits, and jobs. Even law enforcement has used it positively. It has played a major role in recent elections and has helped many groups organize and accomplish things. It has contributed to significant social changes and there are many stories about its help to charities and noble social actions. I add as an academic that social media is being used to disseminate a great deal of academic knowledge.

Social media has also produced negative effects. It can negatively affect social relations. It causes people to spend less time in face-to-face interactions, especially in their homes (a small percent of young people even respond to social media during sex). Social networking has been found to make some children more prone to depression and loneliness and can lead to stress. It correlates with personality disorders like ADHD, difficulty in face-to-face conversations, self-centered personalities, anxiety, and addictive behaviors. It encourages people to waste time. Heavy social media users have lower grades. It can cause many troubles for users including inadvertently engaging in criminal behavior including some cases of "sexting," assisting criminal actions against users (e.g., travel plans informing criminals when to rob their house), loss of privacy, being targeted by scam artists or other criminals, use of the Internet by potential employers or universities who find reasons not to hire potential employees or admit potential students, having revealing pictures and unattractive information widely distributed, facilitating cyberbullying, and reducing some workers' productivity. It often provides misinformation and questionable and even dangerous amateur advice. It can facilitate and spread hate groups and organized crime. It is impossible to weigh these and other negative effects of social media against the positive effects, but most people are avid users in spite of the risks, so consumers believe the net effects are clearly positive.

The pros and cons of social media is a vast topic with many angles and vast changes in the past few years. The rapid speed of change of these phenomena has limited the lessons from empirical research on its effects. When empirical research is sparse, the opinions of experts provide useful guidance and that is what Anderson and Rainie provide us. Overall these 2021 experts were positive but "were fairly evenly split as to whether the younger generation's always-on connection to people and information will turn out to be a net positive or a net negative by 2020." Aaron Smith is much more positive about the use of social media. His respondents used social media to increase social connections and facilitate their activities.

YES

Aaron Smith

Why Americans Use Social Media

$\mathbf{S}$ocial networking sites are appealing as a way to maintain contact with close ties and reconnect with old friends.

Why Americans Use Online Social Media Tools

Two-thirds of online adults (66%) use social media platforms such as Facebook, Twitter, MySpace or LinkedIn.[1] These internet users say that connections with family members and friends (both new and old) are a primary consideration in their adoption of social media tools. Roughly two thirds of social media users say that staying in touch with current friends and family members is a major reason they use these sites, while half say that connecting with old friends they've lost touch with is a major reason behind their use of these technologies.

Other factors play a much smaller role—14% of users say that connecting around a shared hobby or interest is a major reason they use social media, and 9% say that making new friends is equally important. Reading comments by public figures and finding potential romantic partners are cited as major factors by just 5% and 3% of social media users, respectively.

Staying in touch with family members is a major factor across a range of social media users, but it's especially important to women.

Those who say that keeping up with family members is a major consideration in their use of social networking sites are a demographically diverse group. Two-thirds of all social media users cite family connections as a major reason for their use of these tools, and there are no major differences on this question in terms of age, income, education, race/ethnicity, parental status or place of residence. The primary difference on this topic pertains to gender, as female social media users are more likely than male users to cite family connections as a major reason for using these sites (72% vs. 55%).

Staying in touch with current friends and reconnecting with old friends is most relevant for those under the age of 50.

Compared with older adults, social media users under the age of 50 are especially likely to say that these tools help them keep up with existing friends and reconnect with old ones—roughly seven in ten users under the age of

---

[1]Throughout this report the term "social media users" refers to individuals who "use a social networking site like MySpace, Facebook or LinkedIn"(65% of online adults do this) and/or "use Twitter" (13% of online adults).

Motivations for Using Social Networking Sites

Based on adults who use social networking sites such as Facebook, MySpace, Linkedin and/or Twitter

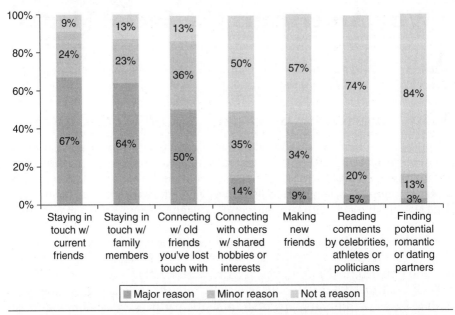

Source: The Pew Research Center's Internet & American Life Project, Apirl 26–May 22, 2011 Spring Tracking Survey; *n* = 2,277 adults ages 18 and older, including 755 cell phone interviews. Interviews were conducted in English and Spanish. Margin of error is ±3 percentage points for SNS users (*n* = 1,015).

fifty say that staying in touch with current friends is a major reason they use online social platforms, and just over half say that connecting with old friends they've lost touch with is equally important. Each of these is significantly higher than comparable figures for users ages 50 and older, although a relatively large number of older adults point to connections with friends as a major reason for their social networking site usage as well.

In addition to age, gender and parental status are linked with users' attitudes towards social media as a way to maintain connections with friends. Women are slightly more likely than men to say that staying in touch with current friends is a major reason for using online social tools (70% vs. 63%) while parents are more likely than non-parents to say that connecting with old friends is a major reason behind their use of these sites (56% vs. 47%).

Compared with keeping tabs on current friends or old acquaintances, users place much less emphasis on using social platforms to make entirely new friends—just 9% say this is a major reason they use these sites, and 57% say that it is not a reason at all for their online social networking activity. Groups that are more likely than average to use social media to make new friends include men (12% say that making new friends is a major reason for using these sites), African Americans (15%), those who have a high school diploma but have not attended college (16%) and those with an annual household income under $30,000 (18%).

Staying in Touch with Current Friends and Reconnecting with Old Ones

% of social networking site users within each group who say the following are a "major reason" for their use of social networking sites

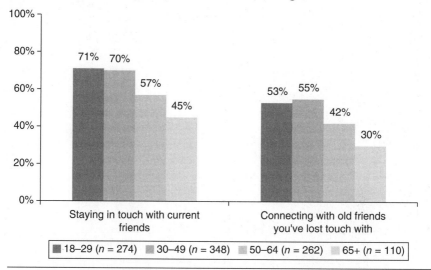

Source: The Pew Research Center's Internet & American Life Project, April 26–May 22, 2011 Spring Tracking Survey; *n* = 2,277 adults ages 18 and older, including 755 cell phone interviews. Interviews were conducted in English and Spanish. Margin of error is ±3 percentage points for SNS users (*n* = 1,015).

Middle-aged and older adults place a relatively high value on social media as a tool to connect with others around a hobby and interest.

Compared with maintaining or rekindling friendships, the ability to connect with others who share a hobby or interest using social media resonates with a slightly older cohort of users. Sixteen percent of 30–49 year olds and 18% of 50–64 year olds cite connecting with others with common hobbies or interests as a major reason they use social networking sites, compared with 10% of 18–29 year olds.

Additionally, men are a bit more likely than women to use these sites to connect around a hobby or interest—56% of male users say that this is either a major or minor reason for their usage of these sites, compared with 44% of female users.

Connecting with public figures online is relatively popular among Twitter users, as well as African Americans and Latinos.

Among social media users as a whole, the ability to read comments by public figures such as politicians, celebrities or athletes does not come into play as a major factor—fully three quarters of users say that this plays no role whatsoever in their decision to use these sites. And while connecting with public figures has a relatively modest impact on users across a range of groups, both African Americans and Latinos show more interest in this activity than white users. One in ten black social media users (10%) and 11% of Latinos say that

Reading Comments by Celebrities, Politicians or Athletes

Based on adults who are Twitter and/or social networking sites such as Facebook, MySpace or LinkedIn

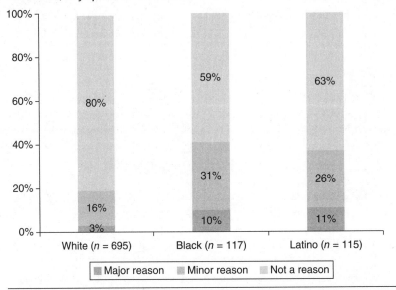

Source: The Pew Research Center's Internet & American Life Project, April 26–May 22, 2011 Spring Tracking Survey; *n* = 2,277 adults ages 18 and older, including 755 cell phone interviews. Interviews were conducted in English and Spanish. Margin of error is ±3 percentage points for SNS users (*n* = 1,015).

reading comments from public figures is a major reason for using these sites (compared with just 3% of white users). Black and Latino social media users are also more likely to say that this is a minor factor (31% of blacks and 26% of Latinos say this, compared with 16% of whites).

Additionally, Twitter users are more interested in connecting with public figures than are social media users who do not use Twitter. One in ten Twitter users (11%) say that reading comments by politicians, celebrities or athletes is a major reason they use online social networks, and 30% say that this is a minor reason for their usage of these sites. Each of these is notably higher than the average for social media users who do not use Twitter (4% of these users say this is a major reason for using these sites, with 11% citing it as a minor reason).

Finding potential dating partners is at most a minor element of the social media experience.

Very few social media users say that finding potential romantic partners or people to date plays a role in their use of these sites—overall more than eight in ten (84%) do not use these sites for that purpose at all. Most of the remainder say that the prospect of romance is only a minor reason. Most differences on this question are quite modest—for example, men are twice as likely as women to say that finding potential dating or romantic partners is a minor reason for using online social platforms (17% vs. 9%) but overall few men say that this is a major factor (just 4% do so).

To be sure, many Americans are currently in relationships or may not otherwise be seeking dating or romantic partners in any venue (on social networking sites or otherwise). Among those users who identify themselves as single, separated or divorced, 6% say that finding romantic or dating partners is a major reason why they use these sites (an additional 27% say that this is a minor reason for their social media usage).

About this survey

The results reported here are based on a national telephone survey of 2,277 adults conducted April 26–May 22, 2011. 1,522 interviews were conducted by landline phone, and 755 interviews were conducted by cell phone. Interviews were conducted in both English and Spanish. For results based on social networking site users, the margin of error is ±3 percentage points (*n* = 1,015).

Janna Quitney Anderson
and Lee Rainie

 **NO**

Millennials Will Benefit *and* Suffer Due to Their Hyperconnected Lives

Analysts generally believe many young people growing up in today's networked world and counting on the internet as their external brain will be nimble analysts and decision-makers who will do well. But these experts also expect that constantly connected teens and young adults will thirst for instant gratification and often make quick, shallow choices. Where will that leave us in 2020? These survey respondents urge major education reform to emphasize new skills and literacies.

Overview

In a survey about the future of the internet, technology experts and stakeholders were fairly evenly split as to whether the younger generation's always-on connection to people and information will turn out to be a net positive or a net negative by 2020. They said many of the young people growing up hyperconnected to each other and the mobile Web and counting on the internet as their external brain will be nimble, quick-acting multitaskers who will do well in key respects.

At the same time, these experts predicted that the impact of networked living on today's young will drive them to thirst for instant gratification, settle for quick choices, and lack patience. A number of the survey respondents argued that it is vital to reform education and emphasize digital literacy. A notable number expressed concerns that trends are leading to a future in which most people are shallow consumers of information, and some mentioned George Orwell's *1984* or expressed their fears of control by powerful interests in an age of entertaining distractions.

These findings come from an opt-in, online survey of a diverse but non-random sample of 1,021 technology stakeholders and critics. The study was fielded by the Pew Research Center's Internet & American Life Project and Elon University's Imagining the Internet Center between August 28 and October 31, 2011.

The survey question about younger users was inspired by speculation over the past several years about the potential impact of technology on them. Looking toward the year 2020, respondents to this survey were fairly evenly split on whether the results will be primarily positive or mostly negative. They were asked to read two statements and select the one they believe that is most likely to be true and then explain their answers.

Some 55% agreed with the statement:

In 2020 the brains of multitasking teens and young adults are "wired" differently from those over age 35 and overall it yields helpful results. They do not suffer notable cognitive shortcomings as they multitask and cycle quickly through personal- and work-related tasks. Rather, they are learning more and they are more adept at finding answers to deep questions, in part because they can search effectively and access collective intelligence via the internet. In sum, the changes in learning behavior and cognition among the young generally produce positive outcomes.

Some 42% agreed with the opposite statement, which posited:

In 2020, the brains of multitasking teens and young adults are "wired" differently from those over age 35 and overall it yields baleful results. They do not retain information; they spend most of their energy sharing short social messages, being entertained, and being distracted away from deep engagement with people and knowledge. They lack deep-thinking capabilities; they lack face-to-face social skills; they depend in unhealthy ways on the internet and mobile devices to function. In sum, the changes in behavior and cognition among the young are generally negative outcomes.

While 55% agreed with the statement that the future for the hyperconnected will generally be positive, many who chose that view noted that it is more their hope than their best guess, and a number of people said the true outcome will be a combination of both scenarios. The research result here is really probably more like a 50-50 outcome than the 55-42 split recorded through survey takers' votes. Respondents were asked to select the positive or the negative, with no middle-ground choice, in order to encourage a spirited and deeply considered written elaboration about the potential future of hyperconnected people.

We did not offer a third alternative—that young people's brains would not be wired differently—but some of the respondents made that argument in their elaborations. They often noted that people's patterns of thinking will likely change, though the actual mechanisms of brain function will not change.

Survey participants did offer strong, consistent predictions about the most desired life skills for young people in 2020. Among those they listed are: public problem-solving through cooperative work (sometimes referred to as *crowd-sourcing* solutions); the ability to search effectively for information online and to be able to discern the quality and veracity of the information one finds and then communicate these findings well (referred to as *digital literacy*); synthesizing (being able to bring together details from many sources);

being strategically future-minded; the ability to concentrate; and the ability to distinguish between the "noise" and the message in the ever-growing sea of information.

Here is a sampling of their predictions and arguments:

- The environment itself will be full of data that can be retrieved almost effortlessly, and it will be arrayed in ways to help people—young and old—navigate their lives. Quick-twitch younger technology users will do well mastering these datastreams.
- Millennials' brains are being rewired to adapt to the new information-processing skills they will need to survive in this environment.
- "Memories are becoming hyperlinks to information triggered by key-words and URLs. We are becoming 'persistent paleontologists' of our own external memories, as our brains are storing the keywords to get back to those memories and not the full memories themselves," argued **Amber Case**, CEO of Geoloqi.
- There is evidence now that "supertaskers" can handle several complicated tasks well, noted communications expert **Stowe Boyd**. And some survey respondents noted that it is not necessarily only young adults who do this well.
- Young people accustomed to a diet of quick-fix information nuggets will be less likely to undertake deep, critical analysis of issues and challenging information. Shallow choices, an expectation of instant gratification, and a lack of patience are likely to be common results, especially for those who do not have the motivation or training that will help them master this new environment. One possible outcome is stagnation in innovation.
- Another possibility, though, is that evolving social structures will create a new "division of labor" that rewards those who make swift, correct decisions as they exploit new information streams *and* rewards the specialists who retain the skills of focused, deep thinking. New winners and losers will emerge in this reconfigured environment; the left-behind will be mired in the shallow diversions offered by technology.
- There are concerns about new social divides. "I suspect we're going to see an increased class division around labor and skills and attention," said media scholar **Danah Boyd**.
- A key differentiator between winners and losers will be winners' capacity to figure out the correct attention–allocation balance in this new environment. Just as we lost oral tradition with the written word, we will lose something big in the coming world, but we will gain as well. "As Sophocles once said, 'Nothing vast enters the life of mortals without a curse,'" noted **Tiffany Shlain**, director of the film *Connected* and founder of the Webby Awards.
- "The essential skills will be those of rapidly searching, browsing, assessing quality, and synthesizing the vast quantities of information," wrote **Jonathan Grudin**, principal researcher at Microsoft. "In contrast, the ability to read one thing and think hard about it for hours will not be of no consequence, but it will be of far less consequence for most people."
- Some argued that technology is not the issue as much as bedrock human behavior is. The "moral panic" over digital technology "seems

to be wired into us,"—it parallels previous concerns about media that have not led to the downfall of civilization, noted **Christopher J. Ferguson**, a professor from Texas A&M whose research specialty is technologies' effects on human behavior.

- Reform of the education system is necessary to help learners know how to maximize the best and minimize the worst. Reform could start by recognizing that distractions of all kinds are the norm now. Educators should teach the management of multiple information streams, emphasizing the skills of filtering, analyzing, and synthesizing information. Also of value is an appreciation for silence, focused contemplation, and "lessons in ignoring people," as futurist **Marcel Bullinga** put it.
- Others noted research that challenges the idea that people can be "multitaskers." People really toggle between tasks and "time slice" their attention into ever-smaller chunks of time, argued Nikki Reynolds, director of instructional technology services at Hamilton College.

Futurist **John Smart**, president and founder of the Acceleration Studies Foundation, recalled an insight of economist Simon Kuznets about evolution of technology effects known as the Kuznets curve: "First-generation tech usually causes 'net negative' social effects; second-generation 'net neutral' effects; by the third generation of tech—once the tech is smart enough, and we've got the interface right, and it begins to reinforce the best behaviors—we finally get to 'net positive' effects," he noted. "We'll be early into conversational interface and agent technologies by 2020, so kids will begin to be seriously intelligently augmented by the internet. There will be many persistent drawbacks however [so the effect at this point will be net neutral]. The biggest problem from a personal-development perspective will be motivating people to work to be more self-actualized, productive, and civic than their parents were. They'll be more willing than ever to relax and remain distracted by entertainments amid accelerating technical productivity.

"As machine intelligence advances," Smart explained, "the first response of humans is to offload their intelligence and motivation to the machines. That's a dehumanizing, first-generation response. Only the later, third-generation educational systems will correct for this."

Another comprehensive insight came from **Barry Chudakov**, a Florida-based consultant and a research fellow in the McLuhan Program in Culture and Technology at the University of Toronto. He wrote that by 2020, "Technology will be so seamlessly integrated into our lives that it will effectively disappear. The line between self and technology is thin today; by then it will effectively vanish. We will think with, think into, and think through our smart tools but their presence and reach into our lives will be less visible. Youth will assume their minds and intentions are extended by technology, while tracking technologies will seek further incursions into behavioral monitoring and choice manipulation. Children will assume this is the way the world works. The cognitive challenge children and youth will face (as we are beginning to face now) is integrity, the state of being whole and undivided. There will be a premium on the skill of maintaining presence, of mindfulness, of awareness in the face of persistent and pervasive tool extensions and incursions into our lives. Is this my intention, or is the tool inciting me to feel and think this way? That question, more than multitasking or brain atrophy due to accessing collective intelligence via the internet, will be the challenge of the future."

Main Findings: Teens, technology, and human potential in 2020

Total Responses	Tension pair on youth and tech effects
55%	In 2020 the brains of multitasking teens and young adults are "wired" differently from those over age 35 and overall it yields helpful results. They do not suffer notable cognitive shortcomings as they multitask and cycle quickly through personal- and work-related tasks. Rather, they are learning more and they are more adept at finding answers to deep questions, in part because they can search effectively and access collective intelligence via the Internet. In sum, the changes in learning behavior and cognition among the young generally produce positive outcomes.
42%	In 2020, the brains of multitasking teens and young adults are "wired" differently from those over age 35 and overall it yields baleful results. They do not retain information; they spend most of their energy sharing short social messages, being entertained, and being distracted away from deep engagement with people and knowledge. They lack deep-thinking capabilities; they lack face-to-face social skills; they depend in unhealthy ways on the Internet and mobile devices to function. In sum, the changes in behavior and cognition among the young are generally negative outcomes.
3%	Did not respond

Respondents' Thoughts

Hyperconnected. Always on. These terms have been invented to describe the environment created when people are linked continuously through tech devices to other humans and to global intelligence. Teens and young adults have been at the forefront of the rapid adoption of the mobile internet and the always-on lifestyle it has made possible.

The most recent nationally representative surveys of the Pew Internet Project show how immersed teens and young adults are in the tech environment and how tied they are to the mobile and social sides of it. Some 95% of teens ages 12–17 are online, 76% use social networking sites, and 77% have cell phones. Moreover, 96% of those ages 18–29 are internet users, 84% use social networking sites, and 97% have cell phones. Well over half of those in that age cohort have smartphones and 23% own tablet computers like iPads.

People are tuning in to communications technologies at an ever-expanding level. Some recent indicators:

- Nearly 20 million of the 225 million Twitter users follow 60 or more Twitter accounts and nearly 2 million follow more than 500 accounts.
- There are more than 800 million people now signed up for the social network Facebook; they spend 700 billion minutes using Facebook

each month, and they install more than 20 million apps every day. Facebook users had uploaded more than 100 billion photos by mid-2011.

• YouTube users upload 60 hours of video per minute and they triggered more than 1 trillion playbacks in 2011—roughly 140 video views per person on earth.

When asked to choose one of the two 2020 scenarios presented in this survey question, respondents were asked to, "Explain your choice about the impact of technology on children and youth and share your view of any implications for the future. What are the positives, negatives and shades of grey in the likely future you anticipate? What intellectual and personal skills will be most highly valued in 2020?"

Following is a selection from the hundreds of written responses survey participants shared when answering this question. The selected statements are grouped under headings that indicate the major themes emerging from these responses. The headings reflect the varied and wide range of opinions found in respondents' replies.

This Is the Next Positive Step in Human Evolution: We Become "Persistent Paleontologists of Our External Memories"

Most of the survey respondents with the largest amount of expertise in this subject area said changes in learning behavior and cognition will generally produce positive outcomes.

One of the world's best-known researchers of teens and young adults—Danah Boyd of Microsoft Research—said there is no doubt that most people who are using the new communications technologies are experiencing the first scenario as they extend themselves into cyberspace. "Brains are being rewired—any shift in stimuli results in a rewiring," she wrote. "The techniques and mechanisms to engage in rapid-fire attention shifting will be extremely useful for the creative class whose job it is to integrate ideas; they relish opportunities to have stimuli that allow them to see things differently. . . ."

Negative Effects Include a Need for Instant Gratification, Loss of Patience

A number of the survey respondents who are young people in the under-35 age group—the central focus of this research question—shared concerns about changes in human attention and depth of discourse among those who spend most or all of their waking hours under the influence of hyperconnectivity.

Alvaro Retana, a distinguished technologist with Hewlett-Packard, expressed concerns about humans' future ability to tackle complex challenges. "The short attention spans resulting from the quick interactions will be detrimental to focusing on the harder problems, and we will probably see a stagnation in many areas: technology, even social venues such as literature," he predicted. "The people who will strive and lead the charge will be the ones able to disconnect themselves to focus on specific problems. . . ."

[Stephen] Masiclat said social systems will evolve to offer even more support to those who can implement deep-thinking skills. "The impact of a future 're-wiring' due to the multitasking and short-term mindset will be mostly negative not because it will reflect changes in the physical nature of thinking, but because the social incentives for deep engagement will erode," he noted. "We will likely retain deep-thinking capability if we just reward it sufficiently in many of our social institutions. . . ."

Dana Levin, a student at Drexel University College of Medicine, wrote, "The biggest consequence I foresee is an expectation of immediacy and decreased patience among people. Those who grow up with immediate access to media, quick response to email and rapid answers to all questions may be less likely to take longer routes to find information, seeking 'quick fixes' rather than taking the time to come to a conclusion or investigate an answer. . . ."

Many anonymous respondents focused their responses on what one referred to as "fast-twitch" wiring. Here's a collection of responses along those lines: "My friends are less interested in genuine human interaction than they are at looking at things on Facebook. People will always use a crutch when they can, and the distraction will only grow in the future."

"Parents and kids will spend less time developing meaningful and bonded relationships in deference to the pursuit and processing of more and more segmented information competing for space in their heads, slowly changing their connection to humanity. . . ."

"'Fast-twitch' wiring among today's youth generally leads to more harm than good. Much of the communication and media consumed in an 'always-on' environment is mind-numbing chatter. While we may see increases in productivity, I question the value of what is produced."

"There is less time for problems to be worked out, whether they are of a personal, political, economic, or environmental nature. When you (individual or collective) screw up (pollute, start a war, act in a selfish way, or commit a sexual indiscretion as a public person) everyone either knows very quickly or your actions affect many people in ways that are irreversible. . . ."

The Result Is Likely to Be a Wide-Ranging Mix of Positives and Negatives—and Not Just for Young People

. . . Youth expert Winograd said the Millennial generation will drive positive change in the next decade. "When Millennials remake our educational institutions so that they reflect this internet-based architecture, rather than the broadcast, 'expert in the center' framework of today's K-doctorate educational systems," he wrote, "then their ability to process, if not actually absorb, a greater amount of information will be used to produce positive outcomes for society. But that will take longer then eight years to accomplish."

"I made the optimistic choice, but in reality, I think that both outcomes will happen," noted Hal Varian, chief economist at Google. "This has been the case for every communications advance: writing, photography, movies, radio, TV, etc. There's no reason to believe that the internet is any different. It will provide ways to save time, and ways to waste time, and people will take advantage of both opportunities. In balance, however, I lean toward the more optimistic view since a larger fraction of the world's population will now be able to access human knowledge. This has got to be a good thing. . . ."

Jerry Michalski, founder and president of Sociate, asked, "What if we're seeing a temporary blip in behavior because an Aleph has suddenly opened in the middle of civilization, a Borges-like hole through which anyone can talk to anyone, and anyone can see everything that ever happened and is happening now? Because this has never existed, all the way back through prehistory, of course we're seeing addictive and compulsive behaviors. Naturally. The big question seems to me to be whether we'll regain our agency in the middle of all this, or surrender to consumerism and infotainment and live out a *WALL-E* world that's either Orwell's or Huxley's misanthropic fantasies in full bloom. I think we're figuring out how to be human again amid all this, and that we'll all learn how to use the new technologies to multitask as well as to dive deep into materials, weaving contexts of meaning that we haven't seen before. Call me an optimist."

Tiffany Shlain, director of the film *Connected* and founder of the Webby Awards, quoted Sophocles. "We are evolving and we are going to be able to access so much knowledge and different perspectives that we will come up with new ideas and new solutions to our world's problems," she responded. "The key will be valuing when to be present and when to unplug. The core of what makes us human is to connect deeply, so this always will be valued. Just as we lost oral tradition with the written word, we will lose something big, but we will gain a new way of thinking. As Sophocles once said, 'Nothing vast enters the life of mortals without a curse. . . .'"

Widening Divide? There's a Fear the Rich Will Get Richer, the Poor Poorer

Teens expert Danah Boyd raised concerns about a looming divide due to the switch in how young people negotiate the world. "Concentrated focus takes discipline, but it's not something everyone needs to do," she wrote, "unfortunately, it is what is expected of much of the workingclass labor force. I suspect we're going to see an increased class division around labor and skills and attention."

Barry Parr, owner and analyst for MediaSavvy, echoed Boyd's concern about a widening divide. "Knowledge workers and those inclined to be deep thinkers will gain more cognitive speed and leverage," he said, "but, the easily distracted will not become more adept at anything. History suggests that on balance people will adapt to the new order. The greatest negative outcome will be that the split in adaptation will exacerbate existing trends toward social inequality. . . ."

No Matter What the Tech, It All Comes Down to Human Nature

Human tendencies drive human uses of technology tools. Many of the people participating in this survey emphasized the importance of the impact of basic human instincts and motivations.

Some survey respondents observed that all new tools initially tend to be questioned and feared by some segment of the public. Socrates, for instance, lamented about the scourge of writing implements and their likely threat to the future of intelligent discourse. In his response to this survey question, Christopher J. Ferguson, a professor from Texas A&M whose research specialty is technologies' effects on human behavior, noted, "The tendency to moralize and fret over new media seems to be wired into us."

He added, "Societal reaction to new media seems to fit into a pattern described by moral panic theory. Just as with older forms of media, from dime novels to comic books to rock and roll, some politicians and scholars can always be found to proclaim the new media to be harmful, often in the most hyperbolic terms. Perhaps we'll learn from these past mistakes? I think we may see the same pattern with social media. For instance the American Academy of Pediatrics claims for a 'Facebook Depression' already have been found to be false by independent scholarly review. New research is increasingly demonstrating that fears of violent video games leading to aggression were largely unfounded. Youth today are the least aggressive, most civically involved, and mentally well in several generations. Independent reviews of the literature by the US Supreme Court and the Australian Government have concluded the research does not support links between new technology and harm to minors. I think on balance we'll eventually accept that new media are generally a positive in our lives. . . ."

EXPLORING THE ISSUE

Does Social Media Have Largely Positive Impacts on Its Users?

Critical Thinking and Reflection

1. Should social media be considered simply a tool that users can use for either good or evil? Thus, it is neither good nor bad in itself.
2. How can the negative consequences of social media be reduced?
3. What role can education play in reducing the negative aspects of social media and increasing its positive aspects?
4. What have been the positive and negative results of your own use of social media?
5. What activities have been reduced by the time spent on social media?
6. How has social media impacted your community? Your nation?
7. Have you or your friends been embarrassed or harmed through your use of social media?

Is There Common Ground?

Both YES and NO selections recognize many of the benefits of social media. Anderson and Rainie also emphasize the many negative impacts of social media and Smith does not. Smith would not deny that social media does have negative impacts but treats them as less important than the positive impacts. Both selections consider the impacts on social connectedness as the key issue to examine, especially on family and close friends. Both agree that it is also useful for news, information, and helping conduct personal business. It also stimulates the economy and facilitates business, governments, and civil sector activities. For example, I just conveniently paid property taxes online 2 hours ago.

Additional Resources

PEW Internet (pewinternet.org), a project of the PEW Research Center, produces many articles a year including the two articles selected for this issue. Another major resource is socialnetworking.procon.org. It is the most informative website on the pros and cons of social media with 173 footnotes, but it does not provide useful links. Its useful references include LexisNexis Risk Solutions, "Role of Social Media in Law Enforcement Significant and Growing," www.lexisnexis.com, July 18, 2012; Mary Wilks, "Online Social Networking's Effect on Adolescent Social Development," www.eckerd.edu

(accessed December 5, 2012); Levi R. Baker and Debra L. Oswald, "Shyness and Online Social Networking Services," *Journal of Social and Personal Relationships* (November 2010); "Economist Debates: Social Networking," *The Economist,* www.economist.com, February 13, 2012; Tony Dokoupil, "Is the Onslaught Making Us Crazy?" *Newsweek,* July 16, 2012; Stephen Marche, "Is Facebook Making Us Lonely?" *Atlantic Monthly*, May 2012. Other useful references are José van Dijck, *The Culture of Connectivity: A Critical History of Social Media* (Oxford University Press, 2013); Tim Jordan, *Internet, Society and Culture [electronic resource]: Communicative Practices Before and After the Internet* (Bloomsbury Publishing, 2013); Francis L.F. Lee, ed., *Frontiers in New Media Research* (Routledge, 2013); Allison Cerra, *Identity Shift: Where Identity Meets Technology in the Networked-Community Age* (John Wiley & Sons, 2012); Andrew Keen, *Digital Vertigo: How Today's Online Social Revolution Is Dividing, Diminishing, and Disorienting Us* (Constable, 2012); Pamela Lund, *Massively Networked: How the Convergence of Social Media and Technology Is Changing Your Life,* 2nd ed. (PLI Media, 2012); Hana S. Noor, Al-Deen, and John Allen Hendricks, eds., *Social Media: Usage and Impact* (Lexington Books, 2012); Nora Young, *The Virtual Self: How Our Digital Lives Are Altering the World Around Us* (McClelland & Stewart, 2012).

Contributors to This Volume

EDITOR

KURT FINSTERBUSCH is a professor of sociology at the University of Maryland at College Park. He received a BA in history from Princeton University in 1957, a BD from Grace Theological Seminary in 1960, and a PhD in sociology from Columbia University in 1969. He is the author of *Understanding Social Impacts* (Sage Publications, 1980), and he is the co-author, with Annabelle Bender Motz, of *Social Research for Policy Decisions* (Wadsworth, 1980) and, with Jerald Hage, of *Organizational Change as a Development Strategy* (Lynne Rienner, 1987). He is the editor of *Annual Editions: Sociology* (McGraw-Hill/Contemporary Learning Series); *Annual Editions: Social Problems* (McGraw-Hill/Contemporary Learning Series); and *Sources: Notable Selections in Sociology*, 3rd ed. (McGraw-Hill/Dushkin, 1999).

AUTHORS

CONSTANCE AHRONS is co-chair of the Council on Contemporary Families. She is a therapist and author of three books: *The Good Divorce, Divorced Families,* and *We're Still Family.* She is Professor Emerita from the Department of Sociology and former director of the Marriage and Family Therapy Doctoral Training Program at the University of Southern California in Los Angeles.

GRAHAM ALLISON is an American political scientist and professsor at the John F. Kennedy School of Government at Harvard. He is renowned for his book *Remaking Foreign Policy: The Organizational Connection,* co-written with Peter Szanton, which was published in 1976 and had some influence on the foreign policy of the administration of President Jimmy Carter. Since the 1970s, Allison has also been a leading analyst of U.S. national security and defense policy.

DAVID A. ANDERSON is a Blazer Associate Professor of Economics. He teaches many courses including law and economics, as well as the economics of crime. He is the author of *Environmental Economics* (Southwestern, 2004).

JANNA QUITNEY ANDERSON is an associate professor at Elon University's School of Communications and is the director of Imagining the Internet, a web-based foresight and history public-good project, which has won international acclaim. She is the lead author of the "Future of the Internet" book series published by Cambria Press. She is the author of *Imagining the Internet: Personalities, Predictions, Perspectives* (Rowman & Littlefield, 2005).

MIRKO BAGARIC is a professor of law at Deakin University; he is a Croatian-born Australian-based author and lawyer who writes on law and moral and political philosophy. He is the author of 20 books and over 100 refereed scholarly articles.

FRED BARNES was the executive editor of *The Weekly Standard* from 1985 to 1995. He has a news TV talk show.

GARY S. BECKER is a university professor in the Department of Economics and Sociology and professor in the Graduate School of Business at the University of Chicago. He is a senior fellow at the Hoover Institution and past president of the American Economic Association.

DAVID C. BERLINER is a Regents' Professor of Education at Arizona State University and a fellow of the Center for Advanced Study in Behavioral Sciences.

LAWRENCE D. BOBO is the Martin Luther King Jr. Centennial Professor at Stanford University, where he is also director of the Center for Comparative Study in Race and Ethnicity and director of the Program in African and African American Studies. He is a founding co-editor of the *Du Bois*

Review: Social Science Research on Race, published by Cambridge University Press. He is co-author of the award-winning book *Racial Attitudes in America: Trends and Interpretations* (Harvard University Press, 1997). He has authored *Prejudice in Politics: Group Position, Public Opinion, and the Wisconsin Treaty Rights Dispute* (Harvard University Press, 2006).

LESTER R. BROWN was the founder and president of the Worldwatch Institute, a nonprofit organization dedicated to the analysis of the global environment. He served as advisor to Secretary of Agriculture Orville Freeman and served as administrator of the International Agricultural Service in that department. In 1969, he helped James Grant establish the Overseas Development Council. He is the author and co-author of numerous books.

JOSEPH A. CALIFANO JR. is founder and chairman of the National Center on Addiction and Substance Abuse (CASA) at Columbia University.

STEVEN A. CAMAROTA is director of research at the Center for Immigration Studies and an expert in economics and demographics.

JULIE CLARKE is a researcher and professor of law at Deakin University.

DAVID COATES is the Worrel Professor of Anglo-American Studies in the Political Science Department at Wake Forest University. He has published *The Liberal Toolkit: Progressive Answers to Conservative Arguments,* from which the reprinted articles were taken.

PHILIP E. DEVINE is a professor of philosophy at Providence College. He received a fellow in law and philosophy from Harvard University, a PhD in philosophy from the University of California at Berkeley, and a BA degree from Yale University.

G. WILLIAM DOMHOFF is a research professor at the University of California at Santa Cruz.

BARBARA EPSTEIN was a writer and founding co-editor of *The New York Review of Books.*

GEORGE W. BUSH WHITE HOUSE released white papers on immigration policy during the Bush administration.

PETER GORMAN is an investigative journalist and former editor-in-chief of *High Times* magazine.

LINDA HIRSHMAN is a retired professor of philosophy and women's studies at Brandeis University. She holds a PhD in philosophy and a law degree from the University of Chicago.

JOSHUA HOLLAND is a freelance writer and editor-at-large at AlterNet. He is also the author of "The 15 Biggest Lies About the Economy."

HUMAN RIGHTS CAMPAIGN is the largest national gay, lesbian, bisexual, and transgender political organization, with members throughout the country.

IMF STAFF began on December 27, 1945, in an effort to stabilize exchange rates and assist with the reconstruction of the world's international payment system.

BRIAN MICHAEL JENKINS, a senior advisor to the president of the Rand Corporation and director of the Transportation Security Center, is an expert on terrorism and transportation security.

SHELDON KAMIENIECKI is dean of the Division of Social Sciences and a professor in the Department of Environmental Studies at the University of California, Santa Cruz.

ROBERT F. KENNEDY JR. is an environmental and political activist. He is an environmental lawyer and co-host of *Ring of Fire* on the Air America Radio Network and also serves as a senior attorney for the Natural Resources Defense Council.

ANTHONY B. KIM researches international economic issues, with a focus on economic freedom and free trade, at the Heritage Foundation.

HERBERT KLEBER has been a pioneer in research and treatment of substance abuse for over 35 years. From 1968 to 1989, he founded and headed the Drug Dependence Unit at Yale University. Kleber is the author of more than 200 papers and the co-editor of the *American Psychiatric Press Textbook of Substance Abuse Treatment*. He has received numerous prestigious awards and two honorary degrees, is listed as one of the "Best Doctors in America" and "Best Doctors in New York," and was elected in 1996 to be a member of the Institute of Medicine of the National Academy of Science.

MARK KRIKORIAN is heading the Center for Immigration Studies since 1995. He holds a master's degree from the Fletcher School of Law and Diplomacy and a bachelor's degree from Georgetown University, and spent 2 years at Yerevan State University in then-Soviet Armenia. Before joining the Center he held a variety of editorial and writing positions.

PAUL KRUGMAN is a noble laureate economist and professor of economics and international affairs at the Woodrow Wilson School of Public and International Affairs at Princeton University. Several times a week he posts an op-ed in *The New York Times* and often appears on television, mainly MSNBC. His recent book is *End This Depression Now!* (W.W. Norton, 2013).

JAMES KURTH is the Claude Smith Professor of Political Science at Swarthmore College, where he teaches defense policy, foreign policy, and international politics. He is also editor of *Orbis*.

DWIGHT R. LEE is a research fellow at The Independent Institute and the William J. O'Neil Endowed Chair in Global Markets and Freedom and Scholar in Residence at Southern Methodist University. He is former president of the Association of Private Enterprise Education and president of the Southern Economic Association.

HILARY M. LIPS is professor and chair of the Department of Psychology and director of the Center for Gender Studies at Radford University.

BJORN LOMBORG is a statistician at the University of Aarhus and the author of the controversial book *The Skeptical Environmentalist: Measuring the Real State of the World* (Cambridge University Press, 2001).

ELIZABETH MARQUARDT is the director of the Center for Marriage and Families and authored *Between Two Worlds: The Inner Lives of Children of Divorce* (Crown, 2005).

STEPHANIE MENCIMER is a contributing editor of *The Washington Monthly*. She was previously an investigative reporter for *The Washington Post* and a staff writer for *Legal Times*. A native of Ogden, Utah, and a graduate of the University of Oregon, Mencimer won the 2000 Harry Chapin Media Award for reporting on hunger and poverty.

KEVIN M. MURPHY is the George J. Stigler Distinguished Service Professor of Economics at the University of Chicago Booth School of Business and a senior fellow at the Hoover Institution. He is the author of over 50 published articles.

SHARON L. NICHOLS is an assistant professor at the University of Texas at San Antonio. She has authored several publications in the area of youth development, policy, and motivation.

KATE O'BEIRNE is the editor of *National Review* and a frequent panelist on TV news shows.

DIANNE PICHÉ is an attorney and the executive director of the Citizens Commission on Civil Rights.

ALVIN POUSSAINT is a noted professor of psychiatry at Harvard Medical School. Poussaint has authored several books on the subject of child psychiatry.

PRESIDENT'S COUNCIL ON BIOETHICS (PCBE) was created in 2001 to advise the Bush administration on bioethics.

LEE RAINIE is the director of the Pew Research Center's Internet & American Life Project, which has studied the social impact of digital technologies since 2000. He is a co-author of *Networked: The New Social Operating System* and five books about the future of the Internet that are drawn from Pew Internet research. Prior to launching the Pew Internet Project, he was managing editor of *U.S. News & World Report*.

ROBERT B. REICH is a professor of public policy at the Goldman School of Public Policy at the University of California at Berkeley. He has served in three national administrations, most recently as secretary of labor under President Bill Clinton. He has written 11 books, including *The Work of Nations*, which has been translated into 22 languages; the best-sellers *The*

Future of Success and *Locked in the Cabinet;* and his most recent book, *Aftershock: The Next Economy and America's Future.*

JEFFREY REIMAN is the William Fraser McDowell Professor of Philosophy at American University in Washington, DC. He is the author of *Justice and Modern Moral Philosophy* (Yale University Press, 1992) and *The Rich Get Richer and the Poor Get Prison: Ideology, Class, and Criminal Justice*, 6th ed. (Allyn & Bacon, 2001). He is also editor, with Paul Leighton, of *Criminal Justice Ethics* (Prentice Hall, 2001).

RAVINDER RENA is coordinator of the Joint African Masters Programme in Local Development (JAMP) at the Harold Pupkewitz Graduate School of Business, Polytechnic of Namibia. Rena has written and published six research books, four textbooks, 18 book chapters, and more than 90 refereed journal articles.

JASON L. RILEY is a member of the editorial board at *The Wall Street Journal*, where he has worked since 1994. He appears regularly on the *Journal Editorial Report* on Fox News.

MICHAEL J. SANDEL is the Anne T. and Robert M. Bass Professor in the Political Science Department at Harvard. His most recent book is *Public Philosophy: Essay on Morality in Politics* (Harvard University Press, 2005).

J. R. SHACKLETON is a professor at the University of East London.

AARON SMITH is a senior researcher for the Pew Research Center's Internet & American Life Project, whose primary areas of research with the Project include the role of the Internet in the political process, technology in civic life, and online engagement with government. He has also authored research on mobile internet usage, the role of the Internet in family life and demographic trends in technology adoption.

PETER SPRIGG serves as vice president for policy at the Family Research Council and oversees FRC research, publications, and policy formulation. He is also the author of the book *Outrage: How Gay Activists and Liberal Judges Are Trashing Democracy to Redefine Marriage* (Regnery, 2004) and the co-editor of the book *Getting It Straight: What the Research Shows about Homosexuality.*

JOSEPH E. STIGLITZ is an economist and a professor at Columbia University. In 2001, he received the Nobel Memorial Prize in Economic Sciences.

PAMELA STONE is a professor of sociology at Hunter College and the Graduate Center of the City University of New York. She is a fellow of Hunter's Gender Equity Program to promote women in science.

WALTER WILLIAMS is the John M. Olin Distinguished Professor of Economics at George Mason University. He holds a BA from California State University at Los Angeles and an MA and a PhD in economics from UCLA. He has received numerous fellowships and awards, including a Hoover Institution National Fellowship and the Valley Forge Freedoms Foundation

George Washington Medal of Honor. A nationally syndicated columnist, his articles and essays have appeared in publications such as *Economic Inquiry, American Economic Review, National Review, Reader's Digest, Policy Review,* and *Newsweek.* Williams has authored six books, including *The State Against Blacks* (later made into a PBS documentary entitled *Good Intentions*) and *Liberty versus the Tyranny of Socialism.*